HIGH WIRE

HIGH WIRE

HOW CHINA REGULATES BIG TECH AND GOVERNS ITS ECONOMY

ANGELA HUYUE ZHANG

OXFORD
UNIVERSITY PRESS

Oxford University Press is a department of the University of Oxford. It furthers
the University's objective of excellence in research, scholarship, and education
by publishing worldwide. Oxford is a registered trade mark of Oxford University
Press in the UK and certain other countries.

Published in the United States of America by Oxford University Press
198 Madison Avenue, New York, NY 10016, United States of America.

© Oxford University Press 2024

All rights reserved. No part of this publication may be reproduced, stored in
a retrieval system, or transmitted, in any form or by any means, without the
prior permission in writing of Oxford University Press, or as expressly permitted
by law, by license, or under terms agreed with the appropriate reproduction
rights organization. Inquiries concerning reproduction outside the scope of the
above should be sent to the Rights Department, Oxford University Press, at the
address above.

You must not circulate this work in any other form
and you must impose this same condition on any acquirer.

Library of Congress Control Number: 2024001054

ISBN 978–0–19–768225–8

DOI: 10.1093/oso/9780197682258.001.0001

Printed by Sheridan Books, Inc., United States of America

To my son Alan, who told everyone in his class that his mom was writing a book about platforms.

Contents

Introduction	1
1.1. The Dynamic Pyramid Model	8
1.1.1. Hierarchy	9
1.1.2. Volatility	12
1.1.3. Fragility	14
1.2. A Road Map	17

PART I. ANALYTICAL FRAMEWORK

1. Hierarchy	25
1.1. Top Leadership	26
1.2. Regulators	28
1.3. Firms	31
1.3.1. Regulatory Arbitrage	32
1.3.2. "Fake It Till You Make It"	33
1.3.3. Crony Capitalism	34
1.4. Platform Participants	36
1.5. Summary	37
2. Volatility	42
2.1. Phase One: Lax Regulation	43
2.2. Phase Two: Harsh Crackdown	47
2.2.1. The Tipping Point	49
2.2.2. Agency Overreach	54
2.3. Phase Three: Regulatory Easing	57
2.4. Summary	61
3. Fragility	64
3.1. China's Covid Control	65
3.2. The 2021 Energy Crisis	70

viii   CONTENTS

3.3. The Property Crackdown   73
3.4. The One-Child Policy   76
3.5. Reflections   80
3.6. Decentralized Policy Experimentation   82
3.7. Summary   85

PART II. PLATFORM REGULATION

4. Antitrust Regulation   89
   4.1. Regulatory Challenges   90
     4.1.1. The Great Firewall   90
     4.1.2. Disorderly Expansion   92
     4.1.3. Unruly Competition   95
   4.2. Applying the Dynamic Pyramid Model   98
     4.2.1. Top Leadership   98
     4.2.2. Firms   101
     4.2.3. Platform Participants   107
     4.2.4. Regulators   109
   4.3. Future Trend   117
   4.4. Summary   120

5. Data Regulation   121
   5.1. Regulatory Challenges   122
     5.1.1. Underground Industry   122
     5.1.2. The Government   124
     5.1.3. Tech Firms   127
   5.2. Applying the Dynamic Pyramid Model   128
     5.2.1. Top Leadership   128
     5.2.2. Firms   132
     5.2.3. Platform Participants   140
     5.2.4. Regulators   142
   5.3. Future Trend   150
   5.4. Summary   154

6. Labor Regulation   155
   6.1. Regulatory Challenges   157
     6.1.1. Algorithmic Exploitation   157
     6.1.2. Lack of Social Protection   159
     6.1.3. Barriers to Collective Action   161
   6.2. Applying the Dynamic Pyramid Model   163
     6.2.1. Top Leadership   164
     6.2.2. Firms   166

CONTENTS   ix

6.2.3. Platform Participants	172
6.2.4. Regulators	173
6.3. Future Trend	185
6.4. Summary	187

PART III. PLATFORM SELF-REGULATION

7. Platforms as Quasi-Regulators	193
7.1. Building (Faking) a Reputation Mechanism	195
7.2. Credible Enforcement Mechanisms	198
7.2.1. The Demand for Self-Regulation	198
7.2.2. The Law of Taobao	200
7.2.3. Co-Regulation with the State	205
7.3. Summary	213
8. Decentralizing Platform Governance	215
8.1. Forms of Decentralization	218
8.1.1. Weak Decentralization	218
8.1.2. Semi-Strong Decentralization	220
8.1.3. Strong Decentralization	223
8.2. Legitimacy Crises	225
8.2.1. User Riot	225
8.2.2. Corruption	227
8.2.3. Case Ambiguity	229
8.3. Decentralization to Enhance Legitimacy	232
8.3.1. Procedural Justice	233
8.3.2. Norm Searching	235
8.4. Summary	238

PART IV. THE PATH FORWARD

9. Is China Exceptional?	241
9.1. Antitrust	242
9.1.1. Western Trend	242
9.1.2. Impact on China	245
9.2. Data	248
9.2.1. Western Trend	248
9.2.2. Impact on China	250
9.3. Labor	253
9.3.1. Western Trend	253
9.3.2. Impact on China	256
9.4. Summary	258

CONTENTS

10. Assessing the Impact   259
    10.1. The Retreat of the Private Sector   260
        10.1.1. Exit and Restructuring   260
        10.1.2. The Unintended Consequences   262
    10.2. The Advancement of the Administrative State   266
        10.2.1. Golden Share and State Investment   267
        10.2.2. The Shift from Soft to Hard Tech   270
    10.3. Summary   275

11. Regulating Generative AI   277
    11.1. Applying the Dynamic Pyramid Model   279
        11.1.1. Top Leaders   279
        11.1.2. Industry Stakeholders   281
        11.1.3. The Public   283
        11.1.4. Regulators   284
    11.2. Is China Exceptional?   286
    11.3. Future Trend   289
    11.4. Summary   290

Notes   293
Acknowledgments   409
Index   411

Introduction

How does China regulate its Big Tech? Far from being of interest only to academics, this is a trillion-dollar question with profound implications for Chinese businesses and international investors. Indeed, China is the only country to have succeeded in fostering tech giants that can rival those of the United States. Companies such as Alibaba, Tencent, ByteDance, Meituan, and Pinduoduo are among the world's top 10 largest internet firms in terms of market capitalization.[1] In 2017, Tencent overtook Meta (then called Facebook) to become the world's fifth largest publicly traded company.[2] China is also home to the largest unicorns (privately held start-ups worth over USD 1 billion) in the world. In 2020, the country boasted 227 unicorns, second only to the United States with 233.[3] Of the world's top 10 unicorns in 2020, 6 came from China, with 4 Chinese companies topping the chart. For years, Chinese regulatory authorities have adopted a very lax and tolerant stance toward regulating its Big Tech, with the goal of cultivating tech titans capable of outperforming their foreign rivals.

However, starting in October 2020, against the political backdrop of President Xi Jinping's "common prosperity" campaign, Beijing has unleashed a seemingly unrelenting blizzard of regulatory measures against Chinese tech firms in areas ranging from antitrust to data and labor. This massive regulatory campaign started with the sudden debacle of Ant Group's initial public offering (IPO) and has since spread like wildfire, affecting a wide range of industries—from fintech and e-commerce to social media, food delivery, ride-hailing, and even tutoring. In 2021, China's antitrust authority imposed a combined fine of USD 3.3 billion on Alibaba, the nation's largest e-commerce company, and Meituan, its largest food-delivery company. That same year, the ride-hailing behemoth Didi found itself subject to a surprise cybersecurity review two days after its IPO listing

High Wire. Angela Huyue Zhang, Oxford University Press. © Oxford University Press 2024.
DOI: 10.1093/oso/9780197682258.003.0001

in New York. Tencent, owner of the ubiquitous messaging app WeChat, also saw some of its mergers restricted or blocked. By March 2022, Chinese tech giants had suffered an extraordinary USD 2 trillion loss in value from their peak in early 2021, with shares of major tech firms such as Alibaba, Meituan, and Didi slumping more than 50 percent.[4] Alarmed by these developments, and seeking to stave off further political pressure, Chinese tech bosses and digital giants are now funneling vast sums of money into socially beneficial projects and charities.[5]

China's tech crackdown has also alarmed the White House. As the rising Asian economic superpower reorients its Big Tech firms toward developing more hardcore, cutting-edge technologies to stay competitive with the United States, profound questions have been raised about the future of the US–China tech rivalry. Will Chinese national champions such as Tencent and Alibaba, which thrive on producing video games and selling clothes online, be able to help China close the technological gap with the United States? What might the future hold for Chinese tech firms eager to access the US capital market? At the time of writing, Chinese firms seeking to list in the United States are struggling to overcome strict cross-border data-transfer rules recently imposed by the Chinese government. A prominent example is Didi, which delisted from the United States—vividly illustrating the intensity of the pressure exerted on domestic firms by China's cyber watchdog. In light of these developments, it is unsurprising that Chinese Big Tech regulation has garnered intense attention from the media, the business community, and academia. There is, however, no established consensus on how to interpret these trends. Two primary views have surfaced in response to the government's recent tech crackdown, representing critics and proponents of China's regulatory initiatives.

Critics of China's regulatory campaign have mostly traced its underlying impetus to the politics of the Chinese Communist Party (CCP), in particular the internal power struggle leading up to the 20th CCP Congress and the CCP's broader ambition to assert unbridled and pervasive control over Chinese society.[6] Such critics are also alarmed by the common prosperity campaign, whose central ethos calls for a more equal distribution of wealth. They see China's recent regulatory actions as an attempt to roll back decades-long market reforms and restore the country's socialist roots, thereby fulfilling Mao Zedong's ultimate vision.[7] Although some critics acknowledge the existence of sound regulatory logic underpinning the new measures, they remain skeptical about the underlying motivation of the crackdown.[8] China experts Barry Naughton and Jude Blanchette underscore that China's income inequality is hardly a new issue, and regulatory gaps that exacerbate these disparities have existed for years.[9] Pointing to the upcoming 20th CCP Congress as a determining factor, they suggest that the launch of this sudden and multifaceted legal campaign against tech firms was primarily driven by the desire of the Xi administration to give its cadres an opportunity "to demonstrate their loyalty and competence."[10] Overall, these critics cast a bleak outlook not only for China's tech sector, but for its economy as a whole, warning that the crackdown is driving China into the unknown and will strangle its greatest source of economic dynamism.[11]

On the other hand, another group of observers views Chinese regulation in a more favorable light, viewing the latest measures as China's attempt to "catch up" with the West by correcting the excesses of capital expansion.[12] Thinkers in this camp believe that the Chinese government has been more responsive than its Western counterparts in curbing tech monopolies and their exploitation of the public.[13] Indeed, the ongoing digital transformation of the world's societies and economies is posing unprecedented challenges for mankind: although innovation generally enhances productivity growth and social mobility, it has also become a source of income and wealth inequality.[14] In the United States, superstar tech firms such as Google, Amazon, Meta, Apple, and Microsoft have so pervasively invaded multiple sectors and product lines that they have discouraged other firms from entering the market, thus foreclosing potential avenues for innovation.[15] The fact that yesterday's innovations can entrench today's incumbents demonstrates the power that tech giants have in deterring new entrants, thereby undermining productivity growth and social mobility in the long run.[16] Such market dominance is particularly worrying as there is increasing evidence that big businesses are capturing Western governments, making it ever more difficult to push forward reforms.[17] Prominent economists, including Raghuram Rajan and Luigi Zingales, now call for protecting capitalism from the capitalists.[18] This, however, is far from easy. As Katharina Pistor observes in *The Code of Capital*, the ultra-rich are adept at leveraging the highly complex legal codes of different jurisdictions to create, preserve, and pass on their wealth.[19] The level of complexity in the interplay of state law and private legal ordering has led her to question whether the current form of global capitalism has become ungovernable.[20] Similarly, David Ellwood, a Harvard economist, points out that even though many solutions have been proposed in the West, they all "stumble on both the question of whether they can ever be achieved politically and whether the scale and speed of the changes are sufficient to achieve real changes in inequality."[21]

Both of the above viewpoints—that is, both critics and supporters of China's recent wave of tech regulation—have their merits. However, neither viewpoint is complete. Critics are correct that the harsh regulatory crackdown has afforded the government a much greater regulatory arsenal, thus strengthening its grip over the tech sector. Critics also have good reasons to be concerned about the common prosperity campaign, which could curb entrepreneurial spirits and sap business confidence. But supporters are also rightly concerned about income inequality. China's transformation from a poor country into the world's second-largest economy brought a dramatic increase in its level of inequality.[22] As China enters its own "Gilded Age," to borrow a term originally used to describe the late-nineteenth-century United States, inequality is becoming a worrying trend.[23] China's Gini coefficient, a measure of income inequality, has been hovering around 0.46 to 0.49 for decades, which is above the 0.40 red line for inequality.[24] In 2015, those with incomes in the top 10 percent of China's earners accounted for approximately 41 percent of the total national income, while the top 1 percent accounted for around 14 percent, according to a study by Thomas Piketty and co-authors.[25] Inequality in China is now worse than in Europe and is fast approaching the level seen in the United States.[26] Indeed, China's wealth gap seems only to have widened in recent years, with the wealthiest 1 percent of Chinese people holding 30 percent of the country's wealth in 2020.[27]

The Chinese tech boom has deepened the chasm between rich and poor in China.[28] Encouraged by a lax regulatory environment, Chinese tech firms have enjoyed rapid growth in the past two decades. In the wake of the Covid-19 outbreak, these platforms have surged into ever greater prominence, and their influence now pervades many aspects of people's daily lives. Tech firms leverage the vast amount of data collected from their consumers and employ smart algorithms in order to extract more surplus from Chinese consumers. At the same time, Chinese tech giants have taken advantage of cheap labor to aggressively expand their businesses. In addition to leveraging their monopoly positions to exploit consumers, large online platforms can also behave like monopsonies—that is, a single buyer dominating the demand for goods or services—by exploiting their suppliers, contractors, and employees. Top executives and engineers in Chinese Big Tech are rewarded with generous paychecks and lucrative options, while the vast population of frontline workers, including delivery workers and ride-hailing drivers, earn little.

In their book *Combating Inequality*, prominent economists Oliver Blanchard and Dani Rodrik categorize economic policies aimed at targeting income inequality into three types, according to the stage of the economy they target.[29] Some policies focus on the preproduction stage by shaping the endowments with which people enter the workforce (e.g., education, health, and financial-access policies). Some policies focus on the production stage by affecting the composition and organization of production, as well as the bargaining power of those with claims on outputs, including workers, shareholders, managers, and suppliers. The third kind of policy focuses on the postproduction stage, which involves the redistribution of income and wealth. China's wide-ranging efforts to fight income inequality via the common prosperity campaign do seem to correspond to these various policy types.

Viewed in this light, the seemingly random policies that the Chinese government has ushered in since 2020 are all connected by a common desire to combat inequality. For instance, China's shutdown of the online tutoring industry focuses on the preproduction stage by narrowing the education gap between the rich and the poor. The myriad laws and regulations that were introduced to regulate the tech sector focus on the production stage by rebalancing the bargaining power of tech firms and online platform participants, respectively. The property-tax reforms that were to be introduced in some Chinese cities, the crackdown on tax evasion by live-streaming celebrities, as well as the political and media pressures on tech bosses to donate, all belong to the postproduction phase of redistributing wealth.

Moreover, critics of China's regulatory campaign tend to downplay the market chaos that has been the result of technological transformation. There is plenty of evidence, as I will demonstrate in Part II (Chapters 4–6) of this book, that the Chinese platform economy has grown to be very unruly, and the country faces a strong need to regulate. These serious regulatory issues, which arise from long-standing conflicts between the platforms and their users, have been growing ever more severely over time as Chinese platforms grow. In fact, both Washington and Brussels have long voiced strong criticisms over the undue influence of major tech companies over their economies and societies, and Beijing is actually a late-comer in joining a global push to regulate Big Tech.

Critics who attribute China's recent reforms to political jockeying within the CCP have also questioned the timing of the regulatory campaign, given that many of the problems it claims to address have existed for a long time.[30] In doing so, they appear to overlook the crucial role the regulatory agencies have played in such reforms, notwithstanding the fact that they are the ones in charge of the day-to-day implementation of policies from the top policymakers. As self-interested rational actors, regulators have an incentive to maximize their own bureaucratic interests, which are not necessarily aligned with the wishes of their superiors. In fact, the severity of the regulatory problems arising from the platform economy partly stems from bureaucratic inertia, which has contributed to a near absence of regulatory intervention in many areas in the past. Critics also fail to realize the randomness in Chinese regulation, or, as Nassim Taleb puts it, "Black Swan events."[31] Above all, they fail to appreciate the importance of a tipping point that can trigger a dramatic reversal in Chinese platform regulation, as I will further explain in Chapter 2.

Some critics have suggested that China should have used progressive taxation and social welfare to mitigate inequality.[32] But such critics appear to underestimate the difficulties of taxing China's ultra-rich. Like the United States, China already imposes a progressive income tax, with the top bracket subject to a tax of up to 45 percent of their income. However, personal income tax only contributes about 6.5 percent of China's total tax revenue and is mostly borne by the middle class.[33] Because they earn most of their income through investments, many of China's ultra-rich are hardly affected by income taxes.[34] Although reforming this tax system could potentially improve equality, it presents significant political hurdles.[35] At present, the Chinese government relies heavily on indirect taxes, such as the value-added tax, rather than direct taxation in the form of personal income tax.[36] As Changdong Zhang observes, increases in direct taxation can increase citizens' tax consciousness, which could in turn generate social discontent and hurt the legitimacy of the CCP.[37] Moreover, many of China's ultra-rich hold the vast majority of their wealth not as individuals, but rather through offshore entities located in tax havens.[38] Unless the offshore entities distribute wealth to the tech bosses and their families, these assets are technically not subject to Chinese taxes. Even when such distributions occur,

INTRODUCTION

it is difficult for China to police overseas transactions that are processed by foreign banks. In this respect, China is in a weaker regulatory position than the United States, which has more leverage to regulate the overseas income of its own citizens. Given the dollar's preeminent and dominant position in the global financial system, international banks are very mindful of their compliance duties relating to US tax law, since failing to do so risks incurring US sanctions.

Notwithstanding all these weaknesses in the arguments of the critics, the staunch supporters of China's regulatory measures are overly optimistic and fail to consider two fundamental challenges to Chinese regulation. First, advocates of regulation appear to assume that Chinese policymakers are infallible. Yet human beings are prone to making errors, and personalities can change over time. A case in point is the series of policy mistakes that Chairman Mao made after 1948, which led the country into disastrous calamities. To provide the necessary safeguards for making the top leadership more reliable and responsible, institutional constraints are crucial to prevent excessive concentration of power. Andrew Nathan, a renowned political scientist, has attributed the resilience of the Chinese authoritarian regime to four formal and informal rules: the peaceful, orderly transition of leadership; an increasing emphasis on meritocracies over factional considerations; increasing agency autonomy; and growing citizen participation in political processes.[39] These institutional safeguards have, however, been waning in the past decade.[40] Instead of an institutionalized collective leadership, there has been an increasing emphasis on ideological discipline and a growing consolidation of power in President Xi since 2012.[41] In 2018, China abolished the constitutional term limits for presidents and vice presidents, representing a radical break from previous norms. Small leadership groups, comprising the country's most powerful leaders, have increased in number over recent years. Although these groups have advantages in terms of their ability to coordinate agency action, cut through bureaucratic roadblocks, and bypass entrenched interests, their proliferation is also shrinking the autonomy of individual agencies.[42] Meanwhile, tightened control of media discourse, pervasive censorship of the internet, and a more aggressive purge of activists have left citizens with fewer opportunities to voice grievances.[43] As Susan Shirk observes, Chinese regulatory governance has returned to more personalistic ruling under the leadership of President Xi.[44]

The other challenge to Chinese regulation stems from the execution of policies by administrative agencies. Agencies' execution is never perfect and their performance is notoriously difficult to observe. Although a regulatory agency can tout the number of cases it has brought and the number of fines it has levied, these quantitative measures are often poor indicators of quality. The Chinese government has long recognized this problem and, in response to it, created the Administrative Litigation Law, which has served as an avenue for citizens to challenge the government since 1989. However, this law lacked teeth, and many plaintiffs relying on it have been known to withdraw their lawsuits without going to trial.[45] In 2014, the Administrative Litigation Law was amended by the Chinese government, making it much easier for ordinary citizens to win in their legal challenges against government authorities.[46] Yet such increased judicial constraints on agency performance are limited in scope and have not yet affected those high-stakes cases decided by large central ministries wielding pervasive policy control over large businesses.[47] Indeed, despite improvements in administrative law, businesses in China remain reluctant to publicly confront governmental agencies or challenge them in court.[48] This has bolstered Chinese regulatory agencies, which place greater emphasis on substantive rather than procedural justice.[49] A good example can be found in the recent regulatory crackdown. When Alibaba received a hefty fine of USD 2.8 billion from the State Administration for Market Regulation (SAMR), the firm did not appeal but rather expressed gratitude to the authority and vowed to improve compliance. Without proper checks and balances, the Chinese approach to regulation raises serious concerns about agency overreach, heightening suspicions about selective enforcement and political targeting, and casting doubts upon the legitimacy of administrative actions.

I.1. The Dynamic Pyramid Model

In a departure from the above two competing viewpoints, I introduce a new analytical framework, termed the "dynamic pyramid model," to elucidate China's distinct regulatory system. As the title of this book suggests, there is a remarkable resemblance between Chinese regulation and a "pyramid on high wire" circus act, in which a team of acrobats form a human pyramid while navigating a tightrope. High-wire walking in itself is

INTRODUCTION   9

a highly risky act. With their feet touching a thin wire while dangling over the ledge, performers need to carefully maintain their balance, usually with a long balancing pole, as they move forward. As the wire tends to rotate, each step along the wire could cause it to spin, disrupting the performer's balance.[50] The "pyramid on high wire" act further amplifies the challenge, as it requires a group of performers to maintain their balance while synchronizing their moves. Even a small tumble by any performer can cause the entire pyramid to collapse, making this act one of the most perilous and suspenseful acts in a circus.

Chinese regulation shares three striking similarities with the "pyramid on high wire" act in terms of hierarchy, volatility, and fragility. Specifically, hierarchy illustrates the structure of the regulatory institutions, volatility underscores the erratic nature of the regulatory process, and fragility characterizes the outcome of these regulations. These three features also interact with each other through various channels, forming a complex network via multiple feedback loops, as will be illustrated in Figure I.2 later in this Introduction. Each of these three features, as well as the interactions among them, are highlighted below and further discussed throughout the entire book. Although this book primarily focuses on the intricacies of Chinese tech policy, the dynamic pyramid model has wider applications and could potentially shed light on a range of regulatory actions within China, as will be explored in greater depth in Chapter 3. Indeed, China's unprecedented tech crackdown between 2020 and 2022 may have taken the world by surprise, yet it fits perfectly within the long-standing patterns in Chinese regulatory governance. I should also clarify at the outset that my focus on "tech" in this book primarily encompasses consumer tech businesses, as opposed to those that involve hardware components such as semiconductors.

I.I.I. Hierarchy

Hierarchy is the first and foremost feature of the dynamic pyramid model. The policymaking process involves interactions between actors from four tiers of the Chinese society, including the top leaders, the regulatory agencies, the firms, and platform participants. This four-tier hierarchy creates a complicated, multilayer principal–agent problem.

At the apex of the hierarchy is the Politburo Standing Committee of the CCP, hereinafter referred to as China's top leadership, which enjoys the highest authority and wields tremendous power. At the same time, the top leadership lacks the expertise to make concrete decisions and has limited time to devote to specific regulatory issues. It thus delegates most of its decision-making power to regulatory agencies, which are filled with technocrats. Chinese regulatory agencies are nested within every level of China's vast bureaucratic machine, and they derive their legitimacy from the delegation of power by the central authority.[51] Because officials are evaluated through a top-down nomenklatura process, the whole bureaucracy is organized based on an upward accountability system.[52] Xueguang Zhou, a renowned China expert, has characterized China's bureaucratic system as an extremely "tightly coupled" system in that all local governments are coordinated by the same chain of command under the leadership of the central government.[53] Chinese regulators thus need to carefully tread the lines laid down by the top when carrying out their enforcement duties. The information asymmetry between the top leaders and the bureaucrats leads to a familiar agency problem in that the latter have incentives to maximize their bureaucratic interests at the expense of their superiors. The potential misalignment of interests between the top leaders and the agencies thus forms the first layer of the principal–agent relationship in Chinese regulation.

Meanwhile, Chinese tech firms are not on an equal footing with regulators due to the strong power imbalances between government and businesses in China. Although companies can theoretically challenge government actions in court, few choose to do so.[54] Instead, businesses under investigation tend to exhibit an unusual level of cooperation with regulators.[55] At the same time, there exists an information asymmetry between regulators and firms when it comes to understanding tensions arising from tech platforms. Due to their capacity constraints and their lack of access to the internal operations of platform systems, regulators cannot possibly identify or monitor every tension that might arise. Instead, most governance functions are delegated to the platform itself, which plays the role of quasi-regulator, as will be elaborated in Chapter 7. However, what is good for the platforms is not always good for society as a whole. Firms can behave in a way that deviates from the ideal of a benevolent social planner to maximize their own interests. This then forms the second layer of the principal–agent relationship.

At the bottom of the hierarchy are the platform participants. These typically include customers, merchants, drivers, delivery workers, contractors, and employees. Platform participants are not restricted to only those who engage willingly; they also include those who interact with the platforms involuntarily. This is attributed to the operation of platforms potentially generating negative externalities, thereby affecting third parties unassociated with the platform. For example, pedestrians might unwittingly become platform participants if involved in traffic accidents caused by a gig worker's speed driving during deliveries, as will be illustrated in Chapter 6. In the meantime, tech companies create the rules that determine access to platforms, allocate wealth among participants, regulate content and activities, enforce penalties for violations of platform rules, and arbitrage disputes that arise from the platform. As Shoshana Zuboff, the author of "Surveillance Capitalism," encapsulates, "platforms are the government we didn't elect."[56] However, platforms also encounter significant constraints when acting in this quasi-governmental capacity. The legitimacy of their centralized model of governance is called into question when platforms, particularly those wielding monopoly power, exert considerable influence over people's lives. Such issues have come to the fore in recent public debates, exemplified by Facebook's challenges in regulating hate speech and other damaging content. As I will delve into in Chapter 8 of this book, many large online platforms, threatened by potential governmental regulation, are gradually decentralizing their governance by transferring some responsibilities to their platform participants. This creates a third tier in the principal–agent relationship. Figure I.1 illustrates the relationship among these four key actors involved in the regulatory process.

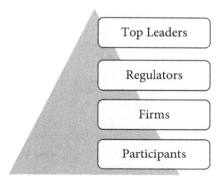

Figure I.1. The hierarchy of Chinese platform regulation.

I.1.2. Volatility

The second feature of the dynamic pyramid model is that Chinese regulation tends to be volatile, often characterized by cycles of regulatory tightening and easing. The instability of Chinese regulation is derived from three major sources.

First, the Chinese top leadership has a very complex utility function and needs to deftly navigate ever-changing societal and economic landscape to maintain its legitimacy, as will be further elaborated in Chapter 1. As the supreme leader in China's regulatory polity, the top leadership obtains its legitimacy from three primary sources—growth, stability, and nationalism. But these three sources of legitimacy are not always consistent with each other. For instance, economic growth can lead to market chaos, which threatens social stability. Heavy-handed state intervention can weaken the confidence of Chinese entrepreneurs, which in turn stifles investment and growth. Overemphasis on techno-nationalism risks discouraging foreign investment in the domestic tech industry, which could adversely affect technological growth and development. Strong government intervention to foster critical technologies could also lead to the misallocation of resources and could curb market incentives to develop other sectors. Similar to the acrobats on the high wire, the Chinese leadership thus needs to constantly balance potentially competing interests and objectives and must try to meet demands from various interest groups in the society. Indeed, Sebastian Heilmann and Elizabeth Perry have described Chinese policymaking as "guerrilla-style" adaptive governance rooted in the revolutionary times of the CCP.[57]

The second source of volatility within the Chinese regulatory system stems from the near absence of checks and balances, an inherent feature of the hierarchical regulatory structure. While the adaptability of Chinese policymakers allows them to react very quickly, their agility can also introduce further volatility into the regulatory system. The absence of formal checks and balances gives Chinese policymakers and regulators wide latitude to intervene. This enables the top leadership to quickly mobilize various bureaucratic departments to tackle regulatory problems. Meanwhile, the overwhelming power of the Chinese government means that few Chinese businesses will dare to challenge a powerful agency in court; instead, they exhibit unusual levels of cooperation with government authorities and readily accede to the latter's demands. In the absence of strong institutional constraints, agencies are able to move forward swiftly, which also entails a grave risk of administrative abuse and overreach. Indeed, as systems-theory expert Donella Meadows reminds us, quick reactions often introduce more volatility into systems, particularly when decision-makers' haste causes them to overreact, requiring ever more drastic actions to reverse the resulting impact.[58]

The third source of volatility derives from an inefficient information-transmission system. As the Chinese leadership needs to constantly balance different interests and objectives during policymaking, it is vital for them to receive accurate and timely feedback about policy implementation. However, China's hierarchical regulatory system tends to impede the free flow of information to decision-makers, making the system more prone to failures. Hayek's well-known argument favoring decentralization over centralized systems as a more effective method of integrating knowledge to resolve social issues still resonates in the Chinese context.[59] Since local authorities are much closer to the information sources, they are better situated to take prompt action to solve problems arising in their jurisdictions. However, since Xi Jinping's ascendency, decision-making in China has become notably centralized and tightly coupled. This consolidation of power at the top deprives local authorities and agencies of both the incentives and autonomy necessary to tackle vexing regulatory issues; instead, they prefer to wait for clear instructions from above. When local authorities receive clear policy signals from above, however, they tend to overact in order to demonstrate loyalty to the top. In either scenario, the agencies have strong incentives to hold back information from the top leaders.

Furthermore, in a highly charged political environment, agencies are averse to revealing bad news which might challenge the policy decisions of top leaders. As such, the top leadership may be too complacent or myopic to realize the long-term side effects of its policy initiatives. This information deficit at the top is further exacerbated by the suppression of public information in an autocratic system, making it exceedingly challenging for disempowered citizens to voice their concerns. These factors collectively contribute to delayed government responses. As will be demonstrated in Chapter 3 of the book, by the time top leaders intervene, regulatory problems have usually become very entrenched and severe, meaning that any attempt at reversal can cause significant volatility in the system.

The instability of the market then touches a sensitive nerve of the Chinese top leadership, causing it to quickly reverse course by offering to ease regulation. However, as regulatory agencies ease their oversight, the market descends into chaos again, introducing fresh regulatory challenges that could cause even more instability in the Chinese market. The Chinese adage "loosening causes chaos, tightening up causes death" (一放就乱, 一抓就死) aptly encapsulates the volatility inherent in China's regulatory cycle. This constant state of flux places Chinese regulatory authorities in an unending cycle of crisis management.

I.1.3. Fragility

The third striking characteristic of the dynamic pyramid model is the fragility manifested in regulatory outcomes. I propose evaluating policy intervention resilience through two dimensions: side effects and information lag. Side effects, or unintended consequences, denote the undesirable outcomes inadvertently resulting from governmental regulation. Greater side effects naturally lead to increased resistance toward a given regulatory measure. It's important to clarify that the severity of a side effect is not an absolute measure, but rather is assessed relative to the benefits of the corresponding regulation. As such, a regulation may lead to considerable side effects, but these can be deemed minor if the benefits derived from the regulation vastly overshadow the costs.

Information lag, or delayed awareness, refers to the interval between the implementation of a regulatory measure and the recognition of its side effects by top leadership. Several factors can contribute to this lag. For instance, side effects may not manifest immediately but gradually develop into long-term systemic issues. Consequently, there is a delay between the introduction of a regulation and the emergence of its side effects. Inefficiency in information transmission also plays a crucial role in information lag. It may be challenging to gather accurate data due to either an initial lack of relevant information or because the available data are "noisy," obfuscating the actual impact. Notably, side effects and information lag are also correlated. Everything else being equal, a prolonged information lag tends to result in larger side effects. Ultimately, the more pronounced the side effects and the longer the information delay, the more challenging it becomes to reverse course and alleviate risks, thereby generating

INTRODUCTION 15

significant unintended outcomes that undermine the original intent of regulation.

Meanwhile, hierarchy and volatility, the other two major features of the dynamic pyramid model, tend to engender fragility in regulatory outcomes. Despite the pyramidal model's unique advantage of resource mobilization for swift intervention, it can quickly become a liability in our complex, interconnected world. Measures initially intended to correct market failures can bring about enormous consequences that may not have been fully contemplated by regulators. This is particularly the problem in China given the prevalence of administrative overreach and the near absence of institutional constraints on administrative action. As a result, unforeseen consequences can easily result from well-intentioned but excessive government interventions. The hierarchical and tightly coupled system further impedes efficient information transmission when it's most needed, leading to prolonged information lag. Coupled with these information lags, the potent side effects of such regulations can precipitate severe and potentially irreparable damage.

Meanwhile, the volatility in regulatory policies can dampen investor confidence and undermine entrepreneurial spirit. Sudden policy changes can sow confusion and incite panic among both Chinese citizens and global investors. This turmoil is amplified by the opacity in law enforcement and the absence of regulatory checks and balances, causing policy shocks to potentially trigger significant repercussions in both domestic and international financial markets. Indeed, a dramatic reversal of regulatory approach can create uncertainty for investors who might misinterpret or overreact to these policy adjustments in China. This propensity for risk aversion can further amplify the side effects. As we will discuss further in Chapter 3, applying a remedy to address one problem can often provoke further problems, leaving Chinese policymakers playing a constant game of "whack-a-mole" as they try to manage ongoing crises.

Not only do hierarchy and volatility induce fragility, but fragility, in turn, can reinforce both hierarchy and volatility. First, fragile regulatory outcomes may fuel additional volatility, subsequently leading to further fragility. In the aftermath of a regulatory crisis, private businesses become more susceptible to regulatory shocks, thereby rendering any regulatory intervention potentially more disruptive in the market. While mass mobilization can aid the government in managing immediate crises, capricious and unpredictable policies undermine its credibility. Consequently, even if top leadership vows to ease stringent regulations, trust in state–business relations may not fully recover. Investors, having endured unexpected severe crackdowns, will demand a significantly higher risk premium to invest in the Chinese market. Hence, even small regulatory changes could provoke overreactions, further escalating market volatility and fragility.

Second, fragile regulatory outcomes can strengthen the hierarchy in the regulatory process, thereby creating more volatility and potentially more fragility. The retreat of the private sector in the wake of regulatory crises creates opportunities for the state sector to expand, reinforcing the hierarchy within the Chinese regulatory system, as will be demonstrated in Chapter 10. Indeed, though law enforcement campaigns may be temporary, they can catalyze lasting institutional changes, often typified by new laws with stronger legal sanctions, increased agency budgets, and expanded enforcement capacity, all of which enhance the administrative state. This expanded administrative state can foster powerful interest groups that may manipulate or withhold information to further their bureaucratic objectives, as illustrated in Chapters 3 and Chapter 9. Moreover, the suppression of private businesses creates more opportunities for the state to invest and expand, further strengthening state control. Thus, when the next crisis calls for strong state intervention, there is an even greater likelihood of agency overreach and administrative abuse. Consequently, Chinese regulatory governance becomes trapped in a self-perpetuating cycle of increasing fragility. Figure I.2 visually depicts the interconnection between these three major features of the dynamic model of regulation.

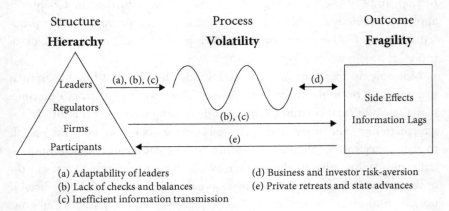

Figure I.2. The dynamic pyramid model of regulation.

INTRODUCTION

In conclusion, a complex network of feedback loops exists within the dynamic pyramid model, interlinking hierarchy, volatility, and fragility. First, the hierarchical regulatory structure can directly influence volatility in regulatory outcomes. Three main contributors to volatility in China's regulatory process—the complex utility function of the top leadership, the absence of checks and balances, and inefficient information transmission—all stem from the top-down nature of policymaking.

Second, hierarchy and volatility can jointly contribute to fragility in regulatory outcomes. The absence of institutional constraints often magnifies the unintended consequences, while the inefficient information transmission exacerbates the time lag within the regulatory hierarchy. Additionally, the unpredictable nature of Chinese regulatory policy can provoke overreaction from businesses and investors, creating a strong aversion toward the Chinese market that could further amplify the side effects.

Third, the fragility in regulatory outcomes can reciprocally impact both volatility and hierarchy. As a regulatory crisis weakens the private sector, businesses and investors grow increasingly risk-averse and sensitive to regulatory changes, thereby inducing greater volatility in future regulatory actions. Additionally, the retreat of the private sector creates more opportunities for the advancement of the administrative state, further reinforcing the hierarchical structure. This dynamic pyramid model thus predicts a direct correlation between hierarchy, volatility, and fragility. The more tightly coupled the regulatory hierarchy, the more volatile the regulatory process will become, pointing toward an increase in fragility. Thus, even if the Chinese authorities can survive the current crisis, their ability to weather future crises can deteriorate over time.

I.2. A Road Map

This book consists of four parts.

Part I, encompassing Chapters 1 through 3, lays down the analytical framework. Chapter 1 delineates the hierarchy within the Chinese regulatory process by introducing its principal actors: the top leadership, the regulators, the firms, and the platform participants. Each of these actors possesses a complex utility function. The top leadership displays considerable adaptability, skillfully balancing conflicting interests and objectives to sustain its legitimacy. Chinese regulators, on the other hand, vie relentlessly for expanded influence while simultaneously striving to sidestep political risks linked with contradicting Beijing's initiatives. This dichotomy often results in agencies either taking minimal action or overextending their reach. Chinese firms, meanwhile, demonstrate remarkable flexibility and acumen to thrive within China's unique institutional landscape. As for the platform participants, their grievances often remain unexpressed, or when articulated are often muted due to censorship and suppression.

Chapter 2 delves deeper into volatility, the second fundamental characteristic of the dynamic pyramid model of regulation. It explores the interactions between the major players and the resulting feedback loops to understand the dramatic regulatory swing as exemplified by the recent tech crackdown. Chapter 3 shifts focus to fragility, the third salient feature of the dynamic pyramid model of regulation. This chapter employs this model to analyze the dynamic complexity in the most critical policy challenges that have confronted the Chinese leadership in recent years. These include China's Covid-control measures, the energy crisis, the property crackdown, and the one-child policy. Through the analysis of the side effects and information lag during these regulatory interventions, the chapter illustrates how the dynamic pyramid model of regulation tends to culminate in fragile regulatory outcomes. Additionally, this chapter examines China's decentralized policy experiments undertaken by local governments, which have been lauded as the key contributor to the resilience of Chinese policymaking. Regrettably, in recent years, the more centralized and personalistic decision-making has replaced local reforms, contributing to increased fragilities in regulatory outcomes.

Part II, encompassing Chapters 4 through 6, applies the dynamic pyramid model to explain three major areas of regulation that have been affecting the Chinese tech sector: antitrust, data, and labor regulation. After diving deeply into each area, I find a strikingly similar pattern of enforcement dynamics: regulation was initially quite lax until Chinese regulators suddenly turned up the heat in late 2020. Although enforcement intensity has subsided since early 2022, Chinese authorities set up chilling precedents and promulgated new rules that are expected to leave long-lasting impacts on the tech industry. Moreover, in each of these areas of law, the Chinese tech firms are not the only ones at fault. The challenges in tech regulation are often exacerbated by the weak institutional environment and the government's abusive practices or inactions. As such, even with perfect regulation,

INTRODUCTION 19

it will be insufficient to provide enhanced protection for Chinese citizens and businesses.

Despite these overarching similarities, there exist variances among these enforcement areas. First, central enforcement agencies typically respond more promptly and decisively to Beijing's directives compared to local courts. As highlighted in Chapters 4 and 5, central enforcement agencies seize the initiative, undertaking aggressive actions to further their bureaucratic interests. This starkly contrasts with the responses from local courts, which tend to be symbolic, lacking substantial changes, as evidenced by my empirical evaluation of judicial decisions in labor cases in Chapter 6. Second, agencies with expansive enforcement mandates generally give more thoughtful consideration to the economic implications of their actions compared to those with narrower purviews. For example, labor regulators in China, entrusted with both labor policy formulation and job creation, typically exercise restraint in enforcement to avert drastic actions that could adversely impact employment. Conversely, data regulators, whose mandates are primarily concerned with data security and information control, have instituted sweeping regulatory measures, often without fully considering their economic consequences.

Part III, encompassing Chapters 7 and 8, examines how Chinese tech firms self-regulate in the shadow of the dynamic pyramid model of regulation. Chapter 7 addresses the limits of public regulation and explores how Chinese tech firms act as quasi-regulators of their own platforms in practice. Contrary to the common perception of the predatory nature of Chinese state intervention, Part III reveals the tremendous judicial resources that have been invested to prop up the digital economy. In fact, the Chinese judiciary and online platforms could be more accurately described as having closely co-regulated to create a credible enforcement system for online platforms. This stands in a sharp contrast to Part II, where Chinese regulators often act in a predatory nature by advancing their bureaucratic interests at the expense of the firms. Here the participation of the Chinese judiciary in the regulatory process actually proves beneficial to the growth of the platform economy. Inasmuch as the Chinese state extends vital judicial support for private internet businesses, it demonstrates another important facet of public regulation—the "helping hand," in that the government is intimately involved in promoting business activities.

Chapter 8 studies an intriguing phenomenon of how Chinese online platforms are increasingly decentralizing their governance to enhance the efficiency and legitimacy of their decision-making. Using the innovative dispute-resolution schemes recently adopted by leading Chinese online platforms as examples, this chapter illustrates how Chinese tech firms have attempted to use crowd-sourcing mechanisms to increase user participation and improve due process. These legal innovations have significantly improved the efficiency of dispute resolution. They also help platforms enhance their legitimacy by diffusing tensions while proactively shaping the policy debate. Compared with their Western peers, Chinese online platforms have a greater incentive to delegate their authority to platform participants to stave off unfavorable regulation. Hence arises the key dichotomy in platform regulation: the more authoritarian the state regulation is, the more democratic the platform's self-regulation will be. Volatile and unpredictable public regulation can therefore incentivize online platforms to commit to more transparent and engaged self-regulation.

Part IV, encompassing Chapters 9 through 11, assesses the impact of the tech crackdown and examines the path forward. Chapter 9 delves into the evolving legal landscapes of the United States and the European Union concerning antitrust, data, and labor regulation. This comparative analysis reveals that China is, in fact, a late arrival in reigning in Big Tech, with many of its regulatory measures mirroring those of its Western counterparts. The understanding of global regulatory trends also sheds light on the future direction of Chinese legal developments. First, there is regulatory interdependence between nations. For instance, in response to the trend of aggressive assertions of data sovereignty in Western jurisdictions, China has increasingly used data outflow control as a negotiation tool with other countries. Second, the global drive to regulate Big Tech could exert strong spillover effects in China. Dynamic legal developments overseas could provide persuasive arguments for interest groups to push for more stringent regulation, despite the easing of tech regulation since early 2022.

Chapter 10 assesses the impact of China's great reversal in regulating its platform economy. This chapter shows that a significant repercussion of the regulatory crackdown has been the retreat of the private sector and the rise of the administrative state. Over the past few years, Chinese Big Tech firms have strategically withdrawn from non-core operational areas and have undertaken massive restructuring in a bid to alleviate Beijing's concerns about their widespread influence. While many of these actions were driven by valid regulatory concerns, the crackdown has resulted in substantial unintended consequences without significantly enhancing competition or facilitating new sector entries. Simultaneously, the state sector has benefited by acquiring more strategic stakes and gaining more leverage in directing investment flows toward cutting-edged technologies.

Chapter 11 looks ahead, providing cautious predictions about the future of tech governance in China. As China rallies societal efforts to foster the advancement of cutting-edge technologies, it raises a profound question regarding the future trajectory of Chinese tech regulation. To navigate this issue, we probe into China's recent foray into regulating the rapidly growing sphere of generative artificial intelligence (AI). Applying the dynamic pyramid model of regulation, this chapter scrutinizes the motives and conduct of the key players involved in the regulatory process. It proposes that the Chinese government is unlikely to adopt a stringent stance that could obstruct the progression of its AI industry. Instead, it predicts that regulatory attention will primarily concentrate on information and content control, aiming to mitigate threats to societal and political stability. Consequently, even though the Cyberspace Administration of China is introducing seemingly strict and comprehensive measures to regulate generative AI, they actually afford Chinese tech companies significant leeway to innovate and prosper within the sector.

PART I

Analytical Framework

This Part, consisting of Chapters 1–3, establishes the analytical framework by elaborating on the three unique features of China's dynamic pyramid model of regulation: hierarchy, volatility, and fragility. Chapter 1 elucidates the hierarchical structure of the Chinese regulatory system, introducing its primary actors: the top leadership, regulators, firms, and platform participants. Chapter 2 delves into the volatility of China's regulatory process by examining the interactions between these major players and the resulting feedback loops, using the recent tech crackdown as a detailed case study. Chapter 3 examines the consequences of Chinese regulation by explaining its tendency to yield fragile policy outcome, as evidenced by the significant policy challenges that have confronted the Chinese leadership in recent years.

1

Hierarchy

The dynamic pyramid model is inspired by systems thinking, which sees our world as a highly interconnected and dynamic system. As Donella Meadows explains, a system is not just a random set of things, but rather an interconnected set of elements that is coherently organized for a particular purpose.[1] Examples that Meadows gives include our digestive system, a football team, a school, a city, an animal, a tree, a forest, and a corporation, all of which have interconnected elements that achieve a specific purpose. I similarly view a country's regulatory governance as a system in that it comprises multiple players who are interconnected via the society's formal and informal rules. In the case of tech regulation, the regulatory system consists of four major players: the top leaders that sit at the apex of Chinese political hierarchy; the regulators overseeing a particular industry sector; the tech firms subject to regulation; and the various platform participants at the bottom of the hierarchy.

Given the constant interactions and feedback among these four major players, Chinese regulatory governance is inherently complex; a major goal of the dynamic pyramid model is to unravel this complexity and clarify the intricacies of the regulatory process.[2] Indeed, the fluid regulatory outcomes that we observe on the surface are not the result of the actions of a single actor's, but rather stem from the interaction among multiple actors with complicated utility functions and simultaneously overlapping and conflicting interests, as well as from the accompanying feedback loops. As such, how information flows through these different tiers of actors becomes an overarching factor affecting the efficiency of this governance model, a topic I will discuss further in Chapter 2.

It is also important to note that while the dynamic pyramid model emphasizes the four major players in the tech regulation process, there may

High Wire. Angela Huyue Zhang, Oxford University Press. © Oxford University Press 2024.
DOI: 10.1093/oso/9780197682258.003.0002

1.1. Top Leadership

The contemporary Chinese leadership derives its legitimacy primarily from three main sources: growth, social stability, and nationalism.[3] These three goals are not necessarily consistent with each other, and in some circumstances may well undercut each other. Indeed, governing a large country like China is a daunting task, and the Chinese Communist Party (CCP) needs to constantly balance competing interests and objectives stemming from these three sources of legitimacy. This demands a high degree of adaptability from the top leadership. As Andrew Nathan once observed: "the authoritarian regime must perform constantly like a team of acrobats on a high wire, staving off all crises while keeping its act flawlessly together."[4]

To begin with, economic growth is crucial for the performance legitimacy of the CCP. However, after decades of double-digit GDP growth, there is increasing evidence that aggregate growth matters less for the CCP's performance legitimacy than the growth for individual citizens.[5] Bruce Dickson, a renowned political scientist, found that neither the level of per capita GDP growth nor the rate of total GDP growth increases trust and support for the CCP.[6] Instead, those individuals who have seen their incomes increase in recent years and are optimistic about such growth prospects are more likely to support the regime.[7] This led him to conclude that slower economic growth is not necessarily a threat to public support as long as the prospect of increased individual income continues to exist. Dickson's analysis helps explain the growing emphasis on "common prosperity" by the top leadership. Although growth is the prerequisite for prosperity, the emphasis on common prosperity also shows that the government is shifting its priority from creating wealth to redistributing wealth.

The second main pillar of the CCP's performance legitimacy is stability. Economic growth tends to bring about market disorder, which pushes society toward more government intervention and stronger state control.[8]

Yet state control is not always benign, and can easily be abused. As a result, countries need to make a delicate trade-off between the two goals of controlling market disorder and restraining the abuse of state intervention.[9] The rapid growth of the Chinese platform economy has brought about market chaos that is spiraling into a series of social and economic crises. As we will see in Chapters 4–8, consumer fraud, monopolistic practices, infringements of consumer privacy, and unfair exploitation of workers and employees are rampant in China. Unfortunately, the existing regulatory framework appears inadequate for dealing with issues arising from the new economy. What also worries Chinese policymakers is that Big Tech companies have the power to sway public opinion by commanding the attention of a large population of Chinese citizens. Concurrently, large and powerful platform businesses also have the incentive and ability to lobby and capture the regulators. This partly explains the CCP's strong urge to regulate the platform economy. The rise of the Chinese regulatory state, however, has not been accompanied by strong institutional checks on agency performance. As the Chinese regulatory authorities acquire more responsiveness capacity, their capacity for repressiveness increases simultaneously.[10]

The last pillar of the CCP's performance legitimacy is nationalism.[11] Research has long identified a close link between patriotic sentiments and regime support.[12] When the CCP rose to power in 1949, it vowed to end the "century of national humiliation" inflicted on China by Western powers and portrayed itself as the only modern Chinese political party with the power to stand up to foreign aggression.[13] President Xi Jinping's call for a great rejuvenation of the Chinese nation is aimed at instilling pride in the shared identity of the Chinese people. In recent years, however, aggressive US sanctions and restrictions on Chinese tech firms such as Huawei and ZTE have exposed China's vulnerability in the global technological supply chain. These incidents were a wake-up call for the Chinese leadership, which has since placed greater emphasis on technological self-sufficiency. US economic sanctions have also generated a "sputnik moment" for China, spurring a wave of Chinese investment in foundational science and technologies to close the technological gap with the United States.[14]

In the meantime, these three sources of legitimacy are not always consistent with each other. For instance, economic growth can lead to market chaos, thereby undermining social stability. Heavy-handed state intervention can weaken the confidence of Chinese entrepreneurs, which in turn stifles investment and growth. Overemphasis on techno-nationalism risks discouraging foreign investment in the domestic tech industry, which could adversely affect technological growth and development. Strong government intervention to foster critical technologies could also lead to the misallocation of resources and could curb market incentives to develop other sectors.

In recent years, falling GDP growth and slowing economic achievement in China appear to have incentivized the CCP leadership to seek legitimacy in other ways. These include beefing up nationalistic achievements and imposing stricter social controls and surveillance to ensure stability in recent years. Similar to the acrobats on the high wire, the Chinese leadership thus needs to constantly balance potentially competing interests and objectives and try to meet demands from various interest groups in the society. Indeed, Sebastian Heilmann and Elizabeth Perry have described Chinese policymaking as "guerrilla-style" adaptive governance rooted in the revolutionary times of the CCP.[15] They attributed the resilience of the CCP ruling to its adaptability, which enables it to effectively meet challenges in changing times.[16]

1.2. Regulators

While policies from the top leadership tend to capture most of the attention, it is the regulators that are doing most of the work since they are in charge of implementing the day-to-day enforcement of the law. Understanding the bureaucratic politics within these agencies is therefore crucial for us to understand the regulatory outcomes. To begin, China has a vast bureaucracy. The official organizational chart reveals that the Chinese bureaucracy is divided into a central government, including the State Council and various ministries, and local governments, including provinces, cities, counties, and townships. In practice, however, both central ministries and the local governments are subordinate to the top leadership in Beijing.[17] Using a principal–agent model, Yasheng Huang divides the Chinese bureaucracy into two levels. The "control level" consists of the Politburo and State Council, which sit at the top of China's political hierarchy, while the "controlled level" comprises various ministerial and local agencies.

The logic behind this division is twofold: first, the agencies at the control level decide who runs the agencies at the controlled level; second, the preference divergence is sharpest between these two levels.[18] Each of the ministries has well-defined functions and each of the provinces has its own territorial interests. Accordingly, these distinct actors often pursue their own interests at the expense of the interests of the system as a whole.[19] Moreover, each of the ministries and provinces has relative autonomy in managing its own affairs, including the control of its own personnel. Since 1984, the CCP has allowed the control level to appoint only the top-level officials at the controlled level (i.e., ministers and provincial heads).[20] In other words, according to this so-called one-rank-down nomenklatura system, the appointments to all but the top-level positions are controlled from within the controlled level.

At the central level, China has 45 ministerial-level agencies, institutions, and organizations in charge of various aspects of the social, economic, and political governance of the country. Based on the data I have gathered from public sources (which do not include those relating to foreign policies and security), the largest ministries include the National Development and Reform Commission (NDRC), with 1,029 staff members; the China Banking and Insurance Regulatory Commission (CBIRC), with 925; the Ministry of Commerce (MOFCOM), with 905; the General Administration of Customs, with 847; the State Administration for Market Regulation (SAMR), with 805; the People's Bank of China (PBOC), with 779; the Ministry of Industry and Information Technology (MIIT), with 731; the Ministry of Finance, with 698; the Ministry of Natural Resources, with 691; and the Ministry of Transport (MOT), with 664.[21] Given that the staff quota is a crucial administrative resource for a ministry, staffing numbers represent a useful proxy to gauge a given ministry's political clout.

As many Chinese scholars have observed, power is very fragmented within the Chinese bureaucracy.[22] While each regulatory agency is responsible for overseeing a specific area, their regulatory functions frequently overlap. In the most recent round of the law-enforcement campaign against Big Tech, at least 14 central ministries joined the Supreme People's Court and a number of other CCP and social organizations in helping to devise new legislative proposals and implement policy guidance from above (see Appendix 1.1). In the area of antitrust, the main authority in charge is the SAMR. But this agency is not completely independent, and other agencies such as the NDRC and the MIIT can also interfere with its policymaking.[23] In the area of fintech regulation, the two major financial regulators, the PBOC and the CBIRC, are concurrently involved. In the area of data regulation, the Cyberspace Administration of China (CAC) is the main agency coordinating enforcement among several central ministries including the MIIT, the Public Security Bureau (PSB), and the SAMR, as well as a vast array of sector regulators.[24] In the area of labor regulation, a patchwork of central authorities are involved, including the Ministry of Human Resources and Social Security (MOHRSS), the MOT, the Ministry of Emergency Management (MEM), the State Post Bureau (SPB), the Supreme People's Court (SPC), and the All-China Federation of Trade Unions (ACFTU).

The above division of labor and organizational setup is roughly replicated at the local level. In the area of antitrust, a number of SAMR's provincial agencies such as those in Jiangsu, Zhejiang, and Shanghai have been quite active in antitrust enforcement. In the areas of data regulation, local authorities including those in Shanghai and Shenzhen have both rolled out new data legislation governing their local regions. Local governments and courts have been the dominant players behind the enforcement of Chinese labor regulations. For instance, wealthy regions such as Zhejiang and Guangdong were the first to initiate experiments to improve insurance protections for gig workers. Each of the relevant enforcement frameworks in data, antitrust, and labor regulation will be elaborated upon in Chapters 4 through 6.

This power fragmentation has given rise to relentless competition among Chinese regulators vying for policy control.[25] In China, policy control is a crucial asset because it enables regulatory authorities to gain political support from their patronage networks and increases rent-seeking opportunities. The more control an agency has over an important policy area, the more likely it is that the agency can capitalize on its control to accumulate administrative merit, thus paving the way for the agency head to rise to the top level of the CCP hierarchy. In these ways, Chinese regulators are naturally inclined toward maximizing their bureaucratic interests within their specific scope of responsibility. The prioritization of these bureaucratic interests also helps explain why regulators tend to focus on short-term and narrow objectives without necessarily considering their broader implications for the whole society.

And yet, paradoxically, while Chinese regulators have significant incentives to expand their turf, they also have a strong incentive to do little, in an attempt to avoid political risk, particularly when they are concerned that their regulatory actions might contravene central initiatives. Since President Xi came into power, his administration has significantly tightened control over the bureaucratic apparatus. The Xi administration also invigorated ideological training and imposed stricter disciplinary measures over government officials.[26] In line with this trend, government officials have faced greater pressures to demonstrate loyalty and adherence to the top Chinese leadership in recent years. Since 2012, the Xi government has also launched a massive anti-corruption crackdown that is unprecedented in terms of its scale and scope. Over the past decade, the Central Commission for Discipline Inspection, the CCP's anti-graft agency, has investigated 4 million cadres, including 500 senior officials, and has expelled 900,000 of them from the CCP.[27] Studies have shown that the chilling effects of the anti-corruption campaign has contributed to bureaucratic slack.[28] With officials struggling to figure out how to please their bosses, reluctance to implement new initiatives and facilitate policy implementation has permeated the regulatory apparatus. "Lazy governance" became commonplace as officials opted to do as little as possible in order to avoid blame and punishment.[29] "Not hoping for merit, just avoiding risk" has become a popular survival strategy among Chinese bureaucrats.[30]

At the same time, when agencies receive clear signals about policy tightening from the top leadership, they subsequently try to actively display their loyalty to the top leadership by taking swift legislative and enforcement actions. Due to the power imbalance between businesses and the state in China, administrative authorities are seldom challenged publicly and thus are subject to little judicial scrutiny. Ambitious administrative authorities tend to overreach in order to obtain more political credits, which can be cashed in for more policy control. Paradoxically, this dynamic has meant that Chinese officials either do too little or too much, in what amounts to a dramatic regulatory pendulum swing.

1.3. Firms

Like most businesses, Chinese tech firms have a simple goal—increase their market shares by gaining more user attention and then boost their profits. In order to survive and even thrive in China, Chinese tech firms have learned to be very flexible. Many of them adapt to China's weak institutional environment through three major survival strategies: regulatory arbitrage, "fake it till you make it," and crony capitalism, each of which is elaborated below.

1.3.1. Regulatory Arbitrage

Regulatory arbitrage is a practice whereby firms try to circumvent unfavorable laws by exploiting legal loopholes. Chinese tech firms are very adept at regulatory arbitrage by innovating at a very rapid speed to take advantage of the gaps in existing regulations. This phenomenon is certainly not unique to Chinese firms—Elizabeth Pollman and Jordan Barry have shown that US tech firms such as Uber and Airbnb have resided in legal gray areas and have engaged in aggressive lobbying to change the law.[31] Although Chinese tech firms do not necessarily aim to change the law, they have similarly adopted an "invest first and get approval later" strategy. As many of their products or services seem not to fit neatly into the frameworks of existing regulation, it is not entirely clear which regulator is in charge of overseeing the problems they create. The bureaucratic inertia we observe in the Chinese context thus further contributes to a regulatory vacuum. Because timing is crucial for tech firms to capture the market, it is extremely important for Chinese tech firms to gain first-mover advantage by entering the market and becoming the market leader. They can then start lobbying the government for its support and endorsement the moment their businesses start to expand and grow. Even when tech firms take the initiative without gaining the necessary approval from the government, their legal violations will not cause significant disruption to their businesses as long as the resultant legal penalties are manageable.

The Chinese fintech sector offers excellent examples of this strategy. Alipay, one of the two major online payment platforms in China, provides consumer-to-merchant money transfers on its e-commerce platform. It also provides escrow services for Taobao consumers, only releasing payments to sellers after buyers receive the goods they have ordered. This important innovation has facilitated Taobao's exponential growth by resolving the intrinsic mistrust between the transacting parties. However, before Alipay's arrival, third-party payment had been a legal gray area in China. Jack Ma, the platform's founder, was even prepared to go to jail for launching this service.[32] But Ma's gamble paid off. Alipay became widely popular and ultimately won the endorsement of the regulators. In 2010, the PBOC issued administrative measures on non-financial payment services and their implementation, thus retroactively recognizing the legal status of online payment platforms such as Alipay.[33] The following year, Alipay obtained a payment business license as one of the first non-financial institutions to conduct payment operations.[34]

Yu'e Bao, an online money-market fund introduced by Alibaba in 2013, offers another example. Yu'e Bao allowed Alipay customers to deposit the money left in their accounts to earn interest rates higher than those offered by banks.[35] It soon became China's largest online market fund, one whose explosive growth surprised industry participants and stimulated new entrants from other tech firms such as Baidu and Tencent.[36] Although Chinese financial regulators were under pressure to impose regulatory restrictions on Yu'e Bao, it wasn't until 2017 that the PBOC started to impose limits to regulate the fund.[37] In effect, the central bank was supporting the growth of Yu'e Bao during its early days as a means of pushing forward financial-market liberalization.[38]

1.3.2. "Fake It Till You Make It"

The second important survival strategy for Chinese firms is "fake it till you make it." This refers to a business culture in which entrepreneurs pretend to be successful until they can finally provide proof of actual success. To be sure, Silicon Valley is full of "fake it till you make it" stories, as epitomized by the conviction of Elizabeth Holmes, the founder of the bogus blood-testing startup Theranos.[39] Fraud is much more prevalent in China, however, due to its weak legal institutions, a point I will further illustrate in Chapters 7 and 8.

Consider the example of Taobao, China's largest e-commerce retailer. Just as other online retailers have done, Taobao set up a reputation mechanism, allowing customers to post reviews of their purchases. Unfortunately, fake promotional reviews are extremely common in China.[40] In 2014, an executive at Alibaba disclosed that 17 percent of all merchants on Taobao had forged close to 500 million transactions, adding that these were only the "tip of the iceberg" and that there were tens of thousands of people in China contributing to fake sales online.[41] Certain estimates indicate that 80 percent of Taobao sellers have committed trust fraud at some stage of their business operations.[42] The pervasiveness of this problem has led to situations in which top sellers feel they have no choice but to use fake promotional reviews in order to defend themselves and maintain their rankings.[43]

Chinese e-commerce platforms are also notorious for selling counterfeit products. China's massive copycat industry has been incredibly quick at churning out *shanzhai* products—that is, products that typically imitate the visual appearance and function of leading luxury fashion brands as well as high-end electronic products.[44] A recent well-known example of a platform selling *shanzhai* products is Pinduoduo, which has been heavily criticized in the Chinese media for hawking low-price knockoffs resembling well-known brands. Days after Pinduoduo listed on the Nasdaq stock exchange in 2018, the SAMR, China's market-supervision watchdog, announced probes into the firm amid reports of rampant counterfeits on its website.[45] Huang Zheng, the platform's founder and CEO, responded by saying that his firm had stepped up its efforts to tackle the sale of counterfeit products, but also stressed that *shanzhai* products should not be confused with counterfeits.[46]

1.3.3. Crony Capitalism

As a result of their regulatory arbitrage and "fake it till you make it" strategies, Chinese businesses are particularly vulnerable to regulatory attacks.[47] This inherent insecurity has driven them to seek political protection. Although China's legal institutions have significantly improved since the country embarked on market reforms, formal institutional protection for private firms remains weak. The World Bank's index of Doing Business Indicators ranked China near the bottom in terms of the ease of starting a business.[48] Nevertheless, private businesses have been able to flourish in China despite poor legal-institutional protection. Economists have attributed this paradox to the prevalence of informal institutions, which they call "special deals," facilitated by local political leaders.[49] Chong-En Bai, Chang-Tai Hsieh, and Michael Song have shown that local governments possess tremendous administrative capacity, which enables them to give a "helping hand" to favored firms, for instance in the form of an exemption from regulation.[50] Local regulators have an enormous incentive to provide such "special deals," given that the support of local champions can form part of their administrative merit, while also allowing officials to extract more rent from favored firms.[51]

Such "special deals" are observed not only among local officials, but also among senior leaders in Beijing.[52] One common form of crony capitalism can be seen in the way in which Chinese businesses share ownership stakes with the so-called princelings and state-owned enterprises (SOEs).[53] Because princelings have strong personal connections with the top leadership while SOEs enjoy high bureaucratic status, both can act as political intermediaries more easily able to provide Chinese firms with opportunities to lobby for favorable government policies In fact, many princelings who work in private equity or venture capital are offered the opportunity to invest in tech firms at an early stage, thus allowing them to reap bonanzas when the firms become public.[54] As Lulu Chen, a veteran journalist covering Chinese tech, wrote in her new book *Influence Empire*: "Tech has been a goldmine, especially in the mobile internet, for a plethora of the princelings operating within China's political apparatus. Venture capital firms actually make a point of hiring those luminaries to amass political clout."[55] Investments by these political intermediaries offer an important form of protection for Chinese tech firms. Since any harsh regulatory interventions into the activities of tech firms will negatively impact investments made by political intermediaries, the regulatory authorities tend to be more reluctant to act against them, especially in the absence of a strong and clear policy signal from the top. As one official put it, regulating Chinese internet businesses is like poking a hornet's nest as "every company has a powerful investor who has powerful allies even higher up."[56] This "ownership-sharing scheme" effectively aligns the interests of Chinese tech firms with those of the political elites who can exert influence on the bureaucracy.

Ant Group, China's largest fintech giant, offers a notable example of this trend. According to reports, one reason why the CCP leadership decided to suspend Ant's initial public offering (IPO) was growing unease regarding the firm's complex ownership structure.[57] An investigation by the central government revealed that a group of well-connected Chinese political elite entities had invested in Ant, as had China's national pension fund and several large state-owned banks and investment companies.[58] Alibaba is another example. When Alibaba first went public in 2014, the *New York Times* ran a sensational report about investment from Chinese political elites in the e-commerce giant.[59] As one analyst put it: "It would take, at this point, a seismic effort to topple an Alibaba. They've got so many different allies across so many different ministries."[60]

1.4. Platform Participants

Generally speaking, platform participants do not play a prominent role in China's regulatory process. Because many of the transactions that occur online only involve small-value claims, consumers generally do not find it worthwhile to make formal complaints to public institutions such as administrative agencies or courts.[61] As Van Loo succinctly observes: "for these [small-value transactional disputes], unlike in contexts typically studied, the corporation is the closest thing to a courthouse that most consumers will encounter."[62] As I will further elaborate in Chapters 4 and 5, most platform participants rely very heavily on a platform's internal dispute-resolution process to settle their conflicts, thus making the platform a quasi-regulator.

When high-stakes disputes between platforms and their participants arise, the latter have a strong incentive to speak out about their grievances. However, widespread censorship and suppression of human rights make it extremely difficult for platform participants to voice dissent. As a result, they need to cry out their grievances or make violent protests for their claims to be noticed and heard by the regulators.[63] Interestingly, platform participants in China often do not resort to formal public institutions, but rather protest through informal institutions. For instance, when Taobao raised the access fees for its online merchants in 2013, thousands of merchants protested by sabotaging and paralyzing Taobao's online review mechanism. This attracted attention from the regulator, who eventually intervened and resolved the matter in favor of the merchants, an incident I will discuss further in Chapter 8. The victory of the Taobao merchants was, however, a rare success. Very often, the collective actions of platform participants are suppressed in China due to tight and pervasive censorship and intolerance of civic organizations. As will be illustrated in Chapter 6, delivery drivers have in the past organized unions or strikes in order to collectively negotiate with the tech giants or enhance their bargaining position.[64] And yet, local governments have been known to crack down on such efforts for fear of social instability.[65] The suppression of protests from informal labor unions has made it even harder for delivery workers to voice grievances. Some helpless delivery workers have resorted to extreme measures. In early 2021, a delivery worker set himself on fire after a dispatch agency employed by the food-delivery platform Ele.me refused to pay him his wages because he switched to another platform.[66] This tragic news went viral on social media, further fueling public discontent with delivery platforms. It should be noted that platform workers in Western countries have also faced hurdles in their attempts to challenge platform practices. However, as compared with their counterparts in China, civic associations and activists in the West have generally been more successful in pushing for institutional changes to regulate businesses.[67]

Pervasive censorship notwithstanding, the top Chinese leadership is responsive to public demands and allows limited political participation.[68] This is primarily due to the following factors: first, the top leadership needs to collect information from its citizens in order to curb agency problems;[69] second, as scholars have found, only specific kinds of dissent can threaten the survival of the authoritarian regime.[70] As such, the central government limits its censoring of politically sensitive information, which can in fact help the government stay responsive to public discontent before it erupts into crises.[71] In fact, Chinese regulatory authorities may tolerate or even provoke nationalistic sentiments in order to rally popular support and enhance the legitimacy of its regulatory actions.[72] To be sure, the Chinese leadership recognizes that nationalism is a double-edged sword that can also reveal the weakness of the regime and might pose a threat to political and social stability.[73] The top Chinese leadership must therefore strike a delicate balance between allowing public grievances to be aired while suppressing those that might be viewed as a threat to its rule.

1.5. Summary

This chapter began by introducing the four major actors in the dynamic pyramid model: the top leadership, the regulators, the firms, and the platform participants. The top leadership has a complicated utility function. In order to stay in power, they need to maintain their performance legitimacy derived from three main sources: economic growth, social stability, and national cohesion. These objectives often undercut each other and thus the top leaders need to constantly balance different interests and objectives in the society. Chinese regulators, on the other hand, are nested within a vast bureaucracy where power is highly fragmented. While agencies are in a relentless competition for policy control, they are also extremely risk-averse.

Until agencies receive clear signals from the top leadership, they avoid taking drastic enforcement actions that might be deemed contradictory to the central policy initiatives. However, once these agencies are mobilized to take action, they tend to overreach. This results in a paradoxical phenomenon that regulators either do very little, or do too much.

In the face of harsh regulatory crackdowns, Chinese firms have appeared much more obedient than their Western counterparts. However, they are far from being passive actors. In order to adapt to China's unique institutional environment plagued by endemic fraud and corruption, Chinese tech firms have relied upon three main strategies to survive and thrive in the Chinese market: regulatory arbitrage, "fake it till you make it," and crony capitalism. Platform participants typically don't express their grievances as most online disputes involve only low-value claims. However, when embroiled in high-stake disputes with a platform or other participants, their voices tend to be stifled due to censorship and suppression. That said, Chinese regulators can tolerate or even provoke nationalistic sentiments in order to bolster their own legitimacy. In the next chapter, we will explore how the interactions between these major actors and the accompanying feedback loops can lead to extreme volatility in the regulation of Chinese Big Tech.

Appendix 1.1 Central Ministries and Other Organizations in Charge of Platform Regulation

Bureaucratic Status	Name of Organization	Functions & Responsibilities	Areas of Regulation
Central Ministry	General Office of the State Council of the People's Republic of China	Preparing meetings of the State Council, assisting the State Council leadership in reviewing or drafting official State Council documents, studying and reviewing issues between governments at all levels and departments of the State Council, and making recommendations to the State Council leadership.	Overseas listing
Central Ministry	State Administration for Market Regulation (SAMR)	Comprehensive supervision and management of the market and unified registration of market entities, unified enforcement of antitrust, and supervision and management of product quality.	Antitrust, Data, Labour
Central Ministry	National Development and Reform Commission (NDRC)	Formulating and organizing the implementation of planning for national economic and social development, reforming and opening up the economic system, drafting relevant laws and regulations, and promoting the implementation of sustainable development strategies and innovation-driven development strategies.	Antitrust, Data, Labour
Central Ministry	China Banking and Insurance Regulatory Commission (CBIRC)	Supervising and managing the banking and insurance sectors nationwide and conducting systematic studies on their open management, participating in the drafting of relevant laws and regulations, and formulating rules for the prudential regulation, and conducting supervision of the banking and insurance sectors.	Fintech, Data
Central Ministry	People's Bank of China (PBOC)	Formulating and implementing monetary policy and credit policy, formulating plans for the reform, opening up, and development of the financial sector, supervising financial markets, formulating and implementing exchange-rate policy, issuing the RMB, and managing the State Treasury.	Fintech, Data

(continued)

Bureaucratic Status	Name of Organization	Functions & Responsibilities	Areas of Regulation
Central Ministry	Ministry of Commerce (MOFCOM)	Formulating strategic plans for national finance and taxation, drafting relevant laws and regulations, drafting the central financial budget and final accounts, supervising the central financial expenditure, and auditing the budget and accounts of the state capital and the national social insurance fund.	Data, Labour
Central Ministry	Cyberspace Administration of China (CAC)	Implementing Internet information-dissemination guidelines and policies, strengthening internet information-content management, approving and supervising network news businesses, and investigating and dealing with illegal and non-compliant websites.	Data
Central Ministry	Ministry of Industry and Information Technology (MIIT)	Studying and proposing industrial-development strategies; formulating industry planning and industrial policies and organizing their implementation; directing the formulation of technical regulations and industry standards for industry; and approving fixed-asset investment projects in industry, communications, and information technology.	Data, Antitrust
Central Ministry	Ministry of Public Security (MPS)	Undertaking functions including counter-espionage, intelligence gathering, and maintaining political and overseas security.	Data
Central Ministry	Ministry of Transport (MOT)	Planning and coordinating the integrated transport system; guiding the planning and management of transport hubs; and supervising the implementation of industry planning, policies, and standards for highways, waterways, and civil aviation.	Labour
Central Ministry	Ministry of Emergency Management (MEM)	Organizing the preparation of overall national emergency plans and planning, guiding the work of all regions and departments in responding to emergencies, promoting the construction of emergency plan systems and plan exercises, and building disaster prevention and relief systems	Labour

Central Ministry	Ministry of Human Resources and Social Security (MOHRSS)	Formulating human-resources and social-security policy-development plans, promoting employment, establishing a multi-level social security system in urban and rural areas, and formulating income policies for personnel in institutions.	Labour
Central Ministry	Ministry of Education (MOE)	Formulating guidelines for educational reform and development, teaching requirements and relevant laws and regulations, and guidelines for national language and writing work.	Online tutoring
Central Ministry	China Securities Regulatory Commission (CSRC)	Managing the securities and futures markets; formulating relevant policies, laws and regulations; and regulating listed companies, securities, and futures exchanges, as well as the issuance of shares and overseas listings of domestic enterprises.	Overseas listing
Vice Presidential Status	Supreme People's Court (SPC)	Hearing certain types of cases, formulating judicial interpretations, supervising the trials of local people's courts at all levels and of specialized people's courts, and managing the judicial administration of the courts nationwide.	Labour
Vice Ministry	State Post Bureau (SPB)	Overseeing the national postal industry as well as national postal enterprises, formulating postal-industry development strategies and policies and drafting relevant laws and regulations, and managing the postal market.	Labour
Equivalent to Central Ministry	Central Propaganda Department (CCPPD)	Overseeing ideological and press work nationwide; guiding national theoretical research; directing public opinion; planning overall ideological and political tasks; and censoring national press, publishing, television, and film.	Labour
Social organization under CCP Leadership	All China Federation of Trade Unions (ACFTU)	Leading local trade unions and industrial unions, conducting investigations and studies on major issues relating to the legitimate rights and interests of workers, formulating relevant laws and regulations, and assisting trade-union leaders at all levels.	Labour
Central Ministry	State Taxation Administration (STA)	Drafting and implementing tax laws and regulations, making tax-policy recommendations, collecting taxes, and organizing and implementing reforms to the tax collection and management system.	Tax

2

Volatility

In Chapter 1, I introduced the four major players in the dynamic pyramid model. I argued that Chinese tech regulation should be viewed as a complex system involving dynamic interactions between and among four players from different tiers of the Chinese polity. This chapter will delve further into these interactions. I will show that changes in one player's behavior can immediately affect how other actors in the system behave, thus creating a chain reaction. A reaction of this kind need not solely impact the targeted industry, but can also have strong ripple effects across many other parts of the economy. A feedback loop is formed when the player who first initiates the action receives information regarding its action that might cause it to change or adjust its behavior. Such changes in how actors behave give rise to the volatility that is the focus of this chapter.

Indeed, the dynamic pyramid model of regulation is inherently unstable, with its volatility stemming from three major sources. The first source of volatility derives from the complex utility function of the top leadership, whose performance legitimacy hinges upon their achievements in three dimensions: economic growth, social stability, and national cohesion. While each of these three goals is vital for their legitimacy, the top leadership will often need to strike a delicate balance between and among them. High economic growth could lead to market chaos that threatens social stability. Harsh government intervention to curb market disorder, on the other hand, can undermine investor sentiments and curb economic growth. Similarly, strong emphasis on national cohesion can deter foreign investment, and nationalism can threaten social stability. Consequently, the top Chinese leadership will need to constantly adapt their goals according to the changing political and economic circumstances.

High Wire. Angela Huyue Zhang, Oxford University Press. © Oxford University Press 2024.
DOI: 10.1093/oso/9780197682258.003.0003

The second source of volatility is the absence of institutional checks and balances in China's regulatory system. During a severe regulatory crisis, Chinese policymakers mobilize the country's vast bureaucracy to tackle a particular regulatory challenge. Without strong institutional safeguards, regulatory agencies are able to move forward quickly. But quick and unconstrained agency intervention often comes with a grave risk of administrative abuse. Although informal institutions can eventually counteract agency overreach, as I will explain below, the overreaction of an agency already results in a dramatic policy swing, which means that a course correction could introduce further volatility in the system.

The third source of volatility arises from the inefficient information transmission within the regulatory hierarchy. The top leadership, despite possessing supreme power, remains distant from the sources of emerging problems. As such, Chinese leaders will need to rely on the information passed on from the bureaucracy before making decisions. As discussed in Chapter 1, in a highly politically charged environment, bureaucrats are extremely risk-averse and try to err on the side of caution by doing as little as possible when the policy signal is unclear. As soon as they receive clear signals from above, they tend to act zealously to demonstrate their loyalty to the top. This results in a paradoxical phenomenon that sees bureaucrats either do very little or do too much. In either case, bureaucrats have the strong incentive to delay or distort the information, creating noisy feedback. The suppression of public grievances in China further aggravates the information deficit at the top, causing the top leaders to become too complacent with their policy decisions. By the time the top leaders realize their policy missteps, the existing problem has often already loomed into a crisis. The top leadership must then intervene rapidly, sending strong signals of either policy tightening or loosening, which introduces dramatic policy swings.

The tech crackdown in China, which extended from late 2020 to early 2022, provides an excellent example of the volatility inherent in the dynamic pyramid model of Chinese regulatory governance.

2.1. Phase One: Lax Regulation

As Avinash Dixit is fond of reminding us, the law is never complete, as it cannot possibly anticipate all contingencies.[1] This is particularly the case for disruptive technologies such as online platforms, which have grown so rapidly that existing rules and regulations often fail to cover their innovative products or services.[2] Moreover, when a new product or service is introduced into the market, it takes time for industry participants and regulators to understand and assess its impact. Human beings are cognitively limited when it comes to foreseeing and estimating the risks that new products and services bring, and regulators often remain unaware of minor problems until they become serious. Even when regulators do become aware of problems, it takes time for the legislature and law-enforcement agencies to formulate a unified and coherent response.

This lag in the regulation of online platforms is certainly not unique to China; other countries, including the United States and those in Europe, are similarly ramping up scrutiny over their tech giants. Nevertheless, the unique structure of Chinese regulation makes a distinct contribution to lax enforcement during the early stages of online platform development. After decades of double-digit growth, the Chinese economy has gradually slowed down since 2008. The government thus needs to identify new economic drivers to jump-start the economy. The emergence of major online platforms was seen as an important means for China to upgrade its traditional manufacturing and service industries, and, for this reason, the central government was very supportive of innovation and entrepreneurship early on.

In 2015, the State Council promoted the "Internet Plus" initiative, a five-year plan to upgrade the traditional manufacturing and service industries by integrating them with big data, cloud computing, and other "internet of things" technologies.[3] The State Council also released five guidelines for implementing the initiative, detailing policy support in various areas such as cross-border e-commerce, commerce circulation, rural e-commerce, innovation, and entrepreneurship.[4] For three consecutive years between 2018 and 2020, the annual government reports by the State Council advocated a "tolerant and cautious" approach in regulating the Chinese platform economy.

Given the hierarchical nature of Chinese regulation, it is not surprising that various central ministries and local governments quickly followed up with concrete guidelines to implement the "Internet Plus" initiative.[5] The Ministry of Commerce, for example, first formulated various action plans in 2015.[6] Sector regulators ranging from the Ministry of Agriculture to the People's Bank of China (PBOC) were also busy promoting this initiative in their relevant sectors.[7] In the following year, the National Development and

Reform Commission (NDRC) announced a three-year plan for building an application market for artificial intelligence that would be worth over RMB 100 billion.[8] The Chinese tax department further offered preferential tax schemes to encourage mass entrepreneurship and innovation.[9] In July 2017, eight Chinese ministries jointly issued a guiding opinion to promote the sharing economy, laying down comprehensive measures for market access, regulatory supervision, and the creation of a nurturing environment.[10] Meanwhile, local governments responded to Beijing's call by issuing measures accelerating the development of e-commerce.[11] Local governments also ran pilot programs to explore the implementation of the "Internet Plus" initiative in various sectors such as logistics, social security, healthcare, and other government services.[12] During this period, government-sponsored incubators for start-ups mushroomed in large cities such as Beijing and Shenzhen.[13] These government efforts created a very supportive and favorable policy environment for Chinese tech firms. When Premier Li Keqiang addressed the Summer Davos Forum in 2017, he touted "an accommodating and prudent regulatory approach toward new industries, new business forms, and models" that, he argued, had facilitated the healthy development of China's tech companies.[14]

Meanwhile, Chinese tech firms are very adept and know how to take advantage of a favorable policy environment to lobby for political support. These firms exert influence over the political process through two main channels. The first is through the use of formal institutional channels such as those accessible through party membership or other legislative and consultative conferences.[15] For instance, Jack Ma, the founder of Alibaba and Ant Group, has been a Chinese Communist Party (CCP) member since the 1980s.[16] Some tech entrepreneurs serve in the National People's Congress (NPC), China's top legislative body, or in the Political Consultative Conference, the top advisory body (the two bodies are known collectively as the "two sessions"). Top executives from large Chinese tech firms have actively participated in the "two sessions" and have submitted proposals for the digital economy.[17] Pony Ma, the CEO and founder of Tencent, has reportedly submitted over 50 proposals to the NPC during the past decade.[18] Commentators note, however, that these proposals serve more "as gestures of fealty to the Communist government than as real policy initiatives," mainly because the NPC is a toothless rubber-stamp parliament.[19] Other scholars have suggested that legislative membership signals a tech company's political capital, thus helping it receive preferential treatment and fend off property appropriation by the government bureaucracy.[20]

The second channel through which Chinese tech firms exert political influence is via informal institutions. In Chapter 1, I noted how Chinese tech firms rely on political elites or SOE partners—essentially, political intermediaries—to exert influence over the regulatory process. Tech firms also resort to former government officials or academics, who are either hired as in-house staff or are engaged or sponsored through academic or research organizations. As this type of intermediary mainly facilitates information exchange between firms and regulators, I call them "information intermediaries." In the past few years, several of China's largest tech firms, including Tencent, Alibaba, ByteDance, Didi Chuxing, and Meituan, have poached former regulatory officials and offered them generous payouts.[21] Seeing little prospect for career advancement in their departments, many officials either move to positions in research centers or government-relations departments at Chinese tech giants.[22] Chinese academics, many of whom advise government departments in drafting new laws or provide expert opinions for investigations, also play a very important role in facilitating this process.[23] Given the lack of transparency in China's legislative and enforcement processes, it is critically important for Chinese tech firms to have access to valuable information so they can gain first-mover advantage in shaping their responses to new policy developments.[24] Because information intermediaries are also legal experts in their relevant policy areas, they can help Chinese tech firms lobby against unfavorable legislative changes and obtain favorable treatment during ongoing investigations. However, it is also well known that this revolving door can distort the incentives of regulators, resulting in regulatory capture.[25]

Given the policy endorsement from the top leadership and the aggressive lobbying from the tech firms, Chinese regulators are disincentivized from taking an aggressive stance to tackle problems in the tech sector. Consequently, even though tensions were building up between the platforms and their participants, the regulators were slow to report this information to the top leadership. Meanwhile, public grievances tend to be dampened by censorship and crackdowns stemming from local governments and regulators. The slow information transmission from both the regulators and the public contributes to an information deficit at the top echelon of China's leadership. Figure 2.1 presents the dynamics among the major actors.

VOLATILITY 47

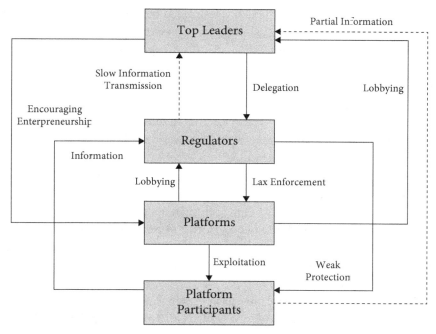

Figure 2.1. Lax regulation.

2.2. Phase Two: Harsh Crackdown

Favorable government initiatives and lax regulation initially created a very supportive and favorable policy environment for Chinese tech firms. Armed with troves of data, deep coffers, and an influence that spans the lives of millions of people, the Chinese internet giants have enjoyed exponential growth in the past decade. During the same period, however, regulatory tensions began to surface and attract public attention. Serious cases involving personal safety, as well as financial-stability issues capable of threatening the social harmony, started to appear soon after the introduction of new platform products and services. Given the outsized influence of Big Tech, even a seemingly small probability of operational failure can generate strong regulatory repercussions. Take Didi Chuxing, for example. In 2015, Didi launched Shunfengche, a "hitchhiking" service that matched car owners willing to offer a free ride with those needing a lift.[26] Within a few years, problems started to emerge when a few female passengers using the

Shunfengche service were raped and murdered by their drivers.[27] Although these incidents were low-probability events, they triggered a massive public uproar, leading Didi to shut down the Shunfengche service.[28] Regulators from various major cities also tightened their oversight, ordering Didi to overhaul its screening mechanisms for drivers and improve safety protections for passengers.[29] Another example is the series of scandals that erupted in the peer-to-peer (P2P) industry. In 2015, Ezubao, one of China's largest P2P lenders, was found to have been engaging in a Ponzi scheme.[30] As of January 2016, Ezubao had defrauded over 900,000 users who lost almost RMB 50 billion.[31] Angry protests erupted in 34 Chinese cities in response to the scandal.[32] The collapse of Ezubao generated a domino effect, with 50 percent of the P2P platforms being identified as "problematic" on the basis of serious operational difficulties in 2016.[33] A series of subsequent regulatory crackdowns gave rise to another wave of scandals and defaults in 2018.[34] By late 2020, the Chinese banking regulators had all but shut down the P2P platforms.[35]

Meanwhile, Chinese regulators have grown increasingly wary of the potential for moral hazard associated with platform operation. Because online platforms serve as intermediaries connecting buyers and sellers, it is often not entirely clear what their legal responsibilities are with respect to conflicts arising from their platforms. As a result, online platforms have an incentive to engage in excessively risky transactions without bearing any liabilities. Consider an example from the food delivery industry. Two of China's leading food-delivery companies, Meituan and Ele.me, have been criticized for using smart algorithms to set up routes and impose tight deadlines on delivery drivers, resulting in many traffic accidents.[36] As most of these drivers are crowdsourced couriers rather than full-time employees, they cannot receive social-security benefits or compensation for work-related injuries.[37] The absence of formal legal protection for drivers has resulted in many labor disputes, some of which escalated into strikes.[38] In one tragic instance, a driver who was unable to receive compensation protested by setting himself on fire.[39] Incidents of this kind generated a public outcry, leading to considerable debate in China about the liabilities of online platforms. Another example stems from the world of micro-lending, a popular financial service introduced by Chinese fintech companies. Ant Group, China's largest fintech company, partnered with Chinese state-owned banks to extend microloans to hundreds of millions of small businesses and

VOLATILITY   49

individuals.[40] According to Ant's IPO filing, banks were responsible for extending almost 98 percent of the loans.[41] The fact that Ant bore almost none of the risk of default generated concerns that it might engage in excessively risky lending. Indeed, it was discovered that Ant had employed deceptive tactics to encourage spending on Taobao by providing convenient borrowing to young students through its micro-lending channels.[42]

Finally, the Chinese digital economy has become highly concentrated, giving rise to a whole host of antitrust and competition issues. In the past few years, Tencent and Alibaba have become China's most formidable competitors, operating like a duopoly in the Chinese digital economy.[43] Tencent is a mega entertainment firm with strong market positions that span social media, music, and gaming. Alibaba is a conglomerate with its core business in e-commerce but also invests heavily in social media, entertainment, logistics, and cloud computing. Each of these two tech giants owns a few super-apps—that is, highly popular apps that are not only used by vast user populations, but which also provide access to countless "mini-programs" that can be launched instantly.[44] Over the years, the intense rivalry between Alibaba and Tencent has carved up China's tech sector into two competing ecosystems, each side blocking users from sharing content to the other's ecosystem, as I will further elaborate in Chapter 6.[45] For instance, users of WeChat couldn't open a link to a product from Taobao, and had to copy and paste the URL into a browser to access the content. Taobao, on the other hand, does not allow Tencent's WeChat Pay as a payment service. Because of the lack of interoperability between these two ecosystems, most new start-ups have no choice but to join either the Alibaba or the Tencent camp in order to survive.[46] Seeking to further entrench their own dominant positions, leading e-commerce firms such as Alibaba and Meituan have also imposed restrictive conditions to force merchants to stay on their platforms.

2.2.1. The Tipping Point

Although regulatory tensions in the tech sector had been building up for many years, they did not tip the balance between innovation and regulation until mid-2020. The State Council's annual work report, released in May of that year, continued to emphasize applying a "cautious and tolerant" approach in regulating the platform economy.[47] That autumn, however, one random, unforeseen event directly triggered a dramatic reversal of China's regulatory approach. On October 24, 2020, Jack Ma made a highly controversial speech at the Bund Financial summit in Shanghai. Ma scathingly criticized Chinese financial regulation, chiding state banks for operating with a "pawn shop" mentality.[48] He also referred to the Basel Accords, a set of agreements on banking regulation issued by the Basel Committee on Banking supervision, as a "club for the elderly."[49] On November 3, 2020, the Shanghai Stock Exchange halted Ant's IPO, citing changes in the regulatory environment.[50] From this point on, the balance was tipped decisively toward increased regulation. But how did Jack Ma's speech and Ant's mega-IPO, which would have brought China tremendous pride, become the tipping point for regulating the Chinese platform economy?

Similar to other Chinese tech firms, Ant is well adapted to the nation's weak institutions and knows how to navigate a complex regulatory environment and grow its business in legal gray areas. Since its establishment in 2014, Ant has created many new financial products in microlending, insurance, and wealth management, none of which seems to fall within existing regulatory frameworks. Although almost 90 percent of Ant's revenue is derived from financial services, the firm has been trying hard to maintain its label as a technology company.[51] Doing so has allowed Ant to seek arbitrage among different regulatory authorities and find room to grow and expand very quickly. For example, Ant saw a good opportunity when the Trump administration threatened to delist many Chinese companies from the US stock exchanges.[52] To lure Chinese tech firms to trade back home, China launched the Technology and Innovation Board (the "STAR market"), a new Chinese technology stock market similar to the Nasdaq.[53] Knowing that Ant's IPO debut could give the STAR market a significant boost, the China Securities Regulatory Commission fast-tracked the listing process for the firm.[54] Ant's IPO was highly oversubscribed, granting the firm a high valuation as a technology company rather than as a bank.[55]

However, Ant's cunning tech-firm pitch directly clashed with the regulatory mission of the PBOC. Unlike other regulatory authorities, which tend to bear few consequences from their regulatory failures, the PBOC, as the lender of last resort, needs to bear the residual risk of bailing out troubled banks.[56] Concerned about the potential for moral hazards, the PBOC has long been pressing for legislation to regulate Ant as a financial holding company. In 2018, the central bank was already drafting a proposal to increase regulation of fintech companies via stricter capital-reserve requirements and risk-management rules.[57] During the summer of 2020, the PBOC issued a spate of regulations, guidelines, and notices to try to curb excessive risk stemming from digital finance.[58] Even after Ant filed for its IPO, the PBOC issued draft guidelines indicating that it would regulate Ant and other fintech companies as financial holding companies.[59] During Ant's IPO process, the PBOC and other financial regulators grew more alarmed, as Ant's high valuation as a tech firm, as opposed to a bank, stoked fears of a bubble.[60] Viewed in this context, Jack Ma's controversial speech in Shanghai appears to have been the entrepreneur's final attempt at lobbying for favorable regulatory treatment in anticipation of tightening regulation of his business.

Ma's speech backfired, however, as it violated the taboo against directly challenging the authority and legitimacy of existing financial regulations. As explained in Chapter 1, all of China's central ministries and local governments ultimately derive their legitimacy from the delegation of power by the top leadership in Beijing.[61] Determined to defend their own bureaucratic interests, the financial regulators went out of their way to wage a regulatory war against the fintech giant. A few days after Jack Ma's controversial speech in Shanghai, *Finance News*, a newspaper affiliated with the PBOC, published three days of commentaries rebutting Ma's Shanghai speech point by point.[62] The fact that the PBOC took such a high-profile approach also demonstrates the resolution and determination of the central bank in its efforts to rein in Ant Group. As such, it provides strong evidence that the direct trigger of the law-enforcement campaign was the mounting regulatory tension between Ant Group and the financial regulators, and not merely the loose lips of a billionaire. After all, it was those very tensions that Ma chafed against in his speech.

Beyond their media campaign, the Chinese financial regulators also reported this matter to President Xi Jinping, who gave instructions to halt Ant's IPO.[63] On October 31, 2020, the Financial Stability and Development Committee headed by Liu He decided that all kinds of financial activities and similar businesses should be regulated in the same way, thus clearing a path for regulators to tighten their scrutiny of Ant.[64] This message was further reiterated by the Politburo on December 11, 2020, when it declared "strengthening antitrust regulation and preventing the disorderly expansion of capital" to be a work priority.[65] Although the top leaders place a strong emphasis on growth, they are very sensitive to any perceived risk to financial stability. In recent years, the Chinese financial regulators have grown increasingly wary of opaque ownership structures and the regulatory arbitrage that non-financial institutions engage in when they provide financial services.[66] It was in this context that, amid the financial fallout from the bankruptcy and demise of HNA Group and Anbang Insurance Corp. Co., respectively, as well as the rampant fraud that erupted in the world of P2P lending, the central leadership implemented a series of organizational shake-ups to exercise comprehensive oversight.[67]

After the debacle of Ant Group's IPO, the Chinese central leadership initiated a massive law-enforcement campaign, mobilizing various legislative and administrative resources as well as propaganda to tighten regulation over Chinese tech firms. Such campaigns, a tactic employed by the CCP across diverse legal realms such as crime, anti-corruption measures, environmental conservation, and financial regulation, have historical origins dating back to the revolutionary period.[68] During this era, mass mobilization, or *yundong*, was an integral facet of Mao's governance strategy.[69] Although mass campaigns have largely vanished after Mao, the Chinese government continues to employ campaign techniques, for instance by mobilizing grassroots party networks along with propaganda blitzes intended to enlist mass support.[70] Once regulators from different ministries had received a clear signal from the top leadership to tighten oversight over the tech sector, they had a strong incentive to demonstrate their loyalty by taking an aggressive stance in regulating these firms. Much as they had done in previous law-enforcement campaigns, the Chinese regulators hastily introduced a myriad of laws and regulations and imposed swift and severe legal sanctions on the domestic tech firms.[71]

While public grievances tend to be suppressed, when the pendulum swings the other way, regulators tend to tolerate or even provoke them in order to enhance the legitimacy of their actions, as mentioned in Chapter 1. A couple of weeks after Jack Ma made his controversial speech in Shanghai, the PBOC published three commentaries that elaborated on the systemic financial risks posed by Ant and other fintech companies.[72] These commentaries also chided Ant for branding itself as a technology company, an action they saw as the company's attempt to seek regulatory arbitrage—as well as one that let them encourage wanton consumption among young students, collect excessive amounts of consumer data, and infringe on personal privacy.[73] In response, the authors called for tightened control of market access, enhancement of consumer and data protections, and general regulatory improvement.[74] These three commentaries presented a strong rebuttal to Jack Ma's speech; in having them published, it would appear that the PBOC seized the first-mover advantage in shaping the public narrative about the case. However, this was not the only action taken to rally public support. Soon enough, an explosion of negative coverage about Jack Ma and Ant's business also started to emerge on Chinese social media. Mr. Ma, who used to be revered as a successful national hero, was now portrayed as a "villain" and a "bloodsucking ghost."[75] Ant Group, which had been providing small loans to consumers and small businesses, was now seen as a "loan shark" in disguise.[76] The turn of popular opinion against Jack Ma and Ant helped top leaders cultivate mass support to further advance the common prosperity initiative. Meanwhile, Chinese tech firms continued to lobby the regulators for lenient treatment, all the while reorienting their businesses to adapt to the new policy initiatives from the top leadership.[77] Figure 2.2 presents the dynamics among the four major actors as described above.

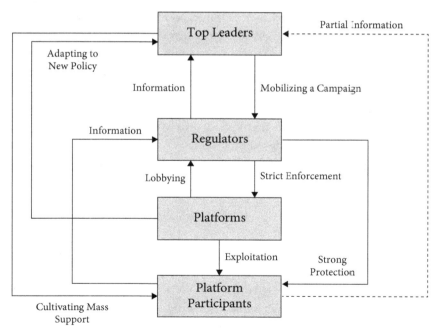

Figure 2.2. Harsh crackdown.

2.2.2. Agency Overreach

Once the regulatory pendulum swings from lax to harsh, the dynamic pyramid model of regulation strongly tends toward agency overreach. First, in contrast to the bureaucratic inertia during the first stage of lax regulation, government authorities now have a strong incentive to take aggressive action. As noted in Chapter 1, the top leaders are generalists and do not necessarily possess expertise in every area of governance. As such, they only set out broad and vague initiatives, while the agencies need to formulate detailed plans to implement them. The agencies therefore still enjoy significant discretion over execution. In the face of uncertainty about the exact preferences of the top leadership, agencies prefer taking a tough stance as a demonstration of loyalty to those at the top. In fact, if any agencies fail to act at this point, their inaction is likely to be perceived as incompetence or even regulatory capture.

The overnight suspension of the private tutoring industry is one such example. In recent years, after-school tutoring has flourished in China due to the severe academic pressures facing Chinese children and the scarcity of public resources to address them. This phenomenon worried Chinese policymakers, who believed that the high cost of education and excessive competition could deter anxious parents from having more children—an important priority for an aging China struggling with population decline.[78] According to a report in *The Wall Street Journal*, the crackdown began when President Xi issued brief instructions to the Ministry of Education to reform the country's private tutoring businesses.[79] The education officials first responded by drafting plans that included new limits on tutoring for children, but this plan was dismissed by President Xi as "too soft."[80] In response, the Ministry not only significantly tightened the limits, but took the extreme step of mandating that all private education businesses be registered as nonprofits. Just like that, the USD 100 billion private tutoring industry was wiped out overnight, triggering a brutal sell-off of Chinese education companies listed overseas.[81]

Second, during an intense law-enforcement campaign, administrative enforcement agencies often engage in significant rivalry with each other. At such times, power fragmentation in the Chinese bureaucracy incentivizes agencies to take a tough stance not only as an expansion strategy to increase their bureaucratic turf, but also as a survival strategy to preempt the encroachment of others on their own turf. The competition between two regulators, the SAMR (China's market watchdog) and the MIIT (China's telecom sector regulator), offers us a glimpse into such inter-agency tensions. As will be further elaborated in Chapter 4, Tencent and Alibaba have each created their own ecosystem, providing companies within their systems with convenient access to their super-apps WeChat, Taobao, and Alipay. But each has also restricted access to its rival's apps, creating an interoperability issue that imposes high barriers to entry for smaller rivals. During the summer of 2021, the MIIT initiated a six-month rectification program aimed at tackling a whole host of consumer-protection and unfair-competition violations, including the interoperability issues.[32] Although the MIIT lacks the power to enforce China's Anti-Monopoly Law, it can rely on its own departmental guidelines to request that firms rectify their behavior. As interoperability is a form of exclusionary conduct in violation of China's antitrust law, the MIIT's aggressive intervention indirectly encroached upon the turf of China's antitrust watchdog, the SAMR.[83]

Third, aggressive intervention in the industry could further expand rent-seeking opportunities for officials working at enforcement agencies, as well as enhance their career opportunities upon leaving their government jobs. Given the high stakes involved, tech companies have strong incentives to lobby regulators, which creates lucrative rent-seeking opportunities not only for agency officials, but also for a large network of information intermediaries, including former regulators, think tanks, academics, and lawyers who can play a role exerting their influence on the process. As Wentong Zheng has observed, officials have incentives to increase the market demand for their services when they exit the government.[84] In the enforcement setting, this may result in more enforcement actions, broadened jurisdictional reach, and higher penalties.[85] In the rule-making setting, this may result in expanded legislative authority, more flexible standards, and a preference for complex rather than simple rules. The actions taken by regulators during the latest wave of crackdowns appear to bear out Zheng's thesis, as agencies imposed record fines on Chinese tech firms while actively churning out new rules and regulations to expand the scope of their enforcement.

Fourth, although in theory Chinese administrative law gives businesses and citizens the opportunity to challenge agency actions, in practice few choose to do so, as they perceive that the costs would exceed the benefits of winning. Because agencies face little institutional resistance from targeted businesses, they enjoy almost unbridled discretion in enforcing the law. As I elaborate in my book *Chinese Antitrust Exceptionalism*, Chinese regulatory authorities have a variety of legal and extralegal tools at their disposal to pressure firms to accede to their demands.[86] Any firm that is deemed un-cooperative could face retaliation in the form of higher penalties and fines. At the same time, those firms that readily yield to agency demands are re-warded with lower penalties or even immunity. Meanwhile, Chinese agen-cies are adept at strategically leveraging the media to advance their policy objectives. All media outlets, including official state media and commer-cial media outlets, are subject to tight control by the Chinese government. In the past, Chinese antitrust regulators have been observed to employ a strategy of inflicting reputational damage on firms by exposing them to negative publicity.[87] This puts significant pressure on firms to conform, es-pecially when their stock prices suffer dramatic losses as a result of officially sanctioned naming and shaming.

The antitrust investigation against Alibaba serves as an excellent example of these varied forms of pressure. On Christmas Eve, 2020, the SAMR an-nounced on its website that it had launched an investigation into Alibaba's business practices. Only 10 minutes after the announcement, the *People's Daily* published a long commentary endorsing the investigation. This com-mentary, which appears to have been prepared in advance, was seemingly designed to secure first-mover advantage and shape public perception of the case.[88] The SAMR's one-sentence announcement caused huge panic among investors. Alibaba's stock price tumbled more than 13 percent in one day, wiping out almost USD 100 billion of its market capitalization.[89] Although there was nothing wrong about the SAMR announcing an im-minent investigation on its website, the Alibaba case marked the first time the agency had done so. In fact, the SAMR had always kept a very low pro-file in investigating cases precisely because it feared damaging stock prices. The timing of the announcement was planned well in advance, with the Christmas holiday break giving the agency room to moderate the market reaction if its statement were felt to be too harsh. The need for moderation might explain why the agency released positive news on the Sunday before the next trading day, stating that it had completed evidence gathering and mentioning that the firm had been very cooperative during the process.[90] The same announcement strategy was also used in the SAMR's investiga-tion of Meituan, China's largest food-delivery platform.

The SAMR was, however, not the only agency to adopt such a media strategy. On July 2, 2021, China's Cyberspace Administration (CAC) announced on its website that it had launched a cybersecurity review into Didi Chuxing, China's largest ride-hailing company. As the CAC had only established the cybersecurity measures a year prior, there were minimal public disclosures or precedents about such reviews at the time of the announcement. The CAC's surprise announcement, which came just two days after Didi's IPO debut in New York, appeared to be a deliberate attempt by the agency to inflict reputational damage on the ride-hailing company. A few months earlier, Didi had reportedly received a warning from the agency to postpone its IPO in the United States in order to undertake a thorough self-examination of cybersecurity risks associated with its service. However, Didi failed to heed the agency's advice and rushed ahead to complete its IPO at lightning speed. The market reacted very badly to the agency announcement, causing Didi's stock to plummet more than 10 percent in one day.[91]

Unlike US tech firms which actively challenge regulators in the United States and Europe, Chinese tech firms appear much more obedient throughout the regulatory process. Both Alibaba and Meituan accepted the record fines imposed by the SAMR without making any appeal and vowed their dedication to achieving compliance. As for Didi, the firm that initially defied the CAC's order against listing in New York, it eventually moved to delist from the United States to assuage the concerns of the regulators.

2.3. Phase Three: Regulatory Easing

As shown above, Chinese regulation can lead to extreme scenarios that swing from very lax regulation during the first stage to very strict regulation during the second stage. At the same time, regulation is also a constant learning process, with each actor absorbing feedback from the system. This leads me to the third stage, in which agency overreach can be moderated, especially after the top leadership receives strong negative feedback about the consequences of its policies. Indeed, despite the lack of formal institutional constraints on agency power, informal institutions in Chinese regulation can counteract agency overreach.

Let's start with the tech firms. Even though none of the Chinese tech firms dared to publicly challenge the antitrust agency's actions, they actively resorted to informal methods, such as internal lobbying, to exert influence over the agency. Given the high stakes involved, firms are ready to invest significant resources into counteracting agency overreach. Because the Chinese regulatory process is very opaque, intermediaries who are in close proximity to the agency become important information brokers. Chinese academics and think tanks, as well as some organizations affiliated with agencies, are often closely involved with providing advice and consultation about the legislative and enforcement process. Such actors become highly sought-after information brokers who can help Chinese tech firms influence regulatory outcomes. Indeed, many tech groups had already lured ex-regulators to serve on their in-house teams, even before the crackdown began.[92] With the increasingly challenging regulatory environment, these struggling Chinese tech firms seem even more determined to tempt government officials working at the relevant regulatory authorities with incredibly lucrative pay packages.[93] As reported by Bloomberg, in some instances these have approached almost half a million dollars, dwarfing the standard civil servant salary by almost 60-fold.[94]

In fact, Chinese tech companies appeared successful in fending off some unfavorable legislative proposals in some instances, even amidst the enforcement campaign.[95] One such example is the draft antitrust enforcement guidelines proposed by the SAMR in November 2020.[96] The guidelines included several provisions which could have reduced the burden of proof that the antitrust regulator must meet when establishing the dominance of an online platform. This would have made it much easier for the agency to prosecute firms.[97] For instance, the draft guidelines allowed regulators to avoid defining the relevant market in difficult cases.[98] The draft also indicated that the possession of data can be used as a consideration in deciding whether a platform constitutes an essential facility.[99] However, the final version of the guidelines removed all of these controversial provisions, added many potential business justifications to be taken into account when considering claims of abusive conduct, and gave more room for tech firms to defend themselves when subject to antitrust scrutiny.[100]

The second type of informal constraint on agency overreach lies in the fragmentation of administrative power, a distinct feature of China's vast bureaucracy. As explained in the previous chapter, each Chinese ministry is allocated specific functions, corresponding to various aspects of the nation's regulatory governance. However, the division of labor is not always clear, and there are often several agencies with overlapping responsibilities overseeing a particular sector. Such power fragmentation acts as an informal system of checks and balances among Chinese agencies. For example, aggressive agency intervention in the tech sector can cause economic and financial turmoil, which adversely affects the parochial interests of financial regulators. In early July 2021, the CAC's sudden inspection of Didi Chuxing two days after its debut on the New York Stock Exchange spooked international investors.[101] Later that month, the Ministry of Education's decision to turn swaths of booming after-school tutoring firms into nonprofits and ban them from raising foreign capital further shocked international investors, triggering a massive sell-off of Chinese stocks. In response to these stock routs, the China Securities Regulatory Commission (CSRC) hastily arranged a meeting with international bankers in an attempt to calm the market. The securities regulator assured investors that those earlier regulatory actions were sector-specific and that China still welcomed foreign investment.[102] The CSRC's move was perfectly aligned with the agency's primary responsibility of overseeing the stock market and ensuring its stability.

Meanwhile, local authorities are more mindful than their central counterparts about the consequences of their policies, despite their need to respond to top-down initiatives through enforcement measures. Officials in local governments are generalists and need to balance different priorities in running the local economy. Intensive regulatory intervention may undermine the competitiveness of local businesses, which could in turn reduce regional GDP and cause massive unemployment. However, it is not just concern about the potential impact on the economy that constrains local authorities and prevents them from taking a very aggressive stance in tackling regulatory problems. Because they need to please two bosses simultaneously—the top leadership in Beijing and the local government— local regulatory agencies must maintain an extremely delicate balance in trying to respond to central policy mandates without causing significant local disruption.

The most important countervailing force against agency overreach, however, is the top leadership. As discussed earlier, the regulatory pendulum swings from lax to strict once top leaders become informed about the severity of regulatory issues and then mobilize the entire bureaucratic machine in response to them. However, when top leaders receive strong negative feedback about the resulting policy consequences, the pendulum can swing back again. As noted in Chapter 1, the top leaders are very adaptable and need to balance different sources of legitimacy. Ambitious and well-intentioned regulatory reforms often have the potential to bring severe economic consequences, creating a downturn that can endanger the legitimacy of the top leadership.[103]

Toward the end of 2021, Chinese policymakers became alarmed by a sharp slowdown of economic growth—the result of market reactions to a combination of different policy measures including tech regulation, stringent Covid measures, and the property crackdown instigated by Beijing. Battered by successive regulatory attacks, most Chinese tech firms were starting to lay off workers.[104] Video-streaming companies such as iQiyi, Kuaishou, and ByteDance, ride-hailing companies such as Didi, as well as after-school tutoring businesses, all underwent massive restructuring and had laid off employees.[105] Both Alibaba and Tencent announced large-scale layoffs in March 2022, with Alibaba estimated to have cut more than 15 percent of its workforce that year, or about 39,000 staff, and Tencent cutting staff in its video-gaming, search, and cloud units by 10–15 percent.[106] During this economic downturn, Chinese policymakers faced tremendous pressures to deregulate in order to stabilize the economy and increase employment. Indeed, although "common prosperity" is heralded as an important priority, this egalitarian goal is built upon the premise of prosperity.

Russia's invasion of Ukraine in early 2022 created further uncertainties for the outlook of Chinese tech stocks. International investors, whose sentiments were already fragile after months of negative news about Chinese tech regulation, grew increasingly wary that Chinese companies could be subject to sanctions due to China's close ties with Russia. Thus, when some Chinese companies were placed on a provisional list for delisting from US stock exchanges in mid-March, it triggered a massive sell-off across Chinese stocks. On March 15, 2022, the Hang Seng China Enterprises Index, which tracks Chinese stocks listed in Hong Kong, plummeted more than 6 percent, worse than it had during the 2008 financial crisis.[107] Meanwhile, the Nasdaq Golden Dragon China Index, which tracks Chinese stocks listed on Nasdaq, saw more than USD 1 trillion worth of value wiped out from its peak the previous year.[108]

This relentless sell-off of Chinese stocks in overseas equities markets evoked memories of the 2008 crash during the financial recession and touched a sensitive nerve for Chinese policymakers. The top leadership responded quickly. On March 16, the day after the massive sell-off of Chinese stocks, Vice Premier Liu He held an emergency meeting of the State Council, sending the strongest signal since late 2020 of its intention to rally support for Chinese stocks. In addition to pledging to introduce market-friendly policies to reassure investors, Liu also called on various government departments to better coordinate their policies with the financial regulators and avoid introducing measures that might cause the market to shrink.[109] Liu also vowed to increase the transparency and predictability of platform regulation, thereby suggesting that agencies should return to their routine enforcement. The Hang Seng Tech Index jumped 22 percent on the day of that meeting, with Alibaba and Tencent bouncing back more than 20 percent before the closing bell.[110] With these announcements, the unprecedented law-enforcement campaign against Big Tech, which had lasted for almost 18 months, ended abruptly. After the State Council's meeting, various ministries convened internal meetings to pass down the central directive. In June 2022, Chinese data regulators finally concluded their yearlong investigation into Didi, while China's National Press and Public Administration approved 60 video-game titles that had previously been condemned as "spiritual opium" for Chinese youth. These proactive moves sent a further strong signal to the market that the regulatory tightening was easing.[111] The regulatory pendulum swung again, and China's tech regulation officially entered its third stage (see Figure 2.3).

2.4. Summary

In this chapter, I have explained how a dynamic pyramid model of regulation can lead to extreme volatility, using the 2020–2022 tech crackdown as a detailed case study. At first, the top Chinese leadership provided strong policy support for entrepreneurship and innovation as a way to upgrade and boost the Chinese economy. Domestic tech firms took advantage of this loose policy environment and aggressively lobbied for support from the top leadership and regulators—the latter of whom, fearful of contravening the national economic agenda, were predisposed against taking tough action.

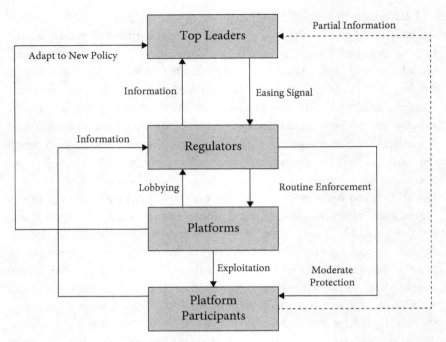

Figure 2.3. Regulatory easing.

The result of this bureaucratic inertia was a very light-touch regulatory environment, which proved conducive to the growth of China's domestic tech giants. However, agency inaction and tolerance also allowed tensions to build up, thus further exacerbating regulatory problems. Information about these issues flowed very slowly to the top leaders, who often became aware of them only when they erupted into social or economic crises.

As soon as the top leaders became informed of the severity of these problems, the pendulum of regulation swung back toward harshness. In swift order, the top leaders mobilized all of their considerable administrative resources for stringent regulation of the tech sector. Bureaucratic mobilizations of this kind often trigger cascading effects, as all of the relevant agencies flock to respond to the top leaders' call. Without strong institutional safeguards, the resulting agency actions easily lead to overreach, giving rise to unintended effects that hurt business growth and affect unemployment. In the most recent case, the slowdown of the Chinese economy and the massive sell-off of Chinese stocks during the regulatory crackdown quickly exerted great pressure on the top leaders to relax their policies. Eager to eliminate the threats to their legitimacy that come with economic and financial turmoil, the top leaders vowed to calm the market by ending the law-enforcement campaign. And so, the regulatory pendulum swung once again. Chinese tech regulation then entered a third phase, with agencies unwinding some of their previous measures and returning to routine enforcement.

3
Fragility

In the preceding chapters, we delved into the hierarchy and volatility in Chinese tech regulation. This chapter pivots to the discussion of fragility, the third main characteristic of the dynamic pyramid model of regulation. As proposed in the Introduction, the resilience of a regulatory policy can be assessed through two dimensions: side effects and information lag. The greater the side effects, the more policy resistance there is. The longer the information lag, the more costly it is for decision-makers to revert course. Table 3.1 outlines the consequences associated with four potential scenarios of regulation.

Scenario I (minor side effects and short lag): This scenario represents the ideal conditions for regulation. Here, the regulatory policy produces minimal side effects, and top leaders can promptly receive feedback and adjust accordingly.

Scenario II (minor side effects and long lag): Regulation also works well in this scenario. Although it takes a long time for top leaders to realize that their policy is leading to unintended side effects, those effects are rather minor.

Scenario III (strong side effects and short lag): In this case, the regulation becomes fragile due to the major negative side effects of the policy. However, the regulation retains some resilience, as top leaders can quickly access feedback and instigate corrective measures.

Scenario IV (strong side effects and long lag): This is the scenario where regulation is at its most vulnerable. The detrimental effects of the policy, combined with a significant lag in the top leaders' awareness of these problems, can lead to irreparable damage.

Unfortunately, the dynamic pyramid model of regulation is inherently fragile, primarily due to its tendency for inducing substantial side effects

High Wire. Angela Huyue Zhang, Oxford University Press. © Oxford University Press 2024.
DOI: 10.1093/oso/9780197682258.003.0004

FRAGILITY

Table 3.1. Consequences of Regulation

	Minor Side Effects	Strong Side Effects
Short Lag	Scenario I	Scenario III
Long lag	Scenario II	Scenario IV

and, at times, long information lag. This vulnerability is closely linked to the hierarchy and volatility, the other two important features of the model. Specifically, the absence of institutional checks and balances, a defining trait of China's hierarchical regulatory structure, often leads to agency overreach. Hence, when policymakers eventually decide to intervene, they may inadvertently trigger a cascade of unintended consequences. Simultaneously, inefficiencies in the information transmission system exacerbate the information lag, potentially amplifying the side effects. Volatility can render investors hyper-responsive to perceived negative news, thereby further amplifying any unintended consequences.

To elucidate these dynamics, I will employ the dynamic pyramid model to unpack the intricate complexity of four severe policy challenges that the Chinese leadership has faced in recent years: China's Covid control, the energy crisis, the property-market crackdown, and the one-child policy. In the past, numerous observers have voiced concerns over the various policy crises confronting Chinese leadership, with some prognosticating the collapse of the regime.[1] And yet, time and time again, China has demonstrated remarkable resilience in navigating the multifaceted challenges posed by these crises. As detailed in the ensuing discussion, the top Chinese leadership has managed to do so due to the relatively short information lags, enabling policymakers to quickly alter their course when necessary. Nevertheless, sometimes side effects are so strong that even a dramatic policy U-turn is not sufficient to get the crisis under control. In the worst-case scenario, the intervention comes so late that the problematic policy results in irreparable damage.

3.1. China's Covid Control

In late December 2019, health professionals in Wuhan identified an unknown infectious disease and called for a rapid response to what would later become known as Covid-19.[2] Similar to what we observed with China's tech regulation, the initial policy response to the Covid outbreak was so lax as to be almost nonexistent. Residents in Wuhan did not receive any warning about the disease, and large social gatherings continued to be held without any precautions such as mask wearing or social-distancing measures being taken.[3] On one occasion, over 10,000 families gathered together for a banquet in Wuhan, sharing dishes to celebrate the forthcoming Chinese New Year.[4]

To be fair, Covid-19 was a new disease and it took a while for health experts to understand it and make proper judgments about how to respond. There was even initial confusion among experts about whether the disease could be spread between humans.[5] Human cognitive limitations were thus an important factor that contributed to delaying an effective policy response; other countries, including the United States, experienced similar problems.[6] Nevertheless, in the Chinese context, this delay was further exacerbated by the *hierarchical* feature of the dynamic pyramid model of regulation. Specifically, there are three major players in the regulatory process of Covid control: the top leadership, the government authorities in charge of pandemic control, and the general public. Consistent with the prediction of this model, information transmission between and among these players was initially very slow. Local authorities, including hospital management, health officials, and local government leaders, suppressed relevant information for weeks.[7] Given the lack of certainty about the contagiousness of the disease, local officials were concerned that aggressive intervention at an early stage would cause public panic, particularly when the disease's initial discovery coincided with the then-annual meetings of the local legislature and the Chinese New Year travel season.[8]

Local authorities in Wuhan accordingly took a two-pronged strategy to protect their own bureaucratic interests. First, they covered up information from the bottom by punishing whistleblowers and censoring social media.[9] A group of doctors who warned their friends and colleagues about the disease were reprimanded by the police and forced to admit wrongdoing in spreading rumors.[10] After a number of frontline doctors were infected, it became an open secret among Wuhan health professionals that the disease was contagious.[11] However, they were afraid to make this information public, as it contradicted the local authorities' official line that the disease's ability to spread between humans was yet to be determined.[12] To be sure, since the outbreak of SARS in 2002, China has significantly improved its reporting mechanism for contagious diseases; the reporting time from grassroots health workers to the China Center for Disease Control and Prevention (China CDC) has been shortened from 15 days to a mere 4 hours. Unfortunately, local officials in Wuhan intercepted the upward flow of information, requiring administrative approval from experts or health officials before grassroots workers could report confirmed cases to the China CDC.[13]

Second, the local authorities in Hubei, the province of which Wuhan is the capital, reported the matter to higher levels of government and refrained from taking any action until they had received clear instructions from above.[14] These local agencies seemed to believe they wouldn't be punished for this delay, since it wasn't within their control. Indeed, if the Hubei officials had taken drastic measures that ended up contravening the direction taken by the top policymakers, their careers could have been in jeopardy. From their standpoint, the safest approach was to leave the decision-making to the top. In the face of a public-health crisis, local authorities and health professionals found themselves lacking the autonomy to make crucial decisions.[15] As Stanford's Zhou Xueguang, a renowned expert in Chinese bureaucracy, has put it: "at the frontline of the outbreak, political considerations took precedence over professional judgment, to override professional authority and stifle professional voice [sic]."[16]

The initially lax stance taken by the Wuhan authorities led to severe unintended consequences. Within a couple of weeks, the disease had spread throughout the country, and, subsequently, to the rest of the world. Upon being informed of the severity of the matter, the top Chinese leadership immediately mobilized all administrative resources and, in late January 2020, imposed draconian lockdown measures. These belatedly decisive actions echo the "volatility" feature of Chinese regulation, with China's Covid control entering into the second phase. As it turned out, the lockdowns were highly effective. While the rest of the world struggled to control the Covid outbreak, China almost eliminated the disease within its borders. Within a few months, Chinese factories had resumed operations, and the daily lives of Chinese citizens had almost returned to normal. Although the lockdowns were very costly, there was a wide consensus that the benefits outweighed the costs, since China was able to keep its total number of infections and deaths at an extremely low level.[17] Despite initial cover-ups by local authorities, the top leaders salvaged the situation, albeit at huge cost, by controlling the pandemic effectively via mass mobilization and draconian lockdowns.

At the same time, the ongoing health crisis facing China is also highly dynamic: what has worked in the past might not work in the future. As Covid-19 mutated to become more contagious and less deadly, countries around the world rapidly adjusted their strategies. When Omicron, another more transmissible but less deadly variant, began to emerge, the increasing costs of China's zero-Covid strategy became apparent.[18] While the shift from lax to strict was relatively easy, returning from strict to lax proved more difficult. This is not to deny that opening up China entails significant health concerns. Omicron is highly contagious and has the potential to cause a very high death toll in a country of China's size, particularly in the many cities whose healthcare capacity is severely lacking. At the same time, however, politics appears to be an important factor in maintaining China's zero-Covid strategy. China's government touted its initial successful control of Covid-19 as an example of the superiority of the Chinese regime in contrast to the chaos and mismanagement in other, especially Western, countries. As soon as local infections began to drop in 2020, China began touting the "China solution" for tackling the virus to other countries in need of support.[19] The zero-Covid policy then became a signature policy of the Chinese top leadership, which helped bolster its legitimacy among its people. Accordingly, when some local officials suggested relaxing the zero-Covid strategy, their proposals were immediately dismissed by the top leadership.[20] A Politburo meeting presided over by President Xi in May 2022 pledged to resolutely adhere to the zero-Covid policy.[21] Responding to this signal, local officials doubled down on strict quarantine measures. It thus appears that, in some ways, China has become a victim of its own success.

In the run-up to the 20th Party Congress, there were growing anxieties and frustrations from the general public who were fed up with the government's strict lockdowns.[22] Although many had expected a loosening of the pandemic restrictions by the end of the Party Congress, little changed after President Xi secured his third term. In mid-October 2022, harsh pandemic restrictions and precarious living conditions for migrant workers in a Foxconn factory in Zhengzhou drove hundreds of thousands to flee the factory campus. This mass exodus of workers paralyzed the operation of Foxconn's assembly line for Apple, creating a massive disruption of its operation. Foxconn's founder Terry Gou reportedly submitted a letter to the Chinese leadership, urging the government to dismantle the Covid restrictions and warning that strict lockdowns would threaten China's position in global supply chains.[23] Then in late November, a deadly fire occurred in a Xinjiang apartment block which sparked a national outcry over the Covid-control measures. News of fatalities caused by the fire triggered an eruption of angry protests in major Chinese cities, alarming the top Chinese leadership. As the economic and political crises loomed, the Chinese leadership took a dramatic U-turn, scrapping almost all Covid restrictions in early December.[24] The dizzying policy whiplash of China's Covid control perfectly fits into the volatile policy cycle as elaborated in Chapter 2.

China's Covid policy vividly illustrates the fragility of the dynamic pyramid model of regulatory governance. Although forced quarantine and strict lockdowns were able to temporarily subdue the outbreak, they had severely infringed upon personal liberty and caused massive disruption to the economy. At the same time, the abrupt loosening of Covid restrictions without well-thought-out preparation triggered a panic among the Chinese public, paralyzed the public healthcare system, and caused a high death toll among Chinese elderly.[25] Although the Chinese economy experienced a sharp rebound after the government's abandonment of its zero-Covid policy, the government's Covid-control policy has done irreparable damage to the Chinese society. The government's policy missteps significantly undermined investor confidence and curbed entrepreneurial spirits, while the leadership's failure to plan for an orderly Covid exit severely eroded public trust in the government.[26] In addition to strong side effects, the information transmission between the key players during the regulatory process of the Covid control has been highly inefficient. During the first phase, cover-ups by the local authorities created a lag that prevented the top leadership from realizing the seriousness of the problem. In the second phase, regulators were slow to report the dire consequences resulting from the continuation of the zero-Covid policy, causing the complacency seen among the top leadership. By the time the top leadership fully realized the severity of the problem, the situation had become so bad that a gradualist approach with a Covid exit had become almost impossible.[27] The government's mishandling of the zero-Covid policy has left indelible scars on both the Chinese economy and society. In fact, this crisis has catalyzed an exodus of wealth from the country. Numerous affluent individuals, disillusioned by the government's handling of the pandemic, have chosen to "vote with their feet" by moving overseas.[28]

3.2. The 2021 Energy Crisis

In late September 2021, several northeastern Chinese provinces experienced severe electricity outages. These failures, stemming from a shortage of coal, soon spread to 20 provinces and regions, disrupting industry production as well as the daily lives of ordinary Chinese households.[29] Given that China is the world's factory, its energy crisis threatened to throw the global supply chain into massive disorder.[30] This nationwide power cut came as a shock to many industry observers. How did China, the world's largest coal producer, descend into power rationing?

A variety of factors contributed to China's coal shortage. China is heavily dependent on coal, which accounts for 56 percent of its energy production.[31] In recent years, the central government in Beijing has set ambitious targets to lower energy consumption and increase energy efficiency. Speaking virtually to the UN General Assembly, President Xi pledged that China would hit peak coal consumption by 2030 and reach carbon neutrality by 2060.[32] This top-down initiative was quickly passed down to various levels of the Chinese bureaucracy, echoing the "hierarchy" feature of the dynamic pyramid model. There followed a nationwide effort to reduce overcapacity, forcing the closure of many small and dirty coal mines.[33] Several major coal-producing provinces, including Shaanxi, Inner Mongolia, and Shanxi, then imposed strict administrative caps on coal output, resulting in miners producing at less than full capacity.[34] Meanwhile, the central government set a goal to reduce energy consumption per unit of GDP by 3 percent in 2021 and by 14 percent from 2021 to 2025, all while reducing carbon emissions by 18 percent per unit of GDP during the same period.[35] However, a third of China's provinces failed to meet this dual target in the first half of 2021. Local authorities then took aggressive measures, including power rationing, to meet Beijing's carbon-reduction targets.[36]

Besides agency overreach, a variety of external and internal factors further exacerbated the energy shortage. In early 2020, the CCP initiated a sweeping anti-corruption campaign in Inner Mongolia to punish coal-related corruption going back as far as two decades. This retroactive probe, which has since been applied to the entire country, has had the effect of deterring coal producers from overproducing in hopes of avoiding anti-corruption investigations. Furthermore, in 2020, China's Criminal Law was amended to impose tougher sanctions (including potential imprisonment) for violations of safety standards in mining-related accidents.[37] The prospect of heightened punishment further deterred mining companies from boosting coal supplies in response to a supply shortage, as they feared incurring potential criminal liabilities.[38] An additional source of pressure came from the significant surge in demand for Chinese exports amid the global pandemic recovery over the summer of 2021, which led to increased energy consumption. Meanwhile, energy prices skyrocketed in overseas markets. To make matters worse, Australia was banned from shipping its coal to China due to diplomatic disputes.

When power companies reduced their output as a result of higher coal prices, the impact was immediately felt across China. This sent a strong feedback signal to the top leaders, who called upon various authorities to intervene immediately. The Chinese top leadership immediately shifted priorities from the long-term target of reducing carbon emissions to the more urgent necessity of meeting the energy demand from China's industries and households. In response to the energy crisis, the National Development and Reform Commission (NDRC), the country's economic planner and price regulator, relaxed its control of electricity prices and ordered power companies to secure energy supplies at all costs.[39] Notably, the NDRC initially didn't allow electricity price hikes, the coal shortage notwithstanding. Indeed, at the beginning of 2020, the NDRC introduced a mechanism to control electricity prices; this granted provincial authorities limited discretion to raise the price of electricity by 10 percent from a fixed starting point.[40] Under these circumstances, power companies were reluctant to produce more electricity as the surge of coal prices cut into their profit margins.

The NDRC then coordinated efforts by local governments to relax its previous strict enforcement of environmental standards by reviving old and dirty coal mines to boost the production of coal supplies.[41] Inner Mongolia, which had previously shut down many coal mines, got approval to expand 72 coal mines in October 2020.[42] The Chinese tax authority provided special incentives to allow coal-fired power plants to defer tax payments, thus alleviating their financial difficulties.[43] Banks were encouraged to prioritize lending to qualified mines and power plants in order to boost the supply of coal and electricity.[44] Meanwhile, the Chinese government allowed a small increase in imports of Australian coal.[45] Within a few weeks, the energy crisis was abated.[46] Such abrupt reversal of the energy policy echoes the "volatility" feature of the dynamic pyramid model of regulation as discussed in Chapter 2.

China's 2021 energy crisis is also a perfect illustration of the complex dynamics of the dynamic pyramid model of regulation. The nation's top leaders were very adaptable in that they were able to quickly dial back their ambitious energy policy in the face of a serious power crunch that affected the livelihoods of a large portion of the population and caused significant damage to the Chinese economy. Central ministries and local governments guarded their parochial interests by first rationing power to meet Beijing's emission targets and then curbing coal production to avoid anti-corruption probes. Once they received clear instructions from the top to boost energy supplies, officials from various ministries and sub-national governments then took extraordinary measures to boost production. Power companies and coal miners were very flexible and acute as they deftly adapted to the changing regulatory environment. Meanwhile, public grievances were kept tightly under control by the government during this process.

The energy crisis also demonstrates how important it is for us to adopt systems thinking when analyzing Chinese regulatory governance. The energy crisis is a result not only of energy policies (such as the Xi administration's carbon-reduction initiatives), but also of a wide range of seemingly unrelated policy measures, including anti-corruption measures, criminal-law amendments, the global pandemic recovery, and the Australia–China diplomatic row. Examining the impact of these factors reveals the interdependence of the global economic system, as a small change in one area can be amplified and felt in other areas. Indeed, few would have anticipated that an obscure amendment to the criminal law aimed at increasing punishments for safety-standard violations would create the strong ripple effects on coal supplies witnessed during the energy crisis.

Just like China's Covid control, China's energy policy results in strong side effects—the initially ambitious carbon-emission targets and subsequent agency overreach directly contributed to China's most severe electricity shortage in decades. Fortunately, the information lag in this instance was relatively short; the top policymakers soon felt the impact of their decisions, prompting them to quickly reverse course and take extraordinary efforts to boost the coal supply. Despite the severe economic toll caused by the energy crunch, the problem was alleviated within just two months. Yet the resumption of the energy supply did not merely come at the expense of China's environmental progress; the rush to increase coal output also worried industry executives, who warned that it could lead to dangerous practices that might cost lives.[47] Those concerns would eventually become reality. In the first two months of 2022, 29 miners died in accidents, nearly doubling the number from the previous year.[48] As fatalities go up, the regulatory pendulum could swing again, thereby further challenging China's energy security.

3.3. The Property Crackdown

In early December 2021, Evergrande, China's second largest property developer, officially declared it was in default. As the world's most indebted property firm, Evergrande has a liability of more than USD 300 billion on its balance sheet. It also has nearly 800 projects under construction in more than 200 cities across China and may still need to deliver as many as 1.6 million properties to homebuyers. The firm also owed hundreds of billions to its employees, contractors, and suppliers. There is a wide consensus that Evergrande's dramatic collapse was directly triggered by Beijing's tightening policies in the property sector.

These policies date back to 2016, when President Xi commented, during the Nineteenth Party Congress, that "houses are for living in, not for speculation." Following this strong call from President Xi, government ministries and local authorities introduced a series of tough measures to cool down the housing market.[49] This quick bureaucratic response recalls the "hierarchy" feature of dynamic pyramid model of regulation. The most stringent measures were rolled out in 2020, when the central government introduced the so-called three-red-lines policy to curb perilous borrowing by property firms.[50] Under this policy, property developers have to ensure a liability-to-asset ratio of less than 70 percent, a net gearing ratio of less than 100 percent, and a cash-to-short-term debt ratio of at least one. If a company passes all three tests, it can increase its debt by a maximum of 15 percent in the next year. Companies that fail to stay within these limits are restricted from borrowing more money.

Evergrande crossed all three red lines, triggering a liquidity crisis that eventually led to its insolvency. But the dynamic complexity in Chinese regulation reminds us that Evergrande didn't fail solely because of Beijing's tightening policies. The firm's reckless expansion over the years also sowed the seeds of its subsequent downfall. Evergrande saw a huge opportunity in China's rapidly expanding housing market, in which soaring house prices were fueling speculative activity and increasing market demand. The firm then resorted to high-debt and high-leverage tactics to expand its business empire, which already spanned real estate, entertainment, football, and even electric vehicles. In addition, Evergrande was one of the most active Chinese property developers in the global bond market, offering lucrative yields to international junk-bond investors. After Beijing initiated a massive deleveraging campaign in 2016, traditional funds became less accessible for property developers.

Evergrande's next move in its quest to fund its ambitions for greater expansion was a turn to supply-chain finance. The company first tapped into its customers by requesting advance payments to make pre-sales of unfinished apartments. Meanwhile, it significantly expanded its borrowing from suppliers and contractors and requested an extension of payment terms. These short-term loans from suppliers are not technically classified as debts in China and thus evade the strict scrutiny of regulators. A considerable number of these loans were further packaged into asset-backed securities and sold to investors. At the same time, Evergrande was also leaning heavily on its employees to purchase its wealth-management products. When Chinese financial regulators eventually noticed the serious risks associated with these loans, Evergrande was already on the brink of bankruptcy, leaving a vast network of employees, suppliers, homebuyers, and customers in severe financial distress.[51]

Local governments were also complicit in facilitating the wild growth of companies like Evergrande. Land sales have been a major source of local-government revenue. In 2020, 59.8 percent of property-sales revenue went to the government.[52] During the same year, revenues from land transfers and special taxes on real estate together accounted for 37.6 percent of local-government revenue.[53] These figures have also increased over the years.[54] Between 2012 and 2020, land transfers and special real-estate taxes increased from 20 percent and 27.1 percent of government revenue to 30.4 percent and 37.6 percent, respectively. Evergrande also partnered with local governments to sell houses and build factories and theme parks.[55] Despite the repeated financial red flags, local governments turned a blind eye to the risks and kept critics at bay.[56] The inaction and tolerance of local governments are a further illustration of the parochialism of Chinese regulators.

Yet Evergrande is not alone. Similar high-leverage problems exist in many other Chinese developers, with the result that the Evergrande crisis was merely the first to send shockwaves across the country's property sector. Data shows that 343 developers, most of them small real-estate enterprises, declared bankruptcy nationwide in 2021.[57] Meanwhile, an increasing number of major developers, including Yango, Kaisa Group, Sinic Holdings, Fantasia, and Modern Land, have declared defaults since 2021.[58] The real-estate downturn has directly contributed to a slowdown of the Chinese economy not seen in decades. In 2021, the Chinese property market accounted for an estimated quarter of China's GDP, and nearly 70 percent of Chinese household wealth is invested in property.[59] A pullback in mortgage lending and a dramatic drop in property sales dragged down the pace of investment spending.[60] Consequently, the global growth forecasts for China have been cut to below 5 percent in 2022.[61]

These spillover effects on the economy are creating strong resistance to the central government's tightening policies. In the face of enormous financial distress in the property sector and damage to the economy, Chinese policymakers had no choice but to gradually loosen up some measures. In doing so, however, the top leadership also faced an acute dilemma. Over the past two decades, the Chinese government has conducted several rounds of policy tightening over its property sector. In fact, prior to 2017, the tightening policies all gave rise to an anomaly, namely, "more regulation, higher house prices." This anomaly was due to the central government's wavering between economic growth and house-price control as its primary aim.[62] Developers and home buyers continued with their investments, as they believed that the central government would eventually loosen up its policy, given the strong backlash such measures could generate for the rest of the economy.

To appear more credible this time, the Chinese government needed to impose tougher measures without pulling back too quickly, as they had done before. But this was easier said than done, given the heavy toll the property crisis had taken on the Chinese economy. Toward the end of 2021, the central government started to roll out fiscal policies to stabilize economic growth and support businesses in making infrastructure investments "appropriately."[63] Around the same time, the People's Bank of China (PBOC) started to loosen up its monetary policy to inject liquidity into the financial system.[64] Concurrently, the government relaxed the three-red-lines policy, giving developers more leeway to finance their loans, buy out distressed developers, and survive.[65] Thus, in January 2022, several large developers received notice from the Chinese government that merger-and-acquisition loans could be excluded from their declared debt level and also that they could increase their debt level by 5 percent.[66] In April 2022, more than 60 municipal governments loosened home-buying restrictions.[67] In the following months, the China Securities Regulatory Commission vowed to support easier financing for property firms, while the PBOC cut the interest rate for mortgages for first-time home buyers.[68] In early 2023, China reportedly dialed back the stringent three-red-lines policy in order to restore market confidence to shore up the ailing Chinese economy.[69]

China's crackdown on the property sector fits neatly into a typical Chinese regulatory cycle of "loosening causes chaos, tightening up causes death," further demonstrating the volatility and fragility of the dynamic pyramid model of regulation. Chinese policymakers have clear legitimate reasons to curb speculation in the property market and reduce the economy's reliance on this sector. However, they also face imminent threats of an economic slowdown and social unrest as a result of the crackdown. The complexity and interdependence of the various components of the property supply chain have created severe challenges for China to tackle deep structural and economic reforms. Beijing is carefully balancing all of these interests, which explains why its policy has remained very nimble. At the same time, Beijing's agility has also made the Chinese government less credible in its commitment to cooling down the property sector.

3.4. The One-Child Policy

China first announced its one-child policy in 1980. Widely viewed as one of the world's most radical experiments in demographic control, this controversial household birth quota remained in effect for almost 35 years. The dynamic pyramid model of regulation can help us understand the dynamic complexity in China's birth-control policy, as well as the reasons for its persistence.

The one-child policy was adopted against a backdrop of political transition after the death of Chairman Mao and the removal of the Gang of Four.[70] After experiencing years of political chaos and economic calamity during the Cultural Revolution, the post-Mao leadership saw economic growth and development as its first priority for re-establishing political legitimacy.[71] One particularly strong advocate for such policies was Deng Xiaoping, who saw population control as a method of raising GDP per capita in China.[72] When Deng assumed power in 1978, he and other top leaders decided to vigorously pursue this aim.[73] The top Chinese leaders believed that birth-control policies—a notable departure from the policies pursued under the previous administration—were essential for economic growth and the improvement of living standards in China.[74] That said, although there was growing recognition among the top leaders that a birth-control policy was essential for achieving China's modernization drive, there was disagreement regarding its ideal speed and scope.[75] It was in the midst of these disputes that Song Jiang, a military scientist at China's Ministry of National Defense, predicted doom unless the country took decisive and drastic birth-control measures.[76] Jiang's neo-Malthusian warning about an uncontrollable population explosion that would threaten the survival of the Chinese people was instrumental in persuading senior leaders to adopt a strict one-child policy.[77] Song's alarming study also enhanced the legitimacy of the top leaders' decision, an important factor in gaining mass public support for the policy.[78]

As a top-down initiative, the one-child policy was quickly put into effect across China. The central government set demographic targets and guidelines, and delegated their implementation to local governments.[79] Because GDP per capita is viewed as an important criterion in evaluating the performance of a CCP cadre, local Chinese officials saw control of population size as an important task in meeting their political and economic objectives.[80] In 1991, the central government made family-planning targets a direct responsibility of local governments.[81] As the policy directives made their way down through the layers of local government, those in charge of implementation at the grassroots level felt sharp pressure to meet their targets.[82] The local government's faithful execution of the mandates from the central government illustrates the hierarchical feature of the dynamic pyramid model. Unsurprisingly, strict implementation of the policy inflicted enormous trauma and pain on Chinese families, with violent abuse frequently used to achieve birth-control targets.[83] Yet the mass suffering of Chinese families was seldom heard.[84]

In retrospect, many scholars have questioned the effectiveness of the one-child policy. China has indeed experienced sharp declines in fertility since the 1970s, yet some scholars argue that China's fertility rate would have declined even without the drastic policy.[85] Such critics have instead pointed to increased socioeconomic development as a crucial factor in China's demographic slowdown.[86] Meanwhile, some scholars have held the middle ground, noting that while the one-child policy may have accelerated the trend, economic development played the more decisive and fundamental role in China's fertility decline, in a pattern similar to what has been observed in other countries.[87] Whatever its role in the decline in fertility, the one-child policy brought about severe unintended consequences. Mandatory birth control is a fundamental violation of human rights, and has caused irreparable harm to many families and individuals.[88] The policy has also led to many social problems, including an imbalanced sex ratio as many Chinese couples prefer to have boys rather than girls.[89] Furthermore, China now faces an acute problem with its aging population. Yong Cai recently predicted that China's elderly will increase to 30 percent or more of the total population in the near future.[90] This disproportion not only creates a huge burden for society, but also for those in China's working class, who need to support their parents despite having no siblings.[91]

Meanwhile, China achieved astounding economic growth during the period in which the one-child policy came into effect, with GDP per capita more than quadrupling between 1980 and 1994, an outcome that far exceeded the initial goal set by Deng Xiaoping.[92] Given that increasing GDP per capita was an important motivation behind the adoption of the one-child policy and economic performance far exceeded expectations, it is puzzling why China had to wait until 2015 to retract the policy.[93] Indeed, experts have suggested that this retraction came at least a decade too late.[94] The inefficiency information transmission in the regulatory hierarchy was an important factor holding back China's reversal of the policy. Thirty-five years of enforcing the strict quota fostered a vast bureaucracy in charge of birth control: the National Population and Family Planning Commission.

The Commission was a nationwide administrative organization that commanded vast resources and half a million employees, along with another six million workers who helped with implementation.[95] As the Commission's agenda grew bigger and bigger over the years, officials working there eventually became one of the strongest interest groups opposing changes to the one-child policy.[96]

Spokesmen from the Commission often touted how the one-child policy helped China avert 400 million births, which they posited as a key contributor to the nation's economic boom and success.[97] Demographic experts sharply contested such estimates, deriding them as false and misleading.[98] Starting in the early 2000s, scholars from leading Chinese population-research institutions collectively and actively appealed to Chinese policymakers to relax or end the one-child policy.[99] In 1990, the reported fertility rate was 2.3. This dropped to 1.2 by the year 2000, according to the official population census. As the policy was not always implemented strictly, some experts disputed this official statistic, arguing that the stated figure was too low to be true, and that a large number of out-of-plan births had gone underreported.[100] This controversy among experts generated a great deal of noise that hindered understanding of the true fertility situation in China. Meanwhile, with its own bureaucratic interests at stake, the Family Planning Commission started to conceal the precipitous population decline—a paradoxical endeavor given that reducing fertility was, in principle, its main objective. By comparing the official statistics with school registration and other measures, experts found that the Commission's estimates were inflated by an average of 25 percent.[101] In 2004, an academic advocacy group submitted years of field-study findings about the worrying decline of fertility rates to the Commission and other government authorities. The experts had hoped that their findings would support the creation of experimental zones in which couples would be allowed to have two children.[102] But the Commission rejected this proposal, reaffirming the official doctrines that the one-child policy was critical to maintaining a low fertility rate in China, and that a low fertility rate was crucial for economic growth.[103]

In addition to stoking debate over China's actual fertility rate, the Family Planning Commission took advantage of the controversy surrounding remedial measures to hold on to the one-child policy. Over the years, the Commission enlisted support from conservative scholars who supported a gradual approach to reforming the policy.[104] One such scholar was Huo Zhenwu, a leading professor of demography from Renmin University. Huo served on the expert committee of the Family Planning Commission, which frequently commissioned him to conduct studies on the one-child policy.[105] In 2014, Huo and his students published an influential study predicting that the Chinese population would have increased by more than 160 million within four years if the one-child policy had been replaced with a two-child policy in 2012.[106] In reality, in the four years after China relaxed the one-child policy in 2016, the Chinese population only increased by less than 65 million, about 40 percent of Huo's estimate. Although other Chinese experts fiercely disputed its findings, the study by Huo's team provided support and legitimacy for the Commission's decision to postpone introducing the two-child policy.[107]

The one-child policy represents the worst form of the dynamic pyramid model of regulation, in that it has resulted in strong negative side effects with a very long information lag. By the time the authorities finally decided to relax birth-control measures, it was too late. In 2016, the Chinese government started allowing couples to have two children. However, the fertility rate of Chinese women dropped to 1.3 in 2020, far below the replacement level of 2.1 needed for a stable population.[108] In 2021, concerns about an aging population and a shrinking labor force led the government to further relax its birth-control measures by allowing each couple to have three children. But experts are not optimistic that this will be effective in preventing a further population decline.[109]

3.5. Reflections

As illustrated above, the dynamic pyramid model of regulation is inherently unstable and creates significant volatility. Similar to its regulation of the tech sector, China's efforts at Covid control and at addressing the property crisis were both characterized in their initial stages by tolerance and inaction at the sub-national level. After this lax regulation created huge social and economic chaos, the central government took drastic action and imposed strict regulations. The birth-control and energy crises, on the other hand, went in the other direction; namely, from strict to lax regulation, as they both originated from top-down measures to improve economic or environmental conditions for the Chinese population. Both policies created strong unintended consequences, however, eventually forcing the central government to unwind its measures.

A common theme across the examples above is that forceful and well-intentioned intervention to correct social ills can create strong side effects, giving rise to additional severe challenges for Chinese policymakers. Whether Chinese policymakers are able to quickly adapt and reorient their policies depends heavily on the information lag. This is extremely important, as accurate and timely information helps policymakers better weigh the costs and benefits of their policies. The top leaders felt the pains of the energy crisis almost immediately and boosted coal supplies to alleviate the electricity shortage. In the case of Covid control, however, the top leaders appeared to receive inadequate feedback on its policies, hence becoming too complacent to realize the disastrous impact on the society and the heavy toll it took on the Chinese economy. The one-child policy represents the worst example of information lag as it took Chinese policymakers decades to realize the severe side effects of their policy. One important contributing factor for the delay came from the difficulties in understanding China's true fertility rate—a source of fierce debate among experts. Meanwhile, the Commission in charge of overseeing the one-child policy created significant noise by supporting misleading research from conservative academics and disseminating misinformation about China's demographic realities.

One key takeaway from the above policy crises is that policymakers should learn to minimize the side effects of their policies as much as possible. Given that side effects cannot be anticipated in advance, one strategy for predicting the impact of radical policy changes is to take incremental steps via gradual experimentation. As Deng Xiaoping famously said, "cross the river by touching the stones." There are great benefits to this approach, which allows policymakers to observe the consequences of a small-scale operation and understand the side effects that could result from a larger-scale application. This mode of policymaking is similar to the development of a drug or vaccine, which likewise needs to go through several phases of trials in order for scientists to observe the impact of a particular treatment. Just as important as controlling side effects is getting timely and accurate information about the impact of a policy experiment. As the cases of the Covid control and the one-child policy illustrate, a dynamic pyramid model of regulation is fatal in circumstances where policymakers are not able to receive quick feedback. By the time they realize the severity of a given problem, it is usually far too late to address it, making reversing the situation extremely costly. In the following discussion, I will turn to China's strategy of policy experimentation, which has often been credited as the key factor that contributes to the resilience of Chinese policymaking during market-ization reforms.[110]

3.6. Decentralized Policy Experimentation

Many historians and economists have pointed to decentralized policy in-novations, which tap into local knowledge and mobilize bottom-up ini-tiatives, as the key reason for China's phenomenal economic success.[111] Isabella Weber, who delved into the historical record on China's debate on marketization, found that the country avoided the shock therapy adopted by many post-Communist countries and instead gradually relaxed its price controls.[112] In addition to price liberalization, the creation of China's special economic zones, the privatization of SOEs, the creation of the stock mar-kets, and the reforms of rural health systems and land management were all initiated via policy experimentation.[113] In fact, the CCP has a long tradition of policy experimentation which dates back to its revolutionary period.[114] Scholars have traced the influence of John Dewey, who delivered a signifi-cant series of lectures in China in the 1920s to Chinese intellectuals and activists, including the founders of the Party.[115] Mao attended Dewey's lec-ture in Shanghai and a number of academic works have since found a direct link between Mao's pragmatic writings and Dewey's advocacy for learning through practical experience.[116] In a related vein, Harvard's Elizabeth Perry has also argued that the experience of China's revolutionary past has actu-ally furthered China's successful market reforms.[117]

Typically, a decentralized experiment unfolds in three stages. The pro-cess commences when local officials carry out spontaneous experiments backed by higher authorities to solve a pressing problem in their respective jurisdictions.[118] Local-government officials have a strong incentive to en-gage in policy innovations because reforms not only help them advance their political careers, but also expand their rent-seeking opportunities.[119] The second step involves higher-level policymakers identifying successful projects and then cautiously broadening them into wider-scale operations. During this stage of the process, local governments that engaged in policy experiments need to regularly report their progress to high-level government bodies, who then send inspectors on a regular basis to conduct official evaluations.[120] In the third step, after thorough testing in real-life administrative environments, successful policies are implemented nationwide via legislation.[121] One famous example of a decentralized policy experiment is the rural de-collectivization experiment initiated by 18 farmers from the small village of Xiaogang in Anhui province—an experiment that was later hailed as a model and replicated all over China.[122]

It is important to bear in mind that there are two distinct types of policy experiments: decentralized and top-down. The former originates from the experience of local authorities tackling pressing problems in their regions, and the latter derives from policy initiatives from the top leadership. While the former type of experiment played an instrumental role during the marketization of the Chinese economy, the latter type has had a mixed track record. In fact, some of the top-down policy experiments imposed during ideologically and politically charged periods resulted in epic failures. The Great Leap Forward, a radical industrialization campaign initiated by Mao in the late 1950s, is one such example. At its core, that campaign sought to achieve rapid economic growth and encourage regional competition so that China could catch up with and overtake Great Britain within 15 years. In order to achieve this ambitious goal, a large population of peasants abandoned farming and moved to urban areas to boost industrial output. The campaign led to the worst man-made famine in history, with an estimated 30 million people having died in excess of the normal mortality rate.[123]

But why do these two types of policy experiments lead to drastically different outcomes? Top-down policy experiments are more likely to lead to agency overreach than decentralized ones because lower-level officials have strong incentives to take radical and excessive measures to implement the top officials' initiatives, without regard for potential consequences. In an empirical study, James Kung and Shuo Chen explored the variation of mortality rates among different provinces during the Great Leap Forward and identified a link between the career incentives of officials and mortality rates.[124] Specifically, they found that provinces where provincial leaders could see greater prospects for promotion were more likely to take drastic actions to signal commitment to the Great Leap Forward movement, resulting in a higher death toll.

Furthermore, top-down policy experiments are more likely to result in slower information transmission from the bottom to the top, because local officials have strong incentives to conceal the negative consequences of experiments in order to display fealty to their superiors' initiatives. Driven by the desire to meet their performance targets based on the cadre evaluation system, local officials in China also tend to distort information about their work achievements.[125] While local officials have similar incentives to inflate their performance with respect to decentralized experiments, these policies are usually subject to more robust supervision and checks before they are transplanted to other areas. Indeed, it sometimes takes years or decades for a local policy experiment to make it into national legislation. One such example is China's Bankruptcy Law, which took a total of 23 years to make it into law, starting from an early experiment with the insolvency of Chinese state-owned enterprises in 1984, and followed by many experimental regulations tested in controversial policy areas including cities, industries, and companies.[126]

In contrast, top-down policy experiments lack this process of trial and error. During the Great Leap Forward, local officials inflated local grain-output numbers, which further encouraged Mao's plan and misled the central government into setting excessive procurement targets. These information distortions were exacerbated by the purge of Peng Dehuai, who criticized Mao's radical plan. Discouraged from revealing the truth, lower-level officials continued to cover up and conceal the situation, despite precipitous drops in grain output and increasing death tolls.[127] It wasn't until two years later that the central government became informed and started famine-relief efforts.[128] Scholars have identified information distortion as the critical factor that resulted in this long information lag.[129] After learning bitter lessons from the Great Leap Forward, the Chinese government took countermeasures to bypass lower-level officials and go directly to the providers of raw data in an attempt to avoid information distortion.[130] The effectiveness of such bypassing strategies is limited, however, and information distortion remains a serious and ongoing concern for Chinese policymakers.[131]

While decentralized policy experiments have better prospects for improving regulation, local authorities still need political support and endorsement from the central authorities before they can launch incremental reform. In her book *How China Escaped the Poverty Trap*, Yuen Yuen Ang relates a vivid analogy employed by a local official, who described the Chinese bureaucracy as a "stack of briquettes"—a block of coal dust used for cooking in China—and noted how air needs to flow through it from top to bottom.[132] In recent years, however, the flow of "air" seems to be waning. In contrast to his predecessors Deng Xiaoping and Jiang Zemin, President Xi Jinping has preferred to use centralized decision-making from a small group of top leaders and trusted advisors.[133] As was discussed in Chapter 1, Beijing's tightening control over the bureaucratic apparatus has created a strong aversion among government officials to engage in risky policy innovations. Instead, the Xi administration's extensive anti-corruption campaign and efforts to enforce intra-party discipline have contributed to lazy governance in China, where local officials try to avoid mistakes by doing less. Sebastien Heilmann has observed widespread misgivings in many party organs and government bodies about decentralized experiments and their associated political risks.[134] Barry Naughton similarly observed a pattern of excess caution regarding policy responsibilities among lower-level officials.[135]

Nassim Taleb and Gregory Treverton have astutely highlighted that while centralization reduces deviation from the norm, it magnifies the consequences of those deviations that do arise.[136] This is due to the concentration of disruption it creates, leading to increased systemic risks.[137] As observed by Heilmann, a number of central policies imposed during the period from 2014 to 2016—including fiscal reform, stock-market regulation, and internet security—prompted very negative market reactions and drew heavy criticism from local governments, leading to their eventual withdrawal.[138] Heilmann further attributed the "more impulsive or even aggressive style of decision-making" in China's foreign and security policy to Xi's leadership style.[139] Consequently, China's simultaneous increase in personalistic and centralized decision-making and a decrease in decentralized policy experimentation have further contributed to fragility in Chinese regulatory governance.

3.7. Summary

This chapter has introduced a framework for us to assess the consequences of regulation, highlighting two important determinants that affect the resilience of China's regulatory governance: side effects and information lag. In short, the greater the side effects, the more resistance there will be to a particular policy; and the longer the information lag, the greater the damage a policy can do, making it potentially more difficult to remedy the situation. To be sure, the dynamic pyramid model of regulation has clear strengths when policy side effects are minor compared to the benefits. More often than not, however, Chinese regulation leads to undesirable outcomes when a regulatory policy creates serious unintended consequences. Indeed, Chinese regulation is most fragile when there is a long lag before top policymakers realize the scale and magnitude of side effects. To illustrate my assessment framework, I looked at four vexing policy challenges facing the Chinese leadership—China's Covid policy, the energy crisis, the property crackdown, and the one-child policy—to explain the fragilities of the dynamic pyramid model of regulation. This then led me into a discussion about how policymakers can better reduce side effects and information lags during policymaking. I noted that China's successful marketization reforms were built upon a series of decentralized policy experiments by local governments, whose incentives for doing such experiments have dwindled in recent years with Xi's increasingly heavy-handed approach toward bureaucratic control. As a consequence, centralized decision-making has replaced local reforms, contributing to more fragilities in Chinese regulation.

The evolution of China's governance approach as described above thus raises an important question about the prospects for regulation in the tech sector. Given the volatility in Chinese tech regulation, how resilient will China's tech policies be? To answer this question in detail, the following chapters proceed via three steps. First, I will apply the dynamic pyramid model to analyze how Chinese tech firms have been regulated in different areas of law, including antitrust, data, and labor regulation. Then I will examine how these tech firms conduct self-regulation in the shadow of an increasingly tightened regulatory environment. I will also compare the developments in major jurisdictions such as the United States and the European Union to help readers better gauge the future direction of Chinese reforms. I will leave the most important question in assessing the impact of the Chinese tech regulation to Chapter 10.

PART II

Platform Regulation

In this part, spanning chapters 4–6, I apply the dynamic pyramid model to expound upon the three major pillar of Chinese tech regulation: antitrust, data, and labor regulation. In each of these chapters, I first investigate the major challenges faced by regulators in their respective areas, highlighting how a fragile institutional environment, coupled with the government's abusive practices or inaction, often exacerbate these issues. I then closely examine the incentives and behaviors of the four major actors involved in the regulatory process, explaining how their interactions have culminated in the regulatory cycles Chinese tech firms have experienced. Looking ahead, I offer some predictions regarding the future trajectory of enforcement in each respective area.

4

Antitrust Regulation

China promulgated the Anti-Monopoly Law (AML), its first modern and comprehensive antitrust law, in 2007. Much like antitrust laws in other jurisdictions, such as the European Union and the United States, China's AML comes with high-powered sanctions and has great potential to deter abusive practices. Since the AML became effective in 2008, however, the law has mostly been applied to foreign multinational firms rather than to the country's state-owned behemoths or domestic tech giants.[1] Indeed, despite the fact that complaints about the anti-competitive practices of Chinese tech giants emerged long before the AML was adopted, it wasn't until 2020 that these firms came under the close scrutiny of China's antitrust law.

Indeed, antitrust enforcement was a major stick wielded by the Chinese government to bring its Big Tech firms into line during the law enforcement campaign, as described in Chapter 2. Between late 2020 and the end of 2021, the State Administration for Market Regulation (SAMR), China's main antitrust enforcer, hastily adopted tough antitrust guidelines targeting the platform economy, proactively vetted a large number of previously unscrutinized merger transactions, and quickly initiated several high-profile antitrust cases against firms such as Alibaba, Tencent, and Meituan. The antitrust bureau at the SAMR emerged as a clear winner from this regulatory campaign, not least because it was elevated to vice-ministerial status, a change that enabled it to significantly expand its personnel and budget. Moreover, the SAMR has also conveniently leveraged its antitrust powers to strengthen its policy control in other areas of market regulation, thus further solidifying its status as a "super regulator."

In the following discussion, I will first delve into the regulatory challenges in the Chinese consumer tech sector, which has witnessed both

High Wire. Angela Huyue Zhang, Oxford University Press. © Oxford University Press 2024.
DOI: 10.1093/oso/9780197682258.003.0005

a high concentration of market power and frenetic competition between major tech firms. I will then apply the dynamic pyramid model to analyze the incentives and behavior of each of the four major actors in the antitrust regulatory process, thereby elucidating the dramatic swing of the regulatory pendulum between 2020 and 2021. Since regulation started to ease in early 2022, I will conclude with an analysis and forecast of the future enforcement trend.

4.1. Regulatory Challenges

For years, the Chinese tech sector has been a "Wild West" with little government intervention, and this has allowed for the unruly growth of tech titans. This competitive landscape is attributed to three primary factors that have presented significant regulatory challenges in the consumer tech sector, each of which will be elaborated below.

4.1.1. The Great Firewall

The Chinese government's efforts to filter out foreign content in the name of maintaining social order and safeguarding national security were, ironically enough, the first regulatory challenge. Since 1998, China has operated the world's most extensive and technologically advanced internet filtering system, widely known as the "Great Firewall," to censor online content. Although China is not unique in controlling information within its border, the scale and sophistication of its operation are unprecedented. A 2020 study shows that China's Great Firewall blocks around 311,000 domains.[2] An estimated 50,000 people have been employed to enforce such censorship.[3] By blocking "unwelcome websites" to protect the country's internet from undue Western influence, the Great Firewall acts like a non-tariff trade barrier that has largely shut out competition from some of the Chinese firms' most formidable rivals, notably Google, Meta, and Twitter. Although some US businesses, such as Microsoft's Bing, continue to operate in China, they have only limited access given their need to adapt to the country's increasingly tight censorship requirements. Home-grown tech firms quickly filled the void by gaining economies of scale within the domestic market, without needing to expand overseas. The result is that China has created its own parallel universe of consumer internet businesses: there is Didi instead of Uber; WeChat instead of WhatsApp, Facebook, and PayPal; Meituan and Ele.me instead of Deliveroo; and Youku instead of YouTube.

Google's unexpected exit from China in 2010 offers a prime example. The search giant entered the Chinese market in 2006 and provided censored search results in compliance with the Chinese government. At that time, Google was engaged in a fearsome rivalry with Baidu, China's homegrown search engine. The two firms constituted a duopoly in China's internet-search market, with Google possessing 33 percent market share and Baidu 64 percent in 2009.[4] In 2009, Google believed it was hit by a sophisticated and targeted cyber-attack launched from China on its corporate infrastructure. In light of the attack and further government censorship, Google went into negotiations with Beijing about how it might operate without censorship in China.[5] When these negotiations failed, Google moved its searching server to Hong Kong. In the months following Google's exit, Baidu's profits doubled, its market share soared, and it quickly became the dominant search engine in China.[6]

To be sure, the lack of foreign competition is not the only reason why Chinese tech firms thrive. Chinese tech firms are very good at so-called micro-innovation, wherein they adapt products or services to the local market. In 2004, Microsoft decided to expand its MSN services, an instant-messaging product, in China. Within two years, Tencent's QQ outcompeted MSN, largely because the former's small and nimble operation offered a competitive advantage over the latter's protracted and bureaucratic internal decision-making process.[7] Another example is Alibaba, which took on and vanquished fearsome US rivals such as eBay. Many commentators have credited Taobao's success to its ability to adapt to the Chinese market, particularly its strategy of enabling direct communication between merchants and consumers and its ability to leverage communities to develop mutual trust among online users.[8] As Jack Ma famously said: "eBay is a shark of the sea, but a crocodile can beat a shark in the Yangtze River."[9] Indeed, even in those areas where the Great Firewall has limited foreign entry, the absence of foreign competition can only partially account for the success of domestic firms. Baidu, for example, outcompeted Google before the latter's exit because its various business strategies more effectively catered to the interests of Chinese consumers.[10] That said, there is little doubt that Google's exit was an important gift to Baidu and other Chinese rivals. Even though Baidu's market share has been eroded in recent years by other domestic competitors such as Sogou, no other foreign rival penetrated the Chinese market as effectively as Google.[11] Indeed, Microsoft's Bing is now the only foreign search engine available in the country, with a mere 2 percent market share.[12]

4.1.2. Disorderly Expansion

The regulatory challenge was the frenetic expansion of leading Chinese tech firms such as Alibaba and Tencent in the platform economy, which enabled them to build partnerships and exert influence over a wide array of internet-based products and services. Such disorderly expansion was also partly facilitated by the inaction of the antitrust authorities when it came to intervening in anti-competitive mergers, as will be further elaborated later. Within the past decade, the in-house investment teams at Chinese Big Tech firms have grown to be on par with leading venture-capital powerhouses in China.[13] As of the end of 2021, Tencent and Alibaba had made more than 1,180 and 706 investments, respectively.[14] Tencent alone had invested in at least 160 companies that later became unicorns and 70 companies that went public as of January 2020.[15] Even in the midst of a tech crackdown in 2021, Tencent and Alibaba snapped up 250 and 75 companies, respectively.[16] Chinese tech giants' aggressive investments have significantly dwarfed those of their American peers. Based on their public filings, Alibaba and Tencent spent between 80 and 100 percent of their revenue on investing between 2014 and 2019, whereas the largest five US Big Tech firms, GAMAM (Google, Amazon, Meta, Apple, and Microsoft) invested only 30 to 66 percent of their revenue.[17]

Through these active acquisitions and investments, Alibaba and Tencent have extended their tentacles into almost every aspect of people's lives in China. Among the top 10 most widely used apps in China in 2021 (based on active user numbers), 7 were owned by Alibaba and Tencent, while the rest were owned by Baidu and ByteDance.[18] Among the top 30 apps in China, 70 percent were either owned by or affiliated with Alibaba or Tencent. Indeed, these two tech giants have together or separately invested in many top players in China's consumer tech sector. These include Didi Chuxing, with almost 80 percent market share in the ride-hailing business; Meituan and Ele.me, with a combined 98 percent market share in the food-delivery business; Taobao, JD.com, and Pinduoduo, with a combined market share of 84 percent in e-commerce; and Alipay and WeChat Pay, with over 90 percent market share in the third-party mobile payment market.[19] Not surprisingly, Tencent and Alibaba are often dubbed the "duopoly" that dominates China's technology landscape.

On the other hand, these two Big Tech firms have different investment styles: Alibaba prefers to purchase controlling stakes and maintain control in businesses, while Tencent is usually content to hold minority ownership in an attempt to form alliances or acquire technologies.[20] Nonetheless, the investment strategies of both firms are driven not just by short-term profits, but more importantly by competition. As Zhaohui Li, Tencent's investment executive has put it, "a project that has strategic value will eventually bring financial value."[21] Li considers the strategic value of an investment as consisting of three major aspects: first, the ability to help enhance the core competitiveness of Tencent; second, the ability to coordinate and integrate with Tencent's businesses; and last but not least, the ability to help Tencent enter into new and promising areas of products and services.[22] Through investing, Tencent is strengthening its own core competence as an ultimate connector that links everything with the internet, while preemptively tackling threats from emerging rivals by investing in them at an early stage.

Given the two firms' pervasive influence over Chinese internet businesses, smaller rival companies have often felt they have no choice but to accept their investment.[23] To be sure, having Alibaba or Tencent as an investor is very appealing for smaller firms for two important reasons: capital and traffic. First, the deep coffers of these two tech titans are an important source of financing for smaller start-ups. Second, investment from Alibaba or Tencent enables startups to better integrate with the two firms' "super-apps," which can rapidly channel gargantuan traffic to these smaller companies.

Generally speaking, super-apps are large integrated ecosystems that enable users to access a wide variety of services within their walled gardens. Tencent's WeChat, an instant-messaging app used by 90 percent of the Chinese population, is a quintessential example. Since its launch, WeChat has pushed beyond being a simple messaging app by introducing various social-media functions, by encouraging user-generated content such as public accounts from individuals and companies, by launching mini-programs that enable users to access a wide range of services without downloading separate apps, and by adding WeChat Pay, which allows users to conveniently pay for goods and services accessed within the app.[24] This strategic expansion has enabled WeChat to grow into an all-purpose platform on which Chinese internet users spend, on average, a fifth of their time.[25] Ant Group's Alipay is another example. The third-party mobile payment tool affiliated with Alibaba is used by more than 900 million Chinese people and offers numerous mini-programs for users.[26] However, investments from these two tech giants can deprive small start-ups of their freedom, leaving their founders with little choice but to run their businesses in a way that serves the strategic interests of the tech giants.[27] Over the years, through the alliances they have created with the hundreds of firms in which they invested, Alibaba and Tencent have each created a massive ecosystem with strong network effects, effectively carving the Chinese consumer internet space into two separate "walled gardens."

In addition to these investments across different sectors, Alibaba and Tencent also hold common ownership in several sectors. For instance, Tencent has invested deeply in gaming and the music industry. The firm owns 47 percent of Huya[28] and 38 percent of Douyu,[29] China's two largest live-streaming gaming firms with a combined market share of more than 80 percent.[30] Alibaba has also holds common ownership in major logistics firms, including Cainiao Network, YTO Express, RRS Supply Chain, Best Inc., ZTO Express, STO Express, Yunda Express, and Singapore Post.[31] Publicly available data suggest that the combined market share of YTO Express, Best Inc., ZTO Express, STO Express, and Yunda Express exceeded 73 percent of the express delivery market in 2020.[32] Recent economic literature has suggested that common ownership could soften competition and facilitate collusion among firms in the common owner's portfolio.[33]

In the United States, the overlapping interests of financial investors in a wide range of industries such as airlines, banking, aluminum, soft drinks, and mobile phones have been viewed as an additional source of market power for these investors.[34] And there has been an ongoing intense debate as to how to limit the anti-competitive power by these institutional investors.[35] One can find a similar case in China. Sequoia Capital, a large venture-capital firm, is the largest investor in Chinese consumer internet businesses. As of the end of 2020, the firm had invested in 339 Chinese tech firms, including the largest players, such as Alibaba, JD.com, Pinduoduo, Meituan, Didi, and ByteDance.[36] One of Sequoia's distinctive investment strategies is to bet simultaneously on several players competing in the same sector, and then push for their consolidation at the right moment.[37] According to Chinese media, Sequoia was reportedly one of the investors that pushed forward the tie-ups between the largest players in the e-commerce sector, including the mergers of Meituan and Dianping, Uber China and Didi, and VShop and Lefenghui.[38]

4.1.3. Unruly Competition

With Alibaba and Tencent becoming the twin pillars dominating China's tech landscape, the cutthroat competition between them and other rivals has given rise over the years to a wide range of antitrust issues The first major issue is that of interoperability, as leading Chinese tech firms carefully guard their traffic by blocking competitors from accessing their ecosystems. One of the earliest examples of this problem dates back to 2008, when Alibaba decided to shut out Baidu so that products listed on its e-commerce platforms such as Taobao could no longer be found on Baidu's search engine. Alibaba justified its decision on the basis of protecting consumers (i.e., to prevent merchants from manipulating search results on Baidu). To be sure, Taobao is not the only website that blocked Baidu's search engine; other major social-networking services such as blog.sohu.com, 51.com, Xiaonei, and Hainei have done the same.[39] All these sites claimed to have blocked Baidu to protect user privacy, even though analysts believe that their real motivation lay in concerns over Baidu's dominant position in the search market.[40] Indeed, Alibaba was worried that once consumers got used to searching for shopping results on Baidu, this would eventually divert traffic from Taobao. At that time, Baidu was also starting to step into Alibaba's turf by creating Youa, an e-commerce platform similar to e-Bay. As almost 20 percent of Taobao's traffic then came from Baidu, some analysts viewed Alibaba's decision as quite risky.[41] But Alibaba's gamble paid off, as it protected its turf by fending off potential competition from Baidu. However, consumers suffered in that they were deprived of the convenience of searching for Taobao products outside of Taobao's site. More importantly, Taobao's move to lock in its users may have delayed the emergence of rival e-commerce platforms from Baidu.

The scale of acrimonious blocking between platforms escalated more and more as Alibaba and Tencent expanded their business empires. In 2013,

Taobao started blocking sellers from subscribing to marketing and promotion apps linked with WeChat.[42] Taobao also invested in the Twitter-like Weibo, which offered to provide Taobao sellers with marketing services and better integrate the services of its shopping and the microblog sites.[43] WeChat retaliated by actively blocking Taobao's content in its app. Of course, WeChat announced that it had only done this following its own internal governance rules prohibiting falsehoods and misinformation.[44] The online payment tools developed by these two tech giants—Tencent's WeChat Pay and Alibaba's Alipay—are also not interoperable. For instance, WeChat is not available on Taobao, whereas WeChat doesn't support Alipay.

In addition to blocking each other, these two tech giants also blocked start-ups in their rivals' camps. In 2013, JD.com, the major rival to Alibaba's Taobao site, terminated cooperation with Sina Weibo, China's Twitter, after the latter's sale of a minority stake to Alibaba.[45] JD.com also stopped using Alipay, a third-party payment platform developed by Alibaba. A year later, Tencent acquired a 15 percent stake in JD.com; since then, JD.com has officially joined the Tencent camp to compete head-to-head with Taobao.[46] In 2014, Kuaidi, a ride-hailing business backed by Alibaba, complained that certain functions of their app were blocked by WeChat. Meanwhile, Didi, which was backed by Tencent, experienced no such problems. Tencent's mini-programs have given JD.com and Pinduoduo, both backed by Tencent, a huge edge since 2017. Yet Taobao has not been allowed to have a presence there.

When ByteDance, a fiercely competitive rival, stepped into the fray, it kicked off another round of war between the tech titans. ByteDance, which owns a portfolio of entertainment, news, and short-video apps, had already amassed an active user population of over 500 million by 2018.[47] Given that Tencent and ByteDance have many overlapping content-related businesses, Tencent felt particularly threatened by ByteDance's rapid growth. In 2018, Tencent started to block ByteDance's apps, such as Toutiao, Douyin, and Feishu, from its flagship networking apps WeChat and QQ.[48] Tencent also began aggressively promoting short-video streaming features within its ubiquitous WeChat app. When ByteDance introduced several instant-messaging apps, such as Duoshan and Feiliao, in 2019, Tencent quickly blocked external links to these apps.[49] ByteDance then launched several unfair-competition and antitrust lawsuits against Tencent.[50] In response to the accusations, Tencent argued that Douyin and other apps from ByteDance had used illegal means to access WeChat's user data. Tencent retaliated by launching its own unfair-competition and defamation countersuits against ByteDance.[51]

In addition to directly restricting rivals from accessing their own ecosystems, Chinese Big Tech giants also restrict users of their platforms from accessing rivals' platforms. This has given rise to exclusionary practices such as forcing merchants to "choose-one-from-two" between leading platforms.[52] The earliest such incident dates back to 2010, when users of Tencent's QQ, a popular instant-messaging app, were presented with a tough choice between QQ and 360, an antivirus service. Qihoo, the developer of 360, alleged that QQ was scanning the private data of its users and released software that could block these invasions into personal privacy. Tencent responded by blocking access to users who had downloaded Qihoo's 360 software.[53] This incident caused an uproar among Chinese netizens, who saw themselves as the victims in this "cat-and-dog" fight between the two firms. Another well-known case involved JD.com, which made complaints about Alibaba in 2015. JD.com accused Alibaba of forcing its merchants to choose between JD.com and Tmall, an e-commerce platform owned by Alibaba. The food-delivery business, which was dominated by a duopoly—Meituan and Ele. me—has also experienced similar competitive dynamics. Over the past few years, Ele.me, China's second largest food-delivery business with almost 30 percent market share, has repeatedly accused Meituan, China's largest food-delivery business, of exclusionary practices. Ironically, Ele.me was also fined in several Chinese cities for similar "choose-one-from-two" practices.[54] It is, of course, Chinese consumers who have been the ultimate victims, since these restrictive practices limit their choices and deprive them of potential innovations.

A broad survey of the three above-mentioned regulatory challenges clearly demonstrates a strong demand for antitrust intervention in China's unruly tech sector. But it is also clear that tech firms are only partial contributors to these challenges, given that the Chinese government's censorship policies also act as a trade barrier shielding domestic firms from foreign competition. Meanwhile, Chinese consumer internet businesses have become so concentrated that it is not clear whether any regulatory intervention at this point can fundamentally change the competitive dynamics. In the following section, I will shift my focus from identifying the problems with the competitive environment among Chinese Big Tech firms to analyzing the regulatory process for tackling them. As we will see, the dynamic pyramid model will again prove very useful in explicating the complex dynamics in Chinese antitrust regulation.

4.2. Applying the Dynamic Pyramid Model

For nearly two decades, China's top leadership was a strong proponent of developing Chinese consumer internet businesses. But the country's priorities for industrial policy have started to shift in recent years, after the United States began imposing hefty sanctions on Chinese tech firms and cut off their access to critical manufacturing components. Faced with this escalating pressure, Beijing hastened its pursuit of technological self-sufficiency. In this process, it became evident that its consumer tech giants were falling short in helping the country fulfill its industrial ambitions. Meanwhile, Chinese tech firms have been lobbying aggressively for favorable legal treatment, and have sought regulatory arbitrage by operating in legal gray areas. The Chinese public in general lacks opportunities to voice its discontent except through litigation. Yet plaintiffs rarely prevail in antitrust lawsuits, resulting in a limited deterrent effect on the Chinese tech titans. Chinese antitrust regulators initially tried to guard their bureaucratic interests by refraining from taking an aggressive stance in regulating the tech firms. They changed their position, however, from late 2020 onward, when they rolled out tough antitrust guidelines and took aggressive enforcement actions against leading Chinese tech firms. In the ensuing discussion, I will delve deeper into the motivations and actions of these four major players, as well as explore the intricate dynamics of their interactions.

4.2.1. Top Leadership

As has been elaborated in Chapter 2, there was a time when Chinese internet businesses won the strong endorsement of the Chinese top leadership, who saw them as saviors of the country's flagging industrial economy. Indeed, McKinsey described the Chinese government as simultaneously "an investor, developer, and consumer" of the digital economy.[55] Beijing invested heavily in building infrastructure to support the digital sector, calling on various government institutions to provide funding for artificial-intelligence projects. The government also encouraged mass innovation, setting up incubators, offering tax incentives, and promoting venture-capital funding in the internet sector.[56] In 2016, the government also launched a pilot program allowing a few commercial banks to invest in high-growth tech firms, removing a previous prohibition on commercial banks directly investing in equities of non-bank firms.[57] The move was intended to channel more support for the Chinese tech sector by bringing more capital to the market.

During this period, Chinese policymakers actively promoted laws to provide crucial institutional support for the growth of the tech industry. Take the example of the Chinese e-commerce sector, the sector that was hit with the largest antitrust fine in 2021. In 2004, China adopted the Electronic Signature Law, based largely on the United Nations model, which encouraged the use of electronic signatures in e-commerce settings.[58] In the years that followed, the Chinese government amended the Contract Law, the Advertising Law, and the Consumer Protection Law, and promulgated the E-Commerce Law to regulate the e-commerce sector.[59] In a departure from the usual top-down, command-and-control approach, the top leadership endorsed an open and participatory approach in drafting the E-Commerce Law.[60] This enabled participation from a wide variety of non-state institutions, particularly Chinese tech businesses.[61] The law was finally passed in August 2018, after five years of intensive debate among various stakeholders.[62] The top leadership's strong endorsement of the tech sector fostered a light-touch regulatory environment that was very conducive to the growth of the domestic e-commerce market, the world's largest since 2013. China's homegrown e-commerce firms such as Alibaba, JD.com, and Pinduoduo have become fiercely competitive with each other. Even though the Chinese e-commerce sector is open to foreign investors, none of the large US players such as Amazon or eBay have been able to capture a large percentage of the Chinese consumer market.

In 2018, the Trump administration launched a number of investigations into Chinese tech firms and imposed hefty sanctions on Huawei and ZTE. This series of regulatory onslaughts on Chinese firms was a rude awakening for the top Chinese leadership. Facing an increasingly hostile geopolitical environment, the Chinese leadership felt a great sense of urgency to catch up with the United States and address its supply-chain shortage in critical components such as semiconductors.[63] Since then, the Chinese government's strategic priorities have started to shift from the consumer internet to hardcore technology. Domestic tech giants such as Alibaba, Tencent, and Baidu, however, have fallen short of fulfilling these industrial ambitions. Instead of producing the foundational science and technologies that can help China stay competitive with the United States, these large domestic tech champions all thrived by catering to the vast Chinese consumer market. Policymakers in Beijing have therefore grown increasingly dissatisfied with the business orientation of its booming tech giants.

Signs of Beijing's discontent were revealed through state media propaganda during the 2020–2021 law enforcement campaign. In December 2020, the *People's Daily*, a party mouthpiece, published a commentary criticizing Chinese tech firms for their excessive mutual competition in the area of community group-buying businesses. The author argued that this competition was threatening the survival of many small and medium-size firms. The piece urged these tech giants to shift their gaze from "the cabbage" to the "starry sky," urging them to set higher ambitions to advance China's technological innovation.[64] Another instance surfaced in August 2021, when *Economic Information Daily*, a Chinese newspaper affiliated with China's official news agency Xinhua, lambasted Tencent's online gaming as "spiritual opium" that is poisoning Chinese teenagers.[65] All of these developments illustrate how Beijing's attitude toward its domestic tech giants has shifted in response to the changing geopolitical environment, echoing the element of *adaptability* of the top leadership in the dynamic pyramid model.

Meanwhile, the top Chinese leadership has grown to appreciate the significant potential of antitrust law as a mighty weapon for disciplining its domestic tech giants. In March 2021, President Xi Jinping declared that China would strengthen its antitrust enforcement to ensure the healthy and sustainable development of its platform economy.[66] This strong endorsement from the highest leadership facilitated two important institutional changes. First, the bureaucratic status of China's antitrust agency was upgraded. In November 2021, China appointed Lin Gan as the new chief of the antitrust bureau of the SAMR. As Ms. Gan is a vice minister of the SAMR overlooking a vast portfolio of market regulations, her appointment signified the antitrust bureau's upgrade to vice-ministerial status. Industry participants viewed this move as a major development in Chinese antitrust enforcement. Indeed, the lack of administrative resources has been a perennial concern for the SAMR, which has only around 40 staff members dedicated to antitrust enforcement. With the new upgrade, the agency is expected to increase its budget and expand its manpower to 100 within two years and 150 within five years.[67]

The second important institutional change is the amendment of the AML, which saw its first major overhaul in June 2022. The amended law includes explicit language targeting the digital economy, such as "preventing undertakings from using data and algorithms, technologies, capital advantages, platform rules and others to engage in monopolistic behavior."[68] The amendment also significantly increases the punitive power of the AML. For instance, the maximum fine for merger-control violations has been augmented from RMB 500,000 to up to 10 percent of a firm's turnover in the previous year.[69] The amendment further introduces a superfine: in cases of serious violation, the fine can be increased to between two and five times the original amount.[70] The new amendment also mentions criminal penalties, leaving room for the potential criminalization of anti-competitive conduct.[71] These two important institutional changes clearly demonstrated the top leadership's commitment to further strengthening antitrust as a tool for regulating the digital economy.

4.2.2. Firms

As the dynamic pyramid model of regulation suggests, businesses operating in China are very flexible and know how to adapt to China's unique institutional environment and work it to their favor. Because policy support is incredibly important in China and often trumps the law itself, Chinese tech firms have resorted to both formal and informal institutional channels to lobby for high-level endorsements of their businesses. Chinese tech firms have also sought regulatory arbitrage and taken advantage of legal loopholes to circumvent antitrust laws in order to expand their business empires, thus inadvertently making themselves vulnerable to regulatory attack.

4.2.2.1. Lobbying

Chinese tech firms engage in lobbying through both formal and informal institutional channels. As mentioned in Chapter 2, many tech entrepreneurs have served in the "two sessions": the National People's Congress (NPC), China's top legislative body, or the Political Consultative Conference (CPPCC), the top advisory body. Participation in such political events is an important channel for tech executives to lobby the top Chinese leadership to support their entrepreneurship. One of the most active entrepreneurs is Pony Ma, the founder and chairman of Tencent. Between 2013 and 2022, Pony Ma made a total of 55 proposals, with many closely related to Tencent's business interests.[72] For instance, during the 2015 NPC meeting, Ma submitted a report advocating for the "internet plus" initiative.[73] The concept, originally proposed by Ma in 2013, envisions a cohesive network linking together people, content, goods, and services. This "Internet Plus" initiative aligns directly with Tencent's key competence of connecting its portfolio companies with its vast sea of users, particularly through its ubiquitous and all-purpose WeChat app. Ma envisaged the initiative toppling and revolutionizing traditional industries, boosting mass entrepreneurship, improving the efficiency of public infrastructure, and stimulating the sharing economy.[74] Ma's proposal later received national recognition, culminating in its inclusion in the State Council's Annual Government Report in 2015. Gaining recognition from the highest executive body of the Chinese government was of upmost strategic importance to Tencent. The successful lobbying has not only bolstered Tencent's position, but has also enhanced the bargaining power of Chinese tech firms vis-à-vis the regulators, deterring the latter from taking forceful regulatory actions that might thwart the national economic agenda.

In 2015, Pony Ma put forth an important proposal to facilitate the amendment of the Copyright Law, which would improve protection of online content and enhance the social recognition of original creation. Notably, Ma's suggestion was strategically aligned with Tencent's ambitions in the music industry. By then, Tencent Music Entertainment had signed exclusive licensing arrangements with the world's four largest music labels. Starting in 2013, the firm sent thousands of legal warnings to numerous online music portals in China, accusing them of infringing on the content it had paid for.[75] In 2014, Tencent launched a copyright-infringement lawsuit against its major competitor, NetEase, leveraging the suit to pressure the latter to start sub-licensing the music rights from Tencent.[76] This sub-licensing arrangement later became the template used by other online music platforms in China. By levying high sub-licensing fees, Tencent gained a huge competitive edge over its rivals, paving the way for its subsequent dominance in the domestic online music-streaming business.[77] Interestingly, Ma's call to strengthen copyright protection coincided with China's crackdown on copyright infringements in domestic music-streaming services. In 2015, the National Copyright Administration issued a mandate requiring all domestic online music portals to remove unlicensed music by the end of July of that year, cautioning severe sanctions would be imposed for noncompliance.[78]

Besides lobbying through formal political participation, Chinese tech firms are also very good at lobbying via informal institutional channels. This is particularly important when a tech firm has gained significant market power, as they are then likely to face complaints from their consumers or competitors, making them prone to antitrust investigations. Not surprisingly, each of the major tech firms has invested tremendous resources aimed at fending off antitrust complaints and unfavorable legislation. In the meantime, power imbalances between businesses and regulators in China have heavily influenced lobbying dynamics in China. Instead of directly challenging the antitrust agency in court, tech firms rely heavily on antitrust scholars or former regulators (whom I called "information intermediaries" in Chapter 2) to exert influence over the regulatory process.

Let's start with the academics. Because the Chinese antitrust authorities suffer from severe capacity constraints and lack the time and expertise to draft rules and tackle difficult cases, they frequently engage academics to provide consulting services. Engaging academics in the regulatory process also helps enhance the legitimacy of regulatory decisions by showing that they have incorporated inputs from a wide range of independent sources. Meanwhile, Chinese antitrust scholars are keen to get involved, despite the lack of compensation, as doing so offers valuable insights into China's opaque regulatory process. Senior scholars are invited to sit on the prestigious Expert Advisory Committee of the Anti-Monopoly Commission (AMC), an independent supervisory commission directly under the State Council, which gives them a peek into the inner workings of the SAMR.

In fact, Liu Xu, an independent Chinese scholar and vocal critic of Chinese antitrust enforcement, describes Chinese antitrust academics as operating in a "two-sided market."[79] On one side of the market, Chinese antitrust scholars provide free services for Chinese regulators and gain privileged access to information about antitrust cases while building personal connections with the case handlers. On the other side, Chinese antitrust scholars are compensated with high consulting fees by tech firms or law firms who want to shape a particular piece of legislation or regulatory decision. As I explained in my last book, *Chinese Antitrust Exceptionalism*, Chinese antitrust scholars' connections with and proximity to antitrust regulators directly translate into influence and prestige.[80] Thus, the more services a scholar renders for regulators, the more influence they can exert over the regulatory process, and the more valuable they then become for Chinese tech firms. A couple of leading Chinese antitrust scholars, particularly those who sit on the Expert Advisory Committee of the AMC, have become highly sought-after expert consultants for businesses and frequently make public comments or contribute essays in defense of large Chinese tech firms.

For instance, in May 2019, the Competition Law Center of the University of International Business and Economics (UIBE) organized a workshop on the "choose-one-from-two" practices of Chinese internet platforms that engaged scholars from several leading universities, regulators, and legislators, as well as representatives from leading internet platforms.[81] Professor Huang Yong from UIBE, a renowned antitrust scholar who had been serving on the AMC, argued that such exclusive practices should not be deemed illegal per se, noting that regulators should take a case-by-case approach. Several other senior professors from leading Chinese universities echoed his thoughts. By the end of the conference, the experts had seemingly come to a consensus that the regulation of internet platforms should abide by the principle of being "tolerant and cautious." Rather than rushing to penalize an internet platform for its exclusive practices, it is better to "let the bullet fly a bit longer" (i.e., take a wait-and-see approach).

It is not only academics, however, who serve as "information intermediaries" in the regulatory process; former government officials also play a crucial role in assisting the lobbying efforts of Chinese tech firms. For years, the antitrust bureau at the SAMR, a small bureau with fewer than 40 staff members, tried in vain to lobby for higher bureaucratic status so it could expand its capacity. Meanwhile, many mid-level antitrust officials, seeing little prospect of being promoted within the bureau, moved to work for large tech firms. A 2021 *Financial Times* report identified 11 former regulators or judges who had recently joined tech giants.[82] According to news reports, tech firms offer such former public servants lucrative salaries, bonuses, and stock options that can sometimes amount to 60 times their government salary.[83] When the Chinese government initiated its tech crackdown, the demand for ex-regulators soared even higher, with some corporate clients offering more than RMB 3 million or even "an unlimited budget" for a suitable candidate.[84]

In addition to hiring them, Chinese tech firms have also informally engaged former regulators to lobby on their behalf.[85] However, because these retired officials were not formally employed by the tech firms, the details of these relationships are largely shrouded in mystery and difficult to verify. That said, it is certainly true that several senior retired antitrust officials have been actively advocating for a more tolerant and cautious approach in regulating tech monopolies.[86] One recent example is the controversy regarding the monopoly status of Alipay and WeChat Pay. In the summer of 2020, the People's Bank of China (PBOC) made a formal recommendation to the Anti-Monopoly Commission (AMC) that it look into the abuse of dominance by Alipay and WeChat Pay, the two major online payment platforms owned by Alibaba and Tencent, respectively.[87] The AMC started to gather information but ultimately did not open a formal probe into these two firms, which could potentially have derailed Ant Group's initial public offering planned for late 2020. Three senior ex-regulators, including Zhang Qiong, who used to chair the advisory body of the AMC, Zhang Hangdong, who used to head the antitrust bureau at the National Development and Reform Commission (NDRC), and Li Qing, formerly the deputy director general of the NDRC, collectively contributed an article to Caijing in September 2020 arguing that Ant and Tencent did not possess a monopoly in the online payment industry.[88] Besides this contribution from three high-profile ex-regulators, several academics have also contributed articles defending these two digital payment platforms.[89]

4.2.2.2. Regulatory Arbitrage

Regulatory arbitrage is the other important survival strategy for Chinese tech firms seeking to avoid antitrust regulation. Over the past two decades, almost all Chinese tech firms have structured themselves as variable interest entities (VIEs) to raise capital overseas and circumvent the Chinese government's restrictions on foreign investment. In a typical VIE structure, foreign investors acquire stakes in an offshore holding company, usually based in tax havens such as the Cayman Islands. The holding company then sets up a Chinese subsidiary, which signs contracts with a third-party company in charge of running the business; the third-party company then pledges to send profits to the Chinese subsidiary. From the start, the legal status of such

VIE structures has been highly controversial, with various Chinese regulatory authorities expressing conflicting views regarding their legitimacy.[90] Chinese tech entrepreneurs, on the other hand, have lobbied for relaxation of the various investment and regulatory restrictions on this novel legal structure.[91] Because VIEs operate in a legal gray area, few Chinese bureaucratic departments want to directly challenge their legality or recognize their legitimacy.[92]

The antitrust authority's inaction dates back to 2009, when Sina.com, a leading Chinese news portal, indicated interest in acquiring Focus Media, a digital media company. As it met the threshold for submitting a merger notification to China's antitrust authority, the parties notified the Ministry of Commerce (MOFCOM), the merger authority at the time, of their planned transaction. However, despite the parties' repeated requests for approval, the authority apparently refused to consider it, leading to the deal being scuttled.[93] This outcome gave rise to market speculation that the agency didn't want to vet deals involving VIE structures so as to avoid taking a stance on their legitimacy.[94] Notably, MOFCOM is also one of the gatekeepers of China's foreign-investment regulation. From that point on, Chinese tech firms avoided notifying the MOFCOM of their transactions, even when the latter clearly met the mandatory notification thresholds.[95]

As a result of MOFOCM's inaction and inertia, Chinese tech acquisitions went almost unchecked for more than a decade. This included the consolidation of the largest players in the Chinese consumer internet sector. In May 2015, Qunar complained to MOFCOM that Ctrip failed to notify the authorities of its acquisition of eLong, despite having met the notification thresholds.[96] According to news reports, the combined market share of these firms could exceed 50 percent of the online hotel-booking sector. Ironically, five months later, Ctrip acquired Qunar, its major competitor in the online travel industry, with the result that the newly merged entity reportedly held almost 70 percent market share in the online travel industry.[97] The year 2015 also saw a tie-up between China's two largest group-buying businesses, Meituan and Dianping, both of which are Chinese shopping platforms for local services and products, with an estimated combined market share exceeding 80 percent in the group-buying sector.[98] During the same year, 58.com, often dubbed the Craigslist of China with 47 percent market share in online classifieds (a multi-content category), acquired its main rival, Ganji, which held a 34 percent share in the same market.[99]

The next year saw Tencent, the owner of QQ music, which held a 33 percent market share in the online music industry, acquire China Music, the number one player with an almost 49 percent share.[100] All of these transactions flew under the radar of Chinese antitrust review.

In addition to taking advantage of legal ambiguities, Chinese tech firms also exploited the loopholes in Chinese antitrust law to obviate their legal obligations. In 2015, Didi Chuxing, a firm with the largest market share of 56 percent in the online ride-hailing market, merged with Kuaidi, the number two player with a 43 percent share in the same market.[101] Despite potential anti-competitive concerns, the Chinese antitrust authority wasn't notified of this transaction. According to Chinese merger rules, companies with a revenue of less than RMB 400 million are not required to submit a filing with the antitrust authority.[102] These two firms argued that they were loss-making, and thus that their transaction did not meet the notification thresholds.[103] Didi explained that it had received little revenue because it applied an incentive scheme that heavily subsidized drivers and riders.[104] A year later, Didi merged with Uber China without undergoing merger review, using a similar justification.[105] Immediately before the merger, Didi's market share in the ride-hailing sector was about 86 percent, followed by Uber's 15 percent.[106] This merger thus cleared almost all competitive hurdles for Didi and further solidified its dominance in the ride-hailing business.

4.2.3. Platform Participants

In the area of antitrust law, there are three major types of complainants against the large tech platforms: consumers, merchants, and competitors. Because administrative enforcement was dormant for years, the Chinese public had to turn to the judiciary for damages and remedies. However, Chinese courts have set up a very high burden of proof for antitrust plaintiffs, thus deterring complainants from bringing antitrust lawsuits against the tech giants.

To be fair, the vast majority of Chinese consumers have benefited tremendously from the cheap prices and conveniences brought by the Chinese tech giants. The cash-burning model of heavily subsidizing merchants and consumers has been a template for competing in Chinese tech sectors ranging from e-commerce and ride-hailing to bike-sharing and food delivery.[107] As a result, many leading tech firms with significant market power have struggled to make profits. Didi, for instance, had been loss-making for years.[108] Even after the firm merged with Uber China, thus ending their long-standing price war, it continued to subsidize rides for a long period of time due to competitive pressures from smaller rivals.[109] Accordingly, despite their growing dominance, Chinese consumers welcome the expansion of China's Big Tech firms and enjoy the convenience of a one-stop-shop brought about by the integration of their super-apps with other services offered by companies in the same portfolio. At the same time, the downsides of the exclusive practices of the Chinese tech firms, including the potential to degrade the quality of their services for consumers and reduce innovation, have been less observable to Chinese consumers.

It is not surprising, then, that few Chinese consumers bother to directly challenge the abusive behavior of dominant platforms. The only exceptions are activist lawyers, who occasionally bring lawsuits against China's tech giants. One such activist is Zhang Zhengxin, a lawyer from Beijing who sued Tencent for improperly blocking his sharing of links from Taobao and Douyin, both of which were major rivals to Tencent's services, on his WeChat account in 2019.[110] Zhang also observed that Tencent adopted self-preferencing practices, as it did not block similar apps such as JD.com, Pinduoduo, or Wesee, which belonged to the Tencent camp. He claimed that Tencent's conduct was inhibiting competition in both the e-commerce and short-video markets and hoped that the lawsuit could change Tencent's practices.[111] The case, however, was subsequently withdrawn from the court. Big Tech firms also occasionally face complaints and lawsuits from merchants. In 2020, Galanz, a top electronics company, sued Alibaba for allegedly abusing its market dominance by forcing it to pick sides when choosing where to sell its wares online. The case was later withdrawn after Galanz reached a settlement with Alibaba.[112] In the same year, Ele.me faced complaints from 20 merchants who alleged that the food-delivery firm had forced them to choose sides by threatening to punish those merchants who failed to comply with the rules.[113]

The most vocal complainants against Chinese Big Tech firms are actually their peer firms, and the clashes between these tech titans have often been spotlighted by the media as "cat-and-dog" fights. In 2017, JD.com hired ChinaLabs, a provider of consulting services headed by Fang Xindong, a well-known media commentator, to attack Tmall's exclusive practices.[114] JD reportedly paid ChinaLab to first initiate research and host media seminars to draw attention to Alibaba's abusive practices, and then incite the Chinese antitrust authority to investigate Tmall. Although ChinaLab's efforts did draw some media attention, it ultimately failed to pressure the authority to open a formal investigation into Alibaba. Such inaction of Chinese administrative agencies drove the Big Tech firms to Chinese courts where they exchanged fire with each other. However, because the burden of proof for plaintiffs is very high in antitrust lawsuits, in most cases Chinese tech firms choose to file their cases under the Anti-Unfair Competition Law (AUCL) instead.

Since 2018, ByteDance and its affiliates have brought at least five unfair-competition lawsuits against Tencent, alleging that the latter was blocking their content.[15] Thus far, none of the cases has reached a final substantive judgment, largely due to disputes about jurisdiction. Tencent, on the other hand, retaliated with two lawsuits, accusing ByteDance and its affiliates of using WeChat and QQ user profiles without authorization and illegally crawling data from public WeChat accounts.[116] Tencent appears to have had more luck in court, as it succeeded in receiving an injunction to stop ByteDance and its affiliates from continuing with its infringements. Ele. me and Meituan, the online food-delivery duopoly, have also been suing each other under the AUCL for engaging in exclusionary practices by forcing merchants to choose sides. As of October 2022, Ele.me had launched five lawsuits and won four against Meituan in Zhejiang, Jiangsu, Shandong, Tianjin, and Guangdong, receiving damages of RMB 2.48 million.[117] Meituan has also launched four suits against Ele.me and won two cases in Zhejiang and Anhui, receiving a total compensation of RMB 160,000.[118] Despite the proliferation of these unfair-competition lawsuits, their protractedness and the low value of the penalties awarded mean they fail to serve as an effective deterrent against the exclusive practices of Chinese tech firms.

4.2.4. Regulators

For over a decade, Chinese antitrust agencies and the judiciary took a conservative approach in dealing with cases arising from the domestic tech sector. As elaborated earlier in this chapter, the absence of antitrust scrutiny over Chinese tech firms has indirectly encouraged their frenetic expansion and resulted in disorderly competition. Since late 2020, however, the attitude of the Chinese antitrust authority has shifted dramatically. To demonstrate its fealty and value to the top leadership, the SAMR hastily introduced new antitrust guidelines, retroactively vetting transactions for which they had not previously been notified, and imposing remedies and prohibition on large merger transactions. This series of enforcement actions, however, ended up being "too little, too late," as it fell short of addressing the fundamental problem of high concentration in the sector. Chinese courts, meanwhile, have appeared slower to react due to the protractedness of the litigation process.

4.2.4.1. Administrative Agencies

Before the SAMR was formally established in 2018, the responsibility for enforcing the AML was split between three different antitrust authorities: MOFCOM was in charge of merger enforcement, while the NDRC and the State Administration for Industry and Commerce (SAIC) were jointly responsible for conducting investigations. This fragmented structure gave rise to overlapping duties during enforcement, while also creating competition between these agencies as they vied for greater policy control. At the same time, the three agencies were all very thinly staffed, with fewer than 50 employees in charge of antitrust enforcement between them. Selective enforcement was therefore inevitable, as each agency tried to prioritize those cases that would best maximize its bureaucratic interests.[119] Because the Chinese agencies prioritized defending national economic interests, foreign large multinational companies with strong market power often found themselves the main targets of antitrust enforcement. In the first decade of its enforcement, the MOFCOM prohibited two mergers and imposed remedies in 36 transactions, all of which involved foreign multinational companies.[120] In the meantime, despite perennial complaints from businesses and consumers, the Chinese antitrust authorities were reluctant to take any action against large domestic tech firms.

As mentioned earlier, such firms took advantage of ambiguities in Chinese law by ignoring the notification requirements in Chinese merger-control rules. While, in theory, MOFCOM had the power to intervene at any time, regardless of whether a transaction had met the notification thresholds, the agency failed to take an aggressive stance. For instance, upon receiving complaints from rivals about Didi Chuxing's acquisition of Uber China, MOFCOM conducted several administrative interviews, an informal type of administrative enforcement.[121] Similarly, in its response to the press's inquiries about its investigation, MOFCOM stressed that it would "adhere to the principle of encouraging innovation and science-based regulation to maintain a level playing-field and promote the innovative development of ride-hailing businesses."[122] Until this day, however, no penalty has been levied against these firms.

Besides its near absence of scrutiny of mergers within the tech sector, the Chinese antitrust authority has also been extremely cautious in the investigations that it has conducted. As mentioned earlier, many of Alibaba's rivals, including JD.com and Pinduoduo as well as several online merchants, have made complaints about Tmall's exclusive practices to the Chinese antitrust authority since 2015.[123] Similarly, Ele.me has also complained to the market watchdog about Meituan's exclusive practices and vice versa. However, China's antitrust regulators failed to take aggressive antitrust action and instead applied more lenient regulatory tools, such as some anti-unfair-competition laws and the E-Commerce Law, to discipline the tech firms.[124] But the weak sanctions provided for by those laws failed to deter the tech giants, who continued with their abusive practices, viewing the punishments simply as part of the cost of doing business.[125] In November 2019, the SAMR summoned 20 Chinese tech firms for an administrative interview in an attempt to persuade them to discontinue abusive practices during the Singles Day Shopping Festival.[126] The authority apparently threatened to invoke the AML to punish firms who continued to engage in such practices. However, no real action was taken until late 2020, when the enforcement campaign started.

From that point onward, in sharp contrast with their previously lax enforcement, the Chinese antitrust authorities, particularly the SAMR, took drastic legislative and enforcement actions. Their first move was to release a set of antitrust guidelines targeting online platforms in November 2020; these were put into effect in February 2021.[127] These guidelines represent a significant step forward in strengthening enforcement in the digital economy. The new rules clarify that a VIE structure will no longer be exempted from merger review, and that the SAMR is prepared to investigate acquisitions of emerging platforms even when the parties' turnover does not meet the notification thresholds. Since November 2020, the antitrust bureau at the SAMR has begun actively vetting a large number of past mergers and acquisitions involving VIE structures. As of the end of 2021, the agency had published 107 cases of parties failing to disclose their trans-actions, a sharp increase from the previous year's 13 cases.[128] Notably, nearly half of these cases involved the acquisition of minority interests (probably with controlling rights), showing that the authority is now paying closer attention to de facto controlling rights.[129]

At the same time, the fines imposed were very low, as the statutory limit is still only RMB 500,000; the authority also did not unwind any of the past deals.[130] As of the time of writing, the SAMR has not pub-lished any penalty decisions regarding large merger transactions involv-ing leading players such as Didi–Kuaidi, Didi–Uber, Meituan–Dianping, Ctrip–eLong, or Ctrip–Qunar. Moreover, the SAMR did not impose structural remedies in any of the penalty decisions it has released—even in cases where the transacting parties had significant and direct over-laps in the market. Consider, for example, the agency's prohibition of the merger between Huya and Douyu, the two largest live-streaming video-game platforms in China, commanding 40 and 30 percent market share, respectively, in the livestream gaming market.[131] A close look at this case reveals that Tencent already possessed sole control over Huya and joint control over Douyu, so that this proposed transaction would merely change its control of Douyu from joint to sole control.[132] In the end, the SAMR prohibited the merger transaction.[133] However, no fur-ther remedies were imposed on either party to the transaction, despite Tencent's common ownership over both companies and the attendant risk of coordination.

In 2021, the SAMR also imposed remedies on the merger between Tencent Music and China Music Corporation.[134] According to the SAMR's analysis, the two firms had respectively captured 30 and 40 percent of the online music broadcasting market.[135] However, instead of directly addressing the concerns over horizontal overlap brought to light in the merger review, the SAMR imposed behavioral remedies on Tencent Music, requiring the firm to end its exclusive arrangements with leading global record labels.[136] The SAMR had, in fact, launched an investigation into these exclusive licensing arrangements back in 2019; however, that investigation was sus-pended after a year without any further disclosure from the administrative authority.[137] It appears that the SAMR tried to avoid directly addressing the concentration issue by imposing remedies that treated it like a case of abuse of dominance.

In fact, the SAMR cleared every case in which the incumbent tech giants acquired a competitor in an adjacent market without imposing any remedies. For instance, the SAMR unconditionally approved Tencent's acquisition of Sogou, the second-largest search engine in China, in July 2021.[138] With its user base of over 700 million, Sogou could pose a competitive threat to Tencent.[139] And yet, because Tencent is mostly active in the social-media and gaming sectors, it has few direct overlaps with Sogou—making the SAMR's approval of the acquisition consistent with its typically rather conservative approach, which tends to focus on direct competition between the transacting parties.[140] By adopting such a lenient approach toward such acquisitions, the SAMR could further entrench the dominance of the incumbents without fundamentally tackling the market-concentration problem in the digital economy.

In addition to active merger enforcement, the SAMR also initiated a few high-profile conduct investigations. On Christmas Eve of 2020, the SAMR announced an investigation into Alibaba for its "choose-one-from-two" business practices.[141] The regulator concluded its investigation within four months and imposed a fine on Alibaba of almost RMB 18.2 billion, equivalent to 4 percent of the firm's revenue in 2019.[142] This hefty fine was the largest ever imposed by China's antitrust authority; the lightning speed of the investigation also deviated sharply from previous practices, which saw regulators take years to complete an abuse-of-dominance investigation.[143] Together with the fine, the agency also issued Alibaba an unprecedented "administrative guidance," requiring the firm to submit annual compliance reports to the agency for the next three years. This notice, though not legally binding, set out the regulator's expectations for the tech giant. In addition to antitrust, it covers a wide range of areas such as platform self-governance, data protection, fair competition, consumer protection, dispute resolution, and improvement of the merchant experience. Not coincidentally, these areas of compliance also fall within the broader mandate of the SAMR, a vast conglomerate that oversees various aspects of market regulation.[144] It thus appears that the SAMR is trying to leverage its antitrust functions to enhance its authority in other areas of market regulation.

After imposing the fine on Alibaba, the SAMR and other regulators summoned 34 leading Chinese tech firms and required them to conduct self-examinations and submit rectification plans within a month.[145] As the public statements released by these tech firms reveal, the agencies ordered them to improve compliance in a wide range of areas that go far beyond their antitrust obligations.[146] For instance, JD.com vowed to improve compliance with the Consumer Protection Law, the E-Commerce Law, the AML, the Advertising Law, and the Price Law, all of which fall within the broader mandate of the SAMR.[147] Six months later, the SAMR imposed a fine of approximately RMB 3.4 billion on Meituan for its "choose-one-from-two" business practices, equivalent to 3 percent of the firm's 2020 revenue.[148] The firm was also required to create an internal compliance system and produce annual compliance reports similar to Alibaba's.

In the summer of 2021, the Ministry of Industry and Information Technology (MIIT), China's telecom regulator, initiated a six-month rectification program aimed at tackling a whole host of consumer-protection and unfair-competition violations, including interoperability issues.[149] A few months later, the authority summoned executives from the major tech firms, warning them that they could no longer block external links that direct traffic to rival companies.[150] Notably, although the MIIT lacks the power to enforce the AML, it can rely on its own departmental guidelines to request firms to rectify their behavior. Since that summer 2021 meeting, leading Chinese tech firms have been gradually tearing down parts of their walled gardens. Since late 2021, WeChat users have been able to access links from Taobao and Douyin.[151] Meanwhile, several of Alibaba's affiliated platforms, including the food-delivery firm Ele.me, video-streaming website Youku, and online ticket-sales platform Damai, have started to offer WeChat Pay as one of their payment options.[152] However, as of now, WeChat Pay is still not available on Alibaba's flagship e-commerce sites, such as Taobao and Tmall. Alibaba and Tencent are reportedly close to reaching a deal that will see the former launch several mini-programs on WeChat, including Taobao Deal, Idle Fish, and Freshippo, all of which will accept online payment from WeChat Pay.[153] There are also rumors that Tencent is divesting some of its portfolio investments in e-commerce and online food-delivery companies to appease Beijing's concerns that the firm's presence in a wide variety of services can give rise to interoperability issues. In December 2021, Tencent announced that it would distribute its shares in JD.com as a special dividend to investors in a move to weaken its tie to the e-commerce platform.[154]

Thus far, hectic enforcement actions by the Chinese antitrust authority have done little to fundamentally change the competitive landscape in China. To be sure, the two exclusivity cases against Alibaba and Meituan have created strong deterrence against similar abusive practices in the future.

ANTITRUST REGULATION

Chinese tech firms have also taken preliminary steps to address interoperability issues. However, while the SAMR is seemingly busy vetting past transactions in which they weren't notified, it hasn't imposed any substantive remedies to restore competition, as the Huya–Douyu and Tencent–China Music cases illustrate. Meanwhile, the SAMR continues to follow traditional antitrust thinking in its analysis of the digital economy, a rigid approach that has made it difficult to prove dominance or identify the anticompetitive effects of Big Tech firms. All in all, China's consumer internet sector remains highly concentrated, in which it is almost impossible for newcomers to effectively challenge the duopoly of Alibaba and Tencent.

4.2.4.2. Courts

Chinese courts have long been a battleground for China's Big Tech rivals. According to Judge Zhu Li of the Supreme People's Court. Chinese courts accepted 700 cases and completed 630 during the first decade of enforcement of the AML.[155] However, because the evidentiary requirements in antitrust lawsuits are very high, the plaintiffs only prevailed in less than 1 percent of cases.[156] Even when firms press ahead with antitrust cases, the litigation process is extremely protracted and generally fails to provide effective and timely remedies for plaintiffs. Compared with the administrative authorities, Chinese courts also face more institutional constraints in responding to changing initiatives from Beijing, which makes any responsiveness on their part to those policies difficult to observe. In the following discussion, I will highlight the significance of the *Qihoo v. Tencent* case, as well as a few recent important litigations.

In 2012, Qihoo launched a case against Tencent, alleging that the latter had abused its dominant position in the instant-messaging software and services market. As mentioned earlier, Tencent made its QQ instant messaging service incompatible with Qihoo's security software, hence forcing users to choose between QQ's and Qihoo's products. In 2013, the Guangdong High Court decided that Tencent did not hold a dominant position in the relevant market and dismissed Qihoo's claims. Upon dismissal, Qihoo appealed the case to the Supreme People's Court, but the highest court continued to uphold the lower court's decision. Despite Tencent's high market share—almost 80 percent—in the instant-messaging market for the previous seven years, the court put little weight on such evidence, noting that Tencent operated in a highly dynamic internet sector, where the boundary of the relevant market is not clear. The court noted that Tencent lost a significant number of users immediately after it tried to force them to choose between its services and Qihoo's app, whereas Tencent's major competitors experienced a significant increase in users. Economists pointed out that the court's analysis was misleading, as it relied upon data on the change in users for a given month rather than the exact week of the implementation of the "choose-one-from-two" policy.[157] The correct data revealed that none of these competitors experienced significant increases in usage, suggesting that they had failed to constrain QQ's dominance.[158] On the other hand, the fact that Tencent had the ability to significantly reduce Qihoo 360's position without suffering tremendous loss was indicative of its market dominance.[159] Just as importantly, the court focused solely on the market for instant-messaging and computer security, while overlooking the two firms' potential competition in other, complementary markets.[160] This was a particularly significant oversight given that Qihoo was trying to compete with Tencent by expanding into mobile games and online searches, both of which are strategic complements to its security software.

Widely hailed as a landmark antitrust decision by the Supreme Court, the *Qihoo v. Tencent* case attracted tremendous media attention and was live-streamed on the judiciary's website.[161] The Supreme People's Court also listed this case as one of the guiding cases to be studied by lower courts. Even though precedents are not legally binding in China, guiding cases have some precedential value, especially given the fact that Chinese courts operate like a bureaucracy, and lower courts thus tend to give some deference to the highest court.[162] Since that 2013 ruling, few plaintiffs have chosen to invoke the AML to challenge a Big Tech firm, the challenges surrounding proof of market dominance having come to be widely perceived as insurmountable.[163]

In 2017, JD.com filed an antitrust lawsuit against Alibaba in Beijing, accusing the two firms of abusing their dominance in the e-commerce market by forcing merchants to choose Tmall over other platforms. Alibaba challenged the jurisdiction of the Beijing court, arguing that the case should be handled by a Hangzhou court, which is where Alibaba is based under Chinese law. The case went through two trials, in the second of which the Supreme People's Court endorsed the position of the Beijing High Court that it had jurisdiction over the case. The case then went into substantial trial phase in 2020, with VShop and Pinduoduo also applying to join the suit.[164] On December 29, 2023, the Beijing High Court delivered a landmark ruling in favor of JD.com, ordering Alibaba to pay RMB 1 billion in damages.[165] Given the historically low success rate of plaintiffs in antitrust cases, this groundbreaking decision indicates a potential shift towards more proactive judicial intervention in future antitrust cases. Notably, this decision was made after the SAMR's 2021 record fine on Alibaba for its "choose-one-from-two" business practice. As such, JD.com's victory is likely to encourage other antitrust plaintiffs to file similar follow-on damage claims. In the meantime, this decision will incentivize businesses to challenge administrative penalty decisions due to the elevated risk of follow-on damage lawsuits. In 2021, ByteDance filed an antitrust suit against Tencent in Beijing, accusing the latter of abusing its dominant position by blocking users from sharing Douyin videos on WeChat and QQ. Like Alibaba, Tencent objected to the jurisdiction of the Beijing court; these jurisdictional issues remain unresolved, and the case is currently pending. As the dynamic pyramid model predicts, Chinese Big Tech firms are very savvy in employing litigation tactics to delay legal challenges from rivals. They also have a strong preference for handling litigations in their home jurisdictions. In fact, Tencent's tendency to win in Shenzhen's Nanshan Court, located in the same city where its company headquarters are based, has won it the nickname "Nanshan Indomitable."[166] While some have chalked these victories up to local protectionism, it is also possible that companies' tendency to win locally is driven by information advantages enjoyed by Chinese Big Tech firms, which simply understand the preferences and beliefs of the local judges better.[167]

4.3. Future Trend

In 2022, Chinese antitrust enforcement against Big Tech firms had softened markedly, with there being no major investigations into large domestic tech firms since then. As regulatory dynamics in other jurisdictions evolve, Chinese market regulators are adopting novel toolkits to tackle Big Tech firms in a bid to expand their influence. One significant instrument under deliberation by Chinese regulators is the ex ante regulation of Big Tech firms. Traditional antitrust assessment has relied on an ex post approach, which demands intervention only in cases of market failure. However, this case-by-case analysis has proven insufficient and too sluggish to effectively address anti-competitive harm in the digital market. To bridge this enforcement gap, Western regulators have introduced ex ante regulation by designating certain large online platforms as gatekeepers, subjecting them to a comprehensive set of rules and obligations. The newly enacted Digital Markets Act (DMA) from the European Union serves as a prime example, while several other countries are in the process of introducing similar regulations, as will be further elaborated in Chapter 9.

Chinese regulators have taken cues from EU legislation. In October 2021, the SAMR released two sets of draft guidelines: Guidelines for the Classification and Grading of Online Platforms, and Guidelines for the Implementation of Online Platforms' Obligations. Seemingly modeled after the DMA, the former guidelines propose classifying Chinese online platforms into three categories (super-large, big, and mid-to-small), while the latter guidelines aim to impose strict obligations on the super-large platforms.[168] Super-large platforms are expected to comply with an extensive range of legal obligations spanning across various areas, including data, competition, content, intellectual property, and more, covering an even broader scope than the DMA. Notably, these two sets of guidelines were proposed by the Bureau of Online Transaction Regulation (Online Transaction Bureau) rather than the Anti-Monopoly Bureau within the SAMR. While the latter focuses on antitrust enforcement, the former specializes in developing and implementing measures for supervising e-commerce transactions and online markets. Unsurprisingly, these two sets of guidelines encompass a vast scope of regulatory compliance overseen by the Online Transaction Bureau.

Another significant toolkit that the SAMR is considering is the deployment of unfair competition law to tackle Big Tech. China's Anti-Unfair Competition Law (AUCL), first enacted in 1993, serves as the primary law regulating unfair business practices that disrupt market competition and order. The AUCL also contained several antitrust provisions, such as abuse of monopoly power by public utilities, administrative monopolies, predatory pricing, tying, and bid rigging. As there is no requirement to prove a dominant position under the AUCL, it is much easier to satisfy the burden of proof for an unfair competition case than an antitrust case. This explains why Chinese tech firms have preferred to file their cases under the AUCL rather than the AML. In 2017, the AUCL was amended to remove all the aforementioned antitrust provisions to avoid potential overlaps with the AML.

However, 2022 saw the SAMR attempting to reverse previous legislative efforts. In November 2022, the SAMR released a set of draft amendments to the AUCL, intending to introduce a wide range of measures to regulate malicious and unfair competition in the digital economy.[169] For instance, the new draft proposed adding a provision prohibiting business operators "with relatively advantageous positions" from engaging in exclusionary practices such as exclusivity, tying, price discrimination, and others.[170] Since these exclusionary practices also fall within the ambit of the AML, these new amendments under the AUCL provide an additional avenue for regulators to challenge tech firms. Indeed, it is much easier to establish the "relatively advantageous position" enjoyed by a business operator than to prove its dominance under the AML. The former is a concept borrowed from Japan and Germany, which is broadly defined under the law as the advantage enjoyed by business operators based on their technology, capital, number of users, impact on the industry, and reliance on other business operators.[171] Unlike the AML, there is no need to prove anti-competitive effects under the AUCL, making it much easier for regulators to prove their cases that might otherwise be difficult to establish under the AML.

Meanwhile, the new amendments propose raising the maximum fines for violations from RMB 3 million to RMB 5 million. Most strikingly, in cases of severe violations, the fine is now capped at 5 percent of the previous year's turnover, effectively removing the ceiling for fines since it is now proportional to the firm's revenue. This proposal significantly increases the sanctioning power of the AUCL, bringing it much closer to the AML, which caps the fine at 10 percent of the previous year's turnover. If these proposed amendments are adopted, the SAMR will be able to tackle antitrust cases by satisfying a much lower burden of proof under the AUCL while subjecting the firm to a similar level of high sanctions. Notably, the agency leading the revision of the AUCL is the Price Supervision and Anti-Unfair Competition Bureau (Price Bureau), which has been responsible for enforcing the AUCL since its promulgation. The adoption of these new amendments will significantly expand its jurisdiction in regulating competition in the digital market, potentially leading to clashes with other departments such as the Anti-Monopoly Bureau and the Online Transaction Bureau.

As of now, neither the guidelines for classifying platforms nor the draft amendments to the AUCL have been enacted. However, these changes, each driven by different departments within the SAMR other than the antitrust bureau, demonstrate the intense regulatory competition within the central ministry. As a result, it is likely that Chinese Big Tech firms will face antitrust scrutiny not only from the antitrust bureaus but also from other government departments within the SAMR, particularly the Price Bureau and the Online Transaction Bureau, in the near future.

4.4. Summary

This chapter began by presenting the challenges to Chinese antitrust regulation in the tech sector and identified three main regulatory challenges. The first derives from the Chinese government's efforts to filter foreign content, which effectively act as a trade barrier that shields domestic tech firms from foreign competition. The second challenge was the unchecked expansion of leading Chinese tech firms such as Alibaba and Tencent into a wide range of consumer internet sectors, enabling these firms to build their own ecosystems that capture huge amounts of attention from the public. The third challenge arose as the Chinese market became highly concentrated, when Chinese Big Tech firms started to erect walled gardens to exclude rivals, among other unruly competitive practices.

Echoing the regulatory dynamics described in Chapter 2, Chinese antitrust authorities were slow to intervene in anti-competitive merger transactions and failed to take forceful actions to stop abusive practices. Since the initiation of the tech crackdown in late 2020, however, Chinese antitrust enforcement has taken a dramatic U-turn, with the SAMR quickly churning out antitrust guidelines while taking aggressive enforcement actions. This unprecedented law-enforcement campaign brought about two important institutional changes to the Chinese antitrust regulatory landscape. The first was the upgrade of the antitrust bureau of the SAMR to vice-ministerial status, which will enable the agency to double or even triple its current capacity in the coming years. The second was the facilitation of the AML amendment, granting regulators much greater punitive power and more discretion during enforcement. These two changes have also significantly emboldened the SAMR, a super-regulator with a wide mandate over many areas of market regulation. Although this enforcement intensity subsided in 2022, interdepartmental rivalry within the SAMR has catalyzed diverse strategies to combat monopolies in China's platform economy. The institutional changes and the bureaucratic rivalry within the SAMR will therefore cast a long shadow over Chinese antitrust regulation in the years to come.

5
Data Regulation

Along with antitrust regulation, data regulation provides the Chinese government with an important set of means for keeping its tech firms on a tight leash. That said, it is not fair to view Chinese data law simply as a disciplinary weapon to tame its unruly tech giants. Nor is it accurate to portray Chinese tech firms as mere tools in the hands of the Chinese government. As will be elaborated below, data thefts and leaks are rampant in China, and there is indeed significant demand within the nation to enhance the protection of personal information. The question of who bears the blame for this situation, however, is a complicated one As we will see, savvy Chinese tech firms should only be held partially responsible, not least because abusive government practices and the illicit information industry are also important contributors to data breaches.

Much like the dynamics in antitrust regulation, Chinese data regulation used to be light-touch. China has long been a strong advocate for internet sovereignty and has placed greater emphasis on cybersecurity than personal-data protection. Meanwhile, the national industrial policy oriented toward encouraging the big-data economy inhibited the data authorities from taking a tough stance on enforcement. Chinese tech firms took advantage of this preferential policy environment to lobby against regulation while advocating for favorable legal treatment. By proactively cooperating with various government authorities and providing technical support for their big-data projects, Chinese tech firms earned the authorities' goodwill and increased the appeal of their own products and services in the latter's eyes. The Chinese public, meanwhile, lacked either the incentives or sufficient access to complain about data violations except through sporadic media coverage, occasional enforcement campaigns, and rare litigation. Then, in 2021, the regulatory pendulum swung toward harshness with the promulgation of two national data laws and a whole host of departmental rules, significantly broadening the scope of enforcement while increasing the punishment for data violations.

Before delving deeply into this dramatic regulatory swing in the data sphere, I will first examine the major regulatory challenges that have beset China's labor governance and regulation. I will then apply the dynamic pyramid model of regulation to analyze the incentives and behavior of each of the four major actors involved in the regulatory process, thus unraveling the dynamic complexity in Chinese data regulation. With the notable easing of regulation that began in early 2022, I will culminate my analysis with a forecast of the anticipated trajectory of enforcement trends in the near future.

5.1. Regulatory Challenges

There is little doubt that China has a great need to enhance data and privacy protection for its citizens, who have suffered from three major sources of regulatory challenges, each of which is elaborated below.

5.1.1. Underground Industry

China is home to a large organized underground industry that specializes in misappropriating and illegally selling personal data. A report from the Shanghai Academy of Social Science estimated that over 560,000 people were engaged in the underground data industry in the first half of 2016 alone.[1] The same report estimated that the annual economic loss resulting from online data theft and leakage amounted to RMB 92 billion.[2] A 2018 survey by the China Consumer Association indicated that 85 percent of people had previously suffered some sort of data leak.[3] High-profile data leaks are frequently exposed in Chinese media. In 2016, hackers attempted to access over 20 million user accounts on Taobao, Alibaba's e-commerce site.[4] In another instance, the account details of 500 million users of Sina Weibo, essentially China's version of Twitter, were posted for sale on the dark web in 2020.[5]

The exponential growth of China's internet finance was an important contributor to the growth of the underground data industry. To improve their assessment of the probability of default among potential borrowers, peer-to-peer (P2P) firms and other internet financial companies rely heavily on risk-management services provided by big-data companies. These companies in turn source their data not only from large online platforms, but also from unscrupulous sources such as the underground data industry.[6] This means that shadowy data traders from the underground economy not only trade with scammers and fraudsters, but also, indirectly, with various P2P businesses, insurance companies, and banks.[7]

In fact, this underground industry obtains its data through two major illegal channels—hacking and collusion. Data theft and data leaks are rife in China. Advanced encryption technologies such as HTTPS, an acronym for Hyper-Text Transfer Protocol (Secured), help ensure that a visitor's connection to a website is confidential.[8] Though this encryption technology has been widely used in many Western countries to improve network security, the Chinese government has blocked some HTTPS traffic because permitting its use would make it difficult for Chinese censors to monitor the internet traffic of Chinese users.[9] For instance, all messages on WeChat, the messaging app used by almost 90 percent of the Chinese population, need to pass through a central network as unencrypted plain text to allow for content moderation in accordance with official censorship requirements.[10] As a consequence, Chinese internet networks have become less secure and more vulnerable to manipulation, spying, and exploitation by cyber criminals.[11] In 2018, Ruizhi Huasheng, a publicly listed online marketing company, was caught up in a massive scandal on account of its involvement in cybercrime. The firm had infiltrated networks run by Chinese telecom operators and had stolen a massive amount of personal account details.[12] The firm then used these account details to crawl over 3 billion pieces of transaction data from 96 e-commerce and social-media sites in China, including Taobao, Weibo, and JD.[13]

In addition to hacking, black-market operators have also leveraged the employees of data-rich firms, particularly those from delivery and hotel-catering businesses, to exfiltrate huge amounts of personal information. In 2018, one of the largest data breaches in Chinese history saw over 500 million lines of personal data from 13 hotel chains operated by Huazhu Hotel Group stolen and posted for sale on a Chinese dark-web website.[14] Experts believe that the data leak, which affected an estimated 130 million customers, was engineered by one of Huazhu's own employees.[15] In 2016,

employees of SF Express, one of the largest delivery companies in China
were found to be selling consumer data in an incident that compromised
the personal details of over 100 million customers.[16] Similar cases occurred
again in 2018, when a Chinese court in Hubei sentenced 11 SF Express employees to jail for selling the data of over 10 million users in over 20 provinces.[17] In 2018, Chinese authorities arrested 22 people linked to Apple's
affiliate companies in China for selling the personal details of Apple users
in a scam worth more than RMB 50 million.[18]

5.1.2. The Government

Beyond the illicit information industry, the Chinese government itself is
an important contributor to the challenges in Chinese data regulation. It
is well-known that the Chinese government closely monitors and censors online expression and works to guide public opinion.[19] Since the late
1990s, the Chinese government has been investing heavily in digital surveillance tools to track and analyze the activities of its citizens.[20] In 1998,
the Ministry of Public Security created the Golden Shield Project, a domestic surveillance and filtering system that integrates online government
population databases with databases that closely monitor and control citizens who are deemed to pose a potential threat to the stability of society
and the regime.[21] Recent technological advancements in high-definition
cameras, facial recognition, and big-data processing have further enhanced
the government's surveillance capacity. Since 2016, the Ministry of Public
Security has started to integrate the street-surveillance camera system into
its Golden Shield Project database.[22] Almost 200 million CCTV cameras
were built across China, making it the country with the world's biggest
camera-surveillance network.[23] Chongqing, a city in southwestern China
with a reputation for being "the most surveilled city in the world," now
boasts of having one camera for every six of its 30 million citizens.[24] In recent years, the Chinese government's surveillance capacity has been further
heightened by the proliferation of smart-city initiatives that deploy a host
of information and communication technologies to boost mobility and
connectivity.[25]

China is not alone, of course, in conducting mass surveillance programs
that intrude upon the privacy of its own citizens.[26] In 2013, former US intelligence consultant Edward Snowden exposed a mass surveillance program

conducted by the US government on its own people and those in other countries. And, to be fair, the Chinese government has legitimate crime-prevention and national-security interests it wishes to safeguard. An empirical study has shown that the Chinese central government uses information on its social media to better monitor local officials.[27] However, surveillance not only can protect people and deter corruption, but also can be used to censor and police the population, as has been shown by another empirical study.[28] Using data on its expenditure on local security and political prisoners, Xu Xu has found that the government's digital surveillance increases targeted repression in China.[29]

The Chinese government's mass surveillance activities in Xinjiang represent its most controversial data-security project to date.[30] In response to rioting and violent protests by Turkic Muslims in 2009, the government implemented a sophisticated, multilayered network of mass surveillance in the region.[31] These efforts have only accelerated since 2016, when Chen Quanguo, the then-newly appointed regional CCP secretary, advocated for a more proactive and systematic approach in combating opposition forces.[32] Some residents in Xinjiang are reportedly required to install a surveillance app called Jingwang, or "clean internet," on their smart phones.[33] The app, which is meant to help residents detect terrorists and filter religious electronic content, also spies on citizens when they post on social-media sites such as Weibo and WeChat.[34]

In addition to mass surveillance, China's social-credit system, an ambitious project in social management that tracks the activities of individuals and provides assessments of its citizens and enterprises, also intrudes into personal privacy. Launched in 2014, the social-credit system aimed to restore trust and promote creditworthiness by raising the costs of unethical behavior. Indeed, an empirical study has shown that the social-credit system does encourage positive behavior among citizens.[35] Empirical studies also show that the system is generally well received by the Chinese population.[36] However, there is no clear legal guidance as to the scope of the information that the government can collect.[37] One striking example is Rongcheng, a small city in Shandong province that has been operating as a laboratory for the social-credit system since 2013.[38] Each of its 740,000 adult residents was allocated an initial 1,000 points and could gain additional points for good deeds or lose points for dishonest behavior, according to the authority's precise reward and punishment mechanisms.[39] Western experts worry about the intrusiveness of this local experiment, in which every move in the city is captured by a camera, especially if the Rongcheng experiment is to be transformed into national standard practice in the future.[40]

Worries about potential government abuse of surveillance data became a reality during a protest in response to a financial scandal in Henan.[41] In May 2022, four rural banks in Henan Province suddenly suspended cash withdrawals, prompting street protests by thousands of desperate depositors.[42] Starting in June, many depositors of these four banks found themselves unable to join planned protests because their health QR codes, which are used by the Chinese government to conduct Covid contact tracing, mysteriously turned red. A red QR code restricts the citizen's access to public places during a Covid outbreak. This incident ignited public fear that local government authorities had misused citizens' public health data for purposes of security control.[43]

Not only can the Chinese government's proactive surveillance harm the data privacy of its citizens, its inaction can equally lead to infringements on personal data. The Chinese government is the country's largest data controller, and is actively engaged in collecting, processing, and using personal data. Its failure to secure the data it collects can lead to massive data leaks. In China, 90 percent of personal-identification information is collected through three official sources: the search center affiliated with the Public Security Bureau, the three state-owned telecom operators, and the state-owned banks.[44] In June 2022, it was widely reported that Shanghai police records containing the personal-identification information of nearly one billion Chinese citizens were left open online for over a year due to negligence by the relevant authorities.[45] The police failed to notice their data-security vulnerability until they received a ransom request from a cybercriminal. Meanwhile, affiliates of the three state-owned telecom operators have all tried to capitalize on their troves of personal-identification data by creating subsidiaries that specialize in credit information and big-data analysis.[46] Employees at large state-owned telecom companies have also been exposed for illegally selling vast amounts of personal data.[47] Local governments, who often lack the necessary legal awareness for adequate data protection, are another major source of data leaks. In order to improve the transparency of their work, some local government departments disclosed the personal details of their administrative-enforcement teams online, including team members' names, personal identification, and affiliations.[48]

5.1.3. Tech Firms

Chinese tech firms are only the third source of harm to data and privacy protection in China. Unlike the underground industry, which engages in clear legal violations, Chinese tech firms operate in legal gray areas. Because Chinese legislation protecting personal information has historically been very weak, many large Chinese tech firms, particularly online platforms, thrived by harvesting troves of consumer data through the free services they provided. As there was no clear Chinese law defining the scope of personal information and what consumer consent actually meant in practice, online platforms tried to collect excessive user data on the basis of uninformed consent. As a result, consumers were often unaware of just how much consent they had inadvertently given to online platforms.

The scandal involving Alipay, a leading online payment platform in China owned by Ant Group, offered a glimpse into the reckless data strategies of Chinese tech firms. Alipay provides its users with "annual reports," giving each of them a summary of their consumption patterns over the past year. However, when some users tried to access their annual reports in 2017, they found that they had inadvertently agreed to share their data with Sesame Credit, a credit-scoring system operated by Ant Group.[49] Alipay is certainly not alone in such practices. In 2018, Robin Li, Baidu's CEO, triggered an online uproar after suggesting that Chinese people were willing to give up their privacy in return for convenience.[50] Although Li's bluntness was controversial, many industry analysts believe that his statement reflects an industry norm—one that has provided an extremely low level of data protection in China.[51]

Notably, Chinese online platforms harvest data not only from their own apps, but also from third-party apps via software development kits (SDK).[52] An SDK is a set of programming tools or frameworks that app developers can import from a third party to avoid having to build their products from scratch.[53] Some SDKs are particularly popular among developers because they enable their users to access apps via large platforms and help provide a ready-made payment infrastructure.[54] Thus, the SDKs of WeChat, QQ, ByteDance, and Alipay are especially popular for app developers because users like to access new apps using their existing account details from these large platforms. In return, SDK owners receive fees or collect data from the apps or the users.[55] Because there was little regulation about the use of

SDKs and ambiguity about how to delineate the proper scope of data collection through them, some SDKs have been able to facilitate abusive practices such as accessing and crawling through contact lists, online messages, bank-account details, and geographical location data.[56]

A broad survey of the three main challenges that has beset Chinese data regulation reveals strong demand among Chinese citizens for enhanced protection of their rights. But it is also clear that tech firms are only partial contributors to this chaos, as deep-seated institutional problems, such as the pervasive underground economy and abusive government practices, present a significant threat to data and privacy protection. In other words, even if regulation targeted at the platform economy worked perfectly (which is never the case, as will be revealed later in this chapter), it would not be sufficient to enhance data protection for Chinese citizens and businesses. In the following section I will switch my focus from identifying legal challenges to analyzing the regulatory process for tackling these problems. As we will see, the dynamic pyramid model again proves very useful in explicating the complicated regulatory dynamics in the Chinese data regime.

5.2. Applying the Dynamic Pyramid Model

For decades, China's top leadership has placed great emphasis on protecting cybersecurity while underplaying the importance of protecting personal information. Meanwhile, Chinese tech firms sought legal arbitrage by taking advantage of loopholes and lobbying aggressively for favorable treatment while proactively cooperating with the Chinese government to earn its goodwill and support. The Chinese public, on the other hand, generally lacks opportunities for voicing its discontent, except in a few instances of litigation and media coverage of big-data leaks and scandals. Chinese regulators initially tried to guard their bureaucratic interests by refraining from taking an aggressive stance in regulating the tech firms. Their position changed dramatically starting in late 2020, however, when they took aggressive enforcement actions against Chinese tech firms.

5.2.1. Top Leadership

As suggested by the dynamic pyramid model of regulation, China's top leadership is very adaptable and constantly needs to balance three sources

DATA REGULATION

of legitimacy: growth, stability, and nationalism. As cybersecurity is deemed essential to safeguarding social stability and national security, it is seen as an utmost priority for Chinese data regulation. At the same time, the Chinese government also views data as an important production factor in boosting the data economy. As a result, China's ambitious industrial policy agenda slowed down the legislative development of personal-data and privacy protections. But the attitude from the top leadership shifted dramatically in late 2020, a change that then provided a significant boost to Chinese data legislation and enforcement.

China has long been a vocal proponent of cyber sovereignty.[57] As President Xi Jinping remarked in 2014, there is no national security without cybersecurity.[58] Given the already mentioned vulnerability of the Chinese internet network, the top leadership is concerned about cyberattacks and data leaks, particularly in light of the 2013 Snowden revelations about extensive US intelligence activities in China. In 2014, the CCP formed the Cybersecurity and Information Leading Group, chaired by President Xi Jinping, thus further demonstrating the top leadership's commitment to enhancing the protection of cybersecurity in China.[59]

Legislative developments during this period further reflected China's security-centered approach to data. From 2015 to 2016, a number of laws relating to national security were issued, granting the government sweeping powers to collect personal data.[60] For instance, the Anti-Espionage Act adopted in 2014 grants regulators broad authority to inspect the electronic equipment and infrastructure of individuals and organizations.[61] The Anti-Terrorism Act promulgated in 2015 mandates that telecom operators and internet service providers must provide assistance and support to public-security agencies for the purpose of combating terrorism.[62] The law also empowers the public-security authority to delete online information or shut down websites. That same year, China adopted the National Security Law, which contains provisions on enhancing cybersecurity to prevent threats to national security.[63] A year later, China adopted the Cybersecurity Law, a broad and comprehensive piece of legislation that addressed cybersecurity and data-governance issues.

Parallel to the leadership's emphasis on data security, Chinese policymakers also actively promoted the development of the big-data economy, which potentially conflicts with the public demand for enhancing personal-data protection. In 2006, the State Council issued the "State Informatization Development Strategy 2006–2020," in which the government highlighted data as an important "production factor."[64] In 2015, the State Council issued "An Outline of Actions to Promote Big Data Development," its first top-down strategy.[65] One of the action plans was to apply big data to boost economic growth and promote mass innovation and entrepreneurship, particularly in new development areas such as internet finance and mobile payment. A year later, the National People's Congress adopted the thirteenth Five-Year Plan, which dedicated an entire chapter to the strategy for national big-data development. The Fourth Plenary Session of the Nineteenth Central Committee of the CCP, held in 2019, further characterized data as a factor of production alongside land, labor, capital, and technology.[66] The following year saw an announcement by the State Council calling for more market-oriented allocation of factors of production, including data.[67] In response to these initiatives from the top leadership, a large number of Chinese central ministries issued guidelines and directives to initiate the construction of big-data centers or facilitate big-data management in their particular sectors.[68] As of the end of 2021, 25 provinces had established various forms of big-data management agencies, under the authority either of regional governments or of the National Development and Reform Commission (NDRC).[69] Data marketplaces have also proliferated in China.[70]

Policy support from the top leadership provided a significant boost to the big-data businesses, despite much concern about unscrupulous sources of data from the underground economy.[71] Scholars pointed out that these strong policy initiatives for the digital economy posed serious challenges for developing data-protection law in China.[72] As Bo Zhao and Yang Feng noted, although many of these policies mention the enhancement of laws for regulating big data, the language used is scant and vague.[73] In any case, the ambitious goals set by these policies for developing the data economy incentivize the government bureaucracy to lean toward industrial development rather than data protection.[74]

Unsurprisingly, legislation for protecting personal information was slow to develop. Although the first draft proposal for a law protecting personal information was completed in 2005 and submitted to China's Political Consultative Conference in 2006, its progress then stalled for many years.[75] Furthermore, while the Cyber Security Law set up a broad framework for cyber-governance in China, the law focuses heavily on cybersecurity rather than personal-information protection. It only contains five vague provisions on the obligations of platform operators with regard to data.[76]

As a consequence, the system for protecting personal data and privacy continued to rely on a patchwork of national laws and regulations, as well as on departmental laws, guidelines, and measures, and on regional rules and regulation.[77] In 2017, the Standardization Administration of China promulgated the Information Security Technology–Personal Information Security Specification Standard (GB/T 35273-2018). Although the Standard lays out detailed requirements for data collection and processing, it is not legally binding and only serves as a recommendation for best practices.

Another problem with this piecemeal data legislation is that it generally lacks teeth. In 2009, China amended its Criminal Law to create a very low threshold for the prosecution of data crimes.[78] However, the Criminal Law only applied to malicious cybercrimes and illegal data sales; the penalty for data misuse by tech firms under other areas of law has remained negligible. For instance, the highest fine that can be levied on e-commerce operators in violation of data-protection provisions in the E-Commerce Law is a paltry RMB 100,000. The maximum fine that can be imposed on platforms for data-privacy violations under the 2017 Cybersecurity Law is likewise very low: either RMB 1 million if there are no illegal gains, or 10 times the amount of the illegal gains. The enforcement strength of departmental guidelines is even weaker. One example is the Ministry of Industry and Information Technology (MIIT)'s 2011 regulation on internet information services, which establishes its highest punishment as a fine of RMB 30,000.

As explained in Chapter 2, the attitude of the top Chinese leadership toward the nation's major internet businesses underwent a significant shift after Jack Ma's provocative speech criticizing Chinese fintech regulation during a financial summit in Shanghai in late October 2020. Strong opposition from the financial regulator convinced the top echelon of the CCP leadership to scuttle Ant's IPO and subsequently mobilized the entire bureaucratic machine to rein in the unruly tech sector. It was against this political backdrop that China promulgated two national laws on data security and privacy in 2021: the Data Security Law (DSL) and the Personal Information Protection Law (PIPL).[79] Specifically, the DSL classifies data into different categories and provides corresponding levels of protection, whereas the PIPL, modeled after the European Union's General Data Protection Regulation (GDPR), is China's first comprehensive law that focuses on protecting individual data rights. These two laws, combined with the Cyber Security Law that became effective in 2017, form the three pillars of China's data legislation.[80] To be sure, these two laws have long been on the legislative agenda and would probably have been implemented regardless of the crackdown.[81] Nonetheless, the crackdown appears to have accelerated the legislative process. The adoption of the DSL and PIPL represented a significant step forward, as both are national laws promulgated by the National People's Congress Standing Committee and carry severe sanctions. For instance, the highest fine that can be imposed under the DSL is RMB 10 million—10 times the maximum fine that can be levied under the Cyber Security Law. The maximum penalty under the PIPL is even higher: a fine of up to RMB 50 million or 5 percent of a firm's revenue from the previous year (whichever is higher). As the fine is no longer capped and is now proportional to a firm's revenue, this creates a strong deterrent for large tech firms.

5.2.2. Firms

As the dynamic pyramid model of regulation suggests, businesses operating in China are very flexible and know how to adapt to China's unique institutional environment and work it to their favor. In the realm of data regulation, Chinese tech firms aggressively sought regulatory arbitrage, lobbied for favorable legal treatment, and actively supported the government's various data projects to gain its support while further enhancing the appeal of their products and services. In response to the recent tightened legislation, large Chinese tech firms also appeared particularly responsive in adapting to new legislation.

5.2.2.1. Regulatory Arbitrage

Until recently, Chinese law was vague about the meaning of personal information and the consumer consent needed for data collection. As such, Chinese tech firms aggressively sought regulatory arbitrage by narrowly interpreting the meaning of personal information while adhering to an expansive notion of consumer consent in order to circumvent data regulation. As illustrated by the Alipay example discussed earlier in this chapter, Chinese tech firms tried to take advantage of the vagueness and ambiguity in Chinese law to collect user data. Cross-platform sharing and processing were also very common, which were made easier by the prevalent use of SDK technologies.

Baidu's cookie policy offers a good example of the haziness surrounding how personal information was defined. In 2013, internet user Zhu Ye sued Baidu for infringing on her personal privacy through its use of cookie technology.[82] Cookie technology is widely used among internet platforms to track the preferences of users, which are then used by advertisers to make targeted recommendations. After Ms. Zhu prevailed in the court of first instance, Baidu appealed the case to the Nanjing Intermediate People's Court in 2014. In a surprising reversal, the appellate court held that the information collected by Baidu was not personal information and that the company had fulfilled its obligation to provide notice and gain consent from consumers.[83] This decision was highly controversial, as the judge appeared to have misunderstood the proper meaning of personal information.[84] Indeed, subsequent laws, such as the Cybersecurity Law, clearly prescribe that personal data are information, alone or with other information, that can be used to identify a data subject.[85] Nonetheless, Baidu was able to take advantage of the earlier legal ambiguity to harvest vast amounts of consumer data and win legal battles against its users.

Sesame Credit provides another example of how tech firms sought arbitrage by taking advantage of the legal ambiguity around the acquisition of consumer consent. In 2015, Alibaba introduced Sesame Credit to give ratings based on the spending habits of Alipay users. Sesame Credit sources its data not only from Alipay, but also from public credit-information platforms operated by local governments.[86] According to local data regulations, Alipay needed to obtain authorization and consent from individuals before it could seek access to their data through the government platforms.[87] In practice, however, Sesame Credit appears to have collected data from users without their prior authorization, as users' credit scores are immediately available to them as soon as they subscribe. Although users of Sesame Credit retroactively grant access to their credit information, this still raises a serious question about the infringement of personal privacy.[88]

5.2.2.2. Lobbying

Chinese Big Tech is also an active participant in the legislative process relating to Chinese data protection. Many large tech firms, such as Alibaba, Tencent, and Meituan, have created their own research institutes that not only promote research in technology and innovation, but also operate as government-relations and lobbying arms.[89] As noted in Chapter 1, Chinese

Big Tech has tried to lure many former regulators to work for their research centers or in-house legal teams. For instance, a number of senior researchers working at the Tencent Research Institute used to work for the data-policy think tanks affiliated with the MIIT and Cyberspace Administration of China (CAC). These researchers closely track the legal developments at home and abroad and actively engage in academic and policy debates to influence policymaking and public opinion. They also work closely with Chinese academics to fend off unfavorable legal developments while lobbying on behalf of legal arguments that are favorable to themselves.

5.2.2.2.1. Against Unfavorable Laws

Shortly after China promulgated the Cyber Security Law, the CAC proposed two important guidelines on cross-border data transfer.[90] Chinese tech firms were alert to the country's evolving approach to handling data-transfer issues. One example is Alibaba, which has operated its e-commerce and cloud-computing business in multiple jurisdictions. The Ali Research Institute then held a joint symposium with the Beijing Institute of Technology on the challenges of cross-border data-transfer issues.[91] It also published a study advocating the free flow of data, cautioning that burdensome data-transfer rules could create obstacles for Chinese tech firms with the ambitions to develop cloud services, artificial intelligence, and other consumer internet business overseas.[92]

In May 2018, the GDPR, a groundbreaking and comprehensive piece of data-protection legislation, took effect in the European Union. The law was expected to have strong spillover effects on other jurisdictions, as many countries, including China, have been emulating the European Union in the design of their own data-privacy legislation. Anticipating similar legislative developments in China, Chinese tech companies swiftly embarked on preemptive actions to fend off similar legislation.[93] In 2018, Tencent's research institute published a series of articles and commentaries by Chinese and foreign academics on the potential harmful consequences of the GDPR for innovation and growth in the European digital economy.[94] These articles cautioned against directly transplanting the EU model of data regulation into the Chinese context.[95] Researchers from the Tencent institute also contributed an essay on the misunderstandings and controversies within the GDPR.[96] They attempted to clarify how the GDPR not only imposes strict obligations on businesses, but also incorporates several business exemptions that strike a balance between protecting consumer data and legitimate business interests.[97] Similarly, Alibaba's research center published a series of articles on the limits of the GDPR, arguing that the law did little to constrain Big Tech, but instead imposed a disproportionate compliance burdens for small and medium-sized companies.[98] Furthermore, they questioned the GDPR's effectiveness in enhancing consumer welfare, since the vast majority of consumers tend not to read privacy updates.[99]

China's tech firms also successfully watered down their obligations under the E-Commerce Law, a comprehensive piece of legislation that regulates e-retailing. The first draft of the E-Commerce Law, released in 2017, dedicated eight detailed provisions to the protection of e-commerce data.[100] However, after intensive lobbying from the tech firms, most of these provisions were scrapped in subsequent versions.[101] For instance, Article 45 of the first draft of the law required e-commerce operators to explicitly inform users about their rules for collecting, processing, and using data, and for obtaining user consent. Crucially, it prohibited e-commerce operators from forcing user consent by refusing to provide services in case a user declines to consent. It further required operators to obtain user consent if the operators modified their rules for collecting, processing, and making use of data. This provision brought much-needed clarity to the consent requirement and would have significantly enhanced protections for Chinese consumers while disciplining tech firms. However, it was significantly watered down and replaced in the final law with a bland requirement stipulating that e-commerce operators must comply with relevant laws and regulations when collecting and processing data.[102]

5.2.2.2.2. *Advocating Property Protection of Data*

Parallel to the Chinese tech firms' aggressive lobbying against strict data obligations, they also proactively lobbied for the creation of a data-ownership regime to enhance the protection of data harvested from consumers. Data ownership is highly controversial.[103] Proponents argue that the creation of property rights in big data will create incentives for companies to collect, process, and share data, while critics contend that doing so will impede the free flow of data and stifle the growth of the digital economy.[104] Critics are also concerned that strong protections for property rights given to tech companies could accelerate data monopolization, as it opens up the potential for tech giants to hoard data on a large scale in various sectors.[105] Chinese tech companies have been actively participating in the public debate about whether and how to create data-ownership regimes in China.[106] In the absence of clear legislation delineating what rights they have in the troves of data harvested from their users, Big Tech companies have tried to protect their datasets by creatively guarding their interests under China's Anti-Unfair Competition Law (AUCL). Through a few important court battles, they succeeded in convincing judges to recognize their property interests in those data disputes. Overall, Chinese tech firms have behaved as what Julie Cohen terms "legal entrepreneurs," in that they have actively employed the law to empower themselves, seeking to legitimize their own data-collection activities while claiming property rights over the data they have harvested.[107]

Sina Weibo v. Maimai is one of the landmark cases in this area. In 2016, Sina Weibo, a leading micro-blogging platform, sued Maimai, a social-networking company, for collecting Weibo users' data without authorization.[108] Maimai entered into an open Developer Agreement that enabled it to access rich user profiles on Weibo. Weibo later found that Maimai had collected the educational and occupational data of its users without authorization. The Intellectual Property Court held that Maimai had violated the AUCL, noting that Weibo had invested time, manpower, and other resources in collecting and maintaining its user database—an important competitive resource for Weibo.[109] In another case, Dianping.com, a restaurant-rating site, sued Baidu for crawling through its consumer-review data and then integrating users' comments into Baidu's online map products.[110] The court in Shanghai similarly recognized Dianping's efforts in collecting and aggregating user-generated content and held Baidu liable for violating the AUCL.[111] In 2018, Taobao, China's largest e-commerce platform, sued Meijing, a data company, for illegally organizing the sharing of Taobao's big-data analysis of its users.[112] The court in Hangzhou also recognized that Taobao had an exclusive property interest in its big-data analytics of users.[113]

In these cases, although courts avoided directly addressing the property-rights issues, they were receptive to arguments that emphasized creating a property interest in data. Indeed, there is a growing consensus among Chinese scholars and policymakers that a data-ownership regime should allow non-exclusive and joint ownership, allowing data subjects and data processors different rights over data according to their individual roles in generating, maintaining, and using it.[114]

5.2.2.3. Cooperating with the Government

Chinese tech firms not only seek regulatory arbitrage or lobby against data regulation and for protection of their rights over third-party data, they also try to align with the government's agenda by cooperating, facilitating, and supporting its various initiatives. In doing so, they not only earn the government's goodwill, but also help enhance the legitimacy and popularity of their own products and services. At the regional level, tech giants are deemed local champions who provide essential goods and services as well as employment opportunities for millions of Chinese citizens. Their technological prowess is viewed as an important asset for various levels of the Chinese government that are keen on adopting data technologies to improve public services. Subnational authorities also count on the tech firms for technical and infrastructural support for their development of various big-data projects under the social-credit system.[115] In 2013, the National Bureau of Statistics signed strategic-cooperation agreements with 11 major Chinese companies, including tech firms such as Baidu and Alibaba, for a long-term project on the use of big data.[116] Jack Ma, the charismatic entrepreneur and founder of Alibaba and Ant Group, was even invited to give a speech in 2016 to a million judicial officials about how to apply big data to conduct prediction analysis.[117]

The growing influence of online platforms also transformed the government's public-governance strategies. During the Covid-19 outbreak, Alibaba and Tencent were both tapped by the government to design a health-rating system that became one of the main contact-tracing tools for health officials.[118] The health code embedded within Alipay and WeChat became an essential pass for citizens visiting public premises and taking public transportation[119] The government also increasingly relied on the tech firms to guide, manipulate, and moderate online content.[120] WeChat, the ubiquitous online messaging tool used by more than 1 billion people in China, has become a powerful tool used by the Chinese government to monitor and censor public speech and punish dissidents.[121] As WeChat does not use end-to-end encryption, the platform has full access to user data.[122] Indeed, the app routinely removes content that is deemed politically sensitive and blocks user accounts held by those with dissenting political views.[123]

Chinese tech firms have also been an important collaborator in the Chinese government's massive social-credit project. There are two major administrators in charge of implementing the social credit system: the NDRC China's economic planner, and the People's Bank of China (PBOC), China's central bank.[124] In 2018, the NDRC signed data-sharing agreements with 15 credit-information companies, including Ant Group, targeting those individuals who had been identified as trust-breakers.[125] In 2015, the PBOC selected eight private consumer-credit companies, including Sesame Score (owned by Ant Group) and Tencent Credit (owned by Tencent), to develop pilot programs for providing credit ratings of consumers.[126] In the end, however, regulatory concerns about conflict of interest meant that none of these firms was able to obtain a credit license.[127] After all, Tencent and Alipay's dual roles as online payment platforms and credit-rating companies could incentivize them to tweak their credit ratings of their own customers to entice them to use more of their payment and other online services.[128]

Chinese tech firms quickly put forward a new proposal for creating a joint "credit union" between the PBOC and these eight credit firms.[129] This proposal was ultimately adopted by the PBOC, resulting in the birth of Baihang Credit, a joint venture between a PBOC-affiliated company and the eight firms.[130] Notably, despite their investments in the government-controlled credit-rating company, five of the eight credit companies, including Sesame Score and Tencent Credit, refused to share their data with Baihang, citing privacy concerns. Their refusal shows the limits of cooperation between Chinese tech firms and the government: although firms are willing to partner with the government to earn its goodwill, they do so only to advance their own commercial interests.

At the same time, Sesame Credit has aggressively pitched itself as a leading credit-information product that serves the government's goal of creating a social-credit system to restore trust and creditworthiness in society.[131] Its collaboration with various government bodies enhances its legitimacy and increases its appeal among users.[132] For instance, Sesame Credit worked with several airports in China to allow those of its users with a high credit score to get through airport security faster than others.[133] Sesame Credit also worked with the Supreme People's Court by restricting dishonest people (defined as those who had evaded their legal obligations as identified by the court) from shopping on Taobao or using other products owned by Alibaba's affiliate companies.[134] In 2017, the local market regulator in Hangzhou announced an agreement with Sesame Credit to utilize the latter's credit data on small and micro-companies to improve the allocation of regulatory resources.[135] For instance, those companies labeled "high risk" would be subject to more frequent inspection by the market regulator.[136] Some local government authorities also currently accept personal credentials verified by Sesame Credit to facilitate the processing of administrative functions, such as the distribution of pension payments.[137] Dai Xin has observed that the government's incorporation of Sesame Credit's information works "as a subsidy" to the private reputation system, making it more attractive to users.[138]

5.2.2.4. Responsiveness to Regulatory Demands

Leading Chinese tech firms have been highly adapted to the changing regulatory environment in China. When data enforcement was lax, Chinese tech firms prioritized growth at the expense of legal compliance. In 2006, a study of 82 commercial websites in China found that few of them had included a privacy policy, let alone a comprehensive one that follows the most basic principles of privacy protection.[139] Over the following decade, even though enforcement gradually increased, compliance remained far from satisfactory. A study in 2017 found that almost 30 percent of the 500 most popular websites in China still lacked a privacy policy.[140]

In April 2021, Chinese market regulators summoned 34 Chinese tech firms and requested that they improve various aspects of their regulatory compliance.[141] To gauge their responsiveness to such regulatory demands, I reviewed the privacy agreements of all of these firms before and after the promulgation of the PIPL in August 2021. As of June 2022, 28 of the 34 tech firms (82 percent) had updated their privacy policies to ensure their compliance with the new law. The other six firms all updated their privacy policies a few months before the adoption of the PIPL; their updated policies are generally compliant with the new law. In other words, all 34 of the tech firms summoned by the regulators updated their privacy policies in 2021, either in anticipation of the PIPL or in response to its requirements. Twenty-three of these tech firms (67 percent), including Alibaba, Tencent, Meituan, and ByteDance, even amended their privacy policies twice after the PIPL's adoption. Responsive and frequent privacy-policy updates demonstrated the importance leading tech giants have attached to privacy compliance. They also reveal the data-compliance capacity of China's leading

5.2.3. Platform Participants

As the dynamic pyramid model of regulation suggests, consumers don't have much voice in the regulatory process. Indeed, public discontent tends to be muted, except in consumer surveys or as conveyed by news reporting. A 2016 consumer survey revealed that 85 percent of people had suffered some sort of data leak, ranging from their phone number being sold and used by scammers to their bank accounts being stolen.[143] In 2016, an 18-year-old girl named Xu Yuyu died of a heart attack after losing almost all her savings for college tuition in a phone scam.[144] The criminals successfully gained Xu's trust because they had purchased her data from the underground economy. The Chinese media's wide reporting of this story fueled public outcry calling for tighter privacy rules.[145] Occasionally, individual consumers do take actions by complaining to the authorities. But this typically occurs during a temporary law-enforcement campaign when public grievances help enhance the legitimacy of the agency's actions. In March 2019, for example, the Joint APP Governance Task Force launched a WeChat blog for handling consumer complaints relating to apps. By the end of that year, it had received 12,125 complaints involving over 2,300 apps.[146] The complaint channel was closed, however, after the 2019 inspection. This was possibly due to the fact that the authorities no longer wanted to handle so many complaints, or else because too many complaints would leave the impression that their previous enforcement was ineffective.

Chinese citizens have also lodged their cases in court. In 2015, Ren Jiayu sued Baidu because the search engine was unwilling to remove some of his unfavorable search results relating to his former employer.[147] Mr. Ren claimed that Baidu had infringed upon his "right of name," which provides protection against others interfering with a person's name or reputation. Mr. Ren claimed he had the right to have information about him deleted from searches—what is known in the European context as a "right to be forgotten." A Beijing district court decided that there was no such right under Chinese law, noting that the search results were neutral findings based on the search engine's algorithms and that the retention of such information was therefore necessary for the public.[148] But litigation by consumers against platforms is very rare. In the vast majority of circumstances, Chinese consumers don't bother to complain about data violations, either because they have low data-protection awareness or because they don't believe it is worthwhile to go through the trouble.

Using the China Judgement Online database, I looked into the litigations brought by Chinese consumers under the Cyber Security Law. This official database, developed by the Supreme People's Court (SPC), is touted as the world's largest official repository of judicial decisions, housing over 60 million legal documents as of October 2019.[149] One caveat about using it: although the SPC has mandated that local courts upload their opinions since 2014, they have often failed to do so in practice.[150] One empirical study has shown that the China Judgement Online database disclosed between 40 and 48 percent of all judicial opinions between 2014 and 2016.[151] Measured against a sample of cases disclosed by publicly listed firms' financial filings, another empirical study has found that China Judgement Online only disclosed 37 percent of corporate litigations.[152] The authors also found that this selective judicial disclosure was strongly correlated with local protectionism and the incentives of local politicians seeking promotion.[153] Moreover, since China adopted its DSL in June 2021, it has been reported that Chinese authorities have further restricted access to politically sensitive cases.[154] This selective disclosure creates a sampling bias in the database. To be sure, because litigations of these individual claims about data privacy do not appear to be political sensitive, it is less likely that the courts would deliberately suppress their disclosure. Nevertheless, we should bear in mind this limitation of the database when interpreting the relevant results.

My search reveals that as of the end of 2020, there were only nine cases in which Chinese consumers invoked the Cyber Security Law to sue online platforms that had infringed on their privacy and data.[155] Out of these nine cases, four were rejected on either substantive or procedural grounds. In the remaining five cases in which the plaintiffs prevailed, two involved cyber theft,[156] while the other three involved the platform's misuse of personal information.[157] In the three data-misuse cases, however, the court only required the platforms to stop infringing the rights of the individual plaintiffs, rather than ordering them to modify their broader practices of collecting and employing user data. As such, the impact on the platform was minimal.

The case involving WeChat Reading, an app owned by Tencent, serves as a particularly good example of the limits of litigation as a means of regulating data privacy. In 2019, Mr. Huang sued Tencent for using his WeChat contact list to create a connection between him and his friends in WeChat Reading, as well as for disclosing his reading activities to his WeChat friends without his consent.[158] Surprisingly, the court did not find Tencent's treatment of Mr. Huang to be a violation of existing data regulations, noting that mobile reading is not an essential service required by the public and that users can vote with their feet by using competing services. The court agreed with the plaintiff that Tencent failed to properly inform its users about instances in which WeChat Reading shares the reading activities of its users with other WeChat users by default. Yet it did not go so far as to require Tencent to modify the default setting. Rather, it only required Tencent to stop infringing on Mr. Huang's personal information.

5.2.4. Regulators

As the dynamic pyramid framework suggests, Chinese regulators try to maximize their own bureaucratic interests while aligning their enforcement actions with initiatives from the top leadership. Given the overriding industrial policy aimed at developing the data economy and Chinese tech firms' aggressive lobbying, Chinese data regulators initially refrained from taking a tough stance in regulating the tech firms. This problem was further exacerbated by two institutional defects in Chinese data regulation. First, the enforcement structure's high level of decentralization creates significant bureaucratic inertia in agencies. Second, sanctioning powers under the pre-existing data regulations were very weak and thus could not credibly deter tech firms from committing data-privacy violations. The situation changed rapidly in 2021, however, when both the courts and the administrative authorities became significantly more active in churning out strict regulations and undertaking aggressive enforcement.

5.2.4.1. Fragmented and Weak Enforcement

Chinese data enforcement is highly fragmented and relies on a large patchwork of enforcers, including the central administrative authorities and affiliated think tanks, sector regulators, and local authorities, as well as the prosecutorial and judicial system. At the central level, there are four major ministries that have regulatory oversight over data: the CAC, the Ministry of Public Security (MPS), the MIIT, and the State Administration for Market Regulation (SAMR). Of these, the CAC is mainly in charge of cybersecurity and content control, the MPS has primary responsibility for preventing cyber-attacks and runs the massive Golden Shield Project, while the MIIT is mainly in charge of regulating data compliance in the information-technology sector. The SAMR, finally, is mostly in charge of dealing with complaints from consumers about privacy violations. With the exception of the CAC, each of the other three ministries is a large regulatory conglomerate in which data regulation is usually handled by one or two small bureaus.

Because these bureaus tend to be thinly staffed, they have outsourced much of their work to their affiliated think tanks. For example, the bulk of the CAC's regulatory functions are delegated to the China Electronic Technology Standardization Institute, which is in charge of testing the compliance of cybersecurity and data-protection rules.[159] Much of the legislative work and standard-setting of the MIIT is delegated to the China Academy of Information and Communication Technology, which also provides support for the testing and certification of information-technology products.[160] The Standardization Administration, which belongs to the SAMR, has been in charge of promoting basic standards for privacy and data compliance.[161] The Public Security Bureau (PSB)'s Third Research Institute is dedicated to research on internet and cybersecurity law.[162] In addition, the National Information Security Standardization Technical Committee (also known as Technical Committee 260), a standard-setting committee jointly supervised by the Standardization Administration of China and the CAC, has been actively promoting new standards since 2016.[163]

Beyond these four primary ministries, sector regulators that oversee a specific sector are also important players in managing data regulation. For example, the PBOC is instrumental in managing data regulation within the financial industry. Similarly, the Ministry of Transportation exerts its regulatory influence over data protection in the automotive sector. As each ministry has local offices at the regional level, this structure of enforcement is replicated at lower levels of the Chinese bureaucracy. Meanwhile, the prosecutorial system has worked closely with the MPS in punishing the illegal sale of personal data by the underground industry, and the judicial system handles both civil litigations lodged by private complainants and criminal litigation brought by public prosecutors.

This highly decentralized enforcement structure has given rise to several enforcement problems.[164] As many agencies share overlapping functions, the specific responsibility of each agency is not always entirely clear. This combination of weak enforcement and lack of coordination has attracted widespread criticism from businesses and the legal and academic community, as revealed during the meeting convened by the Standing Committee of the National People's Congress on cybersecurity enforcement.[165] To overcome coordination issues, the four major central data regulators started to initiate joint enforcement actions starting in 2017. That year, the CAC, MIIT, MPS, and the National Standard Committee (which is administered by the SAMR) created a joint task force to audit the privacy policies of the 10 most popular platforms, including WeChat, Sina Weibo, Taobao, Alipay, and Didi.[166]

Despite such coordination efforts, the Chinese data authorities refrained from taking aggressive stances during enforcement. Rather than imposing legal penalties on firms for data and privacy violations, regulators mostly applied informal tools such as reprimanding as well as naming and shaming tech firms that failed to rectify their practices after repeated warnings. For instance, after the exposure of several data scandals involving Alipay, Baidu, and ByteDance, the MIIT separately invited representatives from each of these three companies to discuss their data compliance and requested that their firms make rectifications. No penalties, however, were imposed.[167]

In 2019, the four central regulators created a Joint App Governance Task Force to regulate data compliance across Chinese apps.[168] The Task Force promulgated two guidelines, one on implementation and the other on compliance; it then conducted an assessment of over 2,300 apps and followed up with enforcement.[169] During these inspections, the agencies mostly conducted administrative interviews with businesses, requested rectifications, and then selectively published a list of apps that were deemed noncompliant.[170] Only those apps that failed to rectify after a certain deadline were subjected to further penalties. In exceptional cases, the agency removed apps that failed to rectify their data practices after receiving multiple warnings.[171] Among these agencies, only the PSB and the SAMR imposed fines during their enforcement actions. These fines were very low—on average about RMB 13,000 per case.[172] Based on the 10 typical cases disclosed by the SAMR, none concerned large online platforms. The Joint App Governance Task Force continued its work in 2020.[173] However, enforcement slowed

DATA REGULATION 145

down significantly, with the Task Force only publishing one notice publicly criticizing 35 apps.[174]

5.2.4.2. Intensified Enforcement

Since late 2020, the Chinese data authorities quickly adapted to the top leadership's new policy initiatives by churning out tough legislation while conducting strict enforcement actions against Chinese Big Tech firms.

5.2.4.2.1. Legislation

During the massive law-enforcement campaign, all of the four major central data regulators rushed to roll out guidelines and measures on enhancing personal-data protection. The most high-profile regulation currently being deliberated is the Network Data Security Management Regulation, which will provide the major legal guidelines for implementing China's three major national data laws mentioned above. This regulation is particularly noteworthy due to its high legal status: it will ultimately be promulgated by the State Council, China's top executive body. The draft rules attracted much attention, as they introduced many strict obligations for tech firms in the areas of data protection and cross-border data transfer.[175] Besides these implementation guidelines, the Chinese data authorities also stepped into uncharted territory by proposing to regulate cutting-edge technologies such as artificial intelligence (AI). In January 2022, the four major data regulators jointly released the Provisions on the Management of Algorithmic Recommendations for Internet Information Services. This set of provisions aims to prevent the abuse and misuse of algorithmic recommendation technologies and also sets up an Algorithm Review Mechanism. In December 2022, the CAC promulgated measures to regulate deep-synthesis technologies, which use algorithms to automatically synthesize or generate text, photo, audio, and visual scenes.[176]

In January 2022, the CAC, in connection with 12 other central authorities, adopted a revision to the Measures on Cybersecurity Review. This new version significantly expanded the original 2020 scope of the cybersecurity review. Under this new iteration, online platforms with more than 1 million users will need to apply for cybersecurity review if they plan to get listed overseas.[177] In July 2022, the CAC finalized its Measures for Security Assessment for Cross-Border Data Transfer, which further tightens the rules surrounding export of personal data and certain restricted classes of data. By promulgating these measures, the CAC's role has evolved significantly. From its initial position as an internet regulator, it has emerged as a super agency with all-encompassing authority over the entire information industry.

Sector-specific rules also proliferated during this period. In 2021, China's Banking and Insurance Regulatory Commission and the PBOC published three sets of rules: the Guidelines for Data Capacity-Building in the Financial Industry, Financial Data Security–Data Life Cycle Security Specification, and Credit Reporting Management Measures.[178] These rules aim to provide guidance for financial institutions to enhance data protection for their users, strengthen data security, and regulate credit reporting on Chinese businesses and individuals. That same year, the SAMR released the Measures for the Supervision and Administration of Online Transactions, which set out a variety of personal-information requirements for e-commerce operators.[179] Multiple ministries also jointly issued the Interim Provisions on Automatic Data Security Management in 2021, the first comprehensive data-protection regulation specifically targeted at the automatic industry.[180] Importantly, this law offers rare clarification on the definition of "important data," an important concept left undefined under the DSL. Local authorities, including those in Shenzhen, Shanghai, and Zhejiang, have also promulgated data regulations in their respective jurisdictions since 2021.[181]

These newly promulgated guidelines and measures, together with the relevant national laws (including the DSL and the PIPL, as mentioned earlier), significantly broadened the scope of Chinese data regulation and afforded various regulators much more leverage over Chinese tech firms. At the same time, they have not imposed any meaningful constraints on the government's power to collect, process, and use personal data—an important source of chaos in Chinese personal-data protection.[182]

5.2.4.2.2. *Administrative Enforcement*

Since late 2020, both the CAC and the MIIT have intensified their enforcement measures against data violations committed by mobile apps.[183] In 2021, the MIIT published 21 notices publicly criticizing the noncompliance of 2,137 apps, 444 of which it removed from app stores. This represented a fourfold increase of enforcement as compared to 2020, when the agency published 15 notices involving 516 apps and removed 120 of them from app stores. In 2021, the CAC published six notices publicly criticizing

377 apps and removed 26, and the various local offices of the agency published five notices criticizing 255 apps and removed 19. This also represented a sharp increase in enforcement compared with 2020, when the CAC only published one notice criticizing 35 apps and didn't remove any apps during its joint inspection with the other data authorities.

In March 2021, the CAC, MIIT, MPS, and SAMR jointly issued the Measure on the Scope of Necessary Personal information for Common Types of Mobile Internet Apps.[184] This measure aimed to crack down on those Chinese mobile apps that are collecting excessive amounts of user data and forcing users to give uninformed consent for companies to use and share their data. This measure narrowly prescribes the information that consumers are required to provide when using such services and grants the CAC further regulatory leverage in disciplining the data-collection practices of Chinese tech firms.[185] From May to June 2021, the CAC called out 267 mobile applications for their excessive collection of user data.[186] These apps included some of the most popular apps owned by Chinese Big Tech firms such as Tencent, Alibaba, ByteDance, and Baidu.[187] In addition to its more frequent market inspections, the CAC has also launched a few high-profile investigations into Chinese tech firms, as is typical in a law-enforcement campaign.

In early July 2021, the CAC announced that it had initiated cybersecurity reviews of the three companies Didi Chuxing (Didi), Full Truck Alliance, and Boss Zhipin. Notably, the announcement came only two days after Didi completed its IPO filing in New York in early July 2021. As it turned out, the CAC had earlier tried to nudge Didi to postpone its IPO filing so that it could go through a thorough cybersecurity review. However, the firm didn't heed the advice and instead pressed ahead with its IPO filing in New York at lightning speed.[188] The CAC's unprecedented cybersecurity check therefore appears to have been a retaliatory measure to punish the firm's defiance. According to the CAC, the investigation was conducted in accordance with the National Security Law, the Cybersecurity Law, as well as the Measures on Cybersecurity Review, which establish the detailed procedure for conducting such a review. However, the Measures only took effect a year earlier and there were no publicly available precedents before the Didi case. Moreover, the cybersecurity review was originally designed to cope with the supply-chain risks involved in the procurement of network products and services by operators of critical information infrastructure. It thus appears that the CAC was retroactively expanding the scope of the review in order to punish Didi for ignoring its advice about listing overseas.

In addition to conducting a cybersecurity review, the CAC also removed 25 of Didi's apps from its app store for "grave issues of collecting and using personal information in violation of laws and regulations."[189] This was a surprising move. As mentioned earlier, in the past, Chinese data regulators mostly applied informal sanctions, for instance by requesting firms to rectify their behavior. Firms were usually given a few days or weeks to conduct rectification. Only those apps that failed to rectify after repeated warnings were removed from the app store. Moreover, the MIIT regularly inspects apps on the market for data compliance, so it is surprising that Didi's apps were suddenly found to have run afoul of the basic requirements for data collection.

The CAC's surprise cybersecurity inspection of Didi rode a wave of strong nationalistic sentiments directed against the firm and exposed it to severe reputational damage. Chinese netizens suspected that Didi had turned over sensitive data to the US government during its IPO filing and accused the ride-hailing firm of being a "traitor" and a "walking dog of the United States."[190] Not even Liu Chuanzhi, the legendary entrepreneur and the father of Didi's president, Ms. Jean Liu, was spared amid the public outrage. Internet users called for Mr. Liu to be punished for selling out the national interest.[191] Indeed, although Chinese citizens are often muted during the regulatory process, Chinese regulators can induce or even amplify citizens' grievances in order to enhance the legitimacy of their own actions.

After the year-long investigation, the CAC finally completed its probe by imposing a record fine of RMB 8 billion on Didi in July 2022.[192] The CAC did not publish its formal decision, which appears to have been withheld on national-security grounds, but rather released a short statement and held a question-and-answer session with the press. This limited disclosure put most of the emphasis on Didi's excessive data-collection practices and its privacy infringements going back seven years. Although both the DSL and the Cybersecurity Law were mentioned as legal bases for the punishment, it appears that the mega-fine was mostly levied on the basis of the newly promulgated PIPL, which enables the regulator to impose a fine of up to 5 percent of a firm's revenue in the previous year. Indeed, it seems that the CAC has leveraged the PIPL to both punish Didi for cybersecurity violations and retroactively punish it for conduct it engaged in before the PIPL was adopted. This apparently violated the basic legal principle of non-retroactivity as well as the relevant requirement under China's Administrative Punishment Law.[193]

The opacity of the CAC's investigation into Didi, the secrecy of its decision, as well as the agency's blatant disregard for basic legal principles, all raised profound concerns about political influence over administrative enforcement and its public accountability. Commentators noted that the CAC's dual status as an entity spanning the party and the state might have contributed to the peculiar outcome.[194] Indeed, the CAC is no ordinary administrative agency. It derives its authority from the Central Cybersecurity and Information Commission chaired by President Xi Jinping. Its predecessor is the State Internet Information Office, which was part of the CCP propaganda department. The historical origin of the CAC, its dual role as a CCP organ and an administrative organ, and its direct link with the top leadership combine to afford this agency a very unusual bureaucratic status.[195] More worryingly, the Didi case may mark only the beginning of the agency's exploration of its seemingly unlimited regulatory arsenal.

5.2.4.2.3. *Judicial Enforcement*

Parallel to this intensifying administrative enforcement, Chinese judges also appear more willing to directly intervene in online platforms' data policies. A case against Ctrip, China's leading hotel- and flight-booking company, offers a striking example.[196] In July 2020, Ms. Hu, a VIP member of Ctrip, booked a hotel room using the company's app, which offered a lowest price guarantee. Subsequently, Ms. Hu realized that her booking fee was more than twice the price offered by the hotel itself. She then lodged a suit against Ctrip alleging the firm had engaged in sales fraud by using big data to conduct price discrimination. In addition, she argued that Ctrip had exceeded the necessary scope in collecting and sharing her personal information with other affiliated companies and business partners. She alleged that users were forced to agree to Ctrip's privacy agreement and service agreement, which enabled the company to collect excessive amounts of information for the sake of creating user profiles. She requested that the company stop collecting unnecessary information and provide an option for her to continue using the app without being required to agree to Ctrip's service agreement and privacy policy.

In July 2021, the Keqiao District People's Court in Zhejiang ruled in favor of Ms. Hu by holding that Ctrip's business practice had constituted fraud and ordered the company to pay three times the price difference to Ms. Hu as compensation. Strikingly, the court also endorsed Ms. Hu's claims that Ctrip was inappropriately collecting and sharing data with its affiliates and business partners and forcing consumers to agree to such conditions in its privacy policy and service agreement. The court found that Ctrip had overstepped the acceptable boundary of data collection and data sharing. It ordered the firm to either revise its privacy policy and service agreement to reduce its scope of data collection and data sharing or else provide an option for Ms. Hu to continue using the app without agreeing to the privacy policy and service agreement.

The district court's decision stood in sharp contrast to previous judicial practice, wherein courts never intervened directly in an online platform's business practices.[197] For instance, in the aforementioned case involving WeChat Reading, even though the court thought the app had failed to properly inform its users about privacy issues, it did not request that WeChat change any of its settings, nor did it require Tencent to modify its privacy agreement. Indeed, even if WeChat Reading required users to authorize it to share their information before allowing them to use the app, at that time the court did not think such "forced data sharing" was inappropriate, noting that there existed competing products on the market. Upon appeal, however, the intermediate court in Shaoxing modified the lower court ruling in Ms. Hu's case and dropped the requirement for Ctrip to provide a new option for users to log in without agreeing to its user agreement. That said, even though the appellate court disagreed with the remedial measures, it agreed with the lower court that Ctrip had inappropriately processed Ms. Hu's personal information and violated the Cyber Security Law.

5.3. Future Trend

Chinese data regulation enforcement against Big Tech firms notably eased in 2022, and no large investigations into domestic tech firms have been conducted since then. With the exceptions of Didi and China National Knowledge Infrastructure (the largest academic research database in China), the CAC has not imposed any substantial fines on other tech firms for PIPL violations. However, the agency has remained active by creating a number of institutional mechanisms for cross-border data transfers. In July 2022, the CAC unveiled guidelines on security assessments of cross-border data transfers for transfers meeting specific criteria, such as the transfer of important data or personal data by critical information infrastructure operators, or data exporters processing personal data of 1 million or more individuals.[198] For smaller-scale data transfers, companies can opt for standard contracts or third-party certification if their data transfer does not require security assessments.[199] These mechanisms for data transfers create significant compliance costs for companies while overwhelming regulators struggling with high volumes of data-transfer notifications. According to disclosures from the CAC's Beijing office, as of late February 2023, the authority had received filing materials from 48 companies and had approved only two cases.[200] Meanwhile, 142 companies had expressed their intentions to apply, with more than 120 companies having consulted the CAC about the application. Lawyers with whom I spoke noted that the approval process had been extremely slow and questioned whether the agency would have the capacity to handle all security assessment reviews.[201]

Despite the increased costs for businesses, the Chinese government seems determined to adopt an aggressive stance on data security. Leading Chinese legal experts believe that strict control over data outflows can help China gain more bargaining leverage with other jurisdictions during trade negotiations.[202] Indeed, the PIPL makes an exception for overseas data transfers in accordance with international treaties or agreements that China has signed, paving the way for future negotiations with other countries.[203] In other jurisdictions, bilateral agreements or regional trade agreements have been the primary forms of transnational cooperation to establish cross-border data flow interoperability mechanisms. For instance, the European Union has promoted bilateral cooperation and has recognized the adequate level of personal data protection in 15 countries.[204] The United States has leveraged the Asia-Pacific Economic Cooperation (APEC) Cross-Border Privacy Rules (CBPR), a voluntary cross-border privacy mechanism established among its members to expand the scope of free data flows.[205] The United States is also in the process of further expanding the CBPR; it launched a Global CBPR forum in April 2022 with Canada, Japan, South Korea, the Philippines, Singapore, and Chinese Taipei. China has joined the Regional Comprehensive Economic Partnership (RCEP) and has applied to join the Digital Economy Partnership Agreement (DEPA) and the Comprehensive and Progressive Agreement for Trans-Pacific Partnership (CPTPP). However, these regional trade agreements allow for ample exceptions and leave wide loopholes for data localization.[206] As a result, China will still maintain considerable control over data flows, while engaging in trade negotiations and partnerships.[207]

Recently, China has begun wielding its data regulation as a nimble tool to counter a US-led "technology blockade" aimed at Chinese enterprises. In April 2023, the CAC initiated a cybersecurity review of Micron Technology, citing the need to preserve supply-chain security for critical information infrastructure and national security.[208] This investigation is widely regarded as a retaliatory move by Beijing against US attempts to curtail its access to cutting-edge chips.[209] Some industry insiders believed that the Chinese government has cast Micron as a malefactor within China's semiconductor sphere.[210] In 2017, Micron accused Fujian Jinhua Integrated Circuit Co., a Chinese state-owned memory plant manufacturer, of stealing its trade secrets.[211] This led to the US Department of Justice indicting the firm and three individuals, followed by the Trump administration imposing sanctions that severed the company's access to US suppliers.[212] After the Biden administration signed the CHIPS and Science Act, Micron has also emerged as one of the few US companies to intensify lobbying efforts for federal subsidies aimed at enhancing American chip production and innovation.[213] The firm shut down its Shanghai chip design center in 2022, offering 150 Chinese engineers relocation packages to the United States or India.[214] Significantly, the CAC's announcement coincided with Japan's decision to limit the export of advanced chip manufacturing equipment to China, following similar moves by the United States and the Netherlands.[215] Observers surmise that the CAC's investigation serves as a warning to US allies such as Japan, South Korea, and the Netherlands against joining the American campaign to restrict China's access to high-end chips.[216] Consequently, Beijing's stringent data-security measures have morphed into a potent bargaining tool, pressuring the United States and its allies to loosen technology constraints on China.[217]

In tandem with the CAC's assertive regulatory efforts, the Chinese government is making a strong push to facilitate domestic data flows in an attempt to improve the utilization of data resources. In December 2022, the State Council released the "Opinions on Building Basic Systems for

Data to Maximize the Role of Data Elements," commonly referred to as the "Twenty Data Measures."[218] These guidelines outline a new plan for building the infrastructure to support China's emerging data economy. Among other things, the Twenty Data Measures propose dividing data rights into resource-holding rights, data-processing and usage rights, and data-product operation rights.[219] The measures also call for improving and standardizing the regulation of data circulation, building a trading system for data usage and circulation, and integrating domestic and international data trading markets.[220] In March 2023, China proposed establishing a National Data Bureau, a new agency that would consolidate some data governance functions from both the CAC and the NDRC.[221] The new data bureau would oversee the construction of data infrastructure and co-ordinate the integration and utilization of data resources.[222] These institutional changes demonstrate the importance that the government places on using data to spur the growth of the digital economy. However, these efforts could potentially be hindered by the strict enforcement of data regulations.

Overall, recent developments demonstrate that data sovereignty issues remain a top priority for Chinese data enforcers, while it is uncertain whether there is sufficient political will to genuinely tackle many important consumer protection issues. Nevertheless, the CAC's ambitions are not un-checked. Other government departments striving to promote the Chinese digital economy could serve as counterbalancing forces, while savvy tech companies will continue to exploit power struggles among regulators to lobby for more lenient regulation, as will be elaborated in Chapter 11. In September 2023, the CAC released new draft rules rolling back some of the onerous restrictions on cross-border data transfer.[223] According to the proposed rules, the vast bulk of business and personal activity involving cross-border data transfer will no longer need to go through a security assessment.[224] Instead, businesses only need to conduct self-assessment in many situations, making Chinese data transfer rules noticeably more le-nient than those of the EU. Interestingly, these draft rules were introduced amid rumors that Premier Li Qiang had been urging the CAC to ease its stringent data transfer restrictions in response to mounting business complaints.[225] Indeed, China experienced an unprecedented economic downturn in 2023 and Beijing desperately wanted to shore up investor confidence.

5.4. Summary

This chapter began by presenting the regulatory landscape of Chinese data protection, pinpointing three main sources of challenges. The first is the illicit information industry. The development of internet finance in China played a particularly strong role in spurring the development of a thriving black market in personal data, one that is currently supported by an elaborate underground supply chain. Meanwhile, the Chinese government, the largest data controller in the country with an elaborate surveillance mechanism, is another major source of chaos. As illustrated by the recent incident involving the leak from the Shanghai police of the identification information of over 1 billion citizens, the government's negligence and inaction could pose a great threat to personal-data security. Tech firms are only the third source of chaos, in that many of them operate in legal gray areas when they collect excessive amounts of personal data and share that data with their affiliate companies and business partners. As a result, the current regulations targeting tech firms alone can at most alleviate a portion of the existing concerns about infringements on the privacy of personal data in China.

Echoing the regulatory dynamics described in Chapter 2, Chinese personal data protection used to be very lax. Since the initiation of the tech crackdown in late 2020, however, China's data enforcement has experienced a great leap forward. The unprecedented law-enforcement campaign initiated against the Big Tech firms brought about two drastic changes to the regulatory landscape in the data sphere. The first was the promulgation of a host of data laws and regulations, imposing onerous compliance burdens on businesses, particularly in the context of cross-border transfer. The second was the much more intense and frequent enforcement by both the administrative agencies and the judiciary. These two changes have also significantly emboldened the major data regulators, particularly the CAC, a dual party–state authority that has gained pervasive control over the data practices of Chinese tech firms. Although this enforcement intensity subsided in 2022, the new data laws that were promulgated, as well as the legal precedents and administrative enforcement practices that were established, will have long-lasting impacts on Chinese data regulation in the years to come.

6

Labor Regulation

Even though they may not want to admit it, the Chinese internet giants are among the world's biggest employers. Since the early 2010s, China's sharing economy has enjoyed phenomenal growth, with its transactional volume reaching RMB 3.7 trillion in 2021, almost double the amount in 2015.[1] The Chinese sharing economy has benefited immensely from the country's large excess labor force, absorbing workers from its shrinking manufacturing industry and its vast migrant-worker population.[2] Leading Chinese tech firms invest heavily in the sharing economy and indirectly employ a large informal labor force in the ride-hailing and food-delivery businesses. In 2020, more than 800 million people participated in China's sharing economy, 84 million of whom were service providers, while 6 million were employees of platform companies.[3] Most of these service providers offered work on demand—that is, work allocated to individuals in a specific geographic location through location-based apps. For the sake of simplicity, in this chapter, I will generally refer to on-demand workers in the sharing economy as *platform workers*. This term should be understood as covering a broad swath of workers, including formal employees, contractors, and gig workers.

As discussed in Chapter 4, China's platform economy is highly concentrated, being controlled mostly by the Alibaba–Tencent duopoly. Ride-hailing and food-delivery businesses are key assets in these companies' investment portfolios, and both have investment stakes in Didi, China's largest ride-hailing company. Didi merged with Kuaidi in 2016 and then acquired Uber China in 2016, thus cementing an unassailable ride-hailing monopoly in China. Meanwhile, the food-delivery sector experienced a similar wave of consolidation. After Meituan's acquisition of Dazhong Dianping in 2016 and Ele.me's acquisition of Baidu Deliveries in 2017,

High Wire. Angela Huyue Zhang, Oxford University Press. © Oxford University Press 2024.
DOI: 10.1093/oso/9780197682258.003.0007

Meituan (owned by Tencent) and Ele.me (owned by Alibaba) together became a duopoly, collectively controlling an almost 98 percent market share in the food-delivery industry. Since then, competition between Meituan and Ele.me has only intensified, as each of the two food-delivery giants strives to gain market dominance. To win over customers, both firms increased their spending, offering low fees and quick deliveries, while offloading the costs onto the delivery drivers by cutting their compensation and increasing fines for late deliveries.[4]

During the same period, online platforms adopted a variety of strategies for exploiting regulatory arbitrage to shed their employment liabilities. Platforms' adoption of such strategies, coupled with harsh labor exploitation, inevitably resulted in many disputes with workers. What's more, the stringent deadlines the platforms set for food deliveries incentivized speeding, which led to an increase in traffic accidents across China. Much like the dynamics we have already observed in the arenas of antitrust and data regulation, Chinese labor protection in the tech sector used to be light-touch. Then, in 2021, the regulatory pendulum swung toward harshness—with the promulgation of a number of documents on administrative guidance, urging leading Chinese tech firms to relax their algorithmic control over platform workers and enhance labor protections for them. The Chinese judicial system also responded with a propaganda campaign, aggressively promoting cases that offered strong protections to workers.

Before delving deeply into this dramatic regulatory swing, I will first examine the major regulatory challenges that have beset China's labor governance and regulation. I will then apply the dynamic pyramid model of regulation to analyze the incentives and behavior of each of the four major actors involved in the regulatory process. Unlike antitrust and data enforcement, Chinese courts play a major role in adjudicating labor disputes arising from the platform. Using data collected from a Chinese judicial database, I will perform a statistical analysis of the consequences of the recent crackdown on actual judicial practice and assess its impact on labor regulation in the tech sector. Interestingly, my empirical results did not identify a significant shift of judicial approach between 2020 and 2021 within my sample. Instead, Chinese courts appear to have largely responded to Beijing's campaign to enhance labor protection for platform workers with symbolic measures. In a similar vein, labor regulators have demonstrated a noticeable restraint in their regulatory responses, favoring a more lenient regulatory approach. Such tempered responses stand in sharp contrast with the over-zealous enforcement by the administrative authorities in data and antitrust enforcement. This discrepancy in responses, I suggest, can be attributed to their distinct utility functions. Unlike their antitrust and data counterparts, the Chinese judiciary and labor regulators hold a much broader mandate, thus requiring them to delicately balance the twin imperatives of fostering economic growth and maintaining regulatory oversight.

6.1. Regulatory Challenges

Three major regulatory challenges have plagued China's labor regulation: algorithmic exploitation of platform workers, lack of social protection for migrants, and significant barriers preventing workers from forming their own unions. As previously noted, tech firms are not the only ones to be blamed here; in fact, the Chinese government is the single biggest contributor to the latter two types of challenges, as I will explain in detail below.

6.1.1. Algorithmic Exploitation

Unlike traditional businesses, platform companies have invested heavily in software applications and mobile technologies to allocate, optimize, and evaluate the performance of their workers.[5] Algorithmic management and data-driven surveillance have played an indispensable role in controlling the services of platform workers, including by calculating delivery times, setting routes, and tracking the location of drivers and couriers throughout their journey. Platforms have also introduced gamification into the labor process, using both rewards and penalties to motivate workers and increase productivity.[6] For example, food-delivery companies, which rely heavily on crowdsourcing flexible workers, have structured the rate of commission based on the total amount of deliveries, so that the more deliveries an individual worker makes each month, the higher piece rate they are entitled to. These measures have provided workers with a significant incentive to work more, thus helping the platforms attain their goal of building a 24/7 on-demand workforce. Other gamification measures see delivery drivers evaluated on the basis of performance statistics such as their transaction volume, on-time rate, and customer reviews.[7] The better a worker's performance statistics, the more credit they are entitled to, the higher their ranking, and the greater the bonus they receive. During task assignment, platforms also give a higher priority to full-time workers and workers with better performance statistics.[8] Many online platforms require a very high acceptance rate of such automated assignments, and drivers could face serious penalties for rejecting assignments that are undesirable or uneconomical.

As a result of such measures, which have increased workers' dependence on the platforms, supposedly flexible platform workers have become "sticky labor" instead.[9] Indeed, a 2018 survey of 1,888 platform workers showed that more than 30 percent worked more than 40 hours per week, and almost 60 percent worked more than 33 hours per week.[10] Moreover, according to a survey of Beijing delivery drivers by the Yilian Labor Center, 95 percent worked more than 8 hours a day and 66 percent worked more than 11 hours.[11] The same survey also showed that almost 90 percent of the crowdsourced delivery drivers relied on online delivery as their sole source of income.[12] Despite their long hours and dependence on the platforms, however, the delivery drivers are not recognized as formal employees of the food-delivery companies, and they enjoy few labor benefits and protections—a point I will elaborate in detail when discussing the regulatory-arbitrage strategies adopted by Chinese tech firms.

In addition to transforming their "flexible workers" into "sticky labor" without shouldering the corresponding employer responsibilities, online platforms also impose a negative externality on society by incentivizing dangerous driving. Between 2016 and 2019, Meituan cut its delivery time from an hour to 30 minutes.[13] Platforms imposed hefty penalties on delivery drivers for late deliveries. When a Beijing government official conducted a field investigation as an undercover delivery driver in 2021, he was shocked that one late order resulted in a 60 percent deduction of his commission.[14] What's more, the method of algorithmic control has resulted in a race to the bottom. Many deliverymen have complained that when they managed to fulfill an order within less time, the algorithmic system would record this and set it as the new required time, forcing the worker and his colleagues to match it.[15] As delivery drivers race against the clock to complete orders, speeding and running red lights have become routine.[16] The emphasis on speed in the food-delivery business has led to many traffic accidents and deaths. In the 14 months after the beginning of 2020, Shanghai recorded 423 road-traffic accidents involving food-delivery drivers, including seven fatalities and 347 cases of injury.[17] In 2021, Guangzhou recorded more than 130,000 traffic violations in the online delivery sector, 55 of which were traffic accidents.[18] And yet, despite their overwhelming frustration at the pervasive algorithmic control to which they are subjected, platform workers are in a very weak position when it comes to dealing with the large and powerful platforms.[19] The online platforms' growing market power, combined with China's abundant supply of migrant labor, have given the platforms immense bargaining leverage, with many delivery drivers having to compete with each other for orders while experiencing a downward trend in their delivery fees.[20]

6.1.2. Lack of Social Protection

Yet Chinese tech firms are not the only ones at fault in this situation: government failure is a major contributing factor to the chaos observed in labor regulation. The vast majority of platform workers engaged in ride-hailing or food-delivery businesses lack adequate social protections, particularly for work-related injuries. The existing social-insurance scheme in China was not designed with the emergence of flexible employment in mind, leaving many workers without a proper social safety net.[21] Migrant workers are particularly vulnerable in this regard, due to the long-standing institutional barriers they face in obtaining social-welfare benefits in their place of work. A 2020 survey by Beijing's Yilian Labor Center showed that more than 80 percent of China's food-delivery workforce is composed of migrant workers from rural areas.[22] Because rural migrants do not have household registrations (commonly known as *hukou* in China) in urban districts, they have been excluded from the urban social-welfare system that provides support for housing, medical care, education, and other social benefits. While it is true that the government has rolled out policies to improve social protections for migrant workers, these are only available to migrant workers who have signed formal labor contracts with their employers.[23] As Mary Gallagher has observed, there exists a large gap between the labor law on paper and the law in practice.[24] A 2014 study has revealed that many employers have failed to purchase workers' compensation insurance for migrant employees—despite being legally required to do so under the Workers' Compensation Insurance Law.[25] Local governments, meanwhile, often fail to take proactive enforcement measures, prioritizing GDP growth and local employment over social protection.[26] Indeed, official government data from 2017 shows that only 22 percent of migrant workers were protected by a basic pension or medical insurance, while 27 percent were entitled to work-related injury insurance.[27]

Under Chinese labor law, employees are entitled to five types of insurance, including pensions, medical, unemployment, work injury, and maternity insurance; and yet, all of these forms of social insurance are typically provided through formal employment. Because the vast majority of platform workers are not treated as formal employees, few are entitled to any of them. An empirical survey of platform workers in three major Chinese cities, including Beijing, Hangzhou, and Chongqing, has revealed that only 3.7 percent of food-delivery drivers and 1 percent of ride-hailing drivers were entitled to employment-injury insurance.[28] Surveys have shown that many workers report not being bothered by this lack of coverage, either because they are unaware that such coverage exists or have little faith that labor laws will protect them.[29] The fact that the *hukou* system is tied to one's permanent residence, which is not necessarily the location of one's workplace, causes additional problems for migrant workers hoping to receive social welfare.[30] Even if some employers have purchased social insurance for their migrant worker employees in the city or region where their *hukou* is registered, it is not accessible in their place of work as migrants lack the local *hukou* registration. Nor can migrant workers voluntarily contribute to the social-insurance schemes at their place of work without having a local *hukou*.[31] In any case, because many migrant workers expect to work in the sharing economy for only a short period of time, they are often unwilling to make regular contributions to social-insurance programs, as these may not be transferable across jobs or localities.[32] All of these institutional barriers increase the cost of compliance and participation in social insurance for both platform workers and the platform companies.[33]

The predicament faced by Chinese platform workers can be illustrated by a recent incident. In late 2020, a 43-year-old delivery driver surnamed Han from Shanxi province died while on duty delivering food in Beijing for Ele.me.[34] Han signed up for this work via Fengniao Zhongbao, a crowdsourced on-demand logistics service. Ele.me claimed that it had no labor relationship with the worker and only paid RMB 2,000 as compassionate compensation to his family. Ele.me's response sparked an outcry among Chinese netizens, causing Ele.me to increase the compensation to RMB

600,000 to the deceased worker's family. Despite this unexpected outcome, Han's insurance trouble is all too typical among crowdsourced delivery drivers, who are only entitled to the accident insurance that is bought by delivery platforms on behalf of their workers. Unfortunately, the fees that drivers pay for insurance are both paltry and cut into their own incomes. For instance, delivery drivers working for Ele.me and Meituan pay RMB 3 per day for accident insurance, but only RMB 1.06 is used to purchase the insurance, while the rest is a handling fee charged by the platform and the third-party dispatch companies.[35] In Han's case, the delivery driver's family was only entitled to a compensation of RMB 30,000, about 5 percent of the work-related injury compensation they would have been entitled to had he been treated as a formal employee.[36] In practice, many delivery drivers have chosen to resolve minor accidents themselves rather than deal with the hassle of obtaining medical certification, not to mention the low payouts they can expect to receive.[37] Making matters worse, delivery drivers who make insurance claims could end up losing "credit points"—or even having their accounts blocked by the platforms.[38]

6.1.3. Barriers to Collective Action

Because individual workers have little bargaining power when facing powerful tech platforms, collective action has become an extremely important means for them to improve their bargaining position. However, China's strict control of union formation and its suppression of nongovernmental organizations (NGOs) have made it exceedingly hard for platform workers to organize any collective bargaining with their employers.

In China, the All-China Federation of Trade Unions (ACFTU) is the only legal workers' union. With 300 million members and one million full-time officials, the ACFTU is the world's largest national trade union.[39] The ACFTU is organized as a complex hierarchy extending from Beijing to different levels of the Chinese government, with its appointments tightly controlled by the Chinese Communist Party (CCP) at both the national and regional level.[40] At the bottom of the ACFTU hierarchy are the grassroots enterprise unions, which are generally not established by the employees of such firms, but rather by the local trade union officials in consultation with the management of these enterprises. As such, the enterprise unions are largely under the control of the enterprise management, with most union chairs being selected from among the management.[41] Union officials who are appointed above the enterprise level are recruited through the same channels as other government officials and behave like other public officials.[42] Given the government's overriding goal of maintaining social stability, the ACFTU has rarely been a staunch advocate for workers. Instead the union has focused its efforts on maintaining social stability by easing tensions between workers and management to ensure harmonious labor relations and avoid disrupting economic activities.[43] However, by prioritizing the interests of the CCP over those of workers, the ACFTU has become alienated from the working class they are supposed to represent. Indeed, workers seldom actively seek help from the trade unions, nor do they typically have the union as a representative in their disputes.[44] In practice, even when workers resort to the ACFTU for assistance, union officials routinely turn them away, using a variety of excuses, or else pass the responsibility on to other ACFTU unions.[45]

Since 2018, the ACFTU has included food-delivery drivers in its list of eight major groups whose interests the union deems a priority for protecting. Thus far, however, the union has done little other than providing some skills training, legal assistance, and some medical benefits.[46] For instance, in the case of the death of Han the delivery driver, the local trade union refused to get involved, arguing that its union only served union members and that it was unclear whether Han was one of them.[47] The ACFTU usually waits for enterprises to set up their own unions rather than organizing workers from the bottom up. But the vast majority of food-delivery drivers are not formal employees of the online platforms, and so even this option is not open to them.[48] The ACFTU's monopoly on organizing trade unions has meant that the Chinese working class has been deprived of the opportunity to create their own unions that could effectively represent them in genuine collective bargaining with their employers.

In the absence of effective workers' unions, grassroots NGOs focused on labor have proliferated since the 1990s.[49] However, these NGOs have frequently been subject to harassment and crackdowns in recent years, which has placed them in a precarious position.[50] Fearful of more repressive state intervention, the NGOs are reluctant to organize any overt form of labor resistance.[51] In response, platform workers have to resort to strikes or protests to protect their rights.[52] A 2016 nationwide survey of taxi drivers found that 55 percent had participated in strikes, while 2 percent had been involved in organizing them.[53] The rise of app-based ride-hailing appears to have increased the number of drivers involved in strikes. For instance, before the introduction of ride-hailing apps in 2013, there averaged a little over four taxi strikes per month.[54] This number increased to 16 times per month between 2013 and 2016, meaning a protest or strike by taxi drivers took place almost once every two days in China.[55] Demonstrations are also common in the delivery sector. China Labor Bulletin, a nonprofit organization that supports workers' movements in China, documented 138 strikes involving food-delivery drivers between 2015 and 2022.[56] Almost all of these involved Meituan or Ele.me, with workers' demands typically relating either to wage arrears or pay increases. Only 10 percent of these strikes involved over 100 workers, while the others were all small-scale protests or strikes that involved fewer than 100 participants.

The Chinese state is increasingly wary of collective action by platform workers. In 2019, a delivery worker, Tianhe Chen, forged an alliance among food-delivery drivers in Beijing.[57] He first set up a WeChat group, which later expanded to 16 groups including almost 8,000 drivers in Beijing.[58] Chen was not afraid of directly confronting the largest platforms and circulated a video accusing Ele.me of having broken its promises to its drivers. The video went viral, prompting Ele.me to issue an apology to the alliance.[59] Yet just a week later, Chen was arrested by the police, along with some other delivery drivers, and was charged with "picking quarrels."[60] In practice, the charge of "picking quarrels" is often used as an excuse by Chinese authorities who want to arbitrarily criminalize any speech they don't like. Chen's arrest dealt a blow to the nascent forms of collective action initiated by the drivers.[61] In its wake, most drivers were afraid to complain too much. This was in large part because they feared retaliation by the platforms, which prohibit workers from going on strike or protesting.[62] Since the food delivery market is dominated by Meituan and Ele.me, workers have very few options but to work for one or the other.

6.2. Applying the Dynamic Pyramid Model

In the following sections, I will apply the dynamic pyramid model to analyze the four major players involved in the process of labor regulation by focusing on their incentives as well as their interactions with each other. Chinese tech firms used to enjoy a very tolerant regulatory environment due to the strong endorsement they received from the top leadership and their own aggressive lobbying. As competition has intensified in recent years, Chinese tech firms have sought regulatory arbitrage to shed liabilities and cut costs. Meanwhile, Chinese labor regulators refrained from taking an aggressive stance in regulating the tech firms. As a consequence, Chinese workers, who lacked effective channels for voicing their complaints, had to resort to the courts to help themselves in the case of labor infringements. Chinese labor policy only started to pivot in 2021 with the launch of the law-enforcement campaign against Chinese Big Tech.

6.2.1. Top Leadership

As mentioned in Chapter 2, in the aftermath of the financial crisis in 2008, the Chinese government put more emphasis on innovation and technology to jump-start the Chinese economy, with 2015 being regarded as the "epoch-making year" for the sharing economy.[63] That year saw the State Council issuing guidelines to encourage innovation and mass entrepreneurship, as well as announcing opinions to promote the ride-hailing industry.[64] In 2016, the Chinese government officially included the development of China's sharing economy in its thirteenth Five-Year Plan.[65] A year later, eight central ministries released guidelines aimed at creating a more transparent and enabling policy environment to boost China's blossoming sharing economy.[66] At the State Council meeting that approved the guidelines, then-premier Li Keqiang proudly declared that China "has led the world in some fields of the sharing economy" and urged all government departments to adopt an open mindset.[67] As he was quoted saying: "Regulations for the sharing economy should be tolerant while prudent, as there is still much yet to be learned about new business models. We should avoid simply applying traditional methodology on the sharing economy."[68] Between 2018 and 2020, the State Council rolled out a series of policies in support of mass entrepreneurship and innovation as an important engine to boost employment. The State Council also released a circular to promote the stable and healthy development of the platform economy in August 2019.[69] Later that year, the State Council issued opinions to stabilize employment, applauding the sharing economy as a novel form of business that offered plenty of room for employment.[70] When the Chinese economy faced severe downward pressures in early 2020 due to the Covid-19 outbreak, the State Council immediately introduced a circular to promote flexible employment in the sharing economy, particularly for rural and urban low-income groups.[71]

Although the growth of the sharing economy has been incredibly helpful in absorbing the excessive supply of low-skilled labor, it also creates many hidden social and economic problems. First, the expansion of the sharing economy could distort the allocation of investment at the expense of the formal economy. Using the example of Mexico, Santiago Levy has shown that subsidizing the informal economy leads to a misallocation of resources that undermines the formal economy, reducing the government's fiscal ability and weakening public infrastructure.[72] This phenomenon is not confined to Mexico—many other Latin American countries have observed a similar trend that has increased wage polarization, leading to more social tensions and instability, while also producing a vicious cycle that further expands the informal economy.[73] Meanwhile, favorable government policies that encourage more Chinese workers to seek informal employment in the sharing economy can lead to larger-than-optimal levels of informal employment that may well undermine China's long-term productivity and growth.[74]

The second problem with the expansion of the sharing economy is that it could further exacerbate income inequality. Research by a team of Stanford economists indicated a growing trend of wage polarization between high- and low-skilled workers in China.[75] They observed that the drop in employment in China's construction and manufacturing sector since the mid-2010s has driven low-skilled workers to informal employment, including in the sharing economy. As the supply of low-skilled workers has accelerated in recent years, demand has not kept pace, causing wage growth to decline. In the meantime, formal workers in high-skill services such as technology, banking, and education have enjoyed faster wage growth, thus exacerbating income inequality even further. The Stanford team warned that China may be caught in a middle-income trap—that is, the inability to move toward becoming a high-income country—even as it continues to struggle with serious wage polarization.[76]

Against this backdrop, China's unveiling of the "common prosperity" initiative should not come as a surprise. In a highly influential piece published in *Qiushi*, a core CCP journal, President Xi Jinping outlined his vision for a comprehensive social program aimed at reducing China's income inequality.[77] Zhejiang, a rich Chinese coastal province that is home to Alibaba, was the first to roll out a pilot scheme for common prosperity.[78] The plan aims to address three main gaps—the regional gap, the urban–rural gap, and the income gap—by 2025. The central pillar of this program is creating an "olive-shaped" income structure that places the middle-income families at the social core, while alleviating pressures in education, healthcare, housing, elderly care, and childcare. As a contemporaneous opinion piece in a state newspaper put it, striking a harmonious employment relationship, curbing monopolies, and preventing the overexpansion of capital should all be seen as essential steps for achieving common prosperity.[79] By tightening labor regulation and improving the welfare of platform workers, Chinese tech regulation could enhance the bargaining power of platform workers. Not only that: by appealing to the masses, these measures can also enhance the popularity of China's leadership.[80]

6.2.2. Firms

As the dynamic pyramid model suggests, businesses operating in China are very flexible and nimble and know how to adapt to China's unique institutional environment and work it to their advantage. Because policy support is incredibly important in China and often trumps the law itself, Chinese tech firms have resorted to both formal and informal institutional channels to lobby for high-level endorsements for their businesses. Chinese tech firms have also sought regulatory arbitrage and have taken advantage of legal loopholes to circumvent employment liabilities and thereby lower costs.

6.2.2.1. Lobbying

China's ride-hailing businesses started out by operating in a legal gray area.[81] For years, companies such as Didi have argued that they are merely online platforms and therefore not subject to the same regulation as traditional taxi companies. Meanwhile, the explosion of ride-hailing threatens the business of the 1.4 million traditional taxis in China, whose drivers have vehemently protested against the "unfair competition" created by the ride-hailing firms.[82] In October 2015, the Ministry of Transport issued its first draft rules on ride-hailing services. Under the proposed rules, operators of ride-hailing services would need to obtain licenses from the local authorities and their cars would need to be registered for commercial use. This proposal would have forced ride-sharing apps to operate more like traditional taxi companies, potentially slowing down their pace of expansion.[83] Moreover, operators of ride-hailing services would have been required to sign labor contracts with drivers, which would have significantly increased their operating costs. Needless to say, Didi Chuxing and other ride-hailing firms exerted tremendous efforts in lobbying the central government to remove these restrictions.[84]

In 2016, Liu Qing, then CEO of Didi, put forward a proposal to the All-China Federation of Industry and Commerce (ACFIC) for facilitating and standardizing the development of ride-hailing in China.[85] The ACFIC is a nongovernmental chamber of commerce that was established in 1953 to represent the CCP's interests and promote its policies among private entrepreneurs. When the ACFIC submits a formal proposal to the Chinese People's Political Consultative Conference (CPPCC), relevant government ministries or departments are required to investigate the proposal and provide a formal response.[86] This institutional channel enables the ACFIC to exert influence over the policymaking process. Although Liu Qing is not among the ACFIC leadership, her father, the legendary entrepreneur Liu Chuanzhi, served as its deputy chair for almost a decade, starting in 1997.[87] Liu Qing's proposal was not ultimately chosen to be submitted to the CPPCC.[88] However, according to a staff member of the ACFIC, Didi was able—by working through the channel of the ACFIC and with the assistance of the CPPCC—to reach out to the State Council Policy Research Office, which enabled the firm to discuss the ride-hailing regulatory issues with policymakers directly.[89]

In 2016, the State Council issued a national policy on reforming and promoting the development of the taxi industry, thereby setting the tone for positive policy support for the ride-hailing platforms.[90] In November of that year, the Ministry of Transport, along with six other government departments, jointly promulgated the interim measures for regulating ride-hailing businesses—thereby effectively legitimizing the sector.[91] Although the interim measures continued to place restrictions on the ride-hailing operators, they significantly watered down the restrictions that had been proposed the year before.[92] Instead of mandating that only commercially registered vehicles be allowed to provide ride-hailing services, the interim measures explicitly encouraged private car sharing; however, they also required vehicles to install proper safety features. Importantly, the measures allowed ride-hailing firms to enter into different types of contracts with drivers instead of requiring a labor contract, which would have significantly increased the firms' labor costs.

In the meantime, the 2016 guidelines also granted local governments more autonomy in deciding how to regulate the ride-hailing sector. This new empowerment of local governments turned out to be another regulatory headache for Didi, however, as many major Chinese cities such as Beijing, Shanghai, Guangzhou, and Shenzhen started to announce strict regulations that restricted car size and imposed local-residency registration requirements on drivers.[93] Given that most of Didi's drivers do not possess a local *hukou*, this effectively excluded a majority of them from joining the ride-hailing workforce. Didi and Uber reacted very strongly to these aggressive local restrictions, arguing that they would significantly increase the cost of ride-hailing and reduce the efficiency of transportation.[94] In 2016, Didi's executives, including its founder Cheng Wei and president Liu Qing, conducted a 27-city, three-week tour to lobby local governments, offering to share Didi's data with the municipal traffic-control system and to partner with the cities to hire millions of laid-off workers.[95]

Meanwhile, Chinese tech firms in the sharing economy made bold claims about their capacities to stimulate employment and relieve poverty in response to the call from the central government. All of the leading players, including Didi, Meituan, and Ele.me, published annual reports via their own research centers about their contribution to the labor market. Didi, for instance, claimed that its ride-hailing services covered over 565 government-listed poor counties, generating income for over 700,000 local drivers in 2018.[96] The firm was also recognized for its efforts in creating 13.6 million flexible job opportunities, lifting over 350,000 people out of poverty and putting them into the middle-income group in 2019.[97] In 2020, the firm partnered with 16 online platforms to create the "New Economy and New Employment Promotion Alliance," which aims to promote more flexible employment for excess labor in the market.[98] During the Covid-19 pandemic, when tens of millions of factory workers were laid off and many young college graduates were unable to find jobs,

Chinese food-delivery and ride-hailing platforms played a critical role in absorbing the excess labor.[99] For instance, Didi pledged to invest RMB 200 million to promote employment for the unemployed, poor drivers, and those affected by the Covid-19 pandemic.[100] The firm also claimed to have created 10 million flexible jobs for drivers and operational staff through bike-sharing services.[101] As we will see, this formal and informal lobbying by Chinese tech firms paid off—in the form of lenient regulatory treatment.

6.2.2.2. Regulatory Arbitrage

Regulatory arbitrage is another important survival strategy used by Chinese tech firms. Much as in other jurisdictions, the biggest legal challenge for labor regulation in China's sharing economy is how to categorize the platform workers, that is, whether they should be classified as employees or independent contractors, a distinction that has significant implications for their legal status. Chinese labor law demands that employment units enter into employment relationships through the establishment of a labor contract, thereby establishing a "labor relationship."[102] This formal status provides workers with a range of rights and benefits under Chinese labor law and imposes a series of liabilities on employers.[103] While platforms often directly employed workers during the early days of their ventures, later years would see this model gradually fade away. In order to lessen regulatory costs, most Chinese tech firms have adopted a variety of tactics aimed at altering the legal status of their employment relationships with platform workers.

The most common strategy that platforms employ involves expanding their use of outsourced or crowdsourced workers. Outsourced workers are typically directly hired and managed by a third-party intermediary (e.g., a dispatch agency) in addition to their algorithmic management by the platform. This model creates a legal separation between the platform and the worker, eliminating any direct labor relationship and the obligations that would come with it. Meanwhile, starting in 2015, major delivery platforms began introducing an additional model for recruiting workers: crowdsourcing.[104] Crowdsourced workers can sign up directly via apps such as Fengniao Zhongbao (owned by Ele.me) or Meituan Zhongbao (owned by Meituan). Although an intermediary agency is often involved, crowdsourced workers differ from outsourced workers in that they are not directly managed by the agency, but are instead subject to the algorithmic management designed by the platform.[105] In 2018, Meituan's workforce consisted exclusively of either outsourced or crowdsourced workers, with almost 60 percent of them being crowdsourced.[106]

In practice, intermediary agencies often enter into a "labor service agreement" (劳务合同) instead of a "labor contract" (劳动合同) with drivers.[107] And yet, a signed formal labor contract is the only legal document that grants workers legal protection and associated social benefits and insurance under China's Labor Contract Law. While "labor service agreements" offer workers a certain level of benefits and insurance, the employment relationship established through labor service agreements is not protected by the Labor Contract Law and hence does not hold employers accountable for standard worker protections or social insurance.[108] Exploiting this loophole, some intermediary agencies sign service agreements with the drivers that explicitly specify the latter as independent contractors. In some cases, drivers have no agreements at all. Because drivers do not enjoy the protection of China's Labor Law, they are more vulnerable to exploitation by the online platforms.

The other strategy employed by platforms and their dispatch companies involves employing a complex web of legal relationships in order to avoid being identified as a formal employer for the delivery driver.[109] Consider the example of Quhuo, China's largest flexible employment platform that connects workers with major on-demand service platforms such as Meituan, Ele.me, and Didi. Quhuo went public on the Nasdaq stock exchange in 2020. The firm now has over 100,000 registered workers, boasts 60,000 active workers per month on its platforms, and manages approximately 1.3 million orders per day.[110] The legitimacy of Quhuo's business model is entirely contingent on the issue of how to classify workers on its platforms. As disclosed by the firm's 2021 annual report:

> We have established business outsourcing relationships with workers on our platform, pursuant to which we pay service fees to workers engaged in our solutions as independent contractors through third-party labor service companies. . . . [W]e believe the workers on our platform are independent contractors because, among other things, they provide services for orders obtained through our industry customers and get paid primarily based on the number of completed orders. As such, we do not believe that workers on our platform should be deemed as [sic] our employees or dispatch employees under the relevant PRC laws and regulations.[111]

As the above statements reveal, Quhuo often does not engage delivery drivers directly, but rather does so via third-party labor-service companies. There consequently exist multiple layers of contractual relationships between the platforms and workers. In 2020, Zhicheng Law Firm, a leading public-interest legal organization in China, published an influential report about the labor issues in Chinese food-delivery services.[112] The report found that delivery platforms employed a labyrinth of contracting companies based in different jurisdictions in order to shed employment liabilities.[113] In one case they represented, they found that a delivery worker who signed a contract with a logistics company in Chongqing had his wages paid by a restaurant in the same municipality, and his personal taxes paid by a construction company in northern Tianjin and a dispatching company in eastern Shanghai.[114] This tactic of layered dispatch arrangement has proven effective in shielding platforms against liabilities. The study also found that where full-time delivery drivers were engaged by dispatch agencies, only 81.62 percent of the cases decided by courts would recognize employment relationships between the drivers and dispatch agencies.[115] The percentage dropped to 46.89 percent when it came to multilayered dispatch arrangements.[116] Notably, tax evasion is also an important factor motivating platforms to employ layered contractual arrangements as some local regions in Jiangsu and Tianjin offer attractive tax benefits for small and micro-enterprises as well as flexible workers.

Unlike Quhuo, the vast majority of dispatch companies are small and medium-size firms. Of the 904 dispatch companies examined, the study found that more than 60 percent did not contribute capital after registering their company, while 16 percent had already de-registered their company.[117] Thus, even if workers win their cases, they may not be able to recover any damages, since many of the dispatch agencies are in fact judgment-proof. Consider a recent case in Chongqing. In early 2020, 91 delivery drivers in that city sued their dispatch companies, requesting that the latter compensate them for wage arrears and the cost of terminating their labor contracts.[118] Although the delivery drivers prevailed in court, the two dispatch companies, with a combined registered capital of only RMB 1.15 million, were unable to perform their obligations in 99 percent of the cases.[119]

As competition in the delivery business further intensified in 2018, more flexible work-management apps, such as Haohuo and Dinggehuo, have started to emerge, offering to help delivery drivers sign up as self-employed workers. Dispatch companies often asked their delivery drivers to join these apps, claiming that it was a more convenient way to pay them.[120] Some were also persuaded to register as self-employed workers on the premise that this status would help them save on their taxes.[121] The result was that many workers were defrauded and became self-employed without knowing the implications of this change in their legal status.[122] The study from Zhicheng Law Firm estimates that 1.6 million delivery drivers have registered as self-employed using various flexible-employment apps.[123] On the Haohuo app alone may be found almost 600,000 delivery drivers registered as self-employed firms.[124] Almost 1.1 million of these workers were registered in Jiangsu province, thanks to an aggressive push by the companies and the favorable policy environment created by the local government there.[125]

6.2.3. Platform Participants

Workers are the major complainants when it comes to labor exploitation by the online platforms. Their complaints include insufficient orders, low wages, capricious fines, grueling hours, and safety issues.[126] While these problems are significant, the avenues for addressing them are somewhat limited. Indeed, when problems arise, workers have reported difficulties in contacting platform representatives.[127] The ACFTU's monopoly in union representation makes it impossible for workers to create their own unions to effectively represent themselves. Absent legal protection for collective action, workers who participate in strikes do so at their own risk. As discussed earlier in this chapter, workers' protests tend to be localized, small-scale, and short-lived. For instance, in June 2021, a delivery driver in Shenyang accepted 253 orders within four hours and instantly clicked "order fulfilled" for each one.[128] This move was seen as an act of retaliation against Meituan's unreasonable penalties. In 2021, as was previously mentioned in Chapter 1, a 45-year-old delivery driver for Ele.me protested unpaid wages by setting himself on fire. The incident attracted widespread attention and triggered nationwide outrage. In August 2022, another food-delivery driver stabbed himself in front of his delivery hub after being informed by his station manager that he would be subject to a penalty of RMB 1,000 if he resigned.[129]

But these are extreme cases. Delivery drivers tend to organize more low-profile resistance to avoid potential state crackdowns. In Shanghai and Guangdong, delivery drivers organized resistance on a small scale, targeting the station managers of the dispatch companies who directly oversee them.[130] Instead of engaging in traditional forms of protest, the workers organized strikes through WeChat or other communication tools to collectively refuse accepting deliveries online. These mini-strikes were by no means always effective, but they show that workers do sometimes have some leverage in dealing with the station managers. Because the dispatch companies have their performance constantly evaluated by the delivery platforms, station managers fear the bad performance statistics that are the likely result of such strikes.[131]

In early September 2020, *Renwu* (*People*) magazine in China published an exposé about the intense working conditions endured by delivery workers in China.[132] Based on dozens of interviews with drivers, company employees, and academics, the report revealed in detail how workers had become slaves to the algorithms controlled by the platforms. The report found that these algorithms impose almost impossible deadlines for food deliveries. As a result, workers were under extreme pressure to beat traffic and found themselves snared in endless disputes with restaurant owners and customers. This report went viral on the Chinese internet, provoking an intense public outcry. On Weibo (the Chinese Twitter), the article garnered over 3 million views within a month.[133] State media also piled on with further criticism, calling for tighter oversight over the platforms, which needed to treat these workers as "people rather than machines."[134]

In the face of a public-relations crisis, both Meituan and Ele.me quickly responded the day after the publication of the exposé. Meituan added eight minutes of "flexible time" for delivery drivers, while Ele.me provided customers with the option to "wait five minutes more" for their delivery.[135] The public reaction to this response was overwhelmingly negative, with many accusing the platforms of shifting the burden from themselves onto their consumers while failing to address the problem of aggressive algorithmic control over workers.[136] Indeed, despite the public sensation that the *Renwu* article initially caused, scholars have found little change in the conditions of delivery drivers two years after its publication.[137]

6.2.4. Regulators

In the face of emerging regulatory tensions arising from the sharing economy, Chinese administrative regulators took a rather cautious and tolerant approach. Their attitude shifted dramatically, however, from late 2020, as they rushed to take action to pressure the tech firms to improve labor protections for their workers. In the meantime, Chinese courts also responded to the central initiatives by aggressively promoting precedents that offered strong legal protection for platform workers. And yet, in spite of these efforts, there has been little sign so far that the enforcement campaign has resulted in a substantive improvement in rights for these workers.

6.2.4.1. Administrative Enforcement

In China, the Ministry of Human Resources and Social Security (MOHRSS) is the central authority in charge of formulating national labor policies and regulations and managing social security. At the same time, the MOHRSS is tasked with managing the employment market in China and with providing assistance to labor-intensive industries and enterprises to create more employment.[138] As such, the ministry needs to simultaneously take on two potentially conflicting tasks—monitoring the firms to ensure adequate labor protection for workers while prodding them to provide more job opportunities. In practice, the MOHRSS sets its enforcement priority according to the policy mandates from the top leadership and the State Council.

To gauge the enforcement priorities of the MOHRSS, I did a search for all posts containing the word "Meituan" or "platforms" on its website; this allowed me to identify the activities the agency had conducted involving online platform companies by the end of 2022. The search generated 225 posts. After reading through each post, I found that almost 95 percent covered at least one of three major topics: enhancing labor protections, facilitating employment, and aiding poverty relief.

As the Figure 6.1 reveals, labor protections were clearly not a priority for the MOHRSS until the end of 2020; at least, they were not as important as the other tasks the agency focused on: increasing employment opportunities to boost growth, and helping with poverty relief. In the meantime, the MOHRSS has been working closely with Chinese tech firms to boost employment, including by co-organizing job forums with tech firms, promoting job training for platform workers, and encouraging tech firms to stabilize employment, in addition to offering subsidies to migrant workers during the pandemic. As an important form of poverty relief, the MOHRSS also organized the leading tech firms to provide employment

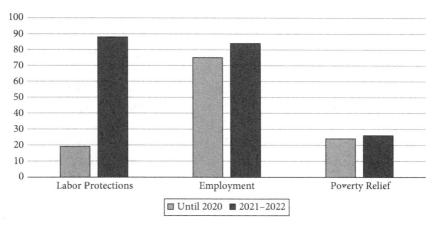

Figure 6.1. MOHRSS's enforcement priorities.

opportunities for targeted groups of peasant workers living in poor areas. As Figure 6.1 shows, it wasn't until late 2020 that the MOHRSS became visibly more active in formulating policies and enforcing relevant rules to enhance labor protections for platform workers.

On the MOHRSS's website, I also identified 25 proposals that the National People's Congress (NPC) and the CPPCC submitted to the agency relating to flexible employment between 2018 and 2021, with almost half submitted in 2021. Clearly, the MOHRSS was aware of the myriad labor issues arising from the platform economy. In response to these proposals, the ministry declared that it had conducted an extensive internal study, had met with leading internet companies, academics, and workers, and had conducted field studies in various regions such as Beijing and Zhejiang.[139] For instance, between 2019 and 2020, the CPPCC twice urged the MOHRSS about the need to recognize the labor relationship between the tech firms and the platform workers.[140] The MOHRSS strongly pushed back against this idea, noting that the classification of platform workers as employees remains a highly controversial issue that is the subject of intense debate both domestically and internationally.[141] It stressed that categorizing platform workers as employees would harm the development of the sharing economy, making it more difficult for it to absorb employment. The MOHRSS also cited several studies by the Chinese Academy of Labor and Social Security (the Academy), its affiliated think tank, as an important basis in shaping its decision.[142] In one study, the Academy urged the authority to take a cautious approach and carefully deliberate over the issues before taking actions, in keeping with the "let the bullet fly a bit longer" (i.e., wait and see) approach advocated by many leading Chinese scholars.[143] As for concerns about the lack of social protections for platform workers (and, in particular, the inadequacy of work-injury insurance), the MOHRSS promised to follow up with research based on observations and trials conducted at the local levels.[144] While the MOHRSS also urged workers to join the ACFTU unions, it stressed that workers cannot create unions based on their professions alone, making it difficult for them to unite together to represent themselves.[145] It appears that, in terms of labor protections, the MOHRSS was trying to maintain the status quo; it seems to have been concerned that tightened enforcement might disrupt the platform economy and hurt the employment prospects of the Chinese labor force.

In early 2020, the MOHRSS coordinated with China's internet association to organize a ceremony celebrating the pledge by 14 leading internet companies, including Alibaba, Tencent, Baidu, JD.com, Meituan, and Didi, to enhance care for platform workers.[146] Among other things, the petition calls on both internet platforms and entrepreneurs to shoulder their responsibilities for laborers and take active measures to prevent accidents and work injuries. These pledges, however, are vague and do not offer any substantive protection for platform workers. Meanwhile, some cities piloted social-insurance programs for platform workers, even though workers would need to contribute to such insurance themselves. In July 2019, the Chengdu city government promulgated measures to enhance the participation of social insurance for gig workers.[147] That same month, the Beijing Post Management Bureau, the MOHRSS, and the Medical Security Bureau jointly promulgated a notice to enhance protections for couriers. In November 2019, Zhejiang MOHRSS promulgated an opinion to enhance protections for gig workers. However, none of these measures is legally mandated and their impact appears limited.[148]

The pivot came only after China initiated a massive crackdown against the tech firms in late 2020. In the summer of 2021, three central ministries, including the Ministry of Transport, the MOHRSS, and the State Administration for Market Regulation (SAMR), led efforts to issue a series of guidance documents or opinions to enhance labor protections for platform workers. On June 23, 2021, seven agencies of the central government, led by the Ministry of Transport, jointly issued a guideline to protect the rights of delivery workers. The Guideline Opinion (also known as "Document No. 59") outlined eight tasks and measures, spanning benefit distribution, labor remuneration, social insurance, the operating environment, the responsibilities of business owners, standardized management, network stability, and career development.[149] In response, many provincial governments, including those in Beijing, Shanghai, Fujian, and Zhejiang, promulgated rules for implementation in accordance with their local conditions.[150]

On July 16, 2021, eight central-level ministries led by the MOHRSS released their Guiding Opinions on Protecting Labor and Social Security Rights and Interests of Workers Engaged in New Forms of Employment ("Document No. 56").[151] Document No. 56 stresses the need to enhance protections for platform workers, particularly with regard to the determination of labor relationships, eliminating employment discrimination, maintaining a minimum wage, establishing a standard for reasonable workload and rest, enhancing safety measures, contributing to social insurance, and preventing occupational injury. Regarding workers who do not fully meet the requirements for a formal employment relationship, Document No. 56 encourages companies to sign written contracts with them and reasonably define the parties' respective rights and obligations.[152] To prevent platforms from shedding their liabilities, Document No. 56 further emphasizes that when tech companies use contractors to hire workers, they should still bear relevant legal liabilities in case of harm to workers' interests.[153] That said, Document No. 56 provides only high-level guidance, and it is left to local governments to work out the details of implementation.

On July 26, 2021, the SAMR and six other government departments jointly published their Guiding Opinions on the Implementation of the Responsibilities of Online Catering Platforms to Effectively Safeguard the Rights and Interests of Food Delivery Drivers ("Document No. 38").[154] Document No. 38 requires delivery platforms to ensure that the actual income of food-delivery drivers does not fall below the local minimum wage and that delivery drivers should have access to basic social security. Most notably, it provides that the "strictest algorithm" shall not be taken as the assessment criterion for delivery drivers. Instead, it calls for platforms to use a moderate version of the algorithms to allow more time for food delivery.[155] In addition, Document No. 38 highlights the duty of platforms to strengthen road safety, urges platforms and dispatch companies to help workers purchase social and commercial insurance, and encourages them to participate in local experiments to protect flexible workers from occupational injuries. Document No. 38 also urges platforms to build union organizations so that workers can better negotiate their labor rights and requires them to create direct and timely dispute-resolution mechanisms for delivery drivers. In the case of disputes about late deliveries, platforms should be able to resolve complaints from delivery drivers within 24 hours.

The ACFTU, China's only legal trade union, also joined the fray. In July 2021, the ACFTU released opinions on enhancing the protection of laborers in the new economy.[156] The opinions urged the ACFTU unions at all levels to enhance their efforts to help platform laborers join unions. In September 2021, the Beijing Municipal Federation of Trade Unions (BMFTU) introduced guidelines to regulate and encourage the unionization of delivery drivers.[157] The guidelines lay out 10 major measures to improve union work to protect China's informal labor force in the new economy.[158] This move represents a significant step by the ACFTU to improve union representation in the sharing economy. Given the ACFTU's dual goal of serving workers and the state, however, labor activists are not optimistic that the establishment of such unions will have a substantive impact on workers' welfare.[159] As grounds for their skepticism, they pointed to a similar union formation in Shanghai and Xiamen, which failed to fundamentally transform the uneven relationship between the workers and the platforms.[160]

On September 10, 2021, the MOHRSS, along with the Ministry of Transport, the SAMR, and the ACFTU, summoned 10 leading internet platforms for a meeting on administrative guidance.[161] During the meeting, the agencies urged these tech firms to lead by example in meeting the labor-protection standards laid down in Document No. 56. In January 2022, the same four central ministries met 11 internet platforms, first acknowledging the improvements these companies had made in the preliminary phase, before also urging their continuing compliance.[162] A similar administrative-guidance meeting was held in September 2022—but this time the same four ministries were joined by the Cyberspace Administration of China (CAC), which apparently had an interest in regulating online platforms' algorithmic control of workers.[163]

As mentioned in Chapter 5, four central ministries, led by the CAC, promulgated some measures for managing the algorithms of internet services in January 2021, which include a provision requiring catering platforms' dispatching algorithms to provide workers with adequate compensation and rest.[164] Companies including Meituan and Ele.me were further required to submit filings on their algorithms with the CAC's newly established filing system. In their filings, both Meituan and Ele.me claimed that they had relaxed their algorithmic control over workers.[165] For instance, Meituan stated that it had chosen the longest estimated delivery time to display on the order page, while Ele.me emphasized that it would not adopt the minimum delivery time and would provide drivers with more time during difficult conditions.[166] An interview with an employee from a food-delivery platform has also shown that adjusting such algorithmic control was a top compliance priority for these catering platforms.[167] In addition to adjusting their algorithms, companies such as Meituan pledged to carry out pilot programs for improving the protection of workers from work-related injuries. Meanwhile, Didi, Meituan, and JD.com set up government-backed unions.[168]

6.2.4.2. Courts

Given the administrative authority's general reluctance to take aggressive action against the tech firms before late 2020, platform workers and related third parties had to rely on themselves to challenge their employers in labor arbitration or in the courts. In China, labor disputes typically first need to go through labor arbitration before going to court. Not all of those with grievances decide to invoke the formal legal processes, however, with many workers being deterred by the fact that they lack a contract with their employers.[169] To assess the judiciary's response during the tech crackdown, I researched cases involving delivery drivers in the China Judgement Online database.[170] In the summer of 2022, I collected a sample of 1,369 cases involving the issue of whether the delivery worker should be deemed an employee of the intermediary agencies or of the platforms. Among these 1,369 cases, 61 percent involved outsourced drivers, with the remainder involving crowdsourced drivers (32 percent) and self-employed drivers (6 percent). This is understandable given that outsourced drivers typically work full-time and are thus more likely to run into traffic accidents than crowdsourced drivers who work part time. Meanwhile, 36 percent of the cases were brought by delivery drivers, while a full 50 percent were brought by pedestrians injured by delivery drivers. This shows that innocent third parties are the major litigants in Chinese court cases involving delivery drivers. At the same time, it is important to note that these cases in my sample represent only a small portion of the cases that were brought to the court, as most are likely resolved through mediation. According to the report from one Shanghai court, 85 percent of the traffic-accident cases involving delivery drivers between 2016 and 2020 were either withdrawn or mediated.[171] The court, which had invested tremendous resources in mediating the conflict, was apparently proud of its achievement, as it explained at great length how it had coordinated with the relevant stakeholders and organizations, including the police, the insurance companies, the injury-identification center, and the law firms.[172]

As mentioned earlier in this chapter, Chinese tech firms have engaged in regulatory arbitrage by either outsourcing or crowdsourcing workers instead of directly employing them. This tactic has proven extremely effective. Within my sample, I found only 36 cases—or 2.6 percent of the total—in which platforms needed to shoulder some employment responsibilities. In the vast majority of cases, courts decided that the platforms were immune from liabilities, either because the workers were independent contractors or employees of intermediary agencies (e.g., dispatch companies, or a human resource management company). In the case of crowdsourcing, platforms typically argue that drivers are not their employees because they do not exert managerial control over them and cannot require them to work. Platforms also argue that they do not set rules for attendance, and drivers can work part-time. Moreover, drivers get remunerated each time they fulfill an order, and this mode of remuneration is inconsistent with the traditional payment of a salary.[173]

Among those 36 cases in which platforms were held liable, 72 percent involved vicarious liabilities, in that the delivery drivers had caused injury to third parties, and two cases involved the deaths of pedestrians. In 53 percent of these 36 cases, the platforms were held solely liable, whereas in the rest, the platforms were held jointly liable with the dispatch companies or the delivery drivers. Of these cases, 67 percent involved Ele.me, and none involved Meituan. Courts in Shanghai decided 44 percent of these cases, all of which involved Ele.me based in the same city. According to my interview with a former judge, some Shanghai courts once attempted some judicial reforms in cases involving delivery workers according to guidance from the Shanghai High Court, but eventually gave up this practice after seeing few similar reforms from other provinces.[174] A close reading of these cases reveals that courts are very reluctant to hold platforms solely liable, except when the third party fails to sue the intermediary agency or the latter is broke. Indeed, even when platforms were found vicariously liable for tortious cases involving physical harm, courts were still reluctant to confirm a labor relationship between the platforms and outsourced workers half of the time.[175]

Although Chinese courts seldom recognize employment relationships between platforms and delivery drivers, they often hold the intermediary agencies liable as an employer. Although many delivery drivers do not enter into any written agreement with the intermediary, a contract is not strictly necessary for courts to establish the existence of an employment relationship.[176] Thus, in the absence of a formal agreement, the intermediary agency could still be held liable for vicarious liabilities or other employment liabilities.[177] Using my sample of cases, I found that Chinese courts are more likely to recognize employment relationships when the delivery driver is outsourced than crowdsourced, and least likely to recognize employment relationships when the worker is self-employed. Moreover, Chinese courts are likely to consider other factors, such as whether the case involves physical injuries or financial loss. Generally speaking, courts are more likely to recognize employment relationships where the worker has caused injuries to third parties than cases in which the worker has incurred a work-related injury, and they are least likely to recognize a labor relationship in cases of wage arrears (see Table 6.1). These results are consistent with the findings of other scholars, who show that Chinese courts are very sensitive to spillover effects of employment relationships on society at large and seem much more willing to intervene in cases involving innocent third parties.[178]

Meanwhile, China is a vast country and there is a significant divergence among courts from different regions in deciding labor cases involving delivery drivers (see Figure 6.2). For instance, the average employment recognition rates between 2020 and 2021 in major provinces such as Guangdong, Beijing, Zhejiang, and Shanghai are above 85 percent, whereas the rates in

Table 6.1. The Rate of Recognition of Employment (2020–2021)

	Crowdsourcing	Self-employed	Outsourced
Third-party injuries	91%	84%	98%
Worker injury	34%	30%	81%
Wage arrears	22%	26%	83%

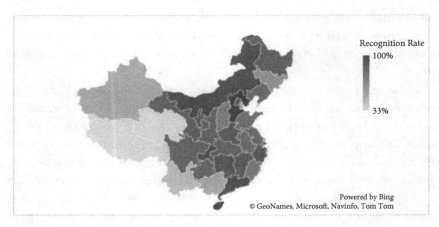

Figure 6.2. Average employment recognition rate (2020–2021).

other provinces such as Jilin, Tianjin, Guangxi, and Yunnan are below 60 percent.

Meanwhile, I found that cases involving self-employed workers increased quite significantly in some provinces. For instance, Beijing had no self-employed cases in 2020, but in 2021 the number jumped to 11, accounting for 19 percent of cases. Similarly, in 2021 Jiangsu saw the number of self-employed cases increase from three cases (3 percent) in 2020, to 11 cases (15 percent). This trend is not consistent across the country, however. Tianjin, for instance, had 26 self-employed cases in 2020 but had no such cases at all in 2021. Overall, the percentage of self-employed cases in both 2020 and 2021 remained at the same level of 6 percent. This suggests that two things could be happening at the same time. First, in some provinces, dispatch companies may be trying to persuade or even force workers into switching from crowdsourcing or outsourcing to a self-employed model to further shed liabilities.[179] Second, platforms have come under increasing public and regulatory scrutiny concerning their engagement of self-employed delivery drivers, especially following the release of the aforementioned Zhicheng report.[180] In response to public criticisms, in September 2021, Meituan and Ele.me both pledged not to force drivers to register as self-employed workers.[181]

Meanwhile, the judicial system has clearly responded with a propaganda campaign. Starting in June 2021, there has been a significant increase of coverage of typical cases and relevant studies within the judicial system's newspapers and magazines. Although there is no stare decisis in China, Chinese courts promote typical cases as a way of nudging lower courts to follow their decisions. Major Chinese cities, including Beijing, Shanghai, Jiangsu, Guangdong, Shandong, and Chongqing, have published typical cases involving flexible employment in the new economy.[182] Most cases published by these provinces recognize the labor relationship between the platform workers and the intermediary firm, thus sending a strong signal to local courts to tighten regulation.[183] This is particularly the case in situations where delivery drivers either lack contracts or have signed up as independent contractors, but are in fact subject to close monitoring by the dispatch companies.[184] In a typical case promoted by the Shanghai High Court, an intermediate court in Shanghai recognized a labor relationship when the dispatch company employed a complex web of legal relationships to avoid being identified as the formal employer of the delivery worker.[185] Courts in Jiangsu and Beijing have also published research reports on how to classify employment relationships in the new economy, advocating a pragmatic approach to enable courts to pierce through the veil of the contract in determining the existence of a labor relationship.[186]

Jiangsu, home to an estimated 1.1 million workers in flexible employment, has been the most active in this regard. In July 2021, the Jiangsu Intermediate Court launched a labor tribunal that specifically handles labor disputes arising from the platform economy.[187] In a landmark ruling in June 2020, the Jiangsu court decided a case in favor of a delivery driver named Meng Jingping, who initially signed up as an independent contractor via the flexible-employment app Haohuo. Like many drivers, Meng apparently didn't understand the legal implications of being an independent contractor rather than a formal employee. The court decided that the dispatch company had exerted de facto management over Meng and recognized a labor relationship in his case. This decision was widely endorsed and promoted by the Jiangsu High Court and the Supreme People's Court (SPC) to deter firms from evading liabilities by registering workers as independent contractors.[188] This case was also featured in a state media television series on the rule of law sponsored by the Supreme People's Court (SPC). This propaganda campaign appears to have been effective. Within my sample of 1,369 cases, the Chinese courts nationwide recognized an employment relationship in 22 percent of cases involving self-employed delivery drivers in 2020; in 2021, this number jumped to 68 percent. That said, the cases involving self-employed drivers account for only 6 percent of the total case in my sample. Thus, even with the improvement of labor protections for self-employed drivers, it can only do little to improve the welfare of the vast majority of drivers in China.

In May 2021, a worker named Liu died of a sudden stroke while delivering food for Ele.me.[189] Mr. Liu had signed an outsourcing service-cooperation agreement with a third-party agency and thus had no direct employment relationship with Ele.me. However, Mr. Liu's family sued both the intermediary firm and Ele.me, arguing that the platform should also be held liable because it failed to exercise due care in regard to Mr. Liu. Ele.me rebutted this argument, saying that the platform had no direct management role over Mr. Liu and only provided him with information services. The platform further claimed that Mr. Liu was a crowdsourced worker, who as such had complete freedom to choose his working time, location, and whether to take any orders. Furthermore, Ele.me maintained that it had already helped Mr. Liu sign up for commercial insurance and thus was not obliged to shoulder any liabilities. In November 2022, the Chaoyang District Court handed down an opinion that strongly favored the delivery driver. The court pierced through the veil of the service-cooperation agreement, noting that the intermediary agency was a de facto employer for Mr. Liu. The court also held the platform partially liable on the basis that it had the capacity to monitor delivery updates, but failed to give timely feedback to the intermediary agency, thus contributing to the delay in rescuing Mr. Liu. As such, the courts held that Mr. Liu was liable for 10 percent of the damages, Ele.me was liable for 20 percent, and the intermediary company was liable for 70 percent.

In a surprising move, the Chaoyang District Court launched a media campaign to promote its decision. Apparently prepared in advance, major Chinese newspapers and social media outlets provided extensive coverage about this case on the day of the trial and the court's announcement of its decision.[190] This proactive publicity approach is quite unusual, particularly as the case might still be appealed, and the verdict is not yet final. It also seems to indicate that the court has already reached its decision before a formal trial. Despite its high publicity, this decision appears to be an outlier thus far. As of February 2023, my search of the China Judgement Online database revealed 11 closely similar cases involving the deaths of delivery drivers in 2022. Platforms were not held liable in any of these cases, while the intermediary agency was held liable in six of them. In the six cases involving crowd-sourced drivers, neither the platform nor any intermediary company was held liable. In fact, the Beijing court didn't hold platforms liable in any of the other cases involving delivery drivers in 2022.

An important question is whether Chinese courts have offered more protection for delivery workers since the initiation of the law-enforcement campaign in late 2020. Overall, I did not identify a significant shift of judicial approach between 2020 and 2021 in my sample. (see the regression analysis in Appendix 6.1) While the rate at which employment relationships are recognized has clearly increased for self-employed workers, there isn't any clear trend of improvement for crowdsourced or outsourced workers. In fact, statistical analysis shows that the rate of employment recognition has actually decreased for crowdsourced delivery workers. Across the country, courts continue to be divided in deciding how to classify labor relations for delivery drivers. While Tianjin clearly improved labor protections for delivery workers, three other provinces, Guizhou, Chongqing, and Qinghai, appear to have gone in the opposite direction.

6.3. Future Trend

Similar to antitrust and data enforcement, labor regulation also saw a loosening in early 2022. However, Chinese labor enforcers have persisted in implementing measures to strengthen labor protection. Simultaneously, they are confronted with the challenging task of establishing appropriate labor standards that do not jeopardize the sharing economy.

In July 2022, China's MOHRSS, in collaboration with nine other central ministries, jointly unveiled a notice initiating a trial scheme for occupational injury insurance targeting platform workers.[191] The pilot program commenced in seven provinces and cities, encompassing Beijing, Shanghai, Jiangsu, Guangdong, Hainan, Chongqing, and Sichuan.[192] Under this arrangement, platforms are obliged to purchase occupational injury insurance for platform workers (e.g., ride-hailing drivers, food-delivery workers, couriers, and truck drivers), with fees ranging between RMB 0.04 and RMB 0.2 per transaction, depending on delivery type.[193]

On February 21, 2023, the MOHRSS issued a notice regarding labor contracts and written contracts for new forms of employment.[194] Echoing the guidance opinion released in July 2021, the notice underscored the importance for companies to sign labor contracts with platform workers, provided their engagement aligns with labor relationship stipulations. Crucially, the notice proffers template contracts for engagement not wholly adhering to employment conditions, including a written agreement between platforms and workers, and a written contract involving the platform, intermediary agency, and worker. This regulatory move represents a significant push for platforms to assume more labor responsibilities for workers. As noted earlier, many platform workers did not sign contracts with intermediary agencies, and few signed contracts directly with platforms. Instead, platforms frequently resorted to employing workers via intricate contractual arrangements with intermediary agencies, skirting labor liabilities. By widely publicizing contract templates, the MOHRSS is exerting social pressure on platforms to conform to its templates. However, the tangible impact of these templates remains nebulous, given the absence of a mandate for platforms to adopt the model contracts.

As the MOHRSS tries to encourage platforms to bear more labor responsibilities, the Chinese courts are also attempting to provide guidance for classifying labor relationships. On December 27, 2022, the SPC published an opinion regarding judicial services and protection to safeguard employment.[195] In this opinion, the SPC outlined five major factors for determining labor relationships in the absence of a prior contractual arrangement between the platform and the worker. These factors include: the working hours and flexibility for workers in deciding their workload; the extent of management and control over the labor process; whether the worker must comply with relevant working procedures, discipline, and award measures; the continuity of the nature of the services provided by the workers; and the workers' ability to determine whether and how to change transactional prices.[196] Despite this attempt to provide clearer guidance to lower courts, the SPC's evaluation criteria remain vague, leaving the boundaries of employee classification undefined. As of mid-2023, the SPC has yet to publish a judicial interpretation on properly classifying platform workers, resulting in continued uncertainty regarding the extent of protection that platform workers may receive in labor disputes.

In the face of mounting pressures for enhanced labor protection, both the MOHRSS and Chinese courts seem to lack a robust commitment for reforms, likely due to the intricate nature of their mandates. As explained earlier in this chapter, the MOHRSS shoulders a plethora of responsibilities, from shaping labor policies and overseeing social security to supervising the employment landscape and fostering job creation. Consequently, the MOHRSS must delicately calibrate its regulation of Chinese tech firms to avoid imposing unduly onerous regulations that could adversely affect employment rates. Indeed, after more than three years of draconian pandemic control measures, the Chinese economy experienced a sharp downturn, with the youth unemployment rate soaring to nearly 20 percent in April 2023.[197] In response, the State Council unveiled an extensive blueprint to invigorate employment, and Premier Li Qiang vowed to bolster market sentiment to preserve employment stability.[198]

Likewise, the Chinese courts must also deftly navigate a complex balancing act, as they contemplate the implications of their dispute adjudications. Faced with an extremely high caseload, Chinese judges have suffered from a perennial problem of capacity constraints.[199] A significant improvement in labor protection for delivery workers by the court will likely cause a sudden influx of cases, bringing additional pressures upon the already highly strained judiciary. More importantly, unlike the central ministries, which only need to answer to Beijing, Chinese courts face much more intense political pressure from the local governments that control their budgets and personnel.[200] In these circumstances, Chinese judges will need to strike a very delicate balance in adhering to Beijing's initiatives while also guarding local economic interests.

6.4. Summary

This chapter began by presenting the status of labor regulation in the Chinese tech sector and identified three main challenges. The first revolves around platforms' algorithmic exploitation of their labor force, which not only harms the interests of workers, but also incentivizes dangerous driving and increases traffic accidents on the road. The second challenge arises from the government's failure to provide sufficient social insurance, particularly for those migrant workers who often work in the informal sector, which offers little in the way of employment protection. The third challenge stems from the government's monopolization of the right to form unions, which creates significant barriers for platform workers seeking to organize collective actions to bargain with the interne giants.

Echoing the regulatory dynamics described in Chapter 2, Chinese labor authorities were slow to intervene in labor violations and failed to take forceful action to stop abusive practices. Chinese courts were also highly divided in cases involving the labor rights of platform workers. Since the initiation of the tech crackdown in late 2020, however, Chinese labor enforcement has taken a dramatic U-turn, with the administrative authorities quickly churning out guidance and measures aimed at enhancing protections for platform workers. The SPC and courts in major Chinese provinces also responded with a propaganda campaign, intensively highlighting precedents that offered strong protection to platform workers. And yet, despite these strong regulatory signals, statistical analysis shows little difference in actual judicial practice, with courts remaining divided as to how to properly classify employment relationships in cases involving platform workers. Although the judicial system has offered more protection for self-employed delivery workers, this improvement has affected only a tiny percentage of cases. In contrast to their counterparts in antitrust and data enforcement, labor regulators—including the judiciary and the administrative authority—appear to exercise a considerably greater degree of restraint in their enforcement actions. This is likely attributable to their intricate and expansive mandates, which demand careful consideration of the economic consequences of their regulatory actions. In fact, if they were to impose excessively stringent standards on tech companies, the potential impact on local employment could pose a serious threat to social stability.

Appendix 6.1 Regression Results on Labor Relationship Recognition

Using a hand collected dataset that includes all cases related to employment relationship recognition in China between 2020 and 2021 (number of cases: 1369), I conducted a regression analysis to estimate the correlation between the temporal changes in the labor relationship recognition rate (from 2020 to 2021) and the identity of the driver ((e.g., crowd-sourced, outsourced, self-employed, others), and geographic regions (provinces). I used a linear probability model with employment relationship recognition (1/0) as the dependent variable, and the main variables of interests are: Year = 2021 (the baseline year is 2020), the interaction terms (Year = 2021)*(Driver Type), which quantifies the temporal change for each driver identity category, and the interaction term (Year = 2021)*Province, which captures the time trend for each province. I also controlled for other variables such as case category (e.g., third-party injury, worker injury, wage arrears, others), platforms (e.g., Meituan, Ele.me, others), whether the accident occurred during delivery, whether insurance is involved in the case, and whether the case was appealed or went through a retrial.

The regression results are shown in the table below, which presents four specifications with different combinations of variables of interest. As Column (1) shows, on average, I did not find a statistically significant increase in labor relationship recognition rate from 2020 to 2021. However, by examining each driver types separately (Columns 2 and 4, Driver = Crowd-sourced is the baseline in the regressions), I found that drivers labeled as "self-employed" see a more than 40 percentage points increase in the labor relationship recognition rate from 2020 to 2021. This increase is both statistically and economically significant. In contrast, I did not observe statistically significant increases for the other driver types.

Regarding geographical differences (Columns 3 and 4, Shanghai is the baseline in the regressions), I found no single province with a statistically significant increase in the labor recognition rate from 2020 to 2021. For exposition brevity, while I included all provinces in the regressions, the table presents only coefficients of the provinces with changes significant at the 5% level. As shown below, four provinces (Anhui, Guizhou, Chongqing, and Qinghai) experienced a significant decline in employment recognition over the two years. Tianjin is the only province that experienced a significant increase in employment recognition in Column (3). However, looking closely, this change can be largely attributed to the fact that the composition of driver types involved in these cases are significantly different between 2020 and 2021. Specifically, out of the 41 cases in Tianjin in 2020, 26 involved drivers identified as self-employed, while this number becomes 0 out of the 24 cases in 2021. Thus, once I controlled for the (Year = 2021)*(Driver type) variables (Column 4), the change becomes insignificant.

Table: Regression Results on Labor Relationship Recognition

Dependent Variable: Employment Relationships Recognition (1/0)

	(1)	(2)	(3)	(4)
Intercept	0.990***	1.016***	0.953***	0.970***
	(0.037)	−0.038	(0.045)	(0.045)
Year = 2021	−0.0197	−0.0828***	0.0523	0.0023
	(0.019)	(0.031)	(0.059)	(0.061)
Driver = Self-Employed	−0.259***	−0.326***	−0.0599	0.304***
	(0.027)	(0.057)	(0.043)	(0.06)
Driver = Outsourced	−0.232***	0.213***	0.223***	0.179***
	(0.066)	(0.028)	(0.02)	(0.028)
Driver = Others	−0.0838	0.160	−0.286	0.194
	(0.141)	(0.316)	(0.222)	(0.31)
(Year = 2021) * (Driver = Self-Employed)		0.467*** (0.080)		0.475*** (0.082)
(Year = 2021) * (Driver = Outsourced)		0.0605 (0.039)		0.0867** (0.04)
(Year = 2021) * (Driver = Others)		−0.892** (0.446)		−0.928** (0.438)
(Year = 2021) * Tianjin			0.211**	0.0785
			(0.103)	(0.104)
(Year = 2021) * Guizhou			−0.676***	−0.782***
			(0.181)	(0.179)
(Year = 2021) * Chongqing			−0.612***	−0.636***
			(0.104)	(0.103)
(Year = 2021) * Qinghai			−0.765**	−0.747*
			(0.387)	(0.382)
(year = 2021) * Anhui			−0.205*	−0.219**
			(0.111)	(0.11)
Other Variables included				
Case Type	v	v	v	v
Platform	v	v	v	v
Timing (delivery or not)	v	v	v	v
Covered by insurance	v	v	v	v
Retrialed	v	v	v	v
Province	v	v	v	v
(Year = 2021) * Province			v	v
Number of Observations	1369	1369	1369	1369
R-squared	0.367	0.385	0.407	0.424

Notes. ***, **, * represent the coefficient is significant at 1%, 5%, and 10% levels respectively.

PART III

Platform
Self-Regulation

This part examines how Chinese tech firms self-regulate in the shadow of the dynamic pyramid model of regulation. It consists of two chapters. Chapter 7 addresses the limits of public regulation and explores how Chinese tech firms become de facto regulators, enforcing internal rules through various sanctioning mechanisms. Contrary to the common perception of the predatory nature of Chinese state intervention, this chapter reveals that Chinese judiciary has actually given a helping hand to Chinese tech firms by offering them indispensable judicial support. Chapter 8 discusses how Chinese online platforms, driven by insecurity about government intervention and rampant market fraud, are decentralizing governance to diffuse tensions arising from their platforms. Drawing on the innovative dispute-resolution schemes adopted by Taobao and other leading Chinese online platforms, this chapter illustrates how Chinese tech firms have attempted to use crowd-sourcing mechanisms to enhances efficiency in dispute resolution and to improve procedural justice.

7

Platforms as Quasi-Regulators

For many Chinese tech firms at an early stage of development, their first priority is not legal compliance, but rather how to move fast and break things in order to grab more user attention and gain market share. Indeed, many leading Chinese online platforms have thrived by operating in legal gray areas—a practice that is vital for them to gain competitive advantage. As observed in previous chapters, Chinese e-commerce firms have tolerated a vast amount of fake promotional reviews and counterfeit products to attract users to their marketplaces, social-media platforms have harvested huge amounts of user data without obtaining proper consent and authorization, and ride-hailing platforms have operated in many Chinese cities without obtaining proper licenses. Meanwhile, the vast majority of these tech firms have structured themselves as variable interest entities (VIEs) to obviate China's foreign-investment restrictions and raise capital overseas. Until the top leadership became concerned about the "overexpansion of capital" and mobilized the entire bureaucracy to rein in its Big Tech firms in late 2020, Chinese tech firms were largely immune from strict regulation and enjoyed vast discretion in running their own platforms.

And yet, paradoxically, the same light-touch regulatory environment that Chinese online platforms exploited during their rise also presented them with acute challenges. Fraud is endemic in China—a problem that has been mentioned in previous chapters, and which will be further elaborated in this chapter. But state law can do little to address many of the problems arising from it. In reality, online consumers rarely resort to the formal legal system for settling their disputes, making state law largely irrelevant to online dispute resolution. Most parties to such disputes were never practically governed by the formal legal system in the first place;

High Wire. Angela Huyue Zhang, Oxford University Press. © Oxford University Press 2024.
DOI: 10.1093/oso/9780197682258.003.0008

they seldom bargain in the "shadow of the law."[1] As Van Loo succinctly observed, "the corporation is the closest thing to a courthouse that most consumers will encounter."[2] The regulatory burden accordingly falls upon the online platforms, which act as middlemen facilitating transactions between buyers and sellers. In essence, online platforms act as for-profit third-party intermediaries, providing contract-enforcement services for transacting parties. That is, not only does a typical e-commerce platform serve as an information intermediary, transmitting the reputation of sellers and buyers through a feedback system; it also operates as an enforcement intermediary, meting out ex post punishments when a party violates transactional rules.

In assuming this role, Chinese online platforms face distinct challenges. In a seminal paper, Molly Cohen and Arun Sundararajan pointed out three factors that might lead to successful governance within self-regulatory organizations: the use of the power of reputation, the establishment of a credible enforcement mechanism, and a perception of legitimacy.[3] These are the three crucial tasks facing Chinese tech firms in governing their own platforms.

First, Chinese online platforms need to build a vibrant reputation mechanism to attract users so as to facilitate transactions between them. Meeting this criterion poses a significant challenge for Chinese platforms given the endemic fraud in the Chinese market. Chinese tech firms turned this challenge into a competitive advantage by quickly installing a major feedback mechanism to grow their market—that is, by tolerating a considerable number of fake promotional reviews, thus echoing the "fake it till you make it" survival strategy discussed in Chapter 1. Second, Chinese tech firms need to create an internal legal system to credibly enforce the rules they create. In practice, Chinese platforms have achieved such credibility by engaging in co-regulation with the Chinese judiciary, which has provided indispensable support for the tech companies' own internal systems of punishment and enforcement. Third, because platforms are only private enforcers and lack the state's legal authority, they are constantly confronted with challenges in asserting their legitimacy. Faced with the threat of stringent regulation, Chinese online platforms have a strong urge to decentralize their governance in order to ease and diffuse tensions arising from the platform. In this chapter, I will focus on the first two aspects of Chinese online platforms' self-governance strategies, drawing frequent references to Taobao, China's premier e-commerce site, owned by Alibaba. I will elaborate on the third point regarding the decentralization of platform governance in the next chapter.

7.1. Building (Faking) a Reputation Mechanism

One of the biggest challenges facing Chinese online platforms in the early days of their business venture was how to build trust between the transacting parties. Without knowing the creditworthiness and reliability of the seller, consumers could be reluctant to place an order, resulting in fewer transactions than the socially optimal level. This can be termed an "adverse selection problem," otherwise known as the "lemons problem" in economics.[4] To overcome this problem, eBay pioneered building an online review mechanism to alleviate information asymmetry between merchants and buyers. This business model was quickly followed by other e-commerce platforms, including those based in China. Chinese tech firms are acutely aware of the value of customer reviews, as positive reviews help merchants attract more customers and thus help facilitate more transactions. Chinese e-commerce platforms therefore have a strong incentive to encourage the proliferation of fake promotional reviews, particularly during the early stages of their development.[5]

Setting up a strong reputation mechanism, however, is far from easy. In an ideal world, online platforms would provide accurate information by building a very clean reputation system. In reality, however, the reputation system is subject to a lot of noise.[6] To begin with, the feedback rate from consumers tends to be very low. Scholars have found, for instance, that even eBay buyers leave feedback on their transactions only 50 percent of the time.[7] After all, writing feedback takes time, and this information only benefits others.[8] As such, user-generated feedback is a public good that is often underprovided.[9] To overcome this problem, Chinese e-commerce businesses such as Taobao have adopted several strategies to encourage and inflate customer reviews. For instance, to encourage consumers to submit reviews after their purchases, Taobao rewards them with consumer credits for contributing reviews that exceed 80 words and contain at least one image.[10] Taobao has also created a default setting that gives a positive rating to the seller if the buyer leaves no review.[11]

Merchants, on the other hand, have a strong incentive to manipulate consumer reviews to boost their sales. For instance, many merchants on Taobao promise to give customers a rebate if they leave a positive review.[12] Although Taobao has explicitly forbidden this practice, the prohibition is hard to enforce because few customers would bother to complain about such "offers" from merchants. Another common form of promotional review is called "brushing," a term that comes from Taobao's feedback system.[13] In a typical brushing transaction, the merchant gives instructions to a "brushing company," who will then place an order and make a payment; the merchants simultaneously either fake an order dispatch on the system or send an empty parcel to complete the transaction.[14] This then gives the brushing company an opportunity to leave a positive review for the merchant. Empirical studies have found that sellers can improve their reputation at least 10 times faster if they use brushing services instead of confining themselves to honest practices.[15] Vendors' desires to boost their reputation expeditiously also birthed an underground industry specializing in review manipulation. Outwardly, all Chinese e-commerce platforms explicitly condemn and prohibit brushing and vow to take drastic measures to combat such fraudulent practices. That said, a strong information asymmetry exists between the platform and its users, and the platform's actual efforts are largely unobservable to outsiders. In this situation, it is easy to imagine an online platform adjusting its enforcement intensity to maximize its own business interests, potentially at the expense of consumers.

Consider the example of Taobao, a business-to-consumer (often called B2C) market founded in 2003 by Jack Ma and his partners. Unlike Amazon, which derives its revenue from a transaction fee for the items sold on its platform, Alibaba initially charged no transaction fee to either buyers or sellers and mainly made money from charging sellers for advertising. In 2008, Alibaba created Tmall, which connects premium brands with customers. Tmall shares Taobao's traffic, as both the Taobao and Tmall listings could be found on Taobao's main mobile app. Of the two, Tmall is more profitable for Alibaba, because it charges merchants a transaction fee. Although brushing is a form of promotion that cuts into Alibaba's advertising profits, it also helps increase the popularity of merchants' products and boosts the volume of transactions conducted on Taobao—a metric that is often used to demonstrate the e-commerce platform's popularity. Boosting the volume of transactions in turn attracts more buyers, which in turn attracts more sellers, thus improving the transaction-fee revenue Alibaba could gain from Tmall. Consequently, if Alibaba adopts a very harsh approach in purging brushing, it could deter many sellers from its platform, particularly those Taobao sellers that rely heavily on brushing to promote their products. Moreover, the loss of Taobao sellers could result in less traffic for Taobao's app, thus reducing Alibaba's overall revenue. To maximize its profits, Alibaba therefore needs to strike a very delicate balance in tolerating some level of brushing to maintain both its profits and its growth.

To be sure, there exist clear legal sanctions against brushing. Brushing is considered a form of false adverting that is prohibited under various Chinese laws, notably the Anti-Unfair Competition Law, Consumer Protection Law, and E-Commerce Rules.[16] The practice can also lead to various criminal charges, including fraud, the destruction of business operations and harming commercial reputation, and infringement of personal information.[17] Moreover, if platforms are aware or should be aware of brushing practices but fail to take proper measures to prevent them, they are held jointly liable.[18] To ward off such liability, Alibaba claimed to have employed an elaborate five-layer risk-prevention framework, punishing sellers who engaged in brushing through online as well as offline channels.[19] In addition to deleting the reviews, imposing a hefty fine, and threatening to close stores, Alibaba has transferred some extreme cases to the police and has lodged complaints against the brushing company in court, as when it sued a scam company for brushing in violation of the Anti-Unfair Competition Law in 2018.[20] The Hangzhou Intermediate Court ruled in favor of Alibaba and held that the culprit firm needed to pay Taobao RMB 2 million in compensation.[21]

Despite this appearance of "tough sanctions" from both the public authorities and the platforms, brushing and other review-manipulation practices continue to be rampant in China.[22] Selective and low-level enforcement helps explain the disappointing enforcement outcome. In one empirical study, the authors examined five underground brushing markets and found that only 2.2 percent of online sellers practicing brushing were identified and penalized by Taobao.[23] In 2015, the State Administration for Industry and Commerce (SAIC), China's market watchdog at the time, accused Alibaba of failing to crack down on the fake products and fake product reviews on its website.[24] In a white paper that was subsequently released on SAIC's website, the market regulator accused the firm of turning a blind eye to these brushing practices. Further evidence of the laxness o͞ the Chinese e-commerce platforms can be gleaned by contrast with the enforcement on US platforms. In 2021, Amazon closed almost 50,000 Chinese online shops on its site in a massive campaign against brushing and other review-manipulation practices.[25] This tough enforcement from Amazon generated strong backlash from Chinese merchants, who had faced little resistance when they adopted the same tactics while selling on Chinese e-commerce platforms.[26]

Although brushing helps boost traffic to e-commerce sites, it also distorts platforms' feedback systems and inevitably leads to more conflict between buyers and sellers. As I will elaborate further below, Chinese platforms face even greater challenges than their Western peers in managing such conflicts between the transacting parties.

7.2. Credible Enforcement Mechanisms

A credible enforcement mechanism is the second important factor for successful self-governance. Although self-regulation of the platform also needs to operate within the boundary of state law, the law is always incomplete. Platforms accordingly often find themselves playing the roles of legislator, prosecutor, and judge all at once. Chinese online platforms have employed two major means for establishing a credible enforcement mechanism: the creation of a sophisticated internal legal system and co-regulation with the state.

7.2.1. The Demand for Self-Regulation

Scholars from various academic disciplines, including sociology, economics, and law, have long identified community self-governance as an alternative to formal state governance. Examples of community self-governance can be found in studies of Maghrebi traders, cattle owners, and herders in eleventh-century Africa; of diamond dealers in modern-day New York; of American whale catchers and lobstermen in Maine; and of cattle rangers in California.[27] The fundamental economic logic of self-governance is based on the game-theoretical insight of repeated interactions.[28] If parties expect repeated interactions in the future, the prospect of establishing a long-term stable relationship will curb their temptation to engage in opportunism for short-term gains. Generally speaking, such self-governance systems rely on only a few commitment devices to ensure cooperation, including timely rewards and punishment in the case of direct reciprocity, and the establishment of social norms in the case of group interactions.[29] Since an important premise for the sustainability of self-governance is repeated interactions, a common feature of the traditional self-governance model is that the communities involved tend to be close-knit, stable, and cohesive groups or networks.[30] This is understandable: the larger the group, the fewer the opportunities for any two members to interact repeatedly with each other. A larger community also makes it costlier to transmit information within the group or network, rendering it difficult to effectively penalize members for opportunistic behavior. As such, self-governance is generally deemed infeasible for large-scale, impersonal market transactions between strangers.

In cases where neither self-governance nor state governance is sufficient for contract enforcement, members of the community can resort to third-party intermediaries to enforce contracts on their behalf.[31] One study by Milgrom, North, and Weingast found that French merchants in the medieval period employed an elaborate alternative dispute-resolution mechanism.[32] In the absence of state legal enforcement, merchants hired private judges, either a local official or another merchant, to adjudicate their disputes. Although no two merchants interacted with each other frequently, each individual traded frequently within the community. For medieval French merchants, therefore, private judges played an important role as information intermediaries, transmitting the reputation of individual merchants to others within the mercantile network. Hiring private judges essentially resolved the information asymmetries associated with having a large trading community, while also promoting honest exchanges. Another intriguing example is provided by Gambetta, who observed that the Sicilian Mafia offered private intermediation services to the community.[33] The Mafia sold protection to parties on both ends of a given transaction and settled conflicts between them by punishing the side that broke its original promises.

Much as private judges in medieval France and the Sicilian Mafia did before them, online platforms act as for-profit, third-party intermediaries providing contract-enforcement services for transacting parties. In their case study of Taobao, Liu and Weingast argue that the company's development of a sophisticated internal legal system was a result of the deficiencies present in Chinese legal institutions.[34] They contend that a variety of political obstacles have prevented developing countries from providing formal legal infrastructure because incumbents are reluctant to foster a legal system that might threaten their regime. This argument, however, stands in stark contrast to the reality. Over the past decade, the Chinese judiciary has provided a sophisticated and efficient infrastructure to support China's thriving e-commerce industry, as evidenced by the introduction of the internet courts and smart-court system, both of which will be elaborated in this chapter. More importantly, Liu and Weingast overstate the importance of state institutions in resolving online consumer disputes. Although state law is generally deemed important for the purposes of facilitating and safeguarding market transactions, the vast majority of online complaints involve low-value claims. Consumers usually find it simply too costly to use formal state institutions to settle them.[35]

To gauge the proportion of online disputes that actually go to the courts, I used the China Judgement Online database. There I found only 371 transactional disputes arising from Taobao and Tmall up to the end of 2021.[36] Of these cases, only 194 (52 percent) were brought by consumers or online merchants, while the rest were brought by the platforms against merchants, from whom they sought damages for violations of platform rules. In view of the millions of disputes Taobao and Tmall handle each year, the percentage of cases in which platform users appeal to the courts is miniscule.[37] Notably, even for those cases that went to court, the claim values involved are very small. Of those 194 complaints brought by merchants or consumers against the platforms, 70 percent involved a claim value of less than USD 1,000, 28 percent involved a claim value of less than USD 100, and there were even 10 cases that involved a claim value of less than USD 10! The paucity of consumer litigation in Chinese courts clearly reveals the limits of regulation. It also demonstrates the importance of online platforms, which have become quasi-regulators in charge of adjudicating most online disputes.

7.2.2. The Law of Taobao

Given the high volume of disputes arising from their platforms, Chinese tech firms have found themselves faced with the urgent task of creating a strong legal system with a highly efficient dispute-resolution mechanism. Taobao, a pioneering e-commerce platform, offers a good example in this regard. Much like a state sovereign, Taobao has exerted tremendous effort in creating a sophisticated legal system. The e-commerce platform even created a dedicated site for the publication of its platform rules and formulated its own constitution—the "General Code."[38] Consisting of 6 chapters and 31 provisions, the General Code prescribes the basic access requirements and obligations of users, the obligations of sellers, and the conflict-resolution mechanism. In addition to the General Code, Taobao has devised numerous transactional rules, standards, guidelines, measures, and announcements in a wide range of categories, including store management, sector regulation, merchandise management, marketing and promotion, content promotion, transaction management, dispute resolution, legal enforcement, environmental issues, and travel and tourism sales.[39] As shown in Figure 7.1, Taobao introduced 180 new rules between 2008 and 2021. The year 2019 saw Taobao introduce the most rules—45 in one year—compared with 33 and 34 in 2020 and 2021, respectively. The most comprehensive law is Taobao's dispute-resolution rules, which contain 10 chapters, 90 provisions, and 8,516 words.[40] This elaborate law, most recently amended in April 2021, addresses important issues at every step of the e-commerce transaction, including acceptance periods; acceptance range; general rules for dispute resolution; rules for dispatching goods, receipts, returns and exchanges, shipping, and gifts; the burden of proof in handling quality; issues

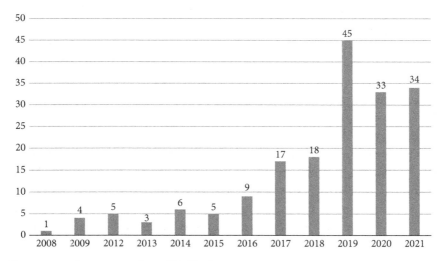

Figure 7.1. Laws promulgated by Taobao.
Source: Taobao's website.

involving counterfeiting and inconsistent descriptions; and revocation anc suspension of disputes.

Much like a state sovereign, Taobao has also frequently amended its laws particularly since 2019. In each of the three years from 2019 to 2021, Taobao amended 16, 16, and 47 laws, respectively. I calculate the rate of amendment for a particular year using the number of amendments in a particular year and the number of laws published in all the preceding years. For the three years between 2019 and 2021, the rate of amendment for Taobao is 24 percent, 14 percent, and 32 percent, respectively. Thus, even if Taobao promulgated the most laws in 2019, the year 2021 actually has the highest rate of amendment. The e-commerce platform's high level of amendment activity in 2021 lends support to the argument about "coerced self-regulation" put forward by Julia Black.[41] As elaborated in Chapter 2, Alibaba was subjected to a hefty fine of USD 2.8 billion in 2021 for abusive business practices. Along with the penalty decision, the accompanying administrative guidance issued by the SAMR requested that the e-commerce giant improve its internal governance. These harsh regulatory pressures appear to have incentivized Taobao to engage more actively in self-regulation.

To improve user compliance, Taobao has also made great efforts in explaining its new rules by means of various explanatory measures, guidelines, and video instructions.[42] The firm also adopted a shaming strategy, publishing the usernames of rule-violating users on its website.[43] While the company's internal legislative process is centralized and opaque, Taobao seems increasingly aware of the importance of public participation in crafting its rules. For example, it has created an online forum for public hearings that engages its users to vote on newly drafted transactional rules before they become effective.[44] The firm also regularly invites experienced users and external legal experts to partake in the legislative and deliberative processes. The voting outcomes, however, are not decisive and are only used as a reference to help guide the company's decision-making.

The key to Taobao's enforcement of its internal law lies in its sanctioning power, which serves as a credible threat against violators of its rules. Alipay, an online payment system that holds consumers' payments in an escrow before releasing them to merchants, plays a vital role in the enforcement process.[45] Alipay will only release the funds once the buyer has received the goods and is satisfied with their purchase. This helps prevent moral hazard in that otherwise merchants might take advantage of their information advantage by behaving more recklessly and expending less effort. If the transaction leads to a dispute and the seller is found to be at fault, Taobao can directly deduct the disputed amount from the seller's account to compensate for the buyer's loss. This mechanism helps reassure buyers and facilitates a higher number of online transactions. It also deters merchants from engaging in fraudulent behavior. In addition to Alipay, Taobao also acquires tremendous enforcement capacity through its decisions regarding resource allocation and dispute resolution, such as how much traffic is allocated to each merchant, whether a negative consumer review should be considered fraudulent and should be removed, whether to downgrade a given store's rating, or even, in some extreme scenarios, whether to remove a user account or product listing, or even close a particular store.

Taobao's handling of malicious and spam reviews can shed light on the ingenuity and sophistication of its internal legal design. While sellers can commit fraud by manipulating online reviews, buyers can also commit fraud by leaving negative reviews in an attempt to blackmail sellers for ransom. In a typical instance of review blackmail, an opportunistic consumer purchases the seller's product, posts a negative review, and then demands a ransom before removing it. The ransom can range from a few yuan in the form of a rebate to a few thousand yuan in the form of discounts. This type of blackmail has proved effective because sellers realize that negative online reviews can significantly impact their sales. In a recent case widely reported in the Chinese media, a malicious customer was able to blackmail a computer vendor into paying RMB 8,888 for the removal of a negative review.[46] This case, however, represents only one small part of a much larger problem, as has been revealed by the significant number of criminal cases handled by Chinese courts over the past few years.[47]

During a series of online public hearings hosted by Taobao in 2018, Taobao vendors complained that review blackmail was so ubiquitous that they needed a dedicated employee to deal with extortion on a daily basis.[48] Sellers have explained that a single negative review can have a drastic impact on their sales in the short term. Although they could have turned to Taobao or the state police when confronted with extortion, these complaint-resolution processes tend to be costly and slow. More importantly, Taobao vendors would suffer significant financial loss while waiting for their case to get to trial. Such pecuniary losses are particularly severe if review extortion takes place during large promotional events. To take one example, the sales

204 HIGH WIRE

volume on Singles Day, the largest shopping event on Taobao, accounted for 4 percent of the platform's total sales in 2018, 13 times higher than an average day's sales.[49] The importance of such events for sellers means that scammers will have higher bargaining leverage if they target vendors and submit fraudulent negative reviews during the festivities. As long as the ransom is lower than the potential financial losses, a vendor will likely agree to pay the ransom. Making matters worse, a recent empirical study drawing on a proprietary dataset from Alibaba found that sellers who had endured blackmail also experienced cascading negative consequences far beyond the requested ransom.[50] This is because the act of blackmail not only decreases the number of orders that a seller receives, but also makes the seller less willing to deal with innocent buyers who have no intention of defrauding them.[51] Sellers might then overreact to declining sales by setting their prices far too low.[52]

To tackle this problem, Taobao launched an innovative dispute-resolution scheme in 2019. This legal innovation enables eligible sellers to delete a limited number of malicious reviews on a daily basis without prior permission from the platform.[53] This new scheme, called the "Golden Cudgel," is named after the magical weapon wielded by the monkey king in *Journey to the West*, a classical Chinese novel.[54] Granting sellers the right to immediately remove a number of fraudulent reviews considerably reduces the ability of malicious reviewers to sabotage sales and, with it, their bargaining leverage. Furthermore, to ensure quality control, sellers are required to pass exams and must receive a score of at least 95 out of 100 before qualifying for the new regulatory scheme. Taobao was cautious in rolling out this idea, initially only allowing sellers with high credit ratings to delete one review each day; eventually, however, the company granted sellers additional rights and opened up the scheme to more of them.

In order to monitor and control sellers' use of the Golden Cudgel scheme, Taobao also implemented a judicial review system: sellers must submit evidence to prove the dishonest nature of each review they remove. If it later becomes apparent that a seller made an erroneous decision, Taobao will reinstate the review on the seller's webpage. Sellers who remove honest reviews are also given a penalty, whereby the number of reviews they are thereafter entitled to remove is drastically reduced. Sellers' rights to delete reviews can even be revoked entirely if they are found to have repeatedly abused the system. Since its launch, this new review-management scheme has become well liked among sellers. Taobao then started applying this scheme to more types of reviews, such as those without meaningful comments, those posted before the product was delivered, or those that were written with the intention of undermining businesses.

In a study I coauthored with Alex Yang and Yiangos Papanastasiou, we discovered that Taobao's introduction of this decentralized review-management scheme can, if used properly, be more efficient than centralized review models.[55] Under a centralized review system, sellers report fake reviews to the platform and request their removal. The platform then examines the evidence and decides whether or not to remove them. We found, however, that the effectiveness of this centralized mechanism can be severely limited by inefficiencies in the platform's investigative process. If the platform's judgments are not relatively quick or accurate, the centralized mechanism might needlessly consume platform resources without offering distinct advantages to sellers. In fact, circumstances could arise in which the bargaining power of the seller might actually decline, allowing malicious customers to extract higher ransoms. The decentralized approach, meanwhile, relies on the accuracy rather than the speed of platform judgments, as sellers can delete fake reviews instantly.

The above example of Taobao's legal innovation in dealing with malicious reviews not only reveals the company's strong enforcement power, but also demonstrates the promise of decentralizing platform governance to allow for more efficient dispute resolution—a topic I will further explore in the next chapter. However, platforms don't always possess such strong capacity in meting out sanctions to punish those who violate their rules. When they lack such capacity, platforms will need to enlist the state to endorse and support their internal legal enforcement.

7.2.3. Co-Regulation with the State

In Part II, we discussed online platforms as subjects to be regulated by the Chinese state. There, Chinese regulation is often seen as "grabbing hands," a term coined by Andrew Shleifer and Robert Vishny to describe an interventionist governance model where bureaucrats pursue their own agendas without necessarily contributing to the broader social welfare.[56] In contrast to the previous discussion, in this chapter we explore how the state actually lends a "helping hand" to internet businesses. Although online platforms handle the vast majority of disputes on their own, their internal regulation can sometimes interact with public regulation. In fact, there are two circumstances in which Chinese tech firms need to enlist the support of the Chinese judiciary to co-regulate their platforms: first, when users disagree with the platform's internal dispute resolution and challenge the decision in state courts; second, when the platform lacks sufficient enforcement capacity to implement its internal decisions. Of course, for the state to provide meaningful support for the platforms' decisions and enforcement, it needs to possess its own capacity to handle a high volume of online disputes. In fact, the Chinese courts have received tremendous technical support from leading Chinese online platforms such as Alibaba. The Chinese state and the internet platforms have thus been close collaborators in the effort to resolve conflicts arising from the platform economy.

7.2.3.1. Judicial Support for Platform Self-Regulation

In the past few years, Chinese courts have provided unparalleled support for Chinese platforms by significantly reducing barriers to litigation while also, crucially, endorsing platforms' self-regulatory decisions. In August 2017, China launched the Hangzhou Internet Court, the first virtual court to specialize in online disputes; this was followed by the launch of the Beijing Internet Court and Guangzhou Internet Court a year later. All the steps involved in adjudicating a case, from case filing, serving court documents, and exchange and examination of evidence to the hearing and execution process, are now conducted online.[57] The creation of the internet courts has greatly enhanced the judiciary's efficiency in handling e-commerce disputes. On average, it takes only 45 minutes to conduct an online trial and 38 days to conclude a case—shorter than half the duration of traditional trials.[58] Following the success of the Hangzhou Internet Court, courts across major cities in China, including Shanghai, Tianjin, Shenzhen, Wuhan, and Chengdu, all set up specialized divisions to handle online disputes.[59]

In addition to the internet courts, the Chinese government also spearheaded efforts to build a "smart court" system, which promotes the use of computer technologies such as artificial intelligence and blockchain to modernize the judicial process and enable quicker and easier access to justice.[60] Unlike the internet courts, the smart-court system is large-scale and complex, spanning more than 3,000 courts and over 10,000 detached tribunals across the country.[61] In 2018, the Supreme Court started to promote the Mobile Micro Court, a mobile app that enables litigants to complete the entire litigation process online.[62] As of March 2020, over 1.3 million users had used this app and over 437,000 cases had been filed on it. The publicly available statistics show encouraging results. In over 70 percent of the cases, the time required for completing the filing process averaged less than 15 minutes.[63] While some lawyers and academics have expressed concern that some of the technologies used to streamline judicial services could come at the expense of achieving a fair and just outcome, there is little doubt that Chinese courts now provide much cheaper and quicker resolution of disputes.[64]

Earlier in this chapter I mentioned that I was able to identify only 371 cases involving the internal disputes of Taobao and Tmall in the China Judgement Online database up to 2021. Strikingly, 86 percent of these cases were decided after 2019. Moreover, 94 percent of the cases in 2019 and 77 percent in 2020 were handled by the Hangzhou Internet Court, thus revealing the importance of this newly created internet tribunal in facilitating dispute resolution for e-commerce platforms. In the meantime, platforms were rarely held liable and almost always prevailed in cases involving their internal dispute resolution. In fact, I have identified only 1 percent of cases in which the court held Taobao or Tmall liable for compensating merchants, and only 2 percent in which the courts overruled the dispute-resolution decisions made by the platforms. Taobao and Tmall's almost unbroken record of courtroom victories may explain the significant drop in complaints that has been observed in 2021, which saw only seven litigations.[65] This seems to suggest that the creation of internet courts has, in fact, significantly bolstered the legitimacy of the internal dispute-resolution mechanisms of the Chinese e-commerce platforms.

Even when the online platforms stepped outside the boundary of the law to mete out punishments against merchants, the Chinese courts seldom intervened in their decisions. For instance, China's E-Commerce Law and Consumer Protection Law both require e-commerce platforms to take proper action if they are aware of or should be aware of the sale of counterfeit goods or other fraudulent behavior by online merchants.[66] In the case of brushing, as discussed above, regulators often accuse Taobao of engaging in selective enforcement and thus doing too little to combat such fraudulent practices. However, Chinese e-commerce platforms also sometimes go beyond the state law's requirements in imposing tougher sanctions on fraudsters in order to enhance deterrence. Online platforms have been able to mete out these tough sanctions through their standard contracts with the merchants, so that the issue then comes down to whether these "extralegal" sanctions should be struck down by law. In practice, however, Chinese courts seldom intervene into these contractual arrangements, thus providing tacit support for extralegal sanctions.

Pinduoduo's anti-counterfeiting measures offer a striking example. Founded in 2015 and backed by Tencent, the firm grew rapidly by encouraging group buying on its app and on WeChat with deep discounts. In just six years, Pinduoduo overtook Alibaba, becoming the largest e-commerce firm in China in 2021. Meanwhile, counterfeit products, many of them knock-off copycats of well-known brands, are ubiquitous on Pinduoduo. Shortly after the firm was listed in New York in 2018, it faced a storm of publicity for selling counterfeit goods on its site. For instance, Skyworth, one of China's largest TV makers, blasted the firm on Chinese media for selling fake products.[67] This onslaught of negative media coverage put pressure on the regulator to act. In 2018, the SAMR conducted an administrative interview with the company, in which it urged the firm to rectify its behavior.[68] It also announced investigations into reports of bogus products sold on the platform and requested that local authorities conduct further investigations. Around that time, several lawsuits were filed against the firm in the United States for misleading investors about its sale of counterfeit products.[69]

Faced with these regulatory demands, Pinduoduo stepped up its internal regulation to crack down on counterfeiting. In 2018, the firm claimed to have removed 10.7 million suspicious products and to have blocked over 40 million suspicious links from its platforms.[70] To reassure consumers, it offered to compensate them 10 times the price of any counterfeit products purchased on its site. The firm also introduced an extremely harsh penalty for merchants: the platform would freeze 10 times the sum of the trading orders for any product found to be a counterfeit. This rule is much more stringent than China's Consumer Protection Law, which only requires merchants to pay three times the product price to compensate consumers.[71] To demonstrate its determination in combating counterfeits, Pinduoduo punished over 200 stores and froze over one hundred million yuan in merchants' accounts in 2018.[72]

This harsh penalty imposed by the e-commerce giant soon generated a backlash among merchants. In June 2018, almost 1,000 angry store owners gathered at the headquarters of Pinduoduo in Shanghai to protest its actions.[73] Their protest grew violent after physical clashes with the firm's security guards. Disgruntled store owners also challenged the firm's penalty clause in court. In the China Judgement Online database, I found 11 cases involving disputes about the penalty clause between merchants and Pinduoduo in 2018.[74] Many sellers asserted that the liquidated damages for selling counterfeits as stipulated in the contract with Pinduoduo were unfair and imposed an extremely onerous burden on small and medium-sized companies in China. Pinduoduo prevailed in 10 of these 11 cases, all of which were decided by courts in its home city of Shanghai. In 2019, China's Supreme People's Court even listed one of those winning cases as a top-10 internet case, signaling a strong endorsement from the judiciary.[75] In this case, the Shanghai Changning District Court distinguished Pinduoduo's penalty clause from traditional liquidated damages clauses, noting that the damages received by the e-commerce platform are all used to compensate consumers, who were guaranteed a compensation of 10 times the original purchase price. Importantly, the court explicitly endorsed the e-commerce platform's self-governance approach to tackling the endemic counterfeits on its platform.

Pinduoduo's all but undefeated record in court has significantly enhanced the legitimacy of its sanction measures and has increased the credibility of its enforcement among merchants. In the years that followed, the number of cases challenging Pinduoduo's penalty clause dropped significantly, with only two in 2019, one in 2020, and three in 2021. In 2021, however, merchants did successfully challenge Pinduoduo's penalty decisions in two cases on the basis of the platform's procedural defects in adjudicating disputes about counterfeit products. This is consistent with the law-enforcement trend we discussed earlier in this book, in that some Chinese courts have appeared noticeably more interventionist in disputes involving online platforms since 2020.

7.2.3.2. *Enhancing Platforms' Enforcement Power*

Although leading e-commerce platforms such as Taobao and Pinduoduo have the ability to vigorously enforce their rules by relying on their own sanctioning power, they occasionally need the assistance of Chinese courts.

For instance, among the 371 cases I identified on the China Judgement Online database of cases involving Taobao and Tmall's dispute-resolution decisions, 48 percent were initiated by the platform against merchants. In those cases, merchants typically refused to repay the platform, or their deposit was not sufficient to cover the damages that the platform had compensated the consumers in advance. Compared with Taobao and Tmall, smaller consumer internet businesses are in an even weaker position when it comes to enforcing their rules. This is particularly the case for fintech platforms specializing in extending small unsecured loans, commonly called micro-loans, to individuals and small businesses. When these loans go into default, these fintech businesses will need to resort to Chinese courts to enforce their decisions. The problem, however, is that state capacity in this arena is very limited, and there is often a long lag before the public authority can resolve the dispute. Both the day-to-day operation and long-term survival of these platforms therefore heavily depend on expanding the state capacity required for efficient dispute resolution.

One particularly notable example is Lakala, an online payment platform that extends micro-loans to individuals online. The firm has experienced a significant surge of defaults since 2017. In the China Judgement Online database, I identified over 132,675 cases relating to Lakala's micro-loan disputes up to 2021, as displayed in Figure 7.2.[76]

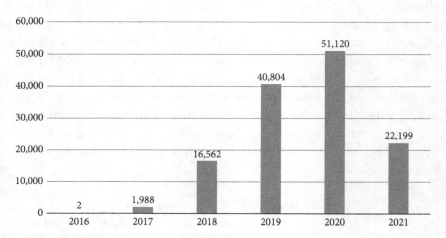

Figure 7.2. Lakala's micro-loan litigations.
Source: China Judgement Online database.

Notably, almost 99 percent of the cases involving Lakala's small loans were decided by three basic courts in Guangzhou, the capital city of the Guangdong province: Yuexiu District Court (70 percent), Haizhu District Court (21 percent), and the Guangzhou Internet Court (8 percent). Based on my search of the China Judgement Online database, the Yuexiu District Court alone handled over 93,000 micro-loan disputes involving Lakala, with a caseload of about 30,000 each year between 2019 and 2020. Public records show that the Yuexiu District Court has only 21 judges dedicated to financial cases.[77] In other words, on average, each judge from Yuexiu decided 1,400 Lakala cases each year! According to the Yuexiu District Court, its quick-resolution court handled about 250,000 cases, and each judge decided 2,400 cases on average each year, reducing the judging cycle to only 42 days for simple cases.[78] In response to such a high volume of cases, the Yuexiu District Court created an online portal specifically for dealing with financial cases involving the internet.[79] This action has significantly streamlined the litigation process, as the case filing, court service, and hearings can all be conducted online. As these financial default cases are routine and strikingly similar to each other, the Yuexiu District Court also tries similar cases in batches using its online templates, thus significantly improving the speed of dispute resolution. Public disclosures regarding the Guangzhou Internet Court also revealed a similar processing procedure for dealing with microloans.[80]

A closer look at the relevant cases decided by the three district courts reveals that about 60–69 percent of cases are civil judgments about repayment obligations, with the rest concerning enforcement of default payments. When I then randomly selected 100 civil judgments each year between 2017 and 2021 from Yuexiu District Court, I found that the court sided with Lakala in every single one of these cases. I did a similar search for enforcement cases during the same period, and found that Lakala similarly prevailed in all of them, except for those in which it had voluntarily withdrawn because the borrowers had repaid their loans. Given this staggering record of victories, it would be reasonable to conclude that Lakala has effectively outsourced its major dispute-resolution function to these three Guangzhou courts.[81] Notably, despite the firm's high volume of defaults, Lakala's lending business continues to thrive: according to its 2020 annual report, the firm's fintech services, including its micro-loan businesses, have a gross margin of 89 percent.[82] In this case, the Chinese judiciary clearly plays the role of a "helping hand" by offering indispensable judicial support for these fintech businesses.

The actions of the Chinese courts as explored in this chapter do stand in striking contrast to what we saw in Part II, where we observed that the central ministries often take the driver's seat in promulgating new rules and taking up aggressive enforcement, particularly in the areas of antitrust and data enforcement. Here the Chinese courts are key actors who co-regulate with the platforms to resolve consumer disputes. But there is no contradiction between the fact that public regulation can simultaneously behave like a "grabbing hand" (as observed in Part II) and like a "helping hand" (as observed in this chapter). Judges working at Chinese courts have a vastly different incentive structure from regulators working at central ministries. As the renowned Chinese legal scholar Qianfan Zhang has observed, Chinese judges lack independence and behave like "an ordinary cadre in the bureaucratic echelon under the party leadership."[83] Although local courts also receive professional guidance and supervision from the Supreme People's Court, local governments assume the primary leadership over local courts as the former control the latter's budget and personnel appointments.[84] Unsurprisingly, there has been much anecdotal evidence of local judicial protectionism in China, as has also been supported by the findings of a few recent empirical studies.[85]

To be sure, China's judicial system underwent massive reform between 2014 to 2017 aimed at curbing judicial favoritism. One of the key reform measures was the recentralization of decisions concerning personnel appointments and fiscal management of the basic and intermediate court in the hands of the provincial governments.[86] A recent empirical study has shown that the move to make Chinese courts more dependent on a higher-tier government has significantly reduced local judicial protectionism.[87] However, provincial governments remain in charge of the court system in their respective regions. Given that leading Chinese tech firms are deemed local champions in their respective provinces, provincial governments have a strong incentive to nurture, support, and prop up these local businesses. That said, Chinese judges are not insulated from the shifting political winds coming from Beijing. It is thus not surprising to see that in more recent cases the district court in Shanghai has appeared more willing to intervene into Pinduoduo's dispute-resolution decisions, as mentioned earlier in this chapter. Nevertheless, for the most part, local courts continue to provide essential judicial support for local tech firms, given their need to support the leadership of their respective provincial governments.

7.3. Summary

This chapter has focused on how Chinese online platforms self-regulate in the shadow of the dynamic pyramid model of regulation. Because most online disputes involve only small-value claims, the vast majority of consumers don't bother to resort to public institutions and instead rely heavily on platforms to resolve their disputes. As such, the vast majority of online disputes actually fall outside the purview of government regulation. Instead, online platforms shoulder much of the regulatory burden, becoming de facto regulators in charge of designing internal rules, which they then enforce through a variety of sanctioning mechanisms to deter noncompliance. As third-party intermediaries, Chinese online platforms are acutely aware of the importance of creating a vibrant reputation system that helps alleviate information asymmetries between buyers and sellers. To entice customers, Chinese tech firms tolerated a large amount of fake promotional reviews, which enabled them to quickly build a large feedback mechanism. These ubiquitous fake reviews boosted sellers' ratings, increased traffic to their sites, and facilitated a higher number of online transactions, thus becoming an important channel for many Chinese e-commerce firms to attain success.

At the same time, this noisy reputation system has inevitably given rise to conflicts among users, creating a strong demand for platforms to improve their dispute-resolution mechanisms. Leading Chinese online platforms have therefore invested tremendous resources in establishing an internal legal system with credible enforcement. Enforcement capacity varies, however, among Chinese platforms. Some platforms possess enormous resources for meting out sanctions to punish violators of their rules, while others rely more heavily on the state's support, especially when their punishment lacks a clear legal basis or they lack the capacity to implement their decisions. Co-regulation between platforms and the Chinese judiciary has thus become indispensable for the growth of the Chinese platform economy. In sharp contrast to the "grabbing hand" tendency of public regulation, as detailed in previous chapters, the Chinese judiciary extends an important "helping hand" to Chinese internet firms when it provides them with vital judicial support that enhances the credibility of platforms' self-regulation.

8

Decentralizing Platform Governance

In the previous chapter, we discussed two important factors affecting Chinese online platforms' ability to self-regulate in the shadow of public regulation: a strong reputation mechanism and a credible enforcement system. In this chapter, we will explore the third factor in how Chinese online platforms enhance the legitimacy of their self-governance: decentralization. In recent years, many leading Chinese platforms have ushered in experiments designed to decentralize their self-governance, either by delegating some degree of authority to users or by exploring better ways to extract information about users' preferences. By turning legislation and enforcement into responsibilities that are shared among a larger number of platform participants, the decentralization of platform governance can become an important tool for Chinese online platforms looking to maintain stability and to avoid making decisions that might result in citizen protests or complaints to the authorities. In this way, platform decentralization not only helps enhance the procedural justice of platforms' internal governance, but also actively shapes policy debate and preempts unfavorable government intervention.

Alibaba, the owner of leading e-commerce sites including Taobao and Tmall, has played a pioneering role in developing a bottom-up approach to governance.[1] In December 2012, Alibaba launched the Public Dispute Resolution Center, which crowdsources both buyers and sellers on its e-commerce platforms to vote on transactional rules and determine the outcome of disputes arising on its platforms.[2] This crowdsourcing mechanism, also known as "crowd-judging," was an instant hit. A year after its establishment, over 480,000 buyers and 330,000 sellers had participated in

High Wire. Angela Huyue Zhang, Oxford University Press. © Oxford University Press 2024.
DOI: 10.1093/oso/9780197682258.003.0009

and adjudicated over 340,000 cases.[3] By the end of 2018, over 4.3 million users were registered as public jurors, with more than 1.7 million volunteers casting their votes; in total, the vote count exceeded 100 million and over 16 million cases had been resolved through this means.[4] Within a relatively short period of time, a large number of Chinese online platforms began emulating Taobao's initiatives. The list of those who experimented with their own decentralized dispute-resolution schemes includes digital flea market Idle Fish, taxi-hailing firm Didi Chuxing, social-media platforms such as WeChat and Bilibili, food-delivery firm Meituan Takeout, restaurant-rating firm Dianping, and question-and-answer company Zhihu (sometimes described as the Chinese Quora), along with several mutual-aid insurance platforms such as Bihu, Waterdrop, and Xianghubao.[5]

Meanwhile, US platforms such as Facebook have experimented with decentralized governance by delegating content-moderation authority to an independent oversight board.[6] However, US tech firms have yet to systematically embrace decentralization schemes similar to those seen in China. The fact that China appears to be emerging at the forefront in creating legal innovations to decentralize platform governance gives rise to an interesting puzzle—why is an authoritarian state breeding online platforms with more democratic and engaged self-governance than those in Western liberal democracies?

The answer lies in China's unique institutional environment. As was elaborated in the previous chapter, fraud is endemic in Chinese consumer internet businesses. Chinese online platforms tolerate more fraud, in the form of counterfeits, fake reviews, and plagiarism, among others, than their US counterparts. When this inevitably gives rise to conflict, crowd-judging is an efficient means to quickly ease tensions and resolve disputes. By helping diffuse tensions, crowd-judging also helps enhance platform legitimacy. As detailed in Part II, the operation of leading tech giants has given rise to an increasing number of public complaints and has attracted a vast amount of public scrutiny. Regulators are therefore under considerable pressure to deal with public discontent arising from the digital economy. Meanwhile, the power imbalance between businesses and the Chinese government makes Chinese tech firms vulnerable to state intervention. As was discussed in Chapter 2, Chinese regulatory authorities have much more leverage in regulating Chinese tech firms than do their Western peers. This is particularly the case for those Chinese tech firms operating in legal gray areas. Indeed, because many of the issues encountered by the platforms are new, there is often no clear answer under existing law. This legal gap has created a significant demand for online platforms to engage with their users in order to understand social norms and community expectations. One thing is clear: the more that platforms tolerate fraud, the greater the public's discontent, the stronger the power imbalance between businesses and government, and the greater the controversy in running online platforms, the more platforms will experience insecurity. And the more insecure are the online platforms, the greater will be their desire to seek protection by adopting decentralization schemes to ease and diffuse tensions arising from their services. These new decentralization initiatives can thus be seen as platforms' proactive response to the perceived threat of public regulation.

In fact, platform decentralization can be viewed as a means to facilitate the tacit bargain between online platforms and the state, which is itself a highly dynamic and interactive process. Two points should be borne in mind here. First, the bargain is made in the shadow of government regulation. Expectations about how the public law will be crafted and enforced greatly influence the way platforms regulate themselves. Yet that policy response itself is highly fluid and uncertain—and contingent on the development of platform self-governance. By delegating their governance authority to platform participants, online platforms are seizing the first-mover advantage to shape the policy debate. Second, the bargain between the platform and the state is tacit, in that it usually does not involve direct and explicit communication. Because it is not entirely clear how the government will regulate the platforms, in practice, platforms are left to figure out thorny regulatory issues on their own. That said, if online platforms fail to address those problems adequately and promptly, regulators can always escalate their actions by creating new laws or bringing formal investigations.

In the following discussion, I will first introduce the various modes of decentralization that Chinese online platforms have introduced into their governance. I will then turn to the legitimacy crises that have confronted Chinese online platforms, and how these crises have spurred them to delegate their governing authority to users as a means of easing and diffusing tensions. In the last section, I will discuss how these platforms have improved procedural justice and explored community norms to stave off potentially unfavorable government regulation.

8.1. Forms of Decentralization

In China, the central underlying mechanism of decentralized platform governance is crowdsourcing, which enables users to participate in rule making and dispute resolution. To clarify, no system is purely centralized or decentralized; decentralization here is relative and only a matter of degree. Generally speaking, the more authority a platform delegates to its users and the less residual control it retains in the rule-making and adjudication process, the more decentralized it is. To simplify the discussion, I classify platform decentralization into three forms—weak, semi-strong, and strong—depending on the extent of the power the platform has delegated to its users.[7]

8.1.1. Weak Decentralization

The weak form of decentralization can be seen when the platform solicits information and feedback from users in an effort to understand the preferences and expectations of the user community. However, this feedback is used only as a reference point. Users' opinions and votes are not regarded as conclusive, and the platform maintains ultimate discretion over the rule-making and adjudication process. Procedurally, this mode of decentralization shares some similarities with due-process requirements under administrative law, such as the possibility of notice-and-comment during rule making and the right for the public to be heard.[8] Online forums, public hearings, and public voting schemes are typical examples of weak forms of decentralization. These mechanisms inject greater transparency into the rule-making process, helping platforms better understand community norms and increasing their capacity to respond to the expectations of users. User feedback also has the benefit of disrupting the status quo, drawing the platform's attention to blind spots or inertia.[9] Above all, the weak form of decentralization allows platforms to more effectively address grievances from disgruntled users, thus mollifying the latter's concerns and forestalling boycotts or protests, as will be mentioned later in this chapter.

Alibaba's Public Dispute Resolution Center offers one such example. In 2012, Alibaba piloted its crowdsourcing mechanism by asking users to vote on market-transactional rules that were going to be adopted by Taobao.[10]

With this approach, after the votes have been solicited, the voting outcomes of the users are then usually used as a reference point by platforms. In 2013 alone, crowd-jurors voted on 22 tentative transactional rules presented to them by Taobao. This input enabled Taobao to improve and adjust its rules based on the votes, together with the public comments made by the jurors.[11] JD.com, the second-largest e-retailer in China, has replicated Taobao's model of rule making. In November 2017, JD.com launched a forum for its vendors to participate in the design and development of transactional rules.[12] Unlike Alibaba's Dispute Resolution Center, this forum only allows vendors to be eligible to act as crowd-jurors, who vote upon invitation from JD.com. If a new transactional rule fails to be endorsed by more than 60 percent of the jurors, then JD.com will postpone promulgation of the discussed rules and consider modifying them after soliciting feedback. Similarly, Didi Chuxing (Didi), the largest taxi-hailing platform in China, set up an online public forum in 2018. The forum seeks user feedback on controversial topics relating to operational, privacy, and consumer-protection issues.[13] Didi will post a topic discussion on its forum, leaving it open for seven days to give users some time to vote and add their comments. The voting results are then used as a reference for Didi's rule making.

Chinese online platforms are not the only ones to have endorsed this weak form of decentralization when designing platform rules. Take eBay, for example. The American e-commerce giant has been running a program called Voices with the intention of using it to develop a detailed understanding of community perspectives.[14] Comparable to Taobao's public hearings, the Voices program comprises standing focus groups that eBay brings to San Jose for multiple-day sessions to initiate dialogue on specific issues, together with product and policy representatives.[15] That said, Taobao's online public hearings are on a much larger scale, as all users are eligible to participate virtually and their comments show up instantaneously. It appears that Taobao has developed a more sophisticated infrastructure for soliciting users' opinions in this respect.

Facebook also once trialed a decentralized model for rule making. In 2009, the social-media platform launched a site for its users to vote on governance issues in response to a controversial proposed policy change.[16] However, instead of employing weak decentralization, Facebook promised to put a new policy into effect if and only if more than 30 percent of active registered users participated in the voting process.[17] As it turned out, some 600,000 users, accounting for only 0.3 percent of the then Facebook user population, had voted, far below the stipulated 30 percent threshold.[18] The *Los Angeles Times* later opined that "Facebook's governance vote is a homework assignment that no one did."[19] It is important to bear in mind that achieving 30 percent user participation was an extremely ambitious target, and it seemed highly unrealistic to suppose that any proposed policy change would be able to garner enough engagement to meet this minimum threshold. After falling short of this goal, Facebook abandoned the idea of having a system that allowed its users to vote on policy changes.[20] The weak form of decentralization is more pragmatic, in that it does not require a minimum level of participation. Although it does not guarantee the democratic representation of the user community, it can still help platforms gather valuable information from users.

8.1.2. Semi-Strong Decentralization

The semi-strong form of decentralization appears when platforms delegate some of the authority to adjudicate disputes to eligible users, but reserve the right to intervene if the parties appeal the decision, or if the platform finds the decision made by its users to be an erroneous one. In this form of decentralization, the platform retains residual control over adjudication. However, unlike the weak form of decentralization, wherein users' opinions are used solely for informational purposes, here users have the power to directly arbitrate individual cases. Companies apply the semi-strong form of decentralization primarily to achieve two goals: to enhance the efficiency of dispute resolution, and to improve the legitimacy of the platform.

The crowd-judging mechanism introduced by Alibaba in 2012 offers an example of semi-strong decentralization. In 2008, e-Bay India launched a community court, which crowdsourced buyers and sellers to adjudicate disputes over online feedback.[21] Inspired by eBay's model, Taobao introduced crowd-judging via its Public Dispute Resolution Center in 2012. Unlike eBay's model, which only dealt with disputes concerning feedback, Taobao's crowd-judging mechanism handles a wide variety of disputes, including disputes between users and the platform, as well as disputes between buyers and sellers. This mechanism significantly improves the speed of dispute resolution. In my recent paper with Alex Yang and Alan Kwan, we find that more than 90 percent of disputes were decided by crowd-jurors within a single day, a task that would take the in-house customer service three to four businesses days.[22]

In July 2016, Xianyu (meaning "idle fish"), a digital flea market owned by Alibaba, replicated Taobao's crowd-judging model by setting up the "Xianyu Small Tribunal" to adjudicate disputes between buyers and sellers of second-hand goods.[23] Unlike Taobao, which attracts professional merchants, Xianyu's dealers are mainly individuals who desire to trade in their used goods, many of whom accumulate very few reviews or none at all. As such, the traditional reputation mechanism based on customer reviews and ratings is less effective on Xianyu. Because customer satisfaction matters less to sellers on Xianyu, it is more common to see Xianyu sellers reject customers' demands for a refund. The resultant disputes between buyers and sellers put pressure on Xianyu to provide redress and protection for consumers.[24] The "Xianyu Small Tribunal" was thus first created as an alternative to customer-service appeals. Previously, Xianyu sent random invitations to crowd-jurors who then vote on a particular case.[25] However, starting in 2023, the firm modified its approach by broadcasting its case online, permitting any crowd-juror to volunteer and participate in the voting process. The first party to receive nine votes wins the case.[26] The losing party can appeal its case by contacting customer service within 24 hours of the decision being released.[27] This backup option offers additional assurance to consumers with regard to effective contract enforcement. In 2021, Meituan Takeout, a food-delivery company, launched its own version of a crowd-judging platform, called Xiaomei Jury Trial, to adjudicate disputes stemming from negative user feedback.[28] According to Meituan, restaurants and other merchants make complaints in response to about 1 percent of negative feedback from users.[29] This controversial feedback is then sent to the Xiaomei Jury Trial, which comprises 30 jurors on average. As of 2022, Xiaomei Jury Trial handled about 90,000 appeals from merchants each month, among which 55 percent were successful.

Social media platforms have also followed the lead of e-commerce platforms in applying the crowd-judging mechanism to content moderation. In June 2017, Bilibili, a video-sharing application, created "Little Dark House," an internal dispute-resolution mechanism that invites users to adjudicate cases relating to rule violations.[30] Two years later, Zhihu, a popular question-and-answer website, launched a tribunal to involve users in content-moderation cases.[31] Crowd jurors are asked to decide cases in which comments have been reported as unfriendly, as well as when a question has been marked as "does not constitute a question." Like Taobao, Zhihu broadcasts its cases online. Once a case has received more than 30 votes within 24 hours, and more than 60 percent of the crowd-jurors have cast their votes in favor of one side, the case is closed.[32] The online crowd's decision can be challenged as well. If other users express doubts about the shared community's decision, they can report the case to Zhihu's customer-service representatives.[33] Zhihu also regularly monitors the decisions of the community and intervenes when it notices an inappropriate decision.

By preserving their ability to intervene in crowdsourced hearings and review the verdicts of crowd-jurors, the semi-strong form of decentralization allows Chinese online platforms to retain some degree of control. There are at least two factors holding them back from offering users absolute authority over governance decisions. One has to do with crowd-jurors' lack of professionalism. To mitigate this issue, users who volunteer to act as jurors on Alibaba's Public Dispute Resolution Center are required to have one year of experience on the platform and a good credit score; furthermore, jurors must pass an exam before working on certain categories of cases. Meanwhile, Alibaba's Public Dispute Resolution Center oversees its jurors' votes on a daily basis.[34] If a juror votes in favor of the seller in 99 out of 100 cases, this could be an indication that a particular juror is biased against the buyer. Alibaba further disciplines crowd-jurors by observing how long they spend on each case. For example, if a juror consistently spends less than one or two seconds on a case, this indicates that the juror does not spend sufficient time deliberating. Despite these basic screening and monitoring mechanisms to ensure the quality of crowd-jurors, however, platforms' schemes for quality control remain quite rudimentary.

The second concern has to do with potential bias. Humans are prone to cognitive bias.[35] Furthermore, experimental evidence has suggested that online crowds are susceptible to well-known cognitive biases, such as anchoring, ambiguity, bandwagon, and decoy effects.[36] Indeed, when platforms crowdsource their users to make decisions, crowd-judging can give rise to a systematic bias whereby one group of users will exhibit a preference for a certain outcome when deciding cases. To be sure, crowd-jurors vote independently without knowledge of how others have approached the case. Nevertheless, even though crowd-jurors are not subject to social influence, they can still be susceptible to in-group bias, whereby jurors who

DECENTRALIZING PLATFORM GOVERNANCE   223

are buyers favor the buyer and jurors who are sellers favor the seller. Indeed, platform users, and particularly sellers, share the perception that in-group bias is prevalent and, because the majority of the crowd-jurors are buyers, this systematically sways case outcomes in their direction, thus undermining the legitimacy of crowd-judging.

I have studied this problem of in-group bias in a recent research project undertaken in collaboration with Alex Yang and Alan Kwan.[37] Using a proprietary dataset from Taobao, we found that sellers' concerns are not completely unfounded: on average, a seller juror was 10 percent likelier than a buyer juror to vote for a seller. Such bias was aggravated among cases that were decided by a thin margin, and when jurors perceived that their in-group's interests were threatened. However, we also found that this bias diminished as jurors gained experience: a user's bias reduced by 95 percent when their experience level grew from zero to that of the sample median. Under Taobao's existing voting policy, we estimated that such in-group bias influences the outcome of no more than 2 percent of cases. This finding can help alleviate the concern about in-group bias and shows the promise of using crowd-judging to decide online disputes.

8.1.3. Strong Decentralization

The strong form of decentralization can be seen when online platforms delegate the ultimate authority of adjudication to users and no longer retain any residual control over the verdict. Under this model, online platforms are often the first arbiter of the dispute, but their decision is subject to judicial review by the crowd-jurors. Platforms adopt strong decentralization when they desire to credibly proclaim to their users that they are committed to the impartial adjudication of cases. This is especially important when users need to invest in the services of a newly launched online platform whose reputation has not yet been established.

Consider the case of Xianghubao, a widely popular mutual-aid insurance platform introduced in 2018 by Ant Group.[38] Xianghubao is an innovative product, whereby participants in the insurance network contribute an equal amount to a payout when a participant falls critically ill.[39] When the participant files a claim, it is first reviewed by Xianghubao. If the platform decides to reject the claim, the participant has the option to appeal their case to the crowd-jurors, all of whom are participants in the insurance network.

Xianghubao randomly sends out an invitation to eligible crowd-jurors, who are informed they must submit their judgment within 24 hours.[40] If a case receives more than 1,000 votes (thereby meeting the minimum sufficient threshold), it is decided by a simple majority decision. If the crowd-jurors decide in favor of the claimant, the platform is obliged to disburse the insured amount. Otherwise, the original decision of the platform is sustained and the claim is rejected.

Xianghubao was not the first to use such a crowd-judging mechanism to decide mutual-aid disputes. Bihu, its rival, began applying crowd-judging to resolve insurance disputes as early as 2015.[41] The use of this decentralized mechanism has also helped allay any remaining doubts that users may have about the platform not honoring their claims, a common complaint made about Chinese insurance companies. Because the platform has delegated its ultimate adjudication authority to the crowd, it has effectively tied its own hands, making its commitments appear more credible to users. A recent case helps to illustrate how crowd-judging enhanced the legitimacy of Xianghubao.[42] In December 2018, Mr. Tang, a participant in the mutual-aid network, succumbed severe injuries after falling into a pit. Xianghubao rejected his claim for insurance on the basis that he had been taking hormone medication. Mr. Tang was not happy with the decision and appealed the case to the crowd-jurors. On March 26, 2019, over 250,000 crowd-jurors cast their votes within five hours, with 57 percent of them voting against the claimant. Seeing that the majority had voted against his claim, Tang's family decided to cancel his petition only five hours after voting. The crowd's reaction to this case, even if not final, clearly enhanced Xianghubao's legitimacy.

Another notable motivation for Xianghubao and other mutual-aid platforms to adopt a strong form of decentralization is that it helps bolster their argument that they should be viewed as mutual-aid companies rather than insurance companies. Obviously, Xianghubao knew that it was operating in a legal gray area—it was providing a type of crowd-funded medical coverage akin to an insurance product. By making a strong commitment to crowd-judging, Xianghubao and its peers were trying to show that they should be distinguished from typical insurance companies, as their users really had the final say in deciding how to run the platform. In this way, these mutual-aid platforms believed that they could avoid needing to obtain the relevant insurance license, and that their services should not fall under the purview of China's banking and insurance regulators. While these arguments were initially useful in helping Xianghubao delay regulatory intervention, the firm wasn't able to escape the tech crackdown launched in late 2020. In the end, Xianghubao suspended its operation in early 2022, as did many other mutual-aid companies in China.[43]

In sum, the strong form of decentralization offers platform operators the strongest legitimacy, followed by the semi-strong form, and finally by the weak form. In terms of efficiency, the semi-strong form offers the greatest improvement in terms of how quickly cases are resolved, followed by the strong form, and then by the weak form of decentralization. Compared with the other two forms of decentralization, which have mostly been used for adjudication, the weak form provides the least legitimacy and efficiency, but it remains very useful for rule making. Although Western online platforms such as eBay and Facebook also experimented with decentralization, the Chinese online platforms have been much more persistent and proactive in adopting decentralization.

8.2. Legitimacy Crises

The proactiveness of Chinese online platforms in decentralizing their governance, as described above, has much to do with their inherent insecurity about public intervention, a fear that has been further exacerbated by the endemic fraud in the Chinese consumer-internet sector. Over the years, leading Chinese online platforms have faced several major challenges to their legitimacy, including user riots, corruption, and case ambiguity, each of which is elaborated below.

8.2.1. User Riot

In many jurisdictions, platforms' self-governance is susceptible to criticisms of opacity, arbitrariness, and lack of accountability during the rule-making and adjudication process.[44] This evident democratic deficit causes dissatisfaction among platform participants, who feel as though they have been disempowered.[45] This has also been the case in China—even though, in most cases, users have very few choices other than to leave the platform. Indeed, users face a classic collective action problem: they are highly dispersed, making it difficult for them to cooperate and form a strong co-alition that can effectively bargain with the platform. However, when users have a lot at stake, they can indeed organize themselves to make public complaints. As mentioned in Part II, the Chinese administrative authorities were reluctant to take an aggressive stance against the online platforms in the early stages of their development. But this did not prevent users from strategically coordinating their efforts online to disrupt the platform's operation. Their virtual protests had the capacity to attract more public scrutiny and thus exert pressure on the regulators to intervene.

The user riot that occurred on Taobao offers a striking example. Recognizing what triggered this protest will require some understanding of the history behind Taobao and Tmall. Alibaba initially operated Taobao as a consumer-to-consumer platform, before introducing Taobao Mall as a new business-to-consumer model, today named Tmall. Unlike Taobao, which provides free listings for vendors and charges zero commission for transactions, Taobao Mall charged vendors a technical service fee, together with a commission for each transaction. Because Taobao and Taobao Mall both operated under the same domain name, many vendors on Taobao were worried that Taobao Mall would divert their traffic, resulting in reduced sales.[46] As a consequence, many had no option but to upgrade and migrate to Taobao Mall. On October 10, 2011, Taobao Mall announced plans to overhaul its business-management system by significantly raising its commission rates and the premium fees it charged vendors.[47] These measures were supposedly aimed at discouraging vendors selling counterfeit goods from joining the platform, thereby revamping Taobao Mall into a high-end marketplace and a premier destination for quality items.[48] However, small and medium-size vendors perceived these rules as Taobao Mall's way of forcing them off the platform.[49] The day after Taobao Mall made the statement, nearly 40,000 small and medium-sized vendors banded together to create an anti-Taobao union, a decision made in a video chat room.[50] Vendors from the anti-Taobao union attacked large Taobao Mall sellers by placing a high number of online orders, leaving many malicious negative reviews with the intention of lowering the large sellers' customer-satisfaction ratings, and then canceling the orders. This unrest massively disrupted the operations of many big vendors on Taobao, leading large Taobao Mall players, such as Hanyidushe, Uniqlo, and Osa, to temporarily halt transactions soon after the attack.

This organized protest not only had immediate financial consequences for Taobao and Tmall, but also severely threatened Tmall's legitimacy, by casting its integrity into doubt.[51] Many commentators attributed this riot to Alibaba's lack of advanced communication with small and medium-size vendors.[52] Because Taobao Mall did not publish its new fees beforehand, vendors were deprived of the opportunity to provide feedback in advance.[53] Small vendors were particularly indignant—they believed that their trust and loyalty to Taobao had played a pivotal role in its early success, by helping the e-commerce giant fend off eBay's expansion in China. However, Taobao appeared to be turning its back on them after it had grown into a thriving platform.[54]

By employing coordinated extralegal schemes as a form of protest, Taobao vendors wanted to enhance their bargaining leverage in dealing with the platform. This illicit approach proved effective. A week later, China's Ministry of Commerce (MOFCOM) intervened, requesting that Alibaba mediate these complaints. It is particularly interesting that MOFCOM's intervention was in no way targeted at the small and medium-sized vendors who had disrupted platform operations. Rather, MOFCOM blamed Alibaba for its poor internal governance, which had promoted social unrest in the first place. Alibaba then sprang into action by initiating online negotiations with representatives of the anti-Taobao group.[55] The firm subsequently made a number of concessions, including an investment of RMB 1.8 billion specifically to help small businesses and improve their experience on its platform, while also promising to postpone the annual service-fee hikes and decrease the deposit amount required to participate on the platform.[56] MOFCOM's intervention thus significantly empowered those small and medium-sized vendors, forcing Alibaba to make compromises under the threat of government regulation.

8.2.2. Corruption

Employee corruption is another acute legitimacy crisis facing many large Chinese online platforms. Agency problems are common in any organization, and online platforms as a form of business organization are no exception. Indeed, because platforms possess supreme authority over the governance of their communities, their employees have access to critical information and possess significant power to allocate important resources to community users. In the absence of a strong monitoring system, plat-form employees may be tempted to engage in illegal and corrupt practices for personal gain at the expense of the platform's reputation. To be sure, this problem is not unique to China. Most recently, six people, including two former Amazon workers, were indicted on charges of bribing Amazon employees to grant unfair competitive advantages to certain third-party sellers.[57] That said, these types of unscrupulous practices are much more ubiquitous in China.

Alibaba again serves as a good example. Employees at Taobao possess vast discretion and power when it comes to making pertinent decisions about the merchants that operate on its e-commerce platforms.[58] Taobao em-ployees have the ability to decide whether a shop can open on the platform, which vendors are allowed to participate in certain promotional events, and whether certain negative reviews can be removed on the basis of fraud. Driven by enormous incentives, Taobao employees can also collude with vendors to defraud customers. This is exactly what happened in 2011, when Alibaba unknowingly got caught in a scandal. As was later revealed by the press, a total of 2,236 dealers with "Gold Suppliers" ratings on Alibaba.com, the company's business-to-business trading platform, swindled more than USD 6 million from overseas buyers.[59] What was even more astonishing was that around 100 Alibaba employees had assisted these vendors in bypassing the company's authentication and verification measures in order to obtain their Gold Suppliers status, the highest ranking for sellers.[60] Ultimately, 36 Taobao employees were arrested, and two senior executives, despite not being involved in the scandal, took responsibility and stepped down.[61]

Even after Alibaba began strengthening its internal monitoring and anti-corruption systems,[62] these efforts still could not dispel public doubts about the severe and endemic nature of corruption within the firm. In 2012, the *IT Times* published a sensational report exposing some of the corruption scandals that had surfaced at Taobao.[63] The report exposed the fact that sev-eral Taobao employees had been working with scam companies engaged in the production of malicious customer reviews, or "brushing." The collusion between these scam firms and company insiders made it more difficult for Taobao to detect or punish these firms. The scam company would first deliberately create a negative review on the vendor's website, then request a small ransom to remove the review. The scammer would also claim that it had connections within Taobao, making it impossible for the vendor to successfully appeal the negative review. In 2011, Taobao discovered that a customer-service employee had conspired with his friend who operated a scam company to delete 993 negative reviews of vendors, obtaining illegal gains of RMB 1.24 million.[64] Both the Taobao employee and his friend were arrested on bribery charges and each subsequently was sentenced to five years in prison.[65] In May 2012, Alibaba released a public letter disclosing that some vendors had bribed its employees to engage in fraudulent behavior.[66] Following this incident, Taobao shut down nine shops, and the police arrested a few Taobao employees.[67] However, given the scale of brushing and other extortionate practices, as mentioned in Chapter 7, the number of penalties imposed by Taobao appears to be rather small. In fact, the vast majority of fraudulent practices go undetected, thus demonstrating the inadequacy of existing monitoring systems. Decentralization, which involves delegating some of the platform's power to users themselves, has been viewed as an alternative means of curbing Alibaba's internal corruption problems.[68]

8.2.3. Case Ambiguity

Beyond the issues of user protests and employee corruption, online platforms often find themselves facing conflicts to which there is no clear answer. This is largely due to the inherent incompleteness of the law, which cannot possibly anticipate all contingencies. Indeed, the emergence of online platforms as a new form of business model has forced legislators to contend with many unforeseen legal issues. It is also difficult for regulators to intervene ex post, which explains the voluntary efforts of many large online platforms to introduce more transparency and self-regulatory reforms.[69] Facebook presents a striking example of such voluntary efforts. On the one hand, Facebook has faced overwhelming criticism for its failure to tackle hate speech and violent content on its network.[70] On the other hand, its content-moderation decisions are considered controversial and the firm has often been accused of censorship for wrongly blocking or eliminating content.[71] The fine balance that the social-media platform needs to strike puts the firm in a difficult spot, which explains why Facebook has been attempting to delegate some of its authority to outside experts to rectify the situation and reduce tensions.[72] In the Chinese context, this issue of case ambiguity is even more severe. Because merchants deliberately take advantage of legal loopholes and engage in activities that might constitute legal infringements in borderline cases, it is difficult for platforms to gauge whether they are facilitating legitimate or illegal transactions. The phenomena known as *shanzhai* and *xigao* offer vivid examples of the legal controversies faced by Chinese online platforms.

In Chinese, the term *shanzhai* (literally "mountain fortress") traditionally referred to bandit nests, but is often used nowadays to refer to China's massive copycat industry.[73] *Shanzhai* products usually imitate the visual and functional similarities of leading luxury fashion brands as well as high-end electronic products. *Shanzhai* first became popular around 2004, when small factories in southern China started producing cheap knockoffs of cell phones from leading brands.[74] It soon became an epidemic.[75] Due to their guerrilla-style modus operandi and agile production processes, *shanzhai* manufacturers have been especially responsive to the local market, often developing additional functions to suit particular consumer demands.[76] While normal counterfeiters try to mislead customers by making their products look like the originals, *shanzhai* businesses often do not conceal the fact that they are producing copycat products, and consumers are typically aware of the differences.[77] Although many *shanzhai* products involve illicit copying and appropriationist practices,[78] some *shanzhai* products operate in a gray zone: it is unclear whether or not they should be considered counterfeit goods that violate Chinese law.

This lack of clarity has in part to do with China's trademark-registration system. China uses the "first-to-file" system for trademarks.[79] Unlike in the United States, where a trademark's proof of use is a requirement for its registration, China does not require trademark applicants to demonstrate its prior use in commerce.[80] This has led to the proliferation of "trademark squatting," rendering it difficult for foreign brand owners to defend their rights in the country.[81] Moreover, many *shanzhai* products are legally registered trademarks in China. As a result, until foreign brand owners successfully challenge *shanzhai* businesses in court, it is not immediately clear that the latter's products should be treated as counterfeits. Furthermore, there have been several well-known cases in which *shanzhai* producers prevailed in lawsuits brought against them by foreign brand owners such as New Balance, Air Jordan, Brooks, and Muji.[82] In those cases, *shanzhai* producers trademarked their "sound-alike" versions of foreign brands before the original foreign producers were able to register theirs.

Shanzhai producers have also gained legitimacy by appealing to their grassroots features.[83] Often known as "grassroots innovations," *shanzhai* businesses imitate high-end brands' products, but also include complementary features that suit the needs of local consumers.[84] Some *shanzhai* products have even acquired their own cultural significance, with some Chinese consumers viewing *shanzhai* goods as acts of rebellion against the consumption of global luxury brands.[85] The increasing popularity of *shanzhai* practices has helped Chinese online operators garner significant attention online, but they also pose considerable legal challenges for them. The E-Commerce Law that China adopted in 2018 holds platforms jointly liable for the sale of counterfeit goods if they had prior knowledge that such goods were being sold.[86] This requirement incentivizes online marketplaces to tighten their scrutiny of *shanzhai* products.[87] Even if firms such as Alibaba have developed cutting-edge technology to detect and remove counterfeit listings, it is often unclear whether *shanzhai* products are indeed counterfeit goods under Chinese law.

Plagiarism is another problem plaguing Chinese online platforms. WeChat, which started out as an instant-messaging application like WhatsApp, offers a wide array of functions, including a public account (also called a "self-media account"), which allows users to independently publish blogs or produce news articles that they can send to subscribers.[88] With user-generated content becoming more popular on WeChat, plagiarism has become an appealing alternative to generating original content.[89] To escape detection by WeChat's sophisticated algorithms for plagiarism detection, some self-media accounts have resorted to a new practice called *xigao* (literally "article laundering"). Instead of duplicating entire paragraphs verbatim from an original work, this new technique involves copying the ideas and creativity of the original work while making substantial changes to the wording.[90] *Xigao* has become so prevalent that it has bred an underground industry specializing in this type of word-theft for clients. According to news reports, ghostwriters typically earn less than RMB 10 for writing these articles, and can produce 100 to 200 articles each day.[91] Some companies also offer automatic services that can generate a fake news article for self-media accounts.[92]

Meanwhile, the existing anti-plagiarism system adopted by online platforms can only detect plagiarism when words are directly copied and pasted from the original article, so it is difficult for online platforms to instantly identify *xigao* articles as copycats.[93] It also is not easy for the original authors to sue for copyright infringement.[94] In practice, it is an arduous task to discern the authors of infringing articles, many of whom are ghostwriters, since self-media accounts receive contributions from many different users. Moreover, the infringing author can easily remove the article from the self-media account, thus impeding the original author's ability to gather proof. Furthermore, because the original authors are usually individuals rather than large companies with deep pockets, few choose to sue the infringing account holder for laundering their articles.[95] Litigation is time-consuming and costly, and plaintiffs usually lack the time and incentive to appeal such cases.[96] Above all, even if a lawsuit is filed in court, it is difficult to determine whether *xigao* has constituted copyright infringement because Chinese copyright law only protects creative expression, rather than ideas.[97] A recent survey indicates that only 6 percent of authors are willing to go to court if they find that their copyrights have been infringed.[98]

In sum, China's massive copycat industry has tried to evade repercussions for intellectual-property infringements by exploiting loopholes in the law and operating in legal gray areas. However, with the Chinese government now applying stricter internet regulations, Chinese online platforms have found themselves in a vulnerable position, as they could be held liable for facilitating illegal activities.

8.3. Decentralization to Enhance Legitimacy

In response to legitimacy crises and the threat of public regulation, Chinese online platforms have reacted with two major reform initiatives to decentralize their governance. The first is to improve procedural justice in their rule-making and adjudication processes by allowing participation from the user community, giving them a say in how the platform is run. This approach has helped platforms address users' grievances and has preempted large user protests. Delegating authority to users also alleviates problems of corruption besetting e-commerce platforms. The second initiative is to encourage platform users to explore community norms, which not only helps the platforms protect themselves from potential legal violations, but also assists them in designing rules and adjudicating conflicts in ways that are consistent with the expectations of community members.

8.3.1. Procedural Justice

Richard Fallon views legitimacy as the extent to which the public views a platform's decisions as justified and appropriate, beyond the fear of sanctions or hope for rewards.[99] John Rawls argued that there will always be disagreement over what is best in a pluralistic society, and that legitimacy is only obtainable when those who disagree with the rules respect the decision-making process, regardless of its outcomes.[100] Tom Tyler has demonstrated that individuals' judgments about legitimacy do not depend on achieving favorable outcomes, but are more strongly influenced by the processes and procedures employed by authorities, including the opportunity for individuals to participate and have their voices heard, disclosure of information regarding the neutrality and impartiality of the decision-makers, respectful treatment, and perceived benevolent motives.[101] Tyler's findings are similar to the conclusions drawn from the business literature. Because customers want to have a say, partake in, and influence decision-making, they view fairness as an important part of their customer experience.[102] In reality, however, corporations acting as courthouses often fail to offer adequate procedural justice to consumers.[103] Chinese online platforms are similarly faced with such legitimacy challenges. Although they typically communicate their rules and regulations in advance, the platforms' legislative and adjudicative processes largely remain a black box for most consumers. As illustrated by the 2011 virtual riot, opacity in platform decision-making can give rise to a huge amount of consumer dissatisfaction. This digital riot marked a major turning point for Taobao's self-governance. To improve its relationship with users, Taobao saw the need to engage its users and provide them with an opportunity to raise their concerns during the rule-making and adjudication process. It was precisely against this background that Taobao launched the Public Dispute Resolution Center in 2012.[104]

Since July 2018, Alibaba has further expanded its decentralized legislative initiatives by introducing its Public Hearing Series. As participants in this program, users can propose hearing topics online, and Taobao will use these hearings as a testing ground before introducing new rules. In each of these hearings, Taobao invites both vendor and buyer representatives to its Hangzhou headquarters, where roundtable discussions are held about new provisions or issues affecting the user experience. These livestreamed discussions are available to all Taobao and Tmall users, many of whom tune in to watch them. Additionally, users can view the recordings of past online hearings, which allows Alibaba to continue to receive feedback even after the hearing is over. Based on Taobao's own estimates, during the hearings held in the second half of 2018, a total of more than 750,000 sellers, 250,000 buyers, and 100 of Taobao's in-house customer-service representatives participated.[105]

Taobao's hearing on dispatch time is an interesting example. In recent years, Alibaba's e-commerce sites have faced stiff competition from JD.com. The competition is primarily fueled by JD's unrivaled nationwide network that promises quick delivery to customers, often within 24 hours. Although many of Taobao's vendors have been able to dispatch products within 24 hours of their being ordered, some tend to take much longer. The difference in dispatch time between vendors on Taobao creates a potential problem of adverse selection. Buyers might be deterred from making a purchase in the first place if they are unsure about how quickly the vendor will dispatch it.[106] In light of this situation, Taobao proposed to shorten its dispatch time from 72 to 48 hours, launching a hearing on its delivery rules on April 18, 2019.[107] In order to solicit opinions from platform participants, Taobao hosted a small hearing composed of employees from Taobao, 20 vendor representatives, and three consumer representatives, who were seated in groups. Members from each group were given the opportunity to state their own opinions during the hearing. The hearing was broadcast online and Taobao users were able to freely access the recording afterward. Overall, about 39,000 users viewed the hearing itself; many others left comments during and after the hearing.

This decentralized lawmaking process helped Taobao gather opinions from different sources and overcome blind spots.[108] Given that no platform can anticipate all the contingencies that could arise from applying its rules, crowdsourcing helps platforms understand the possible exceptions to its laws. For instance, during the hearing on delivery times, some sellers suggested that the platform should allow case-by-case voluntary arrangements between sellers and buyers to allow for longer delivery times, particularly for certain products where a speedy delivery genuinely cannot be guaranteed. Others suggested that the platform should also allow some flexibility if the seller is able to reach an amiable resolution with the buyer by compensating the buyer for any delays. In this way, sellers can avoid having penalties imposed on them by the platform. Some sellers highlighted the fact that it would take them some time to transition from 72 hours to 48 hours. A few vendors argued that the delivery time was not entirely within their control: there could be shipment delays on the part of other intermediaries. Others suggested that Taobao should give sellers some leeway if they occasionally fail to make quick dispatches. For instance, if some products are temporarily out of stock, or are faulty, they argued, it might be a little too harsh to deduct from their credit scores solely based on delivery performance.

Taobao's public-hearing system also aided vendors in understanding their customers' needs. Customer representatives who were interviewed during the hearing indicated that delivery time was a crucial factor in their purchasing decisions. In this particular case, almost all the vendor representatives who spoke at the hearing said that they were usually able to dispatch within 24 hours of receiving an order. However, the hearing also highlighted the imperative for vendors to ensure swift and reliable delivery in order to compete against other platforms that deliver faster. Beyond giving vendors and sellers the opportunity to hear each other's perspectives, Taobao's hearing also helped enhance the legitimacy of Taobao's proposed new rules. Accordingly, when Taobao rolled out a new rule in May 2019, stating that all vendors needed to dispatch their goods within 48 hours of orders being placed, the action was received not as an arbitrary imposition, but rather a response to vendors' and buyers' organically expressed needs and preferences.[109]

8.3.2. Norm Searching

Lawrence Lessig, a renowned scholar of cyber law, has long proposed that systems of control for the digital economy include laws, norms, architecture, and markets.[110] In the absence of clear laws and regulations, judges often decide cases by referring to industry standards or customs—that is, to social norms that have been developed spontaneously.[111] Constitutional experts also note that even if people disagree about an outcome, decisionmakers can still obtain legitimacy when they rely on reasons that have been deemed fair by reasonable people.[112] In the context of online consumer claims, since users seldom resort to formal state institutions, users and platforms resolve disputes mostly in relation to norms.[113] Because customer-service employees are likely to exercise discretion based on their own understanding of social norms, their understanding may not always reflect the actual norms of the community. Furthermore, there is often no clear-cut answer for difficulties that online platforms encounter, making it difficult to decide what is right and what is wrong. As a result, platforms are often asked to make judgment calls on issues that are highly contextual and sensitive. By giving users an avenue to articulate their concerns and by attaching importance to public reasoning, decentralization encourages compliance, allowing the community to collectively set norms while also promoting greater awareness of the rules.[114]

Taobao's policy to handle *shanzhai* products provides a good example of this dynamic. Since 2015, Taobao has tried to use crowd-judging to determine whether *shanzhai* products have tricked its consumers (i.e., made them believe the counterfeit product was the real thing), a major legal criterion in determining trademark and intellectual-property infringements.[115] After using big data to identify *shanzhai* products that closely resemble original luxury-brand products, Taobao uploaded the pictures of *shanzhai* products to the Public Dispute Resolution Center for crowd-jurors to decide whether these products can in fact be confused with the original brands. Each case usually requires the submission of between 800 and 1,000 votes, and the majority decision is then used as a reference point for Taobao's ultimate decision to remove or restrict the sale of *shanzhai* products on its platform. The use of crowd-judging serves two important purposes here: first, it helps shift the blame away from the platform and onto Taobao consumers. Second, it reduces the platform's risk of becoming entangled in potential legal challenges. If certain *shanzhai* products are later found in court to constitute infringements of laws against counterfeiting, the platform might be held jointly liable for having knowingly facilitated transactions of these products. Crowd-judging, on the other hand, preemptively filters out *shanzhai* products that are likely to cause confusion for consumers. Taobao therefore has a strong justification to keep certain *shanzhai* products on its platform—provided that the products in question did not generate confusion when submitted to crowd-judging.

WeChat offers another example of how crowd-judging can facilitate norm discovery. In December 2018, WeChat launched an anti-plagiarism review mechanism to curtail article laundering on user-generated blogs.[116] Drawing on Alibaba's crowd-judging experience, WeChat first uses artificial intelligence to identify articles that could potentially constitute plagiarism. WeChat then recruits professional authors with a solid reputation to act as crowd-jurors and asks them to determine whether an article has been copied. Each crowd-juror must complete their review within 48 hours. A panel is declared to have ruled after more than 10 professional authors have responded and voted. If 70 percent of the jurors rule in favor of the complainant, the article will be categorized as a plagiarized article. According to one report, in about six months, WeChat's crowdsourcing anti-plagiarism system was able to inspect 200 articles.[117] By outsourcing the task of adjudication to users, WeChat neutralizes the decision-making process with democratic support, thereby enhancing the legitimacy of the final decision. In addition to WeChat, other social-media platforms have also applied crowd-judging to moderate content, including Bilibili, a video-sharing application, and Zhihu, a popular question-and-answer website.

Crowd-judging has also been used to facilitate norm discovery in the ride-hailing context. Didi, for instance, receives around 200 emergency requests on a daily basis for passenger itineraries from friends or relatives of passengers who had taken trips with Didi.[118] It is often difficult for Didi to strike a balance between privacy and security. To combat this dilemma, the firm set up an online public forum in November 2018 to seek user feedback on controversial topics related to operational, privacy, and consumer-protection issues.[119] Didi posts topics for discussion on the forum, leaving a given topic open for seven days to give users some time to vote and add their comments. In this instance, 22,804 users cast their votes, with 68 percent deciding that Didi should not give out the personal itinerary of any passenger. This voting outcome allowed Didi to justify its decision not to disclose the personal information of passengers to third parties who have not been identified as emergency contacts of the passenger.[120]

Notably, Didi's decision to create a public forum also appears to have been a proactive move to fend off unfavorable government regulation, similar to when Taobao introduced the Public Dispute Resolution Center after the digital riot. Earlier in the year, a young Chinese woman who used Didi Chuxing's ride-sharing service was raped and killed by a Didi driver. This news triggered a deluge of allegations against drivers on the platform and sparked criticism of the inadequate safety measures undertaken by Didi. Didi and other ride-hailing companies were summoned by six central ministries, including the Ministry of Transportation, to address these safety issues.[121] Didi also suspended its carpooling business.[122] In the face of the biggest public-relations crisis it had ever seen, Didi took a series of measures to salvage its reputation. From this perspective, the public forum seems to aim at winning user confidence while also enhancing the legitimacy of the platform's decisions. In other words, its use is a way to ease and diffuse tensions arising from its platform.[123]

8.4. Summary

This chapter examined how the insecurity about government intervention has strongly incentivized Chinese online platforms to decentralize governance to ease and diffuse the tensions that arise from the platforms. Such platform insecurity is further amplified by the rampant fraud in the Chinese market, which has exacerbated many enforcement crises facing Chinese online platforms, exposing them to more public scrutiny. Alibaba, a pioneer in platform decentralization, was the first to introduce a crowd-judging mechanism to engage users to participate in rule making and dispute resolution in China. Since then, a large number of Chinese online platforms in e-commerce, social media, and ride-hailing have introduced innovative legal schemes to enable user-generated justice.

Drawing on examples from Chinese online platforms, this chapter reveals that crowd-judging can significantly improve efficiency in handling disputes arising from online platforms. In addition, crowd-judging helps platforms improve procedural justice in their internal governance, while also better understanding community standards. China's unique experiment with platform decentralization is showing how technology can be deployed to allow user-generated justice to govern the digital economy. It also reveals an interesting paradox, in that authoritarian state regulation over platforms can actually spur more democratic and engaged platform self-regulation.

PART IV

The Path Forward

This Part, comprising Chapters 9–11, assesses the impact of the tech crackdown and predicts the path forward. Chapter 9 compares China's legal developments with the evolving legal landscapes in the United States and the European Union. Gaining insights into the global regulatory trends helps shed light on the future direction of Chinese legal developments. Chapter 10 evaluate the impact of China's great reversal in regulating its platform economy. While many of these actions were driven by valid regulatory concerns, the crackdown has resulted in substantial unintended consequences without significantly enhancing competition. Simultaneously, the state sector has benefited by acquiring more strategic stakes and gaining more leverage in directing investment flows toward hard tech. As the country rallies societal efforts to foster the advancement of hard tech, it raises a profound question about the future trajectory of Chinese tech regulation. To address this issue, Chapter 11 applies the dynamic pyramid model of regulation by probing into China's recent foray into regulating generative artificial intelligence.

9

Is China Exceptional?

In Parts I–III, we adopted a systems-thinking approach to examine the intricate interplay between the four key stakeholders involved in shaping Chinese platform regulation. As systems thinking reveals, it is essential to contextualize China's tech governance within the broader international regulatory landscape. This chapter takes a deep dive into the trends shaping platform regulation in the United States and Europe, highlighting major areas such as antitrust law, data privacy, and labor rights. As our subsequent analysis reveals, regulatory concern about Big Tech is certainly not unique to China. Both the US and European regulators are simultaneously launching a wide range of regulatory measures aimed at reigning in Big Tech.

Despite this common concern, there are striking differences in the values and objectives that underpin each region's approach. Anu Bradford, a leading scholar on EU law, insightfully articulates these differences: while the United States follows a market-centric strategy, Europe advocates a rights-based philosophy, and China champions a state-centric model.[1] The US model reflects an unwavering confidence in market mechanisms and assigns a relatively limited role to governmental intervention. In contrast, Europe's approach is centered on protecting the rights and interests of users and citizens.[2] Deviating from both of these models, China's strategy places the state as the central figure guiding and regulating the tech industry.[3] Consequently, despite sharing common regulatory concerns about Big Tech, these jurisdictions have crafted remarkably different strategies in their regulatory approaches. Meanwhile, the global drive to regulate Big Tech has created considerable spillover effects on China. Notwithstanding a temporary loosening of tech regulations in China during 2022, the dynamic legal developments occurring internationally have provided compelling arguments for Chinese regulators to advocate for more rigorous regulation.

High Wire. Angela Huyue Zhang, Oxford University Press. © Oxford University Press 2024.
DOI: 10.1093/oso/9780197682258.003.0010

Simultaneously, these global regulatory shifts must be considered against the larger geopolitical context of state rivalry and tech competition. In fact, an intense regulatory interdependence exists among nations.[4] Following the September 11 attacks, the United States enacted laws that empowered intelligence agencies with broad authority to monitor foreign entities. Recent years have seen a further extension of these powers, with US authorities now exerting long-arm jurisdiction over data held overseas by American companies. This expansion has triggered an assertive response from various countries seeking to protect their internet sovereignty, leading to a wave of data localization initiatives and stricter regulations on cross-border data transfers.[5]

China has followed this trend, leveraging data outflow control as both a defensive mechanism against US extraterritorial jurisdiction and as a negotiation tool with the European Union and other nations currently limiting data transfers to China.

In the following discussion, I will first delineate the regulatory developments in the United States and the European Union concerning antitrust, data, and labor regulation. Following this, I will examine their impact on China, elucidating how these international dynamics have influenced domestic regulatory debate and have shaped China's approach to managing its tech industry.

9.1. Antitrust

Chinese antitrust developments cannot be viewed in isolation from the broader trend in Western countries toward their own tightening of antitrust scrutiny over Big Tech. The regulatory debates in the United States and Europe have not only informed Chinese policymakers, but also created compelling reasons for interest groups to push for aggressive enforcement.

9.1.1. Western Trend

In the United States, antitrust enforcement did not become a significant topic of public discourse until recent years. In fact, calls to invigorate antitrust enforcement against Big Tech companies only started to gain momentum across the political spectrum beginning in 2016.[6] Upon assuming office, President Biden appointed several reform-minded individuals to key positions in federal agencies, such as Lina Khan as chair of the Federal Trade Commission (FTC), Jonathan Kanter as the antitrust chief of the Department of Justice (DOJ), and Tim Wu as the special assistant to the president for technology and competition policy. These appointees strongly support a multifaceted approach, moving beyond the consumer welfare standard to address modern antitrust challenges in the tech sector.[7] In July 2021, President Biden signed a sweeping executive order to promote competition in the American economy, directing federal agencies, including the FTC and DOJ, to step up their enforcement efforts against Big Tech firms.[8] Specifically, the order urges the FTC to address issues such as unfair data collection and surveillance practices, and advocates stricter scrutiny of mergers and acquisitions, particularly those involving "nascent competitors" acquired by Big Tech firms. The order also established the White House Competition Council to coordinate and advance federal government efforts to address antitrust issues.

Both US federal agencies and the states have taken a much more aggressive stance toward antitrust enforcement. In 2020, the DOJ and several states filed a case against Google, alleging that the search engine giant had engaged in self-preferencing as well as other exclusive practices. Two years later, the DOJ and a group of states sued Google again, accusing it of abusing its position in online advertising technology. The FTC has also sued Meta (formerly Facebook) for abusing its monopoly power in "personal social networking services" by acquiring WhatsApp and Instagram and imposing restrictions on rivals. Meanwhile, dozens of antitrust legislations have been proposed, but none has been passed at the time of writing. The "American Innovation and Choice Online Act," introduced by Senators Amy Klobuchar and Charles Grassley, has garnered the most bipartisan support but has yet to be voted on due to competing legislative priorities. This bill targets various abusive practices by dominant online platforms, including self-preferencing, competitor data misuse, and interoperability deficiencies. Despite these dynamic legal developments, the US government has not made significant progress in advancing its agenda to rein in Big Tech.

Compared with the relatively sluggish progress in the United States, Europe has achieved more significant strides in digital legislation and enforcement. In 2019, the European Commission published an influential report on competition policy in the digital age, laying the groundwork for a series of legislative initiatives, enforcement priorities, and decision-making practices that would later follow.[9] A year after the report's release, the Commission unveiled its draft proposals for the Digital Markets Act (DMA) and the Digital Services Act (DSA). The DMA focuses on addressing competition issues in the digital economy, while the DSA mainly targets regulation of content on social media platforms. The DMA imposes extensive obligations and prohibitions on large platforms that serve as "gatekeepers" in the digital economy. In a significant departure from the previous regulatory approach that primarily relied on ex post intervention, the DMA introduces ex ante regulation of Big Tech firms such as Google, Apple, Meta, Amazon, and Microsoft. The law scrutinizes their various business practices and prescribes a comprehensive list of dos and don'ts for these companies. The objective of the DMA is to foster innovation and unleash the potential of rivals in a fair and competitive environment, thus achieving fair and competitive prices while increasing consumer choice.[10] Violations of the DMA could result in fines of up to 10 percent of a firm's worldwide turnover, which increases to 20 percent for repeat offenders. The DMA was officially adopted in July 2022 and came into force later that year. Although obligations to notify mergers and acquisitions in the digital economy will take effect immediately, other obligations for gatekeepers will only be legally enforceable after they have been designated. Practitioners anticipate the DMA to be fully enforceable by early 2024.[11]

In tandem with these legislative efforts, the Commission has also intensified its enforcement. Since 2010, the Commission has initiated three investigations into Google, three into Amazon, two into Apple, and one into Meta, imposing record fines on Google and enforcing stringent remedies on both companies. Google has also appealed these decisions to the EU courts. In a landmark 2021 decision, the General Court upheld the Commission's 2017 ruling in the Google Shopping case, which found that Google abused its dominant position by favoring its own comparison-shopping services over competing platforms. The court appeared to have relaxed the standard of proof compared to earlier precedents and Commission guidance papers, effectively lowering the bar for the Commission.[12] National authorities within EU member states have also been actively scrutinizing Big Tech. In 2019, the German Bundeskartellamt issued a decision prohibiting Meta from gathering data from various platforms (e.g., Facebook, WhatsApp, Instagram) and third-party websites, as well as prohibiting the company from combining such data with users' accounts without their consent.[13] The Bundeskartellamt determined that Meta abused its dominant position by collecting, merging, and using data in user accounts, noting that such practices also violated the European Union's General Data Protection Regulation (GDPR). The German authority's position was subsequently endorsed by the EU Court of Justice in 2023.[14] Meanwhile, regulators from Germany, Italy, Austria, and the United Kingdom have all introduced legislative proposals and intensified enforcement actions to tighten regulation over US Big Tech.[15]

9.1.2. Impact on China

Dynamic legal shifts in both the United States and Europe have had a profound influence on China, as evidenced by the recent proposals from the State Administration for Market Regulation (SAMR) concerning market definition and merger control. In traditional antitrust assessments, defining the relevant market boundaries is typically an initial step in evaluating a firm's market power. This process, however, has proven onerous for antitrust regulators and plaintiffs, making it challenging to demonstrate a tech giant's dominant position despite a substantial market share in some sectors. As a result, both the United States and Europe have witnessed growing calls to eschew the need for market definition in antitrust assessments. For instance, the European Commission's 2019 report on competition policy in the digital age ardently championed relaxing the requirement to establish market definition.[16] The DMA introduced ex ante regulation based on revenue and user numbers, effectively eliminating the need to prove market definition and dominance. Although the United States has not yet adopted sweeping legislation, several legislative proposals, such as Senator Amy Klobuchar's Competition and Antitrust Law Enforcement Reform Act and Senator Josh Hawley's Trust-Busting for the Twenty-First Century Act, explicitly state that market definition is not required to demonstrate dominance.[17]

At the onset of China's tech crackdown, the SAMR released a draft set of guidelines on the platform economy. In a move seemingly inspired by its Western counterparts, SAMR proposed dispensing with market definition in certain circumstances due to the challenges of applying traditional antitrust assessments to the platform economy.[18] This proposal stirred the antitrust community, raising concerns about potential arbitrary enforcement.[19] Although the contentious provision was ultimately omitted from the final version, the regulator's initial attempt to include it suggests that Chinese regulators have been closely observing developments in other advanced jurisdictions and are keen to follow global trends, particularly when it aligns with their bureaucratic interests.

Another area where Western influence is apparent in Chinese antitrust enforcement is merger control. In Europe, the United Kingdom is proposing to lower the standard of proof for competitive assessments of mergers involving designated platforms. Germany has introduced a new threshold based on transaction value for reviewing tech start-up acquisitions that would otherwise escape traditional turnover thresholds. The United States is considering the "Platform Competition and Opportunity Act," which proposes a general ban on dominant platforms acquiring existing or potential competitors unless they can demonstrate that the merger will not harm competition. These developments have caught the attention of Chinese regulators.

In a 2020 article published in a newspaper affiliated with the SAMR, Xiao Di (from the merger division of the SAMR) proposed tightening scrutiny over so-called killer acquisitions of start-ups with little or no turnover by Big Tech firms.[20] Referencing the Western trend of enforcement, he suggested revising merger notification thresholds to expand the review of tech acquisitions. In 2022, China amended its Anti-Monopoly Law, formally authorizing the SAMR to intervene in transactions where there is evidence that the concentration may eliminate or restrict competition, even if it does not meet mandatory notification thresholds.[21] This provision closes the legal loopholes that have allowed Chinese tech firms to evade merger control based on little or no target company turnover. The SAMR is also proposing new notification thresholds based on the acquiring party's revenue and the target company's market capitalization to further tighten scrutiny over killer acquisitions.[22]

Although Chinese authorities have been significantly influenced by Western counterparts in introducing new laws and guidelines, their actual enforcement remains relatively conservative. Merger control serves as a prime example. As mentioned in Chapter 4, Alibaba and Tencent have invested in hundreds of start-ups in the past decade. Although some of these investments are only minority interests, the two tech giants' common ownership over a large portfolio of start-ups poses anti-competitive concerns as it facilitates coordination among these companies.[23] Although the antitrust agency started to retroactively review these past acquisitions, it has only levied small fines on the firms for their procedural failures to notify.[24] The agency has not imposed any structural remedies, even in cases with significant direct market overlaps. Tencent Music's acquisition of China Music Corporation is one such example. According to the SAMR's analysis, the two firms respectively possess 30 percent and 40 percent of the market shares in the relevant market of online music broadcasting.[25] Instead of directly addressing the horizontal overlap concern in the merger review, the SAMR imposed behavioral remedies on Tencent Music to end its exclusive dealings with leading record label companies.[26] Notably, the SAMR could have initiated a formal antitrust investigation into China Music Corporation and imposed a substantial fine on Tencent, similar to its actions against Alibaba. However, the SAMR ultimately chose to impose remedies through a merger review and applied a minimal fine for failing to notify the merger, thereby mitigating negative market reactions to its enforcement.

Another example is the SAMR's investigation into the merger between Huya and DouYu, which respectively possess 40 percent and 30 percent market shares in the livestream gaming market.[27] A close look at this case reveals that Tencent actually already possessed sole control over Huya and joint control over DouYu, so this proposed transaction would only change Tencent's control in DouYu from joint control to sole control.[28] In the end, the SAMR prohibited the merger transaction.[29] However, no further remedies were imposed on either transaction party, despite Tencent's common ownership over these two companies and the risk of coordination. Thus far, in cases where the incumbent tech giants have acquired a competitor in an adjacent market, the SAMR has cleared all such cases without imposing any remedies. For instance, the SAMR unconditionally approved Tencent Holding's acquisition of Sogou, the second-largest search engine in China, in July 2021.[30] As Tencent is mostly active in social media and gaming, it has few direct overlaps with Sogou. However, Sogou has a user base of over 700 million that could pose a competitive threat to Tencent.[31] Instead of preemptively banning the incumbent's acquisitions of adjacent firms, the SAMR appears to have taken a conservative approach by focusing on the direct competition between transaction parties.[32] As a result, the SAMR's measures may further solidify the incumbents' dominance without fundamentally addressing the market concentration issue in the digital economy.

9.2. Data

As with antitrust developments, dynamic changes in the United States and Europe have significantly impacted Chinese regulators, leading to substantial spillover effects on China. This is particularly apparent in the case of EU law, which has furnished a convenient model for China's personal data-protection regulations. Simultaneously, global developments of data regulation have directly influenced Chinese legislation as the country increasingly wields its data law as a strategic self-defense measure against United States' long-arm jurisdiction over data held by American companies. It has also served as a bargaining tool with other jurisdictions during international trade negotiation involving global data governance.

9.2.1. Western Trend

Historically, the United States has embraced a laissez-faire approach to data governance, championing free trade and unrestricted internet access.[33] There is, however, an exception for national security and public interest. Following the September 11 attacks, the United States quickly enacted the Patriot Act, which granted sweeping surveillance powers to authorities for the purpose of bolstering national security.[34] The Foreign Intelligence Surveillance Act also allows US authorities to conduct foreign surveillance with limited judicial oversight, as court proceedings under this act are conducted in secret.[35] In 2018, the United States adopted the Clarifying Lawful Overseas Use of Data Act (CLOUD Act), allowing US law enforcement agencies to access data stored outside the country by US-based service providers.[36] The legislation also outlines procedures for creating bilateral agreements with foreign governments to facilitate reciprocal information sharing. Concerned that these laws would grant the United States unfettered access to overseas data, numerous countries have taken measures to keep data within their borders.[37]

In terms of privacy and personal information protection, the US government has traditionally adopted a minimalist approach. Thus far, the United

States lacks a comprehensive federal data law. Instead, a number of sector-specific laws address privacy protection in areas such as telecommunications, health information, credit information, financial institutions, and marketing. By 2022, only five states—California, Colorado, Connecticut, Utah, and Virginia—had enacted their own privacy-protection laws. However, this lax approach on data-privacy protection is evolving as the United States responds to emerging national interests in cyberspace and mounting domestic concerns about Big Tech.[38] In 2020, the Trump administration issued two executive orders accusing WeChat and TikTok of collecting US personal data capable of swaying elections, creating risks to privacy and national security. Trump sought to ban these two apps from app stores, which led to multiple lawsuits from TikTok and its users, as well as WeChat users. US courts eventually blocked these orders.[39] Nonetheless, as TikTok's popularity continues to surge in the United States, it has attracted increasing scrutiny from state governments nationwide. By January 2023, at least 26 states had implemented some form of restrictions on the app, particularly regarding its use on government devices or in lawsuits. In 2023, the State of Montana became the first US state to ban TikTok within its state by next year.

In contrast to the United States, which largely perceives information privacy as a matter of consumer interest, Europe has long regarded consumer privacy and data protection as fundamental human rights.[40] This distinction has its roots in the historical, cultural, and legal contexts of the two regions, with the European outlook shaped by historical experiences with totalitarian regimes, invasions of privacy, and human rights abuses.[41] These experiences have fundamentally shaped Europe's collective consciousness and its interpretation of personal data protection as a crucial human right.

The conceptual difference between the United States and Europe came to the forefront in 2013 following the revelations made by Edward Snowden concerning the United States' vast surveillance operations.[42] The news of such mass surveillance sent shockwaves throughout Europe, stirring deep concerns over American espionage activities on their leaders and citizens. This amplified the European anxieties about the potential misuse of their citizens' data by foreign entities and underscored the need for stricter data protection laws. Since the Snowden revelations, privacy activist Maximilian Schrems has been at the forefront of private litigation challenging the adequacy of EU-US data-protection agreements that govern transatlantic data exchange. Schrems's argument was predicated on the belief that these agreements failed to provide adequate protection to the data of EU citizens against possible intrusion by US surveillance programs.[43] The EU Court of Justice has twice sided with Schrems, citing concerns about potential privacy intrusions from US surveillance programs, and subsequently has invalidated these agreements.[44] These landmark rulings created considerable legal turbulence for transatlantic data transfers, raising questions about the legitimacy and future of such exchanges.

In 2018, the European Union started to implement the GDPR, providing EU citizens with a wide range of protections, such as the right to be informed about data processing transparently, the right to access and understand personal data usage, data portability, the right to erase personal data, the right to rectify errors, and the right to object to automated decision-making. The law also mandates companies to conduct data audits and report data breaches. The GDPR features robust sanction provisions, with maximum fines reaching 4 percent of a firm's revenue. Major US social media companies like Meta, Amazon, and Google have faced substantial fines for GDPR violations. In 2023, the Irish data-protection authority (DPA) imposed a record fine of EUR 1.2 billion on Meta, the social media giant, for transferring personal data from Europe to the United States without providing adequate protection measures for European citizens.[45] The decision not only marked a significant precedent in data-protection law enforcement, but it also threatened the data arrangements of tens of thousands of US businesses that had adopted protocols similar to those of Meta.

9.2.2. Impact on China

The advent of China's data-security regime was significantly shaped by the US mass surveillance program and its increasingly assertive jurisdiction over data stored in other countries. In the aftermath of Snowden's leak, Chinese top leaders formed a Cybersecurity and Information Leading Group in 2014 to address cybersecurity issues.[46] As a defensive strategy against potential foreign surveillance and data collection, China enacted a series of laws and regulations to limit cross-border data mobility.[47] Its first major data law, the 2017 Cybersecurity Law, was characterized by stringent data-localization requirements, which added a new layer of complexity for foreign businesses operating in the country.[48]

In 2021, China implemented the Data Security Law, widely seen as a response to the US CLOUD Act which authorizes extraterritorial access to overseas data.[49] The Data Security Law establishes a data-classification framework based on potential national security impacts. Core data—broadly defined as data related to national and economic security, citizens' welfare, significant public interests, and important data—are subject to extensive data localization and transfer requirements. These requirements not only were aimed at protecting national security interests, but also served to potentially shield Chinese companies from responding to US government requests under the CLOUD Act. This was evident from the law's mandate that any data transfer to foreign law enforcement or judicial agencies must receive official approval.[50] The Personal Information Protection Law (PIPL), enacted in 2021, includes a similar provision countering the CLOUD Act's extraterritorial reach, further reinforcing China's intent to maintain control over its citizens' data.[51] In reaction to escalating export restrictions and sanctions against Chinese tech firms, both the Data Security Law and the PIPL incorporate provisions to counteract foreign export restrictions and sanctions, threatening severe penalties for violations.[52] The Cyberspace Administration of China (CAC) continued this trend into 2022 by releasing additional measures and guidelines related to the security assessment for cross-border data transfers.[53] These developments served to further institutionalize cross-border data-transfer review mechanisms, reinforcing the Chinese government's commitment to maintain stringent control over its data in the face of an increasingly challenging global data-governance regime.

The case involving Didi Chuxing exemplifies the intensifying legal conflict between China and the United States. Notably, this case occurred against the backdrop of deteriorating Sino-US relations and the US government's demand for stricter auditing requirements for Chinese firms listed in the United States. In 2020, President Trump signed the Holding Foreign Companies Accountable Act into law, threatening to delist Chinese firms from US stock exchanges unless Beijing permitted US authorities to inspect the auditing records of Chinese firms. Prior to Didi's initial public offering (IPO) in June 2021, the ride-hailing giant reportedly received advice from the CAC to delay its US filing in order to undergo a comprehensive cybersecurity review. With Didi collecting vast amounts of personal and location data, the CAC was concerned that the firm might hand over personal data and other sensitive information to US authorities during the IPO filing process. The *Wall Street Journal* reported that the CAC feared Didi's server equipment could be vulnerable to security breaches upon disclosure, potentially compromising data security.[54]

Despite this advice, Didi proceeded with its IPO at an accelerated pace, as mentioned in Chapter 5. Two days after its IPO, the CAC announced a cybersecurity review investigation into Didi. The investigation was based on the Cybersecurity Review Measures, an obscure regulatory measure enacted a year earlier, primarily addressing supply-chain risks associated with the procurement of network products and services by operators of critical information infrastructure. To close this potential loophole, Chinese authorities revised the Cybersecurity Review Measures in 2022, adding a new provision requiring online platforms with over one million users to apply for a cybersecurity review if they plan to list overseas.[55]

On the other hand, European data and privacy laws, notably the GDPR, have also had a profound influence on the development of Chinese legislation. Paul Schwartz, a renowned data and privacy expert, observed that the European Union has employed a broad array of strategies to promote the spread of its data protection law.[56] Crucially, the GDPR applies extraterritorially and permits the free flow of data transfers to other countries if the European Union determines that the country has provided an adequate level of data protection. This means that any country wishing to freely engage in data exchange with the European Union must ensure that its data protection standards are in line with the GDPR. Consequently, many countries have rushed to adopt standards similar to the GDPR to fulfill the EU adequacy requirements.

Meanwhile, the European Union has set the gold standard in data regulation, with its strong regulatory capacity and inclination toward strict standards, prompting numerous jurisdictions to model their own regulations on the GDPR.[57] Anu Bradford refers to this as the "Brussels Effect," a term that encapsulates the European Union's far-reaching influence and global regulatory power across a multitude of policy areas.[58] This is a testament to the EU's commitment to uphold high standards of data protection and its clout in the global regulatory landscape. This influence has been particularly pronounced in China. In fact, when drafting the PIPL, the Chinese legislature used the GDPR as a blueprint. The final law not only resonates with the GDPR, but in some areas, it closely mirrors its provisions. Notably, the

PIPL also incorporated the gatekeeper concept from the DMA, imposing certain obligations on large internet platforms with a complex business structure and significant user base. These gatekeeper platforms must fulfill obligations such as establishing a robust compliance system, subjecting themselves to monitoring by independent organizations composed of external experts, and periodically publishing social responsibility reports on personal data protection.[59]

9.3. Labor

In both the United States and Europe, policymakers and enforcers have been grappling with the issue of whether workers in the sharing economy should be classified as independent contractors or employees. Similar to China, tech firms in these jurisdictions have made considerable efforts to resist litigations and legislations that would classify such workers as their employees. Despite aggressive lobbying from tech giants, US and European policymakers have made steady progress in developing specialized rules to enhance labor protection for platform workers. These regulatory developments have inspired Chinese regulators, who are similarly pressuring Chinese tech firms to improve labor protection for platform workers.

9.3.1. Western Trend

In the United States, online platforms and gig workers have been embroiled in a protracted legal battle over the latter's employment status for years. At the state level, ride-hailing companies like Uber and Lyft have faced numerous lawsuits alleging their classification of drivers as independent contractors rather than employees to be bogus.[60] Thus far, many such legal challenges have been settled, preventing courts from making definitive rulings on the issue.[61] For example, Uber settled a lawsuit with 400,000 drivers in California and Massachusetts for approximately USD 100 million before trial in 2016.[62] However, the court rejected the proposed settlement on the grounds that it was insufficient to compensate the drivers.[63] In 2020, a New York federal court ruled that Uber drivers could be treated as employees eligible for unemployment benefits under the law.[64] The State of

Massachusetts also filed suit against Uber and Lyft for misclassifying drivers as independent contractors rather than employees.[65]

Similar to other countries, US courts have adopted some form of a "control" test to determine employee status. There are three major tests, including the common law control test,[66] the ABC test,[67] and the economic realities test,[68] all of which examine the extent to which the firm has the right to control the manner and means by which the workers provide their services. Although the control test was relatively easy to understand in traditional employment relationships, the advent of algorithmic management has blurred the line between employee and independent contractor. Among these tests, the ABC test is the most favorable for platform workers, as it creates a rebuttable presumption of an employment relationship unless the employer can prove that the worker is free from its control and direction, the work is not an integral part of the business, and the worker is free to engage in outside, unrelated work. The second criterion of the ABC test makes it almost impossible for many platforms to demonstrate that the workers' activities do not fall within the company's core competencies.

In addition to court rulings, many state legislatures have taken actions to address worker misclassification. In 2019, California passed AB5, a bill that incorporated the ABC worker classification test into state law, making it more challenging for employers to classify workers as independent contractors.[69] Companies like Uber and Lyft spent tens of millions of dollars on an aggressive campaign to overturn AB5 by introducing Proposition 22, which sought to exempt ride-hailing companies from the ABC test.[70] Although the proposition passed with 59 percent of the vote, the Superior Court of California declared it unconstitutional and unenforceable.[71] The decision was promptly appealed and remains pending. Uber and Lyft launched a similar campaign in Massachusetts, but their efforts were thwarted when a state court deemed their proposed ballots to be in violation of state law.[72] Meanwhile, ride-hailing companies negotiated a deal with drivers in Washington, offering a guaranteed set of benefits while maintaining their status as independent contractors.[73] Similar bills have been proposed in New Jersey, Pennsylvania, Vermont, and Wisconsin.[74] At the federal level, the Biden administration made progress in 2022 when the Department of Labor introduced a new rule making it harder to classify workers as independent contractors, aiming to end the abusive practice of worker misclassification.[75]

This rule replaced a Trump administration regulation that allowed workers to be treated as independent contractors if they owned their businesses or could work for competing firms.

Like the United States, most European countries employ some form of control test to determine labor relations.[76] Some European nations have been particularly active in enhancing labor protections for gig workers. In 2021, the UK Supreme Court ruled that Uber's drivers should be classified as workers rather than independent contractors. This classification grants drivers certain employment rights, such as minimum wage and holiday pay, but does not provide full UK employment rights. French courts have also issued a series of rulings favoring gig workers. In 2020, France's top court classified an Uber driver as an employee, and in 2022, the French Criminal Court convicted Deliveroo of hidden work. A Paris court also ordered the platform to repay EUR 10 million in social payments in 2022.[77] Additionally, the French government adopted an order in 2021 establishing a system of collective representation for independent workers in the digital economy.[78]

In Spain, the Supreme Court ruled against a delivery company called Glovo in 2020 for misclassifying its drivers as contractors rather than employees.[79] Glovo was fined EUR 79 million in 2022 and another EUR 57 million in 2023.[80] In a significant move, the Spanish government codified the Glovo decision and adopted the Riders' Law in May 2021.[81] This new law presumes delivery workers to be employees if they operate under the direct or indirect organization, direction, and control of a digital platform that uses algorithms to manage the service or working conditions. In response to this legislative change, Deliveroo exited the Spanish market entirely, while UberEats opted to subcontract their workers, a practice that may be subject to challenge as it appears to circumvent regulation.[82] Italian authorities have also taken action against food-delivery companies. In February 2021, the Milan public prosecutor fined several food-delivery companies nearly EUR 733 million for misclassifying workers and ordered them to hire all 60,000 delivery workers as "pseudo-subordinate" employees with limited employment rights within 90 days.[83]

Concurrently, the European Commission is working on a series of proposals, including a directive, draft guidelines, and a communication, aiming to address employee misclassification and algorithmic transparency in the gig economy.[84] Part of the proposal involves introducing a legal presumption of employment for misclassified independent contractors. The initial Commission text outlines five criteria that could indicate a subordinate link between a worker and a platform, such as remuneration, uniform requirements, performance oversight, worker scheduling restrictions, and limiting work for competitors. A rebuttable presumption of employment is established if a worker meets two of these five criteria. The Commission also seeks to enhance algorithmic transparency and establish a right to contest algorithmic decision-making.[85] Furthermore, the Commission's DMA imposes obligations on large core platforms deemed "gatekeepers" to provide business users with access to their data, potentially enabling greater transparency concerning decisions affecting the employment relationships of platform workers.[86]

9.3.2. Impact on China

The evolving landscape in both the United States and Europe has significantly influenced the regulatory discourse in China, especially concerning platform worker classification. There is a prevailing consensus among Chinese policymakers and academics that it is imperative to introduce reforms to bolster labor protections for platform workers.

As mentioned in Chapter 6, eight central ministries issued Guiding Opinions on Protecting Labor and Social Security Rights and Interests of Workers Engaged in New Forms of Employment ("Document No. 56") in July 2021.[87] This document specifies that when a platform exercises labor management over workers without fully meeting the conditions for establishing an employment relationship, the platform must enter into written agreements with workers to reasonably clarify their respective rights and obligations. Some scholars have interpreted Document 56 as proposing to introduce a new form of labor relationship wherein platform workers enjoy a hybrid status between an employee and independent contractor. This policy proposal appears to be inspired by recent labor reforms in other jurisdictions, such as the UK Supreme Court's 2021 decision to classify Uber drivers as "workers" rather than contractors. Chinese scholars have also pointed to the experience of Germany, which established an intermediary category of "employee-like persons."[88] This concept refers to workers who are economically dependent (work predominantly for one person or derive half of their total income from one person) and require social protection similar to an employee.[89] This category of workers is entitled to collective bargaining, paid leave, and access to labor tribunals.[90] California's "Proposition 22" adopted in 2020 is another example where platform workers enjoy more labor protections than other independent contractors but are not considered employees.

Meanwhile, some Chinese courts have begun to consider altering the standard of proof during adjudication. In September 2021, a research group from Beijing's First Intermediate People's Court published a report in the People's Court Daily, discussing the legal nature of labor relationships in the platform economy.[91] The study group proposed creating a presumption of labor relationship and shifting the burden of proof from the worker to the platform, drawing inspiration from similar presumptions in favor of platform workers in US and UK cases involving Uber.[92] The Beijing court particularly highlighted the *Berwick v. Uber* case, where the California Labor Commission adopted a two-step approach to determine the labor relationship. First, the worker provides preliminary evidence of service provided to Uber, creating a presumption of employment; second, the employer can offer evidence to rebut the presumption and show that the worker is, in fact, a contractor. Uber lost this case because the court held that it failed to show it exercised minimal control over the plaintiff driver's activities.

Based on the analysis of these foreign precedents, the research group from the Beijing court criticized the existing test widely adopted by Chinese courts in labor cases. As mentioned in Chapter 6, the Ministry of Human Resources and Social Security (MOHRSS) laid out a three-factor test to establish a labor relationship, focusing on employer control, management rules extension, and the integral nature of the employee's services. The research group from the Beijing court observes that the test might be excessively stringent for platform workers, conceding that while workers may not satisfy these conditions they should still qualify as employees. The research group also noted that the informal management by some companies makes it difficult for workers to satisfy the burden of proof. Overall, both Chinese judicial and regulatory authorities are closely monitoring the legal trends in the United States and Europe, as these developments may significantly influence their approach to addressing the complex labor issues arising from the country's dynamic sharing economy.

9.4. Summary

As evidenced by the dynamic developments in platform regulation in both the United States and Europe, China is hardly alone in its efforts to rein in Big Tech. However, driven by distinct values and ideologies, these regions have charted different paths in governing Big Tech within their respective jurisdictions. Concurrently, the vigorous regulatory debates in the West have had a significant impact on Chinese regulation. In many ways, Chinese policymakers are emulating their Western counterparts by introducing similar reforms to address regulatory challenges within China's platform economy.

Apart from these spillover effects, global tech regulation has directly influenced China's regulatory stance. The United States' expansive overseas surveillance and aggressive assertion of jurisdiction over overseas data have prompted various countries, including China, to enforce more stringent data-localization requirements and impose tighter restrictions on data transfers. At the same time, China is attempting to use its data outflow control as a major leverage in negotiations with other nations. This regulatory interdependence between nations adds an additional layer of dynamic complexity to the evolution of Chinese tech regulation. The ever-changing global tech regulatory landscape presents a unique challenge and opportunity for China, and it will be interesting to observe how the country will navigate this complex web of influences in the future.

10

Assessing the Impact

China's relentless law enforcement campaign, which was initiated in October 2020, swept across the entire tech sector and lasted for almost 18 months. As noted in the Introduction, the series of tech policies being rolled out from Beijing, seemingly random and disconnected, all bear the distinct hallmark of a government intent on tackling economic inequality. The extraordinary clampdown on private tutoring, for instance, sought to narrow the educational divide between the rich and poor. Concurrently, the deluge of regulations—spanning antitrust measures to data and labor protections—were designed to bolster the bargaining power of the various platform participants in dealing with the powerful tech firms.

This chapter delves into the short-term implications of this unprecedented enforcement initiative. More specifically, how successful has it been in helping the top leadership to accomplish their ambitious goal of common prosperity? Has it led to any unintended consequences? And how might this enforcement drive shape the future trajectory of tech development in China? As I have outlined in Part II of this book, China's hard-hitting regulatory approach has its great advantages but also fundamental flaws. The broad leeway afforded to the administrative authorities enables them to be agile, reacting quickly to the shifting policy winds. Nonetheless, this also gives rise to systemic issues, such as a lack of political accountability and the potential for overreach in administrative discretion. In past enforcement campaigns, there has been a tendency for "policy overshooting" during the most intense periods. This typically subsides, leaving minimal long-term deterrence as markets adjust to the temporary nature of the campaigns.[1] This cyclical pattern presents a challenge when trying to predict the outcome of the most recent enforcement wave.

High Wire. Angela Huyue Zhang, Oxford University Press. © Oxford University Press 2024.
DOI: 10.1093/oso/9780197682258.003.0011

Still, the tech crackdown, which began to ease in early 2022, has induced lasting institutional changes. The most conspicuous shift lies in the power dynamics between the private sector and the state. The private sector, squeezed by tightening regulations, has ceded ground while the state, emboldened, plays a progressively more assertive role in investing and steering the trajectory of the tech industry. Ironically, the campaign has not really bolstered the bargaining power of the platform participants in their dealings with the tech firms, but the actual result so far has seen the state's position significantly strengthened relative to tech companies. This more assertive role of the Chinese state will likely continue to shape the future of the Chinese tech industry, reshaping power dynamics and recalibrating market forces in ways that could have implications not just for China but for global tech landscape.

10.1. The Retreat of the Private Sector

From the outset, the top Chinese leadership has aimed their enforcement efforts squarely at stemming the unchecked expansion of capital by the country's tech behemoths. In an effort to mollify Beijing, leading tech companies such as Alibaba, Tencent, and ByteDance have undertaken radical measures, from selling off non-core business assets and improving corporate governance to restructuring their businesses. Yet the erratic nature of Chinese tech policy has unnerved investors, precipitating severe and unintended consequences of deterring investment and entry into the consumer tech business. As such, although the campaign ostensibly sought to clear the path for new and innovative entries, its debilitating side effects appear to outweigh the intended benefits.

10.1.1. Exit and Restructuring

In 2021, Tencent distributed USD 16 billion of JD.com to its shareholders, slashing its stake in the e-commerce company from around 17 percent to a mere 2 percent.[2] The following year, Tencent declared that it would dispense nearly USD 22 billion worth of shares in Meituan as dividends to its shareholders, significantly diluting its stake from 17 percent to just 1.5 percent.[3] Although Tencent's retreat from the e-commerce and food-delivery

ASSESSING THE IMPACT   261

sectors may have given room for other businesses to grow, it has also had a chilling effect on investment and market entry.[4] As a powerful and formidable investment force, Tencent has shown a willingness to assume risks that others shy away from.[5] As such, the company's exit from several industries sends an ominous signal to the market. Investors may interpret this withdrawal as indicative of the sector's grim prospects, which in turn could further deter investment.

The corporate empire of Jack Ma has undergone even more profound transformation. In January 2023, Ant Group unveiled sweeping changes to its corporate governance structure.[6] Ma relinquished his control of Ant Group, reducing his voting rights from 50 percent to a modest 6 percent. The restructuring ensured that no single shareholder could exert sole or joint control over the fintech giant, and the board will include an additional independent director. This corporate overhaul was completed by the end of 2023, with the People's Bank of China now listing Alipay as a firm without an actual controller. Undoubtedly aimed at diluting Ma's influence, these changes were touted by the government as steps toward improving transparency and accountability in corporate governance. The regulators' stance is not without merit. As past financial scandals involving the likes of Tomorrow Group and An Bang demonstrate, companies with large shareholders and opaque corporate governance structures are ripe for misconduct. Given Ant's magnitude and reach, Chinese regulators are rightly concerned about the potential fallout if the financial giant is mismanaged.

Concurrently, the dilution of Ma's influence over Ant has the effect of indirectly improving Alibaba's corporate governance. This has to do with the peculiar governance structure of the two firms. After scrutinizing Alibaba's corporate structure, eminent corporate law experts Jessie Fried and Ehud Kamar concluded that Ma could effectively control Alibaba through his control of Ant Group, despite holding only a personal stake of roughly 5 percent.[7] The authors argue that Ma's control over Ant enables him to exercise influence over Alibaba's partnership committee, which in turn allows him to dominate the company's executive team.[8]

Merely two months after Ant Group's structural overhaul, Alibaba announced its decision to splinter into six discrete units, each focusing on a unique domain—cloud computing, Chinese e-commerce, global e-commerce, digital mapping and food delivery, logistics, and media and entertainment.[9] This news emerged concurrent with Jack Ma's return to the public eye after a year-long sojourn overseas, fueling speculation that a pact had been brokered between Beijing and Ma over the reshaping of his corporate empire. Alibaba's CEO, Daniel Zhang, believes this restructuring will render the firm more agile, as each newly independent unit will have increased autonomy in decision-making, bolstering their competitive edge.[10]

In a prior commentary co-authored with Professor Jin Li of the University of Hong Kong, we raised skepticism about Alibaba's restructuring plan, deeming it a costly move.[11] The reorganization risks duplicating company resources, while simultaneously elevating the likelihood of incentives being misaligned across the different units. We argued that an alternative form of organization such as a multi-division form could be adopted to achieve similar purposes of increasing agility without having to endure such high costs. First adopted by DuPont nearly a century ago, and embraced by countless companies since, the M-form structure empowers division heads to make their own personnel, budgeting, and operating decisions, while corporate headquarters offer strategic direction, support, and oversight. Moreover, Alibaba remains the controlling shareholder of these six units. Thus, from an antitrust perspective, the units continue to be viewed as a single entity. As such, Alibaba's move carries significant cost while failing to address fundamental antitrust concerns in any meaningful way. Absent a robust business justification, Alibaba's split appears primarily aimed at placating a Chinese government apprehensive of its growth and influence.

10.1.2. The Unintended Consequences

The orchestrated exits and restructuring undertaken by China's tech titans should, in theory, create more space for competition, enhance these companies' corporate governance, and bolster investor protection. However, these maneuvers have resulted in far-reaching unintended side effects. Fears around the capriciousness of China's regulatory policies, coupled with growing anxieties about the prospects of consumer tech businesses, have dampened investor sentiment and have led to a precipitous decline in investment in the consumer sector. The heightened cost of regulatory compliance disproportionately burdens smaller firms, who lack the extensive in-house resources that larger firms have at their disposal for handling such matters. This disparity in compliance resources inadvertently gives larger tech firms a competitive edge, further cementing their dominance in the market.

For many investors, July 2021 was a tumultuous month that signified a seismic shift in their perception of the Chinese consumer internet market. Two consecutive shocks rocked the market in July, delivering a potent blow to investor confidence. The initial shock stemmed from Didi, the Chinese ride-hailing giant that found itself ensnared in an unexpected cybersecurity investigation. The Didi incident reverberated across the industry, casting a long shadow over Chinese companies seeking to list overseas. As detailed in Chapter 5, the Didi probe prompted the Cyberspace Administration of China (CAC) to mandate cybersecurity checks for internet firms seeking foreign listings. This raised concerns among investors about the feasibility of US listings for such companies, thereby potentially curtailing exit options for US dollar-denominated funds in China.[12] This murky outlook also dampened investor confidence, affecting both early and late-stage start-ups.[13] By the second half of July 2021, the US listing of Chinese firms had practically come to a standstill, due to the uncertainties surrounding the CAC's cybersecurity law requirements.[14] Then came the second blow in late July, when the Chinese government suddenly announced a policy prohibiting for-profit tutoring firms from going public or soliciting foreign capital. As elaborated in Chapter 2, this policy—designed to alleviate excessive competition among Chinese youth and establish a more equitable education system—effectively wiped out the online tutoring sector.[15] The abrupt policy shift sent shock waves across the market, exacerbating investor fears about the capricious and erratic nature of Chinese tech policy.

Data from the China Academy of Information and Communications Technology (CAICT), a think tank affiliated with China's Ministry of Industry and Information Technology, illustrates the chilling effect of these regulatory actions.[16] Investment in China's internet industry plummeted from USD 15 billion to USD 9 billion from the second to the third quarter of 2021, a staggering 40 percent decrease.[17] Moreover, the total investment capital nose-dived from a high of USD 49 billion in 2021 to a paltry USD 10 billion in 2022, an 80 percent reduction. Concurrently, the total market capitalization of Chinese internet companies also shrank from USD 2.5 trillion at its 2020 peak to USD 1.4 trillion in 2022, marking a 44 percent decline. Recent empirical research by Daniel Sokol from the University of Southern California, Feng Zhu from Harvard University, and others have shown that China's tech crackdown fell short of its goal to foster greater competition.[18] Using large-scale industry databases, the authors find that Chinese consumer internet sectors saw 27 percent less monthly investment and 19 percent fewer monthly new entries compared to other sectors not affected by the crackdown.[19] Thus, while the enforcement campaign was ostensibly aimed at curbing the behavior of tech giants, it ended up reinforcing the existing market structure and negatively impacting the industry.[20]

In the meantime, China's tech crackdown has drastically escalated the burden of legal compliance, inadvertently skewing the scales in favor of behemoths and placing smaller, resource-strapped start-ups at a disadvantage. Unlike antitrust laws, which primarily target firms with strong market position, data regulations apply universally to all companies involved in data collection and processing. Consequently, stricter data regulation imposes a disproportionate cost on small businesses. In October 2021, the number of apps available in Chinese app stores fell to just 2.7 million, representing an almost 40 percent decrease from three years prior.[21] Certainly, various factors have contributed to this decline, such as China's maturing consumer internet market and a number of apps falling foul of personal data obligations. Yet, it's indisputable that the increasingly challenging regulatory environment played a substantial role, with the steepest decline coinciding with the crackdown's peak intensity in 2021.[22]

Indeed, even with large tech firms withdrawing from non-core areas of investment, there has been no marked uptick in new entrants into the core businesses currently dominated by titans such as Alibaba and Tencent. In 2020, 70 percent of the most popular apps in China were owned by Alibaba and Tencent, with the remaining 30 percent owned by ByteDance and Baidu.[23] This market structure remained the same for the next two years.[24] In the e-commerce sector, Alibaba's market share ebbed from 54 percent in the first quarter of 2021 to 46 percent by the close of 2022. ByteDance, meanwhile, made inroads, bolstering its share from a meager 4 percent to a sturdy 11 percent.[25] In the realm of food delivery, the duopoly of Meituan and Ele.me remained unchallenged, jointly boasting over 90 percent market share until 2022.[26] The gaming sector echoed a similar pattern, with Tencent and NetEase holding an overwhelming 79 percent of the market in the first quarter of 2023, a slight increase from their 76 percent in 2020.[27] Turning to ride-hailing, despite

ASSESSING THE IMPACT

Didi's shares slipping from 92 percent in mid-2021 to 78 percent by year's end, the ride-hailing giant managed to halt further attrition, stabilizing its market position.[28] On the whole, the tech crackdown has induced minor stumbling among the largest players in some areas such as e-commerce and ride-hailing, with their incumbent rivals seizing the opportunity to bolster their positions. Nonetheless, it hasn't fundamentally changed the competitive landscape, with key sectors still being dominated by these formidable tech giants.

Foreign tech firms operating in China haven't escaped the brunt of the tech crackdown either. An influx of newly implemented rules restricting cross-border data transfer has compelled many companies to either localize their data within China or relocate their operations overseas. Some experts have likened China's new data laws to the proverbial straw that broke the camel's back, compounding the compliance costs for US social media companies already grappling with a heavy censorship burden.[29] LinkedIn, for instance, withdrew from China in late 2021 and instead launched InCareer, a job-posting app devoid of social feeds or post sharing. By entirely disconnecting InCareer from LinkedIn's global platform, the firm tried to sidestep the data export restrictions typically required for multinationals.[30] Yahoo also cited an "increasingly challenging business and legal environment" when it shut down its online services in 2021. The impact has reverberated beyond the tech sector. Banking executives have bemoaned the increasing resources they have to devote to comply with Beijing's data security rules.[31] A senior executive from a US investment bank revealed to me that they shut down their entire global trading platform based in mainland China in 2022.[32] Despite the potential to satisfy cross-border data-transfer rules, the executive remarked that his firm simply did not want to take on those legal risks. Moving their operations out of China was seen as a clean decision.[33]

The campaign has rippled through to the labor market as well. The call to end the "996" work schedule, a prevalent practice in the tech industry that sees employees work from 9 a.m. to 9 p.m., six days a week, drew substantial attention during the enforcement campaign. However, while tech firms pledged to rectify such practices, old habits proved stubbornly persistent.[34] As such, despite many measures having been devised to bolster worker protection, their impact appears negligible. Compounding the issue, revenue losses at leading tech firms have led to significant layoffs, fueling fierce internal competition and heightening worker anxiety. In 2021, more than 35 leading tech firms announced redundancies.[35] Alibaba alone terminated the contracts of 20,000 employees, about 8 percent of its workforce.[36] The following year, Tencent cut 7,300 jobs in the second and third quarter, while Alibaba shed another 11,800 positions.[37] Other firms such as JD.com, ByteDance, Zhihu, Xiaohongshu, Bilibili, and Weibo made similarly drastic cuts.[38] This trend continued into 2023, with Baidu laying off workers in its autonomous driving task force to double down on profitability.[39]

10.2. The Advancement of the Administrative State

Simultaneously, as the private internet sector recedes, the state sector advances. The tech crackdown, though transient in nature, has catalyzed enduring institutional changes. Over the 18-month enforcement campaign, a wave of national and local laws emerged, supplemented by departmental guidelines that further shaped the regulatory landscape. The Anti-Monopoly Law, for instance, was revamped, bestowing upon the agency greater discretionary power and amplified punitive abilities. Newly minted data laws, such as the Personal Information Protection Law and the Data Security Law, also wield significant regulatory force. Consequently, Chinese regulators now command a larger regulatory arsenal and broader administrative discretion. Moreover, the tech crackdown has significantly bolstered regulatory agencies by augmenting their enforcement capabilities. The antitrust unit of the State Administration for Market Regulation (SAMR), having been elevated from a bureau to an agency, now commands a more generous budget and an expanded workforce. These newly empowered agencies have become formidable interest groups, pressing for more stringent regulation. As mentioned in Chapter 9, the global trend toward tighter tech regulation reinforces these agencies' arguments for stringent controls on domestic tech behemoths. Nonetheless, the administrative state's advance doesn't end there. Some government departments are making a case for state ownership as the ultimate form of regulatory intervention. Simultaneously, the Chinese government is assuming a more proactive role in directing capital to advance its quest for technological self-sufficiency.

10.2.1. Golden Share and State Investment

The Chinese government's desire to own stakes in its tech firms stems from its concerns about foreign sway over its technology sector. In the past two decades, many Chinese tech firms have resorted to the variable interest entity (VIE) form to raise overseas capital while circumventing existing legal restrictions on foreign investment in the internet sector. Despite flouting the spirit of Chinese investment regulation, this VIE structure has been tolerated for years.[40] This strategic ambiguity has allowed Chinese tech firms to raise funding from global investors, while also allowing early venture capital investors to seek initial public offering (IPO) exits on global stock exchanges.[41] Although foreign investors hold no direct control, they can exert indirect influence. The Didi saga, discussed in Chapter 5, provides a telling example. The CAC requested Didi to defer its IPO filing for a more rigorous and comprehensive cybersecurity review. Still, spurred by pressure from foreign investors, the firm surreptitiously proceeded with its public listing. At the time of its IPO, the major shareholders of Didi were Japan's Softbank and America's Uber, together holding a 33 percent stake.[42] An IPO offered these investors a chance to capitalize on their investments, a desire that only intensified amidst fears that Didi might be next in line for a tech crackdown. As noted in Chapter 4, Didi gained its dominance in the ride-hailing market through two important mergers with Kuaidi and Uber, both of which could be deemed anti-competitive under Chinese merger control rules.

Following this event, rumors circulated that the Chinese government might invest a "golden share" in Didi to gain better control over the ride-hailing behemoth.[43] While state ownership has predominated nearly every industry sector critical to China, the consumer technology field is one of the few areas where such ownership hasn't made a significant impact. Golden share arrangements typically involve the state acquiring a nominal stake in a company, thereby granting it influence over corporate decisions through special voting or managerial rights. This setup provides an insider's access to key decisions and veto power, which would go a long way toward assuaging Chinese policymakers' worries about the overexpansion of these firms and the data security issues. For this reason, there is some optimism among policymakers that golden share arrangements could give the government the information and influence it craves while avoiding the potential costs of regulation.

It is worth noting that the use of the golden share investment as a form of regulatory control is not new. Its origin can be traced back to 2014, when Beijing encouraged such setups with online content providers as part of its mixed-ownership reform.[44] By 2017, the government has unveiled plans to invest in online media companies to tighten content control. This strategy gained further traction during the tech crackdown. Since 2020, the China Internet Investment Fund (CIIF), co-founded by the CAC and the Ministry of Finance in 2017, has bought golden shares in leading tech firms such as Sina Weibo, ByteDance, Alibaba, and Tencent.[45] In the wake of the Didi incident, there's even more momentum within the government to expand its golden share investments to all data-rich tech companies operating critical information infrastructure. In late 2021, it was revealed that the government had purchased a golden share in Full Truck Alliance Co., a Chinese platform which arranges trucking services.[46] Notably, Full Truck Alliance was also subjected to a cybersecurity review in tandem with Didi, as detailed in Chapter 5. There is now speculation that a similar investment in Didi could be part of the firm's restructuring plan.[47]

Of all its investments, the CIIF's stake in ByteDance has attracted the most scrutiny. In April 2021, CIIF, along with two other state-owned entities, secured a 1 percent stake in Beijing ByteDance Technology, ByteDance's primary Chinese subsidiary. The state investors, in return, gained the right to nominate a board member. A CAC official, Wu Shugang, who used to head the CAC's division overseeing online commentary, was appointed to the board. Beijing ByteDance Technology's corporate charters and bylaws tell an intriguing tale of governmental influence. According to its bylaws, Wu will have a veto right over the appointment or dismissal of the editor-in-chief, which is the chief censor over content on ByteDance's media platform.[48] Wu will also have the right to chair a "content safety committee" set up within the firm, or to appoint a chair for it.[49] But Wu's domain isn't confined to content issues. As per the corporate charter of Beijing ByteDance Technology, he can also influence business strategy, investment plans, mergers and acquisitions, profit allocation, and the appointment and remuneration of top executives.

To be fair, Chinese social media platforms do stand to gain from golden share investments. A notable advantage of the golden share investment is that it helps firms in acquiring necessary video licenses for regulatory compliance. Back in 2018, the Chinese authorities publicly denounced 19 online short-video platforms for vulgar and illegal content. Of these platforms, 15 had their apps removed from app stores, including ByteDance's Neihanduanzi, and three had their operation suspended.[50] As these video applications previously operated without proper video licenses, a golden share investment can, to some extent, mollify such regulatory concerns. However, state investment is hardly a panacea against all regulatory troubles. First, the golden share only allows the state investor to veto board-level decisions, leaving day-to-day operations mostly untouched, which are often the primary target of regulatory scrutiny. Issues such as competition with rivals, treatment of employees and gig workers, value distribution among platform participants, and user-data handling are unlikely to be vetted by the board. But all these fall under the regulatory gaze.

Furthermore, China's regulatory landscape is a maze of numerous competing government departments. Ownership by one department might not shield a company from interference by others, particularly if the stake is held by a lower-tier entity. A regulatory body might even target a firm in which it has an ownership stake. The CAC has proven this; despite holding a board seat at Weibo since 2020, it slapped the platform with 44 fines, totaling USD 2 million, between January and November 2021.[51] In December, the same agency summoned Weibo executives to impose another fine and reprimand them for their content-moderation failures, in what was apparently a deliberate attempt to inflict reputational damage. The firm's stock fell by almost 10 percent on the day the new fine was announced.[52] Likewise, the CAC's indirect investment in Full Truck Alliance did not spare the firm from a surprise cybersecurity review last July. The CAC's move sent the company's shares plunging, just a fortnight after its New York IPO.

Alongside golden shares, Chinese state-owned entities are actively making corporate investments in homegrown tech companies. To date, the CIIF has snapped up stakes in over 30 of these entities, including notable names like the video app Kuaishou, podcasting company Ximalaya, and AI start-up SenseTime. In late 2022, Hangzhou Jintao Digital Technology Group, a state-owned enterprise managed by the local Hangzhou government—Ant Group's home base—acquired a 10 percent stake in Ant's consumer credit–offering subsidiary based in Chongqing.[53] This investment, combined with contributions from other shareholders, was instrumental in helping Ant expand its capital, a prerequisite to meet the regulatory demands for its consumer credit operations.

While the Chinese government has an interest in infusing capital into domestic tech firms, it is noteworthy that these firms too display a reciprocal interest toward government investors. First, state investment enables firms to align the bureaucratic interests of the government investor with their own commercial objectives. This convergence of interests essentially constitutes a form of crony capitalism, a concept previously discussed in Chapter 1. In fact, the more assertive the state power, the stronger the motivation for Chinese tech firms to forge alliances with influential state actors. Second, government investors can act as intermediaries in navigating the labyrinthine regulatory landscape, leveraging their influence to advocate for policies or enforcement actions that favor the firm. Partnerships with local governments also simplify the procurement of administrative approvals, licenses, and financing.[54] Remarkably, this trend of state investment in consumer tech businesses dovetails with the broader pattern of corporate investment in China.[55] Renowned economists, including Chong-en Bai, Chang-Tai Hsieh, and Zheng Song, have empirically demonstrated that the Chinese state is increasingly investing in large private owners, who, in turn, channel funds into smaller private enterprises.[56] This expansion of mixed ownership has considerably expanded the network of companies and owners with tacit state support, thereby facilitating their navigation through China's complex business landscape.[57]

Meanwhile, tech firms may also seek the endorsement from government-invested funds or private-equity and venture-capital funds with strong ties to the Chinese government, as elaborated in Chapter 1. Ming Liao, a managing partner from private-equity fund Prospect Avenue Capital, puts it succinctly: "China has an extensive and complex regulatory framework ... many of these businesses have yet to familiarize themselves with the agencies regulating them, and often they look to their private equity or venture capital (PEVC) backers to bolster their competence. That's why it's vital that PEVC investors possess the necessary 'guanxi' or personal relationships with the regulatory agencies."[58]

10.2.2. The Shift from Soft to Hard Tech

Daron Acemoglu, an esteemed economist, contends that the most damaging impacts of Big Tech firms stem from their power to steer technological change. Acemoglu believes these firms are incentivized to fund research that aligns with their business strategies, leading to a concentration of efforts that match their interests.[59] Consequently, the overwhelming influence of Big Tech essentially corners smaller players into tailoring their products and services to be compatible with these dominating platforms, thereby resulting in a lack of diversity in research and development.[60] Acemoglu envisages an optimal situation where government fosters a diverse research portfolio, a strategy that could spur higher growth rates.[61] The Chinese government, to some extent, appears to be taking cues from Acemoglu's road map by encouraging variety in the innovation endeavors of its tech firms.

The recent tech crackdown in China has indeed amplified the state's ability to redirect capital from less substantial "soft tech" toward more sophisticated "hard-tech." Hard tech, or deep tech, encompasses areas heavily reliant on sophisticated scientific knowledge, long-term research and development, and sustained investment. Amid the escalating Sino–US tech rivalry, China has rejuvenated the "whole nation" system (*juguo tizhi*) to spur technological progress and breakthroughs.[62] This strategy mirrors those from the era of the planned economy, when the government played a pivotal role in mobilizing and distributing resources to expedite development in prioritized areas. During his speech at the Twentieth Party Congress's opening ceremony, President Xi Jinping highlighted China's development goals for 2035, placing the development of hard tech atop all economic policies.[63] Local officials, major contributors to government research funding, face considerable pressure to support this national agenda.[64]

Chinese Big Tech companies are also experiencing the push to pivot their commercial strategies toward hard-tech. In December 2020, the People's Daily, a party organ, criticized Chinese tech firms for their excessive competition in community group-buying businesses, urging them instead to aim higher to propel China's technological innovations.[65] Indeed, despite their remarkable growth, leading Chinese tech firms like Alibaba and Tencent have yet to spearhead development in hard tech, which is vital for China's competition with the United States. Instead, these firms have prospered by developing smart apps that simplify connections between consumers and merchants. Even though China has emerged at the forefront of e-commerce and digital payment, the success of its Big Tech still owes much to China's vast consumer market. The investment surge in these sectors has led to intense competition among Chinese consumer tech businesses, causing myriad social problems, as detailed earlier in Part II. From the viewpoint of Chinese policymakers, capital should flow to hard-tech sectors instead of fueling the growth and expanding the corrupting influence of Chinese tech titans.

In response to the policy shift from Beijing, China's behemoth tech firms considerably scaled down their corporate venture capital investment. In 2022, the total investment by the country's seven tech titans—Tencent, Alibaba, ByteDance, JD.com, Meituan, Baidu, and Xiaomi (the "top seven")—amounted to RMB 100 billion, marking a precipitous 80 percent plunge from the previous year. ByteDance even took the drastic step of disbanding its entire strategic investment team to trim "low synergy" investments in 2022.[66] The same year also saw Alibaba trimming its investment team from 110 to a leaner 70.[67] Investment by Alibaba in e-commerce retail, which constituted 22 percent of its investment portfolio in 2021, nosedived to a mere 5 percent in 2022.[68] Similarly, Tencent's investment in gaming ebbed from 23 percent in 2021 to 12 percent in 2022.[69]

Paralleling this divestment trend, China's tech powerhouses are placing their stakes heavily in hard tech. In fact, there had been signs pointing in this direction even before the crackdown. In 2020, Tencent made a pledge to funnel USD 70 billion into new digital infrastructure.[70] Alibaba, for its part, unveiled its inaugural artificial intelligence (AI) chip in 2019.[71] Notably, Alibaba has been a driving force behind China's Digital Silk Road, providing the technological backbone to support the initiative. The tech crackdown added further impetus to this shift toward hard tech. In 2022, the proportion of investment in hard tech by the top seven Chinese tech firms nearly doubled, from 21 percent in 2021 to 42 percent.[72] For instance, high-end manufacturing, which made up a mere 3 percent of Tencent's investment portfolio in 2021, swelled to 15 percent in 2022.[73] Similarly, Baidu's investment in the same sector surged from 13 percent in 2021 to nearly 60 percent in 2022.[74] Alibaba, for its part, leaned into AI hardware, which grew from 9 percent of its portfolio in 2021 to nearly 20 percent in 2022.[75] In 2021, Alibaba also earmarked USD 1 billion to nurture 100,000 developers and tech start-ups over the following three years,[76] and committed another USD 28 billion to bolster its cloud-computing division to invest in technologies related to operating systems, servers, chips, and networks.[77] Meituan also raised a record USD 10 billion to develop autonomous delivery vehicles and robotics in 2021.[78]

Beyond direct investments, China's leading tech firms are increasingly making passive investments in the hard-tech sector as limited partners in venture capital firms. A limited partner, often a passive investor, entrusts the capital management to the fund's general partner. Since none of these Big Tech firms specializes in hard-tech companies, it seems strategically prudent for them to delegate investment decisions to venture capital funds well-versed in the field. In 2022, Tencent poured money into SourceCode Capital, while Alibaba and Meituan joined forces to invest in Walden International. Meituan also invested in Hua Capital.[79] These three funds all have a proven track record in investing in cutting-edge hardcore technologies.

The ramifications of the tech crackdown are reverberating not only among leading tech firms, but throughout the venture capital sector. As regulatory uncertainties heightened, the consumer internet sector has become less enticing for global investors. Some industries, such as education technology, have been decimated due to abrupt policy shifts. As a result, global capital has scarcely flowed into consumer internet firms since the government halted Ant's IPO.[80] Many investors are now pivoting toward hard tech, which aligns better with state interests and is thus less susceptible to regulatory turbulence.[81] In 2021, Chinese technology start-ups attracted a record volume of venture funding (USD 130.6 billion), about 50 percent up from the previous year.[82] This investment primarily fueled projects linked to hardcore technologies, such as semiconductors, pharmaceutical and biotechnology, automobile, new energy, and new materials.[83] Neil Shen, Sequoia China Capital's founding and managing partner, revealed that over 80 percent of their recent investments were funneled into high-tech areas, including AI and high-end manufacturing.[84]

Government guidance funds—public-private investment entities which aim for financial returns while advancing state industrial policies—have also felt the impact.[85] During President Xi's tenure, these funds have seen a significant boom, becoming some of the most active investors in hard tech.[86] By early 2023, the Chinese government had established funds worth over RMB 2 trillion since 2015.[87] There are three principal types of state investors in these funds: the national government, local government, and state-owned enterprises. Prominent actors include state-invested funds set up by regions like Shenzhen, Jiangsu, Xi'an, and He'fe.[88] Similar to other venture capital funds, government guidance funds used to channel money into the consumer tech sector, but their investments in this area have virtually dried up since the crackdown.[89] Instead, these funds have focused on strengthening their foothold in the hard-tech sector.

Since early 2023, various municipal governments, including Beijing, Shenzhen, Hangzhou, Guangzhou, Anhui, and Xi'an, have announced plans to set up guidance funds to invest in high-tech industries to help boost China's economic recovery.[90] For instance, Guangzhou, the capital city of Guangdong province, announced that it would invest RMB 200 billions to establish funds promoting semiconductors, renewable energy, and advanced manufacturing.[91] In the area of semiconductors, local governments such as Shanghai, Shenzhen, Zhejiang, Anhui, and Jiangsu have all rolled out a range of new measures and subsidy schemes to support the industry.[92] Meanwhile, municipal cities such as Beijing, Shanghai, Guangdong, Sichuan, Hubei, Jiangsu, and Fujian have set aside guidance funds of more than RMB 30 billion to support the semiconductor industry.[93] By 2022, state-backed funds had either invested in or controlled 48 of the 50 semiconductor unicorns.[94]

Although the US sanctions and export restrictions have triggered a "Sputnik moment" in China, China's "whole nation" approach has run into significant challenges. The heavy price paid by China for relying on state allocation of resources during the planned economy era is a painful lesson, and today the specter of a repeat looms large. The sudden flood of funding into hard tech could inflate start-up valuations, potentially creating a sector-wide bubble. Investing in hard tech typically requires extensive experience and deep technical expertise. Local government initiatives, therefore, risk being undermined by a lack of requisite skills and misguided strategies. This is particularly true for hard-tech sectors such as semiconductors, which require substantial long-term investment. The challenges of assessing long-term returns contribute to a severe information asymmetry between investors (often local governments) and firm executives. The catalog of scandals in the semiconductor sector provides a cautionary tale.

In 2014, the China National Integrated Circuit Industry Investment Fund (commonly known as the Big Fund) was established to reduce the country's dependence on foreign semiconductors. This fund pulled together capital from a plethora of state investors, including the Ministry of Finance, China Tobacco, China Mobile, and the China Development Bank.[95] Yet, in a startling turn of events, several key executives from the Big Fund were under scrutiny for corruption charges in 2022.[96] Other government-backed semiconductor projects experienced similar misfortunes. Tacoma

Semiconductor Technology, which launched a USD 3 billion government-backed semiconductor project, declared bankruptcy in 2020.[97] A USD 100 million plant, a collaboration between US chip foundry GlobalFoundries and the Chengdu government, ceased operations in 2021.[98] That same year, the Wuhan government squandered millions on Hongxin Semiconductor Manufacturing Corporation, which was disbanded in 2021 without producing a single chip.[99] Tsinghua Unigroup, which had been the recipient of generous funding from the Beijing government for years for semiconductor development, also collapsed.[100] Its top executive, Zhao Weiguo, was criminally indicted for taking bribes and securing unlawful gains for his friends and relatives.[101] Notably, despite generous financial backing from the Chinese government, the semiconductor industry's advancement has been disappointingly slow. While China has made some limited progress, the country still lags far behind its Western peers in most segments of semiconductor industry.[102]

10.3. Summary

In the aftermath of the tech crackdown, a significant power shift has unfolded in China: the private sector has begun a tactical retreat, while the administrative state advances with newfound vigor. Since the advent of this regulatory storm in late 2020, tech behemoths have opted for strategic recalibration, divesting stakes, reorganizing corporate structures, and adopting proactive compliance measures. In the meantime, this crackdown has sent shockwaves through investor circles, significantly dampening investor confidence and curbing inflow of capital into the consumer tech sector. The heightened cost of regulatory compliance disproportionately burdens smaller firms, which inadvertently gives larger tech firms a competitive edge. Consequently, the tech crackdown has done little to alter the competitive landscape of China's internet sector, with no newcomers having yet challenged the dominance of the incumbent giants.

In the midst of these developments, the state has embarked on an aggressive campaign of intensifying regulatory scrutiny and securing footholds through strategic stake acquisitions. The "golden share" scheme, which endows the state with enhanced control over content and critical corporate decisions, has gained considerable momentum amid the crackdown. While its deployment has been limited primarily to social media platforms, its potential reach to all data-rich firms looms large on the horizon. Furthermore, given the heightened regulatory costs and uncertainties plaguing the consumer tech sector, the state has gained more leverage in steering investment flows within the tech sphere. The result is a perceptible shift in venture capital investment, with both private and state investors increasingly pivoting to "hard tech."

My findings thus far are primarily based on observations made over the past year. I acknowledge the limitations in my findings since given the confounding variables I have yet to isolate and examine them comprehensively. Furthermore, the long-term effects of this enforcement initiative—its effectiveness in fostering common prosperity and technological self-sufficiency, as well as its unintended consequences—all merit careful investigation and analysis in the future. That said, China's approach to regulating its tech giants provides a salient lesson for other countries aiming to control Big Tech. While many progressive scholars and policymakers in the United States express frustration at the slow legislative progress in curbing Big Tech's influence, China illustrates an extreme scenario in which government intervention is swift and forceful. However, without strong institutional oversight, intense law-enforcement campaigns create the risk of over-enforcement and administrative abuse. Given the high stakes involved, Chinese tech firms will likely exert greater efforts in lobbying agencies in the future, giving rise to concerns about regulatory capture. China's experience with platform regulation could therefore offer some lessons that should inform the global policy debate about how to effectively rein in Big Tech.

11

Regulating Generative AI

In the previous chapter, we discussed how the tech crackdown has afforded the Chinese government more leverage to steer investment flows within the tech sector, resulting in a nationwide pivot from soft tech to hard tech. In the wake of this transformation, an imperative question surfaces regarding the future of tech regulation in China: How will the country regulate its burgeoning and rapidly evolving hard-tech sector, which is poised to assume a more prominent societal role? China's recent endeavor to regulate the rapidly expanding domain of generative artificial intelligence (AI) offers an intriguing case study that sheds light on the future of the country's hard-tech governance.

Generative AI, an innovative and disruptive force that is reshaping the global technological terrain, is giving rise to a multitude of intricate legal dilemmas spanning across diverse fields. Traditional intellectual property laws, grounded in the concept of human authorship, are now put to the test with AI emerging as a potential creator—provoking uncertainties about the ownership of generated content.[1] Privacy and data-protection concerns further exacerbate these complexities, chiefly owing to AI's need to process vast amounts of data, often without obtaining proper consent.[2] Additionally, the content moderation of AI-generated material presents daunting challenges for regulators due to its sheer scale and nuanced complexity.[3] Liability under tort law is another unresolved issue, with responsibility for damages caused by autonomous AI systems blurring regulatory lines.[4] Ethical issues can also emerge when AI systems, even inadvertently, perpetuate or amplify societal biases, potentially leading to discrimination against specific individuals.[5]

In April 2023, the Cyberspace Administration of China (CAC) unveiled draft measures on generative AI, signaling its intent to enforce

High Wire. Angela Huyue Zhang, Oxford University Press. © Oxford University Press 2024.
DOI: 10.1093/oso/9780197682258.003.0012

strict regulations that may disrupt the game for major AI players like Baidu, Alibaba Group Holding, and ByteDance.[6] According to the measures put forth by the CAC, tech companies will be obligated to ensure that AI-generated content upholds the political values of the Chinese Communist Party (CCP). Additionally, they must implement measures to prevent discrimination, respect intellectual property rights, and safeguard user data privacy. Tech firms must also bear legal responsibility for both the training data and content generated by their platforms. The measures further demand AI-generated content to be truthful and accurate, an almost Herculean task considering the technology's propensity for pattern recognition over truth verification. Importantly, the CAC further mandates that providers of generative AI services must submit security assessment reports and obtain approval before making these services publicly available.

Industry observers are fretting over Beijing's hands-on approach to AI regulation and how it might saddle Chinese tech firms with burdens heavier than those borne by their Silicon Valley counterparts. Paul Triolo, a prominent industry expert, believes that stringent regulation may leave Chinese firms lagging behind their American counterparts.[7] He cautions that the strict requirement of aligning AI with the CCP's values could distract them from the crucial task of building working and robust large language models (LLMs) and the applications they power.[8] Helen Toner and Jeffery Ding from Georgetown share a similar concern, warning that CAC's demanding criteria for training data could pose formidable challenges for Chinese firms, especially given the existing data scarcity limiting the advancement of cutting-edge generative AI models.[9]

On July 13, 2023, China unveiled the highly anticipated interim measures on the management of generative AI, which took effect the following month.[10] Unlike the earlier draft released solely by the CAC, the final law was a joint effort by the CAC and six other government departments: the National Development and Reform Commission (NDRC), the Ministry of Education, the Ministry of Science and Technology (MOST), the Ministry of Industry and Information Technology (MIIT), the Ministry of Public Security, and the National Radio and Television Administration. Although the CAC spearheaded the legislative process, the collaboration with these six departments seems to have had a significant impact on the legislative outcome.

Indeed, the final law substantially narrowed its scope and watered down many of the stringent requirements found in the earlier draft. For example, the law specifies that it applies only to "public-facing" AI services, thereby excluding a vast number of generative AI services designed for use by enterprises, public organizations, and universities. Instead of insisting that AI-generated content must be truthful and accurate, the final measures require service providers to enhance the transparency of generative AI services and improve their accuracy and reliability. Likewise, the law eliminates the demanding deadline for service providers to fine-tune their foundation models within three months in case illegal content is generated. The initial imposition of a three-month deadline would have placed immense burdens on providers given the exorbitant costs of training a foundation model.

Additionally, the law introduces several friendly provisions that promote the innovation and development of generative AI services, while instructing the regulators to take a tolerant and cautious approach when regulating these services. Compared with the earlier draft, the final measures clearly strike a more encouraging and supportive tone toward the advancement of the generative AI technologies. What explains China's shift from a strict approach in the initial draft to a more lenient stance in the interim measures?

11.1. Applying the Dynamic Pyramid Model

To address this, we shall utilize the dynamic pyramid model to analyze the incentive structure of each of the key players involved in the regulatory system. As outlined in Chapter 1, hierarchy is the first and foremost feature of Chinese regulation. Typically, the policymaking process involves interactions between actors from four tiers of Chinese society. China's regulation of generative AI is no exception.

11.1.1. Top Leaders

At the apex of the pyramid are the top leaders, who view AI development as a high-priority agenda item. In 2017, China's State Council unveiled an ambitious AI development blueprint, which outlined the goal of attaining global AI supremacy by 2030.[11] Alongside the 2015 "Made in China 2025" initiative, these policy documents encapsulate the essence of China's

AI ambition, garnering extensive attention from the country's top brass.[12] Since then, AI has been a linchpin of China's governance, seamlessly integrating with the state's surveillance and control apparatus.[13] With its large domestic market, vast data resources, and unwavering national determination, China holds a distinctive edge in AI development. Kai-fu Lee, the former head of Google China, believes that the Chinese government can outperform Western countries in AI applications because its economy is so connected in all aspects.[14] PWC, an accounting and consulting firm, estimated that China will benefit the most from AI, with the technology expected to contribute to a 26 percent increase in its GDP by 2030.[15]

Indeed, nurturing AI isn't merely an economic catalyst for China—it's a matter of national esteem and global rivalry. As underscored by Graham Allison and Eric Schmidt, China's emergence as a full-scale rival to the United States in both commercial and national-security AI applications merits keen international scrutiny.[16] In fact, there is a mounting concern within the United States that China's technological ambitions, especially in the use of AI for military and scientific advancements, could tilt the geopolitical balance.[17]

Thus far, China has gained a competitive advantage in specific subdomains of AI, such as facial recognition, voice recognition, and AI-enhanced drones.[18] But the country continues to lag behind the United States in other critical areas of AI capability, including scientific and technological inputs and outputs, different layers of the AI value chain, and different subdomains of AI. The race to close the gap heightened when OpenAI, a US-based firm, began leading the way with innovative generative AI services. While Chinese LLMs are making progress, they still lean heavily on American research and technology.[19] Thus, despite the hype surrounding Chinese models built by Chinese labs, many AI researchers believe that China is trailing behind the United States by two to three years.[20] Moreover, the inability of Chinese AI firms to access high-end AI chips poses a significant risk for Chinese AI development. In October 2022, the US government imposed sweeping restrictions on exports of advanced chips and chip-making tools to China, allegedly out of concerns over national security.[21] The Biden Administration further tightened these export curbs in October 2023, further limiting Chinese AI firms' access to these critical technologies.[22]

Against this background of the Sino-US tech rivalry, it is no surprise that Chinese top leadership has viewed AI as critical to maintaining the country's ascendency. As President Xi Jinping repeatedly highlighted in his speeches, China needs to seize AI opportunities to modernize its industrial system.[23] While risk control was also mentioned during a meeting of the Politburo of the Chinese Communist Party in April 2023, the priority is now decidedly on development rather than regulation.

11.1.2. Industry Stakeholders

Then we turn our focus toward the industry stakeholders who are subject to regulation. Leading tech firms such as Alibaba, Tencent, Baidu, and ByteDance have been major investors in generative AI. The Chinese government, keenly aware of the need to fuel AI progress, has embraced a market-centric strategy.[24] Thus far, a significant share of China's AI advancements has emerged from synergistic collaborations between private firms and academic researchers.[25] Meanwhile, the Chinese government has shown no reticence in nurturing its homegrown titans. In a striking move made in 2018, five private tech companies—Baidu, Alibaba, Tencent, iFlytek, and SenseTime—were officially hailed as China's "AI champions."[26] These firms are far from passive actors in this rapidly evolving landscape. Over time, they have built robust relationships with the government and have formed strategic alliances with leading Chinese universities. These resources can be, and have been, mobilized to advocate for policy changes, as expounded in Chapter 2. Contrasting with the past crackdown on consumer internet businesses, Chinese tech firms now stand on firmer ground in their advocacy endeavors. Their present foray into AI development dovetails precisely with the nation's strategic priorities, significantly strengthening their position.

The explosion of generative AI technology has not just captured the attention of established Big Tech firms but also ignited a fervent scramble among Chinese entrepreneurs eager to leverage this trend.[27] Some of the most prominent names in China's tech industries have joined the AI race, including: Wang Changchu, the former director of ByteDance's AI Lab; Zhou Bowen, ex-president of JD.com's AI and cloud computing division; Meituan's co-founder Wang Huiwen and current boss Wang Xing; and venture capitalist Kai-fu Lee.[28] In addition to these influential figures, venture capital investors in China are also chasing the AI concept, with the belief that AI will shape the technological landscape much like how the internet and smartphone created the global titans. According to Zhang Yaqing, ex-president of Baidu, roughly 50 firms across China are working on LLMs.[29] The potent combination of top talent, robust investment, and strong belief in AI's future signals a shift in China's tech landscape, demonstrating the ambition of Chinese firms to pioneer the next frontier in technology.

However, tech firms aren't the only stakeholders here. A number of central ministries, including the MOST, MIIT, and NDRC, are also fervently propelling AI development forward, each driven by its unique missions and objectives.[30] The MOST is primarily charged with outlining the innovation strategy and facilitating the implementation of pertinent research projects.[31] The MIIT, on the other hand, acts as the nation's central industrial planner, with a specific mandate to foster major tech innovation within the internet sector.[32] The NDRC, often likened to a smaller version of the State Council, also plays a role in advancing innovation-centric developmental strategies.[33] Amid escalating US sanctions, Beijing has responded by instituting the Central Commission for Science and Technology in a sweeping government reshuffle earlier this year. This new body allows senior party leaders to directly supervise key research areas, such as semiconductors, new energy, new materials, and AI. The establishment of this central commission underscores Beijing's resolute commitment to achieving technological self-reliance in the face of global tech challenges.

Local governments are also important stakeholders here. While it is the central government that formulates the strategic plan, it is the local governments who bear the primary onus of executing such strategies. Following the release of the 2017 AI development strategy by the State Council, nearly half of China's provincial governments have crafted AI plans tailored to guide and amplify the private sector's efforts in tech advancement.[34] Many of these local governments have also funded AI technologies through state-led investment vehicles, or by employing incentives such as subsidies to attract talent and businesses. For instance, Tianjin, a northeastern port city close to Beijing, has laid out a plan for RMB 100 billion; Hangzhou and Shenzhen have co-founded generative AI research labs in concert with universities, tech firms, and national ministries. These laboratories amalgamate resources, talent, and financial backing from government, industry, and academia. This differs markedly from conventional research financing, typically reliant on research grants from institutions like the National Natural Science Foundation of China.[35]

Take, for instance, the Beijing Academy of Artificial Intelligence, which birthed China's first large-scale pre-trained language model. The academy has joint sponsorship from the MIIT, the Beijing Communist Party Committee, and the Beijing government. It brings together top scholars from Tsinghua University, Peking University, and the Chinese Academy of Sciences, with industry experts from firms such as Baidu, Xiaomi, and ByteDance.[36] Similarly, the Zhejiang government has established the Zhejiang Lab with Zhejiang University and the Alibaba Group. This close collaboration between the industry and the university enables researchers of fundamental AI to apply it to industry applications.[37] Considering the substantial financial resources and computing power required to develop foundational models for generative AI, experts predict that the Chinese government could play an even more prominent role in the future.[38] For this reason, it's crucial to perceive the Chinese government not just as a regulator, but also as an advocate, benefactor, and investor in AI. Therefore, those government entities propelling AI development could potentially emerge as a potent counterweight against stringent AI regulation in China.

11.1.3. The Public

Our next focus is the public, which is situated at the lowest level of the regulatory hierarchy. Thus far, the Chinese public has expressed a largely optimistic outlook toward AI, as shown by a 2021 survey conducted across 28 countries with 19,504 online adults. This poll placed China at the zenith of techno-optimism: an impressive 78% of the population believes the benefits of AI outweigh its risks.[39] However, lurking beneath this gleaming optimism is a darker, less-publicized truth. As highlighted in Chapter 5, an extensive and clandestine market thrives on the illicit trade and misuse of personal data in China. This exploitation of private information has laid a fertile ground for a burgeoning AI fraud industry, raising significant concerns about data privacy and security.

In May 2023, a man was detained by Chinese police for allegedly using ChatGPT to generate and disseminate false news online.[40] The man reportedly produced a fake news article claiming that nine people were killed in a local train accident in April 2023. The preceding month, a chilling instance of AI-fueled deceit led to a corporate executive being defrauded out of RMB 4.3 million.[41] The criminals utilized AI to impersonate an acquaintance in a video call, exploiting the executive's trust to perpetrate the fraud. That same month, a similar case arose in Anhui, in eastern China.[42] These alarming events sent shockwaves rippling across the nation, sparking a nationwide uproar and the emergence of a trending hashtag, #AIFraudIsEruptingAcrossChina, on Weibo, China's Twitter-equivalent. Yet, the hashtag soon vanished, an indication that Chinese censors were possibly curtailing public discussion on the matter. These two incidents starkly illustrate the potential threats posed by generative AI technology to personal and proprietary security. They reveal the murky side of AI's potential when placed in the wrong hands. However, as we discussed in Chapter 1, the expression of public dissatisfaction is often suppressed by China's stringent censorship and control of information, creating an environment where such issues may not receive the widespread attention and action that they require.

11.1.4. Regulators

Last but not least, we shift our focus to the agencies charged with enforcing AI regulation. The CAC, China's formidable internet watchdog, stands at the epicenter of the policy shift on AI. As mentioned in Chapter 5, the CAC is no ordinary agency. Founded in 2014, with internet censorship and information control as core objectives, the CAC has since stretched its tentacles into many areas of internet governance.[43] The agency derived its authority from the general office of the Central Cybersecurity and Information Commission, a central task force of the CCP.[44] This ambitious agency, driven to propose stringent laws to widen its policy purview, nonetheless faces formidable constraints. One is capacity. In comparison to other well-established ministries such as the MIIT and the NDRC, the CAC wrestles with a scarcity of capacity and resources. Furthermore, generative AI poses novel challenges to regulators globally, as traditional content moderation tools fall short in managing misinformation and fake news. The CAC also faces severe legal constraints, possessing limited legislative power and lacking authority to impose hefty fines under its proposed measures on generative AI.

As elucidated in my first book, *Chinese Antitrust Exceptionalism*, there exists strong path dependence in Chinese law enforcement.[45] Understanding the mission and objectives of an administrative authority is critical to grasping the resulting regulatory outcomes.[46] In the case of the CAC, its principal mandate centers around internet security and content control. Consequently, the CAC is heavily invested in ensuring that AI-generated content does not disrupt political or social stability. Given its capacity constraints, the agency will need to prioritize its limited resources on information and content control, rather than dispersing resources across the broad range of legal areas contained in its measures on generative AI. Should the CAC attempt to expand its regulatory purview into other legal domains beyond content moderation, it would inevitably encroach on the jurisdictions of other agencies, thereby complicating enforcement.

A closer examination of the CAC's measures also reveals its enforcement priority on content. First, the law is applicable only when the products or services of generative AI are provided to the public within China.[47] If these products or services are exclusively used internally within a company or supplied to individual enterprises, the law does not apply. This implies that the CAC's regulatory interest does not lie in the product or services per se, but more in mitigating their potential societal impact. Second, the CAC employs a strong arsenal of content-regulation tools to manage generative AI. It requires firms to undertake a security assessment of their generative AI products in line with the Provisions on the Security Assessment of Internet Information Services with Public Opinion Properties or Social Mobilization Capacity.[48] Enacted in 2018, these provisions represent a significant stride in the CAC's long-standing efforts to quell any destabilization of public opinion or mobilization via online services. Indeed, the security-assessment process functions much like an approval and licensing procedure. Only firms whose filings meet the CAC's standards will be granted permission to provide their service to the Chinese public.

A review of the CAC's past enforcement practices concerning existing AI regulations further shed light on its future enforcement tactics. In December 2021, the CAC, along with three other departments, introduced the regulation on recommendation algorithms, which took effect on March 1, 2022.[49] About a year later, in conjunction with two other agencies, the CAC launched the regulation on deepfakes, which was implemented from January 10, 2023.[50] Though both sets of regulations impose an array of obligations on AI service providers, they primarily underscore the CAC's comprehensive efforts to manage the content-control challenges posed by emerging technologies.[51] So far, enforcement has predominantly relied on algorithm filing, a process requiring the submission of detailed reports on algorithm products via the CAC's internet information service algorithm filing system. This procedure effectively functions as a form of coerced self-regulation, obliging firms to provide comprehensive disclosures about their algorithms' regulatory compliance.[52] Notably, so far, the CAC has not initiated a single case against tech firms for violations of these two measures.

The current interim measures on generative AI services have also imposed a similar filing requirement, which requires firms to disclose details about their AI products in accordance with the regulation on algorithmic recommendation. This requirement, together with the requirement for security assessment, may inadvertently exclude foreign competition from the Chinese market. Indeed, foreign AI companies might be reluctant to divulge the intricate details of their AI systems to Chinese regulators. Moreover, it could deter Chinese companies from utilizing open-source foundation models to provide generative AI services to the public, as the upstream foreign AI developers may not cooperate in providing the required details for the CAC's filing process. Consequently, Chinese firms aiming to offer services to the public may have to develop their own foundation models or pivot toward providing bespoke services to private companies, thereby sidestepping the CAC's measures. This dynamic could significantly influence the Chinese domestic AI landscape, affecting both domestic and foreign participants.

11.2. Is China Exceptional?

As elucidated by the preceding analysis, it becomes evident that the Chinese government is attempting to strike a delicate balance in regulating generative AI. On the one hand, the government has a strong interest to foster its development by offering generous financial and policy support. On the other hand, the government sees an urgent need to control its potential societal impact, hence regulators will focus their efforts on content moderation to forestall any possible disruption to stability. This approach fundamentally diverges from those observed in the European Union and the United States. As astutely noted by Anu Bradford, distinct regulatory paradigms are emerging in the European Union, the United States, and China, each deeply entrenched in the distinct values and motivations intrinsic to these regions.[53] Echoing the regulatory dynamics highlighted in Chapter 9, EU law strongly emphasizes the protection of users and citizens' rights in its regulations. In contrast, the United States perceives AI as a key driver for economic growth and a tool to cement US tech and military supremacy. Meanwhile, China adopts a state-centric approach, viewing AI regulation as a vehicle to maintain political and social control.[54]

Let's first start with the European Union. EU AI regulation is intricate and multilayered, building upon a number of existing pieces of legislation, including the General Data Protection Regulation (GDPR), as well as two newly enacted pieces of legislation targeted at Big Tech, namely the Digital Services Act and Digital Markets Act, as mentioned in Chapter 9. Currently, the European Union is deliberating the Artificial Intelligence Act (AI Act), a groundbreaking piece of legislation designed to mitigate the risks associated with AI while safeguarding the fundamental rights of EU citizens. The proposed AI Act categorizes AI usage by risk levels—unacceptable, high, limited, and minimal or no risk—with a focus on applications that pose the most significant potential harm to humans. The Act plans to ban outright AI systems that present an "unacceptable risk," while imposing strict regulatory requirements on "high-risk" AI systems. Conversely, "low-risk" AI systems would be subject to minimal transparency obligations.

Recognizing the swift advancements in generative AI technology, the version of the AI Act endorsed by the European Parliament in June 2023 introduces extensive obligations for providers of foundation models— LLMs that serve as the base for generative AI services. Among other things, it requires the developers of such models to ensure "adequate performance, corrigibility, safety, and cybersecurity" by design throughout the model's development.[55] Additionally, it necessitates the registration of these AI models in an EU database. However, these requirements have faced scrutiny from industry experts who argue that they could impose onerous burdens on AI providers.[56] The European Parliament's version of the AI Act also imposes a variety of transparency obligations on providers of generative AI. These include disclosing when content is AI-generated, designing the model to prevent the generation of illegal content, and publishing summaries of copyrighted data used for training.[57] This version of the AI Act drew criticism from over 150 executives within the European Union, who signed an open letter contending that the Act's current state could potentially stifle the opportunities available to AI technology providers in Europe.[58]

In late 2023, the AI Act proceeded into intensive negotiation between the European Parliament, the European Commission, and the Council of the European Union. On December 9, 2023, the Parliament and the Council reached a provisional agreement on the AI Act.[59] Specifically, all general purpose AI model providers will need to adhere to transparency requirements as initially proposed by the Parliament. High-impact models that pose systematic risks will be subject to more stringent requirements, including model evaluations, risk assessment, adversarial testing, and reporting. Non-compliance with these rules could lead to a fine of up to 7 percent of worldwide turnover or 35 million EUR—whichever is higher.

Similar to the European Union, the United States also advocates a risk-based approach to AI regulation. However, its risk-management approach is noticeably more laissez-faire and lenient. The regulatory authority in the United States is broadly distributed across federal agencies, with many adapting to the AI landscape without the creation of new legal entities.[60] In July 2023, the Federal Trade Commission (FTC) launched an investigation of OpenAI for potential violations of consumer protection laws, requesting a large amount of information on how the company manages risks associated with its AI models. This move represents the most significant regulatory challenge that OpenAI has confronted in the United States. However, given the prevailing sentiment among US policymakers that comprehensive AI legislation could stifle innovation and jeopardize America's technological dominance, it seems improbable that any substantial regulation will be introduced in the near future.[61] Simultaneously, the United States has been investing in non-regulatory infrastructure, such as an AI risk-management framework, evaluations of facial recognition software, and considerable funding for AI research.[62] In 2022, the Biden administration issued the "Blueprint for an AI Bill of Rights," detailing potential AI threats to economic and civil rights, and laying out five non-binding principles for mitigating these risks.[63] In October 2023, the Biden Administration issued a sweeping executive order aimed at improving the safety and trustworthiness of AI (EO).[64] Although the EO covers a broad spectrum of issues, it has mostly directed federal agencies to develop policies and take actions. The major obligations imposed on private businesses are that developers of powerful AI models must disclose their safety tests and cloud service providers must report foreign customers using large AI models that could be used in malicious cyber activities. Recently, several US states, including

California, Connecticut, and Vermont, have introduced legislation aimed at mitigating algorithmic harms.[65] While these initiatives could enhance AI protections, they could also trigger future preemption issues that mirror the ongoing challenges to passing federal privacy legislation.[66]

The respective regulatory approaches of the United States, the European Union, and China underscore the distinct dynamics previously discussed in Chapter 9. The European Union maintains the most stringent approach with its AI Act, which is expected to apply to all AI service providers, covers various stages of AI development, and carries potentially high penalties for noncompliance. In contrast, Chinese measures apply only when services are offered to the public, and the enforcement focus is primarily on content regulation. The US regulatory approach is the most lenient of the three, with no substantive AI standards imposed and minimal obligations on service providers. At present, the United States and China are locked in a neck-and-neck race in the development of AI technology. The cautious stance of the United States on AI regulation is likely to have spillover effects on China, dissuading the latter from espousing an aggressive regulatory stance so as not to compromise its competitive edge in AI development.

11.3. Future Trend

In essence, AI regulation in China is a complex interplay between the top leaders, the regulatory bodies, industry stakeholders, and the larger public, each constituting a pivotal element in the evolving landscape of AI development and its subsequent regulation. Given the current dynamics, it is no surprise that CAC's proposed measures have been softened to accommodate the growth of China's AI industry. That said, regulation will likely remain broad and vague, granting agencies considerable discretion. This strategic ambiguity could create ample room for Chinese tech companies to not just survive, but also flourish in the AI market. In fact, a complete absence of regulation may not necessarily align with the best interests of large Chinese AI developers. As George Stigler astutely observed over 50 years ago, businesses can strategically manipulate regulation to establish hurdles against potential competitors.[67] Therefore, even if Chinese AI regulation increases compliance costs for incumbent players, it may still work in their favor by disadvantaging rivals and solidifying their dominance. Thus, although the current regulation may impose certain compliance costs, they are unlikely to hinder China's AI progression.

At the same time, it's crucial to recognize another key feature of the dynamic pyramid model of regulation—volatility. A growing chorus of voices in the AI community have warned that the technology could pose an existential threat akin to pandemics or nuclear warfare, leading to calls for tighter regulation.[68] Some highlight the potential dangers of AI missteps leading to catastrophic incidents, from biohazards to infrastructure hacking.[69] While the specifics are often left to the imagination, the call for stringent regulation in the United States is becoming louder.[70] In contrast, such information tends to be muffled in Chinese society. As elucidated in Chapter 2, the inefficient transmission of information within the Chinese regulatory hierarchy often results in substantial delays in regulatory responses. Consequently, regulatory issues often lie dormant for extended periods until a crisis strikes, causing severe loss of life or property. At that juncture, Chinese policymakers typically respond rapidly, adopting a tougher stance to mitigate AI-related threats. Such abrupt regulatory oscillations are likely to result in a fragile regulatory outcome, generating strong negative side effects, such as undermining investor confidence and stifling entrepreneurial spirit. In turn, these can hamper the growth trajectory of China's AI sector.

11.4. Summary

Looking ahead, China is poised to dedicate a substantial portion of resources to boost hard-tech development, potentially adopting a hands-off regulatory approach to expedite this growth. China's efforts to regulate generative AI technology provide an intriguing case study for understanding the trajectory of its hard-tech regulatory trends. Having invested heavily in the AI industry, the Chinese government is unlikely to take a harsh stance that could hinder its progress. Instead, the focus of regulation is likely to be primarily on controlling information and content to mitigate threats to social and political stability. Thus, although the interim measures on generative AI appear extensive in scope, they actually afford Chinese tech firms considerable leeway to expand and flourish within the industry. In this regard, China's approach significantly diverges from the evolving regulatory stances of the United States and the European Union. While the

United States has largely abstained from implementing substantial measures to regulate generative AI, the European Union is vigorously regulating AI by leveraging a complex array of existing legal instruments and introducing the new AI Act.

Yet, the malleability of Chinese law may inadvertently sow the seeds of a future regulatory crisis, necessitating swift and drastic interventions, thereby exemplifying the volatility feature of the dynamic pyramid model of regulation. This sudden pendulum swing between lenient and overreaching regulations may precipitate potent side effects that subvert the original intent of law enforcement, reflecting the inherent fragility of China's regulatory model. In the absence of a robust rule-of-law system, the high volatility in Chinese regulation threatens the long-term evolution of China's legal norms and institutions. As such, China teeters on the precipice of a vicious cycle of regulatory interventions, with each intervention sowing the seed for the next.

Notes

INTRODUCTION

1. J. Clement, *Market Capitalization of the Largest Internet Companies Worldwide as of June 2022*, STATISTA.COM (Jul. 27, 2022), https://www.statista.com/statistics/277483/market-value-of-the-largest-internet-companies-worldwide/.

2. Lulu Yilun Chen & Matthew Burgess, *Tencent Just Overtook Facebook in Market Value: Chart*, BLOOMBERG (Nov. 21, 2017), https://www.bloomberg.com/news/articles/2017-11-21/tencent-overtakes-facebook-and-joins-global-top-five-chart.

3. Suzhou Gaoxinqu • 2020 Hurun Quanqiu Dujiaoshou Bang (苏州高新区•2020胡润全球独角兽榜) [Suzhou New District · Hurun Global Unicorn Index 2020], HURUN.NET (Aug. 4, 2020), https://www.hurun.net/zh-CN/Info/Detail?num=EH5O51YAJB9K.

4. Shidong Zhang, *China Tech Crackdown: After a Trillion-Dollar Rout, Has the Stock Market Drubbing Gone Too Far?*, SOUTH CHINA MORNING POST (Dec. 25, 2021), https://www.scmp.com/business/markets/article/3160993/china-tech-crackdown-after-trillion-dollar-rout-has-stock-market. *The Growing Demand for More Vigorous Antitrust Action*, THE ECONOMIST (Jan. 10, 2022), https://www.economist.com/special-report/2022/01/10/the-growing-demand-for-more-vigorous-antitrust-action; Quentin Webb & Dave Sebastian, *How Chinese Shares Went Haywire: "The Market Is Completely Unstable,"* WALL ST. J. (Mar. 19, 2022), https://www.wsj.com/articles/how-chinese-shares-went-haywire-the-market-is-completely-unstable-11647682202.

5. Venus Feng et al., *Billionaire Donations Soar in China Push for Common Prosperity*, BLOOMBERG (Aug. 26, 2021), https://www.bloomberg.com/news/articles/2021-08-26/billionaire-donations-soar-in-china-push-for-common-prosperity.

6. Barry Naughton & Jude Blanchette, *The Party Politics Driving Xi Jinping*, WIRE CHINA (Oct. 3, 2021), https://www.thewirechina.com/2021/10/03/the-party-politics-driving-xi-jinping/; Barry Naughton, *What's behind China's Regulatory Storm*, WALL ST. J. (Dec. 12, 2021), https://www.wsj.com/articles/what-is-behind-china-regulatory-storm-11638372662; George Magnus, *China's Journey into the Unknown*, PROJECT SYNDICATE (Oct. 22, 2021), https://www.project-syndicate.org/onpoint/xi-china-crackdown-flaws-in-governance-model-by-george-magnus-2021-10.

NOTES

7. Lingling Wei, *Xi Jinping Aims to Rein in Chinese Capitalism, Hew to Mao's Socialist Vision*, WALL ST. J. (Sept. 20, 2021), https://www.wsj.com/articles/xi-jinping-aims-to-rein-in-chinese-capitalism-hew-to-maos-socialist-vision-11632150725.

8. Naughton & Blanchette, see *supra* note 6.

9. Ibid.

10. Ibid.

11. Nathaniel Taplin, *China's Tech Crackdown Could Backfire Badly*, WALL ST. J. (Jul. 30, 2021), https://www.wsj.com/articles/chinas-tech-crackdown-could-backfire-badly-11627627273; Magnus, see *supra* note 6. Stephen S. Roach, *China's Animal Spirits Deficit*, PROJECT SYNDICATE (Jul. 27, 2021), https://www.project-syndicate.org/commentary/chinese-tech-crackdown-crushes-animal-spirits-by-stephen-s-roach-2021-07?barrier=accesspaylog.

12. Ray Dalio is one such representative. See Quentin Webb & Jing Yang, *Bridgewater's Ray Dalio Endorses China's "Common Prosperity" Drive*, WALL ST. J. (Jan. 10, 2022), https://www.wsj.com/articles/bridgewaters-ray-dalio-endorses-chinas-common-prosperity-drive-11641870491.

13. Rana Foroohar, *The Lessons for the US from China's "Common Prosperity" Push*, FIN. TIMES (Dec. 19, 2021), https://www.ft.com/content/0910e0b8-98e1-4d21-b7b8-61c0f7003ddd; *New Economy Conversations: China's Tech Crackdown*, BLOOMBERG (Sept. 8, 2021), https://www.bloomberg.com/news/videos/2021-09-08/new-economy-conversations-china-s-tech-crackdown-video; Keyu Jin, *With Common Prosperity: How China Can Avoid the Excesses of Unrestrained Western Capitalism*, SOUTH CHINA MORNING POST (Dec. 21, 2021), https://www.scmp.com/comment/opinion/article/3160148/common-prosperity-china-can-avoid-excesses-unrestrained-western.

14. Philippe Aghion et al., *Innovation and Top Income Inequality*, 86 REV. ECON. STUD. 1 (2018).

15. Philippe Aghion, *Innovation and Inequality*, in COMBATING INEQUALITY: RETHINKING GOVERNMENT'S ROLE 175 (Olivier Blanchard & Dani Rodrik eds., 2021).

16. Ibid.

17. THOMAS PHILIPPON, THE GREAT REVERSAL: HOW AMERICA GAVE UP ON FREE MARKETS (2021).

18. See RAGHURAM RAJAN & LUIGI ZINGALES, SAVING CAPITALISM FROM THE CAPITALISTS: UNLEASHING THE POWER OF FINANCIAL MARKETS TO CREATE WEALTH AND SPREAD OPPORTUNITY (2003).

19. KATHARINA PISTOR, THE CODE OF CAPITAL: HOW THE LAW CREATES WEALTH AND INEQUALITY (2020).

20. Katharina Pistor, *Is Global Capitalism Governable?: Exploring the Legal, Social, and Economic Complexities of Governance in the 21st Century*, COLUMBIA ACADEMY ON LAW IN GLOBAL AFFAIRS (Sept. 17, 2021), https://parker-school.law.columbia.edu/events/global-capitalism-governable.

NOTES

21. David T. Ellwood, *Making Work Work*, in COMBATING INEQUALITY, *supra* note 15, at 221.

22. Stella Yifan Xie, *China Beat Back Covid-19, but It's Come at a Cost—Growing Inequality*, WALL ST. J. (Oct. 21, 2020), https://www.wsj.com/articles/china-beat-back-covid-19-but-its-come-at-a-costgrowing-inequality-11603281656.

23. Yuen Yuen Ang et al., *Can Xi End China's Gilded Age?*, PROJECT SYNDICATE (Sept. 21, 2021), https://www.project-syndicate.org/commentary/xi-china-gilded-age-crackdown-on-corruption-by-yuen-yuen-ang-2021-09.

24. Andrew Mullen, *What Is China's Common Prosperity Strategy That Calls for an Even Distribution of Wealth?*, SOUTH CHINA MORNING POST (Aug. 26, 2021), https://www.scmp.com/economy/china-economy/article/3146271/what-chinas-common-prosperity-strategy-calls-even?module=inline&pgtype=article.

25. Thomas Piketty et al., *Capital Accumulation, Private Property, and Rising Inequality in China, 1978–2015*, 109 AM. ECON. REV. 2469 (2019).

26. Ibid.

27. Mullen, *supra* note 24.

28. Nikki Sun, *China's Tech Boom Leaves Wide Rich-Poor Chasm*, NIKKEI ASIA (Sep. 18, 2018), https://asia.nikkei.com/Spotlight/Asia-Insight/China-s-tech-boom-leaves-wide-rich-poor-chasm (according to a 2016 study from Peking University, the top 1% of the population controls one-third of the country's wealth while the bottom 25% holds less than 1%). See also Branko Milanovic, *China's Inequality Will Lead It to a Stark Choice*, FOREIGN AFFAIRS (Feb. 11, 2021), https://www.foreignaffairs.com/articles/china/2021-02-11/chinas-inequality-will-lead-it-stark-choice (China's Gini coefficient, which measures wealth and income distribution, was 0.47 in 2019, compared with 0.41 in the United States).

29. Olivier Blanchard & Dani Rodrik, *Introduction: We Have the Tools to Reverse the Rise in Equality*, in COMBATING INEQUALITY, *supra* note 15.

30. Naughton & Blanchette, *supra* note 6.

31. NASSIM NICHOLAS TALEB, THE BLACK SWAN: THE IMPACT OF THE HIGHLY IMPROBABLE (2010).

32. Naughton, *supra* note 6.

33. Xiangwei Wang, *Why It's Time for China to Cut Its 45 Per Cent Income Tax Rate*, SOUTH CHINA MORNING POST (Mar. 6, 2021), https://www.scmp.com/week-asia/opinion/article/3124143/why-its-time-china-cut-its-45-cent-income-tax-rate.

34. Ibid., at 70.

35. Ibid., at 71–73.

36. CHANGDONG ZHANG, GOVERNING AND RULING: THE POLITICAL LOGIC OF TAXATION IN CHINA 69 (2021).

37. Ibid.

NOTES

38. Emmanuel Saez & Gabriel Zucman, *Tax Justice Now*, https://taxjusticenow. org/#/book. This website is an essential companion to their book, THE TRIUMPH OF INJUSTICE (2019).

39. Andrew Nathan, *China's Changing of the Guard: Authoritarian Resilience*, in CRITICAL READINGS ON THE COMMUNIST PARTY OF CHINA 86–99 (Erik Kjeld Brodsgaard ed., 2016).

40. CHINA'S CORE EXECUTIVE: LEADERSHIP STYLES, STRUCTURES AND PROCESSES UNDER XI JINPING (Sebastian Heilmann & Matthias Stephan eds., 2016). See also CHENG LI, CHINESE POLITICS IN THE XI JINPING ERA: REASSESSING COLLECTIVE LEADERSHIP (2016).

41. JOSEPH FEWSMITH, RETHINKING CHINESE POLITICS 157–184 (2021).

42. Cary Huang, *How Leading Small Groups Help Xi Jinping and Other Party Leaders Exert Power*, SOUTH CHINA MORNING POST (Jan. 20, 2014), https://www.scmp. com/news/china/article/1409118/how-leading-small-groups-help-xi-jinp ing-and-other-party-leaders-exert.

43. See Nathan, *supra* note 39.

44. Susan L. Shirk, *The Return to Personalistic Rule*, 29 J. DEMOCRACY 22 (2018).

45. See, e.g., Susan Finder, *Like Throwing an Egg against a Stone: Administrative Litigation in the People's Republic of China*, 3 J. CHIN. L. 1 (1989); Ji Li, *Suing the Leviathan—An Empirical Analysis of the Changing Rate of Administrative Litigation in China*, 10 J. EMPIR. LEG. STUD. 815 (2013); Xing Ying (应星) & Yin Xu (徐胤), *Li'an Zhengzhi Xue yu Xingzheng Susong Lü de Paihuai—Huabei Liang Shi Jiceng Fayuan de Duibi Yanjiu* ("立案政治学"与行政诉讼率的徘徊——华北两市基层法院的对比研究) [Case Registration Politics and the Stagnation of Administrative Litigation: An Empirical Study of Two Northern China Basic Courts], 6 TRIB. POL. SCI. & L. 111 (2009).

46. See Haibo He (何海波), *Cong Quanguo Shuju Kan Xin Xingzheng Susong Fa Shishi Chengxiao* (从全国数据看新《行政诉讼法》实施成效) [Implementing Effects of Administrative Litigation Law of 2014 Based on National Data], 3 *Zhongguo Falü Pinglun* (中国法律评论) [CHIN. L. REV.] 145 (2016).

47. ANGELA HUYUE ZHANG, CHINESE ANTITRUST EXCEPTIONALISM: HOW THE RISE OF CHINA CHALLENGES GLOBAL REGULATION 76–79 (2021).

48. Ibid., at 68–72.

49. David Barboza, *Angela Huyue Zhang on How China Regulates*, WIRE CHINA (Dec. 5. 2021), https://www.thewirechina.com/2021/12/05/angela-huyue-zhang-on-how-china-regulates/.

50. Katie Nodjimbadem, *What Happens to Your Body When You Walk on A Tightrope*, SMITHSONIAN MAGAZINE (Oct. 13, 2015), https://www.smithsonianmag. com/science-nature/what-happens-your-body-when-you-walk-tightrope-180956897/.

51. See Xueguang Zhou, *Organizational Response to Covid-19 Crisis: Reflections on the Chinese Bureaucracy and Its Resilience*, 16 MANAG. ORGAN. REV. 473, 479 (2020).

NOTES

52. Ibid., at 480; see also Sebastian Heilmann, *Regulatory Innovation by Leninist Means: Communist Party Supervision in China's Financial Industry*, 181 CHINA Q. 1, 4 (2005); SUSAN SHIRK, THE POLITICAL LOGIC OF ECONOMIC REFORM IN CHINA 348–349 (1993); YASHENG HUANG, INFLATION AND INVESTMENT CONTROLS IN CHINA 322–324 (1999).

53. See Zhou, *supra* note 51, at 474.

54. Zhang, *supra* note 47, at 68.

55. Ibid. A recent prominent example is Alibaba. Unlike US tech firms that are fighting tooth and nail with regulators in the United States and Europe, Alibaba thanked the regulators after receiving a record fine of almost USD 2.8 billion and vowed to improve compliance. See Matthew Brooker, *It's Easy to Make Tech Titans Kneel. Just Ask China*, BLOOMBERG (Apr. 14, 2021), https://www.blocmberg.com/opinion/articles/2021-04-14/china-brought-alibaba-to-heel-fast-can-the-u-s-take-a-lesson-versus-facebook.

56. See *Harvard's Zuboff on the Dangers of "Surveillance Capitalism,"* BLOOMBERG (Feb. 8. 2021), https://www.bloomberg.com/news/videos/2021-02-09/harvard-s-zuboff-on-the-dangers-of-surveillance-capitalism-video.

57. MAO'S INVISIBLE HAND: THE POLITICAL FOUNDATIONS OF ADAPTIVE GOVERNANCE IN CHINA 11–12 (Sebastian Heilmann & Elizabeth J. Perry eds., 2011) (observing the legacy of Mao on the policymaking in contemporary China).

58. DONELLA H. MEADOWS, THINKING IN SYSTEM: A PRIMER (Diana Wright ed., 2008).

59. Friedrich A. Hayek, *The Use of Knowledge in Society*, 35 AM. ECON. REV. 519, 526 (1945).

CHAPTER 1

1. DONELLA H. MEADOWS, THINKING IN SYSTEMS: A PRIMER (Diana Wright ed., 2008).

2. JOHN D. STERMAN, BUSINESS DYNAMICS: SYSTEMS THINKING AND MODELING FOR A COMPLEX WORLD (2000).

3. Andre Laliberte & Marc Lanteigne, *The Issue of Challenges to the Legitimacy of the CCP Rule*, in THE CHINESE PARTY-STATE IN THE 21ST CENTURY 8 (Andre Laliberte & Marc Lanteigne eds., 2007); see also BRUCE J. DICKSON, THE DICTATOR'S DILEMMA: THE CHINESE COMMUNIST PARTY'S STRATEGY FOR SURVIVAL (2016).

4. Andrew Nathan, *Authoritarian Impermanence*, 20 J. DEMOCRACY 37 (2009).

5. DICKSON, *supra* note 3, at 9.

6. Ibid., at 229.

7. Ibid.

8. Simeon Djankov et al., *The New Comparative Economics*, 31 J. COMP. ECON. 595 (2003).

9. Ibid.

10. MANFRED ELFSTROM, WORKERS AND CHANGE IN CHINA: RESISTANCE, REPRESSION, RESPONSIVENESS 6 (2021).

11. Andrew Nathan, *An Anxious 100th Birthday for China's Communist Party*, WALL ST. J. (Jun. 25, 2021), https://www.wsj.com/articles/an-anxious-100th-birthday-for-chinas-communist-party-11624635205.

12. DICKSON, *supra* note 3, at 236–237.

13. Alison Kaufman, *"The Century of Humiliation" and China's Narratives*, 112TH CONG. 140 US-CHINA ECONOMIC AND SECURITY REVIEW COMMISSION (Mar. 10, 2011), https://www.uscc.gov/sites/default/files/3.10.11Kaufman.pdf.

14. Li Yuan, *ZTE's Near-Collapse May Be China's Sputnik Moment*, N.Y. TIMES (Jun. 10, 2018), https://www.nytimes.com/2018/06/10/technology/china-technology-zte-sputnik-moment.html.

15. MAO'S INVISIBLE HAND: THE POLITICAL FOUNDATIONS OF ADAPTIVE GOVERNANCE IN CHINA 11–12 (Sebastian Heilmann & Elizabeth J. Perry eds., 2011) (observing the legacy of Mao on the policymaking in contemporary China).

16. Ibid. See also Andrew Nathan, *China's Changing of the Guard: Authoritarian Resilience*, in CRITICAL READINGS ON THE COMMUNIST PARTY OF CHINA 86–99 (Erik Kjeld Brodsgaard ed., 2016).

17. See Yasheng Huang, *Managing Chinese Bureaucrats: An Institutional Economics Perspective*, 50 POLITICAL STUD. 61, 66–67 (2002).

18. Ibid., at 67.

19. Ibid.

20. KENNETH LIEBERTHAL, GOVERNING CHINA: FROM REVOLUTION THROUGH REFORM 235–237 (2003).

21. The above statistics are based on publicly available statistics on sources on staffing and administrative duties of Chinese administrative authorities promulgated after 2018. Chinese central ministries typically release their "sanding" (meaning "three determinations") provisions (三定规则) that outline their main duties, structures, and personnel arrangements. However, the personnel data on NDRC was dated in 2008 and I was not able to identify more updated figures. I also lack data on a number of central ministries including the Ministry of Foreign Affairs, Ministry of National Defense, Ministry of State Security, Ministry of State Security, Ministry of Veterans Affairs, China International Development Cooperation Agency, and Xinhua News Agency.

22. See generally BUREAUCRACY, POLITICS, AND DECISION MAKING IN POST-MAO CHINA (Kenneth G. Lieberthal & David M. Lampton eds., 1992); Andrew C. Mertha, *"Fragmented Authoritarianism 2.0": Political Pluralization in the Chinese Policy Process*, 200 CHINA Q. 995, 995–996 (2009). See also CHANGDONG ZHANG, GOVERNING AND RULING: THE POLITICAL LOGIC OF TAXATION IN CHINA 57–63 (2021).

23. ANGELA HUYUE ZHANG, CHINESE ANTITRUST EXCEPTIONALISM: HOW THE RISE OF CHINA CHALLENGES GLOBAL REGULATION 76–79 (2021).

24. Sector regulators are not listed in the table.

25. KENNETH LIEBERTHAL & MICHEL OKSENBERG, POLICY MAKING IN CHINA: LEADERS, STRUCTURES, AND PROCESSES (1988); see SUSAN SHIRK, THE POLITICAL

NOTES

Logic of Economic Reform in China 348–349 (1993): Angela Huyue Zhang, *Bureaucratic Politics and China's Anti-Monopoly Law*, 47 Cornell Int'l L. J. 671 (2014).

26. Anna L. Ahlers & Matthias Stepan, *Top-Level Design and Local-Level Paralysis: Local Politics in Times of Political Centralisation*, in China's Core Executive: Leadership Styles, Structures and Processes under Xi Jinping 34–39 (Sebastian Heilmann & Matthias Stephan eds., 2016).

27. Wang Peng & Yan Xia, *Bureaucratic Slack in China: The Anti-Corruption Campaign and the Decline of Patronage Networks in Developing Local Economies*, 243 China Q. 611 (2019); Xiangwei Wang, *TV Parades of China's Corrupt Officials Snared in Xi Jinping's Anti-Graft Campaign Raise More Questions than Answers*, South China Morning Post (Jan. 22, 2022), https://www.scmp.com/week-asia/opinion/article/3164226/tv-parades-corrupt-officials-snared-xi-jinpings-anti-graft.

28. William Zheng, *Follow the Boss: Can China's Communist Party Ignite Initiative in its Grass-Roots Cadres?*, South China Morning Post (Aug. 21, 2021), https://www.scmp.com/news/china/politics/article/3145822/follow-boss-chinas-communist-party-killing-initiative-top-down; *Xi's Expanding Power Is a Growing Risk for China's Economy*, Bloomberg (Nov. 8, 2021), https://www.bloomberg.com/news/articles/2021-11-08/xi-s-expanding-power-is-a-growing-risk-for-china-s-economy.

29. Wang & Yan, *supra* note 27, at 613.

30. Ibid., at 627.

31. Elizabeth Pollman & Jordan M. Barry, *Regulatory Entrepreneurship*, 90 S. Cal. L. Rev. 383 (2017).

32. Lulu Yilun Chen & Coco Liu, *How China Lost Patience with Jack Ma, Its Loudest Billionaire*, Bloomberg (Dec. 22, 2020), https://www.bloomberg.com/news/features/2020-12-22/jack-ma-s-empire-in-crisis-after-china-halts-ant-group-ipo (Ma was quoted saying the following: "If someone has to go to jail, I'll go").

33. People's Bank of China Decree 2010 No. 2, Fei Jinrong Jigou Zhifu Fuwu Guanli Banfa (非金融机构支付服务管理办法) [Administrative Measures for the Payment Services Provided by Non-financial Institutions], effective from Sept. 1, 2010, http://www.gov.cn/flfg/2010-06/21/content_1632796.htm. The translated version is available at http://www.lawinfochina.com/Display.aspx?lib=law&Cgid=134238.

34. Alizila Staff, *Alipay Receives PBOC License*, Alizila (May 25, 2011), https://www.alizila.com/alipay-receives-pboc-license/.

35. For a good introduction to Yu'e Bao, see Moran Zhang, *Alibaba's Online Money Market Fund Yu'E Bao: 8 Things You Need to Know*, Int'l Bus. Times (Mar. 11, 2014), https://www.ibtimes.com/alibabas-online-money-market-fund-yue-bao-8-things-you-need-know-1560601.

36. Yue Zhang (张玥), Wunian, 1.7 Wan Yi Yu'e Bao Weihe Ji Shache? (五年, 1.7万亿余额宝为何急刹车?) [Why Did the Five-Year-Old, Worth 1.7 Trillion Yu'e

Bao Slow Down Its Pace?], 21 JINGJI.COM (May 18, 2018), https://m.21jingji.com/article/20180518/herald/77243fe42af8b8ed803ea9335bee44b5.html.

37. Shailesh Jha, *How Alibaba's Yue Bao Unearthed "Hidden Treasure" From Digital Wallets*, YOURSTORY (Aug. 2, 2018), https://yourstory.com/2018/08/alibaba-yue-bao-unearthed-hidden-treasure-from-digital-wallets/amp.

38. Allen T. Cheng, *Yu'e Bao Wow! How Alibaba Is Reshaping Chinese Finance*, INSTITUTIONAL INVESTOR (May 29, 2014), https://www.institutionalinvestor.com/article/b14zbky543md42/yue-bao-wow-how-alibaba-is-reshaping-chinese-finance.

39. *Tech Tuesday: Silicon Valley's "Fake It Till You Make It" Culture*, WOSU NEWS (Jan. 11, 2022), https://news.wosu.org/show/all-sides-with-ann-fisher/2022-01-11/tech-tuesday-silicon-valleys-fake-it-till-you-make-it-culture.

40. The term "brushing" comes from Taobao's feedback system, which uses diamonds to denote the seller's ranking. As a seller that obtains one diamond on Taobao's reputation system is deemed trustworthy by buyers, when sellers use artificial orders to boost their reputation this is called a "brush diamond" in Chinese. See Yu Zhang et al., *Trust Fraud: A Crucial Challenge for China's E-Commerce Market*, 12 ELECTRON. COMMER. RES. APPL. 299 (2013).

41. Gillian Wong et al., *Inside Alibaba, the Sharp Elbowed World of Chinese E-Commerce*, WALL ST. J. (Mar. 2, 2015), https://www.wsj.com/articles/inside-alibaba-the-sharp-elbowed-world-of-chinese-e-commerce-1425332447.

42. Zhang et al., *supra* note 40, at 300.

43. Jin Chen et al., *To Brush or Not to Brush: Product Rankings, Customer Search and Fake Orders*, INFO. SYS. RSCH. (May 20, 2022), https://pubsonline.informs.org/doi/10.1287/isre.2022.1128.

44. Wade Shepard, *China's Copycat Manufacturers Are Now Pushing the Boundaries of Innovation*, SOUTH CHINA MORNING POST (May 20, 2015), https://www.scmp.com/native/business/topics/invest-china/article/1802238/chinas-copycat-manufacturers-are-now-pushing; see also William Hennessey, *Deconstructing Shanzhai—China's Copycat Counterculture: Catch Me if You Can*, 34 CAMPBELL L. REV. 609, 611 (2012).

45. Feifei Fan, *Heat Turned Up in Fight against Fake Goods*, CHINA DAILY (Aug. 22, 2018), https://www.chinadailyhk.com/articles/185/184/111/1534930959353.html.

46. Fan Liu (刘帆), Shanzhai Bushi Jiahuo? Shangpin Shifou Qinfan Zhishi Chanquan Cheng Jiaodian (山寨不是假货? 商品是否侵犯知识产权成焦点) [Knockoffs Are Not Counterfeits? Whether Products Infringed Intellectual Property Becomes a Central Issue], CHINACOURT.ORG (Aug. 5, 2018), https://www.chinacourt.org/article/detail/2018/08/id/3443462.shtml.

47. Zhang, *supra* note 23.

48. The World Bank's index of Doing Business Indicators ranked China near the bottom in terms of the ease of starting a business.

NOTES

49. Chong-En Bai et al., *Special Deals with Chinese Characteristics*, 34 NBER MACROECONOMICS ANNUAL 341 (2019). See also YASHENG HUANG, CAPITALISM WITH CHINESE CHARACTERISTICS: ENTREPRENEURSHIP AND THE STATE (2010); Chenggang Xu, *The Fundamental Institutions of China's Reforms and Development*, 49 J. ECON. LIT. 1076 (2011).

50. Bai et al., *supra* note 49.

51. Ibid.

52. DESMOND SHUM, RED ROULETTE: AN INSIDER'S STORY OF WEALTH, POWER, CORRUPTION, AND VENGEANCE IN TODAY'S CHINA (2021).

53. MINXIN PEI, CHINA'S CRONY CAPITALISM: THE DYNAMICS OF REGIME DECAY 116–150 (2016) (explaining how officials cash in on their political power through immediate family members in business or partner with others in the private sector); see generally YUEN YUEN ANG, CHINA'S GILDED AGE: THE PARADOX OF ECONOMIC BOOM AND VAST CORRUPTION (2020) (observing the symbiotic relationship between corruption and performance in China's fiercely competitive political system).

54. Shum, *supra* note 52. See also LULU YILUN CHEN, INFLUENCE EMPIRE: THE STORY OF TENCENT AND CHINA'S TECH AMBITION 201–202 (2022).

55. CHEN, *supra* note 54, at 202.

56. Ibid., at 202.

57. Lingling Wei, *Xi Jinping Aims to Rein in Chinese Capitalism, Hew to Mao's Socialist Vision*, WALL ST. J. (Sept. 20, 2021), https://www.wsj.com/articles/xi-jinping-aims-to-rein-in-chinese-capitalism-hew-to-macs-socialist-vision-11632150725.

58. Ibid.

59. Michael Forsythe, *Alibaba's I.P.O. Could Be a Bonanza for the Scions of Chinese Leaders*, N.Y. TIMES (Jul. 20, 2014), https://dealbook.nytimes.com/2014/07/20/alibabas-i-p-o-could-be-a-bonanza-for-the-scions-of-chinese-leaders/ (noting Alibaba's deep political connection with some of the most powerful members of the CCP).

60. Ibid.

61. Rory Van Loo, *The Corporations as Courthouse*, 33 YALE J. REGUL. 547 (2016).

62. Ibid., at 550.

63. Gary King et al., *How Censorship in China Allows Government Criticism but Silences Collective Expression*, 107 AM. POLIT. SCI. REV. 326 (2013); Bei Qin et al., *Why Does China Allow Freer Social Media? Protests Versus Surveillance and Propaganda*, 31 J. ECON. PERSPECT. 117 (2017).

64. *Report on Food Delivery Unrest (2017–2018)*, HONG KONG CONFEDERATION OF TRADE UNIONS (Oct. 22, 2019), https://en.hkctu.org.hk/china_food_del ivery_rider; see Xueguang Zhou, *Organizational Response to Covid-19 Crisis: Reflections on the Chinese Bureaucracy and Its Resilience*, 16 MANAG. ORGAN. REV. 473, 479 (2020).

65. *The Gig Economy Challenges China's State-Run Labour Unions*, THE ECONOMIST (Jan. 27, 2021), https://www.economist.com/china/2021/01/27/the-gig-economy-challenges-chinas-state-run-labour-unions.

66. Alice Su, *Why a Takeout Deliveryman in China Set Himself on Fire*, L.A. TIMES (Feb. 8, 2021), https://www.latimes.com/world-nation/story/2021-02-08/why-takeout-delivery-man-china-set-himself-on-fire.

67. Marc Schneiberg & Sarah Soule, *Institutionalization as a Contested, Multi-level Process: The Case of Rate Regulation in American Fire Insurance*, in SOCIAL MOVEMENTS AND ORGANIZATION THEORY 122 (Gerald F. Davis et al. eds., 2005).

68. See, e.g., Yongshun Cai, *Managed Participation in China*, 119 POLIT. SCI. Q. 425 (2004); Christopher Marquis & Yanhua Bird, *The Paradox of Responsive Authoritarianism: How Civic Activism Spurs Environmental Penalties in China*, 29 ORGAN. SCI. 755 (2018).

69. Jidong Chen & Yiqing Yu, *Why Do Authoritarian Regimes Allow Citizens to Voice Opinions Publicly?*, 79 J. POLITICS 792, 792 (2017); JEREMY L. WALLACE, SEEKING TRUTH & HIDING FACTS: INFORMATION, IDEOLOGY, & AUTHORITARIANISM IN CHINA (2023).

70. See Qin et al., *supra* note 63, at 137.

71. See generally CHRISTOPHER HEURLIN, RESPONSIVE AUTHORITARIANISM IN CHINA: LAND, PROTESTS, AND POLICY MAKING (2016); DANIELA STOCKMANN, MEDIA COMMERCIALIZATION AND AUTHORITARIAN RULE IN CHINA (2013).

72. See, e.g., SUSAN L. SHIRK, CHINA: FRAGILE SUPER POWER: HOW CHINA'S INTERNAL POLITICS COULD DERAIL ITS PEACEFUL RISE 85 (2007). See generally WENFANG TANG, POPULIST AUTHORITARIANISM: CHINESE POLITICAL CULTURE AND REGIME SUSTAINABILITY (2016). See also Stephen M. Walt, *You Can't Defeat Nationalism, So Stop Trying*, FOREIGN POLICY (Jun. 4, 2019), https://foreignpolicy.com/2019/06/04/you-cant-defeat-nationalism-so-stop-trying/ (observing that nationalism is a powerful and persistent force in many countries including China).

73. Suisheng Zhao, *China's Pragmatic Nationalism: Is It Manageable?*, 29 WASH. Q. 131, 130–142 (2005) (arguing that the CCP uses pragmatic populism to rally political support, while also restraining nationalist sentiments that could jeopardize the stability of the regime). See also Yinxian Zhang et al., *Nationalism on Weibo: Towards a Multifaceted Understanding of Chinese Nationalism*, 235 CHINA Q. 758, 760 (2018)(conducting research on Sino Weibo and finding that the majority of nationalists also profoundly criticized the government from a pro-democracy standpoint).

CHAPTER 2

1. See generally AVINASH K. DIXIT, LAWLESSNESS AND ECONOMICS: ALTERNATIVE MODES OF GOVERNANCE (2007); see also Katharina Pistor & Chenggang Xu, *Incomplete Law*, 35 N.Y.U. J. INT'L L. & POL. 931, 931–932 (2003).

NOTES 303

2. Elizabeth Pollman & Jordan M. Barry, *Regulatory Entrepreneurship*, 90 S. Cal. L. Rev. 383 (2017) (explaining how US tech firms such as Uber and Airbnb try to take advantage of the legal gray area to lobby for favorable legal treatment).

3. *China Unveils "Internet Plus" Action Plan to Fuel Growth*, ChinaDaily.com. cn (Jul. 4, 2015), https://www.chinadaily.com.cn/bizchina/tech/2015-07/04/content_21181256.htm.

4. China Int'l E-Com. Ctr., E-Commerce in China 11 (2015) (hereinafter E-Commerce Report); see also Yongqi Hu, *Startups to Gain Government Funds*, ChinaDaily.com.cn (Jul. 28, 2017), https://www.chinadaily.com.cn/busin ess/2017-07/28/content_30275307.htm.

5. Irene Zhou, *Digital Labour Platforms and Labour Protection in China* 39 (ILO Working Paper 11, Oct. 2020), https://www.ilo.org/wcmsp5/groups/pub lic/---asia/---ro-bangkok/---ilo-beijing/documents/publication/wcms_757 923.pdf (summarizing a list of the government policies).

6. See E-Commerce Report, *supra* note 4, at 11.

7. Ibid. See also *China Issues Guidelines on Development of Internet Finance*, HKTDC Research (Aug. 6, 2015), https://hkmb.hktdc.com/en/1X0A3 4J5/hktdc-research/China-Issues-Guidelines-on-Development-of-Internet-Finance.

8. McKinsey & Company, *China's Digital Economy: A Leading Global Force* 15–16 (Aug. 3, 2017), https://www.mckinsey.com/featured-insights/china/chinas-digital-economy-a-leading-global-force.

9. Ibid., at 16. State Taxation Administration of the People's Republic of China, *SAT Releases the Guidelines on Preferential Tax Policies for Mass Entrepreneurship and Innovation*, chinatax.gov.cn (Apr. 26, 2017), http://www.chinatax.gov. cn/eng/c101269/c2655318/content.html.

10. Liyang Hou, *Sharing Economy in China: A National Report* 2, ssrn.com (Aug. 26, 2018), https://ssrn.com/abstract=3231976 (noting China's National Development and Reform Commission, Office of the Central Cyberspace Affairs, Ministry of Industry and Information, Ministry of Human Resource and Social Security, State Administration of Taxation, State Administration of Industry and Commerce, State Administration of Quality Supervision, Inspection and Quarantine, and National Bureau of Statistics, "Guiding Opinions on Accelerating the Development of Sharing Economy," NDRC High-Tech [2017] 1245).

11. See E-Commerce Report, *supra* note 4, at 31–34 (observing the policy measures promulgated by Fujian, Shanghai, Shandong, Jiangxi, Anhui, Hebei, Jiangsu, Hainan, Hunan, Liaoning, and Zhejiang provinces).

12. See McKinsey Report, *supra* note 8, at 15–16.

13. Ibid., at 16; see Zhongchuang Kongjian 50 Qiang Gongbu, Zhongguo Yi Cheng Quanqiu Fuhuaqi Shuliang Zuiduo de (众创空间50强公布, 中国已成全球孵化器数量最多的) [Top 50 Innovation and Startup Incubators

NOTES

Report: China Has the Most Incubators in the World], Sohu (Sept. 18, 2016), http://www.sohu.com/a/114536039_379992.

14. *Full Text of Premier Li's Address at Opening Ceremony of Summer Davos*, Xinhua News (Jun. 28, 2017), http://chinaplus.cri.cn/news/china/9/20170628/7117_2.html.

15. Bruce J. Dickson, Red Capitalist in China (2009); see also Gilles Guiheux, *The Political "Participation" of Entrepreneurs: Challenge or Opportunity for the Chinese Communist Party?*, 73 Soc. Res. 219 (2006); Yue Hou, The Private Sector in Public Office: Selective Property Rights in China (2019).

16. Arjun Kharpal, *Alibaba's Jack Ma Has Been a Communist Party Member since the 1980s*, CNBC (Nov. 27, 2018), https://www.cnbc.com/2018/11/27/alibabas-jack-ma-has-been-communist-party-member-since-1980s.html.

17. Li Yuan, *The Uncomfortable Marriage between China and Its Tech Giants*, Wall St. J. (Mar. 8, 2018), https://www.wsj.com/articles/the-godfathers-of-chinese-tech-get-an-offer-they-cant-refuse-1520510404.

18. Rita Liao, *What China's Big Tech CEOs Propose at the Annual Parliament Meeting*, TechCrunch (Mar. 5, 2021), https://techcrunch.com/2021/03/04/two-sessions-2021-china-tech/.

19. See Yuan, *supra* note 17.

20. Hou, *supra* note 15, at 157.

21. Sun Yu, *China Tech Groups Hire Ex-regulators to Fend Off Beijing's Crackdown*, Fin. Times (Apr. 20, 2021), https://www.ft.com/content/71daa106-259e-4dc2-b267-b0289177de1f.

22. Ibid.

23. Angela Huyue Zhang, Chinese Antitrust Exceptionalism: How the Rise of China Challenges Global Regulation 106–107 (2021) (observing the close-knit group formed among lawyers, academics, and regulators in China).

24. Ibid., at 105–106.

25. Thomas Philippon, The Great Reversal: How America Gave Up on Free Markets 200–201 (2021); see Haris Tabakovic & Thomas Wollmann, *From Revolving Doors to Regulatory Capture? Evidence from Patent Examiners*, SSRN. com (NBER Working Paper No. w24638, May 2018, last revised Apr. 2022), https://ssrn.com/abstract=3185893. See generally Wentong Zheng, *The Revolving Door*, 90 Notre Dame L. Rev. 1265, 1269 (2015).

26. Ma Si, *Didi Helps Migrant Workers Go Home*, ChinaDaily.com.cn (Jan. 19, 2017), http://www.chinadaily.com.cn/newsrepublic/2017-01/19/content_28004907.htm.

27. Sui-Lee Wee, *Didi Suspends Carpooling in China after 2nd Passenger Is Killed*, N.Y. Times (Aug. 26, 2018), https://www.nytimes.com/2018/08/26/business/didi-chuxing-murder-rape-women.html.

28. Ibid.

29. Yue Wang & Robert Olsen, *China's Didi Chuxing Faces Intense Pressure amid Public Anger over Second Passenger Death*, Forbes (Sept. 1, 2018), https://www.for

NOTES   305

bes.com/sites/ywang/2018/09/01/chinas-didi-chuxing-faces-intense-press ure-amid-public-anger-over-second-passenger-death/?sh=237b08b97a6d.

30. *Ponzis to Punters*, THE ECONOMIST (Feb. 6, 2016), https://www.economist. com/china/2016/02/06/ponzis-to-punters.

31. Ibid.

32. Ibid.

33. Chuanman You, *Recent Developments of FinTech Regulation in China: A Focus on the New Regulatory Regime for the P2P Lending (Loan-Based Crowdfunding) Market*, 13 CAPITAL MARKET L.J. 85, 96 (2018).

34. Chong Koh Ping & Xie Yu, *China Hails Victory in Crackdown on Peer-to-Peer Lending*, WALL ST. J. (Dec. 9, 2020), https://www.wsj.com/articles/china-hails-victory-in-crackdown-on-peer-to-peer-lending-11607515547.

35. Frank Tang, *China's P2P Purge Leaves Millions of Victims Out in the Cold, with Losses in the Billions, as Concerns of Social Unrest Swirl*, SOUTH CHINA MORNING POST (Dec. 29, 2020), https://www.scmp.com/economy/china-economy/arti cle/3115580/chinas-p2p-purge-leaves-millions-victims-out-cold-losses.

36. Carol Huang, *Driven to Death? China Food-Delivery Services Criticised for Pressuring Drivers*, CAMPAIGN ASIA (Sept. 10, 2020), https://www.campaignasia. com/article/driven-to-death-china-food-delivery-services-criticised-for-pre ssuring-drivers/463537.

37. Yuan Yang & Ryan McMorrow, *Chinese Courier Sets Fire to Himself in Protest over Unpaid Alibaba Wages*, FIN. TIMES (Jan.12, 2021), https://www.ft.com/ content/d6189ee8-9aea-41dd-a412-b8daba9cacf2; see also Mimi Zou, *The Regulatory Challenges of "Uberization" in China: Classifying Ride-Hailing Drivers*, 33 INT'L J. COMPARATIVE LABOUR L. & INDUSTRIAL RELATIONS 286 (2017).

38. Zixu Wang, *In China, Delivery Workers Struggle against a Rigged System*, SUPCHINA (Apr. 20, 2021), https://supchina.com/2021/04/20/in-china-deliv ery-workers-struggle-against-a-rigged-system/.

39. See Yang & McMorrow, *supra* note 37.

40. Nan Li & John Darwin Van Fleet, *Ant's Road to Redemption: How the Fintech Giant Can Save Itself*, SUPCHINA (May 18, 2021), https://supchina.com/2021/ 05/18/ants-road-to-redemption-how-the-fintech-giant-can-save-itself/.

41. Ibid.

42. Ibid.

43. *Alibaba and Tencent Have Become China's Most Formidable Investors*, THE ECONOMIST (Aug. 2, 2018), https://www.economist.com/business/2018/08/ 02/alibaba-and-tencent-have-become-chinas-most-formidable-investors.

44. Caleb Foote & Robert D. Atkinson, *Chinese Competitiveness in the International Digital Economy*, INFO. TECH. & INNOVATION FOUNDATION 4 (Nov. 23, 2020), https://itif.org/publications/2020/11/23/chinese-competitiveness-internatio nal-digital-economy. "WeChat, which was released in 2011 as a messaging ser vice akin to WhatsApp (indeed, most major Chinese Internet firms started as copies of U.S. digital products or services), now has nearly 1.2 billion monthly

active users and, as of early 2019, has 2.3 million mini programs—more than the 2.1 million apps on the App Store. WeChat mini programs had transactions worth $115 billion in 2019, all moderated through Tencent's digital payment system WeChatPay, which is accepted by 79 percent of small and medium-sized Chinese retailers. . . . Alipay, owned by Alibaba affiliate Ant Financial, and led by Alibaba's founder Jack Ma, is a strong second with 647 million monthly users mid-2019, 401 million of whom used mini programs."

45. Louise Lucas, *Long Freeze between Tencent and Alibaba Thaws*, FIN. TIMES (Apr. 30, 2019), https://www.ft.com/content/c3402462-6728-11e9-a79d-04f35 0474d62.

46. Wee, *supra* note 27.

47. Keqiang Li, *Report on the Work of the Government* (May 22, 2020). "To further unleash the creativity of various sectors, we will launch a new round of pilot reforms for making innovations across the board, build more innovation and entrepreneurship demo centers, continue *accommodative and prudential* regulation, and develop the platform economy and the sharing economy." See *Full Text: Report on the Work of the Government*, XINHUA NEWS (May 30, 2020), http://english.www.gov.cn/premier/news/202005/30/content_WS5ed19 7f3c6d0b3f0e94990da.html.

48. Jing Yang & Lingling Wei, *China's President Xi Jinping Personally Scuttled Jack Ma's Ant IPO*, WALL ST. J. (Nov. 12, 2020), https://www.wsj.com/articles/ china-president-xi-jinping-halted-jack-ma-ant-ipo-11605203556.

49. Ibid.

50. Ibid.

51. See Li & Van Fleet, *supra* note 40 (noting that six months before the IPO, Ant changed its name from Ant Financial to Ant Group to avoid regulatory scrutiny).

52. Sun Yu & Tom Mitchell, *The Man Taking on Jack Ma Cements His Status as a Rising Star*, FIN. TIMES (Feb.2, 2021), https://www.ft.com/content/f44fae66-21c0-48ff-9dd7-bb85ec0e9cf2.

53. Lingling Wei, *Ant IPO-Approval Process under Investigation by Beijing*, WALL ST. J. (Apr. 27, 2021), https://www.wsj.com/articles/ant-ipo-approval-process-under-investigation-by-beijing-11619532022.

54. See Yu & Mitchell, *supra* note 52.

55. See Li & Van Fleet, *supra* note 40 (noting that the price-to-earnings ratio of tech firms are four times of that of banks).

56. See generally Logan Wright & Daniel Rosen, *Credit and Credibility: Risks to China's Economic Resilience*, CSIS (Oct. 3, 2018), https://www.csis.org/analy sis/credit-and-credibility-risks-chinas-economic-resilience.

57. Stella Yifan Xie & Chao Deng, *China to Tighten Rules on Five Financial Giants*, WALL ST. J. (Nov. 3, 2018), https://www.wsj.com/articles/china-to-tighten-rules-on-five-financial-giants-1541246489.

58. Yang & Wei, *supra* note 48.

NOTES

59. Stella Yifan Xie, *China's New Financial Rules to Cover Jack Ma's Ant Group*, WALL ST. J. (Sept. 13, 2020), https://www.wsj.com/articles/chinas-new-financial-rules-to-cover-jack-mas-ant-group-11600013259.

60. See Angela Huyue Zhang, *China's Regulatory War on Ant*, PROJECT SYNDICATE (Mar. 12, 2021), https://shorturl.at/npJNV.

61. See Xueguang Zhou, *Organizational Response to Covid-19 Crisis: Reflections on the Chinese Bureaucracy and Its Resilience*, 16 MANAG. ORGAN. REV. 473, 479 (2020).

62. Feiyu Zhang (张非鱼), Guanyu Jinrong Chuangxin yu Jianguan de Ji Dian Renshi (关于金融创新与监管的几点认识) [A Few Points Regarding Financial Innovation and Regulation], CHINA BUSINESS NETWORK (Oct. 31, 2020), https://www.financialnews.com.cn/hg/202010/t20201031_204309.html; Yu Shi (时雨), Zai Jinrong Keji Fazhan Zhong Xuyao Sikao he Liqing de Jige Wenti (在金融科技发展中需要思考和厘清的几个问题) [A Few Questions That Deserve Clarification in the Course of FinTech Development], CAIXIN (Nov. 2, 2020), https://opinion.caixin.com/2020-11-02/101622 131.html; Jueshou Zhou (周矍铄), Daxing Hulianwang Qiye Jinru Jinrong Lingyu de Qianzai Fengxian yu Jianguan (大型互联网企业进入金融领域的潜在风险与监管) [Potential Risks for Big Tech to Enter Financial Industry and the Regulations], FINANCIALNEWS.COM.CN (Nov. 2, 2020), https://www.financialnews.com.cn/gc/gz/202011/t20201102_204376.html.

63. Yang & Wei, *supra* note 48.

64. Ibid.

65. Zhongyang Yizhou Liang Ti Qianghua Fan Longduan he Fangzhi Ziben Wuxu Kuozhang Dui Ziben Shichang 27 Zi Yaoqiu (中央一周两提强化反垄断和防止资本无序扩张 对资本市场27字要求) [The Central Government Emphasized Reinforcing Antitrust Efforts and Preventing Capital from Expanding in a Disorderly Fashion Twice in a Week and Made a 27-Word Request], EASTMONEY.COM (Dec. 18, 2020), https://finance.eastmoney.com/a2/202012181742994213.html.

66. Ibid. See also Zhang, *supra* note 60.

67. Barry Naughton, *Xi's System, Xi's Men: After the March 2018 National People's Congress*, 56 CHINA LEADERSHIP MONITOR (Spring 2018), https://www.hoover.org/research/xis-system-xis-men-after-march-2018-national-peoples-congress.

68. See, e.g., Susan Trevaskes, *Severe and Swift Justice in China*, 47 BRIT. J. CRIMINOL. 23 (2007); Peng Wang, *Politics of Crime Control: How Campaign-Style Law Enforcement Sustains Authoritarian Rule in China*, 60 BRIT. J. CRIMINOL. 422 (2019); BENJAMIN VAN ROOIJ, REGULATING LAND AND POLLUTION IN CHINA: LAWMAKING, COMPLIANCE AND ENFORCEMENT: THEORY AND CASES (2006); Duoqi Xu et al., *China's Campaign-Style Internet Finance Governance: Causes, Effects, and Lessons Learned for New Information-Based Approaches to Governance*, 35 COMPUT. L. SECUR. REV. 3 (2019).

NOTES

69. Xin Frank He, *Sporadic Law Enforcement Campaigns as a Means of Social Control: A Case Study from a Rural-Urban Migrant Enclave in Beijing*, 17 Colum. J. Asian L. 121, 134 (2003) (noting that "during the revolutionary period, the CCP had to rely on mass movements and campaigns to implement its policies because it had no state institutions"); see Shiping Zheng, Party v. State in Post-1949 China: The Institutional Dilemma 154 (1997).

70. Elizabeth J. Perry, *Mass Campaigns to Managed Campaigns: "Constructing a New Socialist Countryside,"* in Mao's Invisible Hand 50 (Elizabeth J. Perry & Sebastian Heilmann eds., 2011) (quoting Zhao Ziyang, the former general secretary of the CCP: "I specifically stated that The Third Plenum resolved that there would be no more mass campaigns. However, people are accustomed to the old ways, so whenever we attack anything, these methods are still used.").

71. See, e.g., Van Rooij, *supra* note 68; see also Trevaskes, *supra* note 68.

72. See *supra* note 62.

73. Ibid.

74. Ibid.

75. Li Yuan, *Why China Turned against Alibaba's Jack Ma*, N.Y. Times (Dec. 24, 2020), https://www.nytimes.com/2020/12/24/technology/china-jack-ma-alibaba.html.

76. Greg James, *Public Opinion on Jack Ma Swings Wildly after China Calls Off Ant Group's IPO*, SupChina (Nov. 4, 2020), https://supchina.com/2020/11/04/public-opinion-on-jack-ma-swings-wildly-after-china-calls-off-ant-groups-ipo/.

77. Angela Huyue Zhang, *Agility over Stability: China's Great Reversal in Regulating the Platform Economy*, 63 Harv. Int'l L. J. 301, 344–345 (2022).

78. Laurie Chen, *Chinese Parents Spend up to US$43,500 a Year on After-School Classes for Their Children*, South China Morning Post (Dec. 4, 2018), https://www.scmp.com/news/china/society/article/2176377/chinese-parents-spend-us43500-year-after-school-classes-their.

79. Josh Chin, *Xi Jinping's Leadership Style: Micromanagement That Leaves Underlings Scrambling*, Wall St. J. (Dec. 15, 2021), https://www.wsj.com/articles/xi-jinpings-leadership-style-micromanagement-that-leaves-underlings-scrambling-11639582426.

80. Ibid.

81. *Why China Is Cracking Down on After-School Tutoring*, Bloomberg QuickTake (Jun. 9, 2021), https://www.bloomberg.com/news/articles/2021-06-09/why-china-s-cracking-down-now-on-education-tech-firms-quicktake.

82. Stephanie Yang, *China's Tech Regulator Orders Companies to Fix Anticompetitive, Security Issues*, Wall St. J. (Jul. 26, 2021), https://www.wsj.com/articles/chinas-tech-regulator-orders-companies-to-fix-anticompetitive-security-issues-11627304021; see also Gongxin Weibao (工信微报) [Ministry of Industry and Information Technology News], Gongxin Bu Qidong Hulianwang Hangye Zhuanxiang Zhengzhi Xingdong (工信部启动互联网行业专项整治行动)

NOTES

309

[Ministry of Industry and Information Technology Launched Special Rectification Campaign for Internet Industry], WEIXIN.QQ.CCM (Jul. 25, 2021), https://mp.weixin.qq.com/s/GZkFr4DVxPPRvp0_RP8mAQ.

83. Notably, Chinese antitrust agencies and the MIIT have a history of turf war in the past; see Zhang, *supra* note 23, at 97.

84. See *generally* Zheng, *supra* note 25, at 1269.

85. Ibid.

86. See Zhang, *supra* note 23, at 71–73.

87. Ibid., at 95–105.

88. Angela Huyue Zhang, *In China, Behave or Face a Campaign*, BLOOMBERG (Jan. 6, 2021), https://www.bloomberg.com/opinion/articles/2021-01-06/china-s-regulators-turn-to-communist-style-campaigns-to-keep-things-in-line.

89. Jeremy Bowman, *Why Alibaba Just Lost $100 Billion in Market Value*, THE MOTLEY FOOL (Dec. 24, 2020), https://www.fool.com/investing/2020/12/24/why-alibaba-just-lost-100-billion-in-market-value/.

90. Zhang, *supra* note 88.

91. *China Investigates DiDi over Cybersecurity, Shares Drop More than 10 Percent on New York Stock Exchange*, ABC NEWS (Jul. 3, 2021), https://www.abc.net.au/news/2021-07-03/china-investigates-ride-sharing-didi-over-cybersecurity/100265196.

92. See Yu, *supra* note 21.

93. *Ex-Regulators Draw Top Pay to Help Firms Decode China Crackdown*, BLOOMBERG (Aug. 15, 2021), https://www.bloomberg.com/news/articles/2021-08-15/ex-regulators-earn-460-000-to-help-firms-decode-china-crackdown.

94. Ibid.

95. Raymond Zhong, *China Fines Alibaba $2.8 Billion in Landmark Antitrust Case*, N.Y. TIMES (Apr. 9, 2021), https://www.nytimes.com/2021/04/09/technology/china-alibaba-monopoly-fine.html.

96. KING & WOOD MALLESONS, *10 Highlights of the Antitrust Guidelines for Platform Economy* (Nov. 18, 2020), https://www.chinalawinsight.com/2020/11/articles/compliance/10-highlights-of-the-antitrust-guidelines-for-platform-economy/.

97. Ibid.

98. Ibid.

99. Ibid.

100. Jane Zhang & Iris Deng, *China Issues Final Version of Anti-Monopoly Guidelines as Beijing Moves to Rein in Big Tech*, SOUTH CHINA MORNING POST (Feb. 8, 2021), https://www.scmp.com/tech/policy/article/3120977/china-issues-final-version-anti-monopoly-guidelines-beijing-moves-rein.

101. Xiangwei Wang, *From Ant to Didi and Private Education Firms, China Stock Rout Is a Mess of Its Own Making*, SOUTH CHINA MORNING POST (Aug. 7, 2021), https://www.scmp.com/week-asia/opinion/article/3144146/ant-didi-and-private-education-firms-china-stock-rout-mess-its.

310 NOTES

102. *China Stocks Rally as Beijing Intensifies Effort to Calm Market*, BLOOMBERG (July 28, 2021), https://www.bloomberg.com/news/articles/2021-07-29/china-stocks-rise-as-beijing-escalates-effort-to-calm-market.

103. Kevin Rudd, *China's Economic Downturn Gives Rise to a Winter of Discontent*, WALL ST. J. (Jan. 21, 2022), https://shorturl.at/bgxCI.

104. Julie Zhu et al., *Reeling from China's Crackdown, Alibaba and Tencent Readying Big Job Cuts-sources*, REUTERS (Mar. 16, 2022), https://www.reuters.com/technology/reeling-chinas-crackdown-alibaba-tencent-readying-big-job-cuts-sources-2022-03-16/.

105. Yuko Kubota, *In China, Job Cuts Mount in Sectors Hit by Tighter Regulations*, WALL ST. J. (Dec. 19, 2021), https://www.wsj.com/articles/in-china-job-cuts-mount-in-sectors-hit-by-tighter-regulations-11639915203?mod=article_inline.

106. Houston Scott, *Tencent and Other Tech Firms Downsize, Stocks Recover*, SupCHINA (Mar. 17, 2022), https://supchina.com/2022/03/17/tencent-and-other-tech-firms-downsize-stocks-recover/.

107. *Relentless Selling in China Stocks Evokes Memories of 2008 Crash*, BLOOMBERG (Mar. 14, 2022), https://www.bloomberg.com/news/articles/2022-03-15/china-tech-stocks-tumble-after-historic-rout-as-risks-mount.

108. Ibid.

109. Rebecca Feng & Clarence Leong, *China Shares Soar after Beijing Signals Support; Alibaba Jumps 37%*, WALL ST. J. (Mar. 16, 2022), https://www.wsj.com/articles/china-markets-rebound-on-supportive-government-comments-11647416023?reflink=e2twmkts.

110. Ibid.

111. Raffaele Huang & Cao Li, *Chinese Internet Stocks Hit Three-Month High*, WALL ST. J. (Jun. 8, 2022), https://www.wsj.com/articles/chinese-internet-stocks-hit-three-month-high-11654685396.

CHAPTER 3

1. GEORGE MAGNUS, RED FLAGS: WHY XI'S CHINA IS IN JEOPARDY (2018); GORDON G. CHANG, THE COMING COLLAPSE OF CHINA (2001); THOMAS ORLIK, CHINA: THE BUBBLE THAT NEVER POPS (2020); DINNY MCMAHON, CHINA'S GREAT WALL OF DEBT: SHADOW BANKS, GHOST CITIES, MASSIVE LOANS, AND THE END OF THE CHINESE MIRACLE (2018).

2. Jingqi Gong (龚菁琦), *Ren Wu* — Fa Shaozi de Ren (《人物》— 发哨子的人) [*People* — Whistleblowers], MATTER NEWS (Mar. 10, 2020), https://shorturl.at/mvHI7.

3. Lingling Wei & Chao Deng, *China's Coronavirus Response Is Questioned: "Everyone Was Blindly Optimistic,"* WALL ST. J. (Jan. 24, 2020), https://www.wsj.com/articles/china-contends-with-questions-over-response-to-viral-outbreak-11579825832.

NOTES

311

4. Ibid.

5. Chris Buckley et al., *25 Days That Changed the World: How Covid-19 Slipped China's Grasp*, N.Y. TIMES (Dec. 30, 2020), https://www.nytimes.com/2020/12/30/world/asia/china-coronavirus.html.

6. Ian Johnson, *China Bought the West Time. The West Squandered It*, N.Y. TIMES (Mar. 13, 2020), https://www.nytimes.com/2020/03/13/opinion/china-response-china.html.

7. Ci Zhang (张慈), Zhong Mei: Dangju Ceng Gaojie Yiyuan "Zhuyi Zhengzhi Yingxiang" (中媒：当局曾告诫医院"注意政治影响") [Chinese Media: Authorities Warned Hospitals to "Beware of Political Influence"], DEUTSCHE WELLE (Apr. 13, 2020), https://shorturl.at/iwHN2.

8. See Wei & Deng, *supra* note 3.

9. Yanzhong Huang, *China's Public Health Response to the COVID-19 Outbreak*, CHINA LEADERSHIP MONITOR (Jun. 1, 2020), https://www.prcleader.org/huang.

10. Stephanie Hegarty, *The Chinese Doctor Who Tried to Warn Others about Coronavirus*, BBC NEWS (Feb. 6, 2020) https://www.bbc.com/news/world-asia-china-51364382.

11. Huang, *supra* note 9.

12. Buckley et al., *supra* note 5.

13. Yinchan Yan (鄢银婵), Di Yi Ge Ganran de Xinguan Feiyan Fangzhi Zhuanjia Zu Chengyuan Yu Changping: Chuanran Bing Zhi Bao Xitong Baocuo Meiguanxi, Lou Bao Shi Da Wenti (第一个感染的新冠肺炎防治专家组成员余昌平：传染病直报系统报错没关系, 漏报是大问题) [Yu Changping, Member of the First Coronavirus Prevention Expert Taskforce: It Doesn't Matter if the Infectious Disease Direct Reporting System Reports an Error, Underreporting Is a Big Problem], NDB.COM (Mar. 26, 2020), http://www.nbd.com.cn/articles/2020-03-26/1420446.html.

14. Huang, *supra* note 9.

15. Xueguang Zhou, *Organizational Response to Covid-19 Crisis: Reflections on the Chinese Bureaucracy and Its Resilience*, 16 MANAG. ORGAN. REV. 473 (2020); Yuen Yuen Ang, *When Covid-19 Meets Centralized, Personalized Power*, 4 NAT. HUM. BEHAV. 445 (2020).

16. Zhou, *supra* note 15, at 480.

17. Kinling Lo, *Zero-COVID Is Still the Best Choice for China Now, Top Adviser Says*, SOUTH CHINA MORNING POST (Jan. 22, 2022), https://www.scmp.com/news/china/science/article/3164386/zero-covid-still-best-choice-china-now-top-adviser-says.

18. Ezekiel J. Emanuel & Michael T. Osterholm, *China's Zero-Covid Policy Is a Pandemic Waiting to Happen*, N.Y. TIMES (Jan. 25, 2022), https://www.nytimes.com/2022/01/25/opinion/china-covid-19.html?smid=tw-share.

19. Richard McGregor, *China's Deep State: The Communist Party and the Coronavirus*, LOWY INSTITUTE (Jul. 23, 2020), https://www.lowyinstitute.org/publications/china-s-deep-state-communist-party-and-coronavirus#_ftn7.

20. Josh Chin, *Xi Jinping's Leadership Style: Micromanagement That Leaves Underlings Scrambling*, WALL ST. J. (Dec. 15, 2021), https://www.wsj.com/articles/xi-jinpings-leadership-style-micromanagement-that-leaves-underlings-scrambling-11639582426.

21. Lingling Wei & Jonathan Cheng, *Why Xi Jinping Reversed His Zero-Covid Policy in China*, WALL ST. J. (Jan. 4, 2023), https://www.wsj.com/articles/why-xi-jinping-reversed-his-zero-covid-policy-in-china-11672853171?st=ozb320jcplduln5.

22. Ibid.

23. Keith Zhai & Yang Jie, *Letter from Apple Supplier Foxconn's Founder Prodded China to Ease Zero-Covid Rules*, WALL ST. J. (Dec. 8, 2022), https://www.wsj.com/articles/letter-from-top-apple-supplier-foxconn-prodded-china-to-ease-zero-covid-rules-11670504366.

24. Wei & Cheng, *supra* note 21.

25. Katsuji Nakazawa, *Analysis: China's Elderly Pay Ultimate Price for COVID Missteps*, NIKKEI ASIA (Jan. 12, 2023), https://asia.nikkei.com/Editor-s-Picks/China-up-close/Analysis-China-s-elderly-pay-ultimate-price-for-COVID-missteps.

26. Lynette H. Ong, *China's Epidemic of Mistrust: How Xi Jinping's COVID-19 U-Turn Will Make the Country Harder to Govern*, FOREIGN AFFAIRS (Jan. 11, 2023), https://www.foreignaffairs.com/china/china-epidemic-mistrust-xi-jinping-covid-19?utm_campaign=tw_daily_soc&utm_medium=social&utm_source=twitter_posts; Clara Ferreira Marques, *Beware the Aftershocks of China's Covid Earthquake*, BLOOMBERG (Jan. 10, 2023), https://www.bloomberg.com/opinion/articles/2023-01-09/beware-the-aftershocks-of-china-s-covid-earthquake#xj4y7vzkg.

27. Ibid.

28. Pak You & Echo Wong, *Wealthy Chinese Ramp up Efforts to Shift Fortunes Overseas*, NIKKEI ASIA (Feb. 12, 2023), https://asia.nikkei.com/Economy/Wealthy-Chinese-ramp-up-efforts-to-shift-fortunes-overseas2.

29. Alfred Cang, *An Obscure Chinese Mining Law Is Hobbling Global Energy Security*, BLOOMBERG (Sept. 29, 2021), https://www.bloomberg.com/news/articles/2021-09-29/an-obscure-chinese-mining-law-is-hobbling-global-energy-security.

30. Primrose Riordan et al., *China's Energy Crisis Threatens Lengthy Disruption to Global Supply Chain*, FIN. TIMES (Oct. 16, 2021), https://www.ft.com/content/5174e592-1f0b-4334-91ab-aa89ceff3821.

31. Matthew Silberman, *How China's Energy Crisis Happened, in Six Steps*, SUPCHINA (Sept. 28, 2021), https://supchina.com/2021/09/28/how-chinas-energy-crisis-happened-in-six-steps/.

32. Matt McGrath, *Climate Change: China Aims for "Carbon Neutrality by 2060,"* BBC NEWS (Sept. 22, 2020), https://www.bbc.com/news/science-environment-54256826.

NOTES 313

33. Cang, *supra* note 29.

34. Orange Wang, *China's Power Crisis "Man-Made," and Miscalculations by Beijing Serve as "a Very Painful Lesson," Coal Insiders Say*, SOUTH CHINA MORNING POST (Nov. 10, 2021), https://www.scmp.com/economy/china-economy/article/3155584/chinas-power-crisis-man-made-and-miscalculations-beijing.

35. Amanda Lee, *China's Power Crisis: Why Is It Happening, How Bad Is It, and What if It Continues into the Freezing Winter Months?*, SOUTH CHINA MORNING POST (Oct. 10, 2021) https://www.scmp.com/economy/china-economy/article/3151710/chinas-power-crisis-why-it-happening-how-bad-it-and-what-if.

36. Ibid.

37. Cang, *supra* note 29.

38. Ibid.

39. Muyu Xu & Shivani Singh, *China Liberalises Coal-Fired Power Pricing to Tackle Energy Crisis*, REUTERS (Oct. 12, 2021), https://www.reuters.com/world/china/china-liberalise-thermal-power-pricing-tackle-energy-crisis-2021-10-12/.

40. Lee, *supra* note 35.

41. *China Tears Up the Rule Book in the Race to Fix Its Energy Crisis*, BLOOMBERG (Oct. 21, 2021), https://www.bloomberg.com/news/articles/2021-10-21/inside-the-race-to-fix-china-s-energy-crisis-without-missing-climate-goals.

42. *China Orders Coalmines to Raise Production to Address Power Crunch*, THE GUARDIAN (Oct. 8, 2021), https://www.theguardian.com/world/2021/oct/08/china-orders-coalmines-to-raise-production-to-address-power-crunch.

43. Zoey Zhang, *China to Defer Tax Payments for Manufacturing MSMEs, Coal-Fired Power Plants, and Heating Firms*, CHINA BRIEFING (Nov. 1, 2021), https://www.china-briefing.com/news/china-to-defer-tax-payments-for-manufacturing-msmes-coal-fired-power-plants-and-heating-firms/.

44. *China Orders Banks to Ramp Up Funding to Boost Coal Output*, BLOOMBERG (Oct. 5, 2021), https://www.bloomberg.com/news/articles/2021-10-05/china-bans-loans-to-speculate-in-commodities-some-luxury-goods-kudmrl57.

45. Yujie Xue, *Climate Change: China's Power Crisis May Cast a Shadow over Its New Climate Commitments Expected to Be Announced at COP26 in Glasgow*, SOUTH CHINA MORNING POST (Oct. 24, 2021), https://www.scmp.com/business/china-business/article/3153501/climate-change-chinas-power-crisis-may-cast-shadow-over-its.

46. Luna Sun, *China's Energy Crisis Is Easing, but Beijing Says "Results Must Be Consolidated" as Winter Months Loom*, SOUTH CHINA MORNING POST (Nov. 17, 2021), https://www.scmp.com/economy/china-economy/article/3156386/chinas-energy-crisis-easing-beijing-says-results-must-be.

47. See Xu & Singh, *supra* note 39.

48. *China's Coal Mine Safety Problem Is Back at the Worst Time*, BLOOMBERG (Mar. 8, 2022), https://www.bloomberg.com/news/articles/2022-03-09/china-s-coal-mine-safety-problem-is-back-at-the-worst-time.

NOTES

49. Barry Wilson, *Xi Jinping Says Houses Are "for Living In, Not for Speculation." But Is Hong Kong Listening?*, South China Morning Post (Nov. 12, 2017), https://www.scmp.com/comment/insight-opinion/article/2119306/xi-jinping-says-houses-are-living-not-speculation-hong-kong.

50. *What China's Three Red Lines Mean for Property Firms*, Bloomberg QuickTake (Oct. 8, 2020), https://www.bloomberg.com/news/articles/2020-10-08/what-china-s-three-red-lines-mean-for-property-firms-quicktake.

51. S. Alex Yang & Angela Zhang, *Evergrande and Energy Crises Show Beijing's Need for Systems Thinking*, Nikkei Asia (Oct. 7, 2021), https://asia.nikkei.com/Opinion/Evergrande-and-energy-crises-show-Beijing-s-need-for-systems-thinking.

52. Zeping Ren (任泽平), Fangdichan Dui Jingji Jinrong Yingxiang de Lianghua Cesuan (房地产对经济金融影响的量化测算) [Quantitative Study on the Impact of Real Estate on the Economy and Finance], Sina Finance (Oct. 29, 2021), http://finance.sina.com.cn/zl/china/2021-10-29/zl-iktzscyy2363864.shtml.

53. Ibid.

54. Ibid.

55. Brian Spegele et al., *How Evergrande Grew and Grew, Despite Years of Red Flags*, Wall St. J. (Oct. 8, 2021), https://www.wsj.com/articles/how-evergrande-grew-and-grew-despite-years-of-red-flags-11633685400.

56. Ibid.

57. Xiao Su (苏晓), 2021 Nian Chao 340 Jia Fang Qi Shenqing Pochan! (2021年超340家房企申请破产！) [More than 340 Real Estate Companies File for Bankruptcy in 2021!], FangChan.com (Jan. 28, 2021), http://m.fangchan.com/news/320/2022-01-28/6892687084315021633.html.

58. Tianxiang Hu (胡天祥), Fang Qi Da Xi Pai: Jinnian Pingjun Meitian You 1 Jia Pochan, Zhexie Zhiming Qiye Ye Nanyi Xingmian (房企大洗牌: 今年平均每天有1家破产, 这些知名企业也难以幸免) [Real Estate Company Reshuffle: On Average, 1 Company Goes Bankrupt Every Day This Year, and These Well-Known Companies Are Not Immune], Time-Weekly.Com (Sept. 6, 2021), https://www.time-weekly.com/post/284791; Iris Hong, *China Evergrande Debt Crisis: Five Developers on the Brink*, Asia Financial (Feb. 22, 2022), https://www.asiafinancial.com/china-evergrande-debt-crisis-five-developers-on-the-brink.

59. Jennifer Jet, *What Is Evergrande? The Chinese Property Giant Behind Global Sell-off Fears*, NBC News (Sept. 23, 2021), https://www.nbcnews.com/news/world/what-evergrande-chinese-property-giant-behind-global-selloff-fears-n1279929.

60. Quentin Webb & Stella Xie, *Beyond Evergrande, China's Property Market Faces a $5 Trillion Reckoning*, Wall St. J. (Oct. 10, 2021), https://www.wsj.com/articles/beyond-evergrande-chinas-property-market-faces-a-5-trillion-reckoning-11633882048 (showing that the 10 biggest developers, including China

NOTES 315

Evergrande, Country Garden Holdings Co., and China Vanke Co., saw sales down 44 percent from a year ago).

61. Tom Hancock & Enda Curran, *China's Property Crackdown Is Dragging Economy to Lows of 1990*, BLOOMBERG (Nov. 15, 2021), https://www.bloomberg.com/news/articles/2021-11-16/china-s-property-crackdown-is-dragging-economy-to-lows-of-1990.

62. Zhengxun Tan et al., *The Effect of Monetary Policy on China's Housing Prices before and after 2017: A Dynamic Analysis in DSGE Model*, 113 LAND USE POLICY 105927 (2022), https://doi.org/10.1016/j.landusepol.2021.105927.

63. Gabriel Crossley & Stella Qiu, *China to Roll Out Fiscal Policies Proactively to Stabilise Growth Next Year*, REUTERS (Dec. 27, 2021), https://www.reuters.com/markets/rates-bonds/china-roll-out-fiscal-policies-proactively-stabilise-growth-next-year-2021-12-27/.

64. Sylvia Sheng, *No U-Turn on China's Regulatory Crackdown in 2022, but Policy Easing Should Lift Investor Spirits*, SOUTH CHINA MORNING POST (Dec. 17, 2021), https://www.scmp.com/comment/opinion/article/3159942/no-u-turn-chinas-regulatory-crackdown-2022-policy-easing-should.

65. Lingling Wei, *China Weighs Moderating Property Curbs to Help Troubled Developers Unload Assets*, WALL ST. J. (Nov. 10, 2021), https://www.wsj.com/articles/china-weighs-moderating-property-curbs-to-help-troubled-developers-unload-assets-11636572669?mod=article_inline.

66. Arendse Huld, *Explainer: What's Going on in China's Property Market?*, CHINA BRIEFING (Jan. 14, 2022), https://www.china-briefing.com/news/explainer-whats-going-on-in-chinas-property-market/.

67. *How China Is Seeking to Revive a $2.4 Trillion Property Market*, BLOOMBERG (May 25, 2022), https://www.bloomberg.com/news/articles/2022-05-25/how-china-is-seeking-to-revive-a-2-4-trillion-property-market.

68. Ibid.

69. *China Property Crisis: Beijing May Ease "Three Red Lines" Rules in Big Shift*, BLOOMBERG (Jan. 6, 2023), https://www.bloomberg.com/news/articles/2023-01-06/china-may-ease-three-red-lines-property-rules-in-drastic-shift?utm_source=website&utm_medium=share&utm_campaign=twitter#xj4y7vzkg.

70. Feng Wang et al., *Population, Policy, and Politics: How Will History Judge China's One-Child Policy?*, 38 POPUL. DEV. REV. 115 (2012).

71. Ibid.

72. PENG XIZHE, DEMOGRAPHIC TRANSITION IN CHINA: FERTILITY TRENDS SINCE THE 1950S (1991).

73. Junsen Zhang, *The Evolution of China's One-Child Policy and Its Effects on Family Outcomes*, 31 J. ECON. PERSPECT. 141 (2017).

74. PEIYUN PENG (彭佩云), ZHONGGUO JIHUA SHENGYU QUAN SHU (中国计划生育全书) [A COMPLETE BOOK OF CHINA'S FAMILY PLANNING] (1997).

75. Wang et al., *supra* note 70; see also SUSAN GREENHALGH, JUST ONE CHILD: SCIENCE AND POLICY IN DENG'S CHINA (2008).

76. See GREENHALGH, *supra* note 75.

77. Wang et al., *supra* note 70; see also GREENHALGH, *supra* note 75, at 273–278.

78. See GREENHALGH, *supra* note 75, at 294–295.

79. See Zhang, *supra* note 73; M. Giovanna Merli et al., *Adaptation of a Political Bureaucracy to Economic and Institutional Change under Socialism: The Chinese State Family Planning System*, 32 POLITICS SOC. 231 (2004).

80. Wang et al., *supra* note 70.

81. See Merli et al., *supra* note 79, at 235.

82. Ibid.

83. Feng Wang, *The Future of a Demographic Overachiever: Long-Term Implications of the Demographic Transition in China*, 37 POPUL. DEV. REV. 173 (2011).

84. See Greenhalgh, *supra* note 75.

85. See Zhang, *supra* note 73.

86. Ibid.

87. Zhang, *supra* note 73, at 151–152 [citing Yong Cai, *China's Below-Replacement Fertility: Government Policy or Socioeconomic Development?*, 36 POPULATION & DEVELOPMENT REV. 419 (2010); Wang et al., *supra* note 72; Martin King Whyte et al., *Challenging Myths about China's One-Child Policy*, 74 CHINA JOURNAL 144 (2015)].

88. Feng Wang et al., *The End of China's One-Child Policy*, 47 STUD. FAM. PLAN. 83 (2016).

89. Zhang, *supra* note 73.

90. Yong Cai (蔡泳), Lianheguo Yuce Zhongguo Kuaisu Zou Xiang Laoling Hua (联合国预测中国快速走向老龄化) [China's Demographic Prospects: A UN Perspective], INT'L ECON. REV. 73 (2012).

91. Wang, *supra* note 83.

92. Wang et al., *supra* note 70, at 125.

93. Ibid.

94. Fei Wang et al., *China's Family Planning Policies and Their Labor Market Consequences*, 30 J. POPUL. ECON. 31 (2017).

95. Mara Hvistendahl, *Has China Outgrown the One-Child Policy?*, 329 SCI. 1458 (2010), http://image.sciencenet.cn/olddata/kexue.com.cn/upload/blog/file/2010/9/2010917535739887.pdf; see also Wang et al., *supra* note 94.

96. Ibid.; see also Merli et al., *supra* note 79, at 233–234.

97. Andrew Mullen, *China's One-Child Policy: What Was It and What Impact Did It Have?*, SOUTH CHINA MORNING POST (Jun. 1, 2021), https://www.scmp.com/economy/china-economy/article/3135510/chinas-one-child-policy-what-was-it-and-what-impact-did-it.

98. Wang et al., *supra* note 70, at 120–125.

99. Hvistendahl, *supra* note 95.

100. Yong Cai, *An Assessment of China's Fertility Level Using the Variable-r Method*, 45 DEMOGRAPHY 271 (2008).

101. Ibid.

102. Hvistendahl, *supra* note 95.

NOTES

317

103. Ibid.

104. Jianzhang Liang (梁建章), Xianzai Lian Zhai Zhenwu Dou Zhichi Quanmian Fang Kai Shengyu Le? (现在连翟振武都支持全面放开生育了?) [Now Even Zhai Zhenwu Supports the Full Liberalization of Fertility?], 163.COM (Dec. 23, 2020), https://www.163.com/money/article/FUHGIGRR00258 J1R.html.

105. Wenchen Cao (曹玟梦), Zhai Zhenwu: "Zhongguo You Renkou Xue Fazhan he Yanjiu de Feiwo Turang" (翟振武: "中国有人口学发展和研究的肥沃土壤") [Zhai Zhenwu: "China Has Fertile Soil for Demographic Development and Research"], RUC NEWS (May 19, 2015), https://news ruc.edu.cn/archi ves/105091.

106. Zhenwu Zhai (翟振武) et al., Liji Quanmian Kaifang Er Tai Zhengce de Renkou Xue Houguo Fenxi (立即全面开放二胎政策的人口学后果分析) [Demographic Consequences of an Immediate Transition to a Universal Two-child Policy], 38 POPULATION RSCH 3 (2014).

107. Xiaochun Qiao (乔晓春), Zhongguo Jihua Shengyu Zhengce de Yanbian (中国计划生育政策的演变) [The Evolution of China's Family Planning Policy], OYJJ-OYS.ORG (2016), http://www.oyjj-oys.org/UploadFile/Site Content/FJList/sigfgj5s.pdf.

108. Mullen, *supra* note 97.

109. Jane Cai et al., *"Too Much Pressure": Mixed Reaction to China's New 3-Child Policy*, SOUTH CHINA MORNING POST (Jun. 3, 2021), https://www.scmp.com/ news/china/politics/article/3135815/too-much-pressure-mixed-reaction-chi nas-new-3-child-policy.

110. Sebastian Heilmann, *From Local Experiments to National Policy: The Origins of China's Distinctive Policy Process*, 59 CHINA J. 1, 25–30 (2008).

111. SEBASTIAN HEILMANN, RED SWAN: HOW UNORTHODOX POLICY-MAKING FACILITATED CHINA'S RISE 5 (2018); JUSTIN YIFU LIN ET AL., THE CHINA MIRACLE: DEVELOPMENT STRATEGY AND ECONOMIC REFORM 321–325 (2003); Thomas G. Rawski, *Implications of China's Reform Experience*, 144 THE CHINA QUARTERLY 1150 (1995); Dani Rodrik, *Growth Strategies*, in 1 HANDBOOK OF ECONOMIC GROWTH 967–1014 (Philippe Aghion & Steven Durlauf eds., 2005).

112. ISABELLA M. WEBER, HOW CHINA ESCAPED SHOCK THERAPY: THE MARKET REFORM DEBATE (2021).

113. Heilmann, *supra* note 111, at 96–106; see also GÉRARD ROLAND, TRANSITION AND ECONOMICS: POLITICS, MARKETS, AND FIRMS (COMPARATIVE INSTITUTIONAL ANALYSIS) 63 (2000); DAVID ZWEIG, INTERNATIONALIZING CHINA: DOMESTIC INTERESTS AND GLOBAL LINKAGE (2002); SUSAN YOUNG, PRIVATE BUSINESS AND ECONOMIC REFORM IN CHINA (1995); CARL E. WALTER & FRASER J.T. HOWIE, PRIVATIZING CHINA: INSIDE CHINA'S STOCK MARKETS (2nd ed., 2011).

114. Heilmann, *supra* note 110, at 25–30.

115. Ibid., at 18.

116. Ibid., at 19.

117. Elizabeth J. Perry, *Studying Chinese Politics: Farewell to Revolution?*, 57 CHINA J. 1 (2007).
118. CHINA'S POLITICAL SYSTEM (Sebastian Heilmann ed., 2016).
119. Heilmann, *supra* note 111, at 87, 110.
120. Ibid., at 87–90.
121. Ibid., at 67, 90.
122. Roland, *supra* note 113, at 63.
123. James Kai-Sing Kung & Shuo Chen, *The Tragedy of the Nomenklatura: Career Incentives and Political Radicalism during China's Great Leap Famine*, 105 AM. POLIT. SCI. REV. 27 (2011).
124. Ibid.
125. Jie Gao, *"Bypass the Lying Mouths": How Does the CCP Tackle Information Distortion at Local Levels?*, 228 CHINA Q. 950 (2016).
126. See Heilmann, *supra* note 118.
127. Ziying Fan et al., *Information Distortion in Hierarchical Organizations: A Study of China's Great Famine* (Feb. 2016) (working paper, Princeton University).
128. Ibid.
129. Ibid.
130. Gao, *supra* note 125, at 956.
131. Ibid., at 967.
132. YUEN YUEN ANG, HOW CHINA ESCAPED THE POVERTY TRAP 74–75 (2016).
133. Heilmann, *supra* note 111, at 210.
134. Sebastian Heilmann, *Introduction to China's Core Executive: Leadership Styles, Structures and Processes under Xi Jinping, in* 1 MERICS PAPERS ON CHINA, CHINA'S CORE EXECUTIVE: LEADERSHIP STYLES, STRUCTURES AND PROCESSES UNDER XI JINPING 9 (Sebastian Heilmann & Matthias Stepan eds., 2016).
135. Barry Naughton, *Shifting Structures and Processes in Economic Policy-Making at the Center, in* CHINA'S CORE EXECUTIVE, *supra* note 134, at 40.
136. Nassim Nicholas Taleb & Gregory F. Treverton, *The Calm before the Storm: Why Volatility Signals Stability and Vice Versa*, FOREIGN AFFAIRS (Jan. 16, 2015), https://www.foreignaffairs.com/articles/africa/calm-storm.
137. Ibid.
138. Heilmann, *supra* note 111, at 210.
139. Ibid., at 211.

CHAPTER 4

1. ANGELA HUYUE ZHANG, CHINESE ANTITRUST EXCEPTIONALISM: HOW THE RISE OF CHINA CHALLENGES GLOBAL REGULATION 29 (2021) (quoting a senior lawyer saying: "foreign firms are soft persimmons that are much easier to squeeze than the SOEs").
2. Catalin Cimpanu, *China's Great Firewall Is Blocking Around 311k Domains, 41k by Accident*, THE RECORD (Jul. 11, 2021), https://therecord.media/chinas-great-firewall-is-blocking-around-311k-domains-41k-by-accident/.

NOTES 319

3. *The Great Firewall of China*, BLOOMBERG (Nov. 6, 2018), https://www.bloomberg.com/quicktake/great-firewall-of-china.

4. *Google Loses Market Share to Baidu*, CHINA.ORG.CN (Jul. 20, 2010), http://www.china.org.cn/business/2010-07/20/content_20535620.htm.

5. Jessica E. Vascellaro et al., *Google Warns of China Exit over Hacking*, WALL ST. J. (Jan. 13, 2010), https://www.wsj.com/articles/SB126333757451026659.

6. *Google Exit from China a Predictable Gift: Baidu Chief*, ECONOMIC TIMES (Nov. 16, 2010), https://m.economictimes.com/tech/internet/google-exit-from-china-a-predictable-gift-baidu-chief/articleshow/6934003.cms.

7. LULU YILUN CHEN, INFLUENCE EMPIRE: THE STORY OF TENCENT & CHINA'S TECH AMBITION 31–36 (2022).

8. Carol X. J. Ou et al., *Beyond Institutional Based Loyalty: Building Effective Online Marketplaces with Social Mechanisms*, 31ST INTERNATIONAL CONFERENCE ON INFORMATION SYSTEMS 2 (2010). See also Helen H. Wang, *How EBay Failed in China*, FORBES (Sep. 12, 2010), https://www.forbes.com/sites/china/2010/09/12/how-ebay-failed-in-china/?sh=206ebf3d5d57.

9. Eleanor Olcott, *Alibaba Faces New Crocodiles in the Yangtze* FIN. TIMES (Nov. 30, 2021), https://www.ft.com/content/1b161dfb-4927-49fa-a0a7-06bb7ad15534

10. Josh Horwitz, *Why Internet Users Chose Baidu over Google When It Was in China*, QUARTZ (Aug. 9, 2018), https://qz.com/1352137/why-internet-users-chose-baidu-over-google-when-it-was-in-china/.

11. Cresty Lee, *Most Popular Search Engines in China–2021*, THE EGG (Sept. 9, 2021), https://www.theegg.com/seo/china/most-popular-search-engines-in-china-2021/.

12. Robyn Dixon & David Pierson, *Bing Comes Back Online in China, but There Are More Questions than Answers*, L.A. TIMES (Jan. 23, 2019), https://www.latimes.com/world/asia/la-fg-china-bing-20190124-story.html.

13. Jasmine Zheng & Ward Zhou, *Chinese Corporate Venture Capital: A Golden Decade and a Looming Fall*, TECHNODE (Feb. 15, 2022), https://technode.com/2022/02/15/chinese-corporate-venture-capital-a-golden-decade-and-a-looming-fall/.

14. Ali Touzi Shinian Mailuo: Qichacha Shuju Xianshi 2021 Nian Qi Touzi Shoujin, Jujiao Dianshang Wuliu Deng San Da Zhu Saidao (阿里投资十年脉络: 企查查数据显示2021年其投资收紧, 聚焦电商物流等三大主赛道) [Tracking Alibaba's 10-Year Investment: Qichacha Data Shows It Tightened Investment in 2021, Focusing on Three Major Sectors Including E-commerce and Logistics], SOHU NEWS (Mar. 9, 2022), https://www.sohu.com/a/528324753_422199; Zheng & Zhou, *supra* note 13.

15. Liu Chiping "Shai" Tengxun Touzi Chengji Dan: 70 Duo Jia Shangshi Gongsi, 160 Duo Jia Dujiaoshou (刘炽平"晒"腾讯投资成绩单: 70 多家上市公司, 160 多家独角兽) [Liu Chiping "Showed Off" Tencent's Investment Records: More than 70 Public Companies and 160 Unicorns], SINA NEWS (Jan. 20, 2020), https://tech.sina.com.cn/roll/2020-01-20/doc-iihnzhha3696779.shtml.

NOTES

16. Zheng & Zhou, *supra* note 13.

17. Juan Tao (陶娟), Shouge Zhe: Tengxun Ali de 20 Wan Yi Shengtai Quan (收割者: 腾讯阿里的20万亿生态圈) [The Reaper: Tencent and Alibaba's 20-Trillion-RMB Ecosystems], SINA NEWS (Nov. 10, 2020), https://finance.sina.com.cn/china/2020-11-10/doc-iiznctke0726290.shtml.

18. Ibid.

19. *China Internet Report 2021*, SOUTH CHINA MORNING POST (Aug. 31, 2021), https://multimedia.scmp.com/infographics/china-internet-2021/.

20. Adam Lashinsky, *Alibaba v. Tencent: The Battle for Supremacy in China*, YAHOO (Jun. 21, 2018), t.ly/jST6M; see also CHEN, *supra* note 7, at 52.

21. IT Juzi: 2021 Nian Zhongguo CVC Touzi Binggou Baogao (IT桔子: 2021年中国CVC投资并购报告) [IT Juzi: 2021 Report on China's CVC Merger & Acquisition], 199IT (Nov. 9, 2021), http://www.199it.com/archives/1339446.html.

22. Ibid.

23. CHEN, *supra* note 7, at 66.

24. Ibid., at 51.

25. Ibid., at 92.

26. Karishma Vaswani, *The Race to Create the World's Next Super-App*, BBC NEWS (Feb. 5, 2021), https://www.bbc.com/news/business-55929418.

27. Zheng & Zhou, *supra* note 13.

28. Huya 2021 Annual Report 119, https://ir.huya.com/Annual-Reports.

29. Douyu 2021 Annual Report 123, https://ir.douyu.com/Annual-Reports.

30. Shichang Jianguan Zong Ju Guanyu Jinzhi Huya yu Douyu Hebing An Fan Longduan Shencha Jueding de Gonggao (市场监管总局关于禁止虎牙与斗鱼合并案反垄断审查决定的公告) [Announcement of the State Administration for Market Regulation on the Anti-Monopoly Review Decision on Prohibiting the Merger of Huya and DouYu], SAMR.GOV (Jul. 10, 2021), https://www.samr.gov.cn/xw/zj/202107/P020210710327201713322.pdf.

31. Hai Wang (王海), Ali Za Xia 233 Yi, Jiang Cainiao Chigu Bili Cong 51% Sheng Zhi 63% (阿里砸下233亿, 将菜鸟持股比例从51%升至63%) [Alibaba Spent RMB 23.3 Billion to Raise Its Shares in Cainiao from 51% to 63%], YICAI (Nov. 8, 2019), https://www.yicai.com/news/100396471.html; YTO Express 2021 Annual Report 109, http://www.sse.com.cn/disclosure/listedinfo/announcement/c/new/2022-04-27/600233_20220427_32_vpOBR9fa.pdf; RRS Supply Chain 2021 Annual Report 243, http://pdf.dfcfw.com/pdf/H2_AN202203041550536889_1.pdf; Best Inc. 2021 Annual Report 131, https://sec.report/Document/0001104659-22-046848/; ZTO Express 2021 Annual Report 182, https://fscdn.zto.com/fs21/M03/9A/3B/CgRRhWJqobmAToWfADqAeCQoKG0174.pdf; STO Express 2021 Annual Report 92, 216, http://static.cninfo.com.cn/finalpage/2022-04-30/1213262585.PDF; Yunda Express 2021 Annual Report 135, http://www.szse.cn/disclosure/lis

NOTES 321

ted/bulletinDetail/index.html?8d7259f3-0478-470e-8a46-198db0425712; Singapore Post 2021/22 Annual Report 42, https://www.singpost.com/sites/default/files/upload/publications/SingPost-AR-202122_0.pdf.

32. Shi Zhang Tu Liaojie 2021 Nian Zhongguo Kuaidi Hangye Shichang Guimo, Jingzheng Geju ji Fazhan Qushi Kuaidi Hangye Weichi Gao Zengzhang (十张图了解2021年中国快递行业市场规模、竞争格局及发展趋势 快递行业维持高增长 [Ten Pictures to Understand the Market Size, Competition Pattern and Development Trend of China's Express-Delivery Industry in 2021, Express-Delivery Industry Maintains High Growth], QIANZHAN.COM (Jul. 10, 2021), https://bg.qianzhan.com/trends/detail/506/210709-5bfb2f45.html.

33. José Azar et al., *Anticompetitive Effects of Common Ownership*, 73(4) J. FINANCE 1513 (2018).

34. Ian R. Appel et al., *Passive Investors, Not Passive Owners*, 121(1) J. FIN. ECON. 111 (2016); Einer Elhauge, *Horizontal Shareholding*, 129 HARV. L. REV. 1267 (2016); Eric A. Posner et al., *A Proposal to Limit the Anticompetitive Power of Institutional Investors*, 81(3) ANTITRUST L. J. 669 (2017).

35. Jonathan B. Baker, *Overlapping Financial Investor Ownership, Market Power, and Antitrust Enforcement: My Qualified Agreement with Professor Elhauge*, 129 HARV. L. REV. F. 212 (2016).

36. Shen Nanpeng Mai Xia Ban Ge Zhongguo Hulianwang, Hongshan Zhongguo Nengfou Wen Zuo "Fengtou Zhi Wang"? (沈南鹏买下半个中国互联网，红杉中国能否稳坐"风投之王"?) [Shen Nanpeng Has Bought Half of China's Internet, Can Sequoia China Secure Its Place as the "King of Venture Capital"?], 36KR.COM (Nov. 30, 2020), https://36kr.com/p/99058477 1814021.

37. Zhe Ge Nanren, Jushuo Yijing Qiaoqiao Mai Xia Le Zhongguo Ban Ge Hulianwang (这个男人，据说已经悄悄买下了中国半个互联网) [This Man Is Said to Have Bought Half of China's Internet], CENTER FOR CHINA AND GLOBALIZATION (Jun. 23, 2016), http://www.ccg.org.cn/archives/29480.

38. Wei, You Ren Zhuyi Dao Meituan yu Dianping Hebing de Muhou Tuishou Le Ma? Zhe Bing Fei Shen Nanpeng (Hongshan) de Diyi Ci (喂，有人注意到美团与点评合并的幕后推手了吗？ 这并非沈南鹏(红杉)的第一次) [Hey, Has Anyone Noticed the Driving Force Behind the Merge of Meituan and Dianping? This Is Not the First Time for Shen Nanpeng (Sequoia)], HUXIU.COM (Oct. 8, 2015), https://www.huxiu.com/article/127604.html.

39. Ron Haruni, *Why Are Chinese Social Networks Blocking Baidu's Search Engine Spiders?*, SEEKING ALPHA (Sept. 16, 2008), https://seekingalpha.com/article/95715-why-are-chinese-social-networks-blocking-baidus-search-engine-spiders.

40. Ibid.

41. Alex Moazed, *What You Can Learn from Alibaba's Battle with the Google of China*, INC.COM (Jul. 9, 2015), https://www.inc.com/alex-moazed/why-alibaba-shut-out-the-google-of-china-and-all-that-referral-traffic.html.

42. *Alibaba Bans Sellers from Using WeChat, Launches New Weibo Feature*, WALL ST. J. (Aug. 1, 2013), https://www.wsj.com/articles/BL-CJB-18364; Xuemei Yang (杨雪梅), Weixin Qi Nian "Feng Lian" Shi (微信七年"封链"史) [WeChat's Seven-Year History of "Blocking Links"], SINA NEWS (Mar. 6, 2020), https://tech.sina.com.cn/i/2020-03-06/doc-iimxxstf6775344.shtml.

43. Ibid.

44. Yi Xue & Gu Tian, *Blocking External Links, A Monopoly Issue or Not?*, ZHONG LUN LAW FIRM (Dec. 21, 2021), https://www.zhonglun.com/Content/2021/12-21/1108228652.html.

45. Zhang Ye, *JD Terminates Link with Weibo*, GLOBAL TIMES (Sept. 1, 2013), https://www.globaltimes.cn/content/807875.shtml.

46. Iris Deng & Jane Zhang, *Tencent to Offload US$16 Billion Stake in No 2 E-commerce Player JD.com as China's Antitrust Pressure Mounts*, SOUTH CHINA MORNING POST (Dec. 23, 2021), https://www.scmp.com/tech/big-tech/article/3160765/chinese-internet-giant-tencent-offload-its-us16-billion-stake-no-2-e.

47. See Yang, *supra* note 42.

48. Yating Zhang (张雅婷) & Zhiting Yan (闫智婷), Douyin Su Tengxun Beihou: Cong Shangye Jingzheng dao Fan Longduan Dazhan (抖音诉腾讯背后: 从商业竞争到反垄断大战) [Behind Douyin v. Tencent: From Business Competition to Antitrust War], SFCCN.COM (Feb. 3, 2021), https://m.sfccn.com/2021/2-3/5MMDEoMDdfMTYyNDY5MA.html; See Yang, *supra* note 42.

49. See Zhang & Yan, *supra* note 48.

50. "Tou Teng Dazhan" Chixu San Nian He Yi Shouchang? ("头腾大战"持续三年何以收场?) [How Will the Three-Year Long "Toutiao-Tencent" War End?], SINA NEWS (Feb. 6, 2021), https://finance.sina.com.cn/tech/2021-02-06/doc-ikftpnny5380113.shtml#.

51. Rita Liao, *China Court Accepts ByteDance Case Filing against Tencent over Alleged Monopoly*, TECHCRUNCH (Feb. 8, 2021), t.ly/amTVi; Celia Chen et al., *Tencent Sues ByteDance for 1 Yuan, Seeks Apology for Defamation*, SOUTH CHINA MORNING POST (Jun. 1, 2018), https://www.scmp.com/tech/china-tech/article/2148906/tencent-sues-chinas-largest-news-aggregator-1-yuan-seeks-apology.

52. Jet Deng & Ken Dai, *Antitrust Enforcement against Digital Platforms in China: Anatomy of "Choose One from Two,"* WHOSWHOLEGAL (Nov. 12, 2020), https://whoswholegal.com/features/antitrust-enforcement-against-digital-platforms-in-china-anatomy-of-choose-one-from-two.

53. Juliet Ye, *QQ-360 Battle Escalates into War*, WALL ST. J. (Nov. 5, 2010), https://www.wsj.com/articles/BL-CJB-11516.

54. "Er Xuan Yi" Jiufen You Xian, Meituan Eleme Hu Su Bu Zhengdang Jingzheng Huo Pei! ("二选一"纠纷又现, 美团饿了么互诉不正当竞争获赔!) [Disputes over "Choose One from Two" Re-emerge, Meituan and Eleme Sued Each Other and Both Got Compensated!], SOHU NEWS (Apr. 14, 2021), https://www.sohu.com/a/460776258_161795.

NOTES

55. *China's Digital Economy: A Leading Global Force* 13–17, McKinsey Global Institute (Aug. 3, 2017), https://www.mckinsey.com/featured-insights/china/chinas-digital-economy-a-leading-global-force.

56. Ibid.

57. Shu Zhang & Matthew Miller, *China to Allow Banks to Directly Invest in High-Growth Tech Firms*, Reuters (Feb. 1, 2016), https://www.reuters.com/article/china-bank-tech-idINKCN0VA1UH.

58. Chu Zhang & Lingfei Lei, *The Chinese Approach to Electronic Transactions Legislation*. 9 Computer L. Rev. & Tech. J. 333 (2005).

59. Chuanman You, *Law and Policy of Platform Economy in China*, 39 Comput. L. Secur. Rev. 1, 6 (2020).

60. Jingting Deng & Pinxin Liu, *Consultative Authoritarianism: The Drafting of China's Internet Security Law and E-Commerce Law*, 26 J. Contemp. China 679, 686 (2017).

61. Ibid.

62. *A Game Changer? China Enacts First E-Commerce Law*, Hogan Lovells (Sept. 2018), https://f.datasrvr.com/fr1/218/46285/Alert_Corporate_A_game_chang er_-_China_enacts_first_e-commerce_law3.pdf.

63. Li Keqiang, *Report on the Work of the Government 2019*, PRC State Council (Mar. 16, 2019), http://english.www.gov.cn/premier/speeches/2019/03/16/content_281476565265580.htm; Hui Zhou (周慧) & Wei Zhao (赵炜), Li Keqiang:Yanxu Jicheng Dianlu he Ruanjian Qiye Suodeshui Youhui Zhengce (李克强:延续集成电路和软件企业所得税优惠政策) [Li Keqiang: Prolong the Preferential Income Tax Policy for Integrated Circuits and Software Companies], 21JINGJI (May 9, 2019), https://m.21jingji.com/article/20190 509/7523b3ad6114aea0145bbdc542e20946.html?from=weibo.

64. Renmin Ribao Ping Shequ Tuangou: Bie Zhi Dianjizhe Ji Kun Baicai, Keji Chuangxin de Xingchen Dahai Geng Lingren Xinchaopengpai (人民日报评论社区团购: 别只惦记着几捆白菜, 科技创新的星辰大海更令人心潮澎湃) [People's Daily Commenting on Community Group Buying: Don't Just Focus on Selling Cabbages; Technology and Innovation Are More Exciting], Wallstreetcn.com (Dec. 11, 2020), https://wallstreetcn.com/articles/3613229.

65. Iris Deng & Xinmei Shen, *Chinese Newspaper Labels Gaming "Spiritual Opium" and Calls Out Tencent, Fanning Fears of a Crackdown*, South China Morning Post (Aug. 3, 2021), https://www.scmp.com/tech/article/3143 609/chinese-newspaper-labels-gaming-spiritual-opium-and-calls-out-tenc ent-fanning.

66. *China to Strengthen Anti-Trust Regulatory Powers*, Reuters (Mar. 15, 2021), https://www.reuters.com/business/media-telecom/china-strengthen-anti-trust-regulatory-powers-state-media-2021-03-15/.

67. Pei Li & Coco Liu, *China Said to Expand Anti-Monopoly Bureau as Crackdown Widens*, Bloomberg (Oct. 12, 2021), https://www.bloomberg.com/news/

324   NOTES

articles/2021-10-12/china-said-to-expand-anti-monopoly-bureau-as-crackd own-widens.

68. Fan Longduan Fa (反垄断法) [Anti-Monopoly Law] (promulgated by the Standing Comm. Nat'l. People's Cong., Aug. 30, 2007, effective Aug. 1, 2008), art. 22.

69. Ibid., art. 58.

70. Ibid., art. 63.

71. *China Passed Amendments to Its Anti-Monopoly Law*, CLIFFORD CHANCE (Jun. 27, 2022), https://www.cliffordchance.com/content/dam/cliffordchance/briefi ngs/2022/06/client%20briefing---china-passed-amendments-to-its-anti-monopoly-law-en.pdf.

72. Based on publicly available information and the author's tally.

73. Ma Huateng: "Hulianwang +" Chengwei Jingji Shehui Chuangxin Yinqing (马化腾: "互联网+"成为经济社会创新引擎) [Pony Ma: "Internet Plus" Has Become the Engine of Economic and Social Innovation], FINANCE.CHINA (Mar. 4, 2015), http://finance.china.com.cn/roll/20150304/2984531.shtml; Ma Huateng Liang Hui San Xiang Ti'an: Chuangxin, Guihua, Zouchuqu (马化腾两会三项提案: 创新, 规划, 走出去) [Pony Ma Submitted Three Proposals during the Two Sessions: Innovation, Planning, and Going Out], SINA NEWS (Mar. 4, 2013), http://tech.sina.com.cn/i/2013-03-04/18398110682.shtml.

74. Guanyu Yi "Hulianwang +" Wei Qudong Tuijin Woguo Jingji Shehui Chuangxin Fazhan de Jianyi (关于以"互联网+"为驱动 推进我国经济社会创新发展的建议) [Advice on Promoting Our Country's Economic and Social Innovation and Development with "Internet Plus" as the Driving Force], CLOUD.TENCENT.COM (Mar. 9, 2018), https://cloud.tencent.com/developer/article/1056389.

75. CHEN, *supra* note 7, at 175–176.

76. Ibid., at 176.

77. Ibid.

78. Poppy Reid, *China's Copyright Watchdog Bans Unlicensed Music Streaming*, THE-MUSICNETWORK.COM (Oct. 27, 2015), https://themusicnetwork.com/chinas-copyright-watchdog-bans-unlicensed-music-streaming/.

79. Xu Liu (刘旭), Fan Longduan Fa Xueshu Shengtai zhi Fansi (反垄断法学术生态之反思) [Reflecting on the Academic Ecology of Anti-Monopoly Law], ZHIHU (Jun. 5, 2015), https://zhuanlan.zhihu.com/p/19975945.

80. See ZHANG, *supra* note 1, at 106.

81. Qianlin Yang (杨茜麟), Rang Zidan Fei Yihuier? Hulianwang Pingtai "Er Xuan Yi" Falü Shiyong Sibian (让子弹飞一会儿? 互联网平台"二选一"法律适用思辨) [Let the Bullet Fly a Bit Longer? Reflections on the "Choose One from Two" Practice of Internet Platforms], QQ.COM (Jun. 7, 2019), https://mp.weixin.qq.com/s/JiK_OR2Yc4QJoQAbu6c5YQ.

82. Sun Yu, *China Tech Groups Hire Ex-Regulators to Fend Off Beijing's Crackdown*, FIN. TIMES (Apr. 21, 2021), https://www.ft.com/content/71daa106-259e-4dc2-b267-b0289177de1f.

NOTES

83. *Ex-Regulators Draw Top Pay to Help Firms Decode China Crackdown*, BLOOMBERG (Aug. 16, 2021), https://www.bloomberg.com/news/articles/2021-08-15/ex-regulators-earn-460-000-to-help-firms-decode-china-crackdown.

84. Ibid.

85. Xu Liu (刘旭), Cong Fan Longduan Fa Xuezhe Jieshou Hulianwang Qiye Weituo he Zizhu Bixu Baochi Touming Tan Qi——Zai Tan Fan Longduan Fa Xueshu Shengtai (从反垄断法学者接受互联网企业委托和资助必须保持透明谈起——再谈反垄断法学术生态) [Antitrust Legal Scholars Must Be Transparent about Accepting Offers and Funds from Internet Companies—Rediscuss the Academic Ecology of Antitrust Law], ZHIHU.COM (Mar. 16, 2021), https://zhuanlan.zhihu.com/p/357557531.

86. Xu Liu (刘旭), Zhang Qiong, Zhang Handong, Li Qing de Shuming Wenzhang <Shen Yan Wangluo Zhifu Fan Longduan> Yuanyin de Hexin Shuju Cun Yi (张穹、张汉东、李青的署名文章《慎言网络支付垄断》援引的核心数据存疑) [The Core Data Cited in Zhang Qiong, Zhang Handong, and Li Qing's Article "Talk Cautiously about Online Payment Monopoly" Is Doubtful], QQ.COM (Sept. 17, 2020), https://mp.weixin.qq.com/s/mqmDFpELqLOdFzHZ7ALccw.

87. Keith Zhai & Julie Zhu, *Urged on by Central Bank, China Weighs Antitrust Probe into Alipay, WeChat Pay*, REUTERS (Jul. 31, 2020), https://www.reuters.com/article/alipay-wechat-pay-china-idCNL5N2F13EV.

88. Qiong Zhang (张穹) et al., <Cai Jing> Xin Meiti: Shen Yan Wangluo Zhifu Longduan (《财经》新媒体: 慎言网络支付垄断) [Caijing New Media: Talk Cautiously about Online Payment Monopoly], QQ.COM (Sept. 17, 2020), t.ly/RvCsu.

89. Ke Xu (许可), Wangluo Zhifu Longduan de Zhen yu Wei (网络支付垄断的真与伪) [The Truth and Falsehood of Online Payment Monopoly], QQ.COM (Jun. 7, 2020), t.ly/QikAG; Weigang Fu (傅蔚冈), Wangluo Zhifu: Shichang Guimo Bu Dengyu Longduan Xingwei (网络支付: 市场规模不等于垄断行为) [Online Payment: Market Size Does Not Equal Monopolistic Behaviour], QQ.COM (Sept. 28, 2020), t.ly/mwtxb; see also Xu Liu (刘旭), Hui Zong: Zhiyi huo Zhuzhang Yanhuan Zhongguo Hulianwang Hangye Fan Longduan Zhifa de Xuezhe Guandian (汇总: 质疑或主张延缓中国互联网行业反垄断执法的学者观点) [Summary: Viewpoints of Scholars Who Doubt or Advocate Postponing Antitrust Enforcement in China's Internet Industry], QQ.COM (Oct. 18, 2021), t.ly/WBz8m.

90. Marcia Ellis et al., *The VIE Structure: Past, Present and Future—Part I*, HONG KONG LAWYER (Jun., 2020), https://www.hk-lawyer.org/content/vie-structure-past-present-and-future-%E2%80%93-part-i.

91. Song Xue (薛松), VIE Haiwai Shangshi Guli Haishi Xianzhi Yinfa Re Lun (VIE海外上市 鼓励还是限制引发热论) [VIE Overseas Listing: To Encourage or Restrict? A Hot Debate Is Provoked], FINANCE.CE.CN (Mar. 5, 2013), http://finance.ce.cn/rolling/201303/05/t20130305_240255.shtml.

92. Fa Chen, *Variable Interest Entity Structures in China: Are Legal Uncertainties and Risks to Foreign Investors Part of China's Regulatory Policy?*, 29(1) ASIA PAC. L.

Rev. 1–24 (2021), https://www.tandfonline.com/doi/pdf/10.1080/10192
557.2021.1995229?needAccess=true. There have been a few isolated incidents
where the regulator restricted the use of VIE structure within a certain industry. See David Roberts & Thomas Hall, *VIE Structures in China: What You
Need to Know*, O'MELVENY & MYERS LLP (Oct. 2011), http://www.docin.
com/p-288038261.html; see also Thomas Y Man, *Policy above Law: VIE and
Foreign Investment Regulation in China*, 3 PEKING UNIV. TRANSNATIONAL L. REV.
215, 218 (2015).

93. Melanie Lee, *Sina, Focus Media Drop Merger Plan*, REUTERS (Sept. 28, 2009),
https://www.reuters.com/article/us-sina-focus-idUSTRE58R3O620090
928; David Barboza, *Sina.com Pulls Out of Deal after Delay*, N.Y. TIMES (Sept. 28,
2009), https://www.nytimes.com/2009/09/29/business/global/29sina.html.

94. Interview with an antitrust law firm partner in Dec. 2021; Chen Ma et al., *First
Unconditional Approval Granted to Merger Filing Involving VIE Structure-Related
Concentration of Undertakings*, HAN KUN LAW OFFICES (Sept. 7, 2020), https://
www.hankunlaw.com/downloadfile/newsAndInsights/0fac3e6b1db93e1ad
46e7eb151b80784.pdf.

95. Xiaoye Wang (王晓晔), Zhongguo Shuzi Jingji Lingyu Fan Longduan
Jianguan de Lilun yu Shijian (中国数字经济领域反垄断监管的理论
与实践) [Theory and Practice of Antitrust Supervision in China's Digital
Economy], QQ.COM (Jun. 10, 2022), t.ly/2zEn3.

96. Shangwu Bu: Zheng Zai Diaocha Qunaer Jubao Xiecheng Shougou
Fan Longduan An (商务部: 正在调查去哪儿举报携程收购反垄断案)
[Ministry of Commerce: Currently Investigating Qunar's Report on Ctrip's
Monopolistic Aquisition], QQ.COM (Aug. 20, 2015), t.ly/3_BvZ.

97. Yi Wang (王一), Xiecheng Hebing Quna'er Baidu "Zuo Yong" Zaixian
Lüyou Qi Cheng Fen'e (携程合并去哪儿 百度"坐拥"在线旅游七成份额)
[Ctrip Merged with Qunar, Baidu Holds 70% of Online Travel Market], CE.
CN (Oct. 27, 2015), http://www.ce.cn/cysc/tech/dt/201510/27/t20151027_
6812226.shtml.

98. Hua Lin (林华), Meituan Dianping Liang Da Guatou Hebing: Zhe
Longduan, Shi Gai "Fan" Bu Gai "Fan" Ne (美团点评两大寡头合并: 这垄
断, 是该"反"不该"反"呢) [Two Oligarchs, Meituan and Dianping, Merged:
Should the Monopoly Be "Anti" or Not], HUXIU.COM (Oct. 9, 2015), https://
www.huxiu.com/article/127633.html.

99. *Chinese Classified Ad Site 58.com to Buy 43 Percent of Rival Ganji*, REUTERS (Apr.
17, 2015), https://www.reuters.com/article/us-58-com-inc-ganji-idUSKB
N0N80V820150417.

100. Weishan Chen (陈惟杉), Fan Longduan Zhongjie "Dujia Banquan," Weihe
Meiyou Chaifen Tengxun Yinyue? (反垄断终结"独家版权", 为何没有拆
分腾讯音乐?) [Anti-Monopoly Ends "Exclusive Copyright," Why Hasn't
Tencent Music Been Split?], QQ.COM (Sept. 13, 2021), https://new.qq.com/
rain/a/20210912A0230W00.

NOTES

327

101. 2014 Nian Di 4 Jidu Zhongguo Dache APP Shichang Geju Yi Ding Zhongdian Zhuanxiang Zhuanche Shichang (2014年第4季度中国打车APP市场格局已定 重点转向专车市场) [2014 Q4 Market Landscape of Ride-Hailing App Has Taken Shape, Focus Has Shifted to the Premier Market], ANALYSYS (Jan. 22, 2015), https://www.analysys.cn/article/detail/6381.

102. Don Weinland & Charles Clover, *China's Antitrust Launches Inquiry into Didi-Uber Deal*, FIN. TIMES (Sept. 2, 2016), https://www.ft.com/content/41b69c58-70fb-11e6-a0c9-1365ce54b926.

103. Jingjiao Zeng (曾静娇), Didi Huiying Shangwu Bu "Binggou Shenbao" Wenti: Wei Da Shenbao Biaozhun (滴滴回应商务部"并购申报"问题: 未达到申报标准) [Didi Responded to the Ministry of Commerce's Inquiry about "M&A Filing": Not Meeting the Filing Threshold], 21JINGJI.COM (Aug. 2, 2016), https://m.21jingji.com/article/20160802/herald/29df68176ebf184049383a9735a96a939.html.

104. Fengliang Jin, *The Challenges of Applying Turnover Threshold to the Sharing Economy for Control of Concentrations between Undertakings in China*, 35 COMPUT. L. & SECUR. REV. 59 (2019); He Zhang (张翕), Wangyueche Pingtai de Yingye'e Jisuan Wenti Yanjiu—Didi Chuxing Shougou Youbu Zhongguo An Zai Tantao (网约车平台的营业额计算问题研究——滴滴出行收购优步中国案再探讨) [Research on the Calculation of Turnover of Ride-Hailing Platforms—Rediscuss Didi Chuxing's Acquisition of Uber China], SINA NEWS (Jun. 17, 2019), https://cj.sina.com.cn/articles/view/6289104432/176dc1e3001900hsn4?from=finance&.

105. Dongye Ji (汲东野), Pinglun: Didi Kuaidi Hebing Longduan Zhi Shuo Nan Chengli (评论: 滴滴快的合并 垄断之说难成立) [Comment: Didi and Kuaidi Merged, Hard to Establish Monopoly], SINA NEWS (Mar. 5, 2015), http://tech.sina.com.cn/i/2015-03-05/doc-icczmvun6506193.shtml; Yufang Liu (刘玉芳), Didi Huiying Shangwu Bu "Binggou Shenbao": Meiyou Dadao Shenbao Biaozhun (滴滴回应商务部"并购申报": 没有达到申报标准) [Didi Responded to the Ministry of Commerce's "M&A Filing": Not Meeting the Filing Threshold], IFENG.COM (Aug. 2, 2016), https://finance.ifeng.com/a/20160802/14669159_0.shtml.

106. Chenxi Wang (王晨曦), 2016 Nian Di 1 Jidu Zhongguo Zhuanche Fuwu Jiakuai Guojihua Jincheng Fuwu Xiang Duoyuanhua Fazhan (2016年第1季度中国专车服务加快国际化进程 服务向多元化发展) [China's Premier Ride-Hailing Service Accelerated the Process of Internationalization and Diversification in 2016 Q1], ANALYSYS (Jun. 3, 2016), https://www.analysys.cn/article/detail/1000036.

107. See CHEN, *supra* note 7, at 86.

108. Sarah Dai, *Didi Reveals It Is Still Making Losses on Many Fares Charged in China as It Discloses Costs Breakdown*, SOUTH CHINA MORNING POST (Apr. 24, 2019), https://www.scmp.com/tech/start-ups/article/3007439/didi-reveals-it-still-making-losses-many-fares-charged-china-it.

109. Charles Clover, *China Ride-Hailing Subsidies to Continue*, FIN. TIMES (Aug. 4, 2016), https://www.ft.com/content/3a917e2e-59fa-11e6-8d05-4eaa6 6292c32.

110. Jing Li (李静), Yi Wei lüshi Dui Tengxun de Liang Nian Fan Longduan Susong Zhi Lu (一位律师对腾讯的两年反垄断诉讼之路) [A Lawyer's Two-Year Antitrust Battle with Tencent], SINA.CN (Feb. 19, 2021), https://finance.sina.cn/2021-02-20/detail-ikftpnny8290519.d.html; Xuejiao Cai, *Lawyer Sues Tencent for Restricting Competitors' Links in WeChat*, SIXTHTONE.COM (Apr. 25, 2019), https://www.sixthtone.com/news/1003900/lawyer-sues-tencent-for-restricting-competitors-links-in-wechat; Jingli Song, *A Chinese Lawyer Challenges Tencent over Anti-Monopoly Law*, KRASIA NEWS (Apr. 25, 2019), https://kr-asia.com/a-chinese-lawyer-challenges-tencent-over-anti-monopoly-law.

111. Cai, *supra* note 110.

112. Caixin, *China Gets Serious about Antitrust in Cyberspace*, SIXTHTONE.COM (Apr. 26, 2021), https://www.sixthtone.com/news/1007329/china-gets-serious-about-antitrust-in-cyberspace.

113. Peifang Jiang (蒋佩芳) & Shixuan Wang (王施萱), Eleme Wenzhou Chong Cao "Er Xuan Yi," 20 Hu Shangjia Shiming Jubao (饿了么温州重操"二选一," 20户商家实名举报) [Eleme Wenzhou Restarts Its "Choose One from Two" Practice, Twenty Merchants Report with Their Real Names], PEOPLE.COM (Aug. 24, 2020), http://it.people.com.cn/n1/2020/0824/c1009-31833 646.html.

114. Li Tao & Celia Chen, *Alibaba and JD in a War of Words via Lawyers over Claims of Dominating China's E-Commerce*, SOUTH CHINA MORNING POST (Nov. 25, 2017), https://www.scmp.com/tech/article/2121556/alibaba-and-jd-war-words-lawyers-over-claims-dominating-chinas-e-commerce.

115. Beijing Zijie Tiaodong Keji Youxian Gongsi, Yuncheng Shi Yangguang Wenhua Chuanmei Youxian Gongsi yu Shenzhen Shi Tengxun Jisuanji Xitong Youxian Gongsi Bu Zhengdang Jingzheng Jiufen (北京字节跳动科技有限公司、运城市阳光文化传媒有限公司与深圳市腾讯计算机系统有限公司不正当竞争纠纷) [Beijing Bytedance Co., Ltd. and Yuncheng Yangguang Culture Media Co., Ltd. v. Shenzhen Tencent Computer System Co., Ltd., A Dispute over Unfair Competition], Beijing Intellectual Property Ct. No. 578, Oct. 19, 2018; Beijing Zijie Tiaodong Keji Youxian Gongsi yu Shenzhen Shi Tengxun Jisuanji Xitong Youxian Gongsi Bu Zhengdang Jingzheng Jiufen (北京字节跳动科技有限公司与深圳市腾讯计算机系统有限公司不正当竞争纠纷) [Beijing Bytedance Co., Ltd. v. Shenzhen Tencent Computer System Co., Ltd., A Dispute over Unfair Competition], Beijing Intellectual Property Ct. No. 572, Nov. 2, 2018; Beijing Zijie Tiaodong Keji Youxian Gongsi yu Shenzhen Shi Tengxun Jisuanji Xitong Youxian Gongsi Deng Bu Zhengdang Jingzheng Jiufen (北京字节跳动科技有限公司与深圳市腾讯计算机系统有限公司等不正当竞争纠纷) [Beijing Bytedance Co.,

NOTES   329

Ltd. v. Shenzhen Tencent Computer System Co., Ltd., Etc., A Dispute over Unfair Competition], Beijing Intellectual Property Ct. No. 295, Aug. 8, 2019; Yuncheng Shi Yangguang Wenhua Chuanmei Youxian Gongsi yu Shenzhen Shi Tengxun Jisuanji Xitong Youxian Gongsi, Beijing Sougou Keji Fazhan Youxian Gongsi Bu Zhengdang Jingzheng Jiufen (运城市阳光文化传媒有限公司与深圳市腾讯计算机系统有限公司、北京搜狗科技发展有限公司不正当竞争纠纷) [Yuncheng Yangguang Culture Media Co., Ltd. v. Shenzhen Tencent Computer System Co., Ltd. and Beijing Sogou Technology Development Co., Ltd., A Dispute over Unfair Competition], Beijing Intellectual Property Ct. No. 543, Jan. 10, 2020; Fujian Zijie Tiaodong Keji Youxian Gongsi yu Shenzhen Shi Tengxun Jisuanji Xitong Youxian Gongsi Deng Bu Zhengdang Jingzheng Jiufen (福建字节跳动科技有限公司与深圳市腾讯计算机系统有限公司等不正当竞争纠纷) [Fujian Bytedance Co., Ltd. v. Shenzhen Tencent Computer System Co., Ltd., Etc., A Dispute over Unfair Competition], Fujian High People's Ct. No. 26, Mar. 30, 2021.

116. Shenzhen Shi Tengxun Jisuanji Xitong Youxian Gongsi yu Beijing Weibo Shijie Keji Youxian Gongsi Deng Bu Zhengdang Jingzheng Jiufen (深圳市腾讯计算机系统有限公司与北京微播视界科技有限公司等不正当竞争纠纷) [Shenzhen Tencent Computer System Co., Ltd. v. Beijing Microseeding Horizon Technology Co., Ltd., Etc., A Dispute over Unfair Competition], Tianjin Binhai Primary Ct. No. 2091, Mar. 18, 2019; Shenzhen Shi Tengxun Jisuanji Xitong Youxian Gongsi Deng yu Beijing Zijie Tiaodong Keji Youxian Gongsi Deng Bu Zhengdang Jingzheng Jiufen (深圳市腾讯计算机系统有限公司等与北京字节跳动科技有限公司等不正当竞争纠纷) [Shenzhen Tencent Computer System Co., Ltd., Etc. v. Beijing Bytedance Co., Ltd., Etc., A Dispute over Unfair Competition], Chengdu Interm. People's Ct. No. 5468, 2019.

117. Shanghai Lazhasi Xinxi Keji Youxian Gongsi yu Beijing Sankuai Keji Youxian Gongsi Jinhua Fen Gongsi Deng Bu Zhengdang Jingzheng Jiufen (上海拉扎斯信息科技有限公司与北京三快科技有限公司金华分公司等不正当竞争纠纷) [Shanghai Lazhasi Information Science Technology Co., Ltd. v. Beijing Sankuai Online Technology Co., Ltd. (Jinhua Branch), Etc., A Dispute over Unfair Competition], Zhejiang High People's Ct. No. 601, Dec. 8, 2021. Shanghai Lazhasi Xinxi Keji Youxian Gongsi yu Beijing Sankuai Keji Youxian Gongsi Deng Bu Zhengdang Jingzheng Jiufen (上海拉扎斯信息科技有限公司与北京三快科技有限公司等不正当竞争纠纷) [Shanghai Lazhasi Information Science Technology Co., Ltd. v. Beijing Sankuai Online Technology Co., Ltd., Etc., A Dispute over Unfair Competition], Jiangsu High People's Ct. No. 1545, 2021. Shanghai Lazhasi Xinxi Keji Youxian Gongsi yu Beijing Sankuai Keji Youxian Gongsi Deng Bu Zhengdang Jingzheng Jiufen (上海拉扎斯信息科技有限公司与北京三快科技有限公司等不正当竞争纠纷) [Shanghai Lazhasi Information Science Technology Co., Ltd. v. Beijing Sankuai Online Technology Co., Ltd., Etc., A

Dispute over Unfair Competition], Shandong Qingdao Interm. People's Ct. No. 580, Sept. 2, 2021. Shanghai Lazhasi Xinxi Keji Youxian Gongsi yu Beijing Sankuai Keji Youxian Gongsi Deng Shangye Dihui Jiufen, Shangye Huiluo Bu Zhengdang Jingzheng Jiufen (上海拉扎斯信息科技有限公司与北京三快科技有限公司等商业诋毁纠纷、商业贿赂不正当竞争纠纷) [Shanghai Lazhasi Information Science Technology Co., Ltd. v. Beijing Sankuai Online Technology Co., Ltd., Etc., A Dispute over Unfair Competition's Commercial Defamation and Bribery], Tianjin 2nd Interm. People's Ct. No. 971, Jul. 24, 2020. Shanghai Lazhasi Xinxi Keji Youxian Gongsi yu Ganzhou Juyuanmei Canyin Guanli Youxian Gongsi Deng Bu Zhengdang Jingzheng Jiufen (上海拉扎斯信息科技有限公司与赣州聚源美餐饮管理有限公司等不正当竞争纠纷) [Shanghai Lazhasi Information Science Technology Co., Ltd. v. Ganzhou Juyuanmei Catering Management Co., Ltd., Etc., A Dispute over Unfair Competition], Guangdong Meizhou Interm. People's Ct. No. 132, Dec. 24, 2021.

118. Beijing Sankuai Keji Youxian Gongsi yu Shanghai Lazhasi Xinxi Keji Youxian Gongsi Wenzhou Fen Gongsi Deng Bu Zhengdang Jingzheng Jiufen (北京三快科技有限公司与上海拉扎斯信息科技有限公司温州分公司等不正当竞争纠纷) [Beijing Sankuai Online Technology Co., Ltd. v. Shanghai Lazhasi Information Science Technology Co., Ltd. (Wenzhou Branch), Etc., A Dispute over Unfair Competition], Zhejiang High People's Ct. No. 731, Dec. 8, 2021. Beijing Sankuai Zaixian Keji Youxian Gongsi yu Tianchang Shi Eleme Waimai Fuwu Zhan Bu Zhengdang Jingzheng Jiufen (北京三快在线科技有限公司与天长市饿了么外卖服务站不正当竞争纠纷) [Beijing Sankuai Online Technology Co., Ltd. v. Tianchang Ele.me Takeaway Service Station, A Dispute over Unfair Competition], Anhui Chuzhou Interm. People's Ct., 2021. Beijing Sankuai Keji Youxian Gongsi yu Shanghai Lazhasi Xinxi Keji Youxian Gongsi Deng Bu Zhengdang Jingzheng Jiufen (北京三快科技有限公司与上海拉扎斯信息科技有限公司等不正当竞争纠纷) [Beijing Sankuai Online Technology Co., Ltd. v. Shanghai Lazhasi Information Science Technology Co., Ltd., Etc., A Dispute over Unfair Competition], Guangdong High People's Ct. No. 47, Apr. 19, 2021. Beijing Sankuai Keji Youxian Gongsi yu Shanghai Lazhasi Xinxi Keji Youxian Gongsi Deng Bu Zhengdang Jingzheng Jiufen (北京三快科技有限公司与上海拉扎斯信息科技有限公司等不正当竞争纠纷) [Beijing Sankuai Online Technology Co., Ltd. v. Shanghai Lazhasi Information Science Technology Co., Ltd., Etc., A Dispute over Unfair Competition], Beijing Haidian Primary People's Ct. No. 64327, May 25, 2022.

119. See ZHANG, *supra* note 1, at 25.

120. Xu Liu (刘旭), Huimou (2018): Fan Longduan Zhifa Bu Ying Zongrong Hulianwang Guatou (回眸(2018):反垄断执法不应纵容互联网寡头) [Looking Back (2018): Antitrust Enforcement Should Not Condone Internet Oligarchs], QQ.COM (Jul. 7, 2017), t.ly/dXyzp.

NOTES 331

121. *Regular Press Conference of the Ministry of Commerce (July 27, 2017)*, MOFCOM.GOV (Jul. 31, 2017), http://english.mofcom.gov.cn/article/newsrelease/press/201708/20170802619031.shtml.

122. Ibid.

123. Falü Zhujian Chutai, Dan Dianshang "Er Xuan Yi" Weihe Reng Nan Tuichu Lishi Wutai? (法律逐渐出台，但电商"二选一"为何仍难退出历史舞台?) [Laws Have Been Gradually Introduced, But Why Is It Still Difficult to Wipe Out "Choose One from Two" Practices of E-Commerce?], QQ.COM (Nov. 6, 2019), https://tech.qq.com/a/20191106/001891.htm; *JD.com Sues Tmall over Unfair Competition*, CHINA DAILY ASIA (Nov. 6, 2015), https://www.chinadailyasia.com/business/2015-11/06/content_15341220.html.

124. Peng Wu (吴鹏) et al., Dianshang Pingtai "Er Xuan Yi" Xingwei de Falü Shiyong Wenti Tantao (Shang) (电商平台"二选一"行为的法律适用问题探讨(上) [Explore the Legal Application Issue of the "Choose One from Two" Practice of E-Commerce Platforms (Part 1)], ZHONG LUN LAW FIRM (Dec. 11, 2020), https://www.zhonglun.com/Content/2020/12-11/1125284912.html; Eleme Peichang Meituan 8 Wan Yuan Ban Nian Liang Ci Yin Bu Zhengdang Jingzheng Bei Fa (饿了么赔偿美团8万元 半年两次因不正当竞争被罚) [Eleme Compensated Meituan RMB 80,000, Punished Twice Half a Year for Unfair Competition], SINA NEWS (Sept. 13, 2021), https://finance.sina.com.cn/tech/2021-09-13/doc-iktzqtyt5769580.shtml; also see *supra* note 54.

125. See Wu et al., *supra* note 124.

126. Guojia Shichang Jianguan Zong Ju Yuetan Pingtai Qiye Jiang Dui "Er Xuan Yi" Xingwei Yifa Kaizhan Fan Longduan Diaocha (国家市场监管总局约谈平台企业 将对"二选一"行为依法开展反垄断调查) [The State Administration of Market Supervision Held Regulatory Talks with Platform Companies, Will Conduct Anti-Monopoly Investigations into "Choose One from Two" Practice According to Law], GOV.CN (Nov. 5, 2019), http://www.gov.cn/xinwen/2019-11/05/content_5449039.htm; Pei Li & Josh Horwitz, *China Regulator Warns E-Commerce Platforms to Stop Monopolistic Practices*, REUTERS (Nov. 6, 2019), https://www.reuters.com/article/us-china-alibaba-singlesday-idUSKBN1XG1KP.

127. *10 Highlights of the Antitrust Guidelines for Platform Economy*, KING & WOOD MALLESONS (Nov. 18, 2020), https://www.chinalawinsight.com/2020/11/articles/compliance/10-highlights-of-the-antitrust-guidelines-for-platform-economy/.

128. *The Coming Wave of Stringent Enforcement Actions in China*, FRESHFIELDS BRUCKHAUS DERINGER (Mar. 19, 2021), https://www.freshfields.com/en-gb/our-thinking/knowledge/briefing/2021/03/the-coming-wave-of-stringent-enforcement-actions-in-china-4425/.

129. *Antitrust China 2021 Annual Review*, FANGDA PARTNERS (Mar. 2022), https://www.fangdalaw.com/wp-content/uploads/2022/03/%E5%8F%8D%E5%9E%84%E6%96%AD%E5%9B%9E%E9%A1%BE-2021-EN-A4.pdf.

130. Ibid.

131. Shichang Jianguan Zongju Yifa Jinzhi Huya Gongsi yu Douyu Guoji Konggu Youxian Gongsi Hebing (市场监管总局依法禁止虎牙公司与斗鱼国际控股有限公司合并) [The State Administration of Market Supervision Decided to Prohibit the Merger between Huya and Douyu According to Law], SAMR.GOV (Jul. 10, 2021), https://www.samr.gov.cn/xw/zj/202107/t20210710_332525.html.

132. Ibid.

133. Ibid.

134. Yujie Xue & Iris Deng, *China Antitrust: Beijing Orders Tencent to End Exclusive Music Licensing Deals in a First for the Country*, SOUTH CHINA MORNING POST (Jul. 24, 2021), https://www.scmp.com/tech/big-tech/article/3142359/china-antitrust-beijing-orders-tencent-music-relinquish-exclusive.

135. Shichang Jianju Zongju Yifa Dui Tengxun Konggu Youxian Gongsi Zuochu Zeling Jiechu Wangluo Yinyue Dujia Banquan Deng Chufa (市场监管总局依法对腾讯控股有限公司作出责令解除网络音乐独家版权等处罚) [The State Administration of Market Supervision Ordered Tencent Holdings Ltd. to End the Exclusive Copyright of Online Music According to Law, among Other Penalties], SAMR.GOV (Jul. 24, 2021), https://www.samr.gov.cn/xw/zj/202107/t20210724_333016.html.

136. Ibid.

137. See Xue & Deng, *supra* note 134.

138. Iris Deng, *China Antitrust: Beijing Approves Tencent's Acquisition of Search Engine Sogou after Vetoing Huya-Douyu Merger*, SOUTH CHINA MORNING POST (Jul. 13, 2021), https://www.scmp.com/tech/policy/article/3140877/china-antitrust-beijing-approves-tencents-acquisition-search-engine.

139. Henrik Saetre, *Top 5 Chinese Search Engines in 2022 [With Market Share]*, ADCHINA.IO (last visited Feb. 26, 2022), https://www.adchina.io/top-chinese-search-engines/.

140. Mark M. Lemley & Andrew McCreary, *Exit Strategy*, 101 BOSTON U. L. REV. 1, 85 (2021)(calling on antitrust agencies to pay more attention to acquisitions by incumbent monopolists even if the target firms are not direct competitors).

141. See Raymond Zhong, *With Alibaba Investigation, China Gets Tougher on Tech*, N.Y. TIMES (Dec. 23, 2020), https://www.nytimes.com/2020/12/23/business/alibaba-antitrust-jack-ma.html.

142. Coco Liu et al., *China Fines Alibaba Record $2.8 Billion after Monopoly Probe*, BLOOMBERG (Apr. 10, 2021), https://www.bloomberg.com/news/articles/2021-04-10/china-fines-alibaba-group-2-8-billion-in-monopoly-probe.

143. Eustance Huang, *China's Antitrust Push Won't Bring an "Explosion of Cases" against Online Campaigns, Professor Says*, CNBC (Nov. 23, 2020), https://www.cnbc.com/2020/11/24/dont-expect-an-explosion-of-cases-from-chinas-antitrust-push-professor.html.

144. Jigou (机构) [Organization], SAMR.GOV, http://www.samr.gov.cn/jg/ (last visited Feb. 26, 2022).

NOTES

333

145. Baidu, Jingdong, Meituan, 360, Zijie Tiaodong Deng Fabu Hegui Jingying Chengnuoshu (百度、京东、美团、360、字节跳动等发布合规经营承诺书) [Baidu, JD.com, Meituan, 360, and ByteDance etc. Published Commitment Letter for Compliance], SINA NEWS (Apr. 14, 2021), https://finance.sina.com.cn/tech/2021-04-14/doc-ikmxzfmk6691431.shtml.

146. Ibid.

147. Ibid.

148. Minghe Hu, *Meituan Becomes the Focus of China's Antitrust Investigation as Government's Scrutiny of Business Practice Shifts*, SOUTH CHINA MORNING POST (Apr. 26, 2021), https://www.scmp.com/tech/policy/article/3131121/china-antitrust-fury-drops-upon-meituan-after-record-fine-alibaba.

149. Stephanie Yang, *China's Tech Regulator Orders Companies to Fix Anticompetitive, Security Issues*, WALL ST. J. (Jul. 26, 2021), https://www.wsj.com/articles/chinas-tech-regulator-orders-companies-to-fix-anticompetitive-secur ity-issues-11627304021; see Gongxin Bu Qidong Hulianwang Hangye Zhuanxiang Zhengzhi Xingdong (工信部启动互联网行业专项整治行动)[Ministry of Industry and Information Technology Launched Special Rectification Campaign for Internet Industry], GONGXIN WEIBAO (工信微报) (Jul. 25, 2021), https://mp.weixin.qq.com/s/GZkFr4DVxPPRvp0_RP8mAQ.

150. Mengyuan Ge, *Major Tech Companies in China Unbrick Walled Gardens to Integrate Rival Payment Services*, KRASIA NEWS (Sept. 30, 2021), https://kr-asia.com/major-tech-companies-in-china-unbrick-walled-gardens-to-integrate-rival-payment-services.

151. Zheping Huang & Coco Liu, *Tencent Opens WeChat to Rivals' Links as App Walls Crumble*, BLOOMBERG (Sept. 17, 2021), https://www.bloomberg.com/news/articles/2021-09-17/tencent-opens-wechat-to-rivals-links-as-china-app-walls-crumble?leadSource=uverify%20wall.

152. Elles Houweling, *China Forces Open Alibaba for WeChat Payments. Your Move, Apple*, VERDICT (Sept. 29, 2021), https://www.verdict.co.uk/china-forces-open-alibaba-for-wechat-payments-your-move-apple/.

153. Jane Zhang & Iris Deng, *Alibaba Said to Launch Bargain Marketplace Taobao Deals as Mini-Program on Tencent's WeChat*, SOUTH CHINA MORNING POST (Mar. 17, 2021), https://www.scmp.com/tech/big-tech/article/3125781/alibaba-said-launch-bargain-marketplace-taobao-deals-mini-program.

154. See Deng & Zhang, *supra* note 46.

155. Li Zhu (朱理), Fan Longduan Minshi Susong Shi Nian: Huigu yu Zhanwang (反垄断民事诉讼十年: 回顾与展望) [Ten Years of Civil Litigation against Monopoly: Review and Outlook], PEOPLE.CN (Aug. 28, 2018), http://ip.people.com.cn/n1/2018/0828/c179663-30255146.html.

156. Dermot Cahill & Jing Wang, *Addressing Legitimacy Concerns in Antitrust Private Litigation Involving China's State-Owned Enterprises*, 45(1) WORLD COMPETITION 75, 76 (2022), https://doi.org/10.54648/woco2022004.

NOTES

157. David Stallibrass & Sharon Pang, *Clash of Titans: How China Disciplines Internet Market*, 6(6) J. Eur. Compet. 418, 421–422 (2015).

158. Ibid., at 422.

159. *Qihoo v. Tencent: Economic Analysis of the First Chinese Supreme Court Decision under Anti-Monopoly Law*, Charles River Associates, https://media.crai.com/sites/default/files/publications/China-Highlights-Qihoo-360-v-Tencent-0215_0.pdf.

160. Stallibrass & Pang, *supra* note 157, at 423.

161. David Tring, *How the Qihoo v Tencent Case Affects China's Anti-Monopoly Regime*, China Law & Practice (Apr. 18, 2013), https://www.chinalawandpractice.com/2013/04/18/how-the-qihoo-v-tencent-case-affects-chinas-anti-monopoly-regime/.

162. Shucheng Wang, *Guiding Cases and Bureaucratization of Judicial Precedents in China*, 14 U. Pa. Asian L. Rev. 96 (2019).

163. Deng & Dai, *supra* note 52.

164. Honghuan Liu & Xi Zhou, *Antitrust Litigation 2022*, Chambers & Partners (last updated Sept. 15, 2022), https://practiceguides.chambers.com/practice-guides/comparison/693/9487/15271-15274-15281-15285-15289-15293-15296-15300-15303-15306-15309; Deng & Dai, *supra* note 52.

165. Sarah Zheng, *JD Wins 1 Billion Yuan in Damages in Anti-Monopoly Case Against Alibaba*, Bloomberg (Dec. 29, 2023), https://www.bloomberg.com/news/articles/2023-12-29/jd-wins-1b-yuan-in-damages-in-anti-monopoly-case-against-alibaba-as-regulators-deepen-crackdown-on-internet-platforms/.

166. Shen Lu, *China's Big Tech Legal Teams Are Unbeatable on Their Home Courts, Literally*, Protocol (Apr. 30, 2021), https://www.protocol.com/china/china-big-tech-unbeatable-lawyers.

167. Ibid.

168. SAMR, Guanyu Dui "Hulianwang Pingtai Fenlei Fenji Zhinan (Zhengqiu Yijian Gao)" "Hulianwang Pingtai Luoshi Zhuti Zeren Zhinan (Zhengqiu Yijian Gao)" Gongkai Zhengqiu Yijian de Gonggao (关于对《互联网平台分类分级指南（征求意见稿）》《互联网平台落实主体责任指南（征求意见稿）》公开征求意见的公告) [Announcement on Soliciting Public Opinions on the "Guidelines for the Classification and Grading of Online Platforms (Draft for Comment)" and the "Guidelines for the Implementation of Online Platforms' Obligations (Draft for Comment)"] (Oct. 29, 2021), https://www.samr.gov.cn/hd/zjdc/202110/t20211027_336137.html.

169. SAMR, Guanyu Gongkai Zhengqiu "Zhonghua Renmin Gonghe Guo Fan Budang Jingzheng Fa (Xiuding Cao'an Zhengqiu Yijian Gao)" Yijian de Gonggao (关于公开征求《中华人民共和国反不正当竞争法（修订草案征求意见稿）》意见的公告) [Announcement on Soliciting Public Opinions on the "Anti-Unfair Competition Law of the People's Republic of China (Revised Draft for Comment)"] (Nov. 22, 2022), https://www.samr.gov.cn/hd/zjdc/202211/t20221121_351812.html.

NOTES

335

170. Anti-Unfair Competition Law (Revised Draft), *supra* note 169, art. 13.

171. Cheng Liu (刘成) et al., Jiaqiang Quanliantiao Jingzheng Jianguan, Guizhi Shuzi Jingji Buzhengdang Jingzheng (加强全链条竞争监管，规制数字经济不正当竞争) [Strengthening Supervision over Competition in the Entire Supply Chain, Regulating Unfair Competition in the Digital Economy], KING & WOOD MALLESONS (Nov. 25, 2022), t.ly/TYYUB.

CHAPTER 5

1. Cao Yin, *Crackdown Targets Cyber Black Market*, CHINA DAILY (Nov. 29, 2016), https://www.chinadaily.com.cn/business/tech/2016-11/29/content_27510323.htm.

2. Ibid.

3. Yuan Yang, *China's Data Privacy Outcry Fuels Case for Tighter Rules*, FIN. TIMES (Oct. 1, 2018), https://www.ft.com/content/fdeaf22a-c09a-11e8-95b1-d36dfef1b89a.

4. *Hackers Attack 20 Mln Accounts on Alibaba's Taobao Shopping Site*, REUTERS (Feb. 4, 2016), https://www.reuters.com/article/alibaba-cyber-idUSL3N15J1P2.

5. *China's Domestic Surveillance Programmes Benefit Foreign Spies,* THE ECONOMIST (Apr. 22, 2021), https://www.economist.com/china/2021/04/24/chinas-domestic-surveillance-programmes-benefit-foreign-spies.

6. Yuzhe Zhang (张宇哲) et al., Zhengsu Shuju Chanye Lian (整肃数据产业链) [Rectifying the Data Industry Chain], CAIXIN.COM (Aug. 7, 2017), https://topics.caixin.com/zssjcyl/.

7. Engen Tham, *Data Dump: China Sees Surge in Personal Information up for Sale*, REUTERS (Aug. 23, 2018), https://www.reuters.com/article/us-china-dataprivacy-idUSKCN1L80IW.

8. Valentin Weber, *How China's Control of Information Is a Cyber Weakness*, LAWFARE (Nov. 12, 2020), https://www.lawfareblog.com/how-chinas-control-information-cyber-weakness.

9. Catalin Cimpanu, *China Is Now Blocking All Encrypted HTTPS Traffic That Uses TLS 1.3 and ESNI*, ZDNet (Aug. 8, 2020), https://www.zdnet.com/article/china-is-now-blocking-all-encrypted-https-traffic-using-tls-1-3-and-esni/.

10. THE ECONOMIST, *supra* note 5.

11. Ibid.

12. Rui Zhi Hua Sheng Feifa Dao Qu 30 Yi Tiao Geren Wangluo Xinxi Xiangguan Renyuan Huo Xing (瑞智华胜非法盗取30亿条个人网络信息相关人员获刑) [Ruizhi Huasheng Illegally Stole 3 Billion Pieces of Personal Network Information and Related Personnel Were Sentenced], SINA.COM (Nov. 14, 2019), https://finance.sina.com.cn/stock/observe/2019-11-14/doc-iihnzahi0853212.shtml.

13. Xin Sanban Guapai Gongsi She Qiequ 30 Yi Tiao Geren Xinxi Feifa Mouli Chao Qian Wan Yuan (新三板挂牌公司涉窃取30亿条个人信息，非法牟利

超千万元) [New Three Board Listed Company Involved in Stealing 3 Billion Pieces of Personal Information, Illegally Profited over RMB 10 Million], THE PAPER (Aug. 20, 2020), http://m.thepaper.cn/kuaibao_detail.jsp?contid=2362 227&from=kuaibao.

14. 2.4 Yi Tiao Kaifang Xinxi Bei Ren Dabao Chushou! Zhuguo Han Ting Deng de Ren Yao Xiaoxin (2.4亿条开房信息被人打包出售!住过汉庭等的人要小心) [240 Million Pieces of Hotel Booking Information Were Packaged and Sold! People Who Have Lived in Hanting and Others Should Be Careful], SINA.CN (Aug. 29, 2018), https://finance.sina.cn/2018-08-29/detail-ihikcahf 0783619.d.html. Esther Herzfeld, *Data Leak from Huazhu Hotels May Affect 130 Million Customers*, HOTEL MANAGEMENT (Aug. 30, 2018), https://www.hote lmanagement.net/tech/data-leak-from-huazhu-hotels-may-affect-130-mill ion-customers.

15. Yuan Zhou (周源), Huazhu Jiudian Shu Yi Tiao Zhuke Xinxi Shui Zai Xiemi? Heike Hai Shi Neigui? (华住酒店数亿条住客信息谁在泄秘? 黑客还是内鬼?) [Who Was Leaking Hundreds of Millions of Guest Information in Huazhu Hotel? Hacker or Insider?], SINA.CN, (Aug. 28, 2018), https://finance.sina.cn/chanjing/gsxw/2018-08-28/detail-ihiixzkm1866560.d.html; Daniel Ren, *Shanghai Police Investigate Data Leak of 130 Million Hotel Clients Available on Dark Web for 8 Bitcoin*, SOUTH CHINA MORNING POST (Aug. 29, 2018), https://www.scmp.com/business/companies/article/2161800/shang hai-police-investigate-data-leak-130-million-hotel-clients.

16. Wenbo Dong (董文博), Shunfeng Yi Bei Juan Ru Shuju Xielou Shijian, "Yonghu Yinsi" Gai Ruhe Baohu? (顺丰疑被卷入数据泄露事件, "用户隐私"该如何保护?) [SF Express Is Suspected of Being Involved in a Data Breach, How to Protect "User Privacy"?], JWVIEW.COM (Sept. 4, 2018), https://www.jwview.com/jingwei/html/09-04/180307.shtml.

17. Jianting Zhong (钟健挺) & Aili Tian (田爱丽), Shunfeng Bao'an Jiu Chu Gongsi Neibu Shoumai Yonghu Yinsi Wo An 11 Ming Yuangong Huo Xing (顺丰报案揪出公司内部售卖用户隐私窝案 11名员工获刑) [SF Express Reported That 11 Employees Were Jailed for the Company's Internal Sales of User Privacy], SOHU (May. 17, 2018), https://www.sohu.com/a/231935432_ 161795.

18. Mandy Zuo, *Who's Buying, Selling and Stealing Your Personal Data in China?*, SOUTH CHINA MORNING POST (Jun. 9, 2017), https://www.scmp.com/ news/china/society/article/2097629/whos-buying-and-selling-your-sto len-data-china.

19. Gary King et al., *How Censorship in China Allows Government Criticism but Silences Collective Expression*, 107 AM. POLIT. SCI. REV. 1–18 (2013).

20. GEOFFREY CAIN, THE PERFECT POLICE STATE: AN UNDERCOVER ODYSSEY INTO CHINA'S TERRIFYING SURVEILLANCE DYSTOPIA OF THE FUTURE (2021).

21. See Xu Xu, *To Repress or to Co-Opt? An Authoritarian Control in the Age of Digital Surveillance*, 65(2) AM. J. POL. SCI. 309, 316 (2021); see also Zixue Tai,

NOTES

Casting the Ubiquitous Net of Information Control: Internet Surveillance in China from Golden Shield to Green Dam, 2 INT'L J. ADVANCED PERVASIVE & UBIQUITOUS COMPUTING 53, 55 (2010).

22. GREG WALTON, CHINA'S GOLDEN SHIELD: CORPORATIONS AND THE DEVELOPMENT OF SURVEILLANCE TECHNOLOGY IN THE PEOPLE'S REPUBLIC OF CHINA (2001). See also Xu, *supra* note 21.

23. Paul Mozur, *Inside China's Dystopian Dreams: A.I., Shame and Lots of Cameras*, N.Y. TIMES (Jul. 8, 2018), https://www.nytimes.com/2018/07/08/business/china-surveillance-technology.html.

24. Isabel Ivanescu & Robert Carlson, *China's Paper Tiger Surveillance State*, THE DIPLOMAT (Apr. 30, 2021), https://thediplomat.com/2021/04/chinas-paper-tiger-surveillance-state/.

25. Robert Muggah & Greg Walton, *"Smart" Cities Are Surveilled Cities*, FOREIGN POLICY (Apr. 17, 2021), https://foreignpolicy.com/2021/04/17/smart-cities-surveillance-privacy-digital-threats-internet-of-things-5g/.

26. Anita R. Gohdes, Repression in the Digital Age: Communication Technology and the Politics of State Violence (Dec. 19, 2014) (Ph.D. dissertation, Universitat Mannheim), https://madoc.bib.uni-mannheim.de/37902/.

27. Bei Qin et al., *Why Does China Allow Freer Social Media? Protests versus Surveillance and Propaganda*, 31 J. ECON. PERSPECT. 117 (2017).

28. Xu, *supra* note 21.

29. Ibid.

30. James Leibold, *Surveillance in China's Xinjiang Region: Ethnic Sorting, Coercion, and Inducement*, 29 J. CONTEMP. CHINA 46 (2020).

31. Ibid., at 1.

32. Tristan Kenderdine, *Chen Quanguo, Architect of Xinjiang Crackdown, Likely to be Rewarded with Central Position in 2022*, THE DIPLOMAT (Jun. 7, 2021), https://thediplomat.com/2021/06/chen-quanguo-architect-of-xinjiang-crackdown-likely-to-be-rewarded-with-central-position-in-2022/.

33. Roseanne Gerin, *Report: Uyghurs in China Forced to Install Surveillance App That Leaves Their Data Unsecured*, RADIO FREE ASIA (Apr 10, 2018), https://www.rfa.org/english/news/uyghur/report-uyghurs-in-china-forced-to-install-surveillance-app-that-leaves-their-data-unsecured-04102018164341.html.

34. Yi Shu Ng, *China Forces Its Muslim Minority to Install Spyware on Their Phones*, MASHABLE.COM (Jul. 21, 2017), https://mashable.com/article/china-spyware-xinjiang#R66q_PKjlOqG.

35. Genia Kostka & Lukas Antoine, *Fostering Model Citizenship: Behavioral Responses to China's Emerging Social Credit Systems*, 12 POL'Y & INTERNET 256 (2020).

36. Zheng Su et al., *What Explains Popular Support for Government Monitoring in China?*, 19 J. INF. TECHNOL. POLITICS 377–392 (2021); Xu Xu et al., *Information Control and Public Support for Social Credit Systems in China*, 84 J. POLIT. 2230–2245 (2022).

NOTES

37. Charles Clover, *China: When Big Data Meets Big Brother*, FIN. TIMES (Jan. 19, 2016), https://www.ft.com/content/b5b13a5e-b847-11e5-b151-8e15c9a029fb.

38. Simina Mistreanu, *Life Inside China's Social Credit Laboratory*, FOREIGN POLICY (Apr. 3, 2018), https://foreignpolicy.com/2018/04/03/life-inside-chinas-social-credit-laboratory/.

39. Dave Davies, *Facial Recognition and Beyond: Journalist Ventures Inside China's "Surveillance State,"* NPR (Jan. 5, 2021), https://www.npr.org/2021/01/05/953515627/facial-recognition-and-beyond-journalist-ventures-inside-chinas-surveillance-sta.

40. Ibid. See also Charlie Campbell, *"The Entire System Is Designed to Suppress Us." What the Chinese Surveillance State Means for the Rest of the World*, TIME (Nov. 21, 2019), https://time.com/5735411/china-surveillance-privacy-issues/.

41. Phoebe Zhang et al., *Fears of Data Abuse as Chinese Health Code Turns Red for Financial Scandal Protesters*, SOUTH CHINA MORNING POST (Jun. 14, 2022), t.ly/9Whtl.

42. Cheng Leng, *Runs on Chinese Local Banks Spur Fears over Health of Regional Lenders*, FIN. TIMES (Jun. 8, 2022), https://www.ft.com/content/fc0ba3e7-605f-46c3-b388-6bc44968cdda.

43. Zhang et al., *supra* note 41.

44. Zhang et al., *supra* note 6.

45. Karen Hao & Rachel Liang, *China Police Database Was Left Open Online for Over a Year, Enabling Leak*, WALL ST. J. (Jul. 6, 2022), https://www.wsj.com/articles/china-police-database-was-left-open-online-for-over-a-year-enabling-leak-11657119903.

46. Zhang et al., *supra* note 6.

47. Michael Shu, *The Legal Protection over Personal Information in China*, ZHONG LUN (Nov. 4, 2015), t.ly/sqcvc.

48. Feng Lin (林风), Renmin Lai Lun: Zhengfu Guan Wang Xielu Geren Xinxi, Shuo Hao de Xinxi Baohu Ne? (人民来论: 政府官网泄露个人信息, 说好的隐私保护呢?) [People's Comment: Government's Official Website Leaks Personal Information, What about the Promised Privacy Protection?], PEOPLE.CN (Sept. 22, 2020), http://opinion.people.com.cn/n1/2020/0922/c431649-31871150.html; Qi Tang (汤琪), Guowuyuan Yaoqiu Baohu Geren Yinsi Duo Di Zhengfu Wangzhan Reng You Xielou (国务院要求保护个人隐私 多地政府网站仍有泄露) [State Council Requires Personal Privacy Protection, Several Government Websites are Still Leaking], CCTV.COM (May 6, 2018), http://news.cctv.com/2018/05/06/ARTIcnAwuUmNoBfnsxQoYFEs180506.shtml.

49. Kou Jie, *Alipay Apologizes for Illegal Data Collection Scandal*, PEOPLE'S DAILY ONLINE (Jan. 4, 2018), t.ly/Hc9Ea.

50. Liang Jun, *Baidu Chief under Fire for Privacy Comments*, PEOPLE'S DAILY ONLINE (Mar. 28, 2018), http://en.people.cn/n3/2018/0328/c90000-9442509.html.

NOTES

51. Ibid.

52. Jun Wang (王俊) & Yingxue Wen (温莹雪), Gongxinbu Tongbao 13 Kuan Di Sanfang SDK Weigui Wenti Shifang Chu Naxie Xinhao? (工信部通报13款第三方SDK违规问题 释放出哪些信号?) [Ministry of Information and Technology Published 13 Third-Party SDK Violations: What Signals Are Sent?], 21JINGJI.COM (Feb. 22, 2022), https://m.21jingji.com/article/20220 222/herald/3c04435aecee51b7eddb3c6d9e8cd49f.html.

53. Charlie Warzel, *The Loophole That Turns Your Apps into Spies*, N.Y. TIMES (Sept. 25, 2019), https://www.nytimes.com/2019/09/24/opinion/facebook-goo gle-apps-data.html.

54. Jun, *supra* note 50.

55. Ibid.

56. Ibid.

57. Lianrui Jia & Lotus Ruan, *Going Global: Comparing Chinese Mobile Applications' Data and User Privacy Governance at Home and Abroad*, 9 INTERNET POL'Y REV. (Sept. 16, 2020), https://policyreview.info/articles/analysis/going-global-comparing-chinese-mobile-applications-data-and-user-privacy.

58. Ting Yang (杨婷), Xijinping: Ba Woguo Cong Wangluo Daguo Jianshe Chengwei Wangluo Qiangguo (习近平:把我国从网络大国建设成为网络强国) [Xi Jinping: Let's Make Our Country an Internet Superpower], XINHUA NET (Feb. 27, 2014), http://www.xinhuanet.com//politics/2014-02/27/c_119538788.htm.

59. Jyh-Ann Lee, *Hacking into China's Cybersecurity Law*, 53 WAKE FOREST L. REV. 65 (2018).

60. Bo Zhao & Feng Yang, *Mapping the Development of China's Data Protection Law: Major Actors, Core Values, and Shifting Power Relations*, 40 COMPUT. L. SECUR. REV. 13 (2021).

61. Fan Jiandie Fa (反间谍法) [Anti-Espionage Law] (promulgated by the Standing Comm. Nat'l. People's Cong., Nov. 1, 2014, effective Nov. 1, 2014), art. 13.

62. Fan Kongbu Zhuyi Fa (反恐怖主义法) [Anti-Terrorism Law] (promulgated by the Standing Comm. Nat'l. People's Cong., Dec. 27, 2015, effective Jan. 1, 2016), art. 18–19.

63. Guojia Anquan Fa (国家安全法) [National Security Law] (promulgated by the Standing Comm. Nat'l. People's Cong., Jul. 1, 2015, effective Jul. 1, 2015), art. 25.

64. 2006–2020 Guojia Xinxi Hua Fazhan Zhanlue (2006–2020年国家信息化发展战略) [State Informatization Development Strategy 2006–2020], GOV. CN (Mar. 19, 2006), http://www.gov.cn/gongbao/content/2006/content_315 999.htm.

65. Guowuyuan Guanyu Yinfa Cujin Da Shuju Fazhan Xingdong Gangyao de Tongzhi (国务院关于印发促进大数据发展行动纲要的通知) [Notice of the State Council on Issuing the Action Outline for Promoting the

Development of Big Data], Gov.cn (Aug. 31, 2015), http://www.gov.cn/zhen gce/content/2015-09/05/content_10137.htm.

66. Yin Liu (刘垠), Zhongyang Wenjian Jiang Shuju Naru Shengchan Yaosu You He Shenyi? (中央文件将数据纳入生产要素有何深意?)[What Does It Mean for Central Documents to Include Data as Factors of Production?], CAC.gov.cn (Apr. 11, 2020), http://www.cac.gov.cn/2020-04/11/c_15881 49692584407.htm.

67. Guanyu Goujian Gengjia Wanshan de Yao Su Shichang Hua Peizhi Tizhi Jizhi de Yijian (关于构建更加完善的要素市场化配置体制机制的意见) [Opinions on Improving the Systems and Mechanisms for Market-based Allocation of Factors of Production], Gov.cn (Mar. 30, 2020), http://www. gov.cn/zhengce/2020-04/09/content_5500622.htm.

68. Lillian Li, *Abridged: Data as a Factor of Production*, Substack (Nov. 4, 2021), https://lillianli.substack.com/p/abridged-data-as-a-factor-of-product ion?s=r.

69. *Ibid*.

70. Julia Lu, *China's Data Exchanges, Explained*, TechNode (Aug. 17, 2021), https:// technode.com/2021/08/17/chinas-data-exchanges-explained/.

71. Zhang et al., *supra* note 6.

72. Zhao & Yang, *supra* note 60, at 9.

73. Ibid.

74. Ibid.

75. Guanyu Chutai "Geren Xinxi Shuju Baohu Fa" de Ti'an (关于出台《个人信息数据保护法》的提案) [Proposal for the Introduction of the Personal Information Data Protection Law], sina.com.cn (Mar. 8, 2006), http:// tech.sina.com.cn/i/2006-03-08/1751861508.shtml; Wang Yuehong, Geren Xinxi Baohu Fa "Nanchan" 12 Nian Tamen Weihe Hai Shuo Leguan? (个人信息保护法"难产"12年　他们为何还说乐观?) [Personal Information Protection Law Has Been "Difficult to Create" for 12 Years, Why Are They Still Optimistic?], CZTV.com (Mar. 4, 2017), http://i.cztv.com/view/12442 896.html.

76. Wangluo Anquan Fa (网络安全法) [Cybersecurity Law] (promulgated by the Standing Comm. Nat'l. People's Cong., Nov. 7, 2016, effective Jun. 1, 2017), art. 40–44; Shu, *supra* note 47.

77. The key national laws included the Consumer Protection Law, the Criminal Law, the Torts and Liability Law, the Unfair Competition Law, the Civil Code, the E-Commerce Law, and the Law on the Protection of Minors. Various sector regulators also promulgated their own administrative measures in areas such as telecommunications, banking and finance, postal services, healthcare, and credit reporting.

78. Scott Livingston & Graham Greenleaf, *China Whys and Wherefores—Illegal Provision and Obtaining of Personal Information under Chinese Law*, 131 Privacy L. & Bus. Int'l Rep. 1–5 (2014).

NOTES

341

79. Both laws were adopted in a hasty manner and completed three rounds of reviews within a year. See Yi Chang Xinxi Baohu de Boyi (一场信息保护的博弈) [A Game of Information Protection], PEOPLE'S GOVERNMENT OF BEIJING HAIDIAN DISTRICT (Oct. 21, 2021), http://www.bjhd.gov.cn/qyxy/xydt/xydt!link.action?cmsid=12222&titletype=credit_study.

80. One particularly notable provision of the PIPL is Article 58 which introduces a gatekeeper obligation on Chinese tech firms that possess a massive number of users and operate complex types of business activities. This provision, apparently inspired by the EU's Digital Markets Act, affords the Chinese regulatory authorities sweeping power to impose further obligations on Chinese tech firms to ensure compliance.

81. Mark Jia, *Authoritarian Privacy*, 91 U. CHICAGO L. REV. (forthcoming 2023), available at https://papers.ssrn.com/sol3/papers.cfm?abstract_id=4362527.

82. Beijing Baidu Wangxun Keji Youxian Gongsi yu Zhu Ye Yinsi Quan Jiufen An (北京百度网讯科技有限公司与朱烨隐私权纠纷案) [Beijing Baidu Netcom Science & Technology Co., Ltd. v. Zhu Ye, a Dispute over Privacy], Nanjing Interm. People's Ct. No. 5028, May 6, 2015.

83. Ibid.

84. Jie Huang, *COVID-19 and Applicable Law to Transnational Personal Data: Trends and Dynamics*, 21 GER. L. J. 1283 (2020).

85. Ibid.

86. Yongxi Chen & Anne SY Cheung, *The Transparent Self under Big Data Profiling: Privacy and Chinese Legislation on the Social Credit System*, 12 J. COMP. L. 369 (2017).

87. Ibid.

88. Xiaoxiao Li (李小晓), Zhima Xinyong "Mo Shitou Guo He" (芝麻信用"摸石头过河") [Sesame Credit "Crossing the River by Feeling the Stones"], CAIXIN.COM (Feb. 13, 2015), https://weekly.caixin.com/m/2015-02-13/100783997_all.html; see also Chen & Cheung, *supra* note 86, at 369.

89. Zhao & Yang, *supra* note 60.

90. Samm Sacks et al., *Beyond the Worst-Case Assumptions on China's Cybersecurity Law*, NEWAMERICA.ORG (Oct. 13, 2017), https://www.newamerica.org/cybersecurity-initiative/blog/beyond-worst-case-assumptions-chinas-cybersecurity-law/. These include the Personal Information and Important Data Cross-Border Transfer Security Evaluation Measures and the Information Security Technology-Guidelines for Data Cross-Border Transfer Security Assessment. These two measures imposed broad data localization requirements and require operators of "critical information infrastructure" to undergo extensive security reviews.

91. Guonei Shouci "Kua Jing Shuju Liudong" Yantao Hui Zaijing Juxing (国内首次"跨境数据流动"研讨会在京举行) [The First Seminar on "Cross-Border Data Flow" in China Was Held in Beijing], ALI RESEARCH (Nov. 19, 2015), http://www.aliresearch.com/ch/information/informationdetails?articleCode=20701&type=%E6%96%B0%E9%97%BB.

NOTES

92. Sacks et al., *supra* note 90.

93. Both Alibaba and Tencent have published articles; see Jie Jiang (蒋洁), Guanyu GDPR Shixiao Youxian de 4 Ge Guandian (关于GDPR实效有限的四个观点) [Four Views on the Limited Effectiveness of GDPR], Ali Research (May 30, 2018), http://pre.aliresearch.com/Blog/Article/detail/id/21486.html.

94. Jiahao Zhu (朱家豪), GDPR Dui Oumeng Keji Chuangye Touzi de Duanqi Yingxiang (GDPR 对欧盟科技创业投资的短期影响) [The Short-term Impact of GDPR on EU Technology Venture Capital], Tencent Research Institute (Nov. 23, 2018), https://www.tisi.org/15196; Ke Xu (许可), Shuzi Jingji Shiye Zhong de Oumeng "Yiban Shuju Baohu Tiaoli" (数字经济视野中的欧盟《一般数据保护条例》) [EU GDPR from the Perspective of Digital Economy], Tencent Research Institute (Dec. 26, 2018), https://www.tisi.org/15189.

95. Xu, *supra* note 94.

96. Rong Wang (王融), "Oumeng Shuju Baohu Tongyong Tiaoli": Shi Ge Wujie yu Zhengyi (《欧盟数据保护通用条例》：十个误解与争议) [EU GDPR: 10 Myths and Controversies], Tencent Research Institute (Apr. 24, 2018), https://www.tisi.org/15706.

97. Ibid.

98. Jiang, *supra* note 93; Xiaoguo Pinggu: GDPR Jiujing Dai Laile Shenme? (效果评估：GDPR究竟带来了什么？) [Impact Assessment: What Exactly Does GDPR Bring?], Ali Research (Sept. 18, 2018), http://pre.aliresearch.com/Blog/Article/detail/id/21854.html.

99. Ibid.

100. Zhonghua Renmin Gongheguo Dianzi Shangwu Fa Cao An (中华人民共和国电子商务法草案) [Draft of the Electronic Commerce Law of the People's Republic of China], DYHZDL.CN (Jan. 4, 2017), https://www.dyhzdl.cn/k/doc/a83eda6c1611cc7931b765ce050876323112746c.html.

101. Yang, *supra* note 58.

102. Dianzi Shangwu Fa (电子商务法) [E-Commerce Law] (promulgated by the Standing Comm. Nat'l. People's Cong., Aug. 31, 2018, effective Jan. 1, 2019), art. 23.

103. Teresa Scassa, *Data Ownership* (CIGI Paper No. 187, 2018); Katharina Pistor, *Rule by Data: The End of Market*, 83 L. Contemp. Probl. 101–124 (2020); Salomé Viljoen, *A Relational Theory of Data Governance*, 131 Yale L. J. 573–654 (2021).

104. Francesco Banterle, *Data Ownership in the Data Economy: A European Dilemma*, in EU Internet Law in the Digital Era 199–225 (Tatiana-Eleni Synodinou et al. eds., 2020).

105. Camille Boullenois, *China's Data Strategy: Creating a State-Led Market*, EU Institute for Security Studies (Oct. 2021), https://www.iss.europa.eu/sites/default/files/EUISSFiles/Brief_21_2021.pdf.

106. Rong Wang (王融) & Hongqing Yi (易泓清), Shuju Quan Shu Da Taolun Zhong de Gongshi Ningju (数据权属大讨论中的共识凝聚) [Consensus in

NOTES

343

the Debate on Data Ownership], Tencent Research Institute (Jun. 23, 2021), https://tisi.org/18958; Rong Wang (王融), Guanyu Da Shuju Jiaoyi Hexin Falü Wenti—Shuju Suoyou Quan de Taolun (关于大数据交易核心法律问题—数据所有权的讨论) [Discussion on the Legal Core Question of the Data Ownership in Big Data Trade], Big Data Research (2015), http://www.infocomm-journal.com/bdr/article/2015/2096-0271/2096-0271-1-2-00041.shtml; Yuejin Du (杜跃进), Shuju Anquan Zhili de Ji Ge Jiben Wenti (数据安全治理的几个基本问题) [Several Basic Questions about Data Security Governance], secrss.com (Dec. 18, 2018), https://www.secrss.com/articles/6868; Yu Gu (谷雨), Gaohongbing: Shuju Zhi Li Ying Baochi Jingwei he Shenshen (高红冰: 数据治理应保持敬畏和审慎) [Gao Hongbing: Data Governance Should Remain Respectful and Prudent], Xinhuanet (Sept. 7, 2020), http://www.xinhuanet.com/tech/2020-09/07/c_1126463040.htm.

107. Julie Cohen, Between Truth and Power: The Legal Construction of Informational Capitalism (2019).

108. Beijing Weimeng Chuangke Wangluo Jishu Youxian Gongsi Su Beijing Taoyou Tianxia Jishu Youxian Gongsi Deng Bu Zhengdang Jingzheng Jiufen An (北京微梦创科网络技术有限公司诉北京淘友天下技术有限公司等不正当竞争纠纷案) [Beijing Weimeng Chuangke Network Technology Co., Ltd. v. Beijing Taoyou Tianxia Technology Co., Ltd., Etc., a Dispute over Unfair Competition], Beijing Intellectual Property Ct. No. 588, Dec. 30, 2016.

109. The court also established a "tripled authorization" principle, requiring three levels of consent in the case of collecting user data in the open API context, including users' consent to the platform, the platform's consent to the third-party service provider, and users' consent to the third-party service provider. Although this "tripled authorization" principle undoubtedly grants users more control over their data, it has also implicitly recognized the right of the platform in granting third-party service provider access to the user data.

110. Beijing Baidu Wangxun Keji Youxian Gongsi yu Shanghai Hantao Xinxi Zixun Youxian Gongsi Bu Zhengdang Jingzheng An (北京百度网讯科技有限公司与上海汉涛信息咨询有限公司不正当竞争纠纷案) [Beijing Baidu Netcom Science & Technology Co., Ltd. v. Shanghai Hantao Information Consulting Co., Ltd., a Dispute over Unfair Competition], Shanghai Intellectual Property Ct. No. 242, Aug. 30, 2017.

111. Dazhong Dianping Shuju Xinxi Bu Zhengdang Jingzheng Jiufen An (大众点评数据信息不正当竞争纠纷案) [Dianping Data Information Unfair Competition Dispute Case], chinaipmagazine.com (May 21, 2018), http://www.chinaipmagazine.com/topics/InfoShow.asp?47-1932.html.

112. Taobao Ruanjian Youxian Gongsi yu Anhui Meijing Xinxi Keji Youxian Gongsi Bu Zhengdang Jingzheng Jiufen An (淘宝软件有限公司与安徽美景信息科技有限公司不正当竞争纠纷案) [Taobao Software Co., Ltd. v. Anhui Meijing Information Science & Technology Co., Ltd., a Dispute over Unfair Competition], Hangzhou Interm. People's Ct. No.7312, Aug. 16, 2018.

344   NOTES

113. Justina Zhang, *Corporate Property Interest in Data—Emerging Norms in China*, GLOBAL ADVERTISING LAWYERS ALLIANCE (Oct. 22, 2022), http://blog. galalaw.com/post/102ginm/corporate-property-interest-in-data-emerg ing-norms-in-china.

114. Boullenois, *supra* note 105.

115. Xin Dai, Regulating Reputation in China: Privacy, Falsehoods, and Social Credit (Jun. 2018) (J.S.D. dissertation, University of Chicago), 51.

116. Ma Jiantang: Kaichuang Woguo Da Shuju Tongji Yingyong Di Meihao Weilai (马建堂: 开创我国大数据统计应用的美好未来) [Ma Jiantang: Create a Bright Future for the Application of Big Data Statistics in My Country], GOV. CN (Nov. 20, 2013), http://www.gov.cn/gzdt/2013-11/20/content_2531049. htm; see Chen & Cheung, *supra* note 86, at 360.

117. Ma Yun Shouke Bai Wan Zhengfa Ganjing: Shuju Shidai Shi Yuce Weilai de Shidai (马云授课百万政法干警: 数据时代是预测未来的时代) [Jack Ma Teaches Millions of Political and Legal Officials: The Era of Data Is the Era of Predicting the Future], READ01.COM (Oct. 22, 2016), https://read01.com/ zh-sg/OEA2D0.html#.YoWyX6hBxD9.

118. Jing Yang, *WeChat Becomes a Powerful Surveillance Tool Everywhere in China*, WALL ST. J (Dec. 22, 2020), https://www.wsj.com/articles/wechat-becomes-a-powerful-surveillance-tool-everywhere-in-china-11608633003.

119. Ibid.

120. Zhao & Yang, *supra* note 60.

121. Yang, *supra* note 118.

122. Ibid.

123. Ibid.

124. Kendra Shaefer, *China's Corporate Social Credit System: Context, Competition, Technology and Geopolitics* 15, U.S.-CHINA ECONOMIC AND SECURITY REVIEW COMMISSION (Nov. 16, 2020), https://www.uscc.gov/sites/default/files/2020-12/Chinas_Corporate_Social_Credit_System.pdf. The NDRC is mainly in charge of working with other state agencies in aggregating data and coordinating rewards and punishments under the social credit system. The PBOC, on the other hand, mainly focuses on overseeing the collection of credit data in the financial sector.

125. Di Sanfang Liliang—Guojia Fagaiwei Yinru Di Sanfang Xinyong Fuwu Jigiu Canyu Hangye Xinyong Jianshe yu Jianguan Jishi (第三方力量——国家发改委引入第三方信用服务机构参与行业信用建设与监管纪实) [Third-Party Power—National Development and Reform Commission Introduced Third-Party Credit Service Agencies to Participate in Industry Credit Construction and Supervision Records], CREDITCHINA.GOV (May 8, 2018), t.ly/EZ3yF.

126. Chen & Cheung, *supra* note 86, at 361; Wanli Bian (边万莉), Liu Nian Jin You Liang Jia Gongsi Huode Paizhao Geren Zheng Xin Hangye Jiang Wang He Chu Qu (六年仅有两家公司获得牌照 个人征信行业将往何处去)

[Only Two Companies Have Obtained Licenses in Six Years Where Will the Personal Credit Reporting Industry Go?], STCN.COM (Mar. 25, 2021), https://news.stcn.com/news/202103/t20210325_2950854.html.

127. Bian, *supra* note 126; Fei Shen, *The Complex Truth about China's Social Credit Scheme*, GOVINSIDER (Mar. 14, 2019), https://govinsider.asia/connected-gov/the-truth-about-chinas-social-credit-scheme/; John Gapper, *Alibaba's Social Credit Rating Is a Risky Game*, FIN. TIMES (Feb. 20, 2018), https://www.ft.com/content/99165d7a-1646-11e8-9376-4a6390addb44.

128. Shen, *supra* note 127.

129. Dai, *supra* note 115, at 51.

130. Ibid.

131. See Dai, *supra* note 115, at 25.

132. Ibid.

133. Meiti Cheng Yanghang Jiao Ting Zhima Xinyong Shoudu Jichang Kuaisu Anjian Tongdao Yingxiao (媒体称央行叫停芝麻信用首都机场快速安检通道营销) [The Media Reported That the Central Bank Stopped Marketing Sesame Credit's Fast Airport Security Channel of the Capital Airport], SINA (Sept. 24, 2015), http://finance.sina.com.cn/money/bank/bank_hydt/20150924/094923337302.shtml.

134. Ni Liaojie Gang Rehuo de "Zhima Xinyong" Ma? Kaitong You Fengxian Ma? Dui Geren Yingxiang? (你了解刚惹祸的"芝麻信用"吗? 开通有风险吗? 对个人影响?) [Do You Know the "Sesame Credit" That Just Got into Trouble? Is It Risky to Open It? Any Personal Impact?], CREDITCHINA.GOV.CN (Jan. 9, 2018), https://www.creditchina.gov.cn/gerenxinyong/gerenxinyongliebiao/201801/t20180109_105956.html.

135. Qianle! Hangzhou Shi Shichang Jianguan Ju Lianshou Zhima Xinyong Gong Zhu Xiao Wei Qiye Chengxin Tixi (签了! 杭州市市场监管局联手芝麻信用共筑小微企业诚信体系) [Signed! Hangzhou Municipal Bureau of Market Supervision and Sesame Credit Jointly Build an Integrity System for Small and Micro Enterprises], FREEWECHAT (Jan. 11, 2017), https://freewechat.com/a/MzA5NTgwMzYzOQ==/2651410544/1; see also Dai, *supra* note 115, at 28.

136. Ibid.

137. See Dai, *supra* note 115, at 28.

138. Ibid., at 29.

139. Lingjie Kong, *Online Privacy in China: A Survey on Information Practices of Chinese Websites*, 6(1) CHIN. J. INT. L. 157–183 (2007).

140. Yang Feng, *The Future of China's Personal Data Protection Law: Challenges and Prospects*, 27(1) ASIA PAC. L. REV. 62–82 (2019). In recent years, leading Chinese tech firms such as Alibaba, Tencent, and ByteDance have significantly improved their privacy policies, which are now generally compliant with the requirements from Chinese data laws. To strengthen their commitment to data compliance, these tech firms also proactively took steps to

enhance self-regulation. In 2018, Tencent published its first White Paper on Privacy Protection, and invited 14 renowned experts and scholars to serve as privacy inspectors to monitor the firm's privacy protection. Similarly, Alibaba's cloud computing arm released its White Paper on Data Security and Privacy Protection in 2021, aiming to provide more transparency for their data security protection scheme. ByteDance also significantly expanded its data compliance team and created a privacy compliance center to handle various compliance issues.

141. Shichang Jianguan Zong Ju, Zhongyang Wang Xin Ban, Shuiwu Zong Ju Lianhe Zhaokai Guifan Xianshang Jingji Zhixu Xingzheng Zhidao Hui, Yaoqiu Hulianwang Pingtai Qiye Jianchi Yifa Hegui Jingying Qianghua Ziwo Yueshu Guanli Gongtong Cujin Xianshang Jingji Jiankang Guifan Fazhan (市场监管总局、中央网信办、税务总局联合召开规范线上经济秩序行政指导会，要求互联网平台企业坚持依法合规经营 强化自我约束管理 共同促进线上经济健康规范发展) [The State Administration of Market Regulation, the Cyberspace Administration of China and the General Tax Bureau Held a Joint Administrative Guidance Meeting to Regulate the Online Economic Order, Requiring Internet Platforms to Comply with the Law, Strengthen Self-discipline, and Together Promote the Healthy and Standardized Development of Online Economy], SAMR.GOV.CN (Nov. 6, 2020), https://www.samr.gov.cn/xw/zj/202011/t20201106_323156.html.

142. Michal Gal & Oshrit Aviv, *The Competitive Effects of the GDPR*, 16 J. COMPET. L. & ECON. 349–391 (2020).

143. Yang, *supra* note 3.

144. Yin, *supra* note 1.

145. Yang, *supra* note 3.

146. App Weifa Weigui Shouji Shiyong Geren Xinxi Zhuanxiang Zhili Baogao (APP违法违规收集使用个人信息专项治理报告) [Special Governance Report on APP's Illegal Collection and Use of Personal Information], CYBERSPACE ADMINISTRATION OF CHINA (May 2019), http://www.cac.gov.cn/2020-05/26/c_1592036763304447.htm.

147. Nathan Jubb, *Chinese Have No Right to Be Forgotten, Court Rules*, SIXTH TONE (May 5, 2016), https://www.sixthtone.com/news/814/chinese-have-no-right-be-forgotten-court-rules; Ren Jiayu Su Beijing Baidu Wangxun Keji Youxian Gongsi Mingyu Quan, Xingming Quan, Yiban Renge Quan Jiufen An (任甲玉诉北京百度网讯科技有限公司名誉权、姓名权、一般人格权纠纷案) [Ren Jiayu v. Beijing Baidu Netcom Science & Technology Co., Ltd., a Dispute over the Right to Reputation, the Right of Name and General Personality Right], Beijing 1st Interm. People's Ct. No. 09558, Dec. 9, 2015.

148. This ruling stands in contrast with the 2014 decision by the Court of Justice of the European Union that solidified the "right to be forgotten" as a fundamental human right in the EU. Zhengyu Shi, *The Right to Be Forgotten in*

NOTES

China--A Third Way to Construct Public Sphere, SSRN (Apr. 3, 2021), https://papers.ssrn.com/sol3/papers.cfm?abstract_id=3832803.

149. Qi Wang (王琦), *Zhongguo Caipan Wenshu Wang Yi Gongbu Wenshu 4260 Yu Wan Pian* (中国裁判文书网已公布文书4260余万篇) [Over 42.6 Million Judicial Opinions Are Online], Xinhua News (Feb 27, 2018), http://m.xinhuanet.com/2018-02/27/c_129818588.htm.

150. Zhuang Liu et al., *Authoritarian Transparency: China's Missing Cases in Judicial Opinion Disclosure,* 50(1) J. Comp. Econ. 221, 224 (2022).

151. Lei Chen et al., *Judicial Transparency as Judicial Centralization: Mass Publicity of Court Decisions in China,* 31 J. Contemp. China 726 (2022).

152. Ibid., at 222.

153. Ibid.

154. Liza Lin & Chun Han Wong, *China Increasingly Obscures True State of Its Economy to Outsiders,* Wall St. J. (Dec. 6, 2021), https://www.wsj.com/articles/china-data-security-law-ships-ports-court-cases-universities-11638803230.

155. Using the keywords of "online platforms" and "Cyber Security Law," I searched the China Judgement Online database for all relevant cases decided by the end of 2020.

156. Zhou Yuchan Su Guangdong Kuaike Dianzi Shangwu Youxian Gongsi, Dongguan Shi Yide Wangluo Keji Youxian Gongsi Wangluo Qinquan Zeren Jiufen An (周裕婵诉广东快客电子商务有限公司、东莞市易得网络科技有限公司网络侵权责任纠纷案) [Zhou Yuchan v. Guangdong Kuaike E-commerce Co., Ltd. and Dongguan Yide Network Science & Technology Co., Ltd., a Dispute over Network Tort Liability], Guangdong Shenzhen Interm. People's Ct. No. 3954, May 10, 2019; Shen Jin Su Shanghai Xiecheng Shangwu Youxian Gongsi, Zhifu Bao Wangluo Jishu Youxian Gongsi Qinquan Zeren Jiufen An (申瑾诉上海携程商务有限公司、支付宝网络技术有限公司侵权责任纠纷案) [Shen Jing v. Shanghai Ctrip Commerce Co., Ltd. and Alipay Network Technology Co., Ltd., a Dispute over Tort Liability], Beijing Zhaoyang Dist. People's Ct. No. 36658, Dec. 29, 2018.

157. Yu Yanbin Su Zhejiang Tianmao Wangluo Youxian Gongsi Deng Wangluo Qinquan Zeren An (俞延彬诉浙江天猫网络有限公司等网络侵权责任案) [Yu Yanbin v. Zhejiang Tmall Network Co., Ltd., Etc., a Dispute over Network Tort Liability], Beijing Haidian Dist. People's Ct. No. 13661, Dec. 10, 2019; Huang Mou yu Tengxun Keji Youxian Gongsi Deng Wangluo Qinquan Zeren Jiufen An (黄某与腾讯科技有限公司等网络侵权责任纠纷案) [Huang v. Tencent Science & Technology Co., Ltd., Etc., a Dispute over Tort Liability], Beijing Internet Ct. No. 16142, Jul. 30, 2020; Sun Changbao yu Beijing Sohu Hulianwang Xinxi Fuwu Youxian Gongsi Deng Renge Quan Jiufen An (孙长宝与北京搜狐互联网信息服务有限公司等人格权纠纷案) [Sun Changbao v. Beijing Sohu Internet Information Service Co., Ltd., Etc., a Dispute over the Right of Personality], Beijing Internet Ct. No. 10989, Sept. 10, 2020.

348   NOTES

158. Huang v. Tencent, *supra* note 157. Usually, users of WeChat Reading are required to log in using their WeChat account and authorize WeChat Reading to access their WeChat contacts.

159. *Homepage*, CHINA ELECTRONICS STANDARDIZATION INSTITUTE (last accessed on Jul. 4, 2023), http://www.cesi.cn/page/index.html.

160. *About Us*, CHINA ACADEMY OF INFORMATION AND COMMUNICATION TECHNOLOGY (last accessed on Jul. 4, 2023), http://www.caict.ac.cn/english/about/202004/t20200413_279063.html.

161. *Homepage*, STANDARDIZATION ADMINISTRATION (last accessed on Jul. 4, 2023), http://www.sac.gov.cn/.

162. Meiguo Tongguo WTO Yaoqiu Zhongguo Zhanhuan Shishi Wang An Fa Zuizhong Cuoshi (美国通过WTO要求中国暂缓实施网安法最终措施) [United States Asked China to Suspend the Implementation of the Final Measures of the Cybersecurity Law through the WTO], WEIXIN.QQ.COM (Sept. 30, 2017) https://mp.weixin.qq.com/s/aFhlarZsW3zNVP6_c8ZusA.

163. *Homepage*, NATIONAL INFORMATION SECURITY STANDARDIZATION TECHNICAL COMMITTEE (last accessed on Jul. 4, 2023), https://www.tc260.org.cn/.

164. See XINYU LIU (刘新宇), SHUJU BAOHU: HEGUI ZHIYIN YU GUIZE JIEXI (数据保护: 合规指引与规则解析) (2021).

165. Dui Jiancha Wangluo Anquan Fa, Jiaqiang Wangluo Xinxi Baohu de Jueding Shishi Qingkuang Baogao de Yijian he Jianyi (对检查网络安全法、加强网络信息保护的决定实施情况报告的意见和建议) [Opinions and Suggestions on the Implementation Report of the Decision to Review the Cybersecurity Law and Strengthen Cyber Information Protection], NATIONAL PEOPLE'S CONGRESS OF THE PEOPLE'S REPUBLIC OF CHINA (Jan. 24, 2018), http://www.npc.gov.cn/zgrdw/npc/xinwen/jdgz/2018-01/24/content_2036768.htm.

166. Yang Liu (刘杨), Zhongyang Wang Xin Ban Deng Si Bumen Lianhe Kaizhan Yinsi Tiaokuan Zhuanxiang Gongzuo (中央网信办等四部门联合开展隐私条款专项工作) [The Central Cyberspace Administration and Four Other Departments Jointly Carry Out Special Work on Privacy Clauses], GOV.CN (Jul. 27, 2017), http://www.gov.cn/xinwen/2017-07/27/content_5213833.htm. The focus of their assessment includes whether the application has properly informed users about the scope and method of collecting personal information, whether the app has properly informed users about its rules in using personal information (such as personalization and recommendation services), and whether the app has properly informed users about their rights to visit, delete, and modify their personal information; this shows that the largest online platforms were, at the very least, subject to more scrutiny than others from the start.

167. Ni de Geren Xinxi Anquan Ma? Gongxinbu Yue Tan Baidu Mayi Jin Fu Jinri Tou Tiao (你的个人信息安全吗? 工信部约谈百度蚂蚁金服今日头条) [Is Your Personal Information Safe? The Ministry of Industry and

NOTES 349

Information Technology Interviewed Baidu, Ant Financial, and TopBuzz], SINA (Jan. 12, 2018), http://tech.sina.com.cn/roll/2018-01-12/doc-ifyqqciz 5880474.shtml.

168. CYBERSPACE ADMINISTRATION OF CHINA, *supra* note 146.

169. Ibid.

170. Ibid.

171. Ibid.

172. Shichang Jianguan Zongju Zhaokai "Shouhu Xiaofei" Ji Daji Qinhai Xiaofei Zhe Geren Xinxi Weifa Xingwei Zhuanxiang Zhifa Xingdong Zhuanti (市场监管总局召开 "守护消费"暨打击侵害消费者个人信息违法行为 专项执法行动专题新闻发布会) [State Administration for Market Regulation Held a "Guarding Consumption" Press Conference on Special Law Enforcement Actions to Crack Down on Infringement of Consumers' Personal Information], SAMR.GOV.CN (Nov. 18, 2019), https://www.samr.gov.cn/xw/xwfbt/201911/t20191118_308613.html. See also CAC's Special Governance Report, *supra* note 146, at 5.

173. 2020 Nian App Weifa Weigui Shouji Shiyong Geren Xinxi Zhili Gongzuo Qidong Hui Zai Jing Zhaokai (2020年App违法违规收集使用个人信息治理工作启动会在京召开) [The Initiating Meeting for Governing App's Illegal Collection and Usage of Personal Information Will Be Held in Beijing], CYBERSPACE ADMINISTRATION OF CHINA (Jul. 25, 2020), http://www.cac.gov.cn/2020-07/25/c_1597240741055830.htm.

174. Guanyu 35 Kuan App Cunzai Geren Xinxi Shouji Shiyong Wenti de Baogao (关于35款App存在个人信息收集使用问题的通告) [Notice on the Problematic Collection and Usage of Personal Information by 35 Apps], CYBERSPACE ADMINISTRATION OF CHINA (Nov. 17, 2020), http://www.cac.gov.cn/2020-11/17/c_1607178245870454.htm.

175. Luke Dembosky et al., *China Publishes New Draft Regulations on Data Security*, DEBEVOISE DATA BLOG (Dec. 9, 2021), https://www.debevoisedatablog.com/2021/12/09/china-publishes-new-draft-regulations-on-data-security/.

176. Ben Jiang, *China's Internet Censors Target Deepfake Tech to Curb Online Disinformation*, SOUTH CHINA MORNING POST (Dec. 12, 2022), https://www.scmp.com/tech/policy/article/3203000/chinas-internet-censors-target-tec hnology-behind-deepfakes-curb-online-disinformation.

177. Alex Roberts, *China Publishes Revised Cybersecurity Review Measures*, LINKLATERS (Jul. 12, 2020), t.ly/WVels.

178. Yan Luo et al., *Privacy Updates from China: Proliferation of Sector-Specific Rules as Key Legislation Remains Pending—Part 2: Data Protection in the Financial Sector*, INSIDE PRIVACY (May 3, 2021), t.ly/7IujE.

179. Ibid.

180. James Gong et al., *China Tightens Data Protection in Automotive Industry*, BIRD & BIRD (Sept. 12, 2021), https://www.twobirds.com/en/insights/2021/china/china-tightens-data-protection-in-automotive-industry.

NOTES

181. The Shanghai Data Regulation was promulgated by the Standing Committee of the People's Congress of Shanghai on Nov. 25, 2021, effective Jan. 1, 2022. The Shenzhen Data Regulation was promulgated by the Standing Committee of the People's Congress of Shenzhen on Jun. 29, 2021, effective Jan. 1, 2022. The Zhejiang Public Data Measures were promulgated by the People's Congress of Zhejiang Province on Jan. 21, 2022, effective Mar. 1, 2022.

182. Rogier Creemers, *China's Emerging Data Protection Framework*, 8 J. CYBERSECUR. 1, 19 (2022).

183. The data is collected on the CAC's and the MIIT's websites.

184. Guanyu Yinfa "Changjian Leixing Yidong Hulianwang Yingyong Chengxu Biyao Geren Xinxi Fanwei Guiding" de Tongzhi (关于印发《常见类型移动互联网应用程序必要个人信息范围规定》的通知) [Notice on Issuing the "Regulations on the Scope of Necessary Personal Information for Common Types of Mobile Internet Applications"], CYBERSPACE ADMINISTRATION OF CHINA (Mar. 22, 2021), http://www.cac.gov.cn/2021-03/22/c_161799099 7054277.htm.

185. Iris Deng, *Beijing Names and Shames Tencent, Alibaba, Baidu and 81 Other Apps for Excessive Data Collection under New Rules*, SOUTH CHINA MORNING POST (May 10, 2021), https://www.scmp.com/tech/big-tech/article/3132910/beij ing-names-and-shames-tencent-alibaba-baidu-and-81-other-apps.

186. Guanyu Keep Deng 129 Kuan App Weifa Weigui Shouji Shiyong Geren Xinxi Qingkuang de Tongbao (关于Keep等129款App违法违规收集使用个人信息情况的通报) [Announcement on the Illegal Collection and Use of Personal Information by 129 Apps Including Keep], CYBERSPACE ADMINISTRATION OF CHINA (Jun. 11, 2016), http://www.cac.gov.cn/2021-06/11/c_1624994586637 626.htm; Guanyu Dou Yin Deng 105 Kuan App Weifa Weigui Shouji Shiyong Geren Xinxi Qingkuang de Tongbao (关于抖音等105款App违法违规收集使用个人信息情况的通报) [Announcement on the Illegal Collection and Use of Personal Information by 105 Apps Including Douyin], CYBERSPACE ADMINISTRATION OF CHINA (May 21, 2021), http://www.cac.gov.cn/2021-05/20/c_1623091083320667.htm.

187. Companies were given 15 days to rectify their behavior and there was no follow-up action.

188. Minghe Hu et al., *China's Regulators Suspect Didi's US Listing Was "Deliberate Act of Deceit," a Portrayal That Shows Severity of Mistrust, Sources Say*, SOUTH CHINA MORNING POST (Jul. 9, 2021), https://www.scmp.com/tech/policy/article/3140471/chinas-regulators-suspect-didis-us-listing-was-deliberate-act-deceit.

189. Guojia Wang Xin Ban: Xiajia "Di Di Qiye Ban" Deng 25 Kuan App (国家网信办:下架"滴滴企业版"等25款App) [Cyberspace Administration of China: Remove 25 Apps Including "Didi Enterprise Edition"], SINA (Jul. 9, 2021), https://finance.sina.com.cn/tech/2021-07-09/doc-ikqcfnca5945007.shtml.

NOTES

351

190. Li Yuan, *For China's Business Elites, Staying Out of Politics Is No Longer an Option*, N.Y. TIMES (Jul. 6, 2021), https://www.nytimes.com/2021/07/06/technology/china-business-politics-didi.html.

191. Ibid.

192. Graham Webster, *Translation: Chinese Authorities Announce $1.2B Fine in Didi Case, Describe "Despicable" Data Abuses*, DIGICHINA.STANFORD.EDU (Jul. 21, 2022), https://digichina.stanford.edu/work/translation-chinese-authorities-announce-2b-fine-in-didi-case-describe-despicable-data-abuses/.

193. Xingzheng Susong Fa (行政处罚法) [Administrative Punishment Law] (amended by the Standing Comm. Nat'l. People's Cong., Jan. 22, 2021, effective Jul. 15, 2021), art. 37 (providing that administrative punishment should be imposed according to the law stipulated at the time the infringements occur).

194. Vincent Brussee, *Didi Fine Marks New Phase in Beijing's Rectification of Tech Sector*, MERICS (Aug. 9, 2022), https://merics.org/en/short-analysis/didi-fine-marks-new-phase-beijings-rectification-tech-sector. See also Jamie Horsley, *Behind the Facade of China's Cyber Super-Regulator*, DIGICHINA.STANFORD.EDU (Aug. 8, 2022), https://digichina.stanford.edu/work/behind-the-facade-of-chinas-cyber-super-regulator/.

195. Horsley, *supra* note 194. As Jamie Horsley acutely observes: "the CAC lacked many formal attributes of an administrative agency in the Chinese system, including institutional transparency and accountability. While the general principle that merged party-state entities should be treated as administrative agencies when performing state rather than party functions is gaining traction, the line between those two functions is not always clear."

196. Hu Hongfang Su Shanghai Xiecheng Shangwu Youxian Gongsi Qinquan Zeren Jiufen An (胡红芳诉上海携程商务有限公司侵权责任纠纷案) [Hu Hongfang v. Shanghai Ctrip Commerce Co., Ltd., a Dispute over Tort Liability], Zhejiang Shaoxing Interm. People's Ct. No. 3129, Dec. 31, 2021.

197. See Yu Yanbin v. Zhejiang Tmall and others, *supra* note 157.

198. Steve Kwok et al., *New PRC Regulations on Cross-Border Transfer of Data*, SKADDEN (Aug. 23, 2022), https://www.skadden.com/insights/publications/2022/08/new-prc-regulations-on-cross-border-transfer-of-data.

199. Ibid.

200. "Banfa" Shixing Jiang Man 6 Ge Yue Shuju Chujing Xu Yifa Shenbao Pinggu (《办法》施行将满6个月数据出境需依法申报评估) [Implementation of the Measures Approaching Six Months, Outbound Data Transfers Should Undergo Security Assessment According to Law], BEIJING CAC (Feb. 22, 2023), https://mp.weixin.qq.com/s/UCHITtp3dK2KVHtLQFAF2Q.

201. Interview with lawyers based in Beijing (Mar. 2023).

202. Interview with legal experts in Beijing (Mar. 2023).

203. Geren Xinxi Baohu Fa (个人信息保护法) [Personal Information Protection Law] [promulgated by the Standing Comm. Nat'l. People's Cong., Aug. 20, 2021, effective Nov. 1, 2021], art. 38.

NOTES

204. European Commission, *Adequacy Decisions* (last updated Apr. 11, 2023), https://commission.europa.eu/law/law-topic/data-protection/international-dimension-data-protection/adequacy-decisions_en.

205. Anupam Chander & Paul M. Schwartz, *Privacy and/or Trade*, 90 U. Chi. L. Rev. 49, 33–35 (2023).

206. Yik Chan Chin & Jingwu Zhao, *Governing Cross-Border Data Flows: International Trade Agreements and Their Limits*, 11(4) Laws 63, 9 (2022).

207. Ibid.

208. Chang Che & John Liu, *China Strikes Back at Micron Technology Even as It Signals Openness*, N.Y. Times (Apr. 4, 2023), https://www.nytimes.com/2023/04/04/business/micron-china-investigation.html.

209. Ibid.

210. Lilian Zhang, *Why China Launched a Cybersecurity Review into US Memory Chip Maker Micron Technology and What Could Happen Next*, South China Morning Post (Apr. 2, 2023), https://www.scmp.com/tech/tech-war/article/3215742/why-china-launched-cybersecurity-review-us-memory-chip-maker-micron-technology-and-what-could-happen.

211. *Ibid.*

212. US Department of Justice, *PRC State-Owned Company, Taiwan Company, and Three Individuals Charged With Economic Espionage* (Nov. 1, 2018), https://www.justice.gov/opa/pr/prc-state-owned-company-taiwan-company-and-three-individuals-charged-economic-espionage; David Lawder, *U.S. Restricts Exports to Chinese Semiconductor Firm Fujian Jinhua*, Reuters (Oct. 30, 2018), https://www.reuters.com/article/us-usa-trade-china-semiconductors-idUSKCN1N328E.

213. Max A. Cherney, *Intel, AMD, Other Chipmakers Spent $100 Million on Lobbying*, Protocol (Apr. 4, 2022), https://www.protocol.com/enterprise/chip-lobby-spending-washington.

214. Che Pan, *American Chip Firm Marvell "Eliminates" Job Roles in China amid Deepening Tech Rivalry*, South China Morning Post (Oct. 27, 2022), https://www.scmp.com/tech/tech-war/article/3197487/american-chip-firm-marvell-eliminates-job-roles-china-amid-deepening-tech-rivalry.

215. Laura He, *Micron Technology: China Probes US Chip Maker for Cybersecurity Risks as Tech Tension Escalates*, CNN Business (Apr. 3, 2023), https://edition.cnn.com/2023/04/03/tech/china-micron-probe-us-chip-war-intl-hnk/index.html.

216. Zhang, *supra* note 210.

217. *China Starts "Surgical" Retaliation against Foreign Companies after US-led Tech Blockade*, Fin. Times (Apr. 16, 2023), https://www.ft.com/content/fc2038d2-3e25-4a3f-b8ca-0ceb5532a1f3?shareType=nongift.

218. Zhonggong Zhongyang Guowuyuan Guanyu Goujian Shuju Jichu Zhidu Genghao Fahui Shuju Yaosu Zuoyong de Yijian (中共中央 国务院关于构建数据基础制度更好发挥数据要素作用的意见) [The Central Committee

NOTES

353

of the Chinese Communist Party and State Council on Developing Basic Data Systems and Better Utilizing Data as a Factor of Production] (Dec. 2, 2022), http://www.gov.cn/zhengce/2022-12/19/content_5732695.htm.

219. Giulia Interesse, *China Has a New Plan to Strengthen Its Data Economy*, CHINA BRIEFING (Jan. 23, 2023), https://www.china-briefing.com/news/china-has-a-new-plan-to-strengthen-its-data-economy/.

220. Ibid.

221. Qiheng Chen, *China's New National Data Bureau: What It Is and What It Is Not*, THE CHINA PROJECT (Mar. 20, 2023), https://thechinaproject.com/2023/03/20/chinas-new-national-data-bureau-what-it-is-and-what-it-is-not/.

222. Ibid.

223. Jiahui Huang, *China Proposes Easing of Cross-Border Data Controls*, WALL ST. J. (Sep. 29, 2023), https://www.wsj.com/world/china/china-proposes-easing-of-cross-border-data-controls-df3e67e3

224. For instance, the transfer of data relating to international trade, academic collaboration, cross-border manufacturing, and marketing that don't involve personal information or important data would no longer need to undergo security assessment. Moreover, personal data involved in routine commercial and travel transactions, as well as those relating to labor contracts, health and property safety during emergencies, can be exported without the need for a security assessment. The draft rules also specify that data will only be deemed important if explicitly designated by regulators. Furthermore, data exports involving fewer than 10,000 Chinese individuals within a year can be exported without a security assessment. For data exports involving up to 1 million Chinese individuals, exporters can use a standard contract and register with the provincial cyberspace administration. Only for data exports involving over 1 million Chinese persons will a security assessment be mandatory.

225. Martin Chorzempa & Samm Sacks, *China's New Rules on Data Flows could Signal A Shift Away from Security Toward Growth*, Peterson Institute for international Economics (Oct. 3, 2023), https://www.piie.com/blogs/realtime-economics/chinas-new-rules-data-flows-could-signal-shift-away-security-toward-growth

CHAPTER 6

1. Zhongguo Fenxiang Jingji Fazhan Baogao 2016 (中国分享经济发展报告2016) [Report on the Development of China's Sharing Economy 2016], STATE INFORMATION CENTER (Feb. 29, 2016), http://www.sic.gov.cn/News/568/6010.htm; Zhongguo Gongxiang Jingji Fazhan Baogao 2022 (中国共享经济发展报告2022) [Report on the Development of China's Sharing Economy 2022], STATE INFORMATION CENTER (Feb. 22, 2022), http://www.sic.gov.cn/News/568/11277.htm.

2. Ping Sun et al., *From Flexible Labour to "Sticky Labour": A Tracking Study of Workers in the Food-Delivery Platform Economy of China*, WORK, EMPLOYMENT AND SOCIETY (Aug. 27, 2021), https://doi.org/10.1177/09500170211021570.

3. Zhongguo Gongxiang Jingji Fazhan Baogao 2021 (中国共享经济发展报告2021) [Report on the Development of China's Sharing Economy 2021], STATE INFORMATION CENTER (Feb. 19, 2021), http://www.sic.gov.cn/News/557/10779.htm.

4. *Food Delivery Workers Need a Trade Union to Push for Real Change*, CHINA LABOUR BULL. (Sept. 22, 2020), https://clb.org.hk/content/food-delivery-workers-need-trade-union-push-real-change; see also Jenny Chan, *Hunger for Profit: How Food Delivery Platforms Manage Couriers in China*, 23(57) SOCIOLOGIAS 58, 72 (2021).

5. See Chan, *supra* note 4, at 62.

6. Ibid.

7. Waimai Qishou, Kun Zai Xitong Li (外卖骑手，困在系统里) [Delivery Drivers, Stuck in the System], RENWU (人物) [PEOPLE] (Sept. 8, 2020), https://mp.weixin.qq.com/s/Mes1RqIOdp48CMw4pXTwXw.

8. Chan, *supra* note 4, at 9; Ya-Wen Lei, *Delivering Solidarity: Platform Architecture and Collective Contention in China's Platform Economy*, 86(2) AM. SOCIO. REV. 279, 292 (2021); also see PEOPLE, *supra* note 7.

9. Chan, *supra* note 4, at 2.

10. Xuduo Meng (孟续铎), Gongxiang Yonggong Pingtai Shang Congye Renyuan Laodong Jiuye Tezheng Diaocha Fenxi (共享用工平台上从业人员劳动就业特征调查分析) [Investigating and Analyzing the Employment Characteristics of Platform Workers in the Sharing Economy], 4 ZHONGGUO RENLI ZIYUAN SHEHUI BAOZHANG (中国人力资源社会保障) [HUMAN RESOURCES AND SOCIAL SECURITY IN CHINA] 18 (2018).

11. Zixu Wang, *In China, Delivery Workers Struggle against a Rigged System*, THE CHINA PROJECT (Apr. 20, 2021), https://thechinaproject.com/2021/04/20/in-china-delivery-workers-struggle-against-a-rigged-system/.

12. Leping Huang (黄乐平), Wangyue Peisongyuan, Laodong Baohusan Ruhe Chengqilai (网约配送员，劳动保护伞如何撑起来?) [How to Build a Labor Protection Umbrella for On-demand Delivery Workers?], BEIJING YILIAN LEGAL AID AND RESEARCH CENTER OF LABOR (Jan. 13, 2021), http://www.yilianlabor.cn/yanjiu/2021/1902.html.

13. PEOPLE, *supra* note 7.

14. Fu Chuzhang Song Waimai Zhuan 41 Yuan, Zhu Dan Chufa Xia Benpao de Qishou Men, Zhen Neng Yue Ru Guo Wan? (副处长送外卖赚41元, 逐单处罚下奔跑的骑手们, 真能月入过万?) [A Deputy Division Director Earned 41 RMB by Delivering Food, Can Drivers Who Run under the per Order Punishment System Really Earn More than 10,000 RMB a Month?], QQ.COM (Aug. 25, 2021), https://new.qq.com/omn/20210825/20210825A07F0N00.html.

NOTES 355

15. PEOPLE, *supra* note 7.

16. See Chan, *supra* note 4, at 74.

17. Waimai Xiaoge Songcan Yin Jiaotong Shigu Zhi Ren Siwang Shui Fuze? Shanghai Lifa Mingque: Suoshu Qiye Yifa Chengdan Zeren (外卖小哥送餐因交通事故致人死亡谁负责？ 上海立法明确： 所属企业依法承担责任) [Who Is Responsible for the Death in Traffic Accidents Caused by Delivery Workers? Shanghai Legislates to Clarify: The Enterprises Shall Bear Responsibility According to Law], SINA.COM.CN (Feb. 26, 2021), http://finance.sina.com.cn/jjxw/2021-02-26/doc-ikftssap8845480.shtml.

18. Jinnian Yilai Guangzhou Jiaojing Gong Chachu Diandong Zixingche Jiaotong Weifa Xingwei 98.5 Wan Zong (今年以来广州交警共查处电动自行车交通违法行为98.5万宗) [Guangzhou Traffic Police Have Investigated 985,000 Violations by Electric Bicycles This Year], THE PEOPLE'S GOVERNMENT OF GUANGZHOU MUNICIPALITY (Dec. 1, 2021), http://www.gz.gov.cn/xw/jrgz/content/post_7942155.html.

19. See Chan, *supra* note 4, at 78.

20. Ibid., at 70–71 and 78.

21. Jiwei Qian, *Why Informal Workers Are Opting Out of China's Welfare System*, SIXTH TONE (Oct. 9, 2019), https://www.sixthtone.com/news/1004594/why-informal-workers-are-opting-out-of-chinas-welfare-system.

22. Leping Huang et al. (黄乐平等), Xinyetai Congye Renyuan Laodong Quanyi Baohu 2020 Niandu Diaoyan Baogao (新业态从业人员劳动权益保护2020年度调研报告) [2020 Annual Research Report on the Labor Protection of Workers in New Forms of Employment], BEIJING YILIAN LEGAL AID AND RESEARCH CENTER OF LABOR (Jan. 19, 2021), http://www.yilianlabor.cn/yanjiu/2021/1909.html.

23. Li Sun & Tao Liu, *Injured but not Entitled to Legal Insurance Compensation*, 48(7) SOC. POL'Y ADMIN. 905, 906 (2014).

24. MARY GALLAGHER, AUTHORITARIAN LEGALITY IN CHINA: LAW, WORKERS, AND THE STATE (2017).

25. Sun & Liu, *supra* note 23, at 906.

26. Jiwei Qian & Zhuoyi Wen, *Extension of Social Insurance Coverage to Informal Economy Workers in China*, 74(1) INT. SOC. SECUR. REV. 79, 93 (2021).

27. *Migrant Workers and Their Children*, CHINA LABOUR BULL. (May 26, 2022), https://clb.org.hk/content/migrant-workersand-their-children.

28. Bin Chen et al., *The Disembedded Digital Economy: Social Protection for New Economy Employment in China*, 54(7) SOC. POL'Y ADMIN. 1246, 1251 (2020).

29. Lei, *supra* note 8, at 289–290.

30. Jason Hung, *Hukou System Influencing the Structural, Institutional Inequalities in China*, 11(5) SOC. SCI. 194 (2022); see also Chen et al., *supra* note 28, at 1252.

31. Linggong Jingji Xia de 2 Yi "Xiaoge" Shengsi Jingsu Nimen de Shebao Zainali? (零工经济下的2亿"小哥"生死竞速 你们的社保在哪里?) [200 Million "Brothers" in the Gig Economy Are Racing to the Death: Where Is

Their Social Security?], SINA.COM.CN (Jan. 14, 2021), https://finance.sina.com.cn/money/insurance/bxdt/2021-01-15/doc-ikftpnnx7433844.shtml.

32. Qian, *supra* note 21.

33. Qian & Wen, *supra* note 26, at 93.

34. Che Pan & Minghe Hu, *China's Ele.me Stirs Outcry after Initial Low Compensation for Delivery Worker's Death*, SOUTH CHINA MORNING POST (Jan. 8, 2021), https://www.scmp.com/tech/enterprises/article/3117000/chinas-eleme-stirs-outcry-after-initial-low-compensation-delivery.

35. Waimai Qishou "Beimai" de Baoxian Hao Gui (外卖骑手"被买"的保险好贵) [The "Bought" Insurance for Delivery Workers Is So Expensive], SINA.COM.CN (Sept. 9, 2020), https://finance.sina.com.cn/money/insurance/bxyx/2020-09-09/doc-iivhuipp3440387.shtml.

36. SINA, *supra* note 31.

37. Lili Dai (代丽丽), Yiwai Shanghai Fengxian Gao, "Qishou" Quanyi Shui Baozhang (意外伤害风险高, "骑手"权益谁保障) [Who Can Protect the Rights and Interests of "Drivers" Who Bear High Risks of Accidental Injury?], PEOPLE.CN (Jan. 4, 2021), http://capital.people.com.cn/n1/2021/0104/c405954-31988012.html.

38. Chen et al., *supra* note 28, at 1251.

39. *Waiting for Weiquan: Worker Rights Protection at the All-China Federation of Trade Unions*, CHINA LABOUR BULL. (Aug. 8, 2022), https://clb.org.hk/content/clb-report-waiting-weiquan-worker-rights-protection-all-china-federation-trade-unions.

40. Ching Kwan Lee, *China's Precariats*, 16(2) GLOBALIZATIONS 137, 144–145 (2019).

41. Ibid.

42. Ibid.

43. ELI FRIEDMAN, INSURGENCY TRAP: LABOR POLITICS IN POSTSOCIALIST CHINA 55 (2014).

44. CLB, *supra* note 39.

45. Ibid.

46. CLB, *supra* note 4.

47. CLB, *supra* note 39.

48. Ibid.

49. Ibid.

50. Ibid.

51. Chuxuan Liu & Eli Friedman, *Resistance under the Radar: Organization of Work and Collective Action in China's Food Delivery Industry*, 86 CHINA J. 68, 72 (2021).

52. Chan, *supra* note 4, at 65.

53. Julie Yujie Chen, *Thrown under the Bus and Outrunning It! The Logic of Didi and Taxi Drivers' Labour and Activism in the On-Demand Economy*, 20(8) NEW MEDIA SOC. 2691, 2702 (2018).

54. Ibid., at 2693.

55. Ibid.

56. CLB Strike Map, CHINA LABOUR BULL., https://maps.clb.org.hk/.

NOTES

357

57. Jingcheng Qixia Zhuan: Waisong Jianghu Qishi Lianmeng Mengzhu Chen Tianhe he Beijing Shilihe de Qishou Jianghu (京城骑侠传: 外送江湖骑士联盟盟主陈天河和北京十里河的骑手江湖) [Driver-Knight Legend in Peking: Chen Tianhe, Leader of the Jianghu Drivers Alliance, and the Jianghu of Drivers in Peking Shilihe], SINA.COM.CN (Nov. 30, 2020), https://finance.sina.com.cn/chanjing/gsnews/2020-11-30/doc-iiznezxs4471356.shtml.

58. Zixu Wang, *In China, Delivery Workers Struggled against a Rigged System*, THE CHINA PROJECT (Apr. 20, 2021), https://thechinaproject.com/2021/04/20/in-china-delivery-workers-struggle-against-a-rigged-system/.

59. Ibid.

60. Ibid.

61. Emily Feng, *He Tried to Organize Workers in China's Gig Economy. Now He Faces 5 Years In Jail*, NPR (Apr. 13, 2021), https://www.npr.org/2021/04/13/984994360/he-tried-to-organize-workers-in-chinas-gig-economy-now-he-faces-5-years-in-jail.

62. Yanzhong Weigui Guize (严重违规规则) [Rules for Serious Violations], MEITUAN.COM (accessed on Mar. 13, 2023), https://peisong.meituan.com/app/protocolDetail?appType=1&protocolType=33.

63. Ou Lin, *Regulating On-Demand Work in China: Just Getting Started?*, 51(2) IND. L. J. 435, 437 (2022).

64. Guowuyuan Bangong Ting Guanyu Fazhan Zhongchuang Kongjian Tuidong Dazhong Chuangxin Chuangye de Zhidao Yijian (国务院办公厅关于发展众创空间推进大众创新创业的指导意见) [General Office of the State Council Guidance on the Development of Innovation and Promotion of Mass Entrepreneurship], State Council Issued [2015] No. 9, http://www.gov.cn/gongbao/content/2015/content_2835233.htm; Guowuyuan Bangong Ting Guanyu Shenhua Gaige Tuijin Chuzu Qiche Hangye Jiankang Fazhan de Zhidao Yijian (国务院办公厅关于深化改革推进出租汽车行业健康发展的指导意见) [General Office of the State Council Guidance on Deepening Reform and Promotion of the Healthy Development of the Taxi Industry], State Council Issued [2016] No. 58, http://www.gov.cn/zhengce/content/2016-07/28/content_5095567.htm.

65. The 13th Five-year Plan for Economic and Social Development of the People's Republic of China 2016–2020, NATIONAL DEVELOPMENT AND REFORM COMMISSION (Mar. 17, 2016), https://en.ndrc.gov.cn/policies/202105/P020210527785800103339.pdf.

66. Notice on Issuing the Guiding Opinion on Accelerating the Development of Sharing Economy, NATIONAL DEVELOPMENT AND REFORM COMMISSION (Jul. 3, 2017), https://www.chinalawtranslate.com/wp-content/uploads/2017/08/2017-7-28-Sharing-Economy-Opinions-JPH-Tr.pdf.

67. *Premier Li Urges Inclusive Attitude to Further Promote Sharing Economy*, THE STATE COUNCIL (Jun. 22, 2017), http://english.www.gov.cn/premier/news/2017/06/22/content_281475693906896.htm.

68. Xu Wei, *China Takes Measures to Boost Sharing Economy*, THE STATE COUNCIL (Jun. 21, 2017), http://english.www.gov.cn/premier/news/2017/06/21/content_281475693296222.htm.

69. Guanyu Cujin Pingtai Jingji Guifan Jiankang Fazhan de Zhidao Yijian (关于促进平台经济规范健康发展的指导意见) [Guiding Opinions on Promoting the Well-Regulated and Sound Development of the Platform Economy], THE STATE COUNCIL (Aug. 1, 2019), http://www.gov.cn/zhengce/content/2019-08/08/content_5419761.htm.

70. Lin, *supra* note 63, at 451.

71. Sidney Leng, *Coronavirus: China Seeks Solution to Unemployment Crisis with Flexible Jobs*, SOUTH CHINA MORNING POST (Aug. 20, 2020), https://www.scmp.com/economy/china-economy/article/3098011/coronavirus-china-seeks-solution-unemployment-crisis-flexible; Sidney Leng, *Coronavirus: China Faces Historic Test as Pandemic Stokes Fears of Looming Unemployment Crisis*, SOUTH CHINA MORNING POST (May 11, 2020), t.ly/Wy9mK.

72. SANTIAGO LEVY, GOOD INTENTIONS, BAD OUTCOMES: SOCIAL POLICY, INFORMALITY, AND ECONOMIC GROWTH IN MEXICO (2008).

73. Leonardo Gasparini et al., *Income Polarization in Latin America: Patterns and Links with Institutions and Conflict*, 36(4) OXF. DEV. STUD. 461 (2008).

74. LEVY, *supra* note 72, at 2.

75. *"Common Prosperity" in an Era of Wage Polarization?*, STANFORD CENTER ON CHINA'S ECONOMY AND INSTITUTIONS (Mar. 1, 2022), https://sccei.fsi.stanford.edu/china-briefs/common-prosperity-era-wage-polarization.

76. Scott Rozelle, *Moving beyond Lewis: Employment and Wage Trends in China's High- and Low-Skilled Industries and the Emergence of an Era of Polarization*, 62 COMP. ECON. 555, 579 (2020).

77. Jinping Xi (习近平), Zhashi Tuidong Gongtong Fuyu (扎实推动共同富裕) [Promoting Common Prosperity Solidly], QSTHEORY.CN (Oct. 15, 2021), http://www.qstheory.cn/dukan/qs/2021-10/15/c_1127959365.htm.

78. Zhejiang Gao Zhiliang Fazhan Jianshe Gongtong Fazhan Shifanqu Shishi Fang'an (浙江高质量发展建设共同富裕示范区实施方案2021–2025年) [Implementation Plan for Zhejiang's High-Quality Development and Construction of the Common-Prosperity Demonstration Zone 2021–2025], THE PEOPLE'S GOVERNMENT OF ZHEJIANG PROVINCE (Jul. 19, 2021), https://www.zj.gov.cn/art/2021/7/19/art_1552628_59122844.html.

79. Goujian Hexie Laodong Guanxi Zhashi Tuidong Gongtong Fuyu (构建和谐劳动关系 扎实推动共同富裕) [Building Harmonious Labor Relations, Promoting Common Prosperity Solidly], QSTHEORY.CN (Oct. 12, 2021), http://www.qstheory.cn/qshyjx/2021-10/12/c_1127947808.htm.

80. Ryan Hass, *Assessing China's "Common Prosperity" Campaign*, BROOKINGS (Sept. 9, 2021), https://www.brookings.edu/blog/order-from-chaos/2021/09/09/assessing-chinas-common-prosperity-campaign/.

NOTES

359

81. Paul Mozur, *Didi Chuxing and Uber, Popular in China, Are Now Legal, Too*, N.Y. TIMES (Jul. 28, 2016), https://www.nytimes.com/2016/07/29/business/international/china-uber-didi-chuxing.html.

82. *China Plan Seen Dealing Setback to Online Ride-Booking Services*, BLOOMBERG (Oct. 10. 2015), https://www.bloomberg.com/news/articles/2015-10-10/china-to-ban-use-of-private-cars-in-online-taxi-hailing-services?leadSource=uverify%20wall.

83. Ibid.

84. Shai Oster & Jessica E. Lessin, *Didi's IPO Hurdles: Profits and Regulations*, THE INFORMATION (Dec. 6, 2016), https://www.theinformation.com/articles/didis-ipo-hurdles-profits-and-regulations; Catherine Shu, *China Proposes Stricter Laws Targeted at Ridesharing Apps like Didi Kuaidi and Uber*, TECHCRUNCH (Oct. 12, 2015). t.ly/pw6HJ.

85. Dongya Huang & Minglu Chen, *Business Lobbying within the Party-State: Embedding Lobbying and Political Co-optation in China*, 83 CHINA J. 105, 121 (2020).

86. Ibid., at 110.

87. Ibid., at 121.

88. Ibid.

89. Ibid., at 122.

90. State Council Issued [2016] No. 58, *supra* note 64.

91. Interim Measures for the Administration of Online Taxi Booking Business Operations and Services (Order No. 60 [2016] of the Ministry of Transport, the Ministry of Industry and Information Technology, the Ministry of Public Security, the Ministry of Commerce, the State Administration for Industry and Commerce, the General Administration of Quality Supervision, Inspection and Quarantine, and the Cyberspace Administration of China, Jul. 27, 2016, effective Nov. 1, 2016).

92. Wangyueche Huo Hefa Diwei 8 Nian Qiangzhi Baofei Tiaokuan Quxiao (网约车获合法地位 8年强制报废条款取消) [Online Car-Hailing Obtains Legal Status, 8-Year Mandatory Scrapping Clause Is Canceled], TAKUNGPAO (Jul. 28, 2016), http://news.takungpao.com/mainland/focus/2016-07/3351382_wap. html; Mimi Zou, *The Regulatory Challenges of "Uberization" in China: Classifying Ride-Hailing Drivers*, 33(2) INT. J. COMP. LABOUR L. IND. 269, 272 (2017).

93. Oster & Lessin, *supra* note 84.

94. Difang Wangyueche Xize Fenfen Chutai, Didi Dui "Jingren Jingche, Huji Hupai Fanying Qianglie" (地方网约车细则纷纷出台, 滴滴对"京人京车, 沪籍沪牌"反应强烈) [Local Rules for Online Car-Hailing Are Rolling Out, Didi Shows a Strong Reaction to Peking and Shanghai's Requirements on Drivers and Cars Both Being Locals], QQ.COM (Oct. 8, 2016), https://mp.wei xin.qq.com/s/TI239Sob1hicKqJjFBA1YA.

95. Oster & Lessin, *supra* note 84.

NOTES

96. *First City-Level Didi Transportation Brain Went into Full Operation in Jinan*, JUMP-STARTMAG.COM (Jan. 7, 2019), https://www.jumpstartmag.com/didi-transportation-brain-went-into-full-operation-in-jinan/.

97. *Enterprises Support Poverty Alleviation through Industry Creation, Upgrading and Transformation*, GLOBAL TIMES (Feb. 25, 2021), https://www.globaltimes.cn/page/202102/1216611.shtml.

98. Didi Deng Pingtai Chengli "Xinjingji Xinjiuye Cujin Lianmeng" Yi Keji Funeng Jiuye (滴滴等平台成立"新经济新就业促进联盟" 以科技赋能就业) [Didi and Other Platforms Established the "New Economy and New Employment Promotion Alliance" to Empower Employment with Science and Technology], CCTV (Sept. 24, 2020), http://tech.cnr.cn/techph/20200924/t20200924_525275092.shtml.

99. Zhou Xin & Sidney Leng, *Coronavirus: Is China Prepared to Handle an Unemployment Crisis?*, SOUTH CHINA MORNING POST (May 12, 2020), t.ly/Jx6gV.

100. *China's Didi Pledges 200 Mln Yuan in Creating Jobs*, CHINA.ORG.CN (Aug. 15, 2020), http://www.china.org.cn/business/2020-08/15/content_76601459.htm.

101. Ibid.

102. Laodong Fa (劳动法) [Labor Law] (promulgated by the Standing Comm. Nat'l. People's Cong., Jul. 5, 1994, effective Jan. 1, 1995), art. 16 and 19.

103. E.g., Labor Law, *supra* note 102, art. 3.

104. Huang et al., *supra* note 22.

105. Sun et al., *supra* note 2, at 5.

106. Irene Zhou, *Digital Labour Platforms and Labour Protection in China* 10, International Labour Organization Working Paper 11 (Oct. 2020).

107. Sun et al., *supra* note 2, at 7.

108. Ibid. Laodong Hetong yu Laowu Hetong Yizizhicha Yiyi Butong (劳动合同与劳务合同一字之差意义不同) [Labor Contract and Employment Contract are Substantially Different], PEOPLE.COM.CN (May 27, 2021), http://society.people.com.cn/n1/2021/0527/c1008-32114332.html.

109. Peiyue Wu, *Delivery Drivers Can't Figure Out Who Their Boss Is, Lawyers Say*, SIXTH TONE (Jan. 27, 2022), https://www.sixthtone.com/news/1009558/delivery-drivers-cant-figure-out-who-their-boss-is,-lawyers-say; Waimai Pingtai Yonggong Moshi Falü Yanjiu Baogao (外卖平台用工模式法律研究报告) [Legal Research Report on the Employment Model of Food Delivery Platforms], BEIJING ZHICHENG RURAL MIGRANT WORKERS LAW AID AND RESEARCH CENTER (Sept. 2021), https://zgnmg.org/wp-content/uploads/2021/09/zhicheng-report-on-food-delivery-workers.pdf.

110. *Company Overview*, QUHUO TECH COMPANY (last accessed on Mar. 13, 2023), https://www.quhuo.cn/en/#/introduce (Quhuo is the leading tech-enabled workforce operational solution platform in China, providing tech-enabled and end-to-end operational solutions to blue on-demand consumer service companies); see also Quhuo 2021 Annual Report 60, https://ir.quhuo.cn/2022-09-10-Quhuo-Files-Its-Annual-Report-on-Form-20-F.

NOTES

111. Quhuo 2021 Annual Report, *supra* note 110, at 15.

112. ZHICHENG, *supra* note 109.

113. Miao Xu (徐淼) & Xinyi Chen (陈欣怡), Women Yingpin Guo Qishou, Daguo Wodi Dianhua, Kanle 1907 Fen Panjue, Zuihou Pinchule Zhebu Waimai Pingtai Jinhuashi (我们应聘过骑手, 打过卧底电话, 看了1907份判决, 最后拼出了这部外卖平台进化史) [We Worked as Drivers, Made Undercover Phone Calls, Read 1907 Judgments, and Finally Pieced Together the Evolutionary History of Food Delivery Platforms], YIXI (Jan. 23, 2022), https://mp.weixin.qq.com/s/KNLWPjHf6YzTMUNWUkZrUg.

114. Ibid.

115. ZHICHENG, *supra* note 109, at 38.

116. Ibid.

117. Ibid., at 39.

118. Panle! Zheyi Laodong Zhengyi An Sheji 91 Ming Waimai Qishou (判了! 这一劳动争议案涉及91名外卖骑手) [Decided! This Labor Dispute Case Involves 91 Food-Delivery Drivers], UPSTREAM NEWS (May 13, 2021), https://www.cqcb.com/hot/2021-05-13/4134671.html.

119. ZHICHENG, *supra* note 109, at 43.

120. Bei Raokai de Laodongfa: Waimai Pingtai de Fazhan yu Qishou Laodong Guanxi de Bianqian (被绕开的劳动法: 外卖平台的发展与骑手劳动关系的变迁) [Bypassed Labor Law: Development of Food-Delivery Platforms and Change of Drivers' Labor Relations], INITIUM MEDIA (Feb. 27, 2021), https://theinitium.com/article/20210227-notes-platform-economy-labour-webinar/.

121. 2 Yi Linghuo Jiuyezhe Shebao Chuangguan: "Gongshang" Yixing, "Yanglao" Nan Poju (2亿灵活就业者社保闯关: "工伤"易行, "养老"难破局) [200 Million Flexible Workers Are Breaking Through Social Insurance: "Work-Related Injury" Is Easy, "Pension" Is Hard], FJLIB.NET (Jun. 1, 2021), http://fjlib.net/zt/fjstsgjcxx/msgc/202106/t20210601_467030.htm.

122. Huang et al., *supra* note 22.

123. ZHICHENG, *supra* note 109, at 41.

124. Ibid., at 44.

125. Jiangsu Duoguanqixia, Rang Qianwan Shichang Zhuti Huoxiaqu Qiangqilai (江苏多管齐下 让千万市场主体活下去强起来) [Jiangsu's Multi-Pronged Approach Makes Tens of Millions of Market Entities Alive and Stronger], PEOPLE.COM.CN (Sept. 7, 2020), http://js.people.com.cn/n2/2020/0907/c360 301-34275072.html; Jinhui Guo (郭晋晖), Waimai Xiaoge "Bianshen" Getihu, Zhengqi Xietong Funeng Linghuo Jiuyezhe (外卖小哥"变身"个体户, 政企协同赋能灵活就业者) [Delivery Workers Are Turned into Independent Businesses, Governments and Enterprises Work Together to Empower Flexible Workers], YICAI.COM (Jul. 28, 2020), https://m.yicai.com/news/100715970.html.

126. Liu & Friedman, *supra* note 51, at 79–81.

127. Lei, *supra* note 8, at 300.

128. Shenyang Meituan Fasheng Qishou Fankang Shijian: Shenye Daliang Jiedan Yuandi Dianji Songda Zhihou Zhuxiao Zhanghao (沈阳美团发生骑手反抗事件: 深夜大量接单原地点击送达之后注销账号) [Meituan Driver Rebelled in Shenyang: Accepting Numerous Orders Late at Night, Faking Delivery, Then Canceling His Account], SINA.COM.CN (Jun. 25, 2021), https://finance.sina.com.cn/tech/2021-06-25/doc-ikqciyzk1657441.shtml.

129. Zhejiang: Eleme Qishou Zhaoji Cizhi, Beikou Yiqian Hou Qingxu Bengkui, Liantong Ziji Sandao (浙江: 饿了么骑手着急辞职, 被扣一千后情绪崩溃, 连捅自己三刀) [Zhejiang: An Ele.me Driver, Who Was in a Hurry to Resign, Broke Down Emotionally and Stabbed Himself Three Times after 3000 Yuan Was Deducted from Wages], 163.COM (Aug. 26, 2022), https://www.163.com/dy/article/HFNAAATV0553EMFJ.html.

130. Liu & Friedman, *supra* note 51, at 88.

131. Ibid., at 84.

132. PEOPLE, *supra* note 7.

133. Matt Sheehan & Sharon Du, *How Food Delivery Workers Shaped Chinese Algorithm Regulations*, CARNEGIE ENDOWMENT FOR INTERNATIONAL PEACE (Nov. 2, 2022), https://carnegieendowment.org/2022/11/02/how-food-delivery-workers-shaped-chinese-algorithm-regulations-pub-88310.

134. Ibid.

135. Eleme: 5 Fenzhong; Meituan: 8 Fenzhong! Shui Neng Huajie Waimai Jingsu Zhikun (饿了么: 5分钟; 美团: 8分钟! 谁能化解外卖竞速之困?) [Ele.me: 5 mins; Meituan: 8 mins! Who Can Solve the Problem of Delivery Racing?], SINA.CN (Sept. 10, 2020), https://tech.sina.cn/csj/2020-09-10/doc-iivhvpwy5933825.d.html?vt=4&cid=38712&node_id=38712.

136. Eleme de 5 Fenzhong Mei Chengyi, Meituan de 8 Fenzhong Tai Jizei (饿了么的5分钟没诚意, 美团的8分钟太鸡贼) [Ele.me's 5-min Is Insincere, Meituan's 8-min Is Useless], SINA.COM.CN (Sept. 9, 2020), http://tech.sina.com.cn/csj/2020-09-09/doc-iivhuipp3440054.shtml.

137. *Food Delivery Driver Stabs Self in Protest over Fines and Unpaid Wages*, CHINA LABOUR BULL. (Aug. 30, 2022), https://clb.org.hk/content/food-delivery-driver-stabs-self-protest-over-fines-and-unpaid-wages.

138. Weimin Yin, *Ministry of Human Resources and Social Security*, GLOBAL TIMES, https://www.globaltimes.cn/db/government/14.shtml.

139. See, e.g., Renli Ziyuan Shehui Baozhang Bu Dui Zhengxie Dishisanjie Quanguo Weiyuanhui Diyici Huiyi Di 1376 Hao (Shehui Guanli Lei 106 Hao) Ti'an de Dafu (人力资源社会保障部对政协十三届全国委员会第一次会议第1376号(社会管理类106号)提案的答复) [MOHRSS's Reply to No. 1376 Proposal (Social Management No. 106) of the First Meeting of the 13th National Committee of the CPPCC], MOHRSS.GOV.CN (Sept. 30, 2018), http://www.mohrss.gov.cn/xxgk2020/fdzdgknr/zhgl/jytabl/tadf/201812/t20181203_306187.html; Renli Ziyuan Shehui Baozhang Bu Dui Dishisanjie Quanguo Renda Erci Huiyi Di 8033 Hao Jianyi de Dafu (人力资源社会保障部对十三届全国人大二次会议第8033号建议的答复)

[MOHRSS's Reply to No. 8033 Proposal of the Second Session of the 13th National People's Congress], MOHRSS.GOV.CN (Aug. 22, 2019), http://www.mohrss.gov.cn/xxgk2020/fdzdgknr/zhgl/jytabl/jydf/201912/t20191202_344615.html.

140. Renli Ziyuan Shehui Baozhang Bu Dui Zhengxie Dishisanjie Quanguo Weiyuanhui Dierci Huiyi Di 2872 Hao (Shehui Guanli Lei 211 Hao) Ti'an de Dafu (人力资源社会保障部对政协十三届全国委员会第二次会议第2872号(社会管理类211号)提案的答复) [MOHRSS's Reply to No. 2872 Proposal (Social Management No. 211) of the Second Meeting of the 13th National Committee of the CPPCC], MOHRSS.GOV.CN (Sept. 4, 2019), http://www.mohrss.gov.cn/xxgk2020/fdzdgknr/zhgl/jytabl/tadf/201912/t20191205_345297.html; Renli Ziyuan Shehui Baozhang Bu Dui Zhengxie Dishisanjie Quanguo Weiyuanhui Disanci Huiyi Di 4282 Hao (Shehui Guanli Lei 373 Hao) Ti'an de Dafu (人力资源社会保障部对政协十三届全国委员会第三次会议第4282号(社会管理类373号)提案的答复) [MOHRSS's Reply to No. 4282 Proposal (Social Management No. 373) of the Third Meeting of the 13th National Committee of the CPPCC], MOHRSS.GOV.CN (Jan. 13, 2021), http://www.mohrss.gov.cn/xxgk2020/fdzdgknr/zhgl/jytabl/tadf/202101/t20210113_407548.html.

141. Ibid.

142. MOHRSS's Reply to No. 8033 Proposal, *supra* note 139.

143. Wenzhen Wang (王文珍) & Wenjing Li (李文静), Pingtai Jingji Fazhan Dui Woguo Laodong Guanxi de Yingxiang (平台经济发展对我国劳动关系的影响) [The Impact of Platform Economy Development on China's Labor Relations], 6 CHINA LABOUR (2017).

144. Ibid. See also MOHRSS's Reply to No. 1376 Proposal, *supra* note 139.

145. Ibid.

146. Pingtai Qiye Guan'ai Laodongzhe Changyishu (平台企业关爱劳动者倡议书) [Initiative on Platform Enterprises Caring for Workers], INTERNET SOCIETY OF CHINA (Jan. 7, 2020), https://www.isc.org.cn/article/10678001735954432.html.

147. Chengdushi Renmin Zhengfu Bangongting Guanyu Congjin Xinjingji Xinyetai Congye Renyuan Canjia Shehui Baoxian de Shixing Shishi Yijian (成都市人民政府办公厅关于促进新经济新业态从业人员参加社会保险的试行实施意见) [Opinions of the General Office of the Chengdu Municipal People's Government on the Trial Implementation of Promoting the Participation of Workers in Social Insurance in New Economy and New Forms of Employment], CHENGDU.GOV (Jul. 22, 2019), http://gk.chengdu.gov.cn/govInfo/detail.action?id=109659&tn=6.

148. Chang Zhou (周畅), Zhongguo Shuzi Laogong Pingtai he Gongren Quanyi Baozhang (中国数字劳工平台和工人权益保障) [Digital Labor Platforms and Protection of Workers' Rights and Interests in China], INTERNATIONAL LABOUR ORGANIZATION (Nov. 2020), https://www.ilo.org/legacy/chinese/intserv/working-papers/wp011/index.html.

364   NOTES

149. Guanyu Zuohao Kuaidiyuan Qunti Hefa Quanyi Baozhang Gongzuo de Yijian (关于做好快递员群体合法权益保障工作的意见) [Opinions on Safeguarding the Legal Rights and Interests of Courier Groups by the MOT, the SPB, the NDRC, the MOHRSS, the MOC, the SAMR, and the ACFTU], MOT Issued (2021) No. 59, https://www.waizi.org.cn/doc/128625.html.

150. Beijingju Lianhe Duobumen Yinfa Zuohao Kuaidiyuan Hefa Quanyi Baozhang Gongzuo Shishi Fang'an (北京局联合多部门印发做好快递员群体合法权益保障工作实施方案) [Multiple Departments in Beijing Jointly Issued an Implementation Plan to Protect the Legitimate Rights and Interests of Courier Groups], SINA.COM.CN (Dec. 31, 2021), https://news.sina.com.cn/o/2021-12-31/doc-ikyakumx7481595.shtml; Fujiansheng Kuaidiyuan Qunti Hefa Quanyi Baozhang Shishi Fang'an Yinfa (福建省快递员群体合法权益保障实施方案印发) [Fujian Issued the Implementation Plan to Protect the Legitimate Rights and Interests of Couriers], SPB.GOV (Dec. 21, 2021), https://www.spb.gov.cn/ztgz/gjyzjzt/kdxgqybz/sjdt/202112/t20211221_4103553.html; Yixin Chen (陈逸欣), Shanghai Duobumen Lianhe Fawen: Baozhang Kuaidiyuan Heli Laodong Baochou Tigao Shebao Shuiping (上海多部门联合发文: 保障快递员合理劳动报酬提高社保水平) [Multiple Authorities in Shanghai Jointly Announced to Ensure Reasonable Enumeration and Improve Social Security Level for Couriers], THE PAPER (Feb. 16, 2022), http://m.thepaper.cn/newsDetail_forward_16718498; Zhejiang Yindao Yanjiu Shihe Kuaidiyuan de Xinxianzhong (浙江引导研究适合快递员的新险种) [Zhejiang Guided the Study of New Insurance Types Suitable for Couriers], WORKERCN (Jan. 14, 2022), http://www.workercn.cn/34055/202201/14/220114020625227.shtml.

151. Guanyu Weihu Xinjiuye Xingtai Laodongzhe Laodong Baozhang Quanyi de Zhidao Yijian (关于维护新就业形态劳动者劳动保障权益的指导意见) [Guiding Opinions on Safeguarding the Labor Rights and Interests of Workers in New Forms of Employment by the MOHRSS, the NDRC, the MOT, the MOE, the SAMR, the NMIA, the SPC, and the ACFTU], MOHRSS Issued (2021) No. 56, http://www.gov.cn/zhengce/zhengceku/2021-07/23/content_5626761.htm.

152. No. 56 Document, *supra* note 151, art. 1(2).

153. Ibid., art. 1(3).

154. Guanyu Luoshi Wangluo Canyin Pingtai Zeren Qieshi Weihu Waimai Songcanyuan Quanyi de Zhidao Yijian (关于落实网络餐饮平台责任切实维护外卖送餐员权益的指导意见) [Guiding Opinions on the Responsibility of Online Catering Platforms to Safeguard the Rights and Interests of Food-Delivery Workers by the SAMR, the CAC, the NDRC, the MPS, the MOHRSS, the MOC, and the ACFTU], SAMR Issued (2021) No. 38, https://www.samr.gov.cn/xw/zj/202107/t20210726_333061.html.

155. No. 38 Document, *supra* note 154, art. 3.

156. Guanyu Qieshi Weihu Xinjiuye Xingtai Laodongzhe Laodong Baozhang Quanyi de Yijian(关于切实维护新就业形态劳动者劳动保障权益的意

NOTES 365

见) [Opinions on Effectively Safeguarding the Labor Rights and Interests of Workers in New Forms of Employment], ACFTU Issued (2021) No. 12, https://www.acftu.org/wjzl/wjzlzcwj/qzwj/202107/t20210728_784163.html?7OkeOa4k=qAkErAkFCz.FCz.FCPRNhjpnXkyZKFJFi4gSrtc1xhVqqEItIMnlqAqqCG.

157. Beijingshi Zonggonghui Fabu 10 Xiang Cuoshi Tuijin Xinyetai, Xinjiuye Qunti Gonghui Gongzuo (北京市总工会发布10项措施推进新业态、新就业群体工会工作!) [Beijing Federation of Trade Unions Released 10 Measures to Promote the Work of Trade Unions for New Forms of Employment!], THE PAPER (Aug. 31, 2021), https://m.thepaper.cn/baijiahao_14309361.

158. *ACFTU in Beijing Issues Guidelines for Unionizing Gig Workers: What Comes Next?*, CHINA LABOUR BULL. (Sept. 28, 2021), https://clb.org.hk/content/acftu-beijing-issues-guidelines-unionizing-gig-workers-what-comes-next.

159. Ibid.

160. *How Food Delivery Riders in Shanghai Got Their Own Trade Union*, CHINA LABOUR BULL. (Jan. 25, 2018), https://clb.org.hk/content/how-food-delivery-riders-shanghai-got-their-own-trade-union; *High-Level Guidance on Platform Employment Lacks Teeth*, CHINA LABOUR BULL. (Sept. 23, 2021), https://clb.org.hk/content/high-level-guidance-platform-employment-lacks-teeth.

161. Renli Ziyuan Shehui Baozhangbu Deng 4 Bumen Dui Meituan, Eleme, Didi Deng 10 Jia Pingtai Qiye Baozhang Xinjiuye Xingtai Laodongzhe Quanyi Kaizhan Lianhe Xingzheng Zhidao (人力资源社会保障部等4部门对美团、饿了么、滴滴等10家平台企业保障新就业形态劳动者权益开展联合行政指导) [MOHRSS and Three Other Departments Jointly Conducted Administrative Guidance on 10 Platform Enterprises Including Meituan, Ele.me, Didi to Protect the Rights and Interests of Workers in New Employment Forms], MOHRSS.GOV (Sept. 10, 2021), http://www.mohrss.gov.cn/SYrlzyhshbzb/dongtaixinwen/buneiyaowen/rsxw/202109/t20210910_422831.html.

162. Renli Ziyuan Shehui Baozhangbu Deng 4 Bumen Zaici Dui Meituan, Eleme, Didi Deng 11 Jia Pingtai Qiye Baozhang Xinjiuye Xingtai Laodongzhe Quanyi Kaizhan Xingzheng Zhidao (人力资源社会保障部等4部门再次对美团、饿了么、滴滴等11家平台企业保障新就业形态劳动者权益开展行政指导) [MOHRSS and Three Other Departments Carried Out Administrative Guidance Again on 11 Platform Enterprises Including Meituan, Ele.me, Didi to Protect the Rights and Interests of Workers in New Employment Forms], MOHRSS.GOV (Jan. 21, 2022), http://www.mohrss.gov.cn/SYrlzyhshbzb/dongtaixinwen/buneiyaowen/rsxw/202201/t20220121_433318.html.

163. Renshebu Deng 5 Bumen Dui Meituan, Eleme, Didi Deng 11 Jia Pingtai Qiye Baozhang Xinjiuye Xingtai Laodongzhe Quanyi Kaizhan Xingzheng Zhidao (人社部等5部门对美团、饿了么、滴滴等11家平台企业保障新就业形态劳动者权益开展行政指导) [MOHRSS and Four Other Departments Carried Out Administrative Guidance on 11 Platform Enterprises Including Meituan, Ele.me, Didi to Protect the Rights and Interests of Workers in New

Employment Forms], MOHRSS.GOV (Sept. 13, 2022), http://www.mohrss.gov.cn/SYrlzyhshbzb/dongtaixinwen/buneiyaowen/rsxw/202209/t20220913_487123.html.

164. Hulianwang Xinxi Fuwu Suanfa Tuijian Guanli Guiding (互联网信息服务算法推荐管理规定) [Internet Information Service Algorithmic Recommendation Management Provisions], promulgated by the CAC, the MIIT, the MPS, and the SAMR, Dec. 31, 2021, effective Mar. 1, 2022.

165. Sheehan & Du, *supra* note 133.

166. Ibid.

167. Ibid.

168. Yingzhi Yang & Brenda Goh, *Tech Workers Bemoan China's Crackdown on Compulsory Overtime*, REUTERS (Sept. 3, 2021), https://www.reuters.com/technology/not-my-pay-some-tech-workers-bemoan-chinas-crackdown-compulsory-overtime-2021-09-03/.

169. Lei, *supra* note 8, at 296.

170. We used three key words—pingtai (平台) [platform], waimai (外卖) [food delivery], qishou (骑手) [delivery driver]—and searched for cases that were decided between 2020 and 2021. Our searches were conducted between June and July 2022.

171. 2016–2020 Nian She Pingtai Qishou Daolu Jiaotong Shigu Jiufen Anjian Shenpan Baipishu (2016–2020年涉平台骑手道路交通事故纠纷案件审判白皮书) [White Paper on the Judgment of Road Traffic Accident Dispute Cases Involving Platform Drivers in 2016–2020], SHANGHAI PUTUO PEOPLE'S COURT (Dec. 1, 2021), https://www.hshfy.sh.cn/css/2021/12/01/20211201144538411.pdf.

172. Ibid., at 18–19.

173. Legal Research Report on the Employment Model of Food Delivery Platforms, *supra* note 109, at 13.

174. Interview with a former judge from a local court, Beijing, March 5, 2023.

175. Legal Research Report on the Employment Model of Food Delivery Platforms, *supra* note 109, at 14.

176. In 2005, the MOHRSS laid out a three-factor test to determine an employment relationship. First, do the employing unit and employee meet the legal qualification prescribed by laws and regulations (e.g., the employing unit is an enterprise instead of an individual and the employee is at least 18 years old)? Second, are various workplace rules made by the employer in accordance with the law being applied to the employee, and is the employee under the control of the employer and do they perform paid labor assigned by the employer? Third, is the labor provided by the employee part of the employer's business? See Zou, *supra* note 92, at 279 (2017); Guanyu Queli Laodong Guanxi Youguan Shixiang de Tongzhi (关于确立劳动关系有关事项的通知) [Matters Relevant to the Establishment of an Employment Relationship Circular], MOHRSS Issued (2005) No. 12, http://www.moh

rss.gov.cn/ldgxs/LDGXzhengcefagui/LDGXzyzc/2011c7/t20110728_86
296.html.

177. Minfa Dian (民法典) [Civil Code] (promulgated by the Nat'l. People's Cong.,
May 28, 2020, effective Jan. 1, 2021), art. 1191.

178. Legal Research Report on the Employment Model of Food Delivery
Platforms. *supra* note 109; Zou, *supra* note 92.

179. Sanwen Waimai Qishou "Getigongshanghu Hua": Zhuce Hou Yingxiang
Jihe? (三问外卖骑手"个体工商户化": 注册后影响几何?) [Questions on
Food-Delivery Drivers Being Turned into Independent Businesses: What's the
Impact of Registration?], XHBY.NET (Sept. 28, 2021), http://www.xhby.net/
index/202109/t20210928_7250622.shtml.

180. *Chinese Delivery Giants Meituan, Ele.me Pledge to Not Force Drivers to Register
as Independent Businesses*, REUTERS (Sept. 15, 2021), https://www.reuters.com/
world/china/chinese-delivery-giants-meituan-eleme-pledge-not-force-driv
ers-register-2021-09-15/.

181. Ibid.

182. Beijing Fabu Laodong Renshi Zhengyi Zhongcai Shida Dianxing Anli (北
京发布劳动人事争议仲裁十大典型案例) [Beijing Released 10 Typical
Arbitration Cases Regarding Labor and Personnel Disputes], ALL BRIGHT LAW
OFFICES (Nov. 15, 2021), https://www.allbrightlaw.com/CN/10531/c3be7
b1eeed4cacb.aspx; Shui Shi Waimai Xiaoge de Shiji Yongren Danwei (谁是外
卖小哥的实际用人单位?) [Who Is the Actual Employer of Food-Delivery
Workers?], SHANGHAI HIGHER PEOPLE'S COURT (Mar. 7, 2022), https://mp.wei
xin.qq.com/s/34-OyMyINJcw7aB0IV2Sbw; Suzhou Laodong Fating Fabu
Xinyetai Laodong Quanyi Baozhang 8 Da Anli (苏州劳动法庭发布新业态
劳动权益保障8大案例) [Suzhou Labor Court Released 8 Typical Cases of
Labor Rights Protection for Workers in New Employment Forms], SUZHOU
INTERMEDIATE PEOPLE'S COURT (Dec. 28, 2021), https://rbj.jiyuan.gov.cn/rbj_z
cfg/rbj_qwjd/t835830.html; Guangdong Fayuan 2021 Niandu She Hulianwang
Shida Anli Fabu, Rending Laodong Guanxi Baozhang Waimaiyuan Quanyi
(广东法院2021年度涉互联网十大案例发布　认定劳动关系保障外卖员
权益) [Guangdong Court Released 10 Typical Internet-Related Cases in
2021, Recognizing Labor Relationship to Protect Deliverymen], GUANGDONG
HIGHER PEOPLE'S COURT (Feb. 22, 2022), http://www.gdftu.org.cn/xwzx/
rdgz/content/post_752450.html; Waimaiyuan yu Peisong Gongsi Goucheng
Laodong Guanxi, Jiaotong Shigu Rending Gongshang (外卖员与配送公
司构成劳动关系, 交通事故认定工伤) [Labor Relationship Exists be-
tween Deliverymen and Distribution Companies, Work-Related Injury Is
Recognized in Traffic Accidents], SHANDONG HIGHER PEOPLE'S COURT (Jan.
16, 2021), https://www.thepaper.cn/newsDetail_forward_10817975; Hairen
Zhou (周海仁), Waimai Qishou Songcan Tuzhong Shuaishang, Nengfou
Rending Wei Gongshang? (外卖骑手送餐途中摔伤　能否认定为工伤?)
[Can Work-Related Injury Be Recognized for Drivers Who Fell While

Delivering Food?], Chongqing Court Net (Jul. 12, 2021), http://cqgy.cqfyg
zfw.gov.cn/article/detail/2021/07/id/6145229.shtml.

183. Chongqing, however, is a notable exception. E.g., Waimai Qishou yu Pingtai
Gongsi, Peisong Fuwu Gongsi Zhijian Shifou Cunzai Laodong Guanxi? (外卖
骑手与平台公司、配送服务公司之间是否存在劳动关系?) [Does Labor
Relationship Exist between Food-Delivery Drivers, Platform Companies, and
Distribution Service Companies?], Chongqing Court Net (Aug. 19, 2021),
http://cqgy.cqfygzfw.gov.cn/article/detail/2021/12/id/6460445.shtml.

184. Waimai Xiaoge yu Pingtai Hezuo Yonggong Qiye Cunzai Laodong Guanxi
Ma? (外卖小哥与平台合作用工企业存在劳动关系吗?) [Does Labor
Relationship Exist between Deliverymen and Employment Enterprises
Cooperated with Platforms?], Supreme People's Court (Apr. 20, 2022),
https://mp.weixin.qq.com/s/LOZSr1BGZmcGnB6HYWutZg.

185. Shanghai's typical case, *supra* note 182.

186. Guanyu Xinjiuye Xingtai Laodong Yonggong Falü Guanxi Jieding de
Diaoyan Baogao (关于新就业形态劳动用工法律关系界定的调研报告)
[Research Report on the Definition of the Legal Relationship in New Forms
of Employment], Suzhou Intermediate People's Court (Mar. 16, 2022),
https://mp.weixin.qq.com/s/5it_u6b126tFvrBK4kfTJg; Xinjiuye Xingtai
Xia Pingtai Yonggong Falü Guanxi Dingxing Yanjiu (新就业形态下平台用
工法律关系定性研究) [Study on the Evaluation of the Legal Relationship
in New Forms of Employment on Platforms], Beijing First Intermediate
People's Court (Mar. 14, 2022), https://mp.weixin.qq.com/s/5it_u6b126t
FvrBK4kfTJg.

187. Suzhou Laodong Fating: Qishi "Zhiguangda" Luozi "Jinjingwei" (苏州劳动
法庭: 起势"致广大" 落子"尽精微") [Suzhou Labor Court: A Grand Rise,
a Fine Fall], Supreme People's Court (Feb. 8, 2022), https://mp.weixin.
qq.com/s/h-qHc-Ry5QP536GxzlDIKA.

188. Waimai Xiaoge Jiujing Youmeiyou "Danwei"? (外卖小哥究竟有没有"单
位"?) [Do Food-Delivery Drivers Have "Units"?], Supreme People's Court
(Feb. 25, 2022), https://mp.weixin.qq.com/s/R74c0zDJyO4pW7EajmN
yug; Jiangsu Fayuan 2020 Niandu Laodong Renshi Zhengyi Shida Dianxing
Anli (江苏法院2020年度劳动人事争议十大典型案例) [Ten Typical
Cases of Labor and Personnel Disputes in Jiangsu Courts in 2020], Jiangsu
Higher People's Court (Apr. 29, 2021), https://www.jsfy.gov.cn/article/
91653.html.

189. Ka Ding (丁咖), Waimai Qishou Shenye Songcan Tuzhong Cusi, Waimai
Pingtai, Guyong Gongsi Beipan Peichang 500 Wan (外卖骑手深夜送餐途
中猝死, 外卖平台、雇佣公司被判赔偿150余万) [A Driver Died Suddenly
While Delivering Food Late at Night, Platform and Employment Company
Were Ordered to Pay 1.5 Million Yuan], People's Court Daily (Nov. 11,
2022), https://mp.weixin.qq.com/s/74w0HRAee04bu_alukC2vQ.

190. Ibid.

NOTES

191. Waimai Qishou You Shebao Ma? Da'an Lai le! Zhiye Shanghai Baozhang Yi Zai Duo Shengshi Shidian (外卖骑手有社保吗? 答案来了. 职业伤害保障已在多省市试点) [Do Food Delivery Drivers Enjoy Social Insurance? Here's the Answer! Occupational Injury Insurance Has Been Piloted in Multiple Provinces and Cities], SOHU.COM (Apr. 11, 2023), https://www.sohu.com/a/665718699_121630404.

192. Ibid.

193. Guonei Shouge Shidian Fang'an: Xin Jiuye Xingtai de Zhiye Shanghai Baozhang Fang'an Ding Le (国内首个试点方案: 新就业形态的职业伤害保障方案定了) [China's First Pilot Program: A Scheme for Occupational Injury Insurance for New Employment Forms Has Been Established], QQ.COM (Aug. 16, 2022), https://mp.weixin.qq.com/s/GtVYLghdY4ARhBAaupftUg.

194. Renshebu Fabu Xin Jiuye Xingtai Laodong Hetong he Shumian Xieyi Dingli Zhiyin (人社部发布新就业形态劳动合同和书面协议订立指引) [MOHRSS Released Guidelines for the Conclusion of Labor Contracts and Written Agreements for New Employment Forms], ZHIHU.COM (Feb. 21, 2023), https://zhuanlan.zhihu.com/p/614781359.

195. Zuigao Renmin Fayuan Wei Wending Jiuye Tigong Sifa Fuwu he Baozhang de Yijian (最高人民法院关于为稳定就业提供司法服务和保障的意见) [Opinions of the Supreme People's Court on Providing Judicial Services and Guarantees for Stable Employment], SPC Issued (2022) No. 36, https://www.court.gov.cn/zixun-xiangqing-384301.html.

196. Ibid.

197. Mia Nulimaimaiti, *China Jobs: Rise in Youth Unemployment Belies Surprising Economic Growth, as "Weak Confidence Remains,"* SOUTH CHINA MORNING POST (Apr. 19, 2023), https://www.scmp.com/economy/china-economy/article/3217467/china-jobs-rise-youth-unemployment-belies-surprising-economic-growth-weak-confidence-remains.

198. Guowuyuan Bangongting Guanyu Youhua Tiaozheng Wenjiuye Zhengce Cuoshi Quanli Cufazhan Huiminsheng de Tongzhi (国务院办公厅关于优化调整稳就业政策措施全力促发展惠民生的通知) [Notice from the General Office of the State Council on Optimizing Employment Policies and Measures to Fully Promote Development and Improve People's Livelihood], State Council Issued (2023) No. 11, http://www.gov.cn/zhengce/content/2023-04/26/content_5753299.htm.

199. Xin He, *Pressures on Chinese Judges under Xi*, 85 CHINA J. 49 (2021); Jonathan J. Kinkel & William J. Hurst, *The Judicial Cadre Evaluation System in China: From Quantification to Intra-State Legibility*, 224 CHINA Q. 933 (2015).

200. Ying Sun & Hualing Fu, *Of Judge Quota and Judicial Autonomy: An Enduring Professionalization Project in China*, 251 CHINA Q. 866 (2022); see also KWAI HANG NG & XIN HE, EMBEDDED COURTS: JUDICIAL DECISION-MAKING IN CHINA 142–166 (2017).

NOTES

CHAPTER 7

1. Rory Van Loo, *The Corporation as Courthouse*, 33 YALE J. REGUL. 547, 578 (2016).
2. Ibid., at 550.
3. Molly Cohen & Arun Sundararajan, *Self-Regulation and Innovation in the Peer-to-Peer Sharing Economy*, 82 UNIV. CHIC. L. REV. 116, 125–126 (2015).
4. Cite George Akerlof, *The Market for "Lemons": Quality Uncertainty and the Market Mechanism*, 84 Q. J. ECON. 488, 493–494 (1970).
5. Such incentive is certainly not unique to Chinese firms. See also Jens Dammann, *Electronic Word of Mouth and Consumer Protection: A Legal and Economic Analysis*, 94 S. CAL. L. REV. 423 (2021).
6. Ibid.
7. Lingfang Li, *Reputation, Trust and Rebates: How Online Auction Markets Can Improve Their Feedback Mechanism*, 19 J. ECON. & MANAG. STRATEGY 303, 305 (2010); see also Luis Cabra & Ali Hortascu, *The Dynamics of Seller Reputation: Theory and Evidence from eBay*, 58 J. INDUS. ECON. 54 (2010).
8. Nolan Miller et al., *Eliciting Informative Feedback: The Peer-Predication Method*, 51 MGMT. SCI. 1359, 1359 (2005).
9. Jonathan Lafky, *Why Do People Rate? Theory and Evidence on Online Ratings*, 87 GAMES & ECON. BEHAVIOR 554 (2014).
10. See Taobao's hearing with users on meaningless reviews on July 31, 2018. The hearing is available on Taobao's app.
11. Ying Fan et al., *Reputation Premium and Reputation Management: Evidence from the Largest E-Commerce Platform in China*, 46 INT'L J. INDUS. ORG. 63 (2016).
12. Taobao Jinzhi Maijia Haoping Fanxian Deng Fangshi Yao Haoping Huilu Xiaofeizhe Niuqu Pingjia Shuyu Weifa (淘宝禁止卖家好评返现等方式要好评 贿赂消费者扭曲评价属于违法) [Taobao Prohibits Sellers from Trading Cashing for Good Reviews, Bribing Consumers to Distort Reviews Is Illegal], CCTV.COM (Dec. 24, 2021), https://news.cctv.com/2021/12/24/ARTI2r4TDDxkXf4c7Kj3p0Zm211224.shtml.
13. As a seller that obtains one diamond on Taobao's reputation system is deemed trustworthy by buyers, when sellers use artificial orders to boost their reputation this is called a "brush diamond" in Chinese. See Yu Zhang et al., *Trust Fraud: A Crucial Challenge for China's E-Commerce Market*, 12 ELECTRON. COMMER. RES. APPL. 299 (2013).
14. See Sherry Fei Ju & Charles Clover, *China's Ecommerce Sites Try to Sweep Away "Brushing,"* FIN. TIMES (Nov. 23, 2016), https://www.ft.com/content/73572 2e6-aca6-11e6-9cb3-bb8207902122.
15. Zhang et al., *supra* note 13, at 302.
16. Dawei Li (李大伟), Shuadan Ni Lieru Yanzhong Weifa Shixin Mingdan, Shui Hai Zai Dingfeng Zuo'an? (刷单拟列入严重违法失信名单, 谁还在顶风作案?] (Brushing Activities to Be Included on the List of Serious Illegal and Dishonest Acts, Who Are Still Blatantly Breaking the Law?), BEIJING NEWS (Jul. 13, 2019), http://www.bjnews.com.cn/finance/2019/07/13/602916.html.

NOTES

371

Mengting Wang (汪梦婷), Wangluo Shuadan de Falü Zeren Ji Qi Lifa Guizhi (网络刷单的法律责任及其立法规制) [The Legal Responsibility of Online Shopping Brushing and Its Legislative Regulation], 8(4) FA XUE (法学) [L. SCI.] 608–616 (2020).

17. Ibid.

18. Xiaofeizhe Baohu Fa (消费者保护法) [Consumer Protection Law] (promulgated by the Standing Comm. Nat'l People's Cong., Oct. 31, 1993, effective Jan. 1, 1994), art. 44; Dianzi Shangwu Fa (电子商务法) [E-Commerce Law] (promulgated by the Standing Comm. Nat'l People's Cong., Aug. 31, 2018, effective Jan. 1, 2019), art. 38.

19. See Jidong Chen et al., *Big Data Based Fraud Risk Management at Alibaba*, 1 J. FIN. & DATA SCI. 1 (2015). (Online disciplinary action can include reducing the rating of the seller, making the seller's store or products unsearchable for a certain period, or even going so far as to ban the seller's account in extreme cases. For offline action, Taobao might share information with the police, who will then be able to trace the identified suspects that have engaged in brushing.)

20. See Feng Wang (王峰), Shangpin Shiyong Wangzhan "Meili Pa" Zuzhi Shuadan Bei Pan Bu Zhengdang Jingzheng, Peichang Taobao 200 Wan Yuan (商品试用网站"美丽啪"组织刷单被判不正当竞争，赔偿淘宝200万元) [Brushing Activities Conducted by the Product Trial Website "Meili Pa" Were Found to Have Engaged in Unfair Competition, Ordered to Compensate Taobao 2 Million Yuan], 21 JINGJI.COM (Jun. 6, 2019), https://m.21jingji.com/article/20190606/herald/5093a0aab06ea47faa7e271123238d3d.html.

21. Zhejiang Sheng Hangzhou Shi Zhongji Renming Fayuan Minshi Panjue Shu (浙江省杭州市中级人民法院民事判决书) [Zhejiang Hangzhou Intermediate People's Civil Decision], (2018) Zhe 01 Min Chu 3845 Hao ((2018)浙01民初3845号).

22. Gillian Wong et al., *Inside Alibaba, the Sharp-Elbowed World of Chinese E-Commerce*, WALL ST. J. (Mar. 2, 2015), https://www.wsj.com/articles/inside-alibaba-the-sharp-elbowed-world-of-chinese-e-commerce-1425332447.

23. Haitao Xu et al., *E-commerce Reputation Manipulation: The Emergence of Reputation-Escalation-as-a-Service*, *in* PROCEEDINGS OF THE 24TH INTERNATIONAL CONFERENCE ON WORLD WIDE WEB 1296–1306 (2015).

24. Carlos Tejada, *China Raps Alibaba for Fakes*, WALL ST. J. (Jan. 28, 2015), https://www.wsj.com/articles/chinas-saic-criticizes-alibaba-over-fake-goods-1422425378.

25. Tracy Qu, *Amazon Closes 3,000 Chinese-Brand Online Stores in Campaign against Fake Reviews*, SOUTH CHINA MORNING POST (Sept. 17, 2021), https://www.scmp.com/tech/big-tech/article/3149203/amazon-closes-3000-chinese-brand-online-stores-campaign-against-fake; Iris Deng, *"Made in China, Sold on Amazon" Merchants Scramble to Minimise Losses after US platform Closes over 50,000 Chinese Shops*, SOUTH CHINA MORNING POST (Jul. 26, 2021), https://

www.scmp.com/tech/big-tech/article/3142599/made-china-sold-amazon-merchants-scramble-minimise-losses-after-us?module=inline&pgtype=article.

26. Xin Xu, *Amazon the Monopoly Takes on Unruly Chinese Firms*, PANDAILY (Jul. 27, 2021), https://pandaily.com/amazon-the-monopoly-takes-on-unruly-chinese-firms/.

27. Avner Greif, *Reputation and Coalitions in Medieval Trade: Evidence on the Maghribi Traders*, 49 J. ECON. HIST. 857 (1989); JEAN ENSMINGER, MAKING A MARKET: THE INSTITUTIONAL TRANSFORMATION OF AN AFRICAN SOCIETY (1992); Lisa Bernstein, *Opting out of the Legal System: Extralegal Contractual Relations in the Diamond Industry*, 21 J. LEGAL STUD. 115, 126 (1992); Robert C. Ellickson, *A Hypothesis of Wealth-Maximizing Norms: Evidence from the Whaling Industry*, 5 J. L. ECON. & ORG. 83 (1989).

28. AVINASH K. DIXIT, LAWLESSNESS AND ECONOMICS: ALTERNATIVE MODES OF GOVERNANCE 12 (2007).

29. Ibid., at 62.

30. See Greif, *supra* note 27. See also Bernstein, *supra* note 27.

31. DIXIT, *supra* note 28, at 12, 97.

32. Paul R. Milgrom et al., *The Role of Institutions in the Revival of Trade: The Law Merchant, Private Judges, and the Champagne Fairs*, 2 ECON. & POL. 1 (1990).

33. DIEGO GAMBETTA, THE SICILIAN MAFIA: THE BUSINESS OF PRIVATE PROTECTION 19 & 85 (1993).

34. See Lizhi Liu & Barry R. Weingast, *Taobao, Federalism, and the Emergence of Law, Chinese Style*, 102 MINN. L. REV. 1563, 1568–1569 (2018).

35. See Van Loo, *supra* note 1, at 550.

36. To identify the cases relating to the disputes about Taobao and Tmall's decisions, I conducted two searches in China Judgement Online database in June 2022. My first search used keywords of dazong pingshen (大众评审) [public juror] and Taobao to search for cases that are decided by the Public Jury of Taobao. I also used keywords: Taobao kefu (淘宝客服) [Taobao customer service] and wangluo fuwu hetong jiufeng (网络服务合同纠纷) [internet service contract disputes] to search for cases decided by the customer representatives of Taobao. After filtering out the irrelevant cases, my search identifies 371 relevant cases involving disputes regarding the decisions by Taobao and Tmall. In particular, only five cases involved decisions made by the Public Jury, while the rest were all decisions made by the customer representatives.

37. Wanggou Maidao Jiahuo Maijia Zhi Tui Huokuan "Jia Yi Pei San" Xiang Shui Yao (网购买到假货卖家只退货款 "假一赔三"向谁要) [Sellers Only Returned Payment for Counterfeits, Whom to Ask for "One Fake Triple Refund"], CCTV.COM (Jan. 24, 2016), http://jingji.cntv.cn/2016/01/24/ARTInDa1jWRnrLNnguYestb1160124.shtml.

38. Taobao Pingtai Guize (淘宝平台规则) [Taobao Platform Rules], https://zhongyiyuan.alitrip.com/.

NOTES

39. Ibid.
40. Ibid.
41. Julia Black, *Decentering Regulation: Understanding the Role of Regulation and Self-Regulation in a 'Post-Regulatory' World*, 54 CURRENT L. PROBS. 103, 118 (2001).
42. See Taobao Platform Rules, *supra* note 38.
43. Ibid.
44. Ibid.
45. See Alipay Services Agreement, https://render.alipay.com/p/f/agreementpages/alipayserviceagreement.html.
46. Wei Shan Chaping Shangjia Bei Lesuo RMB8888, Zhiye "Chapingshi" Ruhe Guan? (为删差评商家被勒索8888元, 职业"差评师"如何管") [In Order to Delete Bad Reviews Sellers Were Blackmailed RMB8888, How to Regulate Professional "Bad Reviewers"], ECONOMIC DAILY (May 17, 2019), https://www.xhby.net/index/201905/t20190517_6194541.shtml. See also Guangdong Sheng Shenzhen Shi Zhongji Renmin Fayuan Xingshi Caiding Shu (广东省深圳市中级人民法院刑事裁定书) [Guangdong Shenzhen Intermediate People's Court Criminal Decision], (2019) Yue 03 Xin Zhong 809 ((2019)粤刑终809号) (According to the court's findings, two defendants spent RMB 1,589 on a computer from a Taobao vendor. After they received the computer, one of the defendants left a damaging review, questioning the product's authenticity and openly denouncing its quality. The computer vendor reached out to the defendant to explain that the computer was in fact genuine and did not have any of the quality issues alleged by the defendant. The vendor also agreed to a full refund. However, the defendants demanded that the computer vendor transfer RMB 8,888 to them, otherwise they would not delete the comment. Fearing the review's impact on its sales, the computer vendor agreed to their demands. The defendants deleted the comment after the transfer but never returned the computer. Emboldened by their initial success, the defendants applied this tactic again to blackmail other computer sellers on Taobao. It was not until their third attempt that the same defendants were arrested by the police.).
47. E.g., Haicheng Shi Renmin Fayuan Xingshi Panjue Shu (海城市人民法院刑事判决书) [Haicheng Primary People's Court Criminal Decision], (2018) Liao 0381 Xing Chu 438 Hao ((2018)辽0381刑初438号) (three defendants blackmailed more than five Taobao shop-owners for RMB8485 by submitting false negative reviews over the course of three months); Hangzhou Shi Shangcheng Qu Renmin Fayuan Xingshi Panjue Shu (杭州市上城区人民法院刑事判决书) [Hangzhou Shangcheng Primary People's Court Criminal Decision], (2013) Hang Shang Xing Chu Zi 357 Hao ((2013)杭上刑初字第357号) (12 defendants blackmailed Taobao vendors for RMB2995 by threatening to leave bad reviews); Jiangsu Sheng Haimen Shi Renmin Fayuan Xingshi Panjue Shu (江苏省海门市人民法院刑事判决书) [Jiangsu Haimen Primary People's Court Criminal Decision], (2019) Su 0684 Xing Chu 430 Hao ((2019)苏0684刑

初430号) (two married couples allegedly colluded to blackmail a Taobao shop-owner for over RMB11,000); Zhejiang Sheng Yiwu Shi Renmin Fayuan Xingshi Panjue Shu (浙江省义乌市人民法院刑事判决书) [Zhejiang Yiwu Primary People's Court Criminal Decision], (2018) Zhe 0782 Xing Chu 2423 Hao ((2018)浙0782刑初2423号) (the defendant provided a false address, wrote unfavorable reviews and blackmailed the shop-owner for RMB8,500).

48. See Taobao's hearing with users on malicious reviews on Aug. 28, 2018, Oct. 17, 2018, Nov. 15, 2018. Taobao's hearings are available on its app.

49. Manish Singh, *Alibaba's Singles' Day Sales Top $38 Billion*, TECHCRUNCH (Nov. 12, 2019), https://techcrunch.com/2019/11/11/alibaba-singles-day-record/. In 2019, Alibaba's Singles' Day achieved USD 38 billion. Alibaba's e-commerce overall sales volume was USD 853 billion in 2019.

50. Kaifu Zhang et al., *Review Extortion and Online Marketplace* (2016) (unpublished manuscript, on file with the author).

51. Ibid.

52. Ibid.

53. See Taobao's hearing with users on malicious reviews on Oct. 17, 2018. Taobao's hearings are available on its app.

54. For more information about the Golden Cudgel scheme, see Chedi Yu Chapingshi Zaijian! Taobao Shangxian Pingjia Chuli Shenqi "Jingubang" (彻底和差评师再见！淘宝上线评价处理神器"金箍棒") [Say Goodbye to Malicious Buyer! Taobao Launched Review Management Tool "Golden Cudgel"], KK NEWS (Mar. 15, 2019), https://kknews.cc/zh-sg/news/mpyv ly9.html; Taobao Jingubang Zai Nali Shenqing? Neng Shan Suoyou Pingjia Ma? (淘宝金箍棒在哪里申请？能删所有评价吗) [How to Apply for Taobao Golden Cudgel? Can It Delete All Reviews?], ADFM.CN (Sept. 15, 2019), https://www.adfm.cn/250147.html.

55. Yiangos Papanastasiou et al., *Decentralizing Dispute Resolution of Two-Sided Platforms: The Case of Review Blackmail*, MGMT. SCI. (Jan. 23, 2023), available at https://pubsonline.informs.org/doi/10.1287/mnsc.2022.4655 (Taobao's new review-management tool allows sellers to remove malicious reviews immediately, while being subject to ex post penalties for removing truthful negative reviews. The initial results show that this new scheme can be an efficient form of dispute resolution, provided that the penalty for sellers' wrongdoings is chosen appropriately.).

56. Here I use the rhetoric of "grabbling hand" and "helping hand" as seen in economic literature. See Timothy Frye & Andrei Shleifer, *The Invisible Hand and the Grabbing Hand*, 87(2) AM. ECON. REV. 354, 354 (1997).

57. Liangrui Bao & Yifei Gao, *Construction of Online Dispute Resolution Mechanism—Chinese Internet Court under Comparative Law*, 5 J. ADV. SOC. SCI. HUMANIT. 10, 14 (2019).

58. PRC SUPREME PEOPLE'S COURT, CHINESE COURTS AND INTERNET JUDICIARY 64 (2019).

NOTES

375

59. Ibid.

60. Changqing Shi et al., *The Smart Court—A New Pathway to Justice in China?*, 12 INT. J. COURT. ADM. 4 (2021); see also Rachel E. Stern et al., *Automating Fairness? Artificial Intelligence in the Chinese Courts*, 59 COLUM. J. TRANSNATL. L. 515 (2021).

61. Sophia Tang, *How Emerging Technologies Shape the Face of Chinese Courts?*, CONFLICT OF LAWS (Nov. 10, 2021), https://conflictoflaws.net/2021/how-emerging-technologies-shape-the-face-of-chinese-courts.

62. Ibid.

63. "Zhangshang" Sifa Fuwu Jie Yiqing Qijian Susong Zhi Ji ("掌上"司法服务 解疫情期间诉讼之急) [Smart Judicial Services Meet the Urgent Need of Litigation during the Pandemic], COURT.GOV (May 7, 2020), https://www.court.gov.cn/zixun-xiangqing-228161.html.

64. Ibid. Benjamin Minhao Chen & Zhiyu Li, *How Will Technology Change the Face of Chinese Justice?*, 34 COLUM. J. ASIAN L. 1 (2020).

65. It is also possible that a significant decrease of the number of litigations has to do with the reduction of the number of cases that were uploaded to the China Judgement Online database.

66. E-Commerce Law, *supra* note 18, art. 38, 42.

67. Xinmei Shen, *Pinduoduo under Fire for Hosting Counterfeit Goods*, SOUTH CHINA MORNING POST (Jul. 31, 2018), https://www.scmp.com/abacus/tech/article/3028690/pinduoduo-under-fire-hosting-counterfeit-goods.

68. Fan Feifei, *Heat Turned Up in Fight against Fake Goods*, CHINADAILY (Aug. 22, 2018), https://www.chinadailyhk.com/articles/185/184/111/1534930959353.html.

69. Meng Yewen & Han Wei, *Pinduoduo May Face Class-Action Suits in U.S.*, CAIXIN GLOBAL (Aug. 3, 2018), https://www.caixinglobal.com/2018-08-03/pinduoduo-may-face-class-action-suits-in-us-101311128.html.

70. *Pinduoduo Denounced as Online Marketplace for Counterfeits*, ANTI-PIRACY ANALYST (Sept. 26, 2018), https://www.karg-und-petersen.de/anti-piracy-analyst/en/pinduoduo-denounced-as-online-marketplace-for-counterfeits/.

71. Consumer Protection Law, *supra* note 18, art. 55.

72. Xiaochun Zhao, *China's Fastest Growing E-commerce Startup Pinduoduo in Disputes with Merchants*, KRASIA (Jun. 20, 2018), https://kr-asia.com/chinas-fastest-growing-e-commerce-startup-pinduoduo-in-disputes-with-merchants.

73. Ibid.

74. I used the following keywords to conduct my search: jia yi pei shi (假一赔十) [ten times compensation for fake products], shanghai xunmeng (上海寻梦) [Shanghai Xunmeng].

75. Fuzhou Jiunong Maoyi Youxian Gongsi yu Shanghai Xunmeng Xinxi Jishu Youxian Gongsi Fuwu Hetong Jiufen Yishen Minshi Panjueshu (福州九农贸易有限公司与上海寻梦信息技术有限公司服务合同纠纷一审民事判决

书) [Fuzhou Jiunong Commerce Co., Ltd. v. Shanghai Xunmeng Information and Technology Co., Ltd., A Dispute over Service Contract, Civil Decision of First Instance], (2017) 沪0105民初20204号 ((2017) Hu 0105 Min Chu 20204 Hao).

76. I searched for all cases (until 2021) using keywords of Lakala as a party and small loans in the database on May 31, 2022.

77. Yuan'e Faguan (员额法官) [Judges], GUANGZHOU YUEXIU PRIMARY PEOPLE'S COURT, https://court.yuexiu.gov.cn/index.php?s=/List/index/cid/8.html.

78. Quanpiao Tongguo! Yitu Dudong Yuexiu Fayuan 2021 Niandu Gongzuo Baogao (全票通过! 一图读懂越秀法院2021年度工作报告) [Unanimously Approved! One Picture to Understand the 2021 Annual Work Report of Yuexiu Court], THE PAPERS (Jan. 24, 2022), https://www.thepaper.cn/news Detail_forward_16436947.

79. See the Yuexiu Court's website, http://court.yuexiu.gov.cn/fywh/fxtt/2020/10/3000221519344991.html.

80. Fangfan Huajie Jinrong Fengxian: Shou Dixian, Wen Shichang, Qiang Xinxi (防范化解金融风险: 守底线、稳市场、强信心) [Control Financial Risks: Guard the Bottom Line, Stabilize the Market, and Strengthen Confidence], CHINACOURT.ORG (Feb. 25, 2021), https://www.chinacourt.org/article/det ail/2021/02/id/5821357.shtml.

81. Lakala Qixia Chao 10 Wan Pian Caipan Wenshu Beihou, Keji Fuwu Maolilü Gaoda 89% (拉卡拉旗下超10万篇裁判文书背后，科技服务毛利率高达89%) [Behind Lakala's over 100,000 Judicial Rulings, the Gross Profit Margin of Technology Services Can Reach 89%], BAIDU.COM (May 18, 2021), https://shorturl.at/bjnPY.

82. Ibid.

83. Qianfan Zhang, *The People's Court in Transition*, 12 J. CONTEMP. CHINA 69, 77 (2003).

84. Ibid., at 79–82. See also generally KWAI HANG NG & XIN HE, EMBEDDED COURTS: JUDICIAL DECISION-MAKING IN CHINA (2017); RANDALL PEERENBOOM, JUDICIAL INDEPENDENCE IN CHINA: LESSONS FOR GLOBAL RULE OF LAW PROMOTION (2009).

85. Cheryl Xiaoning Long & Jun Wang, *Judicial Local Protectionism in China: An Empirical Study of IP Cases*, 42 INT. REV. L. ECON. 48 (2015). See also Zhenhuan Lei & Yishuang Li, *Making Local Courts Work: The Judicial Recentralization Reform and Local Protectionism in China* (China Center for Economic Research Working Paper E2022016, 2022), https://nsd.pku.edu.cn/docs/202210032 22234994110.pdf.

86. *Decision of the Central Committee of the Communist Party of China on Some Major Issues Concerning Comprehensively Deepening the Reform*, CHINA.ORG.CN (Jan. 16, 2014), http://www.china.org.cn/china/third_plenary_session/2014-01/16/content_31212602.htm.

87. Lei & Li, *supra* note 85.

NOTES 377

CHAPTER 8

1. Alan Kwan et al., *Crowd-Judging on Two-Sided Platforms: An Analysis of In-Group Bias*, MGMT. SCI. (Jun. 7, 2023), https://pubsonline.informs.org/doi/abs/10.1287/mnsc.2023.4818?journalCode=mnsc.

2. Jim Erickson, *How Taobao Is Crowdsourcing Justice in Online Shopping Disputes*, ALIZILA (Jul. 17, 2014), https://www.alizila.com/how-taobao-is-crowdsourcing-justice-in-online-shopping-disputes/.

3. Alibaba Shengtai Xitong Huliangwang Zhiyuan Zhe Yanjiu Baogao (生态系统互联网志愿者研究报告) [Alibaba Ecosystem Internet Volunteers Research Report] (2016) (report on file with the author).

4. Data is available on Taobao's website: *Public Participation in Public Administration*, ALIBABA PUBLIC JURY, https://pan.taobao.com/.

5. Some of these examples have been covered by the Chinese media, while others are based on the author's own observation. See Huliangwang Peishentuan Jianshi: Cong Ali Dazhong Pingshen Dao Zhihu Zhongcai Guan (互联网"陪审团"简史：从阿里大众评审到知乎仲裁官) [Internet Juror History: From Alibaba Public Hearing to Zhihu Tribunal], 163.COM (Jul. 21, 2019), https://dy.163.com/article/EKL6UJJL0518KVNS.html.

6. DRAFT CHARTER: AN OVERSIGHT BOARD FOR CONTENT DECISIONS, FACEBOOK (Jan. 28, 2019). See also Evelyn Douek, *Facebook's "Oversight Board:" Move Fast with Stable Infrastructure and Humility*, 2 N.C.J.L. & TECH. 1, 2–3 (2019).

7. I was inspired by a constitutional law study which divided judicial review into strong form and weak form. See Mark Tushnet, *Judicial Activism or Restraint in a Section 33 World Review Article*, 53 U. TORONTO L.J. 89, 89 (2003).

8. Danielle Keats Citron, *Technological Due Process*, 85 WASH. U. L. REV. 1249, 1281–1291 (2008).

9. See Douek, *supra* note 6, at 56.

10. Alibaba's Report, *supra* note 3.

11. Ibid.

12. Xing Zhou (周兴), Jingdong Shangxian Guize Pingshentuan Shangjia Ke Dui Guize Jinxing Toupiao Pingshen (京东上线规则评审团 商家可对规则进行投票评审) [JD.com Launched Rule Review Committee, Vendors Can Vote], DSB.CN (Nov. 21, 2017), http://www.dsb.cn/70139.html.

13. Didi Shi Yunxing "Gongzhong Pingyi Hui" Yaoqing Gejie Tantao Pingtai Nanti (滴滴试运行"公众评议会" 邀请各界探讨平台难题) [Didi Trial Launched Public Forum, Inviting All Walks of Life to Discuss Issues Faced by the Platform], GLOBAL TIMES (Nov. 2, 2018), https://tech.huanqiu.com/article/9CaKrnKelVc.

14. See GEOFFREY G. PARKER ET AL., PLATFORM REVOLUTION: HOW NETWORKED MARKETS ARE TRANSFORMING THE ECONOMY—AND HOW TO MAKE THEM WORK FOR YOU 169–170 (2016); see also discussion on eBay's community forum, https://community.ebay.com/t5/Professional-eBay-Sellers/PESA-memb

ers-in-eBay-s-Voices-program/gpm-p/7829699; Ina Steiner, *eBay Silences Founding "Voices" Members*, ECOMMERCEBYTES (Aug. 19, 2009), https://www.ecommercebytes.com/C/abblog/blog.pl?/pl/2009/8/1250740707.html.

15. See PARKER ET AL., *supra* note 13, at 169–170.

16. Dieter Bohn, *Facebook Taking User Votes on Proposed Policy Changes, Will Require 270 Million to Be Binding*, THE VERGE (Jun. 1, 2012), https://www.theverge.com/2012/6/1/3057997/facebook-vote-policy-changes.

17. Adi Robertson, *Mark Zuckerberg Wants to Democratize Facebook—Here's What Happened When He Tried*, THE VERGE (Apr. 5, 2018), https://www.theverge.com/2018/4/5/17176834/mark-zuckerberg-facebook-democracy-governance-vote-failure.

18. Ted Ullyot, *Results of the Inaugural Facebook Site Governance Vote*, FACEBOOK (Apr. 23, 2009), https://web.archive.org/web/20090430215524/http://blog.facebook.com/blog.php?post=79146552130.

19. David Sarno, *Facebook Governance Vote Is Homework Assignment No One Did*, *L.A.* TIMES (Apr. 23, 2009), https://latimesblogs.latimes.com/technology/2009/04/facebook-governance-vote-is-a-homework-assignment-no-one-did.html.

20. Kimber Streams, *Facebook Proposes Policy Changes, Will Share User Data with Instagram and Kill User Veto*, THE VERGE (Nov. 21, 2012), https://www.theverge.com/2012/11/21/3676518/facebook-data-use-instagram-filters-vote.

21. But e-Bay discontinued these experiments two years later when the senior management in charge of the project left the company and subsequently delegated all its dispute-resolution procedures to Square Trade, an independent third party. Interview with Colin Rule. See ETHAN KATSH & ORNA RABINOVICH-EINY, DIGITAL JUSTICE: TECHNOLOGY AND THE INTERNET OF DISPUTES 34 (2017).

22. Kwan et al., *supra* note 1.

23. Shihao Luo (罗世浩), "Daoshou Dao" Dao "Jinchan Tuoqiao": Xianyu Shang de Zhiye "E-Ba" ("到手刀"到"金蝉脱壳":闲鱼上的职业"恶霸") [From "Finding Troubles Upon Receiving Product" to "Sloughing Skin like a Cicada": Professional "Bullies" on Xianyu], SINA NEWS (Dec. 28, 2018), https://tech.sina.cn/csj/2018-12-28/doc-ihqfskcn1947290.d.html?from=wap.

24. Jing Guo (郭晶), Cong "Xianyu Xiao Fating" Kan Wanggou Jiufen Jiejue Jizhi Chuangxin (从"闲鱼小法庭"看网购纠纷解决机制创新) [Innovation of Online Shopping Dispute Resolution Mechanism: From the Experience of "Xianyu Small Tribunal"], SZNEWS (Jun. 21, 2018), http://news.sznews.com/content/2018-06/21/content_19349931.htm.

25. Xianyu Xiao Fating Zhibei (闲鱼小法庭指北) [Guide to Xianyu Small Tribunal], BILIBILI (Jul. 15, 2019), https://www.bilibili.com/read/cv3081956/. Buyers can opt to use either the customer-service channel or the crowd-judging system. Normally, if they have solid evidence, users will prefer to complain to customer service. But if they feel their evidence is thin, they

NOTES

will try their luck with the crowd-jurors. If they decide to use the crowd-judging system, then the parties involved need to upload the evidence within 72 hours.

26. Rui Li (李睿) & Honghao Du (杜鸿浩), Wo Rensheng Diyici "Kaiting" Jingran Shi Zai Xianyu Shang (我人生第一次"开庭"竟然是在闲鱼上) [The First "Trial" in My Life Turned Out to Be on Xianyu], NEWS.QQ (Mar. 17, 2021), https://new.qq.com/rain/a/20210317A0CHYL0C.

27. Ibid.

28. See Jie Chen (陈婕) & Yao Zhu (祝瑶), Maijia Youli Haishi Maijia Yuanwang? Hangzhou Wangyou Qinli: Wo Zai Meituan Xianyu "Xiao Fating" Shang Dang Peishenyuan (买家有理还是卖家冤枉? 杭州网友亲历: 我在美团闲鱼"小法庭"上当陪审员) [Is the Buyer Reasonable or the Seller Mistaken? Hangzhou Netizen's Juror Experience in Meituan and Xianyu Tribunals], QIANJIANG WANBAO (钱江晚报), https://www.baobuzz.com/info/608688.html.

29. Zhengyi Chaping Kunrao Shangjia, Meituan Waimai Yinru Gongzhong Pingshen Jizhi (争议差评困扰商家, 美团外卖引入公众评审机制) [Controversial Bad Reviews Plague Merchants, Meituan Introduces Public Review Mechanism], SINA.COM (Sept. 27, 2022), https://finance.sina.com.cn/jjxw/2022-09-27/doc-imqmmtha8948040.shtml.

30. See Xiaoheiwu Chufa Tiaoli V1.6 (小黑屋处罚条例V1.6) [Little Dark House Rules Version 1.6], BILIBILI, https://www.bilibili.com/blackboard/blackroomrule_v16.html.

31. See Zhihu Zhongcai Guifan Shixing (知乎众裁规范试行) [Zhihu Tribunal Rules], ZHIHU, https://www.zhihu.com/court/terms.

32. The case will remain open until one party obtains 60 percent of the votes, but the maximum number of votes that will be drawn is 60. A case will be dropped if one party fails to obtain 60 percent of votes when 60 voters have participated. Ibid.

33. Zhihu Tribunal Rules, *supra* note 31 ("Users can make a complaint through the complaint channel when their posted content has been determined by the jury as consisting a breach of the rules").

34. Information based on the author's interview with an Alibaba employee in Hangzhou (Apr. 2019).

35. See generally Amos Tversky & Daniel Kanneman, *Judgment under Uncertainty: Heureistcis and Biases*, 185 SCI. 1124 (1974).

36. See generally Carsten Eickhoff, *Cognitive Bias in Crowdsourcing*, in PROCEEDINGS OF THE ELEVENTH ACM INTERNATIONAL CONFERENCE ON WEB SEARCH AND DATA MINING 162 (2018).

37. Kwan et al., *supra* note 1.

38. Bloomberg, *Ant Financial Disrupts Old School Health Insurance in China, Attracts 50 Million Users to Its Newly Launched Protection Plan*, SOUTH CHINA MORNING POST (Apr. 11, 2019), https://www.scmp.com/business/companies/article/3005683/ant-financial-disrupts-old-school-health-insurance-china.

380   NOTES

39. There is no membership fee, premiums, or upfront payment. As of June 2020, over 100 million members have signed up for the insurance network. See Xianghubao Canjia Renshu Yijing Tupo Yiyiren, Ni Jiaru Le Ma? (相互宝参加人数已经突破1亿人, 你加入了吗?) [More Than 100 Million People Joined Xianghubao, Have You Joined?], DAILY ECONOMIC (Jun. 28, 2020), http://cn.dailyeconomic.com/roll/2020/06/28/115104.html.

40. See Xianghubao Tribunal Rules, https://render.alipay.com/p/f/fd-jqw9jigf/index.html.

41. Wangluo Huzhu Pingtai Bihu Huzhu Xiying Si Zhounian Li Haibo Tan Gan'en he Baoxian (网络互助平台壁虎互助喜迎四周年 李海博谈感恩和保险) [Online Mutual Aid Insurance Platform Bihu Welcomed Its Fourth Year Anniversary, Li Haibo Discussed Gratitude and Insurance], ZGDYSJ.COM (Jul. 5, 2019), http://www.zgdysj.com/html/news/20190705/38041.shtml.

42. See "Beibao Ren" Yiwai Shuaishang, Zhifubao "Xianghubao" Wei Shenme Bu Pei? ("被宝人"意外摔伤, 支付宝"相互宝"为什么不赔?) [The "Insured" Accidentally Slipped and Was Injured, Why Alipay's "Xianghubao" Rejected the Claim?], JINKU.COM (Apr. 8, 2019), https://www.jinku.com/zixun/36071/.

43. Ant Group Shuts Mutual Aid Platform Xianghubao Amid Crackdown, BLOOMBERG (Dec. 28, 2021), https://www.bloomberg.com/news/articles/2021-12-28/ant-group-shuts-mutual-aid-platform-xianghubao-amid-crackdown#xj4y7vzkg.

44. See, e.g., Kate Klonick, The New Governors: The People, Rules and Process Governing Online Speech, 131 HAR. L. REV. 1598, 1667–1668 (2017); David Kaye, Report of the Special Rapporteur on the Promotion and Protection of the Right to Freedom of Opinion and Expression, U.N. DOC. A/HRC/38/35 (Apr. 6, 2018); James Boyle, A Nondelegation Doctrine for the Digital Age, 50 DUKE L. J. 5, 10 (2000).

45. See Ben Bradford et al., Report of the Facebook Data Transparency Advisory Group 31, THE JUSTICE COLLABORATORY OF YALE LAW SCHOOL (Apr. 2019), https://law.yale.edu/sites/default/files/area/center/justice/document/dtag_report_5.22.2019.pdf.

46. Nan Zhao (赵楠), Taobao Shangcheng Hetan Zaiji: Mishi de Maijia vs Pibei de Ma Yun (淘宝商城和谈在即: 迷失的卖家VS疲惫的马云) [Taobao Mall's Negotiation Is Around the Corner: Lost Sellers v. Tired Jack Ma], TECH.QQ (Oct. 17, 2011), https://tech.qq.com/a/20111017/000103.htm; Taobao Shangcheng Tiaojia Yinfa Shu Wan Maijia "Wangluo Weigong" (淘宝商城调价引发数万卖家"网络围攻") [Taobao Mall Leveled up the Entry Threshold, Tens of Thousands of Sellers Were Provoked to Protest Virtually], XINHUA NEWS (Oct. 13, 2011), https://www.cnfin.com/news-xh08/a/20111014/820082.shtml.

47. See Wei He, Vendors Rebel against Taobao Mall Changes, CHINA DAILY (Oct. 13, 2011), https://www.chinadaily.com.cn/china/2011-10/13/content_13881218.htm; see also Yonghong Han (韩咏红), Waibao: Taobao Zao Weigong Zheshe

Zhongguo Dianzi Shangwu Zhuanxing Kunjing (外报: 淘宝遭"围攻"折射中国电子商务转型困境) [Foreign News: Protests against Taobao Reflected the Transitional Dilemma of China's E-Commerce Industry], CHINA NEWS (Oct. 14, 2011), https://www.chinanews.com.cn/hb/2011/10-14/3390126.shtml.

48. See Han, *supra* note 47.

49. Zhao, *supra* note 47.

50. *China Vendors "Riot" Online over Taobao Fee Hike*, TERRA DAILY (Oct. 13, 2011), https://www.terradaily.com/reports/China_vendors_riot_online_over_Taobao_fee_hike_999.html.

51. More details about the protests have been documented by various online sources, such as Wei He, *Vendors Rebel against Taobao Mall Changes*, CHINA DAILY (Oct. 13, 2011), http://www.chinadaily.com.cn/bizchina/2011-10/13/content_13881570.htm; Bien Perez, *Online Sellers Stage Charges Protest*, SOUTH CHINA MORNING POST (Dec. 16, 2011), http://www.scmp.com/article/987920/online-sellers-stage-charges-protest; Taobao, Shui de Taobao? (淘宝, 谁的淘宝?) [Taobao, Whose Taobao Is It?], HUXIU.COM (Dec 9, 2013), https://www.huxiu.com/article/24377.html.

52. See Han, *supra* note 47; see also Yenei Zhuanjia: Taobao Baodong Laizi Yu Dianzi Shangwu Da Huanjing Hunluan (业内专家: 淘宝暴动来自于电子商务大环境混乱) [Industry Experts: Taobao Protest Arises From Chaotic E-Commerce Industry Environment], IRESEARCH (Oct. 15, 2011), http://report.iresearch.cn/wx/news.aspx?id=152985.

53. Taobao "Baodong" (淘宝"暴动") [Taobao "Protests"], YICAI NEWS (Oct. 15, 2011), https://www.yicai.com/news/1140863.html; Huimin Li (励辉旻), Shenru Jiedu Taobao Shangcheng Baodong Shijian (深入解读淘宝商城暴动事件) [A Deep Analysis of Taobao Mall Protest Incident], FORTUNE CHINA (Oct. 17, 2011), http://www.fortunechina.com/column/c/2011-10/17/content_75641.htm; Taobao Shangjia: Xingui Jue Mei Tiqian Pubian Zhengqiu Yijian (淘宝商家: 新规绝没提前普遍征求意见) [Taobao Vendors: Taobao Never Solicited Opinions from the Public before Publishing the New Rule], YIBANG DONGLI WANG (Oct. 16, 2011), http://www.360doc.com/content/11/1020/11/7950951_157662459.shtml.

54. See Li, *supra* note 53.

55. Taobao Baodong Zanting Shangwu Bu Jieru Shuangfang Huo Hejie (淘宝暴动暂停 商务部介入双方或和解) [Taobao Protests Suspended, Ministry of Commerce Intervened and Parties May Reconcile], CHINA BUSINESS (Oct. 17, 2011), http://www.cb.com.cn/index/show/sd/cv/cv135128441314.

56. Taobao Shangcheng Tiaozheng Xingui Zhixing Banfa Tou 18 Yi Yuan Fuchi Maijia (淘宝商城调整新规执行办法 投18亿元扶持卖家) [Taobao Mall Adjusted Its Implementation Measures of the New Rule, Invested RMB 1.8 Billion to Support Sellers], XINHUA NEWS (Oct. 17, 2011), https://business.sohu.com/20111018/n322535115.shtml.

NOTES

57. Matt Grossman, *Six Charged with Bribing Amazon Employees to Boost Third-Party Sellers*, WALL ST. J. (Sept. 18, 2020), https://www.wsj.com/articles/six-char ged-with-bribing-amazon-employees-to-boost-third-party-sellers-11600460 355. Amazon has also been embroiled in corrupt practices in China. In 2018, Amazon was implicated in a scandal in which its employees in Shenzhen, through the aid of intermediaries, had been leaking data and accepting bribes to help some merchants gain better reputations on Amazon's feedback system. See Jon Emont et al., *Amazon Investigates Employees Leaking Data for Bribes*, WALL ST. J. (Sept. 16, 2018), https://www.wsj.com/articles/amazon-investiga tes-employees-leaking-data-for-bribes-1537106401.

58. Taobao Dian Xiao'er Fubai Heimu Diaocha Taobao de Shui You Duo Shen (淘宝店小二腐败黑幕调查 淘宝的水有多深?) [Investigation on Taobao Employees' Corruption Scandals, How Deep Is Taobao's Water], LINKSHOP (Jul. 17, 2014), www.linkshop.com.cn/web/archives/2014/295382.shtml.

59. Melanie Lee, *Chinese Police Arrest 36 in Alibaba.com Fraud Sting*, REUTERS (Jul. 1, 2011), https://www.reuters.com/article/us-alibaba/chinese-police-arrest-36-in-alibaba-com-fraud-sting-idUSTRE7600JF20110701.

60. Austin Ramzy, *Fraud Scandal Hits China's Online Giant Alibaba*, TIME (Feb. 22, 2011), http://content.time.com/time/world/article/0,8599,2052 971,00.html.

61. Lee, *supra* note 59; see also *Alibaba and the 2,236 Thieves*, ECONOMIST (Feb. 22, 2011), https://www.economist.com/newsbook/2011/02/22/alibaba-and-the-2236-thieves.

62. Alibaba 2011 CSR Report 43, http://www.alijijinhui.org/Uploads/file/20150917/55fa28274817d.pdf.

63. Gang Yuan (袁刚), Taobao Fubai Heimu Diaocha (淘宝腐败黑幕调查) [Investigation on Taobao Corruption Scandal], IT TIME WEEKLY (Apr. 27, 2012), http://www.domarketing.cn/html/2012/observe_0427/4082.html.

64. See Hangzhou Shi Xihu Qu Renmin Fayuan Xingshi Panjue Shu (杭州市西湖区人民法院刑事判决书) [Hangzhou Xihu Primary People's Court Criminal Decision), Hangzhou Xihu Primary People's Ct. No. 703 (2011).

65. Fan Taobao Lianmeng Shengcheng de "Taobao Neibu Renyuan de Fubai Xingwei" Shi Zenme Huishi? (反淘宝联盟声称的「淘宝内部人员的腐败行为」是怎么回事?) [What Is Going on with "the Corruption of Taobao's Internal Staff" as Alleged by Anti-Taobao Alliance?], ZHIHU (Nov. 25, 2011), https://www.zhihu.com/question/19930804/answer/13389924; ibid.

66. Ali "Yanda" Fubai Dian Xiao'er (阿里"严打"腐败店小二) [Alibaba Strikes Hard at Its Corrupted Employees], BEIJING MORNING POST (May 7, 2012), https://tech.huanqiu.com/article/9CaKrnJvi9J; see also Tianmao Xiao'er Shexian Shouhui Bei Xingju Ali Chongshen Ling Rongren (天猫小二涉嫌受贿被刑拘 阿里重申零容忍) [Tmall Employee Detained on Suspicion of Taking Bribes, Alibaba Restates Zero Tolerance), YIBANG DONGLI WANG (Apr. 22, 2016), http://www.ebrun.com/20160422/173403.shtml.

NOTES 383

67. See Alibaba Fanfu Jiu Jia Wangshang Bei Guan (阿里巴巴反腐 九家网商被关) [Alibaba Campaigns against Corruption, 9 Online Stores Were Closed], SHANGHAI MORNING POST (May 5, 2012), http://finance.sina.com.cn/stock/hkstock/ggscyd/20120505/093311993806.shtml. Over the succeeding years, Alibaba has followed up with additional investigations and has sacked more corrupt employees. See Alibaba 2012–2013 CSR Report 22, http://www.alijijinhui.org/Uploads/file/20150917/55fa2540443dd.pdf (disclosing information about how Alibaba's internal anti-corruption department investigated 128 cases and sacked 142 employees); Alibaba 2014–2015 CSR Report 37, http://csr.alibaba.com/Uploads/file/20151127/5657c945e1fa1.pdf (disclosing Alibaba's follow up of 104 investigations, and firing of 108 employees); Song Xue (薛松), Alibaba Guanbi 26 Jia Wangdian (阿里巴巴关闭26家网店) [Alibaba Closed 26 Online Stores], GUANGZHOU DAILY (Mar. 26, 2015) (disclosing Alibaba's closure of 26 stores that were engaging in bribery to obtain illegal benefits from Taobao); Alibaba 2014–2015 CSR Report 37, http://csr.alibaba.com/Uploads/file/20151127/5657c945e1fa1.pdf (disclosing that the firm shut down 36 stores on Taobao in 2017).

68. Taobao Xiao Maijia Lianhe Gongji Tianmao Da Maijia: Jiexi Qianyin Houguo (淘宝小卖家联合攻击天猫大卖家: 解析前因后果) [Small Sellers on Taobao Repelled against Big Sellers on Tmall: Analysis of Its Causes and Implications], HUXIU (Dec. 8, 2013), https://m.huxiu.com/article/24332.html.

69. Douek, *supra* note 6, at 22–23.

70. See, e.g., DANIELLE KEATS CITRON, HATE CRIMES IN CYBERSPACE (2014); Danielle Keats Citron, *Cyber Civil Rights*, 89 B.U. L. REV. 61, 115–125 (2009); Danielle Keats Citron & Helen Norton, *Intermediaries and Hate Speech: Fostering Digital Citizenship for Our Information Age*, 91 B.U. L. REV. 1435, 1456–1468 (2011); Mary Anne Franks, *Sexual Harassment 2.0*, 71 MD. L. REV. 655, 678, 681–683 (2012).

71. See John Koetsier, *Facebook Deleting Coronavirus Posts, Leading to Charges of Censorship*, FORBES (May 17, 2020), https://www.forbes.com/sites/johnkoetsier/2020/03/17/facebook-deleting-coronavirus-posts-leading-to-charges-of-censorship/#6cc9a33d5962.

72. In just the first quarter of 2019, Facebook received 25 million appeals of content-moderation decisions, amounting to 275,000 requests per day. See Monika Bickert, *Defining the Boundaries of Free Speech on Social Media, in* THE FREE SPEECH CENTURY 254, 256 (Lee C. Bollinger & Geoffrey R. Stone eds., 2018). The social media platform currently employs over 30,000 individuals to enforce its community standards. See Ezra Klein, *Mark Zuckerberg on Facebook's Hardest Year, and What Comes Next*, VOX (Apr. 2, 2018), https://www.vox.com/2018/4/2/17185052/mark-zuckerberg-facebook-interview-fake-news-bots-cambridge; Mark Zuckerberg, *A Blueprint for Content Governance and Enforcement*, FACEBOOK (Nov. 16, 2018), https://www.facebook.com/notes/mark-zuckerberg/a-blueprint-for-content-governance-and-enforcement/

10156443129621634/. As Nick Clegg, the vice president of global affairs and communications, acknowledged in the draft charter for the independent oversight board: "when reviewing content on Facebook, some decisions go to the core of how we balance safety and free expression. We believe these decisions are too consequential for Facebook to make alone." See Nick Clegg, *Charting a Course for an Oversight Board for Content Decisions*, FACEBOOK NEWSROOM (Jan. 28, 2019), https://about.fb.com/news/2019/01/oversight-board/.

73. Wade Shepard, *China's Copycat Manufacturers Are Now Pushing the Boundaries of Innovation*, SOUTH CHINA MORNING POST (May 20, 2015), https://www.scmp.com/native/business/topics/invest-china/article/1802238/chinas-copycat-manufacturers-are-now-pushing; see also William Hennessey, *Deconstructing Shanzhai—China's Copycat Counterculture: Catch Me if You Can*, 34 CAMPBELL L. REV. 609, 611 (2012).

74. Barton Beebe, *Shanzhai, Sumptuary Law, and Intellectual Property Law in Contemporary China*, 47. U.C. DAVIS L. REV. 849, 860 (2014).

75. Ibid. In 2008, an estimated 150 million cell phones, or almost 20 percent of all cell phones produced in China, were *shanzhai* products.

76. Wy Cheng, *The Hidden Benefits of China's Counterfeiting Habit*, THE DIPLOMAT (Jul. 8, 2016), https://thediplomat.com/2016/07/the-hidden-benefits-of-chinas-counterfeiting-habit/ (noting that some have attributed the innovative phenomenon of *shanzhai* to the highly competitive structure of the *shanzhai* market, and the fewer bureaucratic constraints that *shanzhai* producers face in developing new products); see also Yao Qin et al., *Neither an Authentic Product nor a Counterfeit: The Growing Popularity of Shanzhai Products in Global Markets*, 36 CAN. J. ADM. SCI. 306, 307 (2019).

77. Qin et al., *supra* note 76, at 309. Notably, *shanzhai* producers are quite creative in the way that they brand their products to mimic the famous brands they copy. For instance, a coffee brand uses "Sunbuck" to mimic "Starbucks," and a shoe company bearing a logo resembling Nike's swoosh has also surfaced with names such as "Like" or "Hike." See Alvin Tsang, *Fake Friday*, CHINALERT (Feb. 25, 2011), http://chinalert.com/category/fake-stuff/page/2/; Olivia, *Photo Hunt Game of Chinese Shanzhai Products*, CHINAHUSH (Jul. 31, 2011), http://www.chinahush.com/2011/07/31/photo-hunt-game-of-chinese-shanzhai-products/.

78. Beebe, *supra* note 74, at 852.

79. Shangbiao Fa (商标法) [Trademark Law] (promulgated by the Standing Comm. Nat'l. People's Cong., Aug. 23, 1982, effective Mar. 1, 1983, last amended Apr. 23, 2019), art. 31; see also Patricia E. Campbell & Michael Pecht, *The Emperor's New Clothes: Intellectual Property Protections in China*, 7 J. BUS. & TECH. L. 69, 78 (2012).

80. US trademark law specifies that the United States Patent and Trademark Office will not issue the trademark registration until the applicant files a verified statement that the mark has been in use in commerce. 15 U.S.C. § 1051(b),

NOTES   385

(d) (2001); see also Leahy-Smith America Invents Act, Pub. L. No. 112-29, 125 Stat. 284 (2011).

81. Sunny Chang, *Combating Trademark Squatting in China: New Developments in Chinese Trademark Law and Suggestions for the Future*, 34 Nw. J. Int'l L. & Bus. 337, 337 (2014).

82. Zhenzhou Ma (马振洲), Cong "Qiaodan Tiyu" Dao "Wuyin Liangpin," Naxie Daying Shangbiao Guansi de Shanzhai Pai Xiachang Ruhe? (从乔丹体育到无印良品, 那些打赢商标官司的山寨牌下场如何?) From "QiaoDan Tiyu" to "Natural Mill," What Happened to Those Knockoffs That Won the Trademark Lawsuits?], The New Lens (Dec. 29, 2019), https://www.then ewslens.com/article/128860; Zhengpai Bu Di Shanzhai: Ni Suo Kanjian de Zhi Shi Qinquan Yijiao (正牌不敌山寨: 你所看见的只是侵权一角?) [The Real Brands Lose to the Knockoffs: What You See Is Only a Corner of the Infringement?], Huyi Global (Dec. 13, 2019), https://huyiglobal.com/zh/2019/12/13/fake-brand-wins-2/.

83. Hennessey, *supra* note 73, at 631.

84. David Ramli & Lulu Yilun Chen, *Alibaba's Jack Ma: Better-than-Ever Fakes Worsen Piracy War*, Bloomberg (Jun. 14, 2016), https://www.bloomberg.com/news/articles/2016-06-14/alibaba-s-ma-fake-goods-today-are-better-than-the-real-thing (as revealed by Jack Ma's comment: "The problem is that the fake products today, they make better quality, better prices than the real products, the real names").

85. Beebe, *supra* note 74, at 863. See also Hua Yu, China in Ten Words 188 (Allan H. Barr trans., 2012) (noting that *shanzhai* "represents a challenge of the grass-roots to the elite, of the popular to the official, of the weak to the strong").

86. Dianzi Shangwu Fa (电子商务法) [E-Commerce Law] (promulgated by the Standing Comm. Nat'l. People's Cong., Aug. 31, 2018, effective Jan. 1, 2019), art. 38.

87. For instance, Huang Zheng, the founder and CEO of Pinduoduo, responded by saying that the firm has stepped up its efforts to tackle the sale of counterfeit products, and that *shanzhai* products should not be confused with counterfeits. See Fan Liu (刘帆), Shanzhai Bushi Jiahuo? Shangpin Shifou Qinfan Zhishi Chanquan Cheng Jiaodian (山寨不是假货? 商品是否侵犯知识产权成焦点) [Knockoffs Are Not Counterfeits? Whether Products Infringed Intellectual Property Becomes a Central Issue], Chinacourt.org (Aug. 5, 2018), https://www.chinacourt.org/article/detail/2018/08/id/3443462.shtml.

88. This form of user-generated content has become widely popular in China since its introduction in 2012. Self-media accounts earn most of their incomes from placed advertisements, which are closely related to the quality of the content and the frequency of the feeds. However, the creation of original content is both time-consuming and costly. See Jason Q. Ng, *Politics, Rumors, and Ambiguity: Tracking Censorship on WeChat's Public Accounts Platform*, Citizenlab

89. *2019 Weixin Intellectual Property Protection Report* 21, TENCENT (Dec. 23, 2019), https://ipr.tencent.com/report/content?id=4 (WeChat removed over 1.5 million articles that it found to have infringed copyrights in 2019 alone).

90. Tao Ni, *Blockchain Entrepreneur Takes Aim at Word Theft and Rumor-Mongering in Cyberspace*, SHINE.CN (Sept. 17, 2018), https://www.shine.cn/opinion/chin ese-views/1809172236/.

91. Jie Shan, *As Self-Media Booms in China, Plagiarism Has Become a Profitable Business*, GLOBAL TIMES (May 15, 2018), http://www.globaltimes.cn/content/ 1102359.shtml.

92. Ibid. These services cost only RMB 199 and enable users to put together a forged article for publication by replacing many words of the original article using synonyms with just a simple click.

93. Yibin Qian & Qing Xu, *Fraud in WeMedia Hurts Content Quality, Reader Trust*, CHINESE SOC. SCI. TODAY (Sept. 20, 2018), http://www.csstoday.com/Print. aspx?id=5977; see also Haichao Fan (范海潮) & Liping Gu (顾理平), Zimeiti Pingtai "Xigao" Xingwei de Falü Kunjing yu Banquan Baohu (自媒体平台"洗稿"行为的法律困境与版权保护) [Legal Dilemma and Copyright Protection for Xigao on Self-Media Platforms], 11 PUBLISHING RSCH. 5 (2018), http://www.cqvip.com/qk/97105x/201811/6100112776.html.

94. Ni, *supra* note 90; Fan & Gu, *supra* note 93.

95. Shan, *supra* note 91.

96. Di Lin (林迪), Weixin Shi Yunxing Xigao Tousu Heyi Jizhi Yanda "Xigao" Xingwei (微信试运行洗稿投诉合议机制严打"洗稿"行为) [WeChat Trial Launched Xigao Complaint Review Mechanism in Combat of Plagiarism], GLOBAL TIMES (Dec. 4, 2018), https://tech.huanqiu.com/article/9CaKrnKf xdP.

97. Fan & Gu, *supra* note 93.

98. 2016 Zimeiti Hangye Banquan Baogao (2016 自媒体行业版权报告) [2016 Self-Media Industry Copyright Report], IPR DAILY (Jan. 7, 2017), http:// www.iprdaily.cn/article_15263.html.

99. Richard H. Fallon, *Legitimacy and the Constitution*, 118 HARV. L. REV. 1787, 1795 (2004).

100. JOHN RAWLS, POLITICAL LIBERALISM 217 (2005); see also RICHARD H. FALLON, LAW AND LEGITIMACY IN THE SUPREME COURT 12 (2018); Lawrence B. Solum, *Procedural Justice*, 78 S. CAL. L. REV. 181, 230 (2004).

101. Tom R. Tyler, *Procedural Justice, Legitimacy, and the Effective Rule of Law*, 3 CRIME & JUST. 283 (2003).

102. Merlin Stone, *Literature Review on Complaint Management*, 18 DATABASE MKTG. & CUSTOMER STRATEGY MGMT. 111 (2011).

103. Rory Van Loo, *The Corporation as Courthouse*, 33 YALE J. REG. 547, 578 (2016).

104. Alibaba's Report, *supra* note 3.

NOTES

387

105. Statistics revealed during the hearing held in Jan. 2019 on enhancing user experience. The hearing is available on Taobao's app.

106. See generally George A. Akerlof, *The Market for "Lemons": Quality Uncertainty and the Market Mechanism*, 84 Q. J. ECON. 488 (1970) (Akerlof demonstrated that when it is difficult to observe the quality of goods or services before the purchase, it is hard for buyers to distinguish between high-quality and low-quality sellers. This would deter buyers from making purchase in the first place, also known as "adverse selection.").

107. Taobao's hearing on shortening its dispatch time on Apr. 18. 2019. The hearing is available on Taobao'a app.

108. Douek, *supra* note 6, at 54.

109. [Zhongyao Tiaozheng] Taobao Fahuo Shixiao 72 Xiaoshi Gaiwei 48 Xiaoshi! ([重要调整]淘宝发货时效72小时改为48小时!) ["Important Adjustment": Taobao's Delivery Time Changed from 72 Hours to 48 Hours!), TAOBAO GUIZE (淘宝规则) [TAOBAO RULES] (May 23, 2019), http://www.shuaishou.com/school/infos38894.html.

110. See LAWRENCE LESSIG, CODE AND OTHER LAWS OF CYBERSPACE (1999).

111. Claus Ott & Hans Bernd Schafer, *Emergence and Construction of Efficient Rules in the Legal System of German Civil Law*, 13 INT'L REV. L.& ECON. 285, 292 (1993).

112. Douek, *supra* note 6, at 68.

113. Van Loo, *supra* note 103, at 577.

114. Ibid., at 72. See also J. Nathan Matias, *Preventing Harassment and Increasing Group Participation through Social Norms in 2,190 Online Science Discussions*, in 116 PROCEEDINGS OF THE NATIONAL ACADEMY OF SCIENCES OF THE UNITED STATES OF AMERICA 9785 (2019).

115. Jin Bacheng Dazhong Pingshen Yi Hunxiao Tianmac Zhudong Zhaipai "Zhongguo Ban Hongsheng" (近八成大众评审易混淆 天猫主动摘牌"中国版红绳") [Almost 80% of the Crowd Jurors Tend to Mix Up, T-Mall Voluntarily Took Down the Chinese Version of Redline], GLOBAL E-BUSINESSMEN (Oct. 8, 2016), http://www.iwshang.com/Post/Default/Index/pid/247603.html; Da Shuju + Dazhong Pingshen Ali Qingli Shanzhai Pinpai (大数据+大众评审 阿里清理山寨品牌) [Big Data + Crowd-judging, Alibaba Cleaned Up Shanzhai Brands], MAIJIA.COM (Apr. 1, 2016), https://www.maijia.com/news/article/23522.

116. Weishenme 10 Wan+ Zimeiti Ren Zuotian Xiang Gei Zhang Xiaolong Song Jinqi? (为什么10万+自媒体人昨天想给张小龙送锦旗?) [Why Did More Than 100,000 Self-Media Workers Want to Compliment Zhang Xiaolong Yesterday?], ZHIHU (Dec. 24, 2018), https://zhuanlan.zhihu.com/p/51513241.

117. See Weixin's Report, *supra* note 88, at 24.

118. Didi Gongzhong Pingyi Hui Di 10 Qi: Qinyou Zhacji Suoyao Xingcheng Xinxi, Kefu Neng Gei Ma? (滴滴公众评议会第10期: 亲友着急索要行程

388 NOTES

信息, 客服能给吗?) [Didi's 10th Public Forum: Can the Customer Service Provide Itinerary Information When Requested Urgently by Family and Friends?], CUNMAN (Sept. 11, 2019), http://www.cunman.com/new/a3559 945f582b0275441e00675886783.

119. See Didi Trial Launched Public Forum, Inviting All Walks of Life to Discuss Issues Faced by the Platform, *supra* note 13.

120. Didi Chuxing, WEIBO (Sept. 10, 2019, 3:40 pm), https://weibo.com/2838754 010/I6ibR3SvM?refer_flag=1001030103_&type=comment#_rnd159816 7675793.

121. Jiaotong Yunshu Bu Deng Liu Bumen Jizhong Yuetan Zhuyao Wangyueche Shunfengche Pingtai Gongsi (交通运输部等六部门集中约谈主要网约车顺风车平台公司) [Six Ministries Including the Ministry of Transport Conducted Intensive Regulatory Talks with Major Online Ride-Hailing Platforms], XINHUA NEWS (Nov. 12, 2019), http://www.gov.cn/xinwen/2019-11/12/content_5451078.htm.

122. Jon Russell, *China's Didi Suspends Carpooling Service after Another Female Passenger Is Murdered*, TECHCRUNCH (Aug. 26, 2018), https://techcrunch.com/2018/08/26/didi-suspends-carpooling-service/?guccounter=1&guce_referrer=aHR0cHM6Ly93d3cuZ29vZ2xlLmNvbS8&guce_referrer_sig=AQAAAFYN5ccJa3Eef1xItIU3k5PblSEdCpKMhq_P--mD0dA6d7gBSQ-e6krcaTnimhjf6c620bAlOjncEiCLxvlhPMQQmR1V_SvhlntbKkmUn1WAjYwVGSJ_WnQNgJCltYl-z0axxX9B4n19DtqcUTpNpuEwBeYobJsYb-tR586r3FPu.

123. See Barclay Bram, *Rocked by Scandal, China's Largest Ride-Sharing App Scrambles to Right Itself*, WIRED (Nov. 8, 2018), https://www.wired.co.uk/article/didi-car-chuxing-uber-china-safety.

CHAPTER 9

1. ANU BRADFORD, DIGITAL EMPIRES: THE GLOBAL BATTLE TO REGULATE TECHNOLOGY (2023).

2. Ibid.

3. Ibid.

4. ANGELA HUYUE ZHANG, CHINESE ANTITRUST EXCEPTIONALISM: HOW THE RISE OF CHINA CHALLENGES GLOBAL REGULATION (2021), chapter 5.

5. Anupam Chander & Uyên P. Lê, *Data Nationalism*, 64 EMORY L. J. 677, 682–706 (2015).

6. Joseph Antel et al., *Effective Competition in Digital Platform Markets*, 6(1) EUR. COMPETITION REGUL. L. REV. 35, 47 (2022).

7. George L. Paul et al., *Key Developments in the United States*, GLOBAL COMPETITION REV. (Nov. 25, 2022), https://globalcompetitionreview.com/guide/digital-markets-guide/second-edition/article/key-developments-in-the-united-states.

NOTES

389

8. The White House, *Fact Sheet: Executive Order on Promoting Competition in the American Economy* (Jul. 9, 2021), https://www.whitehouse.gov/briefing-room/statements-releases/2021/07/09/fact-sheet-executive-order-on-promoting-competition-in-the-american-economy/.

9. Athena Kontosakou, *European Antitrust Enforcement in the Digital Era: How It Started, How It's Going, and the Risks Lying Ahead*, 67(4) THE ANTITRUST BULL. 522, 524.

10. Ibid., at 526.

11. René Grafunder et al., *EU Digital Markets Act: Next Steps and Long-Term Outlook*, DENTONS (Dec. 7, 2022), https://www.dentons.com/en/insights/articles/2022/december/7/eu-digital-markets-act-next-steps-and-long-term-outlook.

12. Case T-612/17, *Google and Alphabet v. Commission*, OJ C 369 from 30.10.2017.

13. Bundeskartellamt, *Bundeskartellamt Prohibits Facebook from Combining User Data from Different Sources* (Feb. 7, 2019), https://www.bundeskartellamt.de/SharedDocs/Meldung/EN/Pressemitteilungen/2019/07_02_2019_Facebook.html.

14. Adam Satariano, *Meta Loses Appeal on How It Harvests Data in Germany*, N.Y. TIMES (July 4, 2023), https://www.nytimes.com/2023/07/04/business/meta-germany-data.html

15. *UK, German and Australian Regulators Unify against Big Tech*, FIN. TIMES (Apr. 20, 2021), https://www.ft.com/content/ae16c27b-54d5-41da-ba20-71518 616f0e4; see also Kontosakou, *supra* note 9, at 534; Jonathan Keane, *Italy Has Quietly Become One of Big Tech's Most Prolific Antagonists*, CNBC.COM (Jan. 18, 2022), https://www.cnbc.com/2022/01/18/european-regulators-in-italy-fra nce-germany-and-uk-rein-in-big-tech-.html.

16. European Commission, *Report on Competition Policy 2019.* https://ec.europa. eu/competition/publications/annual_report/2019/part1_en.pdf; also see Kontosakou, *supra* note 9.

17. Kristen O'Shaughnessy & Jaclyn Phillips, *Senator Josh Hawley Joins Growing Number in Congress Proposing Sweeping Antitrust Reform Legislation*, WHITE & CASE (Apr. 19, 2021), https://www.whitecase.com/insight-alert/senator-josh-haw ley-joins-growing-number-congress-proposing-sweeping-antitrust-reform.

18. King & Wood Mallesons, *10 Highlights of the Antitrust Guidelines for Platform Economy*, CHINA L. INSIGHT (Nov. 18, 2020), https://www.chinalawinsight. com/2020/11/articles/compliance/10-highlights-of-the-antitrust-guideli nes-for-platform-economy/.

19. Jane Zhang & Iris Deng, *China Issues Final Version of Anti-Monopoly Guidelines as Beijing Moves to Rein in Big Tech*, SOUTH CHINA MORNING POST (Feb. 8, 2021), https://www.scmp.com/tech/policy/article/3120977/china-issues-final-vers ion-anti-monopoly-guidelines-beijing-moves-rein

20. Yonnex Li, *"Killer Acquisitions" Call for Revamp of China's Merger-Control Threshold, SAMR Says*, MLEX MARKET Insight (May 26. 2020), https://floria nederer.github.io/china.pdf.

21. Fan Longduan Fa (反垄断法) [Anti-Monopoly Law] (amended by the Standing Comm. Nat'l. People's Cong., Jun. 24, 2022, effective Aug. 1, 2022), art. 26.

22. SAMR, Guanyu Gongkai Zhengqiu "Guowuyuan Guanyu Jingyingzhe Jizhong Shenbao de Guiding (Xiuding Cao'an Zhengqiu Yijian Gao)" Yijian de Gonggao (关于公开征求《国务院关于经营者集中申报标准的规定（修订草案征求意见稿）》意见的公告) [Announcement on Soliciting Public Opinions on the "Regulations of the State Council on the Reporting Standards for Concentration of Business Operators (Revised Draft for Comment)"] (Jun. 27, 2022), https://www.samr.gov.cn/hd/zjdc/202206/t20220625_348149.html.

23. Scholars have long identified the potential anti-competitive harm resulting from common ownership, even in circumstances of passive investment of minority interests. See generally Einer Elhauge, *Horizontal Shareholding*, 109 HARV. L. REV. 1267 (2016); Eric A. Posner, *Policy Implications of the Common Ownership Debate*, 66 ANTITRUST BULL. 140 (2021).

24. Celia Chen & Iris Deng, *Tencent, Didi Chuxing, Other Internet Firms Slapped with Fine by Antitrust Authorities for Failing to Disclose Deals*, SOUTH CHINA MORNING POST (Apr. 30, 2021), https://www.scmp.com/tech/big-tech/article/3131818/tencent-didi-chuxing-other-internet-firms-slapped-fine-antitrust.

25. Shichang Jianguan Zongju Yifa Dui Tengxun Konggu Youxian Gongsi Zuochu Zeling Jiechu Wangluo Yinyue Dujia Banquan Deng Chufa (市场监管总局依法对腾讯控股有限公司作出责令解除网络音乐独家版权等处罚) [SAMR Decided to Impose Penalty and Requested Tencent Holdings to End Exclusive Music Deals] (Jul. 24, 2021), https://www.samr.gov.cn/xw/zj/202107/t20210724_333016.html.

26. *Ibid.*

27. Shichang Jianguan Zongju Yifa Jinzhi Huya Gongsi Yu Douyu Guoji Konggu Youxian Gongsi Hebing (市场监管总局依法禁止虎牙公司与斗鱼国际控股有限公司合并) [SAMR Decided to Prohibit the Merger between Huya and DouYu International Corporation] (Jul. 10, 2021), https://www.samr.gov.cn/xw/zj/202107/t20210710_332525.html.

28. Ibid.

29. Ibid.

30. Iris Deng, *China Antitrust: Beijing Approves Tencent's Acquisition of Search Engine Sogou after Vetoing Huya-Douyu Merger*, SOUTH CHINA MORNING POST (Jul. 13, 2021), https://www.scmp.com/tech/policy/article/3140877/china-antitrust-beijing-approves-tencents-acquisition-search-engine.

31. Henrik Saetre, *Top 5 Chinese Search Engines in 2022 [With Market Share]*, ADCHINA.IO (last visited May 12, 2023), https://www.adchina.io/top-chinese-search-engines/.

32. Mark M. Lemley & Andrew McCreary, *Exit Strategy*, 101 BOSTON U. L. REV. 1, 85 (2021) (calling on antitrust agencies to pay more attention to acquisitions by incumbent monopolists even if the target firms are not direct competitors).

NOTES

33. Douglas W. Arner et al., *The Transnational Data Governance Problem*, 37 BERKELEY TECH. L. J. 623, 6 (2022).

34. US Department of Justice, *The USA PATRIOT Act: Preserving Life and Liberty*, https://www.justice.gov/archive/ll/highlights.htm.

35. Foreign Intelligence Surveillance Act of 1978, 50 U.S.C. § 1802.

36. US Department of Justice, *Cloud Act Resources*, https://www.justice.gov/criminal-oia/cloud-act-resources.

37. Chander & Lê, *supra* note 5.

38. See Arner et al., *supra* note 33.

39. *US WeChat Users Alliance v. Trump*, 488 F. Supp. 3d 912 (N.D. Cal. 2020); *Marland v. Trump*, 498 F. Supp. 3d 624 (E.D. Pa. 2020); *TikTok Inc. v. Trump*, 507 F. Supp. 3d 92 (D.D.C. 2020).

40. Paul M. Schwartz, *Global Data Privacy: The EU Way*, 94 N.Y. U. L. REV. 771, 773 (2019).

41. PRIVACY AND POWER: A TRANSATLANTIC DIALOGUE IN THE SHADOW OF THE NSA-AFFAIR (Russell A. Miller ed., 2017); James Q. Whitman, *The Two Western Cultures of Privacy: Dignity versus Liberty*, 113 YALE L. J. 1151 (2004).

42. Laurens Cerulus & Hans Von Der Burchard, *Snowden's Back: Spying Scandal Clouds EU-US Ties Ahead of Biden Visit*, POLITICO (May 31, 2021), https://www.politico.eu/article/edward-snowden-is-back-spying-scandal-disrupts-eu-us-ties-ahead-of-joe-biden-europe-visit/.

43. C-362/14, *Maximillian Schrems v. Data Protection Commissioner*, ECLI:EU:C:2015:650; C-311/18, *Data Protection Commissioner v. Facebook Ireland Limited and Maximillian Schrems*, ECLI:EU:C:2020:559.

44. Ibid.

45. Adam Satariano, *Meta Fined $1.3 Billion for Violating E.U. Data Privacy Rules*, N.Y. TIMES (May 22, 2023), https://www.nytimes.com/2023/05/22/business/meta-facebook-eu-privacy-fine.html

46. Henry Gao, *Data Regulation with Chinese Characteristics*, in BIG DATA AND GLOBAL TRADE LAW 245–267 (Mira Burri ed., 2021).

47. Xuan Wu (吴玄), Yun Jisuan Xia Shuju Kuajing Zhifa: Meiguo Yun Fa yu Zhongguo Fang'an (云计算下数据跨境执法：美国云法与中国方案) [Law Enforcement over Cross-Border Data Flow under Cloud Computing: The U.S. Cloud Act and the Chinese Approach], INSTITUTE OF RULE OF LAW (Sept. 14. 2023), http://fzzfyjy.cupl.edu.cn/info/1035/14444.htm.

48. Jyh-An Lee, *Hacking into China's Cybersecurity Law*, 53 WAKE FOREST L. REV. 57, 78–83 (2018).

49. Ryan D Junck et al., *China's New Data Security and Personal Information Protection Laws: What They Mean for Multinational Companies*, SKADDEN (Nov. 3, 2021), https://www.skadden.com/insights/publications/2021/11/chinas-new-data-security-and-personal-information-protection-laws.

50. Shuju Anquan Fa (数据安全法) [Data Security Law] (promulgated by the Standing Comm. Nat'l. People's Cong., Jun. 10, 2021, effective Sept. 1, 2021), art. 36.

51. Geren Xinxi Baohu Fa (个人信息保护法) [Personal Information Protection Law] (promulgated by the Standing Comm. Nat'l. People's Cong., Aug. 20, 2021, effective Nov. 1, 2021), art. 41.

52. Data Security Law, *supra* note 50, art. 25–26; Personal Information Protection Law, *supra* note 51, art. 42–43. Lizhi Yuan (袁立志) & Yu Duan (段宇), Geren Xinxi Baohu Fa: Luoji, Zhongdian ji Jianyi (个人信息保护法: 逻辑、重点及建议) [Personal Information Protection Law: Logic, Focus, and Advice], JINGTIAN & GONGCHENG (Aug. 24, 2021), https://www.jingtian.com/Content/2021/08-25/1716461261.html.

53. Barbara Li et al., *Cross-Border Data Transfer Mechanism in China and Practical Steps to Take*, REED SMITH (Oct. 13, 2022), https://www.reedsmith.com/en/perspectives/2022/10/cross-border-data-transfer-mechanism-in-china-and-practical-steps-to-take.

54. Lingling Wei & Keith Zhai, *Chinese Regulators Suggested Didi Delay Its U.S. IPO*, WALL ST. J. (Jul. 5, 2021), https://www.wsj.com/articles/chinese-regulators-suggested-didi-delay-its-u-s-ipo-11625510600.

55. Alex Roberts, *China Publishes Revised Cybersecurity Review Measures*, LINKLATERS (Jul. 12, 2020), https://lpscdn.linklaters.com/knowledge/-/media/digital-marketing-image-library/files/06_ckp/2021/july/210712_linklaters-zhao-sheng-alert_china-publishes-revised-cybersecurity-review-measures.ashx?rev=59a35871-5027-4dbe-b72a-a4b4537d4cdf&extension=pdf.

56. Schwartz, *supra* note 40, at 903.

57. ANU BRAFORD, THE BRUSSELS EFFECT: HOW THE EUROPEAN UNION RULES THE WORLD 30–31 (2020).

58. Ibid.

59. Personal Information Protection Law, *supra* note 51, art. 58.

60. Richard D. Alaniz, *The Independent Contractor Dilemma*, ACHR NEWS (Aug. 9, 2022), https://www.achrnews.com/articles/146882-the-independent-contractor-dilemma.

61. Allison Fiorentino, *American Case Law and the Uberization of Work*, OPENEDITION JOURNALS (Dec. 1, 2019), https://journals.openedition.org/rdctss/1415.

62. Mike Isaac, *Judge Overturns Uber's Settlement with Drivers*, N.Y. TIMES (Aug. 18, 2016), https://www.nytimes.com/2016/08/19/technology/uber-settlement-california-drivers.html.

63. Ibid.

64. Noam Scheiber, *Uber and Lyft Drivers Win Ruling on Unemployment Benefits*, N.Y. TIMES (Jul. 28, 2020), https://www.nytimes.com/2020/07/28/business/economy/lyft-uber-drivers-unemployment.html.

65. Kate Conger & Daisuke Wakabayashi, *Massachusetts Sues Uber and Lyft over the Status of Drivers*, N.Y. TIMES (Jul. 14, 2020), https://www.nytimes.com/2020/07/14/technology/massachusetts-sues-uber-lyft.html.

66. *S. G. Borello & Sons, Inc. v. Department of Industrial Relations*, 48 *Cal. 3d 341* (Cal. 1989).

NOTES

393

67. *Dynamex Operations West, Inc. v. Superior Court*, 4 Cal.5th 903 (Cal. 2018).

68. *Brock v. Mr. W Fireworks, Inc. & Fair Labor Standards Act* (which codified the test), 814 F2d 1042 (5th Cir. 1987).

69. Assemb. B. 5, 2019–2020 Leg., Reg. Sess. (Cal. 2019), https://leginfo.legislat ure.ca.gov/faces/billNavClient.xhtml?bill_id=201920200AB5.

70. Andrew J. Hawkins, *Uber and Lyft Had an Edge in the Prop 22 Fight: Their Apps*, THE VERGE (Nov. 5, 2020), https://www.theverge.com/2020/11/4/21549760/ uber-lyft-prop-22-win-vote-app-message-notifications.

71. Margot Roosevelt & Suhauna Hussain, *Prop. 22 Is Ruled Unconstitutional, a Blow to California Gig Economy Law*, L.A. TIMES (Aug. 20, 2021), https://www. latimes.com/business/story/2021-08-20/prop-22-unconstitutional.

72. Kellen Browning, *Massachusetts Court Throws Out Gig Worker Ballot Measure*, N.Y. TIMES (Jun. 14, 2022), https://www.nytimes.com/2022/06/14/technol ogy/massachusetts-gig-workers.html.

73. Chris Marr, *Uber Driver Compromise in Washington Is Tougher Sell Elsewhere*, BLOOMBERG L. (Aug. 8, 2022), https://news.bloomberglaw.com/daily-labor- report/uber-driver-compromise-in-washington-is-tougher-sell-elsewhere.

74. Ibid.

75. Daniel Wiessner et al., *Biden Labor Proposal Shakes up Gig Economy That Relies on Contractors*, REUTERS (Oct. 12, 2022), https://www.reuters.com/world/ us/new-biden-labor-rule-would-make-contractors-into-employees-2022- 10-11/.

76. Harald Hauben et al., *The Platform Economy and Precarious Work* 22, EUROPEAN PARLIAMENT (Sept. 2020), https://www.europarl.europa.eu/RegData/etudes/ STUD/2020/652734/IPOL_STU(2020)652734_EN.pdf.

77. *Deliveroo Ordered to Pay 9.7 Million Euros for Concealed Work in France*, TELLER REPORT (Sept. 3, 2022), https://www.tellerreport.com/news/2022-09-03- deliveroo-ordered-to-pay-9-7-million-euros-for-concealed-work-in-france. Sk6kVjxls.html.

78. *France: An Executive Order on Representation Rights for Platform Workers*, INDUSTRIAL RELATIONS AND LABOUR LAW (Nov. 25, 2021), https://industrialre lationsnews.ioe-emp.org/es/industrial-relations-and-labour-law-november- 2021/news/article/france-an-executive-order-on-representation-rights-for- platform-workers.

79. *Spain's Supreme Court Rules Food Delivery Riders Are Employees, Not Freelancers*, REUTERS (Sept. 23, 2020), https://www.reuters.com/article/uk-spain-glovo- ruling-idUKKCN26E2NR.

80. Natasha Lomas, *Spain's Delivery Platform Glovo Fined Again for Breaching Labor Laws*, TECHCRUNCH (Jan. 24, 2023), https://techcrunch.com/2023/01/24/ glovo-madrid-labor-law-fine/.

81. Spain *Approves a "Riders Law,"* INDUSTRIAL RELATIONS AND LABOUR LAW (May 31, 2021), https://industrialrelationsnews.ioe-emp.org/industrial-relations- and-labour-law-may-2021/news/article/spain-approves-a-riders-law.

NOTES

82. Cillian Shields, *Deliveroo to Cease Operations in Spain at the End of November*, CATALAN NEWS (Nov. 18, 2021), https://www.catalannews.com/business/item/deliveroo-to-cease-operations-in-spain-at-the-end-of-november.

83. Emilio Parodi, *Milan Prosecutors Order Food Delivery Groups to Hire Riders, Pay 733 Mln Euros in Fines*, REUTERS (Feb. 25, 2021), https://www.reuters.com/business/milan-prosecutors-order-food-delivery-groups-hire-riders-pay-733-mln-euros-fines-2021-02-24/.

84. European Commission, *Commission Proposals to Improve the Working Conditions of People Working through Digital Labour Platforms* (Dec. 9, 2021), https://ec.europa.eu/commission/presscorner/detail/en/ip_21_6605.

85. Ibid.

86. Regulation (EU) 2022/1925 of the European Parliament and of the Council of 14 September 2022 on Contestable and Fair Markets in the Digital Sector and Amending Directives (EU) 2019/1937 and (EU) 2020/1828 (Digital Markets Act), recital 55.

87. Ministry of Human Resources and Social Security et al., Guanyu Weihu Xin Jiuye Xingtai Laodongzhe Laodong Baozhang Quanyi de Zhidao Yijian (关于维护新就业形态劳动者劳动保障权益的指导意见) [Guiding Opinions on Protecting Labor and Social Security Rights and Interests of Workers Engaged in New Forms of Employment], MOHRSS Issued (2021) No. 56, http://www.gov.cn/zhengce/zhengceku/2021-07/23/content_5626761.htm.

88. Tianyu Wang (王天玉), Hulianwang Pingtai Yonggong de "Leiguyuan" Jieshi Lujing ji Qi Guifan Tixi (互联网平台用工的"类雇员"解释路径及其规范体系) [Interpretation Path and Normative Framework for "Quasi-Employees" on Internet Platforms], 3 GLOBAL L. REV. 85 (2020), http://www.globallawreview.org/Admin/UploadFile/Issue/valnitvu.pdf.

89. Christina Hießl, *Case Law on the Classification of Platform Workers: Cross-European Comparative Analysis and Tentative Conclusions* 17, EUROPEAN COMMISSION (Aug. 31, 2022), https://papers.ssrn.com/sol3/papers.cfm?abstract_id=3839603.

90. Ibid.

91. Beijing First Intermediate People's Court Research Group (北京市第一中级人民法院课题组), Xin Jiuye Xingtai Xia Pingtai Yonggong Guanxi Falü Xingzhi de Jieding Guize (新就业形态下平台用工关系法律性质的界定规则) [Rules on Defining the Nature of Legal Relationships for Platform Workers in New Employment Forms], PEOPLE'S COURT DAILY (Sept. 23, 2021), http://rmfyb.chinacourt.org/paper/images/2021-09/23/07/2021092307_pdf.pdf.

92. Beijing First Intermediate People's Court Research Group (北京市第一中级人民法院课题组), Xin Jiuye Xingtai Xia Pingtai Yonggong Falü Guanxi Dingxing Yanjiu (新就业形态下平台用工法律关系定性研究) [Examining the Nature of Legal Relationships for Platform Workers in New Employment Forms], PEOPLE'S JUDICATURE APPLICATION (Mar. 2022), https://mp.weixin.qq.com/s/cbQoi2OmeIA24SrtLtFSsQ.

NOTES

CHAPTER 10

1. Chen Li et al., *The Hybrid Regulatory Regime in Turbulent Times: The Role of the State in China's Stock Market Crisis in 2015–2016*, 16(2) REGUL. GOV. 392, 404 (2022); see also Xin Frank He, *Sporadic Law Enforcement Campaigns as a Means of Social Control: A Case Study from a Rural-Urban Migrant Enclave in Beijing*, 17 COLUM. J. ASIAN L. 121, 134 (2003) (noting that "during the revolutionary period, the CCP had to rely on mass movements and campaigns to implement its policies because it had no state institutions"); SHIPING ZHENG, PARTY V. STATE IN POST-1949 CHINA: THE INSTITUTIONAL DILEMMA 154 (1996).
2. Sophie Yu & Scott Murdoch, *Tencent Hands Shareholders $16.4 Bln Windfall in the Form of JD.com Stake*, REUTERS (Dec. 23, 2021), https://www.reuters.com/business/tencent-distribute-most-jdcom-stake-shareholders-2021-12-23/.
3. *Tencent Divestment Strategy Sends Chill through China's Tech Sector*, FIN. TIMES (Sept. 1, 2022), https://www.ft.com/content/24f7b605-3052-4476-ae2d-a2d0028e70a4.
4. Ibid.
5. Ibid.
6. *Ant Group Announces Further Corporate Governance Optimization*, ANT GROUP (Jan. 7, 2023), https://www.antgroup.com/en/notices/1.
7. Jesse M. Fried & Ehud Kamar, *Alibaba: A Case Study of Synthetic Control*, 11(2) HARV. BUS. L. REV. 279 (2021).
8. Ibid.
9. Raffaele Huang & Clarence Leong, *Alibaba to Split into Six Groups and Explore IPOs in a Departure from Jack Ma Era*, WALL ST. J. (Mar. 28, 2023), https://www.wsj.com/articles/alibaba-to-split-into-six-separate-groups-in-biggest-shake-up-9ce2201f.
10. Ibid.
11. Jin Li & Angela Huyue Zhang, *Alibaba and the Forced Restructuring*, PROJECT SYNDICATE (Apr. 5, 2023), https://www.project-syndicate.org/commentary/alibaba-restructuring-advantages-and-disadvantages-by-jin-li-and-angela-huyue-zhang-2023-04?barrier=accesspaylog.
12. Xinmei Shen, *China's Internet Sector Sees Steep Drop in Funding amid Rising Geopolitical and Regulatory Risks*, SOUTH CHINA MORNING POST (Apr. 27, 2022), https://www.scmp.com/tech/tech-trends/article/3175703/chinas-internet-sector-sees-steep-drop-funding-amid-rising.
13. Ibid.
14. Hudson Lockett, *How Xi Jinping Is Reshaping China's Capital Markets*, FIN. TIMES (Jun. 11, 2022), https://www.ft.com/content/d5b81ea0-5955-414c-b2eb-886dfed4dffe; *Chinese Companies Listed on Major U.S. Stock Exchanges*, U.S.-CHINA ECONOMIC AND SECURITY REVIEW COMMISSION (Jan. 9, 2023), https://www.uscc.gov/research/chinese-companies-listed-major-us-stock-exchanges.

15. Yi-Ling Liu, *The Larger Meaning of China's Crackdown on School Tutoring*, THE NEW YORKER (May 16, 2022), https://www.newyorker.com/culture/culture-desk/the-larger-meaning-of-chinas-crackdown-on-school-tutoring.

16. Shen, *supra* note 12.

17. 2021 Nian Si Jidu Hulianwang Tou-Rongzi Yunying Qingkuang (2021年四季度互联网投融资运营情况) [Internet Sector Investment and Financing Report 2021Q4], CHINA ACADEMY OF INFORMATION AND COMMUNICATIONS TECHNOLOGY (Jan. 24, 2022), http://www.caict.ac.cn/kxyj/qwfb/qwsj/202201/P020220124567191389083.pdf.

18. Ke Rong et al., *Antitrust Platform Tech Regulation and Competition: Evidence from China* (unpublished manuscript on file with the author).

19. Ibid.

20. Ibid.

21. Jane Zhang, *China's Big Tech Crackdown: Number of Apps Falls 40 Per Cent over 3 Years amid New Data Laws and Clean-up Campaigns*, SOUTH CHINA MORNING POST (Dec. 21, 2021), https://www.scmp.com/tech/tech-trends/article/3160457/chinas-big-tech-crackdown-number-apps-falls-40-cent-over-three.

22. Ibid.

23. Hui Zhao (朝晖), Zhongguo Qian 30 Da APP Paiming (中国前30大APP排名) [Ranking of the Top 30 Apps in China], MYDRIVERS.COM (Nov. 13, 2020), https://news.mydrivers.com/1/724/724055.htm#:~:text=近日，新财富杂志统计,合计垄断7成份额%E3%80%82.

24. Zhongguo Ershi Da APP Paiming (中国二十大APP排名) [Ranking of the Top 20 Apps in China], TOUTIAO.COM (Oct. 15, 2021), https://www.toutiao.com/article/7019201333089616423/?channel=&source=search_tab; Zhongguoren Yong de Zuiduo de 20 Kuan APP Paiming (中国人用的最多的20款APP排名) [Ranking of the 20 Most Used Apps in China], QQ.COM (Aug. 3, 2022), https://new.qq.com/rain/a/20220803A0AL7H00.

25. Dianshang Hangye 2022 Nian Q4 Caibao Zongjie (电商行业2022年Q4财报总结) [Summary of the 2022 Q4 Financial Report of the E-commerce Industry], GUOSEN SECURITIES (Apr. 9, 2023), https://pdf.dfcfw.com/pdf/H3_AP202304101585250189_1.pdf?1681135044000.pdf.

26. 2023 Nian Zaixian Waimai Hangye Shichang Guimo Fenxi (2023年在线外卖行业市场规模分析) [Market Size Analysis of Online Food Delivery Industry 2023], CHINABGAO.COM (Mar. 23, 2023), https://www.chinabgao.com/info/1244495.html#:~:text=美团和饿了,逐渐往线上发展%E3%80%82.

27. Youxi Yewu Fenxi (游戏业务分析) [Game Business Analysis], XUEQIU.COM (Jun. 11, 2023), https://xueqiu.com/4263852107/252859370; 2021 Nian Zhongguo Youxi Hangye Jingzheng Geju ji Shichang Fen'e Fenxi (2021年中国游戏行业竞争格局及市场份额分析) [Analysis of the Competition Pattern and Market Share of China's Gaming Industry 2021], QIANZHAN.COM (Dec. 7, 2021), https://bg.qianzhan.com/trends/detail/506/211207-c2029b8c.html.

NOTES

28. 2023 Nian 2 Yue Didi Rijun Danliang Shangzhang 26%, Shichang Fen'e Huifu Zhi 78% (2023年2月滴滴日均单量上涨26%, 市场份额恢复至78%) [Didi's Average Daily Order Volume Rose by 26% and Market Share Recovered to 78% in February 2023], XUEQIU.COM (Mar. 11, 2023), https://xueqiu.com/248 2094753/244172594.

29. Josh Ye & Robert Delaney, *Yahoo Makes Final China Exit amid Tightened Regulation in World's Biggest Internet Market*, SOUTH CHINA MORNING POST (Nov. 2, 2021), https://www.scmp.com/tech/tech-war/article/3154575/ yahoo-makes-final-china-exit-amid-tightened-regulation-worlds-biggest.

30. Taojun Xie et al., *Navigating China's New Cross-Border Data Transfer Rules*, THE BUS. TIMES (Feb. 21, 2023), https://lkyspp.nus.edu.sg/docs/default-source/ aci/thebusinesstimes_21feb2023_navigating-china-s-new-cross-border-data-transfer-rules.pdf.

31. Echo Wong & Kenji Kawase, *China's Data Securities Laws Pose Costly Challenge for JPMorgan*, NIKKEI ASIA (Jun. 6, 2023), https://asia.nikkei.com/Business/ Finance/China-s-data-security-laws-pose-costly-challenge-for-JPMorgan.

32. Interview with a senior bank executive, Beijing, March 2023.

33. Ibid.

34. Interview with five employees from Chinese tech firms based in Hangzhou and Beijing (April 2023).

35. Qunian Chao 35 Jia Hulianwang Gongsi Caiyuan (去年超35家互联网公司裁员) [More than 35 Internet Companies Laid Off Employees Last Year], 21ST CENTURY BUSINESS HERALD (Jan. 25, 2022), https://mp.weixn.qq.com/s/F3N 3bG9TiSejWmxYbROwRw.

36. Ibid.

37. Iris Deng, *Tencent Cuts Nearly 1,900 Jobs in the Third Quarter as Tech Giant Struggles under Beijing Scrutiny in Slowing Economy*, SOUTH CHINA MORNING POST (Nov. 16, 2022), https://www.scmp.com/tech/big-tech/article/3199 840/tencent-cuts-nearly-1900-jobs-third-quarter-tech-giant-struggles-under-beijing-scrutiny-slowing?module=inline&pgtype=article; Tracy Qu & Iris Deng, *Tech Lay-Offs in China Extend into Year-End as Bilibili and Weibo Cut Headcount in Worsening Economy*, SOUTH CHINA MORNING POST (Dec. 8, 2022), https://www.scmp.com/tech/tech-trends/article/3202541/tech-lay-offs-china-extend-year-end-bilibili-and-weibo-cut-headcount-worsening-economy.

38. 2022 Nian Shang Bannian Naxie Caiyuan de Hulianwang "Dachang" (2022上半年那些裁员的互联网"大厂") [Big Tech That Laid Off Employees in the First Half of 2022], 100EC.CN (Jul. 28, 2022), https://www.100ec.cn/detail--6615596.html.

39. Che Pan, *Baidu Said to be Slashing Jobs, Trimming Bonuses at Intelligent Driving Unit*, SOUTH CHINA MORNING POST (Jan. 10, 2023), https://www.scmp.com/ print/tech/big-tech/article/3206302/baidu-said-be-slashing-jobs-trimming-bonuses-autonomous-driving-unit.

40. Fa Chen, *Variable Interest Entity Structures in China: Are Legal Uncertainties and Risks to Foreign Investors Part of China's Regulatory Policy?*, 29(1) Asia Pacific L. Rev. 1–24 (2021).

41. Thomas Y. MAN, *Policy above Law: VIE and Foreign Investment Regulation in China*, 3 Peking U. Transnat'l. L. Rev. 215 (2015).

42. Martin Peers, *Why Didi Global's Delisting Shouldn't Be Forgotten*, The Information (Apr. 18, 2022), https://www.theinformation.com/articles/why-didi-global-s-delisting-shouldn-t-be-forgotten.

43. *Fretting about Data Security, China's Government Expands Its Use of "Golden Shares,"* Reuters (Dec. 16, 2021), https://www.reuters.com/markets/deals/exclusive-fretting-about-data-security-chinas-government-expands-its-use-golden-2021-12-15/.

44. Jiangyu Wang & Tan Cheng-Han, *Mixed Ownership Reform and Corporate Governance in China's State-Owned Enterprises*, 53(3) Vand. J. Transnat'l. L. 1055–1107 (2020).

45. *China Moves to Take "Golden Shares" in Alibaba and Tencent Units*, Fin. Times (Jan. 12, 2023), https://www.ft.com/content/65e60815-c5a0-4c4a-bcec-4af0f76462de.

46. Reuters, *supra* note 43.

47. Ibid.

48. Fin. Times, *supra* note 45.

49. Ibid.

50. Guojia Wangxinban: Yao Rang Wangluo Duan Shipin Chongman Zheng Nengliang (国家网信办：要让网络短视频充满正能量) [Cyberspace Administration of China: Make Online Short Videos Full of Positive Energy], People.cn (Aug. 23, 2018), http://politics.people.com.cn/n1/2018/0823/c1001-30247538.html.

51. Guojia Wangxinban Yifa Yuetan Chufa Xinlang Weibo (国家网信办依法约谈处罚新浪微博) [Cyberspace Administration of China Interviewed and Punished Sina Weibo According to Law], Cyber Administration of China (Dec. 14, 2021), http://www.cac.gov.cn/2021-12/14/c_1641080795548173.htm.

52. *Weibo's Shares Spiral Lower after Fine from Chinese Regulator*, Bloomberg (Dec. 14, 2021), https://www.bloomberg.com/news/articles/2021-12-14/weibo-s-shares-spiral-lower-after-fine-from-chinese-regulator#xj4y7vzkg.

53. Iris Deng, *Ant Group Moves Key Step Forward in Restructuring, as Consumer Finance Unit Wins Approval to Expand Capital Base*, South China Morning Post (Dec. 31, 2022), https://www.scmp.com/tech/article/3205149/ant-group-moves-key-step-forward-restructuring-consumer-finance-unit-wins-approval-expand-capital.

54. Bloomberg, *Betting on Tech Firms like NIO and BOE Pays Off for Communist Officials in China's Eastern City of Hefei*, South China Morning Post (Feb. 7, 2022), https://www.scmp.com/print/tech/tech-trends/article/3166064/betting-tech-firms-nio-and-boc-pays-communist-officials-chinas.

NOTES

399

55. Chong-en Bai et al., *Special Deals with Chinese Characteristics*, 34(1) NBER MACROECON. ANNU. 341 (2019).

56. Chong-en Bai et al., *The Rise of State-Connected Private Owners in China* (Nat'l. Bureau of Econ. Rsch., Working Paper No. 28170, 2021).

57. Ibid.

58. *Preqin Markets in Focus: Private Equity & Venture Capital in Greater China's Innovation Economy*, PREQIN (Dec. 10, 2019), https://www.preqin.com/insig hts/research/reports/preqin-markets-in-focus-private-equity-venture-capi tal-in-greater-chinas-innovation-economy.

59. Daron Acemoglu, *Antitrust Alone Won't Fix the Innovation Problem*, PROJECT SYNDICATE (Oct. 30, 2020), https://www.project-syndicate.org/commentary/ google-antitrust-big-tech-hurdle-to-innovation-by-daron-acemoglu-2020-10?barrier=accesspaylog.

60. Daron Acemoglu, *Diversity and Technological Progress*, in THE RATE AND DIRECTION OF INVENTIVE ACTIVITY REVISITED 319, 345 (Josh Learner & Scott Stern eds., 2012).

61. Ibid.

62. Xiao Tan & Yao Song, *China's "Whole Nation" Effort to Advance the Tech Industry*, THE DIPLOMAT (Apr. 21, 2022), https://thediplomat.com/2022/04/chinas-whole-nation-effort-to-advance-the-tech-industry/.

63. Frank Tang, *China Prioritises Hi-tech at "Top of All Economic Policies" as Xi Jinping Refines 2035 Development Goals*, SOUTH CHINA MORNING POST (Oct. 18, 2022), https://www.scmp.com/economy/china-economy/article/3196263/ china-priorities-hi-tech-top-all-economic-policies-xi-jinping-refines-2035-development-goals.

64. Ruihan Huang & AJ Cortese, *Nanometers over GDP: Can Technocrat Leaders Improve China's Industrial Policy?*, MACROPOLO (May 23, 2023), https://macrop olo.org/analysis/technocrat-leaders-china-industrial-policy/.

65. Renmin Ribao Ping Shequ Tuangou: Bie Zhi Dianjizhe Ji Kun Baicai, Keji Chuangxin de Xingchen Dahai Geng Lingren Xinchaopengpai (人民日报评社区团购: 别只惦记着几捆白菜, 科技创新的星辰大海更令人心潮澎湃) [People's Daily Commenting on Community Group Buying: Don't Just Focus on Selling Cabbages; Technology and Innovation Are More Exciting], WALLSTREETCN.COM (Dec. 11, 2020), https://wallstreetcn.com/articles/ 3613229.

66. *ByteDance Disbands Investment Team amid China's Big Tech Clampdown*, FIN. TIMES (Jan. 19, 2022), https://www.ft.com/content/8de842c5-25fc-4c8c-a4e1-fd27f39c187e.

67. Ibid.

68. Dachang Touzi, Buzai Fengkuang (大厂投资, 不再疯狂) [Big Tech No Longer Crazy about Investment], 36KR.COM (Mar. 10, 2023), https://36kr. com/p/2179082434539776.

69. Ibid.

NOTES

70. Iris Deng & Celia Chen, *Tencent to Invest US$70 Billion in New Digital Infrastructure, Backing Beijing's Economic Stimulus Efforts*, SOUTH CHINA MORNING POST (May 26, 2020), https://www.scmp.com/tech/big-tech/article/3086 162/tencent-invest-us70-billion-new-digital-infrastructure-backing.

71. Coco Liu & Cheng Ting-Fang, *Alibaba Unveils AI Chip to Boost Cloud Plans and Cut Reliance on US*, NIKKEI ASIA (Sept. 25, 2019), https://asia.nikkei.com/Business/China-tech/Alibaba-unveils-AI-chip-to-boost-cloud-plans-and-cut-reliance-on-US.

72. 2022 Zhongguo Keji Touzi Pandian: Zhuizhu Anquangan, Zhuizhu Quedingxing (2022 中国科技投资盘点：追逐安全感，追逐确定性) [China's Technology Investment Summary 2022: Looking for Security and Certainty], LATE POST (Jan. 3, 2023), https://baijiahao.baidu.com/s?id=175400308398 0748008&wfr=spider&for=pc.

73. 36KR.COM, *supra* note 68.

74. Ibid.

75. Ibid.

76. Eileen Yu, *Alibaba Cloud Parks $1B in Skills Development, to Build First Philippine Data Centre*, ZDNET (Jun. 7, 2021), www.zdnet.com/article/alibaba-cloud-parks-1b-in-skills-development-to-build-first-philippine-data-centre/.

77. Arjun Kharpal, *China's Alibaba to Invest $28.2 Billion in Cloud Infrastructure as It Battles Amazon, Microsoft*, CNBC (Apr. 20, 2020), www.cnbc.com/2020/04/20/alibaba-to-invest-28-billion-in-cloud-as-it-battles-amazon-microsoft.html.

78. *China Tech Giants Spend Billions to Fuel Growth after Crackdown*, BLOOMBERG (May 26, 2021), www.bloomberg.com/news/articles/2021-05-26/china-tech-giants-spend-billions-to-fuel-growth-after-crackdown.

79. 2022 Nian, Hulianwang Gongsi Qu Zuo LP Le (2022年，互联网公司去做LP了) [Internet Companies Became Limited Partners in 2022], JIEMIAN.COM (Feb. 17, 2022), https://m.jiemian.com/article/7092547.html.

80. *Investors Pivot from Ecommerce to Chips to Avoid China Crackdown*, FIN. TIMES (Aug. 15, 2021), https://www.ft.com/content/d06e04e0-6a9e-48b5-860d-94208163bbd2.

81. Liza Lin et al., *China's Startups Are Awash with Money as Beijing Shifts Focus to "Hard Tech,"* WALL ST. J. (Jan. 13, 2022), https://www.wsj.com/articles/chinas-startups-attract-record-funding-despite-tech-clampdown-11642000017.

82. Ibid. Coco Liu, *China Venture Funding Hits Record US$131 Billion Despite Crackdown, as Start-ups Pivot to Hard Tech*, BLOOMBERG (Jan. 10, 2022), https://www.bloomberg.com/news/articles/2022-01-09/china-venture-funding-hits-record-131-billion-despite-crackdown.

83. Zhongguo Xinjingji Chuangye Touzi Fenxi Baogao Zhi Touzi Pian (中国新经济创业投资分析报告之投资篇) [Investment Chapter of China's New Economy Venture Capital Analysis Report] 13, ITJUZI (Feb. 2023), https://m.itjuzi.com/mall/95.

NOTES

84. Lin et al., *supra* note 81.
85. Ngor Luong et al., *Understanding Chinese Government Guidance Funds*, CENTER FOR SECURITY & EMERGING TECH. (Mar. 2021), https://cset.georgetown.edu/publication/understanding-chinese-government-guidance-funds/.
86. Lockett, *supra* note 14.
87. Iris Deng, *Tech War: Guangzhou Pours US$29 Billion into Funds for Semiconductors, Other Hi-Tech Fields as Local Governments Boost China's Recovery*, SOUTH CHINA MORNING POST (Feb. 21, 2023), https://www.scmp.com/tech/policy/article/3210888/tech-war-guangzhou-pours-us29-billion-funds-semiconductors-other-hi-tech-fields-local-governments.
88. ITJUZI, *supra* note 83, at 35. Take the example of Shenzhen Capital Group, which was established in 1999 by Shenzhen Municipal government and commercial shareholders. With RMB 434 billion (approximately USD 60 billion) of asset under its management, the fund has made 1,682 investments, of which 248 portfolio companies went public as of April 2023. It primarily focuses on investing in small and medium-sized technology enterprises. The official website of the fund is https://www.szvc.com.cn.
89. Zhongguo Xinjingji Chuangye Touzi Fenxi Pandian 2021–2022 (中国新经济创业投资分析盘点 2021-2022) [China's New Economy Venture Capital Analysis 2021–2022] 71, ITJUZI (Feb. 2022), available at https://www.renrendoc.com/paper/248776530.html.
90. Deng, *supra* note 87.
91. Ibid.
92. Iris Deng & Tracy Qu, *Tech War: Chinese Local Governments Ramp Up Chip Industry Support as US Piles on Export Restrictions*, SOUTH CHINA MORNING POST (Oct. 18, 2022), https://www.scmp.com/tech/tech-war/article/3196406/tech-war-local-governments-china-ramp-support-chip-industry-development-us-piles-export-restrictions.
93. Jane Zhang, *China's Semiconductors: How Wuhan's Challenger to Chinese Chip Champion SMIC Turned from Dream to Nightmare*, SOUTH CHINA MORNING POST (Mar. 20, 2021), https://www.scmp.com/print/tech/tech-trends/article/3126124/chinas-semiconductors-how-wuhans-challenger-chinese-chip-champion.
94. *How to Make It Big in Xi Jinping's China*, THE ECONOMIST (Apr. 24, 2023), https://www.economist.com/business/2023/04/24/how-to-make-it-big-in-xi-jinpings-china.
95. Erchi Zhang et al., *Cover Story: Graft Scandal Casts Long Shadow over China's Chipmaking Ambitions*, CAIXIN GLOBAL (Aug. 8, 2022), https://www.caixinglobal.com/2022-08-08/cover-story-graft-scandal-casts-long-shadow-over-chinas-chipmaking-ambitions-101923281.html.
96. Ibid.
97. Zhang, *supra* note 93.
98. Ibid.

NOTES

99. Ibid.

100. Masha Borak, *Chinese Chip Maker Tsinghua Unigroup Faces Bankruptcy Restructuring after Creditor Takes It to Court*, SOUTH CHINA MORNING POST (Jul. 11, 2021), https://www.scmp.com/tech/tech-trends/article/3140678/chin ese-chip-maker-tsinghua-unigroup-faces-bankruptcy.

101. Min Qin & Wei Han, *Former Chief of Chip Giant Unigroup Charged with Corruption*, CAIXIN GLOBAL (Mar. 21, 2023), https://www.caixinglobal.com/ 2023-03-21/former-chief-of-chip-giant-unigroup-charged-with-corrupt ion-102010136.html#:~:text=Zhao%20Weiguo%2C%20former%20chair man%20and,tycoon%20was%20placed%20under%20investigation.

102. Alex He, *China's Techno-Industrial Development: A Case Study of the Semiconductor Industry* 20 (CIGI Working Paper No. 252, 2021), https://www.cigionline. org/static/documents/documents/no.252%20web.pdf.

CHAPTER 11

1. *Generative AI—The Copyright Issues*, SIMMONS-SIMMONS (Apr. 25, 2023), https://www.simmons-simmons.com/en/publications/clgxkqd5z000utrj8z uuc5cms/generative-ai-the-copyright-issues.

2. Giangiacomo Olivi & Chiara Bocchi, *Generative AI vs Privacy Compliance: Who Doesn't Like a Happy Ending?*, DENTONS (May 4, 2023), https://www.dent ons.com/en/insights/articles/2023/may/4/generative-ai-vs-privacy-complia nce-who-doesnt-like-a-happy-ending.

3. Tate Ryan-Mosley, *Catching Bad Content in the Age of AI*, MIT TECH. REV. (May 15, 2023), https://www.technologyreview.com/2023/05/15/1073019/ catching-bad-content-in-the-age-of-ai/.

4. Giles Pratt et al., *Generative AI: Five Things for Lawyers to Consider*, FRESHFIELDS BRUCKHAUS DERINGER (Feb. 21, 2023), https://technologyquotient.freshfields. com/post/102i82i/generative-ai-five-things-for-lawyers-to-consider

5. Furat Ashraf, *Generative AI Tools: Key Employment Issues and How to Address Them*, BIRD & BIRD (Jun. 30, 2023), https://www.twobirds.com/en/insights/ 2023/global/generative-ai-tools-key-employment-issues-and-how-to-addr ess-them.

6. Guojia Hulianwang Xinxi Bangongshi Guanyu <Shengchengshi Rengong Zhineng Fuwu Guanli Banfa (Zhengqiu Yijian Gao)> Gongkai Zhengqiu Yijian de Tongzhi (国家互联网信息办公室关于《生成式人工智能服务管理办法(征求意见稿)》公开征求意见的通知) [Notice on Soliciting Public Opinions Issued by the Cyberspace Administration of China on the Measures for the Management of Generative Artificial Intelligence Services (Draft for Comment)], MINISTRY OF JUSTICE OF THE PEOPLE'S REPUBLIC OF CHINA (Apr. 11, 2023), http://www.moj.gov.cn/pub/sfbgw/lfyjzj/lflfyjzj/202 304/t20230411_476092.html.

NOTES

403

7. Paul Triolo, *ChatGPT and China: How to Think about Large Language Models and the Generative AI Race*, THE CHINA PROJECT (Apr. 12, 2023), https://thechinaproject.com/2023/04/12/chatgpt-and-china-how-to-think-about-large-language-models-and-the-generative-ai-race/.

8. Ibid.

9. Helen Toner et al., *How Will China's Generative AI Regulations Shape the Future? A DigiChina Forum*, DIGICHINA (Apr. 19, 2023), https://digichina.stanford.edu/work/how-will-chinas-generative-ai-regulations-shape-the-future-a-digichina-forum/; Helen Toner et al., *The Illusion of China's AI Prowess*, FOREIGN AFFAIRS (Jun. 2, 2023), https://www.foreignaffairs.com/china/illusion-chinas-ai-prowess-regulation.

10. Shengchengshi Rengong Zhineng Fuwu Guanli Banfa (生成式人工智能服务管理办法) [The Measures for the Management of Generative Artificial Intelligence Services](hereinafter as "Interim Measures for Generative AI"), OFFICE OF THE CENTRAL CYBERSPACE ADMINISTRATION OF CHINA (July 13, 2023), http://www.cac.gov.cn/2023-07/13/c_1690898327029107.htm.

11. Graham Webster et al., *Full Translation: China's "New Generation Artificial Intelligence Development Plan,"* NEW AMERICA (Aug. 1, 2017), https://www.newamerica.org/cybersecurity-initiative/digichina/blog/full-translation-chinas-new-generation-artificial-intelligence-development-plan-2017/.

12. Gregory C. Allen, *Understanding China's AI Strategy*, CENTER FOR A NEW AMERICAN SECURITY (Feb. 6, 2019), https://www.cnas.org/publications/reports/understanding-chinas-ai-strategy.

13. JOSH CHIN, & LIZA LIN, SURVEILLANCE STATE: INSIDE CHINA'S QUEST TO LAUNCH A NEW ERA OF SOCIAL CONTROL (2022).

14. Mia Nulimaimaiti, *Can AI Give China the Upper Hand to Surpass the US and Become the World's Top Economy after ChatGPT Changed the Game?*, SOUTH CHINA MORNING POST (Jun. 15, 2023), https://www.scmp.com/economy/global-economy/article/3224050/can-ai-give-china-upper-hand-surpass-us-and-become-worlds-top-economy-after-chatgpt-changed-game.

15. *Sizing the Prize: What's the Real Value of AI for Your Business and How Can You Capitalise?*, PwC (Jun. 2017), https://www.pwc.com/gx/en/issues/analytics/assets/pwc-ai-analysis-sizing-the-prize-report.pdf.

16. Graham Allison & Eric Schmidt, *Is China Beating the US to AI Supremacy?* 1, BELFER CENTER (Aug. 2020), https://www.belfercenter.org/publication/china-beating-us-ai-supremacy.

17. Ian King et al., *Nvidia Drops on Report US Plans More AI Chip Curbs for China*, BLOOMBERG (Jun. 28, 2023), https://www.bloomberg.com/news/articles/2023-06-28/nvidia-leads-selloff-after-report-on-us-tightening-ai-chip-curbs.

18. Allison & Schmidt, *supra* note 16, at 7–8.

19. Toner et al. on FOREIGN AFFAIRS, *supra* note 9.

20. Ibid.

21. Ana Swanson, *Biden Administration Clamps Down on China's Access to Chip Technology*, N.Y. TIMES (Oct. 7, 2022), https://www.nytimes.com/2022/10/07/business/economy/biden-chip-technology.html

22. Ana Swanson, *U.S. Tightens China's Access to Advanced Chips for Artificial Intelligence*, N.Y. TIMES (Oct. 17, 2023), https://www.nytimes.com/2023/10/17/business/economy/ai-chips-china-restrictions.html

23. Che Pan, *Chinese Leader Xi Jinping Urges Country to Seize Opportunities in Artificial Intelligence to Modernise Industry*, SOUTH CHINA MORNING POST (May 6, 2023), https://www.scmp.com/tech/tech-war/article/3219623/chinese-leader-xi-jinping-urges-country-seize-opportunities-artificial-intelligence-modernise.

24. Allen, *supra* note 12.

25. Allison & Schmidt, *supra* note 16, at 5.

26. Allen, *supra* note 12.

27. Jane Zhang & Sarah Zheng, *Billionaires and Bureaucrats Mobilize China for AI Race with US*, BLOOMBERG (Jun. 29, 2023), https://www.bloomberg.com/news/articles/2023-06-27/ai-is-next-tech-battle-for-us-and-china-on-chatgpt-frenzy#xj4y7vzkg.

28. Ibid.

29. Ibid.

30. Amanda Lee, *China Launches New AI Programme as Race against the US for Supremacy Heats Up*, SOUTH CHINA MORNING POST (Mar. 28, 2023), https://www.scmp.com/economy/china-economy/article/3215138/china-launches-new-ai-programme-race-against-us-supremacy-heats; Ben Jiang, *China Plans to Set Up Regional AI "Highlands" and Related Technology Platforms as Beijing Pushes to Bridge Hi-Tech Divide with US*, SOUTH CHINA MORNING POST (May 18, 2023), https://www.scmp.com/tech/big-tech/article/3221053/china-plans-set-regional-ai-highlands-and-related-technology-platforms-beijing-pushes-bridge-hi-tech. Gongxinbu: Jiang Jiakuai Rengong Zhineng Dashuju Deng Xinxing Shuzi Chanye Fazhan (工信部: 将加快人工智能大数据等新兴数字产业发展) [MIIT: Accelerate the Development of Emerging Digital Industries like AI and Big Data], GDCA.MIIT.COM (Mar. 3, 2023), https://gdca.miit.gov.cn/xwdt/xydt/art/2023/art_0396391e69154bfa95cfee0841c91f32.html. Fagaiwei: Jiakuai Fazhan Shuzi Jingji Zhongshi Tongyong Rengong Zhineng Fazhan (发改委: 加快发展数字经济 重视通用人工智能发展) [NDRC: Accelerate the Development of Digital Economy and Value the Advancement of General AI], CLS.CN (May 12, 2023), https://www.cls.cn/detail/1348922.

31. *Homepage*, MINISTRY OF SCIENCE AND TECHNOLOGY, https://en.most.gov.cn/organization/.

32. *Homepage*, MINISTRY OF INDUSTRY AND INFORMATION TECHNOLOGY, http://english.www.gov.cn/state_council/2014/08/23/content_281474983035940.htm.

33. *Main Functions*, NATIONAL DEVELOPMENT AND REFORM COMMISSION, https://en.ndrc.gov.cn/aboutndrc/mainfunctions/.

NOTES 405

34. Jeffrey Ding, *China's Current Capabilities, Policies and Industrial Ecosystem in AI*, CENTER FOR SECURITY AND EMERGING TECHNOLOGY (Jun. 7, 2019), https:// cset.georgetown.edu/publication/chinas-current-capabilities-policies-and-industrial-ecosystem-in-ai/.

35. Jeffrey Ding & Jenny Xiao, *Recent Trends in China's Large Language Model Landscape*, CENTER FOR THE GOVERNANCE OF AI (Apr. 28, 2023), https://www.governance.ai/research-paper/recent-trends-chinas-llm-landscape.

36. Ibid., at 8.

37. Ibid.

38. Shaoshan Liu, *Will China Create a New State-Owned Enterprise to Monopolize Artificial Intelligence?*, THE DIPLOMAT (Feb. 27, 2023), https://thediplomat.com/ 2023/02/will-china-create-a-new-state-owned-enterprise-to-monopolize-artificial-intelligence/.

39. *Global Opinions and Expectations about Artificial Intelligence*. IPSOS (Jan. 2022), https://www.ipsos.com/sites/default/files/ct/news/documents/2022-01/ Global-opinions-and-expectations-about-AI-2022.pdf.

40. William Zheng, *ChatGPT: China Detains Man for Allegedly Generating Fake Train Crash News, First Known Time Person Held over Use of AI Bot*, SOUTH CHINA MORNING POST (May 8, 2023), https://www.scmp.com/news/china/ politics/article/3219764/china-announces-first-known-chatgpt-arrest-over-alleged-fake-train-crash-news.

41. *Boss Cheated Out of 4.3 Million Yuan by AI Face-Changing Fraud*, GLOBAL TIMES (May 24, 2023), https://www.globaltimes.cn/page/202305/1291302.shtml.

42. Shen Lu, *China Cracks Down on Surge in AI-Driven Fraud*. WALL ST. J. (Jun. 4, 2023), https://www.wsj.com/articles/china-cracks-down-on-surge-in-ai-dri ven-fraud-c6c4dca0.

43. Nabil Alsabah, *Information Control 2.0: The Cyberspace Administration of China Tames the Internet*, MERICS (Sept. 15, 2016), https://www.merics.org/sites/defa ult/files/2020-05/MERICS_China_Monitor_32_Eng.pdf.

44. Ibid.

45. ANGELA HUYUE ZHANG, CHINESE ANTITRUST EXCEPTIONALISM: HOW THE RISE OF CHINA CHALLENGES GLOBAL REGULATION, 38–39 (2021).

46. Ibid., at 39–44.

47. Interim Measures for Generative AI, *supra* note 10, art. 2.

48. Juyou Yulun Shuxing huo Shehui Dongyuan Nengli de Hulianwang Xinxi Fuwu Anquan Pinggu Guiding (具有舆论属性或社会动员能力的互联网信息服务安全评估规定) [Regulations for the Security Assessment of Internet Information Services Having Public Opinion Properties or Social Mobilization Capacity] (promulgated by the CAC, Nov. 30, 2018, effective Nov. 30, 2018), https://www.gov.cn/zhengce/zhengceku/2018-11/30/cont ent_5457763.htm.

49. Hulianwang Xinxi Fuwu Suanfa Tuijian Guanli Guiding (互联网信息服务算法推荐管理规定) [Internet Information Service Algorithmic

50. Recommendation Management Provisions] (promulgated by the CAC, the MIIT, the MPS, and the SAMR, Dec. 31, 2021, effective Mar. 1, 2022), https://www.gov.cn/zhengce/zhengceku/2022-01/04/content_5666429.htm.

50. Hulianwang Xinxi Fuwu Shendu Hecheng Guanli Guiding (互联网信息服务深度合成管理规定) [Internet Information Service Deep Synthesis Management Provisions] (promulgated by the CAC, the MIIT, and the MPS, Nov. 25, 2022, effective Jan. 10, 2023), https://www.gov.cn/zhengce/zhengceku/2022-12/12/content_5731431.htm.

51. Helen Toner et al., *Experts Examine China's Pioneering Draft Algorithm Regulations*, DIGICHINA (Aug. 27, 2021), https://digichina.stanford.edu/work/experts-examine-chinas-pioneering-draft-algorithm-regulations/.

52. Hulianwang Xinxi Fuwu Suanfa Bei'an Xitong (互联网信息服务算法备案系统) [Internet Information Service Algorithm Filing System], CYBER ADMINISTRATION OF CHINA (launched Mar. 1, 2022), https://beian.cac.gov.cn/#/index.

53. Anu Bradford, *The Race to Regulate Artificial Intelligence*, FOREIGN AFFAIRS (Jun. 27, 2023), https://www.foreignaffairs.com/united-states/race-regulate-artificial-intelligence.

54. Ibid.

55. Ronald Del Sesto et al., *European Parliament Adopts Position on Artificial Intelligence Act*, MORGAN LEWIS (Jun. 16, 2023), https://www.morganlewis.com/pubs/2023/06/european-parliament-adopts-position-on-artificial-intelligence-act.

56. Ulrik Stig Hansen, *What the European AI Act Means for You, AI Developers*, ENCORD (Jun. 26, 2023), https://encord.com/blog/what-the-european-ai-act-means-for-you/.

57. *EU AI Act: First Regulation on Artificial Intelligence*, EUROPEAN PARLIAMENT (Jun. 8, 2023), https://www.europarl.europa.eu/news/en/headlines/society/20230601STO93804/eu-ai-act-first-regulation-on-artificial-intelligence.

58. Jess Weatherbed, *European Companies Claim the EU's AI Act Could "Jeopardise Technological Sovereignty"*, THE VERGE (Jun. 30, 2023), https://www.theverge.com/2023/6/30/23779611/eu-ai-act-open-letter-artificial-intelligence-regulation-renault-siemens.

59. European Parliament, Press Release, *Artificial Intelligence Act: deal on comprehensive rules for trustworthy AI* (Dec. 9, 2023).

60. Alex Engler, *The EU and U.S. Diverge on AI Regulation: A Transatlantic Comparison and Steps to Alignment*, BROOKINGS (Apr. 25, 2023), https://www.brookings.edu/articles/the-eu-and-us-diverge-on-ai-regulation-a-transatlantic-comparison-and-steps-to-alignment/.

61. Bradford, *supra* note 53.

62. Engler, *supra* note 60.

63. The White House, *Blueprint for an AI Bill of Rights* (Oct. 2022), https://www.whitehouse.gov/ostp/ai-bill-of-rights/.

NOTES

64. The White House, *Fact Sheet: President Biden Issues Executive Order on Safe, Secure, and Trustworthy Artificial Intelligence* (Oct. 30, 2023), https://www.whitehouse.gov/briefing-room/statements-releases/2023/10/30/fact-sheet-president-biden-issues-executive-order-on-safe-secure-and-trustworthy-artificial-intelligence/

65. Ibid.

66. Engler, *supra* note 60; Cameron F. Kerry, *Will California Be the Death of National Privacy Legislation?*, BROOKINGS (Nov. 18, 2022), https://www.brookings.edu/articles/will-california-be-the-death-of-national-privacy-legislation/.

67. George J. Stigler, *The Theory of Economic Regulation*, 2 BELL J. ECON. MANAGE. SCI. 3 (1971).

68. Kevin Roose, *AI Poses "Risk of Extinction," Industry Leaders Warn*, N.Y. TIMES (May 30, 2023), https://www.nytimes.com/2023/05/30/technology/ai-threat-warning.html?smid=tw-share.

69. Bill Drexel & Hannah Kelley, *China Is Flirting with Artificial Intelligence Catastrophe*, FOREIGN AFFAIRS (May 30, 2023), https://www.foreignaffairs.com/china/china-flirting-ai-catastrophe.

70. The White House, *FACT SHEET: Biden-Harris Administration Announces New Actions to Promote Responsible AI Innovation That Protects Americans' Rights and Safety* (May 4, 2023), https://www.whitehouse.gov/briefing-room/statements-releases/2023/05/04/fact-sheet-biden-harris-administration-announces-new-actions-to-promote-responsible-ai-innovation-that-protects-americans-rights-and-safety/.

Acknowledgments

My journey with this book project began in early 2022 and came to fruition by the summer of 2023. During this period, I found myself juggling numerous responsibilities: introducing several new courses, navigating the various events at the Centre for Chinese Law at the University of Hong Kong, and tending to my two lively children, Alan and Alice. This balancing act was not without its challenges, especially with China's ever-evolving platform regulation offering more plot twists than an intricate thriller.

Fueling this ambitious endeavor, my daily three-kilometer dash became a reminder to stay as focused and persistent as a marathon runner nearing the finish line. With the breaking of each dawn, I found myself already immersed in my work at the law school, with my book being the first order of the day. As I cross this finish line, I'm filled with gratitude and joy, having managed to exceed my own expectations and complete this marathon.

A troupe of invaluable companions offered their wisdom and camaraderie along this journey. My heartfelt gratitude goes to Anu Bradford, a beacon of unwavering support and cherished friendship. I am also immensely thankful to Sida Liu, Mark Jia, Thomas Streinz, Miao Xu, Yang Feng, and Curtis Milhaupt for their insightful feedback.

I owe a considerable debt of thanks to the participants of the Global Order workshop led by Professors Bill Alford and Mark Wu from Harvard Law School. Their incisive feedback not only sharpened my analysis but expanded the horizons of my thought process. I am grateful to my academic home—the University of Hong Kong Law School—for fostering a stimulating intellectual environment. The early constructive feedback from my colleagues proved instrumental in refining my work. Special mention must go to Professor Jin Li from the HKU Business School, whose economic insights never fail to spark my intellectual curiosity.

In the labyrinth of research that this book entailed, I was extremely fortunate to receive stellar support from an excellent team of research assistants.

ACKNOWLEDGMENTS

I extend my heartfelt thanks to Jingxian Zeng, Daniel Cheng, Kiki Dong, Jonathan Yeung, Muzhi Chen, Yilin Yu, and Qi Wang for their incredible support. My two-week field trip post China's reopening in March proved a veritable treasure trove of insights. My sincere appreciation to all the interviewees for their candid narratives that lent a rich texture to this work.

Last but not least, I extend my deepest gratitude to my husband, Alex, for his sharp and discerning critique. To my beloved children, Alan and Alice, your unconditional love fuels my every endeavor. Alan, this book is dedicated to you. Thank you for spreading the word in your class about your mother's book on platforms. May this book serve as an enduring reminder of the potency of perseverance and dedication.

Index

For the benefit of digital users, indexed terms that span two pages (e.g., 52–53) may, on occasion, appear on only one of those pages.

Tables and figures are indicated by *t* and *f* following the page number

accountability, 9–10, 149, 225–26, 259, 261
Acemoglu, Daron, 270–71
adaptability, 12–13, 16*f*, 17–18, 26, 28, 59–60, 72, 100, 128–29
adaptive governance, 12, 28
administrative guidance or interview, 110–11, 113, 144–45, 156, 178, 202, 208
Administrative Litigation Law, 8
administrative state advances, 16, 16*f*, 17, 20–21, 266–75
adverse selection, 195, 234
Advertising Law, 99, 113–14
agency overreach, 8, 12–13, 15, 16, 43, 54–60, 64–65, 70–71, 72–73, 83–84, 276
Airbnb, 32
algorithm, 4–5, 48–49, 101, 140–41, 145, 156, 157–59, 169–70, 173, 177–79, 187–88, 231, 254, 255–56, 285–86, 288–89
    algorithmic control and exploitation, 157–59, 187–88
Alibaba, 1–2, 8, 33–34, 35, 45–46, 49, 54–55, 56, 57, 60, 61, 89, 91–96, 97, 99–100, 105, 108–9, 111, 113–15, 116–17, 120, 122, 133–35, 137, 138–40, 147, 155–56, 165–66, 176, 194–95, 196–98, 202, 203–4, 205–6, 208, 215–16, 218–19, 220–21, 222, 226–27, 228–29, 231, 233–34, 236–37, 238, 246–47, 260, 261–62, 264–66, 268, 271–73, 277–78, 281, 283

Alipay, 32–33, 54–55, 92–94, 95–96, 105, 127–28, 132 133, 137–38, 144, 202–3
All-China Federation of Industry and Commerce (ACFIC), 167
All-China Federation of Trade Unions (ACFTU), 29–30, 39*f*, 161–62, 172, 175–76, 178
Allison, Graham, 280
Amazon, 3–4, 92, 99, 196–98, 227–28, 243–45, 250
American Innovation and Choice Online Act, 243
Ang, Yuen Yuen, 84–85
Anhui, 82–83, 109, 274, 283–84
Ant Group, 1–2, 35, 45–46, 48–49, 51, 52–53, 93–94, 105, 127, 137, 138, 223–24, 261–62, 269
anti-corruption, 30–31, 52, 70–71, 72, 84–85
Anti-Espionage Act 129
Anti-Monopoly Law (AML), 54–55, 89, 246, 266
Anti-Terrorism Act 129
antitrust and competition, 1–2, 18–19, 20–21, 29–30, 39*f*, 49, 51–52, 54–56, 58, 89–120, 121–22, 155–57, 166–67, 171–72, 185, 188, 212, 241, 242–48, 259, 262–64, 266, 268, 286
Anti-Unfair Competition Law (AUCL), 108–9, 118–20, 135–36, 197
Apple, 3–4, 68–69, 92, 123–24, 243–45

artificial intelligence (AI), 21, 44–45, 134, 145, 206–7, 236–37, 272, 277–91
  generative AI, 21, 277–91
  large language model (LLM) or foundation model, 278, 279, 280, 281–82, 286, 287–88
Australia, 70–72
authoritarian, 7, 20, 26, 37, 216, 238

Bai, Chong-En, 34, 270
Baidu, 33, 91–93, 95, 99–100, 127, 133, 136, 137, 140–41, 144, 147, 155–56, 176, 264–66, 272, 277–78, 281–82, 283
Bankruptcy Law, 84
bargaining leverage or power, 5, 101–2, 151–52, 158–59, 161, 165–66, 203–4, 205, 227, 259, 260
Barry, Jordan, 32
Basel Accords, 49–50
Beijing, 44–45, 108, 116–17, 134, 140–41, 150–51, 158–61, 163, 168, 175–77, 178, 181–83, 184–85, 206, 257, 268, 274–75, 282–83
Biden administration or President Biden, 152, 242–43, 254–55, 280, 288–89
big data, 44, 121–23, 124, 128, 129–30, 135–36, 137, 149, 236
Big Tech, 1, 2, 4–6, 20–21, 26–27, 29–30, 38, 47–48, 61, 89, 92, 93, 97–98, 107–9, 114–15, 116–18, 119–20, 133–36, 145, 147, 150–51, 154, 163–64, 193, 241, 242–45, 246, 248–49, 258, 270–72, 273, 276, 281–82, 287
Bilibili, 215–16, 221–22, 236–37, 265–66
birth-control, 76–78, 80–81
Black, Julia, 202
Blanchard, Oliver, 5
Blanchette, Jude, 2–3
Bradford, Anu, 241, 252–53, 286–87
Brussels Effect, 252–53
bureaucracy, 9–10, 28, 29–30, 35, 37–38, 43, 45–46, 54–55, 58–59, 67, 70, 78–79, 84–85, 116, 130, 143, 193
  bureaucratic inertia, 6, 32, 54, 61–62, 142
  bureaucratic politics, 28
ByteDance, 1, 46, 60, 92–93, 94–95, 96–97, 109, 116–17, 127–28, 139–40, 144, 147, 260, 264–66, 268–69, 272, 277–78, 281–82, 283

California, 198–99, 248–49, 253–55, 256–57, 263–64, 288–89
capital expansion, 3–4, 51–52, 165–66, 193, 260
carbon reduction, 70, 72
censorship, 7, 17–18, 36–37, 46, 90–91, 97–98, 123, 229–30, 265, 283–84
Central Commission for Discipline Inspection, 30–31
Central Commission for Science and Technology, 282
centralized decision-making, 84–86
champion, 2, 34, 99–100, 137, 212–13, 281
check and balance, 8, 12–13, 15, 16f, 17, 43, 58–59, 64–65
  institutional constraint, 7, 12–13, 15, 17, 26–27, 57, 115
Chen, Lulu, 35
Chen, Quanguo, 125
Chen, Shuo, 83–84
Chen, Tianhe, 163
Cheng, Wei, 168
chilling effect, 30–31, 260–61, 263–64
China Academy of Information and Communication Technology (CAICT), 143, 263–64
China Banking and Insurance Regulatory Commission (CBIRC), 29–30, 39f, 146
China Internet Investment Fund (CIIF), 268
China National Integrated Circuit Industry Investment Fund, 274–75
China Securities Regulatory Commission (CSRC), 39f, 50, 58–59, 75–76
Chinese Communist Party (CCP), 2–3, 6–7, 9–10, 12, 26–27, 28–31, 35, 45–46, 52, 70–71, 77–78, 82, 125, 129–30, 131–32, 149, 161–62, 165–66, 167, 277–78, 284
chip, 152, 272, 274–75, 280
  CHIPS and Science Act, 152
  semiconductor, 9, 99–100, 273, 274–75, 282
Chongqing, 124, 160, 171, 182–83, 185, 269
choose-one-from-two, 97, 104, 113, 115–16
Clarifying Lawful Overseas Use of Data Act (CLOUD Act), 248, 251

INDEX   413

coal shortage, 70, 71
cognitive limitation, 43–44, 66, 222–23
Cohen, Molly, 194
collective action, 36–37, 161–63, 172,
   187–88, 225–26
common prosperity, 1–3, 4, 5, 26, 52–53,
   60, 165–66, 259, 276
community norm, 217, 218, 232, 235–38
Competition and Antitrust Law
   Enforcement Reform Act, 245
competitive advantage, 91–92, 139–40,
   193, 194–95, 227–28, 280
consent, 127, 132–33, 135, 141–42, 147, 193,
   244–45, 277
Consumer Protection Law, 99, 113–14,
   197, 207–8
consumer welfare, 134–35, 242–43
content moderation and information
   control, 19, 21, 123, 142–43,
   221–22, 268, 277, 284–85,
   286–87, 289
control test for employee status, 254
copycat industry, 34, 230, 232
   shanzhai product, 34, 229–31, 236
   xigao practice, 229–30, 231–32
corporate governance, 260, 261,
   262–63
court, 8, 10, 12–13, 19, 29–30, 36, 39f, 103,
   107, 108–10, 115–17, 123–24, 133,
   135–37, 138–39, 140–42, 150, 156–57,
   163–64, 171, 173–74, 179–85, 186–87,
   188, 193–94, 197, 199–200, 203, 205–
   13, 220–21, 230, 231–32, 233, 236,
   244–45, 248–50, 253–55, 256–57
Covid control, 65–70, 72–73, 80–82,
   85–86
Criminal Law, 70–71, 72, 131
crisis, 14, 15–16, 17, 18, 26–27, 37, 43, 60,
   61–62, 65, 67, 68–73, 74, 75–76, 80–
   82, 85–86, 164–65, 173, 217, 225–32,
   237–38, 290, 291
crony capitalism, 34–35, 38, 270
cross-border data transfer, 2, 134, 145–46,
   150–52, 242, 250–51, 265
crowd-judging, crowd-jurors, and
   crowdsourcing, 20, 215–17, 218–19,
   220–25, 234–35, 236–37, 238
Ctrip, 106–7, 112, 149–50
cybersecurity, 1–2, 57, 121–22, 128–29,
   130–32, 133, 134, 141, 147–49, 150,

   152, 250, 251–52, 253, 267, 268, 269,
   284, 287
Cybersecurity Law, 129, 130–32, 133, 134,
   141, 143, 147–49, 150, 250, 263
Cyberspace Administration of China
   (CAC), 21, 29–30, 39f, 57, 58–59,
   133–34, 142–43, 144, 145–49, 150–51,
   152, 153, 154, 178–79, 251–52, 263,
   267, 268, 269, 277–78, 284–86,
   289–90

Dai, Xin, 138–39
data-classification framework, 251
data element, 152–53
data outflow control, 20, 242, 258
   data localization, 151–52, 242, 251, 258
data protection and privacy, 26–27, 52–53,
   95, 97, 113, 121–54, 218–19, 237, 241,
   244–45, 248–53, 277–78, 283, 287,
   288–89
data regulation and governance, 29–30,
   121–54, 156, 248–53, 264
data security, 19, 129–30, 131–32, 145, 146,
   151–52, 154, 251–52, 265, 266, 267
Data Security Law (DSL), 131–32, 141,
   146, 148–49, 251, 266
decentralized governance or platform
   decentralization, 215–38
deep-synthesis or deepfake, 145,
   285–86
Deliveroo, 90–91, 255
Deng, Xiaoping, 77, 78–79, 81–82, 84–85
Department of Justice (DOJ), 152,
   242–43
Dewey, John, 82
dichotomy in platform regulation, 20
Dickson, Bruce, 26
Didi, 1–2, 46, 47–48, 57, 58–59, 60, 61,
   90–91, 92–93, 94–95, 96, 107–8,
   110–11, 112, 144, 147–49, 155–56,
   166–67, 168–69, 170, 176, 178–79,
   215–16, 218–19, 237–38, 251–52, 263,
   264–65, 267–68
Digital Markets Act (DMA), 117–18,
   243–44, 245, 252–53, 255–56, 287
Digital Services Act (DSA), 243–44, 287
Digital Silk Road, 272
Ding, Jeffery, 278
discrimination, 118–19, 149, 177,
   277–78

INDEX

dispute resolution, 20, 36, 113, 177–78, 193–94, 199, 200–3, 204, 205–6, 207, 209–10, 211–14, 215–16, 218–19, 220–22, 233, 236, 237–38

Dixit, Avinash, 43–44

duopoly, 49, 91, 92–93, 97, 109, 114–15, 155–56, 264–65

eBay, 91–92, 95, 99, 195, 219, 220–21, 225, 227

E-Commerce Law, 99, 111, 113–14, 131, 135, 197, 207–8, 231

economic dynamism, 2–3

economic growth, 12, 26–28, 37–38, 42, 60, 75–76, 77, 78–79, 83, 129–30, 156–57, 286–87

Electronic Signature Law, 99

Ele.me, 36–37, 48–49, 90–91, 92–93, 97, 108, 109, 111, 114, 155–56, 160–61, 162–63, 168–70, 172, 173, 178–79, 180–81, 182, 184, 188–89, 264–65

Ellwood, David, 3–4

employment liability, 156, 166, 171, 181
vicarious liability, 180–81

encryption and anonymization, 123, 137

energy crisis, 18, 65, 70–73, 81, 85–86

enforcement mechanism, 194, 198–213
Golden Cudgel scheme, 204–5

Eric Schmidt, 280

Europe and European Union, 4, 20, 44, 57, 86, 89, 117–18, 131–32, 134–35, 140–41, 151–52, 241, 242, 243–45, 246, 248, 249–50, 252–53, 255–56, 258, 286–89, 290–91

Evergrande, 73, 74–75

ex ante or ex post regulation, 117–18, 193–94, 229–30, 243–44, 245

exit and restructuring, 20–21, 60, 260–63, 268

facial recognition, 124, 280, 288–89

Fallon, Richard, 233

Fang, Xindong, 108–9

Federal Trade Commission (FTC), 242–43, 288–89

feedback, 9, 13, 17, 18, 25, 38, 42, 43, 57, 59–60, 64, 71, 81–82, 184, 193–96, 198, 213, 218–19, 220–21, 227, 233–34, 237

Feng, Yang, 130

fertility rate, 78, 79–80, 81

Financial Stability and Development Committee, 51–52

first-mover advantage, 32, 46, 52–53, 56, 217

Foreign Intelligence Surveillance Act, 248

Foxconn, 68–69

France, 199–200, 255

fraud, 26–27, 33–34, 38, 47–48, 51–52, 122–23, 149–50, 171–72, 193–95, 196, 197, 202–4, 207–8, 216–17, 225, 228–29, 238, 283–84

Fried, Jessie, 261

Fujian, 152, 176–77, 274

Galanz, 108

Gallagher, Mary, 159–60

Gambetta, Diego, 199

gamification, 157–58

Gan, Lin, 100–1

gatekeeper, 106, 117–18, 243–44, 252–53, 255–56

General Administration of Customs, 29, 39*f*

General Data Protection Regulation (GDPR), 131–32, 134–35, 244–45, 250, 252–53, 287

Germany, 118–19, 244–45, 246, 256–57

Google, 3–4, 90–92, 243–45, 250, 279–80

Gou, Terry, 68–69

government guidance fund, 273–74

Grassley, Charles, 243

Great Firewall, 90–92

Guangdong, 30, 109, 115–16, 172–73, 181–83, 185, 211, 274
Guangzhou, 158–59, 168, 206, 211–12, 274

Hang Seng China Enterprises Index, 60

Hawley, Josh, 245

Hayek, Friedrich, 13

health code, 126, 137

Heilmann, Sebastian, 12, 28, 84–85

helping hand, 19, 34, 205–6, 211–12, 213–14
grabbing hand, 205–6, 212, 213–14

Henan, 126

INDEX

hierarchy, 9–11, 15–18, 16f, 25–38, 43, 64–65, 70, 73–74, 78–79, 161–62, 279, 283, 290
Holding Foreign Companies Accountable Act, 251–52
Holmes, Elizabeth, 33
Hsieh, Chang-Tai, 34, 270
Huang, Yasheng, 28
Huang, Yong, 104
Huang, Zheng, 34
Huawei, 27, 99–100
Huazhu Hotel Group, 123–24
Hubei, 67, 121–22, 274
  Wuhan, 65–68, 206, 274–75
hukou system, 159–60, 168
Huo, Zhenwu, 79–80
Huya and Douyu, 94, 112, 114–15, 247–48

Idle Fish, 114, 215–16, 221
inequality, 2–4, 5, 6–7, 165–66, 259
  wage polarization, 165
informal institution, 34, 36–37, 43, 46, 57
information intermediary or broker, 46, 55, 58, 103, 104–5, 193–94, 199
information transmission, 13, 14–15, 16f, 17, 43, 46, 47f, 64–65, 66, 69–70, 78–79, 84
  information asymmetry, 9–10, 195, 196, 199, 213, 274
  information lag, 14–15, 16f, 18, 64–65, 72–73, 80, 81, 84, 85–86
infrastructure, 75–76, 91, 98–99, 101–2, 127–28, 129, 147–48, 150–51, 152–53, 165, 199–200, 219, 252, 268, 272, 288–89, 290
in-group bias, 222–23
initial public offering (IPO), 1–2, 35, 48–52, 57, 131–32, 147–48, 251–52, 267, 269, 273
Inner Mongolia, 70–72
innovation, 3–4, 20, 32–33, 39f, 44–45, 49–50, 61–62, 82–83, 84–85, 91–92, 97, 98–99, 100, 107–8, 110–11, 129–30, 133–35, 152, 164–65, 204, 205, 216, 231, 243–44, 270–72, 279, 282, 288–89
institutional change, 16, 36–37, 100–1, 120, 260, 266
institutional protection or safeguard, 7, 34, 43, 62–63

intellectual property, 118, 136, 277–78
  copyright, 102–3, 231–32, 288
  trademark, 230, 236
interest group, 12, 16, 20, 28, 78–79, 242, 266
internal governance, 95–96, 202, 215, 227, 238
international trade, 243
internet court, 199–200, 206–7, 211
internet plus, 44–45, 101–2
interoperability, 49, 54–55, 95, 114–15, 151–52, 243
  blocking, 49, 95–96, 97, 108, 109, 116–17
Italy, 244–45, 255

Japan, 118–19, 151–52, 267
JD.com, 92–93, 94–95, 96, 97, 99, 108–9, 111, 113–14, 116–17, 123, 176, 178–79, 218–19, 234, 260–61, 265–66, 272, 281–82
Jiang, Song, 77
Jiang, Zemin, 84–85
Jiangsu, 30, 109, 171–72, 182–84, 185, 273–74
Joint APP Governance Task Force, 140, 144–45

Kamar, Ehud, 261
Kanter, Jonathan, 242–43
Khan, Lina, 242–43
Klobuchar, Amy, 243, 245
Kung, James, 83–84
Kwan, Alan P., 220–21, 223

Labor Contract Law, 170
labor regulation, 18–19, 20, 29–30, 86, 155–90, 242, 253–57
labor service agreement, 170
lax regulation, 43–46, 47–48, 54, 57, 80–81
lazy governance, 30–31, 84–85
Lee, Kai-fu, 279–80, 281–82
legal gray area, 32–33, 50, 98, 105–6, 127, 154, 166–67, 193, 224–25, 232
legitimacy, 6–7, 8, 9–10, 12, 17–18, 20, 26–28, 37–38, 42, 51, 52–53, 59–60, 62–63, 68, 77, 79–80, 103, 105–6, 128–29, 137, 138–39, 140, 148, 170, 194–95, 207, 209, 215, 216–17, 220–21, 222–23, 224, 225–38, 249–50

INDEX

Lessig, Lawrence, 235–36
Levy, Santiago, 165
Li, Jin, 262
Li, Keqiang, 44–45, 164–65
Li, Qiang, 186–87
Li, Qing, 105
Li, Robin, 127
Li, Zhaohui, 93
liberalization, 33, 82
Liu, Chuanzhi, 148, 167
Liu, He, 51–52, 61
Liu, Lizhi, 199–200
Liu, Qing (Jean), 148, 167, 168
Liu, Xu, 103–4
lobbying, 32, 46, 47f, 50–51, 53f, 58, 62f,
    98, 101–5, 128, 133–37, 142, 152,
    163–64, 166–69, 253, 276
local (judicial) protectionism, 116–17, 141,
    212–13
lockdown, 67–70
long-arm jurisdiction, 242, 248

Ma, Jack, 32–33, 45–46, 49–51, 52–53,
    91–92, 131–32, 137, 196–97, 261–62
Ma, Pony, 45–46, 101–3
Mao, Zedong, 2–3, 7, 52, 77, 82, 83, 84
market concentration, 89–90, 109–10,
    112–13, 246, 247–48
market definition, 245–46
Massachusetts, 253–55
Meadows, Donella, 12–13, 25
Meituan, 1–2, 46, 48–49, 56, 57, 89, 90–91,
    92–93, 94–95, 97, 106–7, 109, 111,
    112, 113–15, 133–34, 139–40, 155–56,
    158–59, 160–61, 162–63, 168–70, 172,
    173, 174, 176, 178–79, 180–81, 182,
    188–89, 215–16, 221, 260–61, 264–65,
    272–73, 281–82
Meng, Jingping, 183–84
mergers and acquisitions (M&A), 1–2,
    75–76, 89, 92–93, 94–95, 101, 106–7,
    109–13, 120, 155–56, 242–44, 245,
    246–48, 249–50, 268, 275–76
    killer acquisition, 246
    merger control, 245, 246–47, 267
    notification threshold, 106–7, 110–12, 246
Meta or Facebook, 1, 3–4, 10–11, 90–91,
    92, 216, 219–20, 225, 229–30, 243–45,
    250
Mexico, 165
Micron Technology, 152

Microsoft, 3–4, 90–92, 243–44
    LinkedIn, 265
Milgrom, Paul, 199
Ming Liao, 270
Ministry of Commerce (MOFCOM), 29,
    39f, 44–45, 106–7, 110–11, 227
Ministry of Education, 39f, 54, 58–59, 278
Ministry of Emergency Management
    (MEM), 29–30, 39f
Ministry of Finance, 29, 39f, 268, 274–75
Ministry of Human Resources and
    Social Security (MOHRSS), 29–30,
    39f, 174–77, 178, 185–87, 257
Ministry of Industry and Information
    Technology (MIIT), 29–30, 39f,
    54–55, 114, 131, 133–34, 142–43,
    144, 146–47, 148, 263–64, 278, 282,
    283, 284
Ministry of Natural Resources, 29
Ministry of Public Security (MPS), 39f,
    124, 142–43, 278
Ministry of Science and Technology
    (MOST), 278, 282
Ministry of Transport (MOT), 29, 39f,
    143, 166–68, 176–77, 178, 237–38
monopoly, 4–5, 10–11, 13, 54–55, 89, 103,
    105, 118, 119, 155–56, 162, 172, 243,
    246, 266
monopsony, 4–5
moral hazard, 48–49, 50–51, 202–3
multilayered dispatch arrangement, 171
    Haohuo, 171–72, 183–84
    Quhuo, 170, 171
mutual-aid platform, 223–25

naming and shaming, 55–56, 144, 202
Nasdaq Golden Dragon China Index, 60
Nathan, Andrew, 7, 26
National Bureau of Statistics, 137
National Data Bureau, 152–53
National Development and Reform
    Commission (NDRC), 29–30, 39f,
    44–45, 71–72, 105, 110, 129–30, 138,
    152–53, 278, 282, 284
nationalism or national cohesion, 12, 26,
    27–28, 37–38, 42, 128–29
National People's Congress (NPC),
    45–46, 101–2, 129–30, 131–32, 144,
    175–76
National Population and Family
    Planning Commission, 78–79

INDEX

national security, 90–91, 124–25, 128–29, 147–49, 152, 248–49, 251, 280
National Security Law, 129, 147–48
Naughton, Barry, 2–3, 84–85
negative externality, 10–11, 158–59
Netherlands, 152
New York, 1–2, 57, 58–59, 147–48, 198–99, 208, 253–54, 269
nomenklatura, 9–10, 28–29
nongovernmental organization (NGO), 161, 162–63
North, Douglass, 199

one-child policy, 18, 65, 76–80, 81–82, 85–86
open-source, 286
ownership structure, 35, 51–52
common ownership, 94, 112, 247–48
data ownership, 135–37
state ownership or golden share, 266, 267–70, 275–76

Papanastasiou, Yiangos, 205
paradox or puzzle, 30–31, 34, 37–38, 43, 79, 193–94, 216, 238
Patriot Act, 248
patronage network, 30
peer-to-peer (P2P), micro-lending, micro-loan, 47–49, 51–52, 122–23, 209–12, 210f
Lakala, 210–12, 210f
Peng, Dehuai, 84
People's Bank of China (PBOC), 29–30, 32–33, 39f, 44–45, 50–51, 52–53, 75–76, 105, 138, 143, 146
Perry, Elizabeth, 12, 28, 82
personal information, 121, 123–24, 127, 128, 130–33, 141–42, 147, 148, 149, 150, 197, 237, 248–49, 251, 266
Personal Information Protection Law (PIPL), 131–32, 139–40, 146, 148–49, 150–52, 251, 252–53, 266
picking quarrels, 163
Piketty, Thomas, 4
Pinduoduo, 1, 34, 92–93, 94–95, 96, 99, 108, 111, 116–17, 208–10, 212–13
Pistor, Katharina, 3–4
Platform Competition and Opportunity Act, 226

platform worker, 36–37, 155–90, 253–57
employee or independent contractor, 169, 170, 180, 182–84, 253–57
flexible or sticky labor, 158–59
gig worker, 10–11, 30, 155, 176, 253–54, 255, 268–69
new forms of employment, 177, 185–86, 256–57
outsourced, crowdsourced, or self-employed worker, 157–58, 160–61, 169–70, 171–72, 179–81, 181t, 182, 183–85, 188
worker classification, 175–76, 186, 253–56
policy control, 30, 31, 37–38, 89, 110
policy experimentation, 81–85
policy intervention resilience, 14
Politburo, 9–10, 28, 51–52, 68, 280–81
Political Consultative Conference (CPPCC), 45–46, 101–2, 130–31, 167
political intermediary, 35, 46, 270
Pollman, Elizabeth, 32
power fragmentation 30, 54–55, 58–59
preference divergence, 28–29
Price Law, 113–14
princeling, 35
principal-agent, 9–11, 28
agency problem, 9–10, 37, 227–28
private equity and venture capital (PEVC), 35, 92, 94–95, 98–99, 267, 270, 272, 273, 275–76, 281–82
private retreat, 16, 16f, 17, 20–21, 260–66, 275
procedural justice, 8, 215, 217, 232, 233–35, 238
property crackdown, 18, 60, 65, 73–76, 80–81, 85–86
public good, 195
public grievance, 7, 17–18, 36–37, 38, 43, 46, 52–53, 72, 140, 148, 179–80, 218, 232
public hearing, 202, 203–4, 218, 219, 233–34
Public Security Bureau (PSB), 29–30, 126, 143, 144–45

QQ, 91–92, 96–97, 106–7, 109, 115–17, 127–28

race to the bottom, 158–59
Rajan, Raghuram, 3–4

418   INDEX

Rawls, John, 233
regulatory arbitrage, 32–33, 34, 38, 51–53,
    98, 101, 105–7, 132–33, 137, 156,
    163–64, 166, 169–72, 180
regulatory campaign, 1–3, 5–6, 89
    law-enforcement campaign, 29–30, 51,
        52, 54–55, 61, 62–63, 120, 140, 145,
        154, 163–64, 185, 276
regulatory capture, 46, 54, 276
regulatory easing, 57–61, 62f
regulatory interdependence, 20, 242, 258
regulatory model or model of regulation,
    16, 16f, 18, 19, 21, 42, 54, 61–62, 64–
    65, 66, 71–72, 73–74, 76–77, 80–81,
    85–86, 101, 122, 128–29, 132, 140,
    156–57, 213, 290, 291
regulatory pendulum, 31, 52–54, 59–60,
    61, 62–63, 72–73, 89–90, 121–22,
    156, 291
regulatory tightening, 12, 61
regulatory trend, 20, 117–20, 150–53, 185–
    87, 242–45, 248–50, 253–56, 289–91
regulatory vacuum, 32
relatively advantageous position, 118–19
Ren, Jiayu, 140–41
rent-seeking, 30, 55, 82–83
repeated interaction, 198–99
reputational damage, 55–56, 57, 148, 269
reputation mechanism, 33–34, 194–98,
    215, 221
residual control, 218, 220, 223
review manipulation, 196, 197–98
    fake or promotional review, 33–34, 193,
        194–95, 196, 205, 213, 216–17
revolving door, 46
right to be forgotten, 140–41
ripple effect, 42, 72
risk aversion, 15, 17, 37–38, 43
Rodrik, Dani, 5
Ruizhi Huasheng, 123
rule of law, 183–84, 291

sanction, 6–7, 16, 27, 52, 60, 70–71, 89, 98,
    99–100, 102–3, 111, 119, 131–32, 148,
    152, 197–98, 205, 207–8, 213–14, 233
    sanctioning power, 119, 142, 202–3,
        209–10
Schrems, Maximilian, 249–50
Schwartz, Paul, 252
security assessment and filing, 145–46,
    150–51, 178–79, 251, 277–78, 285–86

self-governance and self-regulation, 20,
    86, 113, 191–238
self-preferencing, 108, 243
Sequoia Capital, 94–95, 273
Sesame Credit, 127, 133, 138–39
SF Express, 123–24
Shandong, 109, 125–26, 182–83
    Rongcheng, 125–26
Shanghai, 30, 49–51, 52–53, 82, 122, 126,
    131–32, 136, 146, 152, 154, 158–59,
    168, 171, 172–73, 176–77, 178, 179–
    83, 185, 189, 206, 209, 212–13, 274
sharing economy, 44–45, 101–2, 155, 160,
    164–65, 168–69, 173–74, 175–76, 178,
    185, 253
Shen, Neil, 273
Shenzhen, 30, 44–45, 116–17, 146, 168,
    206, 273–74, 282
Shirk, Susan, 7
Shleifer, Andrew, 205–6
Sichuan, 185, 274
    Chengdu, 176, 206, 274–75
side effect, 13, 14–15, 17, 18, 64–65, 65t,
    69–70, 72–73, 80, 81–82, 85–86, 260,
    262–63, 290, 291
Silicon Valley, 33, 278
smart court, 199–200, 206–7
Snowden, Edward, 124–25, 129,
    249–50
social-credit system, 125–26, 138–39
social protection and insurance, 39f, 157,
    159–61, 170, 175–78, 185, 187–88,
    256–57
social stability, 12, 26–28, 36–38, 42,
    128–29, 161–62, 188, 284–85
soft tech and hard tech, 270–76, 277
Sokol, Daniel, 263–64
Song, Michael, 34
Song, Zheng, 270
South Korea, 151–52
sovereignty, 20, 121–22, 129, 153, 242
Spain, 255
special deal, 34–35
spillover effect, 20, 75, 134–35, 181, 241,
    248, 258, 289
sputnik moment, 27, 274
standardization, 130–31, 143
start-up, 44–45, 49, 93–94, 96, 246–47,
    264, 269, 272, 273, 274
State Administration for Industry and
    Commerce (SAIC), 110, 197–98

INDEX

State Administration for Market Regulation (SAMR), 8, 29–30, 34, 39f, 54–55, 56–57, 58, 89, 100–1, 103, 104–5, 109–10, 111–15, 118–20, 142–43, 144–45, 146, 147, 176–78, 202, 208, 245–48, 266

State Council, 28, 39f, 44, 49–50, 61, 101–2, 103, 129–30, 145, 152–53, 164–65, 167–68, 174, 186–87, 279–80, 282

state investment, 267–70

state-owned enterprise (SOE), 35, 82, 84, 273–74

State Post Bureau (SPB), 29–30, 39f

Stigler, George, 289–90

stock exchange, 34, 49–50, 58–59, 60, 170, 251–52, 267

strategic ambiguity, 267, 289–90

structural and behavioral remedy, 112, 246–47

Sundararajan, Arun, 194

super-app, 49, 54–55, 93–94, 107–8

Supreme People's Court (SPC), 29–30, 39f, 115–17, 138–39, 141, 183–84, 186–88, 206–7, 209, 212

surveillance, 10–11, 28, 124–26, 154, 157–58, 242–43, 248, 249–50, 258, 279–80

    Golden Shield Project, 124

systems thinking, 25, 72, 241

    systems-theory, 12–13

Taleb, Nassim, 6, 85

Taobao, 32–34, 36–37, 48–49, 54–55, 91–93, 95–96, 108, 114, 122, 123, 136, 138–39, 144, 194–98, 199–205, 207–8, 209–10, 215–16, 218–19, 220–22, 223, 226–27, 228–29, 233–35, 236, 237–38

tech crackdown, 2, 9, 18, 20, 43, 61–62, 92, 104–5, 120, 154, 179–80, 188, 224–25, 245–46, 260, 263–65, 266–67, 268, 271, 272, 273, 275, 277

techno-optimism, 283

technological gap, 2, 27

technological self-sufficiency, 27, 266

technology blockade, 152

tech rivalry, 2, 271, 280–81

tech sector, 2–3, 4, 5, 18–19, 46, 49–50, 52, 58–59, 62–63, 80–81, 86, 89–90, 92–93, 97–99, 107–8, 109–10, 111, 120. 131–32, 156–57, 187–88,

242–43, 259, 255, 271–72, 273–74, 275–76, 277

e-commerce, 1–2, 32–34, 35, 44–45, 49, 92–93, 94–95, 97, 99, 107–8, 111, 113–14, 116–17 122, 123, 131, 135, 136, 146, 193–98, 200–2, 206, 207–8, 209–10, 213, 215–16, 219, 221–22, 227, 228, 231, 232, 234, 238, 260–62, 264–65, 271–72

fintech, 1–2, 29–30, 32–33, 35, 39f, 48–49, 50–51, 52–53, 131–32, 209–10, 211–12, 261

food-delivery, 1–2, 36–37, 48–49, 56, 92–93, 97, 107–8, 109, 114, 155–56, 157–60, 162–63, 168–69, 171, 172, 177–79, 185, 215–16, 221, 255, 260–62, 264–65

gaming, 49, 60, 94, 100, 112, 113, 247–48, 264–65, 272

ride-hailing, 1–2, 4–5, 57, 60, 92–93, 96, 107–8, 110–11, 148, 155–56, 160, 162–63, 164–65, 166–69, 185, 193, 237–38, 251–52, 253–55, 263, 264–65, 267

social media, 1–2, 36–37, 49, 52–53, 66–67, 124–25, 184–85, 221–22, 238, 243–44, 247–48, 250, 265, 268–69, 275–76

tutoring, 1–2, 5, 39f, 54, 58–59, 60, 259, 263

Tencent, 1–2, 33, 45–46, 49, 54–55, 60, 61, 89, 91–94, 95–97, 99–100, 101–3, 105, 106–7, 108, 109, 112–13, 114–17, 120, 133–35, 137–38, 139–40, 141–42, 147, 150, 155–56, 176, 208, 246–48, 260–61, 264–66, 268, 271–73, 281

three-red-lines policy, 73–74, 75–76

Tianjin, 109, 171, 181–82, 185, 206, 282

TikTok, 248–49

T-Mall, 97, 108–9, 111, 114, 116–17, 196–97, 200, 207, 209–10, 215–16, 226–27, 233–34

tolerant and cautious approach, 44, 104, 105, 279

    let the bullet fly a bit longer, 104, 175–76

Tom Tyler, 233

Toner, Helen, 278

trade barrier, 90–91, 97–98, 120

transparency, 46, 61, 126, 218, 229–30, 255–56, 261, 279, 287, 288

Treverton, Gregory, 85

420 INDEX

Triolo, Paul, 278
Trump administration or President Trump, 50, 99–100, 152, 248–49, 251–52, 254–55
Trust-Busting for the Twenty-First Century Act, 245
Twenty Data Measures, 152–53
Twitter, 90–91, 95–96, 122, 173, 283–84

Uber, 32, 90–91, 94–95, 107–8, 110–11, 112, 155–56, 168, 253–55, 256–57, 267
underground data industry, 122–24
unicorn, 1, 92, 274
United States, 1, 2, 3–4, 6–7, 20, 27, 44, 57, 66, 86, 89, 94–95, 98, 99–100, 148, 151–52, 208, 230, 241–44, 245, 246, 248–50, 251–52, 253–54, 255, 256, 258, 271–72, 276, 280, 286–87, 288–89, 290–91
utility function, 12, 17–18, 25, 37–38, 42, 156–57

Van Loo, Rory, 36, 193–94
variable interest entity (VIE), 105–6, 193, 267
Vishny, Robert, 205–6
volatility , 9, 12–14, 15–17, 16f, 18, 38, 42–63, 64–65, 67–68, 71–72, 76, 80–81, 86, 290, 291

walled garden, 93–94, 114, 120
Wang, Changchu, 281–82
Wang, Huiwen, 281–82
Wang, Xing, 281–82
Weber, Isabella, 82
WeChat, 1–2, 49, 54–55, 90–91, 92–94, 95–97, 101–2, 105, 108, 109, 114, 116–17, 123, 125, 127–28, 137, 140, 141–42, 144, 150, 163, 172–73, 208, 215–16, 231, 236–37, 248–49
Weibo, 95–96, 122, 123, 125, 136, 144, 173, 265–66, 268, 269, 283–84
Weingast, Barry, 199–200

White House, 2, 242–43
whole nation system or approach, 271, 274
World Bank's index of Doing Business Indicators, 34
Wu, Shugang, 268

Xi, Jinping, 1–2, 7, 13, 27, 51–52, 54, 68–69, 70, 73–74, 84–85, 100–1, 129, 149, 165–66, 271, 273–74, 280–81
Xinjiang, 68–69, 125
Xu, Xu, 124–25
Xu, Yuyu, 140

Yahoo, 265
Yang, S. Alex, 205, 220–21, 223
Yilian Labor Center, 158, 159–60

zero-Covid, 68, 69–70
Zhang, Changdong, 6–7
Zhang, Daniel, 261–62
Zhang, Hangdong, 105
Zhang, Qianfan, 212
Zhang, Qiong, 105
Zhang, Yaqing, 281–82
Zhang, Zhengxin, 108
Zhao, Bo, 130
Zhao, Weiguo, 274–75
Zhejiang, 30, 109, 146, 150, 165–66, 175–77, 181–82, 274, 283
    Hangzhou, 116–17, 136, 138–39, 160, 197, 206, 207, 233–34, 269, 274, 282
Zheng, Wentong, 55
Zhicheng Law Firm, 171–72
Zhihu, 215–16, 221–22, 236–37, 265–66
Zhou, Bowen, 281–82
Zhou, Xueguang, 9–10
Zhu, Feng, 263–64
Zhu, Li, 115
Zhu, Ye, 133
Zingales, Luigi, 3–4
ZTE, 27, 99–100
Zuboff, Shoshana, 10–11